Ethics Notes

Focus on Process

Tech Tips

Practical Strategies for Technical Communication

Mike Markel
Boise State University

Bedford/St. Martin's

Boston • New York

For Bedford/St. Martin's

Senior Executive Editor: Leasa Burton
Senior Developmental Editor: Caroline Thompson
Production Supervisor: Samuel Jones
Executive Marketing Manager: Molly Parke
Project Management: Books By Design, Inc.
Permissions Manager: Kalina K. Ingham
Senior Art Director: Anna Palchik
Text Design: Books By Design, Inc.
Cover Design: Marine Miller
Cover Photo: Fibre optic lights © UVimages/amanaimagesRF
Composition: Graphic World Inc.
Printing and Binding: RR Donnelley and Sons

President, Bedford/St. Martin's: Denise B. Wydra
Presidents, Macmillan Higher Education: Joan E. Feinberg and Tom Scotty
Editor in Chief: Karen S. Henry
Director of Marketing: Karen R. Soeltz
Production Director: Susan W. Brown
Associate Production Director: Elise S. Kaiser
Manager, Publishing Services: Andrea Cava

Library of Congress Control Number: 2012941482

Manufactured in the United States of America.

7 6 5 4 3
f e d c b

For information, write: Bedford/St. Martin's, 75 Arlington Street, Boston, MA 02116   (617-399-4000)

ISBN 978-1-4576-0940-4 (paperback)
ISBN 978-1-4576-5378-0 (Loose-leaf Edition)

Acknowledgments

Acknowledgments and copyrights are continued at the back of the book on pages 475–76, which constitute an extension of the copyright page.

Preface for Instructors

Practical Strategies for Technical Communication is a shorter version of *Technical Communication*, which for 10 editions has remained a best-selling text for introductory courses in technical communication. *Practical Strategies* focuses on the essential topics, writing strategies, and skills students need to succeed in the course and in their professional lives. Its streamlined and reorganized chapters make it more concise than the larger book, but it remains an accessible and thorough introduction to planning, drafting, designing, and revising technical documents. *Practical Strategies* also offers detailed advice on the most common applications such as proposals, reports, and instructions.

Evident throughout this book is a focus on the expanding role of social media in the world of technical communication. Today, almost everyone in the working world understands that customers and other stakeholders—including the general public, government regulators, and suppliers—play an enormous role in shaping organizations, their products, and their services. Through social media, organizations seek to form relationships with their stakeholders, drawing customers into a community that helps set the values of the organization. Social-media tools also shape the professional identities and roles of technical communicators. Within individual organizations, technical professionals are no longer merely members of one or two project groups. Rather, they offer ideas, comments, and insights to many other people in the organization, thus enlarging the talent pool that contributes to every project.

Practical Strategies for Technical Communication reflects these many exciting developments through many discussions related to how social media have changed the opportunities and responsibilities of workplace communicators. For instance, the first chapter focuses on a new role for everyone in an organization: providing information and resources for others. The chapter on audience analysis contains a discussion of ways to use social media to learn more about an audience's needs and interests. The chapter on research includes a discussion of how to use social media to learn more about a subject. And the chapter on collaboration offers advice for using social-media tools in collaborative projects. From designing Web sites to writing correspondence and other kinds of applications, the text offers guidance in how to use social media responsibly and effectively.

ORGANIZATION AND FEATURES OF THE TEXT

Practical Strategies for Technical Communication is organized into five parts.

- Part 1, "Working in the Technical Communication Environment," orients students to the practice of technical communication, introducing important topics such as the roles of technical communicators, a basic process for writing technical documents, ethical and legal considerations, effective collaboration, and uses for social media in collaboration.

- Part 2, "Planning and Drafting the Document," focuses on rhetorical and stylistic concerns: considering audience and purpose, gathering information through primary and secondary research, and writing coherent, clear documents.

- Part 3, "Designing User-Friendly Documents and Web Sites," introduces students to design principles and techniques and to the creation and use of graphics in technical documents and Web sites.

- Part 4, "Learning Important Applications," offers practical advice for preparing the types of technical communication that students are most likely to encounter in their professional lives: letters, memos, e-mail, and microblogs; job-application materials; proposals; informational reports, such as progress and status reports; recommendation reports; definitions, descriptions, and instructions; and oral presentations.

- The appendix, "Reference Handbook," provides help with paraphrasing, quoting, and summarizing sources; documenting sources in the APA, IEEE, and MLA styles; and editing and proofreading documents.

Help with the writing process is integrated throughout the book in the form of two prominent features.

- Choices and Strategies charts (see page 43, for example) are designed to help students at decision points in their writing. These charts summarize various writing and design strategies and help students choose the one that best suits their specific audience and purpose.

- Focus on Process boxes in each of the applications chapters (see page 275, for example) highlight aspects of the writing process that require special consideration when writing specific types of technical communication. Each Focus on Process box in Part 4 relates back to a complete overview of the writing process in Chapter 1 (see page 14).

In addition to annotated model documents, illustrations, and screen shots throughout the text, *Practical Strategies for Technical Communication* includes integrated e-Pages that offer 10 real-world multimedia models of technical communication such as video instructions, interactive graphics, a student's oral presentation, and a student's online portfolio. Each model is accompanied by questions for analysis, and instructors can add to e-Pages by uploading their own syllabi, links, and assignments. Students receive access to e-Pages automatically with the purchase of a new print book or Bedford e-Book to Go. Students who do not buy a new book can purchase access at <bedfordstmartins.com/ps/epages>. See the inside back cover for more details; see the Index of Features on the inside front cover for a complete listing of e-Pages.

For descriptions of additional helpful features of this book—including Guidelines boxes, Document Analysis Activities, and Writer's Checklists—see the Introduction for Writers on pages xi–xiv.

ACKNOWLEDGMENTS

All of the examples in this book—from single sentences to complete documents—are real. Some were written by my students at Boise State University. Some were written by engineers, scientists, health-care providers, and businesspeople with whom I have worked as a consultant for more than 35 years. Because much of the information in these documents is proprietary, I have silently changed brand names and other identifying information. I thank the dozens of individuals—students and professionals alike—who have graciously allowed me to reprint their writing. They have been my best teachers.

Practical Strategies for Technical Communication has benefited greatly from the perceptive observations and helpful suggestions of my fellow instructors throughout the country. I thank the following reviewers who helped to refine the table of contents for this brief edition: Rebekka Andersen, University of California, Davis; Brian Anderson, Central Piedmont Community College; Katie Arosteguy, University of California, Davis; Juliana Brixey, University of Texas Health Science Center at Houston; An Cheng, Oklahoma State University; Teresa Cook, University of Cincinnati; Paula Coomer, Washington State University; Timothy Cox, Alfred University; Richie Crider, University of Maryland; Ed Cuoco, Wentworth Institute of Technology; Jerry DeNuccio, Graceland University; Melissa Donegan, Santa Clara University; Doris Fleischer, New Jersey Institute of Technology; Ruth Gerik, University of Texas at Arlington; Sarah Hagelin, New Mexico State University; Lee Honeycutt, Iowa State University; Debra Johanyak, University of Akron: Wayne College; Steve Kark, Virginia Polytechnic Institute and State University; Margaret Karsten, Ridgewater College; Lisa Meloncon, University of Cincinnati; Mary Ellen Muesing, University of North Carolina at Charlotte; Ervin Nieves, Kirkwood Community College; Sarah Perrault, University of California, Davis; Ehren Pflugfelder, Purdue University; Lynnette Porter, Embry-Riddle Aeronautical University; Kathleen Robinson, Eckerd College; Stella Setka, Ivy Tech Community College of Indiana; Katherine Tracy, Nicholls State University; Candice Welhausen, Georgia Institute of Technology; Beverly Williams, Westfield State University; and Bill Williamson, Saginaw Valley State University.

I am also grateful to the reviewers who provided helpful comments and suggestions on sample chapters and new features: Tracy Bridgeford, University of Nebraska at Omaha; Tracy Clark, Purdue University; Julia Deisler, Santa Fe Community College; Jessica Edwards, Washington State University; Michael Frasciello, Syracuse University; Elizabeth Monske, Northern Michigan University; Jane Moody, University of Central Florida; Karen Stewart, Norwich University; and Stephanie Zerkel, Metropolitan Community College.

I have been fortunate, too, to work with a terrific team at Bedford/St. Martin's, led by Carrie Thompson, an editor of great intelligence, judgment, and energy. Carrie has helped me improve the text in many big and small ways. I also want to express my appreciation to Joan Feinberg, Denise Wydra, Karen Henry, and Leasa Burton for assembling the first-class team that has worked so hard on this edition, including Andrea Cava, Regina Tavani, Anna Palchik, Judith Riotto, Naomi Kornhauser, Caryn Burtt, and Nancy Benjamin. For me, Bedford/St. Martin's continues to exemplify the highest standards of professionalism in publishing. The people there have been endlessly encouraging and helpful. I hope they realize the value of their contributions to this book.

My greatest debt is, as always, to my wife, Rita, who over the course of many years has helped me say what I mean.

A FINAL WORD

I am more aware than ever before of how much I learn from my students, my fellow instructors, and my colleagues in industry and academia. If you have comments or suggestions for making this a better book, please get in touch with me at the Department of English, Boise State University, Boise, ID 83725. You can phone me at (208) 426-3088, or you can send an e-mail to <mmarkel@boisestate.edu>. I hope to hear from you.

Mike Markel

YOU GET MORE CHOICES FOR *PRACTICAL STRATEGIES FOR TECHNICAL COMMUNICATION*

Bedford/St. Martin's offers resources and format choices that help you and your students get even more out of the book and your course. To learn more about or order any of the products below, contact your Bedford/St. Martin's sales representative, e-mail sales support (<sales_support@bfwpub.com>), or visit <bedfordstmartins.com/ps/catalog>.

Alternative Formats

Bedford/St. Martin's offers a range of affordable formats that lets students choose the one that works for them. For details, visit <bedfordstmartins.com/ps/formats>.

E-book Options   Students can purchase *Practical Strategies for Technical Communication* as a Bedford e-Book to Go and in popular e-book formats for computers, tablets, and e-readers. For more details, visit <bedfordstmartins.com/ebooks>.

Loose-leaf Edition   The loose-leaf edition does not have a traditional binding; its pages are loose and two-hole punched to provide flexibility and a low price to students. To order the loose-leaf edition, use ISBN 978-1-4576-5378-0.

Value Packages

Add more value to your text by packaging one of the following resources with *Practical Strategies for Technical Communication*. To learn more about package options for any of the products below, contact your Bedford/St. Martin's sales representative or visit <bedfordstmartins.com/ps/packages>.

Document-Based Cases for Technical Communication, Second Edition, by Roger Munger, Boise State University, offers realistic writing tasks based on seven context-rich scenarios with more than 50 examples of documents that students are likely to encounter in the workplace. To order the textbook packaged with *Document-Based Cases for Technical Communication*, Second Edition, for free, use ISBN 978-1-4576-3418-5.

Team Writing by Joanna Wolfe, University of Louisville, is a print supplement with online videos that provides guidelines and examples of collaborating to manage written projects by documenting tasks, deadlines, and team goals. Two- to five-minute videos correspond with the chapters in *Team Writing* to give students the opportunity to analyze team interactions and learn about communication styles. Practical troubleshooting tips show students how best to handle various types of conflicts within peer groups. To order the textbook packaged with *Team Writing*, use ISBN 978-1-4576-4635-5.

ix visual exercises for tech comm by Cheryl E. Ball, Illinois State University, and Kristin L. Arola, Washington State University, introduces the fundamentals of design for technical communication in a CD-ROM that extends beyond the printed page. Each of the nine exercises progresses through a three-part sequence, helping students develop a critical vocabulary and method to read and compose all kinds of technical communication. To order the textbook packaged with ix *visual exercises for tech comm* for free, use ISBN 978-1-4576-4633-1.

Student Site <bedfordstmartins.com/ps>

Several free and open resources for *Practical Strategies for Technical Communication* are integrated into the text through cross-references in the margins:

- Document Analysis Activities
- Tutorials on evaluating online sources, creating presentation slides, designing documents, designing Web sites, and creating effective graphics
- Downloadable cases for every chapter in the book
- Downloadable forms for use in completing assignments
- Links to all of the Web resources listed in the book as well as to additional helpful resources
- Flashcards for reviewing key terms from each chapter
- Self-study quizzes to reinforce students' understanding

Instructor Resources

You have a lot to do in your course. Bedford/St. Martin's wants to make it easy for you to find the support you need—and to get it quickly.

Instructor's Resource Manual for Practical Strategies for Technical Communication is available as a PDF file that can be downloaded from the Bedford/St. Martin's companion Web site <bedfordstmartins.com/ps> or the online catalog. In addition to sample syllabi, chapter summaries, and suggested teaching approaches, the *Instructor's Resource Manual* includes suggested responses to every exercise in the book. The manual also includes a unique series of teaching topics: "Making the Transition from Comp to Tech Comm," "Addressing Plagiarism in the Tech-Comm Course," "Integrating Technology in the Tech-Comm Course," "Teaching Distance Education," "Including Service Learning in the Tech-Comm Course," and "Introducing Green Writing in the Tech-Comm Classroom."

Other resources for instructors include additional exercises and cases for every chapter, reading quizzes to download and distribute to students, presentation slides that can be adapted for classroom use, and suggested responses for Document Analysis Activities.

Bedford Coursepacks for the most common course management systems—Blackboard, Canvas, Angel, Desire2Learn, Sakai, and Moodle—allow you to easily download Bedford/St. Martin's digital materials for your course.

Introduction for Writers

The many features of *Practical Strategies for Technical Communication* offer a wealth of support to help you complete your technical-communication projects. For quick reference, many of the following features are indexed on the inside front cover of this book.

Annotated Examples make it easier for you to learn from the many model documents, illustrations, and screen shots throughout the text.

Figure 7.3   Effective Use of Repetition
Source: Myers, 2007, p. 362.

e-Pages notes in the margin of the book refer you to additional examples that use video, audio, interactive graphics, and other multimedia techniques. See the inside back cover of the book for your access code.

A Look at Several Sample Descriptions

A look at some sample descriptions will give you an idea of how different writers adapt basic approaches for a particular audience and purpose.

Figure 14.3 on page 372 shows the extent to which a process description can be based on a graphic. The topic is a household solar array. The audience is the general reader.

Figure 14.4 on page 373 shows an excerpt from a set of specifications.

Figure 14.5 on page 374 is a description of how to convert biomass into useful fuels and other products.

e-Pages
To analyze a mechanism description that uses animated graphics, visit <bedfordstmartins.com/ps/epages>.

Document Analysis Activities allow you to apply what you have just read as you analyze a real technical document. Online versions and additional activities are available on the companion Web site at <bedfordstmartins.com/ps>.

DOCUMENT ANALYSIS ACTIVITY

Analyzing a Page Design

The following page is from a government report. The accompanying questions ask you to think about page design (as discussed on pp. 147–65).

 USAID | SUDAN
FROM THE AMERICAN PEOPLE

MONTHLY UPDATE

March 2010

New Girls' Secondary School in Blue Nile State Honors Fallen USAID Staff

USAID on March 8 officially presented to the Blue Nile State Ministry of Education the new Granville-Abbas Girls' Secondary School in Kurmuk. Designed as a model of girls' education for the region, the school was dedicated on International Women's Day to highlight the importance of educating girls.

USAID Assistance to Sudan FY 2009

A local music group celebrates at the opening of the Granville-Abbas Girls' Secondary School in Kurmuk, Blue Nile state. Photo: Rebecca Debbins/USAID

The school was named in honor of John Granville, an American diplomat who worked for USAID in Sudan, and his Sudanese colleague Abdelrahman Abbas Rahama, who were both assassinated in Khartoum on January 1, 2008. The Granville-Abbas Girls' Secondary School serves as a testimony to their service and commitment to the people of Sudan.

The school, which can accommodate 120 female students, includes three sets of classrooms, a library, theater, cafeteria, dormitories, and teachers' offices. The Health, Education and Reconciliation (HEAR) Program Education Resource Center, a USAID-supported learning center attached to the school, provides students with Internet access and computer training. The school is part of USAID's efforts to increase Sudan's capacity to provide quality primary and secondary

Peace and Security	$6.7
Governing Justly and Democratically	$72.7
Health	$47.1
Education	$25.5
Economic Growth	$140.8
Food Aid	$679.7*
Humanitarian Assistance	$127.6*
Transition	$4.3
TOTAL	**$1,104.4**

Note: Amounts in millions
Includes eastern Chad

U.S. Agency for International Development
www.usaid.gov
1

1. Describe the use of proximity as a design principle on this page. How effective is it?

2. Describe the use of alignment as a design principle on this page. How effective is it?

3. Describe the use of repetition as a design principle on this page. How effective is it?

4. Describe the use of contrast as a design principle on this page. How effective is it?

➤ On the Web

To submit your responses to your instructor, click on Document Analysis Activities for Ch. 7 on <bedfordstmartins .com/ps>.

Source: U.S. Agency for International Development, 2010 <www.usaid.gov/locations/sub-saharan _africa/countries/sudan/docs/mar10_monthly_update.pdf>.

Guidelines boxes throughout the book summarize crucial information and provide advice related to key topics.

Guidelines

Dealing with Copyright Questions

Consider the following advice when using material from another source.

► **Abide by the fair-use concept.** Do not rely on excessive amounts of another source's work (unless the information is your company's own boilerplate).

► **Seek permission.** Write to the source, stating what portion of the work you wish to use and the publication you wish to use it in. The source is likely to charge you for permission.

► **Cite your sources accurately.** Citing sources fulfills your ethical obligation and strengthens your writing by showing the reader the range of your research.

► **Consult legal counsel if you have questions.** Copyright law is complex. Don't rely on instinct or common sense.

Choices and Strategies charts provide help for deciding which writing and design strategies to use to suit your specific audience and purpose.

CHOICES AND STRATEGIES	Choosing Effective Organizational Patterns	
If you want to . . .	**Consider using this organizational pattern**	**For example . . .**
Explain events that occurred or might occur, or tasks the reader is to carry out in sequence	**Chronological.** Most of the time, you present information in chronological order. Sometimes, however, you use reverse chronology.	You describe the process you used to diagnose the problem with the accounting software. In a job résumé, you describe your more-recent jobs before your less-recent ones.
Describe a physical object or scene, such as a device or a location	**Spatial.** You choose an organizing principle such as top-to-bottom, east-to-west, or inside-to-outside.	You describe the three buildings that will make up the new production facility.
Explain a complex situation or idea, such as the factors that led to a problem or the theory that underlies a process	**General to specific.** You present general information first, then specific information. Understanding the big picture helps readers understand the details.	You explain the major changes in and the details of the law mandating the use of a new refrigerant in cooling systems.
Present a set of factors	**More important to less important.** You discuss the most important issue first, then the next most-important issue, and so forth. In technical communication, you don't want to create suspense. You want to present the most important information first.	When you launch a new product, you discuss market niche, competition, and then pricing.

Focus on Process boxes in Part 4 highlight aspects of the writing process that require special consideration when writing specific types of technical communication. Each Focus on Process box in Part 4 relates back to the complete overview of the writing process in Chapter 1.

Focus on Process

When writing a proposal, pay special attention to these steps in the writing process. For a complete process for writing technical documents, see page 14.

- **Planning.** Consider your readers' knowledge about and attitudes toward what you are proposing. Use the techniques discussed in Chapters 4 and 5 to learn as much as you can about your readers' needs and about the subject. Also consider whether you have the personnel, facilities, and equipment to do what you propose to do.

- **Drafting.** Collaboration is critical in large proposals because no one person has the time and expertise to do all the work. See Chapter 3 for more about collaboration. In writing the proposal, follow the instructions in any request for proposal (RFP) or information for bid (IFB) from the prospective customer. If there are no instructions, follow the structure for proposals outlined in this chapter.

- **Revising.** External proposals usually have a firm deadline. Build in time to revise the proposal thoroughly and still get it to readers on time. See the Writer's Checklist on page 296.

Tech Tips for using basic software tools give you step-by-step, illustrated instructions on topics such as tracking changes, creating graphics, and formatting pages. Keywords in each Tech Tip help you use the Help menu in your word-processing software to find additional information.

TECH TIP

How to Insert and Modify Graphics

To highlight, clarify, summarize, and organize information, you can insert and modify graphics by using the **Picture** button and the **Format** tab.

To **insert a graphic** that you have on file—such as a photograph, drawing, chart, or graph—place your cursor where you want to insert the graphic and then select the **Picture** button in the **Illustrations** group on the **Insert** tab.

You can also insert clip art, shapes, charts, screenshots, and SmartArt.

To **modify an image** that is already in your document, double-click on it and then use the **Picture Tools Format** tab. This tab allows you to modify the appearance, size, and layout of a picture.

Buttons in the **Adjust** group allow you to modify many aspects of the picture's appearance.

Buttons in the **Arrange** group allow you to position your graphic and control how text wraps around it.

KEYWORDS: format tab, arrange group, picture style, size, adjust, insert picture, format picture, modify picture, picture style, picture toolbar

Ethics Notes remind you to think about the ethical considerations and implications of your writing.

Pulling Your Weight on Collaborative Projects

Collaboration involves an ethical dimension. If you work hard and well, you help the other members of the team. If you don't, you hurt them.

You can't be held responsible for knowing and doing everything, and sometimes unexpected problems arise in other courses or in your private life that prevent you from participating as actively and effectively as you otherwise could. When problems occur, inform the other team members as soon as possible. Be honest about what happened. Suggest ways you might make up for missing a task. If you communicate clearly, the other team members are likely to cooperate with you.

If you are a member of a team that includes someone who is not participating fully, keep records of your attempts to get in touch with that person. When you do make contact, you owe it to that person to try to find out what the problem is and suggest ways to resolve it. Your goal is to treat that person fairly and to help him or her do better work, so that the team will function more smoothly and more effectively.

Writer's Checklists summarize important concepts and act as handy reminders as you draft and revise your work.

Writer's Checklist

- [ ] Did you abide by copyright law? (p. 28)
- [ ] Did you abide by the appropriate corporate or professional code of conduct? (p. 29)
- [ ] Did you abide by your organization's policy on social media? (p. 29)
- [ ] Did you take advantage of your company's ethics resources? (p. 29)
- [ ] Did you tell the truth? (p. 29)

Did you avoid using
- [ ] false implications? (p. 29)
- [ ] exaggerations? (p. 29)

- [ ] legalistic constructions? (p. 30)
- [ ] euphemisms? (p. 30)

- [ ] Did you use design to highlight important ethical and legal information? (p. 30)
- [ ] Did you write clearly? (p. 30)
- [ ] Did you avoid discriminatory language? (p. 30)
- [ ] Did you acknowledge any assistance you received from others? (p. 30)

On the Web notes in the margins of the book refer you to free resources on the companion Web site, including tutorials, quizzes, downloadable cases, Document Analysis Activities, annotated links, and more.

On the Web
For more about audience analysis, see Writing Guidelines for Engineering and Science Students. Click on Links Library for Ch. 4 on <bedfordstmartins.com/ps>.

Why Is Your Audience Reading Your Document?

For each of your most important readers, consider why he or she is reading your document. Some writers find it helpful to classify readers into categories—such as primary, secondary, and tertiary—each of which identifies a reader's distance from the writer. Here are some common descriptions of three categories of readers:

On the Web

For more about audience analysis, see Writing Guidelines for Engineering and Science Students. Click on Links Library for Ch. 4 on <bedfordstmartins.com/ps>.

. . . sts of people who use the document in carrying . . . . hey might include the writer's team mem- . . . . ut an analysis of a new server configura- . . . . riter's supervisor, who reads it to decide . . . . mmendation; an executive, who reads . . . . server project should have on a list . . . . nalyst, who reads it to determine . . . . project.

. . . le who need to stay aware of devel- . . . . o will not directly act on or respond . . . . managers of other departments . . . . t's broad outlines; and representa- . . . . departments, who need to check . . . . the company's standards and prac- . . . . andards, such as antidiscrimination or

. . . ts of people farther removed from the writer who . . . . an interest in the subject of the report. Examples in-

Brief Contents

Contents

PART 2

Planning and Drafting the Document   55

PART 3

Designing User-Friendly Documents and Web Sites   141

PART 4

Learning Important Applications   217

PART 1

Working in the Technical Communication Environment

1

Introduction to Technical Communication

Teliris Telepresence.

The heart of technical communication is communicating with people.

Although high-tech tools such as this videoconferencing package from Teliris (2011) are becoming more important in the workplace, the heart of technical communication remains what it has always been: communicating with people. All technical-communication documents—whether e-mails, reports, Web sites, or any of a dozen other forms—are meant to help people learn, carry out tasks, and make decisions. This book is about the process of finding and creating technical information and communicating it to others.

The working world depends on written communication. Within most modern organizations, almost every action is documented in writing, whether on paper or online. Here are a few examples:

- a wiki with instructions that explain how to carry out a new task
- a proposal to persuade management to authorize a project
- a report to document a completed project
- an oral presentation to explain a new policy to employees

Every organization also communicates with other organizations, customers, suppliers, and the public, using materials such as these:

- letters to customers, clients, and suppliers
- Web sites to describe and sell products and to solicit job applications
- podcasts, videos, and posts on social-networking sites to introduce new products and services
- research reports for external organizations

WHAT IS TECHNICAL COMMUNICATION?

You can look at technical communication in two ways: as the process of making and sharing information and ideas in the workplace, and as a set of applications—the documents you write.

Technical communication is the process of finding, using, and sharing information. Conversations you have with your colleagues in the hallway, text messages to vendors, phone calls with your project team—all these are examples of technical communication.

In fact, every professional spends most of every workday reading, writing, speaking, and listening. Think of it this way: a professional is a person who communicates with others about a technical subject. An engineer is a person who communicates about engineering. An architect is a person who communicates about architecture.

Professionals create, design, and transmit technical information so that people can understand it easily and use it safely, effectively, and efficiently. Much of what you read every day—textbooks, computer-based training videos, Web sites, owner's manuals—is technical communication.

The purpose of this book is to help you improve your skills in the *process* of technical communication (finding information and developing ideas on your own and with others) and in the *applications* of technical communication (the reports, blogs, and other kinds of documents you will write). The book focuses on the techniques that skilled communicators use to analyze their audience and purpose, create and find the best information on their subject, arrange it skillfully to meet their audience's needs and preferences, and deliver it effectively using the most appropriate application.

Technical communication relies on many of the principles you have studied in your earlier writing courses. The biggest difference between technical communication and the other kinds of writing you have done is that technical communication has a somewhat different focus on *audience* and *purpose*.

In most of your previous academic writing, your *audience* has been your instructor, and your *purpose* has been to show your instructor that you have learned some body of information or skill. By contrast, in the workplace, your *audience* will likely include peers and supervisors in your company, and perhaps people outside your company. Your *purpose* will be to reinforce or change their attitudes toward the subject you are writing about, motivate them to take particular actions, or help them do their own jobs.

For example, suppose you are a public-health scientist working for a federal agency. You have just completed a study showing that, for most adults, moderate exercise provides as much health benefit as strenuous exercise. You might report your results in a journal article for other scientists, in a press release distributed to popular print and online publications, and in a blog and podcast on your agency's Web site. In each case, you will present the key information in different ways to meet the needs of the various audiences.

WHAT ARE YOUR ROLES AS A COMMUNICATOR?

Whether you are a *technical professional* (such as an electrical engineer, a chemist, or an accountant) or a *technical communicator* (a person whose main job is to create applications such as manuals, reports, and Web sites), you are likely to have three major roles as a communicator:

- *The writer of a document.* You will be the main author of documents and oral presentations.
- *A member of a project team.* As a member of a team, you will likely participate in writing documents for various audiences.
- *An information resource for people inside and outside your organization.* You will communicate with your co-workers when they seek advice and information. In addition, you will communicate with vendors, suppliers, and customers to help them understand your industry and your organization's products and services.

This book focuses on the strategies, techniques, and tools that you will use in all three of these roles.

On the Web

For a good introduction to technical communication, see the STC introduction to the subject. Also see Tom Johnson's blog. Click on Links Library for Ch. 1 on <bedfordstmartins .com/ps>.

TECHNICAL COMMUNICATION AND YOUR CAREER

Employers in every industry stress the importance of communication skills. A survey by the Plain English Network found that 96 percent of the nation's 1,000 largest employers say employees must have good communication skills to get ahead (2002). A study of over 400 U.S. companies found that almost all of them felt that the following skills are "very important" for new college graduates (Conference Board, 2006, p. 20):

Skill	Percentage of employers who think the skill is "very important"
Oral communication	95.4
Teamwork and collaboration	94.4
Professionalism and work ethic	93.8
Written communication	93.1

Job ads reflect this reality. The following ad from an organization that manufactures medical instruments is typical:

Design Assurance Engineer. Duties include performing electronic/mechanical product, component, and material qualifications. Requires spreadsheet/word-processing abilities, excellent client-relationship skills, and excellent written/oral communication skills. BSEE or biology degree preferred.

This typical job ad mentions not only computer skills but also communication skills.

Another survey of more than 100 large American corporations suggests that writing is a more important skill for today's professionals than it ever has been (College Entrance Examination Board, 2004, pp. 3–4). Among the major findings of the survey are the following:

- For hiring and promotions, writing is a "threshold skill." If your job-application materials are written poorly, 86 percent of companies surveyed would "frequently" or "almost always" hold it against you. If you somehow get the job, you won't last long enough to be promoted.

▶ **In This Book**
For more about job-application materials, see Ch. 10.

- Two-thirds of professionals need strong writing skills in their daily work. Some 80 percent of companies in the service, finance, insurance, and real-estate industries assess applicants' writing during the hiring process. Fifty percent of all companies in all industries consider writing skills in making promotion decisions.

- Half of all companies "frequently" or "almost always" produce reports, memos, and correspondence. Almost 100 percent of companies use e-mail, and more than 80 percent use PowerPoint presentations.

- Almost half of the largest U.S. companies offer or require training for professionals who cannot write well.

- The companies spent about $900 per employee for writing training.

The facts of corporate life today are simple: if you cannot communicate well, you are less valuable; if you can, you are more valuable.

CHARACTERISTICS OF A TECHNICAL DOCUMENT

Almost every technical document has six major characteristics: it addresses particular readers, helps readers solve problems, reflects the organization's goals and culture, is produced collaboratively, uses design to increase readability, and consists of words or images or both.

Addresses Particular Readers

In This Book

For more about addressing a particular audience, see Ch. 4, p. 57.

Technical documents address particular readers. For instance, if you are planning to write a proposal for your supervisor, you might think about that person's job responsibilities, the level of detail he or she would be interested in reading, and personal factors such as history with the organization and attitudes toward your ideas. These factors help you decide what kind of document to write, how to structure it, how much detail to include, and what sentence style and vocabulary to use.

Even if you do not know your readers personally, you can try to create a profile of them. For example, if readers of your brochure are police officers responsible for purchases, you know that they share a police background and a common responsibility for approving expenditures.

Your writing might also be read by people you never intended as your audience: managers and executives in your organization, the public, or the press. Avoid writing anything that will embarrass you or your organization if other audiences read it.

Often, you will write for people from different cultures or whose native language is different from yours. These readers will react differently to the design, organization, and writing style of documents than people from your own culture will. Therefore, you should consider cultural differences as you write.

A good first step is to read a full-length discussion of intercultural communication, such as one or more of the following respected resources:

Hofstede, G. H., Hofstede, G. J., & Minkow, M. (2010). *Cultures and organizations: Software for the mind* (3rd ed.). New York, NY: McGraw-Hill.

Jandt, F. E. (2012). *An introduction to intercultural communication: Identities in a global community* (7th ed.). Thousand Oaks, CA: Sage.

Lustig, M. W., & Koester, J. (2013). *Intercultural competence: Interpersonal communication across cultures* (7th ed.). Boston, MA: Pearson (Allyn & Bacon).

Neuliep, J. W. (2011). *Intercultural communication: A contextual approach* (5th ed.). Boston, MA: Houghton Mifflin.

Samovar, L. A., Porter, R. E., and McDaniel, E. R. (Eds.). (2012). *Intercultural communication: A reader* (13th ed.). Belmont, CA: Wadsworth.

Another valuable resource is the Intercultural Communication Institute (www.intercultural.org). The articles, training, and resource lists available through this nonprofit organization offer a helpful introduction to the subject.

Helps Readers Solve Problems

Technical documents help readers learn something or carry out a task. For instance, you might watch your company's video on employee benefits to help you select a benefits package. In other words, you watch it because you need information to analyze a situation and solve a problem.

Reflects the Organization's Goals and Culture

Technical documents further the organization's goals. For example, a state government department that oversees vocational-education programs submits an annual report to the state legislature, as well as a lot of technical information for the public: flyers, brochures, pamphlets, radio and television ads, and course materials. These documents help the department secure its funding and reach its audience.

Technical documents also reflect the organization's culture. For example, many organizations encourage their employees to blog about their areas of expertise. Blogging can help an organization establish an identity based on producing high-quality products, using green energy and protecting the environment, helping the community, and many other values.

Is Produced Collaboratively

Although you will work alone in writing short documents, you will probably work as part of a team in producing more-complicated documents because no one person has all the information, skills, or time to create a large document. Writers, editors, designers, and production specialists work with subject-matter experts—the various technical professionals—to create a better document than any one of them could have made working alone.

Collaboration can range from having a colleague review your two-page memo to working with a team of a dozen technical professionals and technical communicators on a 200-page catalog. Social media such as wikis, blogs, and microblogs (such as Twitter) make it convenient for professionals to collaborate inside and outside their own organizations.

▶ **In This Book**
For more about collaboration, see Ch. 3.

Uses Design to Increase Readability

Technical communicators use design features—typography, spacing, color, special paper, and so forth—to accomplish three basic goals:

- *To make the document look attractive and professional.* If it is attractive and creates a positive impression, you are more likely to accomplish your goal.

- *To help readers navigate the document.* Design features such as headings, color, and highlighting help readers see where they are and get to where they want to be.

▶ **In This Book**
For more about design, see Ch. 7.

DOCUMENT ANALYSIS ACTIVITY

Studying How Technical Communication Combines Words, Graphics, and Design

This is a page from a brochure from Xerox describing two products. The questions ask you to consider how technical communication combines words and graphics.

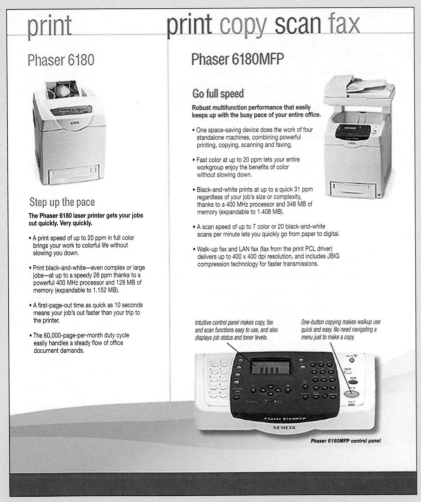

print

Phaser 6180

Step up the pace

The Phaser 6180 laser printer gets your jobs out quickly. Very quickly.

- A print speed of up to 20 ppm in full color brings your work to colorful life without slowing you down.

- Print black-and-white—even complex or large jobs—at up to a speedy 26 ppm thanks to a powerful 400 MHz processor and 128 MB of memory (expandable to 1.152 MB).

- A first-page-out time as quick as 10 seconds means your job's out faster than your trip to the printer.

- The 60,000-page-per-month duty cycle easily handles a steady flow of office document demands.

print copy scan fax

Phaser 6180MFP

Go full speed

Robust multifunction performance that easily keeps up with the busy pace of your entire office.

- One space-saving device does the work of four standalone machines, combining powerful printing, copying, scanning and faxing.

- Fast color at up to 20 ppm lets your entire workgroup enjoy the benefits of color without slowing down.

- Black-and-white prints at up to a quick 31 ppm regardless of your job's size or complexity, thanks to a 400 MHz processor and 348 MB of memory (expandable to 1.408 MB).

- A scan speed of up to 7 color or 20 black-and-white scans per minute lets you quickly go from paper to digital.

- Walk-up fax and LAN fax (fax from the print PCL driver) delivers up to 400 x 400 dpi resolution, and includes JBIG compression technology for faster transmissions.

Intuitive control panel makes copy, fax and scan functions easy to use, and also displays job status and toner levels.

One-button copying makes walkup use quick and easy. No need navigating a menu just to make a copy.

Phaser 6180MFP control panel

Source: Xerox, 2007 <www.office.xerox.com/latest/61CBR-01U.PDF>.

1. How has the company used words and graphics to communicate different kinds of information?

2. How has the company used design to help readers understand that this page describes two different products?

3. How has the company used color to help readers understand the messages that it wishes to communicate?

On the Web

To submit your responses to your instructor, click on Document Analysis Activities for Ch. 1 on <bedfordstmartins .com/ps>.

- *To help readers understand the document.* If all the safety warnings in a manual appear in a color and size different from the rest of the text, readers will be better able to recognize the importance of the information.

Consists of Words or Images or Both

Most technical documents include words and images—both static graphics and moving images. Images help the writer perform five main functions:

- make the document more interesting and appealing to readers
- communicate and reinforce difficult concepts
- communicate instructions and descriptions of objects and processes
- communicate large amounts of quantifiable data
- communicate with nonnative speakers

Figures 1.1, 1.2 (page 10), and 1.3 (page 11) illustrate a number of the characteristics of technical communication discussed in this chapter.

▶ In This Book
For more about graphics, see Ch. 8.

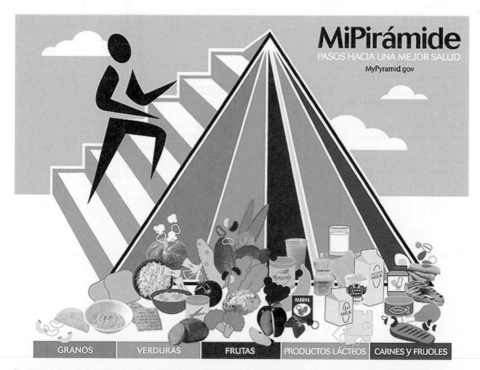

Figure 1.1   A Poster That Shows the Characteristics of Technical Communication
Source: U.S. Department of Agriculture, 2005 <www.mypyramid.gov/downloads/sp-MiniPoster.pdf>.

Characteristics of technical communication:

- *addresses particular readers:* This poster is addressed to Spanish-speaking children and their caregivers in the United States.
- *helps readers solve problems:* It provides information about the elements of a balanced diet.
- *reflects the organization's goals and culture:* It is intended to show that the organization (the U.S. Department of Agriculture) works to improve children's nutrition.
- *is produced collaboratively:* The poster was created by nutrition experts, technical communicators, graphic artists, Web authors, and others.
- *uses design to increase readability:* The width of each color-coded food group is intended to suggest how much of that food group a child requires. Elsewhere on the poster this concept is communicated in more detail.
- *consists of words or images or both:* The words, colors, and graphics are used to make the message clear and easy to understand.

Characteristics of technical communication:

- **Addresses particular readers.** *This page is from a white paper addressed to managers interested in learning about the company's customer relationship management software.*
- **Helps readers solve problems.** *The page explains how the software is easy to use and shows the user interface.*
- **Reflects the organization's goals and culture.** *This white paper focuses on usability: making the product easy to use. The explanations, the image, and the marginal quotation all focus on this goal.*
- **Is produced collaboratively.** *It was created by the product experts, with the help of technical communicators.*
- **Uses design to increase readability.** *The three elements—the textual explanation, the screen shot, and the marginal quotation—work together to make an argument.*
- **Consists of words or images or both.** *The words explain the argument; the graphic shows what the words say.*

Proving Usability and Productivity

While creating ACT! 2010 we emphasized a number of usability and productivity related themes. Our first focus area was on navigation. Navigation is the act of finding your way around in a software product. Similar to navigating when traveling by car, there sometimes are easy paths and sometimes difficult paths depending on the route and the signs provided. Our goal was to make navigation as effortless as possible. We did this by creating simplified "context-driven" menus, by including a familiar "PC-style" navigation scheme to access views, and by augmenting the traditional top-of-screen toolbar with big "easy buttons" to allow instant recognition and access to the most frequently used functions. In addition, we added a persistent Lookup box, so you can search for information more quickly (Figure 1).

ACT! by Sage

"Our goal was to make navigation as effortless as possible."

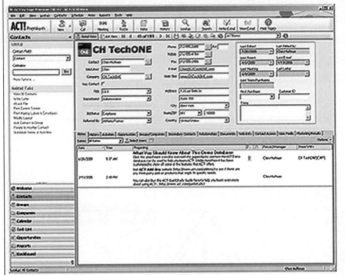

Figure 1: Contact Details Screen Showing New User Interface Elements

Second, we added a customizable Welcome page as a home base for users (Figure 2). This new screen is a navigational aid and a touchpoint for beginning ACT! users. It is also a place for all ACT! users to discover important features and how to use them. It exposes advanced features and provides assistance to experienced users who need to access infrequently used functionality. It also provides a view tailored specifically for Administrators.

ACT! by Sage 2010: Delivering on Usability and Productivity   5

Figure 1.2   A White Paper Page That Shows the Characteristics of Technical Communication
Source: Sage Software, 2009 <http://download.act.com/act2010/docs/act_2010_usability_and _productivity_whitepaper.pdf>.

Figure 1.3   A Q&A That Shows the Characteristics of Technical Communication
Source: Marathon Technologies, 2010 <www.marathon1.com/why_marathon_video.html>.

MEASURES OF EXCELLENCE IN TECHNICAL COMMUNICATION

Eight measures of excellence characterize all technical communication: honesty, clarity, accuracy, comprehensiveness, accessibility, conciseness, professional appearance, and correctness.

Honesty

The most important measure of excellence in technical communication is honesty. For three reasons, you have to tell the truth and not mislead the reader:

- *It is the right thing to do.* Technical communication is meant to help people make wise choices as they live and work in a high-tech culture.
- *If you are dishonest, readers can get hurt.* Misinforming your readers or deliberately omitting important information can defraud, injure, or kill people.

Characteristics of technical communication:

- ***Addresses particular readers.*** *This Web page is addressed to prospective buyers of the company's software.*
- ***Helps readers solve problems.*** *All the elements—the text, the links, and the video—answer readers' questions and show that the product is a good value. A set of links on the right is titled "Solve Your Problem."*
- ***Reflects the organization's goals and culture.*** *This page contains numerous elements—from the photo to the logos from social-media sites such as Facebook—that say that the company will be there to help readers solve their problems.*
- ***Is produced collaboratively.*** *It was created by a writer, with the help of a photographer, a videographer, a designer, and a Web specialist.*
- ***Uses design to increase readability.*** *This page is well designed, with navigation information spanning the top and a balanced three-column design in the main content area of the screen.*
- ***Consists of words or images or both.*** *Like much technical communication, this Web page consists of words and images (such as the photographs, logos, and video).*

▶ **In This Book**
For more about the ethical and legal aspects of technical communication, see Ch. 2.

- *If you are dishonest, you and your organization could face serious legal charges.* If a court finds that your document's failure to provide honest, appropriate information caused a loss or substantial injury, your organization might have to pay millions of dollars.

ETHICS NOTE

You will find Ethics Notes throughout this book. These notes will describe typical ethical problems related to technical communication and suggest ways to think about them.

Clarity

Your goal is to produce a document that conveys a single meaning the reader can understand easily. Technical communication must be clear for two reasons:

- *Unclear technical communication can be dangerous.* A carelessly drafted building code, for example, could tempt contractors to use inferior materials or techniques.
- *Unclear technical communication is expensive.* The average cost of a telephone call to a customer-support center is more than $32 (About.com, 2008). Clear technical communication in the product's documentation—its instructions—can greatly reduce the number and length of such calls.

Accuracy

You need to get your facts straight. A slight inaccuracy can confuse and annoy your readers; a major inaccuracy can be dangerous and expensive. In another sense, accuracy is a question of ethics. Technical documents must be as objective and unbiased as you can make them. If readers suspect that you are slanting information—by overstating or omitting facts—they will doubt the validity of the entire document.

Comprehensiveness

A good technical document provides all the information readers need to follow the discussion and carry out any required tasks. It refers to supporting materials clearly or includes them as attachments.

Comprehensiveness is crucial because readers need a complete, self-contained discussion to use the information safely, effectively, and efficiently. A document also often serves as the official company record of a project, from its inception to its completion.

Accessibility

Most technical documents—both in print and online—are made up of small, independent sections. Because few people will read a document from the beginning to the end, your job is to make its various parts accessible. That is, readers should not be forced to flip through the pages or click links unnecessarily to find the appropriate section.

▶ **In This Book**
For more about making documents accessible, see Chs. 6 and 7.

Conciseness

A document must be concise enough to be useful to a busy reader. You can shorten most writing by 10 to 20 percent simply by eliminating unnecessary phrases, choosing shorter words, and using economical grammatical forms. Your job is to figure out how to convey a lot of information economically.

▶ **In This Book**
For more about writing concisely, see Ch. 6.

Professional Appearance

You start to communicate before anyone reads the first word of your document. If the document looks neat and professional, readers will form a positive impression of it and of you. Your document should adhere to the format standards of your organization or your professional field, and it should be well designed and neatly printed. For example, a letter should follow one of the traditional letter formats and have generous margins.

Correctness

A correct document is one that adheres to the conventions of grammar, punctuation, spelling, mechanics, and usage. Sometimes, incorrect writing can confuse readers or even make your writing inaccurate. The more typical problem, however, is that incorrect writing makes you look unprofessional. If your writing is full of errors, readers will wonder if you were also careless in gathering, analyzing, and presenting the technical information. If readers doubt your professionalism, they will be less likely to accept your conclusions or follow your recommendations.

A PROCESS FOR WRITING TECHNICAL DOCUMENTS

Although every technical document is unique, in most of your writing you will likely carry out the tasks described in the Focus on Process box on page 14.

Focus on Process

Planning	• **Analyze your audience.** Who are your readers? What are their attitudes and expectations? How will they use the document? See Ch. 4 for advice about analyzing your audience.
	• **Analyze your purpose.** After they have read the document, what do you want your readers to *know* or to *do*? See Ch. 4, p. 72, for advice about determining your purpose.
	• **Generate ideas about your subject.** Ask journalistic questions (*who, what, when, where, why,* and *how*), brainstorm, freewrite, talk with someone, or make clustering or branching diagrams.
	• **Research additional information.** See Ch. 5 for advice about researching your subject.
	• **Organize and outline your document.** See Ch. 6, p. 107, for information about common organizational patterns.
	• **Select an application, a design, and a delivery method.** See Ch. 7 for advice about designing your document.
	• **Devise a schedule and a budget.** How much time will you need to complete each task of the project? Will you incur expenses for travel, research, or usability testing?
Drafting	• **Draft effectively.** Get comfortable. Start with the easiest topics, and don't stop writing to revise.
	• **Use templates—carefully.** Check that their design is appropriate and that they help you communicate your information effectively to your readers.
	• **Use styles.** Styles are like small templates that apply to the design of elements such as headings and bullet lists. They help you present the elements of your document clearly and consistently. See the Tech Tip on p. 162.
Revising	**Look again at your draft to see if it works.** Revising by yourself and with the help of others, focus on three questions:
	• Has your understanding of your audience changed?
	• Has your understanding of your purpose changed?
	• Has your understanding of your subject changed?
	If the answer to any of these questions is yes, what changes should you make to the content and style of your document? See the Writer's Checklists in each chapter for information about what to look for when revising.
Editing	**Check your revised draft to improve six aspects of your writing:** grammar, punctuation, style, usage, diction (word choice), and mechanics (matters such as use of numbers and abbreviations). See Appendix, Part B, for more information about these topics.
Proofreading	**Check to make sure you have typed what you meant to type.** Don't rely on the spell-checker or the grammar-checker. They will miss some errors and flag correct words and phrases. See Appendix, Part B, for more information about proofreading.

This writing process consists of five steps: planning, drafting, revising, editing, and proofreading. The frustrating part of writing, however, is that these five steps are not linear. That is, you don't plan the document, then check off a box and go on to drafting. At any step, you might double back to do more planning, drafting, or revising. Even when you think you're almost done—when you're proofreading—you still might think of something that would improve the planning. That means you'll need to go back and rethink all five steps.

As you backtrack, you will have one eye on the clock, because the deadline is sneaking up on you. That's the way it is for all writers. A technical writer stops working on a user manual because she has to get it off to the print shop. An engineer stops working on a set of slides for a conference presentation because it's time to head for the airport.

So, when you read about how to write, remember that you are reading about a messy process that goes backward as often as it goes forward and that, most likely, ends only when you run out of time.

Later chapters will discuss how to vary this basic process in writing various applications such as proposals, reports, and descriptions. The Focus on Process boxes at the beginning of Chapters 9 to 15 will highlight important steps in this process for each application.

Should you use the process described here? If you don't already have a process that works for you, yes. But your goal should be to devise a process that enables you to write *effective* documents (that is, documents that accomplish what you want them to) *efficiently* (without taking more time than necessary).

Exercises

▶ **In This Book**   For more about memos, see Ch. 9, p. 223.

1. **INTERNET EXERCISE** Form small groups and study the home page of your college or university's Web site. Focus on three characteristics of technical communication:

   • It addresses particular readers.

   • It helps readers solve problems.

   • It reflects the organization's goals and culture.

   Identify two or three examples of each characteristic on the home page of the site. For example, for the characteristic that technical communication addresses particular readers, you might point to the section of the site called "For Prospective Students" because it presents information addressed specifically to people who are considering enrolling. Be prepared to share your findings with the class.

2. Locate an owner's manual for a consumer product, such as a coffeemaker, bicycle, or hair dryer. In a memo to your instructor, describe and evaluate the manual. To what extent does it meet the measures of excellence discussed in this chapter? In what ways does it fall short? Submit a copy of the document (or a representative portion of it) with your memo.

3. **INTERNET EXERCISE** Locate a document on the Web that you think is an example of technical communication. Describe the aspects of the document that illustrate the characteristics of technical communication

discussed in this chapter. Then evaluate the effectiveness of the document. Write your response in a memo to your instructor. Submit a copy of the document (or a representative portion of it) with your assignment.

On the Web

For a case assignment, "Using the Measures of Excellence in Evaluating a Résumé," see Cases on <bedfordstmartins.com/ps>.

2

Understanding Ethical and Legal Considerations

Joseph McNally/Getty Images.

Does a bicycle company care about riders' safety?

Ethical and legal issues are all around you in your work life. If you look at the Web site of any bike manufacturer, you will see that bicyclists are always shown wearing helmets. Is this because bike manufacturers care about safety? Certainly. But bike makers also care about product liability. If a company Web site showed cyclists without helmets, an injured cyclist could sue, claiming that the company was suggesting it is safe to ride without a helmet.

Ethical and legal pitfalls lurk in the words and graphics of many kinds of formal documents. In writing a proposal, you might be tempted to exaggerate or lie about your organization's past accomplishments, pad the résumés of the project personnel, list as project personnel some workers who will not be contributing to the project, or present an unrealistically short work schedule. In drafting product information, you might feel pressured to exaggerate the quality of the products shown in catalogs or manuals or to downplay the hazards of using those products. In creating graphics, you might be asked to hide an item's weaknesses by manipulating a product photo electronically.

One thing is certain: there are many serious ethical and legal issues related to technical communication, and all professionals need a basic understanding of them.

A BRIEF INTRODUCTION TO ETHICS

Ethics is the study of the principles of conduct that apply to an individual or a group. For some people, ethics is a matter of intuition—what their gut feelings tell them about the rightness or wrongness of an act. Others see ethics in terms of their own religion or the Golden Rule: treat others as you would like them to treat you. Ethicist Manuel G. Velasquez outlines four moral standards that are useful in thinking about ethical dilemmas (2006):

- *Rights.* This standard concerns individuals' basic needs and welfare. Everyone agrees, for example, that people have a right to a reasonably safe workplace. When we buy a product, we have a right to expect that the information that accompanies it is honest and clear. However, not everything that is desirable is necessarily a right. For example, in some countries high-quality health care is considered a right. That is, the government is required to provide it, regardless of whether a person can afford to pay for it. In other countries, health care is not considered a right.

- *Justice.* This standard concerns how the costs and benefits of an action or a policy are distributed among a group. For example, justice requires that people doing the same job receive the same pay, regardless of whether they are male or female, black or white.

- *Utility.* This standard concerns the positive and negative effects that an action or a policy has, will have, or might have on others. For example, if a company is considering closing a plant, the company's leaders should consider not only the money they would save but also the financial hardship of laid-off workers and the economic effects on the community. One tricky part in thinking about utility is figuring out the time frame to examine. An action such as laying off employees can have one effect in the short run—improving the company's quarterly balance sheet—and a very different effect in the long run—hurting the company's productivity or the quality of its products.

- *Care.* This standard concerns the relationships we have with other individuals. We owe care and consideration to all people, but we have greater responsibilities to people in our families, our workplaces, and our communities. The closer a person is to us, the greater care we owe that person. Therefore, we have greater obligations to members of our family than we do to others in our community.

Although these standards provide a vocabulary for thinking about how to resolve ethical conflicts, they are imprecise and often conflict with each other. Therefore, they cannot provide a systematic method of resolving ethical conflicts. Take the case of a job opportunity in your company. You are a member of the committee that will recommend which of six applicants to hire. One of the six is a friend of yours who has recently gone through a divorce and is currently unemployed. He needs the health benefits the job provides because he has a daughter with a chronic condition who requires expensive medications. Unfortunately, you have concluded that he is less qualified for the position than some of the other applicants.

How can the four standards help you think through the situation? According to the *rights* standard, lobbying for your friend or against the other applicants would be wrong because all applicants have a right to an evaluation process that considers only their qualifications to do the job. Looking at the situation from the perspective of *justice* yields the same conclusion: it would be wrong to favor your friend. From the perspective of *utility*, lobbying for your friend would probably not be in the best interests of the organization, although it might be in your friend's best interests. Only according to the *care* standard does lobbying for your friend seem reasonable.

As you think about this case, you have to consider another related question: should you tell the other people on the hiring committee that one of the applicants is your friend? Yes, because they have a right to know about your personal relationship so that they can better evaluate your contributions to the discussion. You might also offer to recuse yourself (that is, not participate in the discussion of this position), leaving it to the other committee members to decide whether your friendship with a candidate represents a conflict of interest.

Most people do not explore the conflict among rights, justice, utility, and care when they confront a serious ethical dilemma; instead, they simply do what they think is right. Perhaps this is good news. However, the depth of ethical thinking varies dramatically from one person to another, and the consequences of superficial ethical thinking can be profound. For these reasons, ethicists have described a general set of principles that can help people organize their thinking about the role of ethics within an organizational context. These principles form a web of rights and obligations that connect an employee, an organization, and the world in which the organization is situated.

For example, in exchange for their labor, employees enjoy three basic rights: fair wages, safe and healthy working conditions, and due process in the handling of such matters as promotions, salary increases, and firing. Although there is still serious debate about the details of employee rights, such as the freedom from surreptitious surveillance and unreasonable searches in drug investigations, the question almost always concerns the extent of employees' rights, not the existence of the basic rights themselves. For instance, ethicists disagree about whether hiring undercover investigators to identify drug users at a job site is an unwarranted intrusion on the employees' rights, but there is no debate about the right of exemption from unwarranted intrusion.

YOUR ETHICAL AND LEGAL OBLIGATIONS

In addition to enjoying rights, an employee assumes obligations, which can form a clear and reasonable framework for discussing the ethics of technical communication. The following discussion outlines four sets of obligations: to your employer, to the public, to the environment, and to copyright holders.

Obligations to Your Employer

You will be hired to further your employer's legitimate aims and to refrain from any activities that run counter to those aims. Specifically, you have five obligations:

- *Competence and diligence. Competence* refers to your skills; you should have the training and experience to do the job adequately. *Diligence* simply means hard work.

- *Generosity.* Although *generosity* might sound like an unusual obligation, you are obligated to help your co-workers and stakeholders outside your organization by sharing your knowledge and expertise. What this means is that if you are asked to respond to questions or provide recommendations on some aspect of your organization's work, you should do so. If a customer or supplier contacts you, make the time to respond helpfully. Generosity shows professionalism and furthers your organization's goals.

- *Honesty and candor.* You should not steal from your employer. Stealing includes such practices as embezzlement, "borrowing" office supplies, and padding expense accounts. *Candor* means truthfulness; you should report to your employer problems that might threaten the quality or safety of the organization's product or service.

- *Confidentiality.* You should not divulge company business outside of the company. If a competitor finds out that your company is planning to introduce a new product, it might introduce its own version of that product, robbing you of your competitive advantage. Many other kinds of privileged information—such as quality-control problems, personnel matters, relocation or expansion plans, and financial restructuring—also could be used against the company. A well-known problem of confidentiality involves *insider information:* an employee who knows about a development that will increase the value of the company's stock, for example, buys the stock before the information is made public, thus reaping an unfair (and illegal) profit.

- *Loyalty.* You should act in the employer's interest, not in your own. Therefore, it is unethical to invest heavily in a competitor's stock because that could jeopardize your objectivity and judgment. For the same reason, it is unethical to accept bribes or kickbacks. It is unethical to devote considerable time to moonlighting (performing an outside job, such as private consulting) because the outside job could lead to a conflict of interest and because the heavy workload could make you less productive in your primary position. However, you do not owe your employer absolute loyalty; if your employer is acting unethically, you have an obligation to try to change that behavior, even, if necessary, by blowing the whistle.

In This Book
For more about whistle-blowing, see p. 27.

Obligations to the Public

Every organization that offers products or provides services is obligated to treat its customers fairly. As a representative of an organization, and especially as an employee communicating technical information, you will frequently confront ethical questions.

In general, an organization is acting ethically if its product or service is both *safe* and *effective*. The product or service must not injure or harm the consumer, and it must fulfill its promised function. However, these common-sense principles provide little guidance in dealing with the complicated ethical problems that arise routinely.

According to the U.S. Consumer Product Safety Commission (2009), more than 4,500 deaths and 14 million injuries occur each year in the United States because of consumer products—not counting automobiles and medications. Even more commonplace, of course, are product and service failures: products or services don't do what they are supposed to do, products are difficult to assemble or operate, they break down, or they require expensive maintenance.

Who is responsible for injuries and product failures—the company that provides the product or service or the consumer who purchases it? Courts frequently rule that manufacturers are responsible for providing adequate instructions for their products and for warning consumers about safety risks. (Figure 2.1 shows a sample warning label.) A person who operates a chainsaw without reading the safety warnings or instructions is to blame for any injuries caused by the normal operation of the saw. But a manufacturer that knows that the chain on

Figure 2.1   A Warning Label

This warning label uses symbols—such as the orange box, the red circle with the slash, and the image of the heart and pacemaker—and words to visually and verbally warn people with pacemakers to stay away from a device that can hurt them. The warning helps the company do the right thing—and avoid product-liability lawsuits.
Source: Safety Label Solutions, 2010 <http://safetylabelsolutions .com/store/page8.html>.

the saw is liable to break under certain circumstances and fails to remedy this problem or warn the consumer is responsible for any resulting accidents.

Unfortunately, such ideas do not outline a rational theory that can help companies understand how to act ethically in fulfilling their obligations to the public. Today, most court rulings are based on the premise that the manufacturer knows more about its products than the consumer does and therefore has a greater responsibility to make sure the products comply with all of the manufacturer's claims and are safe. Therefore, in designing, manufacturing, testing, and communicating about a product, the manufacturer has to make sure the product will be safe and effective when used according to the instructions. However, the manufacturer is not liable when something goes wrong that it could not have foreseen or prevented.

Obligations to the Environment

We know that we are polluting and depleting our limited natural resources at an unacceptably high rate. Our excessive use of fossil fuels not only deprives future generations of their use but also causes possibly irreversible pollution problems, such as global warming.

But what does this have to do with you? In your daily work, you will often know how your organization's actions affect the environment. For example, if you work for a manufacturing company, you might be aware of the environmental effects of making or using your company's products. Or you might help write an environmental impact statement.

As communicators, we should treat every actual or potential occurrence of environmental damage seriously. We should alert our supervisors to the situation and work with them to try to reduce the damage. The difficulty, of course, is that protecting the environment can be expensive. Clean fuels cost more than dirty ones. Disposing of hazardous waste properly costs more (in the short run) than merely dumping it. Organizations that want to reduce costs may be tempted to cut corners on environmental protection.

Obligations to Copyright Holders

As a student, you are constantly reminded to avoid plagiarism. A student caught plagiarizing would likely fail the assignment or the course or even be expelled from school. A medical researcher or a reporter caught plagiarizing would likely be fired, or at least find it difficult to publish in the future. But plagiarism is an ethical, not a legal, issue. Although a plagiarist might be expelled from school or be fired, he or she will not be fined or sent to prison.

By contrast, copyright is a legal issue. *Copyright law* is the body of law that relates to the appropriate use of a person's intellectual property: written documents, pictures, musical compositions, and the like. Copyright literally refers to a person's *right* to *copy* the work that he or she has created.

On the Web

For more about copyright law, see the U.S. Copyright Office Web site. Click on Links Library for Ch. 2 on <bedfordstmartins .com/ps>.

The most important concept in copyright law is that only the copyright holder—the person or organization that owns the work—can copy it. For instance, if you work for IBM, you can legally copy information from the IBM Web site and use it in other IBM documents. This reuse of information is routine because it helps ensure that the information a company distributes is both consistent and accurate.

However, if you work for IBM, you cannot simply copy information that you find on the Dell Web site and put it in IBM publications. Unless you obtained written permission from Dell to use its intellectual property, you would be infringing on Dell's copyright.

Why doesn't the Dell employee who wrote the information for Dell own the copyright to that information? The answer lies in a legal concept known as *work made for hire*. Anything written or revised by an employee on the job is the company's property, not the employee's.

Although copyright gives the owner of the intellectual property some rights, it doesn't give the owner all rights. You can place small portions of copyrighted text in your own document without getting formal permission from the copyright holder. When you quote a few lines from an article, for example, you are taking advantage of an aspect of copyright law called *fair use*. Under fair-use guidelines, you have the right to use material, without getting permission, for purposes such as criticism, commentary, news reporting, teaching, scholarship, or research. Unfortunately, *fair use* is based on a set of general guidelines that are meant to be interpreted on a case-by-case basis. Keep in mind that you should still cite the source accurately to avoid plagiarism.

> **On the Web**
>
> The U.S. Copyright Office Web site describes work made for hire. Click on Links Library for Ch. 2 on <bedfordstmartins .com/ps>.

Guidelines

Determining Fair Use

Courts consider four factors in disputes over fair use.

▶ **The purpose and character of the use, especially whether the use is for profit.** Profit-making organizations are scrutinized more carefully than nonprofits.

▶ **The nature and purpose of the copyrighted work.** When the information is essential to the public—for example, medical information—fair use is applied more liberally.

▶ **The amount and substantiality of the portion of the work used.** A 200-word passage would be a small portion of a book but a large portion of a 500-word brochure.

▶ **The effect of the use on the potential market for the copyrighted work.** Any use of the work that is likely to hurt the author's potential to profit from the original work will probably not be considered fair use.

Guidelines

Dealing with Copyright Questions

Consider the following advice when using material from another source.

▶ **Abide by the fair-use concept.** Do not rely on excessive amounts of another source's work (unless the information is your company's own boilerplate).

▶ **Seek permission.** Write to the source, stating what portion of the work you wish to use and the publication you wish to use it in. The source is likely to charge you for permission.

▶ **Cite your sources accurately.** Citing sources fulfills your ethical obligation and strengthens your writing by showing the reader the range of your research.

▶ **Consult legal counsel if you have questions.** Copyright law is complex. Don't rely on instinct or common sense.

In This Book

For more about documenting your sources, see Appendix, Part A.

ETHICS NOTE

Distinguishing Plagiarism from Acceptable Reuse of Information

Plagiarism is the act of using someone else's words or ideas without giving credit to the original author. Obviously, it is plagiarism to borrow, buy, or steal graphics, video or audio media, written passages, or entire documents, and then use them without attribution. Web-based sources are particularly vulnerable to plagiarism, partly because people mistakenly think that if information is on the Web it is free to borrow and partly because it is so easy to copy, paste, and reformat it.

However, writers within a company often reuse one another's information without giving credit—and it is completely ethical. For instance, companies write press releases when they wish to publicize news. These press releases typically conclude with descriptions of the company and how to get in touch with an employee who can answer questions about the company's products or services. These descriptions, sometimes called *boilerplate*, are simply copied and pasted from previous press releases. Because these descriptions are legally the intellectual property of the company, reusing them in this way is completely honest. Similarly, companies often *repurpose* their writing. That is, they copy a description of the company from a press release and paste it into a proposal or an annual report. This reuse also is acceptable.

When you are writing a document and need a passage that you suspect someone in your organization might already have written, ask a more-experienced co-worker whether the culture of your organization permits reusing someone else's writing. If the answer is yes, check with your supervisor to see whether he or she approves what you plan to do.

THE ROLE OF CORPORATE CULTURE IN ETHICAL AND LEGAL CONDUCT

We know that organizations exert a powerful influence on their employees' actions. According to a study by the Ethics Resource Center of more than 2,000 employees in various businesses (2010), organizations with strong ethical cultures—organizations in which ethical values are promoted at all levels and employees see that everyone lives up to the organization's stated values—experience fewer ethical problems.

Companies can take specific steps to improve their ethical culture:

- The organization's leaders can set the right tone by living up to their commitment to ethical conduct.

- Supervisors can set good examples and encourage ethical conduct.

- Peers can support those employees who act ethically.

- The organization can use informal communication to reinforce the formal policies, such as those presented in a company code of conduct.

In other words, it is not enough for an organization to issue a statement that ethical and legal behavior is important. The organization has to create a culture that values and rewards ethical and legal behavior. That culture starts at the top and extends to all employees, and it permeates the day-to-day operations of the organization.

One company that has earned praise for its commitment to ethical and legal conduct is Texas Instruments (TI). Its culture is communicated on its Web site, which contains a comprehensive set of materials that describes how TI employees and suppliers are required to act, and why (Texas Instruments, 2010). The materials begin with a statement from the President and Chief Executive Officer, Rich Templeton:

> TI's products and markets have changed through the years, but our determination to maintain the values on which our company was founded remains true to this day. High ethical standards, a respect for individuals, a commitment to long-term relationships, a concern for the environment, and a sense of duty to our communities—these are the principles that bind us together and make TI a company of which we can all be proud.
>
> Innovation lies at the center of all we do, but great products, alone, aren't enough to win in the long run. In our business, trust matters, and a reputation for integrity is our most effective marketing tool. Our customers choose TI, not only for our technology, but also because we treat them with respect, deal with them fairly, and deliver on our promises. We strive to be a company they can count on, and that focus has played a huge role in our success.
>
> Throughout our company history, TI's commitment to high ethical standards has served our people, our customers and our communities. But it has also been good for business. Our determination to do the right thing demands that we look at problems

Notice that this statement outlines the company's core values—respect for people and the environment, trust in business relationships—and links those values to the business success that the company enjoys. Many companies today have a statement of values focusing on issues of character (such as respect, trust, honesty, and commitment).

from many perspectives and consider the full impact of our actions. As a result, we develop solutions that are more efficient, more creative, and more effective.

The TI site also includes a number of other statements and numerous other ethics resources, including the company's formal code of conduct for all employees, its code of ethics for company officers, information about the company's Ethics Office, links to all its ethics publications, its statement of ethics for its suppliers, and detailed information on how to contact the TI Ethics Office confidentially.

Does the culture improve conduct? That question is difficult to answer, but the TI site describes some of the major awards the company has won for its ethics program, presents data from its own employee surveys showing they think the company's ethical culture is good, and describes the company's outreach to communities and other organizations that have established their own ethics programs.

One important element of a culture of ethical and legal conduct is a formal code of conduct. Of the 200 largest corporations in the world, more than half have codes of conduct (Kaptein, 2004). In the United States, most large corporations have them, as do almost all professional societies. Codes of conduct vary greatly from organization to organization, but most of them address such issues as the following:

On the Web

To analyze a company's statement of values, click on Document Analysis Activities for Ch. 2 on <bedfordstmartins .com/ps>.

A code of conduct focuses on behavior, including such topics as adhering to the law.

- adhering to local laws and regulations, including those intended to protect the environment
- avoiding discrimination
- maintaining a safe and healthy workplace
- respecting privacy
- avoiding conflicts of interest
- protecting the company's intellectual property
- avoiding bribery and kickbacks in working with suppliers and customers

Many codes of conduct are only a few paragraphs long; others are lengthy and detailed, some consisting of several volumes.

An effective code has three major characteristics:

On the Web

For links to codes of conduct from around the world, see Codes of Conduct/Practice/ Ethics from Around the World. Click on Links Library for Ch. 2 on <bedfordstmartins .com/ps>.

- *It protects the public rather than members of the organization or profession.* For instance, the code should condemn unsafe building practices but not advertising, which increases competition and thus lowers prices.
- *It is specific and comprehensive.* A code is ineffective if it merely states that people must not steal, or if it does not address typical ethical offenses such as bribery in companies that do business in other countries.
- *It is enforceable.* A code is ineffective if it does not stipulate penalties, including dismissal from the company or expulsion from the profession.

Although many codes are too vague to be useful in determining whether a person has violated one of their principles, writing and implementing a code can be valuable because it forces an organization to clarify its own values and can foster an increased awareness of ethical issues. Texas Instruments, like many organizations, encourages employees to report ethical problems to a committee or a person—sometimes called an *ethics officer* or an *ombudsperson*—who investigates and reaches an impartial decision.

If you think there is a serious ethical problem in your organization, find out what resources your organization offers to deal with it. If there are no resources, work with your supervisor to solve the problem.

What do you do if you have exhausted all the resources at your organization and, if appropriate, the professional organization in your field? The next step will likely involve *whistle-blowing*—the practice of going public with information about serious unethical conduct within an organization. For example, an engineer is blowing the whistle when she tells a regulatory agency or a newspaper that quality-control tests on a company product were faked.

Ethicists such as Velasquez (2006) argue that whistle-blowing is justified if you have tried to resolve the problem through internal channels, if you have strong evidence that the problem is hurting or will hurt other parties, and if the whistle-blowing is reasonably certain to prevent or stop the wrongdoing. But Velasquez also points out that whistle-blowing is likely to hurt the employee, his or her family, and other parties. Whistle-blowers can be penalized through negative performance appraisals, transfers to undesirable locations, or isolation within the company.

COMMUNICATING ETHICALLY ACROSS CULTURES

Every year, the United States exports more than $1.8 trillion worth of goods and services to the rest of the world (U.S. Census Bureau, 2010, p. 1264). U.S. companies do not necessarily have the same ethical and legal obligations when they export as when they sell in the United States. For this reason, communicators should understand the basics of two aspects of writing for people in other countries: communicating with cultures with different ethical beliefs and communicating with countries with different laws.

Communicating with Cultures with Different Ethical Beliefs

Companies face special challenges when they market their products and services to people in other countries (and to people in their home countries who come from other cultures). Companies need to decide how to deal with situations in which the target culture's ethical beliefs clash with those of their own culture. For instance, in many countries, sexual discrimination makes it difficult for women to assume responsible positions in the workplace. If a U.S. company that sells computers, for example, wishes to present product information in such a country, should it reinforce this discrimination by excluding women from photographs of its products? Ethicist Thomas Donaldson argues that doing so is wrong (1991). Under the principle he calls the *moral minimum*, companies are ethically obligated not to reinforce patterns of discrimination in product information.

However, Donaldson argues, companies are not obligated to challenge the prevailing prejudice directly. A company is not obligated to include photographs that show women performing roles they do not normally perform within that culture, nor is it obligated to portray women wearing clothing, makeup, or jewelry that is likely to offend local standards. But there is nothing to prevent an organization from adopting a more activist stance. Organizations that actively oppose discrimination are acting admirably.

Communicating with Cultures with Different Laws

When U.S. companies export goods and services to other countries, they need to adhere to those countries' federal and regional laws. For instance, a company that wishes to export to Montreal must abide by the laws of Quebec Province and of Canada. A company that wishes to export to Germany must abide by the laws of Germany and of the European Union, of which it is a part.

Because exporting goods to countries with different laws is such a complex topic, companies that export devote considerable resources to finding out what they need to do, not only in designing and manufacturing products but also in writing the product information. For a good introduction to this topic, see Lipus (2006).

PRINCIPLES FOR ETHICAL COMMUNICATION

Although it is impossible to state principles for ethical communication that will guide you through all the challenges you will face communicating in the workplace, the following ten principles provide a starting point.

Abide by Copyright Law

When you want to publish someone else's copyrighted material, such as graphics you find on the Web, get written permission from the copyright owner.

Abide by the Appropriate Professional Code of Conduct

Your field's professional organization, such as the American Society of Civil Engineers, is likely to have a code that goes beyond legal issues to express ethical principles, such as telling the truth, reporting information accurately, respecting the privacy of others, and avoiding conflicts of interest.

Abide by Your Organization's Policy on Social Media

Most organizations have written policies about how employees may use social media. These policies address such issues as what kinds of Web sites employees may visit while at work, how employees should represent themselves and the organization both at work and outside of work, and whether employees may set up a blog on the organization's servers. You should abide by your organization's policies related to social media.

Take Advantage of Your Employer's Ethics Resources

Your employer is likely to have a code of conduct, as well as other resources, such as an ethics office or ombudsperson, that can help you find information to guide you in resolving ethical challenges you encounter. Your employer will likely have a mechanism for registering complaints about unethical conduct anonymously.

Tell the Truth

Sometimes, employees are asked to lie about their companies' products or about those of their competitors. Obviously, lying is unethical. Your responsibility is to resist this pressure, going over your supervisor's head if necessary.

Don't Mislead Your Readers

A misleading statement—one that invites or even encourages the reader to reach a false conclusion—is ethically no better than a lie. Avoid these four common kinds of misleading technical communication:

> **In This Book**
>
> For a more detailed discussion of misleading writing, see Ch. 6. For a discussion of avoiding misleading graphics, see Ch. 8.

- *False implications.* If you work for SuperBright and write, "Use only Super-Bright batteries in your new flashlight," you imply that only that brand will work. If that is untrue, the statement is misleading. Communicators sometimes use clichés such as *user-friendly*, *ergonomic*, and *state-of-the-art* to make the product sound better than it is. Use specific, accurate information to back up your claims about a product.

- *Exaggerations.* If you say, "Our new Operating System 2500 makes system crashes a thing of the past," but the product only makes them less likely, you are exaggerating. Provide the specific technical information on the reduction of crashes. Do not write, "We carried out extensive market research," if all you did was make a few phone calls.

In This Book
For techniques for writing clearly, including avoiding discriminatory language, see Ch. 6.

- *Legalistic constructions.* It is unethical to write, "The 3000X was designed to operate in extreme temperatures, from −40 degrees to 120 degrees Fahrenheit," if the product cannot operate reliably in those temperatures. Although the statement might technically be accurate—the product was *designed* to operate in those temperatures—it is misleading.
- *Euphemisms.* If you refer to someone's being fired, say *fired* or *released*, not *granted permanent leave* or *offered an alternative career opportunity.*

Use Design to Highlight Important Ethical and Legal Information

Courts have found that information that is buried in footnotes or printed in very small type violates the company's obligation to inform consumers and warn them about hazards in using a product. If you want to communicate safety information or other facts that readers need to know, use design features to make it easy to see and understand. Figure 2.2 shows how design principles can be used to communicate nutritional information in food labels.

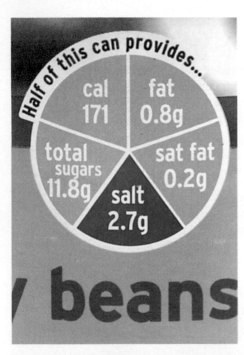

Figure 2.2 Using Design to Emphasize Important Information
This nutritional labeling system is called "traffic light labeling" because it uses red and green to indicate how healthy a food is.
Source: Alamy, 2011 <www .alamy.com>.

Be Clear

Clear writing helps your readers understand your message easily. Your responsibility is to write as clearly as you can to help your audience understand what you are saying. For instance, in writing a product warranty, make it as simple and straightforward as possible. Use tables of contents, indexes, and other accessing devices to help your readers find what they need.

Avoid Discriminatory Language

Don't use language that discriminates against people because of their sex, religion, ethnicity, race, sexual orientation, or physical or mental abilities. Employees have been disciplined or fired for sending inappropriate jokes through the company e-mail system.

Acknowledge Assistance from Others

Don't suggest that you did all the work yourself if you didn't. Cite your sources and your collaborators accurately and graciously. For more about citing sources, see Appendix, Part A.

Writer's Checklist

- ☐ Did you abide by copyright law? (p. 28)
- ☐ Did you abide by the appropriate corporate or professional code of conduct? (p. 29)
- ☐ Did you abide by your organization's policy on social media? (p. 29)
- ☐ Did you take advantage of your company's ethics resources? (p. 29)
- ☐ Did you tell the truth? (p. 29)

Did you avoid using

- ☐ false implications? (p. 29)
- ☐ exaggerations? (p. 29)

- ☐ legalistic constructions? (p. 30)
- ☐ euphemisms? (p. 30)

- ☐ Did you use design to highlight important ethical and legal information? (p. 30)
- ☐ Did you write clearly? (p. 30)
- ☐ Did you avoid discriminatory language? (p. 30)
- ☐ Did you acknowledge any assistance you received from others? (p. 30)

Exercises

▶ **In This Book** For more about memos, see Ch. 9, p. 223.

1. It is late April, and you need a summer job. In a local newspaper, you see an ad for a potential job. The only problem is that the ad specifically mentions that it is "a continuing, full-time position." You know that you will be returning to college in the fall. Is it ethical for you to apply for the job without mentioning this fact? Why or why not? If you feel it is unethical to withhold the information that you plan to return to college in the fall, is there any way you can ethically apply? Be prepared to share your ideas in class.

2. You serve on the Advisory Committee of your college's bookstore, which is a private business that leases space on campus and donates 10 percent of its profits to student scholarships. The head of the bookstore wishes to stock Simple Study Guides, a popular series of plot summaries and character analyses of classic literary works. In similar bookstores, the sale of Simple Study Guides yields annual profits of over $10,000. Six academic departments have signed a statement condemning the idea. Should you support the bookstore head or the academic departments? Be prepared to discuss your answer in class.

3. **INTERNET EXERCISE** Find an article or advertisement in a newspaper or magazine or on the Web that you feel contains untrue or misleading information. Write a memo to your instructor describing the ad and analyzing the unethical techniques. How might the information have been presented more honestly? Include a photocopy or a printout of the ad with your memo.

4. **GROUP EXERCISE** Form small groups. Study the Web site of a company or other organization that has a prominent role in your community or your academic field. Find the information about the organization's commitment to ethical and legal conduct. Often, organizations present this information in sections called "information for investors," "about the company," "values and principles of conduct," or similar titles.

- One group member could identify the section that states the organization's values. How effective is this section in presenting information that goes beyond general statements that ethical behavior is important?

- A second group member could identify the section that describes the organization's code of conduct. Does the organization seem to take ethical and legal behavior seriously? Can you get a clear idea from the description whether the organization has a specific, well-defined set of policies, procedures, and resources available for employees who wish to discuss ethical and legal issues?

- A third group member could identify any information related to the organization's commitment to the environment. What does the organization do, in its normal operations, to limit its carbon footprint or in other ways encourage responsible use of natural resources and limit damage to the environment?

- As a team, write a memo to your instructor presenting your findings. Attach the organization's code to your memo.

On the Web

For a case assignment, "The Ethics of Requiring That Students Subsidize a Plagiarism-Detection Service," see Cases on <bedfordstmartins.com/ps>.

3

Writing Collaboratively and Using Social Media

REUTERS/Thomas Peter/Landov.

Every document calls for a unique kind of collaboration.

The two people shown in this photo are using a touch table to work with digital images. A touch table is typical of new technologies that streamline the process of collaborating in technical communication. The explosive growth of social media over the last decade has greatly expanded the scope of workplace collaboration, reducing earlier barriers of time and space. Today, people routinely collaborate not only with members of their project teams but also with others within and outside their organization, as shown in Figure 3.1.

But how exactly does this sort of collaboration work? In every possible way. For example, you and your project team might use social media primarily to gather information that you will use in your research. You bring this information back to your team, and then you work exclusively with your team in drafting, revising, and proofreading

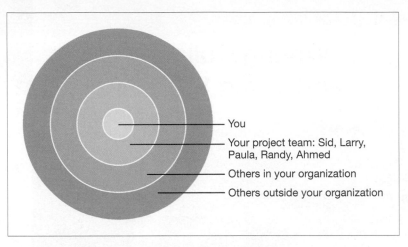

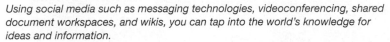

Figure 3.1 Collaboration Beyond the Project Team

Using social media such as messaging technologies, videoconferencing, shared document workspaces, and wikis, you can tap into the world's knowledge for ideas and information.

your document. In a more complex collaboration pattern, you and your team might use social media to gather information from sources around the globe and then reach out to others in your organization to see what they think of your new ideas. Later in the process, you create the outline of your document, in the form of a wiki, and authorize everyone in your own organization to draft sections, pose questions and comments, and even edit what others have written. In short, you can collaborate with any number of people at one or several stages of the writing process.

Every document is unique and will therefore call for a unique kind of collaboration. Your challenge is to think creatively about how you can work effectively with others to make your document as good as it can be. Being aware of the strengths and limitations of collaborative tools can prompt you to consider people in your building and around the world who can help you think about your subject and write about it compellingly and persuasively.

ADVANTAGES AND DISADVANTAGES OF COLLABORATION

As a student, you might have already worked collaboratively on course projects. As a professional, you will work on many more. In the workplace, the stakes might be higher. Effective collaboration can make you look like a star, but ineffective collaboration can ruin an important project—and hurt your reputation. The best way to start thinking about collaboration is to understand its main advantages and disadvantages.

Advantages of Collaboration

According to a recent survey conducted by Cisco Systems (2010), more than 75 percent of employees said that collaboration is critical to their success on the job. Some 90 percent said that collaboration makes them more productive. Writers who collaborate can create a better document and improve the way an organization functions:

- *Collaboration draws on a greater knowledge base.* Therefore, a collaborative document can be more comprehensive and more accurate than a single-author document.

- *Collaboration draws on a greater skills base.* No one person can be an expert manager, writer, editor, graphic artist, and production person.

- *Collaboration provides a better idea of how the audience will read the document.* Each collaborator acts as an audience, offering more questions and suggestions than one person could while writing alone.

- *Collaboration improves communication among employees.* Because many of your collaborators share a goal, they learn about each other's jobs, responsibilities, and frustrations.

- *Collaboration helps acclimate new employees to an organization.* New employees learn how things work—which people to see, which forms to fill out, and so forth—as well as what the organization values, such as the importance of ethical conduct and the willingness to work hard and sacrifice for an important initiative.

- *Collaboration motivates employees to help an organization grow.* New employees bring new skills, knowledge, and attitudes that can help the organization develop. More experienced employees mentor the new employees as they learn from them. Everyone teaches and learns from everyone else, and the organization benefits.

Disadvantages of Collaboration

Collaboration can also have important disadvantages:

- *Collaboration takes more time than individual writing.* It takes longer because of the time needed for the collaborators to communicate. In addition, meetings—whether they are live or remote—can be difficult to schedule.

- *Collaboration can lead to groupthink.* When collaborators value getting along more than thinking critically about the project, they are prone to *groupthink*. Groupthink, which promotes conformity, can result in an inferior document, because no one wants to cause a scene by asking tough questions.

- *Collaboration can yield a disjointed document.* Sections can contradict or repeat each other or be written in different styles. To prevent these problems, writers need to plan and edit the document carefully.

In This Book
For more about the writing process, see Ch. 1.

- *Collaboration can lead to inequitable workloads.* Despite the project leader's best efforts, some people will end up doing more work than others.
- *Collaboration can reduce a person's motivation to work hard on the document.* A collaborator who feels alienated from the team can lose motivation to make the extra effort.
- *Collaboration can lead to interpersonal conflict.* People can disagree about the best way to create the document or about the document itself. Such disagreements can hurt working relationships during the project and long after.

MANAGING PROJECTS

At some point in your academic career, you will likely collaborate on a course project that is just too big, too technical, and too difficult for your team to complete successfully without some advance planning and careful oversight. Often, collaborative projects are complex, lasting several weeks or months and involving the efforts of several people at scheduled times so that the project can proceed. For this reason, collaborators need to spend time managing the project to ensure that it not only meets the needs of the audience but also is completed on time and, if appropriate, within budget.

Guidelines

Managing Your Project

These seven suggestions can help you keep your project on track.

▶ **Break down a large project into several smaller tasks.** Working backward from what you must deliver to your client or manager, partition your project into its component parts, making a list of what steps your team must take to complete the project. This task is not only the foundation of project management but also a good strategy for determining the resources you will need to successfully complete the project on time. After you have a list of tasks to complete, you can begin to plan your project, assign responsibilities, and set deadlines.

▶ **Plan your project.** Planning allows collaborators to develop an effective approach and reach agreement before investing a lot of time and resources. Planning prevents small problems from becoming big problems with a deadline looming. Effective project managers use planning documents such as *needs analyses*, *information plans*, *specifications*, and *project plans*.

▶ **Create and maintain an accurate schedule.** An accurate schedule helps collaborators plan ahead, allocate their time, and meet deadlines. Update your schedule when changes are made, and place the up-to-date schedule in an easily accessible location (for example, on a project Web site) or send the schedule to each team member. If the team misses a deadline, immediately create a new deadline. Team members should always know when tasks must be completed.

▶ **Put your decisions in writing.** Writing down your decisions, and communicating them to all collaborators, helps the team remember what happened. In addition, if questions arise, the team can refer easily to the document and, if necessary, update it.

▶ **Monitor the project.** By regularly tracking the progress of the project, the team can learn what it has accomplished, whether the project is on schedule, and if any unexpected challenges have arisen.

▶ **Distribute and act on information quickly.** Acting fast to get collaborators the information they need helps ensure that the team makes effective decisions and steady progress toward completing the project.

▶ **Be flexible regarding schedule and responsibilities.** Adjust your plan and methods when new information becomes available or problems arise. When tasks depend on earlier tasks that are delayed or need reworking, the team should consider revising responsibilities to keep the project moving forward.

CONDUCTING MEETINGS

Successful collaboration involves meetings because human communication is largely nonverbal. That is, although people communicate through words and through the tone, rate, and volume of their speech, they also communicate through body language. For this reason, meetings provide the most information about what a person is thinking and feeling—and the best opportunity for team members to understand one another.

To help make meetings effective and efficient, team members should arrive on time and stick to the agenda. One team member should serve as secretary by recording the important decisions made at the meeting. At the end of the meeting, the team leader should summarize the team's accomplishments and state the tasks each team member is to perform before the next meeting. If possible, the secretary should give each team member this informal set of meeting minutes.

Whether you are meeting live in a room on campus or using videoconferencing tools, the three aspects of meetings discussed in this section can help you use your time productively and produce the best possible document.

Listening Effectively

Participating in a meeting involves listening and speaking. If you listen carefully to other people, you will understand what they are thinking and you will be able to speak knowledgeably and constructively. Unlike hearing, which involves receiving and processing sound waves, listening involves understanding what the speaker is saying and interpreting the information.

On the Web

For an excellent discussion of how to conduct meetings, see Matson (1996). Click on Links Library for Ch. 3 on <bedfordstmartins.com/ps>.

Guidelines

Listening Effectively

Follow these five steps to become a more effective listener.

▶ **Pay attention to the speaker.** Look at the speaker, and don't let your mind wander.

▶ **Listen for main ideas.** Pay attention to phrases that signal important information, such as "What I'm saying is . . ." or "The point I'm trying to make is. . . ."

▶ **Don't get emotionally involved with the speaker's ideas.** Even if you disagree, keep listening. Keep an open mind. Don't stop listening so that you can plan what you are going to say next.

▶ **Ask questions to clarify what the speaker said.** After the speaker finishes, ask questions to make sure you understand. For instance, "When you said that each journal recommends different printers, did you mean that each journal recommends several printers or that each journal recommends a different printer?"

▶ **Provide appropriate feedback.** The most important feedback is to look into the speaker's eyes. You can nod your approval to signal that you understand what he or she is saying. Appropriate feedback helps assure the speaker that he or she is communicating effectively.

Setting Your Team's Agenda

It's important to get your team off to a smooth start. In the first meeting, start to define your team's agenda.

Guidelines

Setting Your Team's Agenda

Carrying out these eight tasks will help your team work effectively and efficiently.

▶ **Define the team's task.** Every team member has to agree on the task, the deadline, and the length of the document. You also need to agree on more-conceptual points, including the document's audience, purpose, and scope.

▶ **Choose a team leader.** This person serves as the link between the team and management. (In an academic setting, the team leader represents the team in communicating with the instructor.) The team leader also keeps the team on track, leads the meetings, and coordinates communication among team members.

▶ **Define tasks for each team member.** There are three main ways to divide the tasks: according to technical expertise (for example, one team member, an engineer, is responsible for the information about engineering), according to stages of the writing process (one team member contributes to all stages, whereas another participates only during the planning stage), or according to sections of the document (several team members work on the whole document but others work only on, say, the appendixes). People will likely assume informal roles, too. One person might be good at clarifying what others have said, another at preventing unnecessary arguments, and another at asking questions that force the team to reevaluate its decisions.

▶ **Establish working procedures.** Before starting to work, collaborators need answers—in writing, if possible—to the following questions:

— When and where will we meet?

— What procedures will we follow in the meetings?

— What tools will we use to communicate with other team members, including the leader, and how often will we communicate?

▶ **Establish a procedure for resolving conflict productively.** Disagreements about the project can lead to a better product. Give collaborators a chance to express ideas fully and find areas of agreement, and then resolve the conflict with a vote.

▶ **Create a style sheet.** A style sheet defines the characteristics of writing style that the document will have. For instance, a style sheet states how many levels of headings the document will have, whether it will have lists, whether it will have an informal tone (using "you" and contractions), and so forth. If all collaborators draft using a similar writing style, the document will need less revision. And be sure to use styles to ensure a consistent design for headings and other textual features. (See the Tech Tip on page 162.)

▶ **Establish a work schedule.** For example, to submit a proposal on February 10, you must complete the outline by January 25, the draft by February 1, and the revision by February 8. These dates are called *milestones*.

▶ **Create evaluation materials.** Team members have a right to know how their work will be evaluated. In college, students often evaluate themselves and other team members. But in the working world, managers are more likely to do the evaluations.

On the Web

To download a work-schedule form and evaluation forms, click on Forms for Technical Communication on <bedfordstmartins.com/ps>.

ETHICS NOTE

Pulling Your Weight on Collaborative Projects

Collaboration involves an ethical dimension. If you work hard and well, you help the other members of the team. If you don't, you hurt them.

You can't be held responsible for knowing and doing everything, and sometimes unexpected problems arise in other courses or in your private life that prevent you from participating as actively and effectively as you otherwise could. When problems occur, inform the other team members as soon as possible. Be honest about what happened. Suggest ways you might make up for missing a task. If you communicate clearly, the other team members are likely to cooperate with you.

If you are a member of a team that includes someone who is not participating fully, keep records of your attempts to get in touch with that person. When you do make contact, you owe it to that person to try to find out what the problem is and suggest ways to resolve it. Your goal is to treat that person fairly and to help him or her do better work, so that the team will function more smoothly and more effectively.

Communicating and Critiquing Diplomatically

Because collaborating can be stressful, it can lead to interpersonal conflict. People can become frustrated and angry with one another because of personality clashes or because of disputes about the project. If the project is to succeed, however, team members have to work together productively. When you speak in a team meeting, you want to appear helpful, not critical or overbearing.

In collaborating, team members often critique notes and drafts written by other team members. Knowing how to do it without offending the writer is a valuable skill.

Guidelines

Communicating Diplomatically

These seven suggestions will help you communicate effectively.

▶ **Listen carefully, without interrupting.** See the Guidelines box on page 38.

▶ **Give everyone a chance to speak.** Don't dominate the discussion.

▶ **Avoid personal remarks and insults.** Be tolerant and respectful of other people's views and working methods. Doing so is right—and smart: if you anger people, they will go out of their way to oppose you.

▶ **Don't overstate your position.** A modest qualifier such as "I think" or "it seems to me" is an effective signal to your listeners that you realize that everyone might not share your views.

| OVERBEARING | My plan is a sure thing; there's no way we're not going to kill Allied next quarter. |
| DIPLOMATIC | I think this plan has a good chance of success: we're playing off our strengths and Allied's weaknesses. |

Note that in the diplomatic version, the speaker calls it "this plan," not "my plan."

▶ **Don't get emotionally attached to your own ideas.** When people oppose you, try to understand why. Digging in is usually unwise—unless it's a matter of principle—because, although you may be right and everyone else wrong, it's not likely.

▶ **Ask pertinent questions.** Bright people ask questions to understand what they hear and to connect it to other ideas. Asking questions also encourages other team members to examine what they hear.

▶ **Pay attention to nonverbal communication.** Bob might *say* that he understands a point, but his facial expression might show that he doesn't. If a team member looks confused, ask him or her about it. A direct question is likely to elicit a statement that will help the team clarify its discussion.

Guidelines

Critiquing a Colleague's Work

Most people are very sensitive about their writing. Following these three suggestions for critiquing writing increases the chances that your colleague will consider your ideas positively.

▶ **Start with a positive comment.** Even if the work is weak, say, "You've obviously put a lot of work into this, Joanne. Thanks." Or, "This is a really good start. Thanks, Joanne."

▶ **Discuss the larger issues first.** Begin with the big issues, such as organization, development, logic, design, and graphics. Then work on smaller issues, such as paragraph development, sentence-level matters, and word choice. Leave editing and proofreading until the end of the process.

▶ **Talk about the document, not the writer.**

RUDE	You don't explain clearly why this criterion is relevant.
BETTER	I'm having trouble understanding how this criterion relates to the topic.

Your goal is to improve the quality of the document you will submit, not to evaluate the writer or the draft. Offer constructive suggestions.

RUDE	Why didn't you include the price comparisons here, like you said you would?
BETTER	I wonder if the report would be stronger if we include the price comparisons here.

In the better version, the speaker focuses on the goal—to create an effective report—rather than on the writer's draft. Also, the speaker qualifies his recommendation by saying, "I wonder if. . . ." This approach sounds constructive rather than boastful or annoyed.

USING SOCIAL MEDIA AND OTHER ELECTRONIC TOOLS IN COLLABORATION

The tremendous growth of social media such as Facebook, YouTube, and Twitter in the general population is reflected in the working world. Although few of the social media sites were created to be used in the working world, most of them are used by professionals as business tools. Today, entrepreneurs are creating business-specific versions of some of the popular social media, such as Twitter-like microblogs that can be integrated with the rest of the organization's digital infrastructure and protected behind the organization's firewall to reduce security threats.

Managers in business, industry, and government around the world encourage employees to use social media to find information, create and

DOCUMENT ANALYSIS ACTIVITY
Critiquing a Draft Clearly and Diplomatically

This is an excerpt from the methods section of a report about computer servers. In this section, the writer is explaining the tasks he performed in analyzing different servers. In a later section, he explains what he learned from the analysis. The comments in the balloons were inserted into the document by the author's colleague.

The questions ask you to think about techniques for critiquing (as outlined on page 41).

1. What is the tone of the comments? How can they be improved?

2. How well does the collaborator address the larger issues?

3. How well does the collaborator address the writing, not the writer?

4. How well do the collaborator's comments focus on the goal of the document, rather than judge the quality of the writing?

On the Web

To submit your responses to your instructor, click on Document Analysis Activities for Ch. 3 on <bedfordstmartins .com/ps>.

The first task of the on-site evaluations was to set up and configure each server. We noted the relative complexity of setting up each system to our network.

> Comment: Huh? What exactly does this mean?

After we had the system configured, we performed a set of routine maintenance tasks: add a new memory module, swap a hard drive, swap a power supply, and perform system diagnostics.

> Comment: Okay, good. Maybe we should explain why we chose these tests.

We recorded the time and relative difficulty of each task. Also, we tried to gather a qualitative feeling for how much effort would be involved in the day-to-day maintenance of the systems.

> Comment: What kind of scale are you using? If we don't explain it, it's basically useless.

> Comment: Same question as above.

After each system was set up, we completed the maintenance evaluations and began the benchmark testing. We ran the complete WinBench and NetBench test suites on each system. We chose several of the key factors from these tests for comparison.

> Comment: Will readers know these are the right tests? Should we explain?

---

sustain relationships with stakeholders (such as other organizations, customers, suppliers, and the general public), recruit and retain workers, and keep employees informed about the organization's new products, services, and initiatives.

Because social media make it convenient for people to participate in the work of their organizations, they are having a profound effect on the ways that information is created and distributed in the working world. In a traditional organization that relies primarily on face-to-face meetings, only those who are invited to the meeting get to participate fully—and the organization benefits from the knowledge and ideas of only those people. However, an organization that relies on social media can tap into the knowledge and ideas of everyone in the organization—and many others outside the organization.

Different types of electronic tools facilitate the kind of broad, two-way interchange of information and ideas that is fundamental to effective collaboration. Word processors offer three powerful features you will find useful: the comment feature, the revision feature, and the highlighting

CHOICES AND STRATEGIES   Choosing Appropriate Tools for Collaboration

If you want to . . .	Consider using these collaboration tools
Collaborate on documents	**Word-processing tools.** Readers can add electronic comments to your file, highlight portions of the document, and make changes by adding, deleting, and revising text.
	A shared document workspace. Users can write, edit, and share documents that are stored online. Files can be uploaded to and downloaded from the online workspace.
	A wiki. Authorized users can contribute to and edit a Web-based document on an ongoing basis.
Communicate with team members and send files	**E-mail.** You can send and receive text-based messages asynchronously and share files such as documents, photographs, and videos.
	Text messaging. You can exchange brief messages by phone that can include images, audio, and video.
Communicate with team members in real time	**Instant messaging.** You can exchange text-based messages synchronously.
	Videoconferencing. Two or more people at different locations can see and hear each other as well as share documents, video, and other data.
Discuss topics and solicit responses from many people	**A discussion board.** Authorized users can participate in threaded discussions of a topic.
	A blog. Individuals and organizations can publish news, commentary, videos, and other information periodically. Readers can comment on blog entries and respond to others' comments.
	A microblog. You can post quick questions or comments to people in your community and receive responses.

feature. The Tech Tip on page 44 shows how to take advantage of these features. The following discussion highlights the other major technologies that enable collaboration, including messaging technologies, videoconferencing, shared document workspaces, and wikis, discussion boards, and blogs.

Messaging Technologies

Two messaging technologies have been around for decades: instant messaging and e-mail. In the last decade, several new technologies have been introduced that are made to function on mobile devices. Of these, the two most popular are text messaging and microblogging.

▶ **In This Book**
For more about writing e-mail, see Ch. 9, p. 232.

TECH TIP

How to Use the Review Tab

When collaborating with others, you can distribute your document to readers electronically so that they can add comments, revise text, and highlight text. You can then review their comments, keep track of who made which changes, compare two versions, and decide whether to accept or decline changes without ever having to print your document. You can use the **Review** tab to electronically review a document or to revise a document that readers have already commented on.

1. Select the **Review** tab to access the **Comments**, **Tracking**, **Changes**, and **Compare** groups.

2. To **electronically review** a document, highlight the relevant text and do the following:

 Select the **New Comment** button in the **Comments** group to write comments in a bubble in the margin.

Select the **Track Changes** button to distinguish between revised text and original text.

 On the **Home** tab in the **Font** group, select the **Text Highlight** button to emphasize a particular passage.

Answering the Central Research Questions

Regarding the history and background of the white paper genre, we have seen that the white paper began in Britain as a statement of government policy. The term was later applied to technical documents describing aspects of the development and use of atomic weapons in the Manhattan Project of World War II. While white papers continue to be used as descriptive and explanatory documents in various technical fields, the term was applied to research and development documents in the 1960s. These documents were shared with select customers to aid the sales and marketing process. The technology boom of the 1980s and 1990s led vendors to use white papers as technical marketing documents for educating prospective customers. As the technology sector has become

Comment [RW2]: Capitalized

Formatted: Highlight

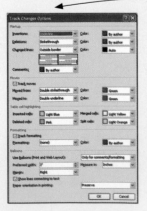 To change the color or design of comment bubbles or markup, select the **Track Changes** button in the **Tracking** group, and select **Change Tracking Options**. The **Track Changes Options** dialog box will appear.

3. To **revise a document** that reviewers have already commented on, you can do the following:

Use the **Tracking** group to change how the document is displayed.

Select buttons in the **Changes** group to see the **previous** or **next** comment and to **accept** or **reject** a change.

Select the **Reviewing Pane** button to review all comments and changes.

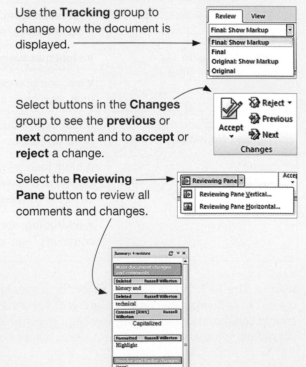

KEYWORDS: review tab, comments group, tracking group, changes group, compare group

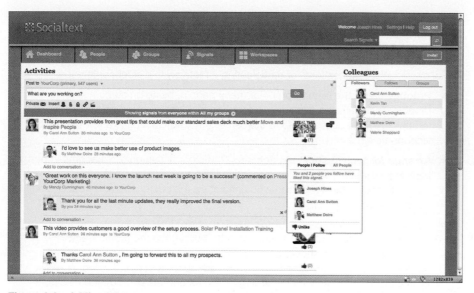

Figure 3.2   A Microblog
Source: Socialtext, 2010 <www.socialtext.com/products/desktop.php>.

Text messaging—a technology for sending messages that can include text, audio, images, and video—is the fastest-growing technology for exchanging messages electronically because most people keep their phones nearby. Organizations use text messaging for such tasks as sending a quick update or alerting people that an item has been delivered or a task completed.

Microblogging is a technology for sending very brief textual messages to your personal network. The world's most popular microblog, Twitter, now has more than half a billion users. Although some organizations use Twitter, many use Twitter-like microblogs such as Yammer, which includes a search function and other features. Figure 3.2 shows a screen from Socialtext, another microblog.

Videoconferencing

Videoconferencing technology allows two or more people at different locations to simultaneously see and hear one another as well as exchange documents, share data on computer displays, and use electronic whiteboards. Systems

Guidelines

Participating in a Videoconference

Follow these six suggestions for participating effectively in a videoconference.

▶ **Practice using the technology.** For many people, being on camera is uncomfortable, especially the first time. Before participating in a high-stakes videoconference, become accustomed to the camera by participating in a few informal videoconferences.

▶ **Arrange for tech support at each site.** Participants can quickly become impatient or lose interest when someone is fumbling to make the technology work. Each site should have a person who can set up the equipment and troubleshoot if problems arise.

▶ **Organize the room to encourage participation.** If there is more than one person at the site, arrange the chairs so that they face the monitor and camera. Each person should be near a microphone. Before beginning the conference, check that each location has adequate audio and video as well as access to other relevant technology such as computer monitors. Finally, remember to introduce everyone in the room, even those off camera, to everyone participating in the conference.

▶ **Make eye contact with the camera.** Eye contact is an important element of establishing your professional persona. The physical setup of some videoconferencing systems means you will likely spend most of your time looking at your monitor and not directly into the camera. However, this might give your viewers the impression that you are avoiding eye contact. Make a conscious effort periodically to look directly into the camera when speaking.

▶ **Dress as you would for a face-to-face meeting.** Wearing inappropriate clothing can distract participants and damage your credibility.

▶ **Minimize distracting noises and movements.** Sensitive microphones can magnify the sound of shuffling papers, fingers tapping on tables, and whispering. Likewise, depending on your position in the picture frame, excessive movements can be distracting.

such as Skype are simple and inexpensive, requiring only a Webcam and some free software. However, there are also large, dedicated systems that require extensive electronics, including cameras, servers, and a fiber-optic network or high-speed telephone lines.

Shared Document Workspaces and Wikis

A *shared document workspace* such as Microsoft SharePoint or Google Docs archives all the revisions made to a file by each of the team members, so that the team can create a single document that incorporates selected revisions. Some shared document workspaces enable a user to download the document, revise it on his or her own computer, and then upload it again. This feature makes it extremely convenient because the user does not need to be connected to the Internet to work on the document.

A *wiki* is a Web-based document that authorized users can write and edit. The best-known example of a wiki is Wikipedia, an online encyclopedia that contains millions of articles written and edited by people around the world. In the working world, wikis are used for creating many kinds of documents, such as instructions, manuals, and policy documents. For instance, many organizations create their policies on using social media by setting up wikis and inviting employees to write and edit what others have written. The concept is that a wiki draws upon the expertise and insights of people throughout the organization and, sometimes, outside the organization. Figure 3.3 shows a portion of a wiki.

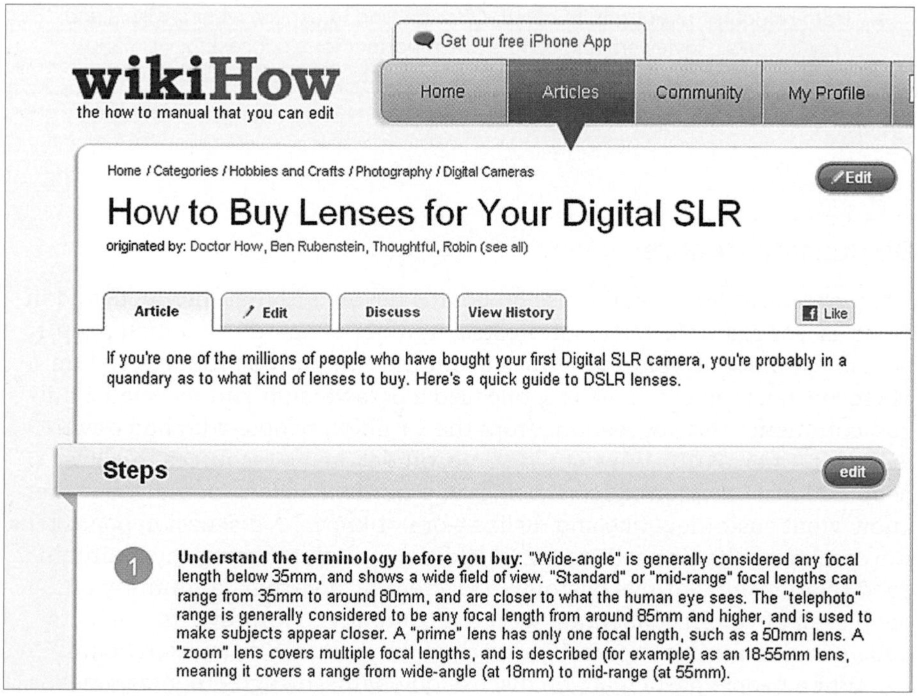

This portion of a screen from wikiHow shows an excerpt from an article about how to buy lenses for a digital SLR camera. Users can click on the Edit tab or Edit buttons to edit the article; on the Discuss tab to post questions and answers; and on the View History tab to see any of the previous versions of the article.

Figure 3.3   A Wiki

Source: wikiHow, 2010 <www.wikihow.com/Buy-Lenses-for-Your-Digital-SLR>.

Guidelines

Using and Participating in Wikis Effectively

These six suggestions will help you get the most from wikis.

▶ **Know your audience.** Find out what your audience needs from your wiki, and then develop a plan to provide it.

▶ **Keep your wiki up-to-date.** Current information is valuable. Check the wiki periodically to correct outdated and inaccurate information and to generate ideas for new content.

▶ **Integrate the wiki with other documentation.** A familiar look and feel will encourage participation from users, and it will help your organization maintain its image.

▶ **Integrate the wiki within your community.** Wikis work best when supported by a community of users who share interests and goals. Get management support to make the wiki a part of your organization's culture.

▶ **Make organization a high priority.** Create category pages to organize content. Contact authors of uncategorized pages to suggest potential locations for their pages.

▶ **Help reluctant users get involved.** Offer training to explain what a wiki is and how it works. Reviewers and editors are important for a successful wiki, and serving in those roles may help users develop into more active participants.

Discussion Boards

Many organizations host discussion boards devoted to their products and industries. For example, Microsoft hosts a number of boards on which people post questions, answers, and gripes about the company's products. Before Microsoft released Office 2010, it released a beta version and received 2 million comments and suggestions from the 9 million people who had downloaded it (Chen, 2010). Why would Microsoft devote its resources to allow people to discuss its products? Well, if you were Microsoft, would you rather know what customers like and dislike—or not know? A discussion board tells the company what it needs to fix. In addition, it helps a company maintain a good relationship with its customers by creating a virtual community of people, all of whom collaborate with the company to improve its products and customer service. Figure 3.4 shows a screen from a discussion board.

When people participate on discussion boards, disagreements sometimes arise. Avoid the temptation to respond to one disparaging comment with another, especially if you are posting as a member of an organization, not just a private citizen.

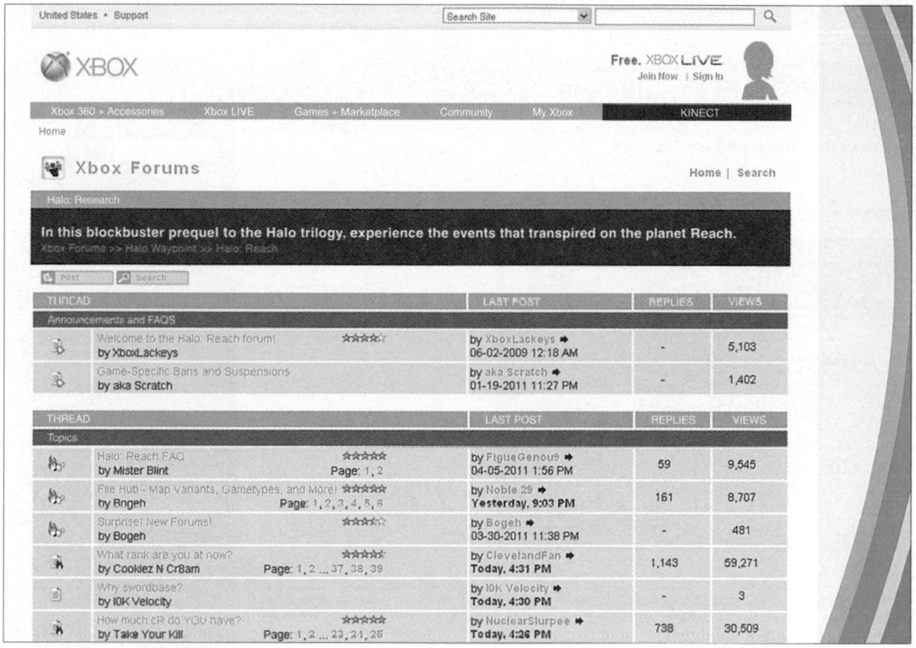

Figure 3.4   A Discussion Board
Source: Microsoft, 2011 <http://forums.xbox.com/1496/ShowForum.aspx>.

This discussion board, for fans of a popular game, begins with announcements and FAQs from the site moderators and then presents threads from users.

Guidelines

Participating in Discussion Boards

The following six guidelines will help you post to discussion boards responsibly.

▶ **Share your knowledge.** Because discussion boards thrive when members share what they know, participate by posting when you can contribute something of value.

▶ **Do your homework before posting a question.** Before you ask a question, search the archives and check other sources to see if an answer is already available.

▶ **Support your claims with evidence.** Provide specific data to back up your statements.

▶ **Stay on topic.** Follow the posted guidelines, and make sure that your posts are relevant to the topic.

▶ **Avoid personal attacks.** Avoid *flame wars*, which are angry exchanges on discussion boards and e-mail lists. No one benefits from them, and other forum participants tire of them quickly.

▶ **Disclose potential conflicts of interest.** If your connection with a person, a company, or a competitor could affect your writing or how readers interpret it, say so.

Because NASA is a taxpayer-supported government agency, its employees blog extensively to help build and maintain public support for its missions.

Figure 3.5   A Blog
Source: National Aeronautic and Space Administration, 2011 <http://blogs.nasa.gov/cm/blog/fragileoasis/posts/post_1307836834103>.

Blogs

Many large organizations host blogs written by their executives as well as by typical workers. Reporters and columnists working for major newspapers such as the *New York Times*, engineers, physicians, athletes—whatever the field, people and organizations are blogging to present information about their workplace and to learn from their readers' comments. Organizations encourage blogging because it can make them seem less impersonal, thereby helping them build relationships with the public. Figure 3.5 shows a blog written by a NASA astronaut.

Guidelines

Being a Responsible Blogger

To blog more effectively, follow these six suggestions.

▶ **Know and follow your company's blogging policies.** Do not start a work blog without approval from management. Ensure that your personal blogging won't jeopardize your employment.

▶ **Provide good content without saying too much.** Information that is current, accurate, and interesting will attract readers, but do not reveal sensitive information such as trade secrets. Bloggers have been disciplined and fired for divulging trade secrets or revealing that the company is being investigated by a government regulatory agency, leading investors to sell their company stock.

▶ **Use an authentic voice.** Readers want to read blogs written by "real people." If you spin the facts or insist that everything is perfect, you will lose your credibility, and then your readers.

▶ **Avoid conflicts of interest.** If your relationship with a person, a company, or a competitor could affect what you write or how readers interpret what they read, disclose it. Some companies try to bribe bloggers. For instance, several software manufacturers have been caught giving bloggers free software—and the hardware on which to run it.

▶ **Manage your time carefully.** Blogging often takes more time than you expect. Take enough time to write effectively, but don't let blogging interfere with your other duties.

▶ **Follow up on negative comments.** Briefly acknowledge any negative comments made on a work-related blog, and then make sure the right people see them. Don't let problems fall through the cracks.

ETHICS NOTE

Maintaining a Professional Presence Online

According to a reputable report from Cisco Systems (2010), half of the surveyed employees claim to routinely ignore company guidelines that prohibit the use of social media for non-work-related uses during company time. When you use your organization's social media at work, be sure to act professionally so that your actions reflect positively on you and your organization. Be aware of several important legal and ethical issues related to social media.

Although the law has not always kept pace with recent technological innovations, a few things are clear. You and your organization can be held liable if you make defamatory statements (statements that are untrue and damaging) about people or organizations, publish private information (such as trade secrets) or something that publicly places an individual "in a false light," publish personnel information, harass others, or participate in criminal activity.

In addition, follow these guidelines to avoid important ethical pitfalls:

- Don't waste company time using social media for nonbusiness purposes. You owe your employer a duty of diligence (hard work).

- Don't divulge secure information, such as a login and password that exposes your organization to unauthorized access, and don't reveal information about products that have not yet been released.

- Don't divulge private information about anyone. Private information relates to such issues as religion, politics, and sexual orientation.

- Don't make racist or sexist comments or post pictures of people drinking.

 **In This Book**
For more about your obligations to your employer, see Ch. 2, p. 20.

If your organization has a written policy on the use of social media, study it carefully. Ask questions if anything in it is unclear. If the policy is incomplete, work to make it complete. If there is no policy, work to create one.

For an excellent discussion of legal and ethical aspects of using your organization's social media, see Kaupins and Park (2010).

Writer's Checklist

In managing your project, did you

- [ ] break down a large project into several smaller tasks? (p. 36)
- [ ] plan your project? (p. 36)
- [ ] create and maintain an accurate schedule? (p. 36)
- [ ] put your decisions in writing? (p. 37)
- [ ] monitor the project? (p. 37)
- [ ] distribute and act on information quickly? (p. 37)
- [ ] act flexibly regarding schedule and responsibilities? (p. 37)

To conduct efficient meetings, do you

- [ ] arrive on time? (p. 37)
- [ ] stick to the agenda? (p. 37)
- [ ] make sure that a team member records important decisions made at the meeting? (p. 37)
- [ ] make sure that the leader summarizes the team's accomplishments and that every member understands what his or her tasks are? (p. 37)

In your first team meeting, did you

- [ ] define the team's task? (p. 38)
- [ ] choose a team leader? (p. 38)
- [ ] define tasks for each team member? (p. 38)
- [ ] establish working procedures? (p. 39)
- [ ] establish a procedure for resolving conflict productively? (p. 39)
- [ ] create a style sheet? (p. 39)
- [ ] establish a work schedule? (p. 39)
- [ ] create evaluation materials? (p. 39)

To communicate diplomatically, do you

- [ ] listen carefully, without interrupting? (p. 40)
- [ ] give everyone a chance to speak? (p. 40)
- [ ] avoid personal remarks and insults? (p. 40)
- [ ] avoid overstating your position? (p. 40)
- [ ] avoid getting emotionally attached to your own ideas? (p. 40)
- [ ] ask pertinent questions? (p. 40)
- [ ] pay attention to nonverbal communication? (p. 40)

In critiquing a team member's work, do you

- [ ] start with a positive comment? (p. 41)
- [ ] discuss the larger issues first? (p. 41)
- [ ] talk about the document, not the writer? (p. 41)

- [ ] If appropriate, do you use the comment, revision, and highlighting features of your word processor? (p. 44)

In participating in a videoconference, do you

- [ ] practice using videoconferencing technology? (p. 46)
- [ ] arrange for tech support at each site? (p. 46)
- [ ] organize the room to encourage participation? (p. 46)
- [ ] make eye contact with the camera? (p. 46)
- [ ] dress as you would for a face-to-face meeting? (p. 46)
- [ ] minimize distracting noises and movements? (p. 46)

Does your wiki

- [ ] show that you understand the specific needs of its audience? (p. 48)
- [ ] present up-to-date information? (p. 48)
- [ ] integrate well with other documentation? (p. 48)
- [ ] have a helpful organizational scheme? (p. 48)

Does your discussion-board post

- [ ] share your knowledge with the group? (p. 49)
- [ ] show that you have already checked relevant archives for answers to your questions? (p. 49)
- [ ] use evidence to support your claims? (p. 49)
- [ ] stay on topic? (p. 49)
- [ ] avoid personal attacks? (p. 49)
- [ ] disclose potential conflicts of interest? (p. 49)

Does your blog

- [ ] adhere to company policies? (p. 50)
- [ ] provide good content without saying too much? (p. 51)
- [ ] use an authentic voice? (p. 51)
- [ ] avoid conflicts of interest? (p. 51)

Exercises

In This Book　For more about memos, see Ch. 9, p. 223.

1. Experiment with the comment, revision, and highlighting features of your word processor. Using online help if necessary, learn how to make, revise, and delete comments; make, undo, and accept revisions; and add and delete highlights.

2. **INTERNET EXERCISE**　Using a search engine, find free videoconferencing software on the Internet. Download the software, and install it on your computer at home. Learn how to use the feature that lets you send attached files.

3. **INTERNET EXERCISE**　Using a wiki site such as wikiHow .com, find a set of instructions on a technical process that interests you. Study one of the revisions to the instructions, noting the types of changes made. Do the changes relate to the content of the instructions, to the use of graphics, or to the correctness of the writing? Be prepared to share your findings with the class.

4. You have probably had a lot of experience working in collaborative teams in previous courses or on the job. Brainstorm for five minutes, listing some of your best and worst experiences participating in collaborative teams. Choose one positive experience and one negative experience. Think about why the positive experience went well. Was there a technique that a team member used that accounted for the positive experience? Think about why the negative experience went wrong. Was there a technique or action that accounted for the negative experience? How might the negative experience have been prevented—or fixed? Be prepared to share your responses with the class.

5. **INTERNET EXERCISE**　Your college or university wishes to update its Web site to include a section called "For Prospective International Students." With the members of your team, first determine whether your school already has information of particular interest to prospective international students. If it does, write a memo to your instructor describing and evaluating the information. Is it accurate? Comprehensive? Clear? Useful? What kind of information should be added to the site to make it more effective?

   If the school's site does not have this information, perform the following two tasks:

   - *Plan.* What kind of information should this new section include? Does some of this information already exist elsewhere on the Web, or does it all have to be created from scratch? For example, can you create a link to an external site with information on how to obtain a student visa? Write an outline of the main topics that should be covered.

   - *Draft.* Write the following sections: "Where to Live on or Near Campus," "Social Activities on or Near Campus," and "If English Is Not Your Native Language." What graphics could you include? Are they already available? What other sites should you link to for these three sections?

   In a memo, present your suggestions to your instructor.

On the Web

For a case assignment, "Accommodating a Team Member's Scheduling Problems," see Cases on <bedfordstmartins.com/ps>.

PART 2

Planning and Drafting the Document

4

Analyzing Your Audience and Purpose

Blend/Glow Images.

Audience and purpose determine everything about how you communicate on the job.

In the workplace you will communicate with many people with different backgrounds and needs. Your challenge is to select the information each person needs and present it so that it helps each person do his or her job.

The key concept in technical communication is that audience and purpose determine everything about how you communicate on the job. As a nurse, for example, you would need to communicate information to both doctors and patients. You'd likely use different language with these two audiences and have different goals in relaying the information to each party. As a sales manager, you would communicate information about your products to potential clients; you'd communicate that same information differently to other sales representatives that you're training to work with you.

What can go wrong when you don't analyze your audience? McDonald's Corporation found out when it printed takeout bags decorated with flags from around the world. Among them was the flag of Saudi Arabia, which contains scripture from the Koran. This was extremely offensive to Muslims, who considered it sacrilegious to throw out the bags. The chain's sales went way down.

Throughout this chapter, the text will refer to your *reader* and your *document*. But all of the information refers as well to oral presentations, which are the subject of Chapter 15, and to nonprint applications.

DETERMINING THE IMPORTANT CHARACTERISTICS OF YOUR AUDIENCE

When you analyze the members of your audience, you are trying to learn what you can about their technical background and knowledge, their reasons for reading or listening to you, their attitudes and expectations, and how they will use the information you provide.

Who Are Your Readers?

For each of your most important readers, consider six factors:

- *The reader's education.* Think not only about the person's degree but also about when the person earned the degree. A civil engineer who earned a BS in 1993 has a much different background from a person who earned the same degree in 2013. Also consider any formal education or training the person completed while on the job.

  Knowing your reader's educational background helps you determine how much supporting material to provide, what level of vocabulary to use, what kind of sentence structure and length to use, what types of graphics to include, and whether to provide such elements as a glossary or an executive summary.

- *The reader's professional experience.* A nurse with a decade of experience might have represented her hospital on a community committee to encourage citizens to give blood and might have contributed to the planning for the hospital's new delivery room. These experiences would have provided several areas of competence or expertise that you should consider as you plan the document.

- *The reader's job responsibility.* Consider the major job responsibility of your reader and how your document will help that person accomplish it. For example, if you are writing a feasibility study on ways to cool the air for a new office building and you know that your reader oversees operating expenses, you should explain how you are estimating future utility costs.

On the Web

For an audience profile sheet, which will help you think of audience characteristics, click on Forms for Technical Communication on <bedfordstmartins.com/ps>.

- *The reader's personal characteristics.* The reader's age might suggest how he or she will read and interpret your document. A senior manager at age 60 is probably less interested in tomorrow's technology than a 30-year-old manager is. Does your reader have any other personal characteristics, such as impaired vision, that would affect the way you write and design your document?

- *The reader's personal preferences.* One reader might hate to see the first-person pronoun *I* in technical documents. Another might prefer one type of application (such as blogs or memos) over another. Try to accommodate as many of your reader's preferences as you can.

- *The reader's cultural characteristics.* Understanding cultural characteristics can help you appeal to your reader's interests and avoid confusing or offending him or her. As discussed later in this chapter (page 63), cultural characteristics can affect virtually every aspect of a reader's comprehension of a document and perception of the writer.

Why Is Your Audience Reading Your Document?

On the Web

For more about audience analysis, see Writing Guidelines for Engineering and Science Students. Click on Links Library for Ch. 4 on <bedfordstmartins.com/ps>.

For each of your most important readers, consider why he or she is reading your document. Some writers find it helpful to classify readers into categories—such as primary, secondary, and tertiary—each of which identifies a reader's distance from the writer. Here are some common descriptions of three categories of readers:

- A *primary audience* consists of people who use the document in carrying out their jobs. For example, they might include the writer's team members, who assisted in carrying out an analysis of a new server configuration for the IT department; the writer's supervisor, who reads it to decide whether to authorize its main recommendation; an executive, who reads it to determine how high a rank the server project should have on a list of projects to fund; and a business analyst, who reads it to determine how the organization can pay for the project.

- A *secondary audience* consists of people who need to stay aware of developments in the organization but who will not directly act on or respond to the document. Examples include managers of other departments who need to be aware of the project's broad outlines; and representatives from the marketing and legal departments, who need to check that the document conforms to the company's standards and practices and with relevant legal standards, such as antidiscrimination or intellectual-property laws.

- A *tertiary audience* consists of people farther removed from the writer who might take an interest in the subject of the report. Examples include interest groups (such as environmental groups); local, state, and federal government officials; and the general public. Even if the report is not intended to be distributed outside the organization, given today's climate of information access and the ease with which documents can be distributed, chances are good that it will be made available to outsiders.

Regardless of whether you classify your readers using a scheme such as this, think hard about why the most important audience members will be reading your document. Don't be content to list only one purpose. Your direct supervisor, for example, might have several purposes that you want to keep in mind:

- to learn what you have accomplished in the project
- to determine whether to approve any of your recommendations
- to determine whether to assign you to a follow-up team that will work on the next stage of the project
- to determine how to evaluate your job performance next month

You will use all of this information about your audience as you determine the ways it affects how you will write your document or plan your presentation. In the meantime, record it so you can refer to it later.

What Are Your Readers' Attitudes and Expectations?

In thinking about the attitudes and expectations of each of your most important readers, consider these three factors:

- *Your reader's attitude toward you.* Most people will like you because you are hardworking, intelligent, and cooperative. Some won't. If a reader's animosity toward you is irrational or unrelated to the current project, try to earn that person's respect and trust by meeting him or her on some neutral ground, perhaps by discussing other projects or some shared interest, such as gardening or science-fiction novels.

- *Your reader's attitude toward the subject.* If possible, discuss the subject thoroughly with your primary readers to determine whether they are positive, neutral, or negative toward it. The Choices and Strategies box on page 60 suggests some basic strategies for responding to different attitudes.

- *Your reader's expectations about the document.* Think about how your readers expect to see the information treated in terms of scope, organizational pattern, and amount of detail. Consider, too, the application. If your reader expects to receive a memo, use a memo unless some other format would clearly work better.

CHOICES AND STRATEGIES   Responding to Readers' Attitudes

If . . .	Try this
Your reader is neutral or positively inclined toward your subject	Write the document so that it responds to the reader's needs; make sure that vocabulary, level of detail, organization, and style are appropriate.
Your reader is hostile to the subject or to your approach to it	• Answer the objections directly. Explain why the objections are not valid or are less important than the benefits. • Organize the document so that your recommendation follows your explanation of the benefits. This strategy encourages the hostile reader to understand your argument rather than to reject it out of hand. • Avoid describing the subject as a dispute. Seek areas of agreement and concede points. Avoid trying to persuade readers overtly. Instead, suggest that there are new facts that need to be considered.
Your reader was instrumental in creating the policy or procedure that you are arguing is ineffective	In discussing the present system's shortcomings, be especially careful if you risk offending a reader. Don't write, "The present system for logging customer orders is completely ineffective." Instead, write, "While the present system has worked well for many years, new developments in electronic processing of orders might enable us to improve logging speed and reduce errors substantially."

How Will Your Readers Use Your Document?

In thinking about how your reader will use your document, consider the following three factors:

- *The way your reader will read your document.* Will he or she
  - — file it?
  - — skim it?
  - — read only a portion of it?
  - — study it carefully?
  - — modify it and submit it to another reader?
  - — try to implement recommendations?
  - — use it to perform a test or carry out a procedure?
  - — use it as a source document for another document?

If only 1 of your 15 readers will study the document for detailed information, you don't want the other 14 people to have to wade through it. Therefore, put this information in an appendix. If you know that your reader wants to use your status report as raw material for a report to a higher-level reader, try to write it so that it requires little rewriting. Make sure the reader has access to the electronic file so that your report can be merged with the new document without being retyped.

- *Your reader's reading skill.* Consider whether you should be writing at all, or whether it would be better to do an oral presentation or use computer-based training. If you decide to write, consider whether your reader can understand how to use the type of document you have selected, handle the level of detail you will present, and understand your graphics, sentence structure, and vocabulary.

- *The physical environment in which your reader will read your document.* Often, technical documents are formatted in a special way or constructed of special materials to improve their effectiveness. Documents that might be exposed to wind, water, and grease often have special waterproof bindings and oil-resistant or laminated paper.

▶ **In This Book**
For more about designing a document for use in different environments, see Ch. 7, p. 143.

TECHNIQUES FOR LEARNING ABOUT YOUR AUDIENCE

To learn about your audience, you figure out what you do and do not already know, interview people, read about them, and read documents they have written. Although you cannot perform extensive research about every possible reader of every document you write, you should learn what you can about your most important readers of your most important documents.

Determining What You Already Know About Your Audience

Start by asking yourself what you already know about your most important readers: their demographics (such as age, education, and job responsibilities); their expectations and attitudes toward you and the subject; and the ways they will use your document. Then list the important factors you *don't* know. That is where you will concentrate your energies.

Interviewing People

For each of your most important readers, make a list of people who have known them and their work the longest or who are closest to them on the job. These people might include those who joined the organization at about the same time your reader did; people who work in the same department as your reader; and people at other organizations who have collaborated with your reader.

Prepare a few interview questions that are likely to elicit information about your reader and his or her preferences and needs. Then, conduct these informal interviews in person, on the phone, or by e-mail.

▶ **In This Book**
For a discussion of interviewing, see Ch. 5, pp. 96–99.

Reading About Your Audience Online

If you are writing for people in your own organization, start your research there. If the person is a high-level manager or executive, search the organization's Web site. Sections such as "About Us," "About the Company," and "Information for Investors" often contain a wealth of biographical information, as well as links to other sources. Also, use a search engine to look for information on the Internet. You are likely to find newspaper and magazine articles, industry directories, Web sites, and blog posts about your audience.

Searching Social Media for Documents Your Audience Has Written

Documents your readers have written can tell you a lot about what they like to see. Again, start in your own organization, searching for documents the person has written. Then broaden the search to the Internet.

Many or even most of your readers might be active participants in social media, such as Facebook. Pay particular attention to LinkedIn, which specializes in professional people. Figure 4.1 is an excerpt from the LinkedIn entry written by Mike Markley, a technical communicator at Aquent.

Mike Markley ①ˢᵗ

Director, Aquent Studios; content development consultant; and technical communication professional

Boise, Idaho Area | Writing and Editing

Current	• **Director, Aquent Studios** at **Aquent** ◻ • **Adjunct Instructor** at **Boise State University** ◻
Past	• Resource Manager / Sr. Project Manager at Sakson & Taylor, Inc. ◻ • Director of Content Design & Development at Lionbridge Technologies, Inc. ◻ • Assembly Documentation Supervisor at Micron Technology, Inc. ◻
Education	• Boise State University • University of Idaho
Recommendations	3 people have recommended Mike
Connections	206 connections
Public Profile	http://www.linkedin.com/pub/mike-markley/0/244/64b

This summary is followed by a much more detailed description of Mike Markley's professional history and education. Even this brief summary suggests that Markley has extensive experience (note the words director, senior project manager, and supervisor).

Figure 4.1   A LinkedIn Bio
Source: Markley, 2010a <www.linkedin.com/pub/mike-markley/0/244/64b>.

Markley begins his LinkedIn biography with these paragraphs:

Mike Markley joined Aquent Studios in 2003. While at Aquent Studios, he has held the positions of Information Developer, Senior Project Manager, and Resource Manager. In 2007 he became the Managing Director for Aquent Studios, overseeing a team of 100 people across studios located in Idaho, Oregon, Colorado, and India. His home office is located in Boise, Idaho.

Mike has worked in professional and technical communication for over 15 years, with a focus on managing projects and directing teams in the development of creative and technical content for commercial and consumer products. His background includes consulting work for several Fortune 500 companies as an author, an editor, a graphics and training developer, and a project manager. With five years' experience in the director role with Aquent and a prior company, he has experience building client relationships, recruiting and managing creative and technical resources, as well as setting up and directing managed-service groups for clients throughout the western United States and India.

These two paragraphs suggest a couple of points about Markley's credentials:

- He has an extensive background, not only in writing and editing but also in various levels of management. You can expect that he knows project management, budgeting, and human resources. He understands both how to make documents and how to lead teams that make documents.

- He has experience overseeing project teams in India. This experience gives him a broad perspective not only on how two very different cultures see the world but also on how to supervise people from those cultures so that they work effectively and efficiently.

In short, Markley's biography on LinkedIn clearly suggests that he is an experienced, versatile, and highly respected technical communicator.

A typical LinkedIn entry also directs you to the person's Web sites and blogs and to the LinkedIn groups to which the person belongs. You can also see the person's *connections* (the list of people whom the person is connected to through work or personal relationships). And if you are a LinkedIn member, you can also see whether you and the person share any connections.

The person you are researching might also have a Twitter account. Reading a person's tweets gives you a good idea of his or her job responsibilities and professionalism, as shown in Figure 4.2 on page 64.

COMMUNICATING ACROSS CULTURES

Our society and our workforce are becoming increasingly diverse, both culturally and linguistically, and businesses are exporting more and more goods and services. As a result, technical communicators and technical professionals often communicate with nonnative speakers of English in the United

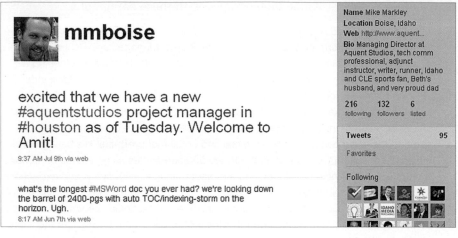

The tweet welcoming Amit shows appropriate professional courtesy. The little bio to the right suggests a well-grounded individual with whom you would likely feel comfortable working.

Figure 4.2   A Twitter Page
Source: Markley, 2010b <http://twitter.com/mmboise>.

States and abroad and with speakers of other languages who read texts translated from English into their own languages. Effective communication requires an understanding of culture: the beliefs, attitudes, and values that motivate people's behavior.

Understanding the Cultural Variables "on the Surface"

Communicating effectively with people from another culture requires understanding a number of cultural variables that lie on the surface. You need to know, first, what language or languages to use. You also need to be aware of political, social, religious, and economic factors that can affect how readers will interpret your documents.

In *International Technical Communication*, Nancy L. Hoft (1995) describes seven major categories of cultural variables that lie on the surface:

- *Political.* This category includes trade issues and legal issues (for example, some countries forbid imports of certain foods or chemicals) and laws about intellectual property, product safety, and liability.

- *Economic.* In many countries, most people cannot afford computers.

- *Social.* This category covers many gender and business customs. In most Western cultures, women play a much greater role in the workplace than they do in many Middle Eastern and Asian cultures. Business customs—including forms of greeting, business dress, and gift giving—vary from culture to culture.

- *Religious.* Religious differences can affect diet, attitudes toward individual colors, styles of dress, holidays, and hours of business.

- *Educational.* In the United States, 40 million people are only marginally literate. In other cultures, that rate can be much higher or much lower. In some cultures, classroom learning with a teacher is considered the most acceptable way to study; in others, people tend to study on their own.

- *Technological.* If you sell high-tech products, you need to know whether your readers have the hardware, the software, and the technological infrastructure to use them.

- *Linguistic.* In some countries, English is taught to all children; in other countries, English is seen as a threat to the national language. In many cultures, the orientation of text on a page and in a book is not from left to right.

In addition to these basic differences, you need to understand dozens of other factors. For instance, the United States is the only major country that has not adopted the metric system. Americans also use periods to separate whole numbers from decimals, and commas to separate thousands from hundreds. Much of the rest of the world reverses this usage.

UNITED STATES	3,425.6
EUROPE	3.425,6

These cultural variables are important in an obvious way: you can't send an e-mail to a person who doesn't have Internet access. However, there is another set of cultural characteristics—those beneath the surface—that you also need to understand.

Understanding the Cultural Variables "Beneath the Surface"

Scholars of multicultural communication have identified cultural variables that are less obvious than those discussed in the previous section but just as important. Writing scholars Elizabeth Tebeaux and Linda Driskill (1999) explain six key variables that are reflected in technical communication.

- *Focus on individuals or groups.* Some cultures, especially in the West, value individuals more than groups. The typical employee doesn't see his or her identity as being defined by the organization. Other cultures, particularly in Asia, value groups more than individuals. The typical employee sees himself or herself more as a member of the organization than as an individual who works there.

    In individualistic cultures, writers use the pronoun *I* rather than *we*. They address letters to the principal reader and sign them with their own names. In group-oriented cultures, writers focus on the organization's needs by emphasizing the benefits to be gained by the two organizations through a cooperative relationship. They emphasize the relationship between the writer and reader rather than the specific technical details of the message. Writers use *we* rather than *I*.

- *Distance between business life and private life.* In some cultures, especially in the West, people separate their business lives from their private lives. In other cultures, particularly in Asia, people see a much smaller distance between their business lives and their private lives. Even after the day ends, they still see themselves as employees of the organization.

   In cultures that value individualism, communication focuses on technical details, with relatively little reference to personal information about the writer or the reader.

   In cultures that are group oriented, communication contains much more personal information—about the reader's family and health—and more information about general topics, for example, the weather and the seasons. The goal is to build a formal relationship between the two organizations.

- *Distance between ranks.* In some cultures, the distance in power and authority between workers within an organization is small. In other cultures, the distance is great. Supervisors do not consult with their subordinates. Subordinates use formal names and titles—"Mr. Smith," "Dr. Jones"—when addressing higher-ranking people.

   In individualistic cultures, communication is generally less formal. Informal documents (e-mails and memos) are appropriate, and writers often sign their documents with their first names only.

   In cultures with a great distance between ranks, writers tend to use their full professional titles and to prefer formal documents (such as letters) to informal ones (such as memos and e-mails). Writers make sure to address their documents to the appropriate person and to include the formal design elements (such as title pages and letters of transmittal) that signal their respect for their readers.

- *Nature of truth.* Some cultures feel that truth is a universal concept. An action is either wrong or right. If facts are presented clearly and comprehensively, all reasonable readers will understand them in the same way. People in other cultures think that truth is more complex and believe that reasonable people can have different perspectives on complex ethical issues.

   In cultures that take a universal approach to truth, such as the United States, documents tend to be comprehensive and detailed, spelling out the details of the communication and leaving nothing to interpretation. In cultures that take a relative view of truth, documents tend to be less detailed and less conclusive.

- *Need to spell out details.* Some cultures value full, complete communication. Writers spell out all the details, and written text contains all the information a reader needs to understand it. These cultures are called *low context.* Other cultures value documents in which some of the details are merely implied. Writers tend to omit information that they consider obvious because they don't want to insult the reader. Implicit information is communicated through other forms of communication that draw upon the personal relationship between the reader and the writer, as well as social and business norms of the culture. These cultures are called *high context*. Low-context cultures tend to be individualistic; high-context cultures tend to be group oriented.

- *Attitudes toward uncertainty.* In some cultures, people are comfortable with uncertainty. They communicate less formally and rely less on written policies. In other cultures, people are uncomfortable with uncertainty. Businesses are structured formally, and they use written procedures for communicating.

   In cultures that tolerate uncertainty, written communication tends to be less detailed. Oral communication is used frequently. In cultures that value certainty, communication tends to be detailed. Policies are lengthy and specific, and forms are used extensively.

As you consider this set of cultural variables, keep four points in mind:

- *Each variable represents a spectrum of attitudes.* Terms such as *high-context* and *low-context* represent the two end points on a scale. Most cultures occupy a middle ground.

- *The six variables do not line up in a clear pattern.* Although the variables sometimes correlate—for example, low-context cultures tend to be individualistic—in any one culture, the six variables do not form a consistent pattern. For example, the dominant culture in the United States is highly individualistic rather than group oriented but only about midway along the scale of attitudes toward accepting uncertainty.

- *Different organizations within the same culture can vary greatly.* For example, one software company in Germany might have a management style that does not tolerate uncertainty, whereas another software company in that country might tolerate a lot of uncertainty.

- *An organization's cultural attitudes are fluid, not static.* How an organization operates is determined not only by the dominant culture but also by its own people. As new people join an organization, its culture changes. The IBM of 1993 is not the IBM of 2013.

For you as a communicator, this set of variables offers questions, not answers. You cannot predict the attitudes of the people in an organization. You have to interact with them for a long time before you understand the culture. The value of being aware of the variables is that they can help you study the communications from people in that organization and become more aware of underlying values that affect how they will interpret your documents.

Considering Cultural Variables as You Write

The challenge of communicating effectively with a person from another culture is that you are communicating with a person, not a culture (Lovitt, 1999). For example, a 50-year-old Japanese-born manager for the computer manufacturer

Fujitsu in Japan has been shaped by the Japanese culture, but he also has been influenced by the culture of his company and of the Japanese computer industry in general. It is also likely that he has worked outside of Japan for several years and has absorbed influences from another culture.

A further complication is that when you communicate with a person from another culture, to that person *you* are from another culture, and you cannot know how much that person is trying to accommodate your cultural patterns. When you write to a large audience, the complications increase. A group of managers for Fujitsu represents a far more complex mix of cultural influences than one manager for Fujitsu.

No brief discussion of cultural variables can answer questions about how to write for a particular multicultural audience. You need to study your readers' culture and, as you plan the document, seek assistance from someone native to the culture who can help you avoid blunders that might confuse or offend your readers. Read some of the basic guides to communicating with people from other cultures, and study guides to the particular culture you are investigating. In addition, numerous Web sites provide useful guidelines that can help you write to people from another culture.

On the Web

For a list of books about intercultural communication, see the Selected Bibliography on <bedfordstmartins.com/ps>.

If possible, study documents written by people in your audience. If you don't have access to these, try to locate documents written in English by people from that culture. Figures 4.3 and 4.4 show two excerpts from documents that provide useful glimpses into cultural variables. Figure 4.3 is an excerpt from a statement by the president of a Japanese electronics company. Figure 4.4 is from a training manual used by Indian Railways. The paragraph describes a training course that new employees are required to take.

Notice how the writer describes his company in terms of its long history and its cutting-edge technology. In Japan, a long history suggests trustworthiness.

He emphasizes the concept of fulfilling customers' needs through high performance, safety, and environmental awareness.

Here he describes his company's commitment to realizing a prosperous and sustainable society. This focus emphasizes the Japanese concept of living in harmony with the physical environment.

This year, FDK marks the 60th anniversary of the founding of the company. Keeping our customers in mind, we supply high performance batteries and electronic devices based on material technology which FDK has cultivated over many years and which increases the value and function of our customers' products.

While the business environment in our product markets has been changing dramatically on a global scale as a result of progress from globalization and network technology, we strive for stable management from a global viewpoint. In response to our customers' needs, we offer products and services created in pursuit of the highest possible performance, accompanied by safety and environmental friendliness.

To contribute to society through manufacturing, we aim to realize the affluent society by pursuing the realization of the 3 Es (Energy Security, Environmental Protection, and Economic Efficiency) to build a sustainable society.

Figure 4.3   Statement by a Japanese Electronics Company President
Source: Ono, 2010 <www.fdk.co.jp/company_e/message-e.html>.

There is no denying the fact that the Combined Civil Services Foundation Course, held for different Services at the Lal Bahadur Shastri National Academy of Administration (LBSNAA), Mussoorie, provides a great and unique opportunity for developing 'spirit de corps' [sic] and fostering appropriate attitudes and values in the young minds of the Probationers belonging to different Services. The importance of imbibing these values right in the beginning of the career of the officers can hardly be overemphasized.

This paragraph from a report by managers of Indian Railways describes a training course that new employees are required to take.

The reference to "esprit de corps" (group spirit) and "fostering appropriate attitudes and values in the young minds of the Probationers" suggests a culture in which age and seniority are considered to be the most important characteristics of a successful employee and in which it is the duty of elders to teach young people proper values.

Figure 4.4   Statement from an Indian Training Manual
Source: Indian Railways, 2010 <www.indianrailways.gov.in/indianrailways/directorate/mgt_ser/training _circulars/report_iras.pdf>.

Using Graphics and Design for Multicultural Readers

One of the challenges of writing to people from another culture is that they are likely to be nonnative speakers of English. One way to overcome the language barrier is to use effective graphics and appropriate document design.

Guidelines

Writing for Readers from Other Cultures

The following eight suggestions will help you communicate more effectively with multicultural readers.

▶ **Limit your vocabulary.** Every word should have only one meaning. For example, use *right* to mean the opposite of *left*; do not use it to mean *correct*.

▶ **Keep sentences short.** Try for an average length of no more than 20 words.

▶ **Define abbreviations and acronyms in a glossary.** Don't assume that your readers know what a GFI (ground fault interrupter) is, because the abbreviation is derived from English vocabulary and word order.

▶ **Avoid jargon unless you know your readers are familiar with it.** For instance, your readers might not know what a graphical user interface is.

▶ **Avoid idioms and slang.** These terms are culture specific. If you tell your Japanese readers that your company plans a "full-court press," most likely they will be confused.

▶ **Use the active voice whenever possible.** The active voice is easier for nonnative speakers of English to understand than the passive voice.

▶ **Be careful with graphics.** The garbage-can icon on the Macintosh computer does not translate well, because garbage cans have different shapes in other countries.

▶ **Be sure someone from the culture reviews your document.** Even if you have had help in planning the document, have it reviewed before you publish and distribute it.

In This Book
For more about voice, see Ch. 6, pp. 126–27.

In This Book
For more about graphics, see Ch. 8.

DOCUMENT ANALYSIS ACTIVITY

Examining Cultural Variables in a Business Letter

These two versions of the same business letter were written by a director of marketing for an American computer company. The first letter was addressed to a potential customer in the United States; the second version was addressed to a potential customer in Japan. The accompanying questions ask you to think about how the cultural variables affect the nature of the evidence, the structure of the letters, and their tone (see pp. 65–67).

July 3, 2012

Server Solutions
Cincinnati, OH 46539

Nadine Meyer
Director of Marketing

Mr. Philip Henryson, Director of Purchasing
Allied Manufacturing
1321 Industrial Boulevard
Boise, ID 83756

Dear Mr. Henryson:

Thank you for your inquiry about our PowerServer servers. I'm happy to answer your questions.

The most popular configuration is our PowerServer 3000. This model is based on the Intel® Xeon processor, ServerSure High-End UltraLite chipset with quad-peer PCI architecture, and embedded RAID. The system comes with our InstallIt system-management CD, which lets you install the server and monitor and manage your network with a simple graphical interface. With six PCI slots, the PowerServer 3000 is equipped with redundant cooling as well as redundant power, and storage expandability to 950 GB. I'm taking the liberty of enclosing the brochure for this system to fill you in on the technical details.

The PowerServer 3000 has performed extremely well on a number of industry benchmark tests. I'm including with this letter copies of feature articles on the system from *PC World*, *InternetWeek*, and *Windows Vista Magazine*.

It would be a pleasure for me to arrange for an on-site demo at your convenience. I'll give you a call on Monday to see what dates would be best for you. In the meantime, please do not hesitate to get in touch with me directly if you have any questions about the PowerServer line.

I look forward to talking with you next week.

Sincerely,

Nadine Meyer

Nadine Meyer
Director of Marketing

Attachments:
    "PowerServer 3000 Facts at a Glance"
    "Another Winner from Server Solutions"
    "Mid-Range Servers for 2012"
    "Four New Dual-Processor Workhorses"

Mr. Kato Kirisawa, Director of Purchasing
Allied Manufacturing
3-7-32 Kita Urawa
Saitama City, Saitama Pref. 336-0002
Japan

Server Solutions
Cincinnati, OH 46539

Nadine Meyer
Director of Marketing

Dear Sir:

It is my sincere hope that you and your loved ones are healthy and enjoying the pleasures of summer. Here in the American Midwest, the warm rays of the summer sun are accompanied by the sounds of happy children playing in the neighborhood swimming pools. I trust that the same pleasant sounds greet you in Saitama City.

Your inquiry about our PowerServer 3000 suggests that your company is growing. Allied Manufacturing has earned a reputation in Japan and all of Asia for a wide range of products manufactured to the most demanding standards of quality. We are not surprised that your company requires new servers that can be expanded to provide fast service for more and more clients.

For more than 15 years, Server Solutions has had the great honor of manufacturing the finest computer servers to meet the needs of our valued customers all over the world. We use only the finest materials and most innovative techniques to ensure that our customers receive the highest-quality, uninterrupted service that they have come to expect from us.

One of my great pleasures is to talk with esteemed representatives such as yourself about how Server Solutions can help them meet their needs for the most advanced servers. I would be most gratified if our two companies could enter into an agreement that would be of mutual benefit.

Sincerely,

Nadine Meyer

Nadine Meyer
Director of Marketing

Attachments:
    "PowerServer 3000 Facts at a Glance"
    "Another Winner from Server Solutions"
    "Mid-Range Servers for 2012"
    "Four New Dual-Processor Workhorses"

2012 July 3

1. How does the difference in the salutation (the "Dear . . ." part of the letter) reflect a cultural difference?

2. Does the first paragraph of the second letter have any function beyond delaying the discussion of business?

3. What is the function of telling Mr. Kirisawa about his own company? How does this paragraph help the writer introduce her own company's products?

4. To a reader from the United States, the third paragraph would probably seem thin. What aspect of Japanese culture makes it effective in the context of this letter?

5. Why doesn't the writer make a more explicit sales pitch at the end of the letter?

▶ On the Web

To submit your responses to your instructor, click on Document Analysis Activities for Ch. 4 on <bedfordstmartins .com/ps>.

▶ **In This Book**

For more about design for multicultural readers, see Ch. 7, p. 173. For more about graphics for international readers, see Ch. 8, p. 212.

However, the use of graphics and design can differ from culture to culture. A business letter written in Australia uses a different size paper and a different format than in the United States. A series of graphics arranged left to right could confuse readers from the Middle East, who read from right to left. For this reason, you should study samples of documents written by people from the culture you are addressing to learn the important differences.

APPLYING WHAT YOU HAVE LEARNED ABOUT YOUR AUDIENCE

You want to use what you know about your audience to tailor your communication to their needs and preferences. Obviously, if your most important reader does not understand the details of DRAM technology, you cannot use the concepts, vocabulary, and types of graphics used in that field. If she uses one-page summaries at the beginning of her documents, decide whether they will work for your document.

The following figures show some of the ways writers have applied what they know about their audiences to their use of text and graphics. Figure 4.5a shows text addressed to a technical audience. Figure 4.5b shows text addressed to decision makers. Figure 4.6 on page 74 shows two examples that combine text and graphics to meet various audiences' needs.

WRITING FOR MULTIPLE AUDIENCES

Many documents of more than a few pages are addressed to more than one reader. Often, multiple audiences consist of people with widely different backgrounds, needs, and attitudes.

If you think your document will have a number of readers, consider making it *modular*: break it up into components addressed to different readers. A modular report might contain an executive summary for managers who don't have the time, knowledge, or desire to read the whole report. It might also contain a full technical discussion for expert readers, an implementation schedule for technicians, and a financial plan in an appendix for budget officers. Figure 4.7 on page 75 shows the table of contents for a modular report.

DETERMINING YOUR PURPOSE

Once you have analyzed your audience, it is time to examine your purpose. Ask yourself this: "What do I want this document to accomplish?" When your readers have finished reading what you have written, what do you

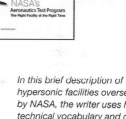

Hypersonic Facilities

8-Foot High-Temperature Tunnel

This combustion-heated, blow-down-to-atmosphere tunnel at LaRC duplicates flight enthalpies at hypersonic conditions Mach 4 to 7 and accommodates large air-breathing propulsion systems and Thermal Protection System components. Tests of note include a Pratt & Whitney and U.S. Air Force test on the Ground Demonstrator Engine No. 2 (GDE–2) to better understand how test conditions influence the internal/external profile shapes of the engine and to document in detail any changes to its form. This landmark test also successfully demonstrated for the first time the use of a closed-loop hydrocarbon-fueled scramjet propulsion system at hypersonic conditions.

Aerothermodynamics Laboratory

The Aerothermodynamics Laboratory at LaRC is a collection of three small, economical hypersonic tunnels used for basic fundamental flow physics research, aerodynamic performance measurements, and aero heating assessment. Many of the studies are aimed at screening, assessing, optimizing, and benchmarking (when combined with computational fluid dynamics) advanced aerospace vehicle concepts. Collectively, these tunnels have contributed to many major hypersonic vehicle programs from the Apollo Space Program to the recent X–43A scramjet that flew at Mach 7 in March 2004 and Mach 9.6 in November 2004. These facilities also provide vital support to the development of NASA's CEV.

In this brief description of hypersonic facilities overseen by NASA, the writer uses highly technical vocabulary and concepts. A reader who would need this level of technical information would understand this passage.

a. Text addressed to a technical audience

Source: National Aeronautics and Space Administration, 2011 <www.aeronautics.nasa.gov/atp /documents/B-1240.pdf>.

There are three recording modes: Video only, audio only, and event (audio & video). The available modes are configurable by the department administrator. For example, in states where audio recording is illegal, the department can configure the AXON unit to always record video only.

These three modes can be selected depending on the circumstances. Video only is the default mode during non-event times. This prevents recording of general conversations when the officer is not involved in an actual event.

The event mode is activated manually by the officer and records both audio and video in addition to increasing the video frame rate for higher quality resolution.

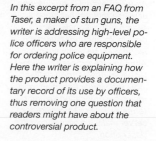

In this excerpt from an FAQ from Taser, a maker of stun guns, the writer is addressing high-level police officers who are responsible for ordering police equipment. Here the writer is explaining how the product provides a documentary record of its use by officers, thus removing one question that readers might have about the controversial product.

b. Text addressed to decision makers

Source: Taser International, 2010 <www.taser.com/research/Pages/LawEnforcementFAQs.aspx>.

Figure 4.5 Using Text to Appeal to Readers' Needs, Interests, and Attitudes

Figure 4.6 Using Verbal and Visual Techniques to Appeal to Readers' Needs, Interests, and Attitudes
Source: Climate Savers Computing, 2010 <www .climatesaverscomputing.org /component/option.com _surveys/act,view_survey /lang,en/survey,3%20Steps%20 to%20Go%20Green/>.

This screen shows a good understanding of general readers who are interested in learning some simple ways to reduce their carbon footprint. The screen presents clear, basic information, followed by a brief interactive feature that prompts the reader to take action.

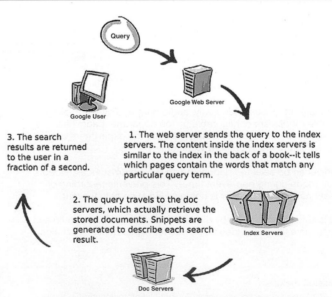

This image, from Google, is addressed to the general reader. Although almost everyone who uses the Internet has done a search using Google, most people do not understand the technology behind a search. Although the process is highly technical, the cartoon drawings, the simple flowchart, and the clear explanations of such terms as index server and doc server make it a very accessible description.

Source: Google, 2010 <www.google.com/corporate/tech.html>.

Contents

Foreword		v
Preface		vii
Summary for Policymakers		1
Technical Summary		19
1	Historical Overview of Climate Change Science	93
2	Changes in Atmospheric Constituents and Radiative Forcing	129
3	Observations: Atmospheric Surface and Climate Change	235
4	Observations: Changes in Snow, Ice and Frozen Ground	337
5	Observations: Ocean Climate Change and Sea Level	385
6	Palaeoclimate	433
7	Coupling Between Changes in the Climate System and Biogeochemistry	499
8	Climate Models and Their Evaluation	589
9	Understanding and Attributing Climate Change	663
10	Global Climate Projections	747
11	Regional Climate Projections	847
Annex I:	Glossary	941
Annex II:	Contributors to the IPCC WGI Fourth Assessment Report	955
Annex III:	Reviewers of the IPCC WGI Fourth Assessment Report	969
Annex IV:	Acronyms	981
Index		989

This table of contents shows the organization of a modular document.

Few readers will want to read the whole document—it's almost 1,000 pages long.

Most readers will want to read the 18-page summary for policymakers.

Some readers will want to read selected sections of the technical summary or "annexes" (appendixes).

Figure 4.7 Table of Contents for a Modular Report
Source: Solomon et al., 2007, p. xix.

want them to *know* or *believe*? What do you want them to *do*? Your writing should help your readers understand a concept, hold a particular belief, or carry out a task.

In defining your purpose, think of a verb that represents it. (Sometimes, of course, you have several purposes.) The following list presents verbs in two categories: those used to communicate information to your readers and those used to convince them to accept a particular point of view.

Communicating verbs

authorize	define	describe
explain	illustrate	inform
outline	present	review
summarize		

Convincing verbs

assess	evaluate	forecast
propose	recommend	request

This classification is not absolute. For example, *review* could in some cases be a *convincing verb* rather than a *communicating verb*: one writer's review of a complicated situation might be very different from another's.

Here are a few examples of how you can use these verbs to clarify the purpose of your document (the verbs are italicized).

- This wiki *presents* the draft of our policies on professional use of social media within the organization.

- This letter *authorizes* the purchase of six new laptops for the Jenkintown facility.

- This memo *recommends* that we revise the Web site as soon as possible.

Sometimes your real purpose differs from your expressed purpose. For instance, if you want to persuade your reader to lease a new computer system rather than purchase it, you might phrase the purpose this way: *to explain the advantages of leasing over purchasing.* Many readers don't want to be *persuaded* but are willing to learn new facts or ideas.

Writer's Checklist

Following is a checklist for analyzing your audience and purpose. Remember that your document might be read by one person, several people, a large group, or several groups with various needs.

In analyzing your audience, did you consider the following questions about each of your most important readers? (p. 57)

- ☐ What is your reader's educational background? (p. 57)
- ☐ What is your reader's professional experience? (p. 57)
- ☐ What is your reader's job responsibility? (p. 57)
- ☐ What are your reader's personal characteristics? (p. 58)
- ☐ What are your reader's personal preferences? (p. 58)
- ☐ What are your reader's cultural characteristics? (p. 58)
- ☐ Why is the reader reading your document? (p. 58)
- ☐ What is your reader's attitude toward you? (p. 59)
- ☐ What is your reader's attitude toward the subject? (p. 59)
- ☐ What are your reader's expectations about the subject? (p. 59)

- ☐ What are your reader's expectations about the document? (p. 59)
- ☐ How will your reader read your document? (p. 60)
- ☐ What is your reader's reading skill? (p. 61)
- ☐ What is the physical environment in which your reader will read your document? (p. 61)

In learning about your readers, did you

- ☐ determine what you already know about them? (p. 61)
- ☐ interview people? (p. 61)
- ☐ read about your audience online? (p. 62)
- ☐ search social media for documents your audience has written? (p. 62)

In planning to write for an audience from another culture, did you consider the following cultural variables:

- ☐ political? (p. 64)
- ☐ economic? (p. 64)
- ☐ social? (p. 64)
- ☐ religious? (p. 64)
- ☐ educational? (p. 65)
- ☐ technological? (p. 65)
- ☐ linguistic? (p. 65)

In planning to write for an audience from another culture, did you consider the other set of cultural variables:

- [ ] focus on individuals or groups? (p. 65)
- [ ] distance between business life and private life? (p. 66)
- [ ] distance between ranks? (p. 66)
- [ ] nature of truth? (p. 66)
- [ ] need to spell out details? (p. 66)
- [ ] attitudes toward uncertainty? (p. 67)

In writing for a multicultural audience, did you

- [ ] limit your vocabulary? (p. 69)
- [ ] keep sentences short? (p. 69)

- [ ] define abbreviations and acronyms in a glossary? (p. 69)
- [ ] avoid jargon unless you know that your readers are familiar with it? (p. 69)
- [ ] avoid idioms and slang? (p. 69)
- [ ] use the active voice whenever possible? (p. 69)
- [ ] use graphics carefully? (p. 69)
- [ ] have the document reviewed by someone from the reader's culture? (p. 69)

- [ ] In writing for multiple audiences, did you consider creating a modular document? (p. 72)
- [ ] Did you state your purpose in writing and express it in the form of a verb or verbs? (p. 72)

Exercises

▶ **In This Book**   For more about memos, see Ch. 9, p. 223.

1. **INTERNET EXERCISE** Choose a 200-word passage from a technical article addressed to an expert audience, one related to your major course of study. (You can find a technical article on the Web by using a directory search engine, such as Yahoo Directory, selecting a subject area such as "science," then selecting "scientific journals." In addition, many federal government agencies publish technical articles and reports on the Web.) Rewrite the passage so that it is clear and interesting to the general reader. Submit the original passage to your instructor along with your revision.

2. The following passage is an advertisement from a translation service. Revise the passage to make it more appropriate for a multicultural audience. Submit the revision to your instructor.

   If your technical documents have to meet the needs of a global market but you find that most translation houses are swamped by the huge volume, fail to accommodate the various languages you require, or fail to make your deadlines, where do you turn?

   Well, your search is over. Translations, Inc. provides comprehensive translations in addition to full-service documentation publishing.

   We utilize ultrasophisticated translation programs that can translate a page in a blink of an eye.

   Then our crack linguists comb each document to give it that personalized touch.

   No job too large! No schedule too tight! Give us a call today!

3. **INTERNET EXERCISE** Study the Web site of a large manufacturer of computer products, such as Hewlett-Packard, Acer, Dell, or Lenovo. Identify three different pages that address different audiences and fulfill different purposes. Here is an example:

   Name of the page: Lenovo Group Fact Page
   Audience: prospective investors
   Purpose: persuade the prospective investor to invest in the company

   Be prepared to share your findings with the class.

4. **GROUP/INTERNET EXERCISE** Form small groups and study two Web sites that advertise competing products. For instance, you might choose the Web sites of two carmakers, two television shows, or two music publishers. Have each person in the group, working *alone*, compare and contrast the two sites according to these three criteria:

   a. the kind of information they provide: hard, technical information or more emotional information

   b. the use of multimedia such as animation, sound, or video

c. the amount of interactivity they invite, that is, the extent to which you can participate in activities while you visit the site

After each person has separately studied the sites and taken notes about the three points, come together as a group to share your findings and discuss the differences. Which aspects of these sites caused the most difference in group members' reactions? Which aspects seemed to elicit the most consistent reactions?

In a brief memo to your instructor, describe and analyze how the two sites were perceived by the different members of the group.

On the Web

For a case assignment, "Reaching Out to a New Audience," see Cases on <bedfordstmartins.com/ps>.

5

Researching Your Subject

Rhoda Sidney/The Image Works.

In the workplace, you will conduct research all the time.

In the workplace, you will conduct research all the time. As a civil engineer, you might need to decide whether to replace your company's traditional surveying equipment with GPS-based gear. As a pharmacist, you might need to determine what medication a patient is taking and find information on potentially harmful drug interactions.

Although you will conduct some of this research by consulting traditional printed sources, most of your research will involve online sources. You will consult Web sites, blogs, and discussion boards, and you might listen to podcasts or watch videos. Like the U.S. Census worker pictured in the photograph, sometimes you will interview people. Regardless of which technique you use, your challenge will be to sort the relevant information from the irrelevant, and the accurate from the bogus.

This chapter focuses on conducting primary research and secondary research. *Primary research* involves creating technical information yourself. *Secondary research* involves collecting information that other people have already discovered or created. This chapter presents secondary research first. Why? Because you will probably do secondary research first. To design the experiments or the field research that goes into primary research, you need a thorough understanding of the information that already exists about your subject.

UNDERSTANDING THE DIFFERENCES BETWEEN ACADEMIC AND WORKPLACE RESEARCH

Although academic research and workplace research can overlap, in most cases they differ in their goals and their methods.

In *academic research*, your goal is to find information that will help answer a scholarly question: "What would be the effect on the balance of trade between the United States and China if China lowered the value of its currency by 10 percent?" Academic research questions are often more abstract than applied. That is, they get at the underlying principles of a phenomenon. Academic research usually requires extensive secondary research: reading scholarly literature in academic journals and books. If you do primary research, as scientists do in labs, you do so only after extensive secondary research.

In *workplace research*, your goal is to find information to help you answer a practical question, usually one that involves the organization for which you work: "Should we replace our sales staff's notebook computers with tablet computers?" Because workplace research questions are often focused on improving a situation at a particular organization, they call for much more primary research. You need to learn about your own organization's processes and how the people in your organization would respond to your ideas.

Regardless of whether you are conducting academic or workplace research, the basic research methods—primary and secondary research—are fundamentally the same, as is the goal: to answer questions.

UNDERSTANDING THE RESEARCH PROCESS

When you perform research, you want the process to be effective and efficient. That is, you want the information that you find to answer the questions you need to answer. And you don't want to spend any more time than necessary getting that information. To meet these goals, you have to think about how the research relates to the other aspects of the overall writing process, as outlined in the chart from Chapter 1.

Focus on Process

Planning	• **Analyze your audience.** Who are your readers? What are their attitudes and expectations? How will they use the document? See Ch. 4 for advice about analyzing your audience.
	• **Analyze your purpose.** After they have read the document, what do you want your readers to *know* or to *do*? See Ch. 4, p. 72, for advice about determining your purpose.
	• **Generate ideas about your subject.** Ask journalistic questions (*who*, *what*, *when*, *where*, *why*, and *how*), brainstorm, freewrite, talk with someone, or make clustering or branching diagrams.
	• **Research additional information.**
	• **Organize and outline your document.** See Ch. 6, p. 107, for information about common organizational patterns.
	• **Select an application, a design, and a delivery method.** See Ch. 7 for advice about designing your document.
	• **Devise a schedule and a budget.** How much time will you need to complete each task of the project? Will you incur expenses for travel, research, or usability testing?
Drafting	• **Draft effectively.** Get comfortable. Start with the easiest topics, and don't stop writing to revise.
	• **Use templates—carefully.** Check that their design is appropriate and that they help you communicate your information effectively to your readers.
	• **Use styles.** Styles are like small templates that apply to the design of elements such as headings and bullet lists. They help you present the elements of your document clearly and consistently. See the Tech Tip on p. 162.
Revising	**Look again at your draft to see if it works.** Revising by yourself and with the help of others, focus on three questions:
	• Has your understanding of your audience changed?
	• Has your understanding of your purpose changed?
	• Has your understanding of your subject changed?
	If the answer to any of these questions is yes, what changes should you make to the content and style of your document? See the Writer's Checklists in each chapter for information about what to look for when revising.
Editing	**Check your revised draft to improve six aspects of your writing:** grammar, punctuation, style, usage, diction (word choice), and mechanics (matters such as use of numbers and abbreviations). See Appendix, Part B, for more information about these topics.
Proofreading	**Check to make sure you have typed what you meant to type.** Don't rely on the spell-checker or the grammar-checker. They will miss some errors and flag correct words and phrases. See Appendix, Part B, for more information about proofreading.

You begin your research as part of your planning. In generating ideas about your subject, consider what you already know about your subject and what you still need to find out. Make a list of the pieces of information you still need to acquire and the questions you need to answer. Then research those questions. Start with secondary research: study journal articles and Web-based sources such as online journals, discussion boards, blogs, and podcasts. Don't forget to evaluate the information you find to be sure it is accurate, comprehensive, unbiased, and current. (See the Guidelines box on pages 92–93.) Then conduct primary research by consulting company records, interviewing people, and distributing questionnaires. Finally, if the information you have acquired doesn't sufficiently answer your questions, or if you think of additional questions while outlining or drafting your deliverable, do more research. When do you stop? Only when you think you have enough high-quality information to create the deliverable.

CHOOSING APPROPRIATE RESEARCH METHODS

Once you have determined the questions you need to answer, think about the various research techniques you can use to answer them. Different research questions require different research methods.

For example, your research methods for finding out how a current situation is expected to change would be different than your research methods for finding out how well a product might work for your organization. That is, if you want to know how outsourcing will change the computer-support industry over the next 10 to 20 years, you might search for long-range predictions in journal and magazine articles and on reputable Web sites and blogs. By contrast, if you want to figure out whether a specific scanner will produce the quality of scan that you need and will function reliably, you might do the same kind of secondary research and then observe the use of the product at a vendor's site; schedule product demos at your site; follow up by interviewing others in your company; and perform an experiment in which you try two different scanners and then analyze the results.

Choosing research methods means choosing the ways in which you'll conduct your research. Start by thinking about the questions you need to answer:

- *What types of research media might you use?* Should you look for information in books, journals, and reports, or online in Web sites, discussion boards, and blogs?

- *What types of research tools might you use?* Are these media best accessed via online catalogs, reference works, indexes, or abstract services?

- *What types of primary research might you conduct?* Should you conduct observations, demonstrations, inspections, experiments, interviews, questionnaires, or other field research?

You are likely to find that your research plan changes as you conduct your research. You might find, for instance, that you need more than one method to get the information you need, or that the one method that you thought would work doesn't.

If you are doing research for a document that will be read by people from other cultures, think about what kinds of evidence your readers will consider appropriate. In many non-Western cultures, tradition or the authority of the person making the claim can be extremely important, more important than the kind of scientific evidence that is favored in Western cultures.

And don't forget that all people pay particular attention to information that comes from their own culture. If you are writing to European readers about telemedicine, for instance, try to find information from European authorities and about European telemedicine. This information will interest your readers and will likely reflect their cultural values and expectations.

Guidelines

Researching a Topic

Follow these three guidelines as you gather information to use in your document.

▶ **Be persistent.** Don't be discouraged if a research method doesn't yield useful information. Even experienced researchers fail at least as often as they succeed. Be prepared to rethink how you might find the information. Don't hesitate to ask reference librarians for help or to post questions on discussion boards.

▶ **Record your data carefully.** Prepare the materials you will need. Write information down, on paper or online. Record interviews (with the respondents' permission). Paste the URLs of the sites you visit into your notes. Bookmark sites so you can return to them easily.

▶ **Triangulate your research methods.** *Triangulating* your research methods means using more than one or two methods. If a manufacturer's Web site says the printer produces 17 pages per minute, an independent review in a reputable journal also says 17, and you get 17 in a demo at your office with your documents, the printer probably will produce 17 pages per minute. When you need to answer important questions, don't settle for only one or two sources.

CHOICES AND STRATEGIES   Choosing Appropriate Research Techniques

Type of question	Example of question	Appropriate research technique
What is the theory behind this process or technique?	How do greenhouse gases contribute to global warming?	**Encyclopedias**, **handbooks**, and **journal articles** present theory. Also, you can find theoretical information on **Web sites** from reputable professional organizations and universities. Search using keywords such as "greenhouse gases" and "global warming."
What is the history of this phenomenon?	When and how did engineers first try to extract shale oil?	**Encyclopedias** and **handbooks** present history. Also, you can find historical information on **Web sites** from reputable professional organizations and universities. Search using keywords such as "shale oil" and "petroleum history."
What techniques are being used now to solve this problem?	How are companies responding to the federal government's new laws on health-insurance portability?	If the topic is recent, you will have better luck using digital resources such as **Web sites** and **social media** than using traditional print media. Search using keywords and tags such as "health-insurance portability." Your search will be most effective if you use standard terminology in your search, such as "HIPAA" for the health-insurance law.
How is a current situation expected to change?	What changes will outsourcing cause in the computer-support industry over the next 10 to 20 years?	For long-range predictions, you can find information in **journal articles** and **magazine articles** and on reputable **Web sites**. Experts might write forecasts on **discussion boards** and **blogs**.
What products are available to perform a task or provide a service?	Which vendors are available to upgrade and maintain our company's Web site?	For current products and services, search **Web sites**, **discussion boards**, and **blogs**. Reputable vendors—manufacturers and service providers—have sites describing their offerings. But be careful not to assume vendors' claims are accurate. Even the specifications they provide might be exaggerated.

Choosing Appropriate Research Techniques (*continued*)

Type of question	Example of question	Appropriate research technique
What are the strengths and weaknesses of competing products and services?	Which portable GPS system is the lightest?	Search for benchmarking articles from experts in the field, such as a **journal article**—either in print or on the Web—about camping and outfitting that compares the available GPS systems according to reasonable criteria. Also check **discussion boards** for reviews and **blogs** for opinions. If appropriate, do **field research** to answer your questions.
Which product or service do experts recommend?	Which four-wheel-drive SUV offers the best combination of features and quality for our needs?	Experts write **journal articles**, **magazine articles**, and sometimes **blogs**. Often, they participate in **discussion boards**. Sometimes, you can **interview** them, in person or on the phone, or write **inquiries**.
What are the facts about how we do our jobs at this company?	Do our chemists use gas chromatography in their analyses?	Sometimes, you can **interview** someone, in person or on the phone, to answer a simple question. To determine whether your chemists use a particular technique, start by asking someone in that department.
What can we learn about what caused a problem in our organization?	What caused the contamination in the clean room?	You can **interview** personnel who were closest to the problem and **inspect** the scene to determine the cause of the problem.
What do our personnel think we should do about a situation?	Do our quality-control analysts think we need to revise our sampling quotient?	If there are only a few personnel, **interview** them. If there are many, use **questionnaires** to get the information more quickly.
How well would this product or service work in our organization?	Would this scanner produce the quality of scan that we need and interface well with our computer equipment?	Read product reviews on reputable **Web sites**. Study **discussion boards**. **Observe** the use of the product or service at a vendor's site. Schedule product **demos** at your site. Follow up by **interviewing** others in your company to get their thinking. Do an **experiment** in which you try two different solutions to a problem, then analyze the results.

CONDUCTING SECONDARY RESEARCH

Even though workplace research often focuses on primary research, you will almost always need to do secondary research as well. Some topics call for research in a library. You might need specialized handbooks or access to online subscription services that are not freely available on the Internet. More and more, however, you will do your research on the Web. As a working professional, you might find most of the information in your organization's information center. An *information center* is the organization's library, a resource that collects different kinds of information critical to the organization's operations. Many large organizations have specialists who can answer research questions or who can get articles or other kinds of data for you.

Using Traditional Research Tools

There is a tremendous amount of information in different research media. The trick is to learn how to find what you want. This section discusses six basic research tools.

Online Catalogs   An online catalog is a database of books, microform materials, films, compact discs, phonograph records, tapes, and other materials. In most cases, an online catalog lists and describes the holdings at one particular library or a group of libraries. Your college library has an online catalog of its holdings. To search for an item, consult the instructions for searching, which explain how to limit your search by characteristics such as the type of media, date of publication, and language. The instructions also explain how to use punctuation and words such as *and*, *or*, and *not* to focus your search effectively.

Reference Works   Reference works include general and specialized dictionaries and encyclopedias, biographical dictionaries, almanacs, atlases, and dozens of other research tools. These print and online works are especially useful when you begin a research project because they provide an overview of the subject and often list the major works in the field.

To find information on the Web, use a library Web site or search engine and go to its "reference" section. There you will find numerous sites that contain links to excellent collections of reference works online, such as Best Information on the Net and ipl2.

Periodical Indexes   Periodicals are excellent sources of information because they offer recent, authoritative discussions of limited subjects. The biggest challenge in using periodicals is identifying and locating the dozens of relevant articles that are published each month. Although only half a dozen major journals might concentrate on your field, a useful article could appear in one of hundreds of other publications. A periodical index, which is a list of articles classified according to title, subject, and author, can help you determine which journals you want to locate.

▶ **On the Web**

For links to reference sources, click on Links Library for Ch. 5 on <bedfordstmartins.com/ps>.

There are periodical indexes in all fields. The following brief list gives you a sense of the diversity of titles:

- *Applied Science & Technology Index*
- *Business Periodicals Index*
- *Readers' Guide to Periodical Literature*
- *Engineering Index*

You can also use a directory search engine. Many directory categories include a subcategory called "journals" or "periodicals" listing online and printed sources.

Once you have created a bibliography of printed articles you want to study, you have to find them. Check your library's online catalog, which includes all the journals your library receives. If your library does not have an article you want, you can use one of two techniques for securing it:

- *Interlibrary loan.* Your library finds a library that has the article. That library photocopies the article and sends it or faxes it to your library. This service can take more than a week.
- *Document-delivery service.* If you are in a hurry, you can log on to a document-delivery service, such as IngentaConnect, a free database of 4.5 million articles in 13,500 periodicals. There are also fee-based document-delivery services.

Newspaper Indexes   Many major newspapers around the world are indexed by subject. The three most important indexed U.S. newspapers are the following:

- The *New York Times* is perhaps the most reputable U.S. newspaper for national and international news.
- The *Christian Science Monitor* is another highly regarded general newspaper.
- The *Wall Street Journal* is the most authoritative news source on business, finance, and the economy.

▶ **On the Web**

For links to online newspapers, click on Links Library for Ch. 5 on <**bedfordstmartins** .com/ps>.

Many newspapers available on the Web can be searched electronically, although sometimes they charge for archived articles. Keep in mind that the print version and the electronic version of a newspaper can vary greatly. If you wish to cite a quotation from an article in a newspaper, the print version is the preferred one.

Abstract Services   Abstract services are like indexes but also provide abstracts: brief technical summaries of the articles. In most cases, reading the abstract will enable you to decide whether to seek out the full article. The title of an article alone is often a misleading indicator of its contents.

CDC Home | About CDC | Press Room | A-Z Index | Contact Us

CDC Department of Health and Human Services
Centers for Disease Control and Prevention   Search: [____] [GO]   CDC en Español

EMERG
INFECT

Journal Con
› Home
› Expedited
› Current Issu
› Ahead of Pri
› Past Issues
› Announcem
General Info
› About Us
› Instructions
  Authors

Latent Tuberculosis among Persons at Risk for Infection with HIV, Tijuana, Mexico

Abstract

Because there is little routine tuberculosis (TB) screening in Mexico, the prevalence of latent TB infection (LTBI) is unknown. In the context of an increasing HIV epidemic in Tijuana, Mexico, understanding prevalence of LTBI to anticipate emergence of increased LTBI reactivation is critical. Therefore, we recruited injection drug users, noninjection drug users, female sex workers, and homeless persons for a study involving risk assessment, rapid HIV testing, and TB screening. Of 503 participants, the overall prevalences of TB infection, HIV infection, and TB/HIV co-infection were 57%, 4.2%, and 2.2%, respectively; no significant differences by risk group ($p > 0.05$) were observed. Two participants had TB (prevalence 398/100,000). Incarceration in Mexico (odds ratio [OR] 2.28), age (OR 1.03 per year), and years lived in Tijuana (OR 1.02 per year) were independently associated with TB infection ($p < 0.05$). Frequent LTBI in marginalized persons may lead to increases in TB as HIV spreads.

Figure 5.1   An Abstract from *Emerging Infectious Diseases*
Source: Garfein et al., 2010 <www.cdc.gov/eid/content/16/5/757.htm>.

Some abstract services, such as *Chemical Abstracts*, cover a broad field, but many are specialized rather than general. *Adverse Reaction Titles*, for instance, covers research on the subject of adverse reactions to drugs. Figure 5.1 shows an abstract from *Emerging Infectious Diseases*.

Government Information   The U.S. government is the world's biggest publisher. In researching any field of science, engineering, or business, you are likely to find that a federal agency or department has produced a relevant brochure, report, or book. Government publications are not usually listed in the indexes and abstract journals. The *Monthly Catalog of United States Government Publications*, available on paper, on CD, and on the Web, provides extensive access to these materials.

Printed government publications are usually cataloged and shelved separately from other kinds of materials. They are classified according to the Superintendent of Documents system, not the Library of Congress system. A reference librarian or a government documents specialist at your library can help you use government publications.

You can also access most government sites and databases on the Internet. The major entry point for federal government sites is USA.gov (www.usa.gov), which links to hundreds of millions of pages of government information and services. It also features tutorials, a topical index, online transactions, and links to state and local government sites.

On the Web

For an excellent guide to using government information, see Patricia Cruse and Sherry DeDecker's "How to Effectively Locate Federal Government Information on the Web." Click on Links Library for Ch. 5 on <bedfordstmartins.com/ps>.

On the Web

For links to USA.gov and to other government information, click on Links Library for Ch. 5 on <bedfordstmartins.com/ps>.

Using Social Media and Other Interactive Resources

Social media and other interactive resources enable people to collaborate, share, link, and generate content in ways that traditional Web sites offering static content cannot. The result is an Internet that can harness the collective intelligence of people around the globe—and do so quickly. As a result, researchers today have access to far more information than they had in the past, and they have access to it almost instantaneously. However, the ease and speed of posting new content, as well as the lack of formal review of the content, creates challenges for people who do research on the Internet. Everyone using social-media resources must be extra cautious in evaluating and documenting their sources.

This discussion covers three categories of social media and Web-based resources used by researchers: discussion boards, wikis, and blogs.

Discussion Boards   Discussion boards—online discussion forums sponsored by professional organizations, private companies, and others—enable researchers to tap a community's information. Discussion boards are especially useful in providing quick, practical advice. However, the advice might or might not be authoritative. Figure 5.2 shows one interchange on a thread related to civil engineering.

Wikis   A wiki is a Web site that makes it easy for members of a community, company, or organization to create and edit content collaboratively. Often, a wiki contains articles, information about student and professional conferences,

DirtPusher (Civil/Environme)   21 Jun 10 9:38

Does anybody have a good rule of thumb for shrinkage factors for sand. The material is described as coarse to fine with "some" clay. Moisture content is unknown. Previous development is unknown but, thought to be original ground. What I am looking for is the difference between the volume of naturally occurring materials vs compacted material.

Thanks

Here, someone with the username DirtPusher asked a question about how to calculate the shrinkage factor for sand.

Check Out Our Whitepaper Library. Click Here.

fattdad (Geotechnical)   21 Jun 10 9:45

Do a Proctor.
Take a nuke test of the native soil.
Determine the in-situ relative compaction.
Contrast that value to what you've specified.
Determine the "shrinkage factor."

You will likely find that the in-situ density is close to what you want to specify. Let's say it's 93 percent and you want 95 to 100. So, that's an increase of about 5 percent.

Usually, shrinkage factors are a more relavent concern when you are trucking in dirt. What's end-dumped in the back of a truck has very low relative compaction. Your shrinkage factor could easily be 15 percent.

Hope this helps.

f-d

Seven minutes after he posted the question, the first responder, fattdad, replied. Within a few hours, a half dozen people had contributed their ideas.

Figure 5.2   A Discussion Board Exchange
Source: Eng-Tips Forums, 2010 <www.eng-tips.com/viewthread.cfm?qid=274942&page=1>.

reading lists, annotated sets of links, book reviews, and documents used by members of the community. You might have participated in creating and maintaining a wiki in one of your courses or as a member of a community group outside of your college.

Wikis are popular with researchers because they contain information about topics that can change day to day, such as medicine or business. In addition, because wikis rely on information contributed voluntarily by members of a community, they represent a much broader spectrum of viewpoints than media that publish only information that has been approved by editors. For this reason, however, you should be especially careful when you use wikis because the information they contain might not be trustworthy. It's a good idea to corroborate any information you find on a wiki by consulting other sources.

How do you search wikis? You can use any search engine and add the word "wiki" to the search. Or you can use a specialized search engine such as Wiki.com.

Blogs   Many technical and scientific organizations, universities, and private companies sponsor blogs that can offer useful information for researchers. Bloggers almost always invite their readers to post comments.

Keep in mind that bloggers are not always independent voices. A Hewlett-Packard employee blogging on an HP-sponsored blog will likely be presenting the company's viewpoint on the topic. Don't count on that blogger to offer objective views about products.

Figure 5.3 is a screen shot of a portion of the blog.AIDS.gov site, which offers information that is likely to be credible, accurate, and timely.

Evaluating the Information

You've taken notes, paraphrased, and quoted material from your secondary research. Now, with more information than you can possibly use, you try to figure out what it all means. You realize that you still have some questions, that some of the information is incomplete, some contradictory, and some unclear. There is no shortage of information; the challenge is to find information that is accurate, unbiased, comprehensive, appropriately technical, current, and clear.

- *Accurate.* If you are researching whether your company should consider flextime scheduling, you might begin by determining the number of employees who would be interested in flextime. If you estimate that number to be 500 but it is in fact closer to 50, you will waste time doing an unnecessary study.

- *Unbiased.* You want sources that have no financial stake in your project. If employees cannot carpool easily because they start work at different times, a private company that transports workers in vans is likely to be a biased source because it could profit from flextime.

▶ **In This Book**

For more about blogs, see Ch. 3, pp. 50–52.

▶ **In This Book**

For more about taking notes, paraphrasing, and quoting, see Appendix, Part A.

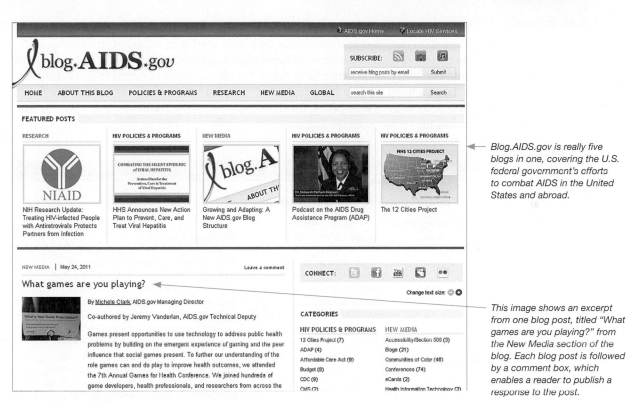

Figure 5.3   A Blog
Source: U.S. Department of Health and Human Services, 2011 <http://blog.aids.gov/>.

Blog.AIDS.gov is really five blogs in one, covering the U.S. federal government's efforts to combat AIDS in the United States and abroad.

This image shows an excerpt from one blog post, titled "What games are you playing?" from the New Media section of the blog. Each blog post is followed by a comment box, which enables a reader to publish a response to the post.

- *Comprehensive.* You want information from different kinds of people—in terms of gender, cultural characteristics, and age—and from people representing all viewpoints on the topic.

- *Appropriately technical.* Good information is sufficiently detailed to respond to the needs of your readers, but not so detailed that readers cannot understand it. For the flextime study, you need to find out whether opening your building an hour earlier and closing it an hour later will significantly affect your utility costs. You can get this information by interviewing people in the Operations Department; you will not need to inspect all the utility records of the company.

- *Current.* If your information is 10 years old, it might not accurately reflect today's situation.

- *Clear.* You want information that is easy to understand. Otherwise, you'll waste time figuring it out, and you might misinterpret it.

The most difficult kind of material to evaluate is information from the Internet, because it rarely undergoes the formal review procedure used for books

On the Web

For links to sources on finding and evaluating Internet information, click on Links Library for Ch. 5 on <bedfordstmartins.com/ps>.

and professional journals. A general principle for using any information you found on the Internet, especially on social media, is to be extremely careful. Because content is unlikely to have been reviewed before being published on a social-media site, use one or more trusted sources to confirm the information you locate. Some instructors do not allow their students to use blogs or wikis, including Wikipedia, for their research. Check with your instructor to learn his or her policies.

Guidelines

Evaluating Print and Online Sources

Criteria	For printed sources	For online sources
Authorship	Do you recognize the name of the author? Does the source describe the author's credentials and current position? If not, can you find this information in a who's who or by searching for other books or other journal articles by the author?	If you do not recognize the author's name, is the site mentioned on another reputable site? Does the site contain links to other reputable sites? Does it contain biographical information—the author's current position and credentials? Can you use a search engine to find other references to the author's credentials? Be especially careful with unedited sources such as Wikipedia; some articles in it are authoritative, others are not. Be careful, too, with blogs, some of which are written by disgruntled former employees with a score to settle.
Publisher	What is the publisher's reputation? A reliable book is published by a reputable trade, academic, or scholarly publisher; a reliable journal is sponsored by a professional association or university. Are the editorial board members well known? Trade publications—magazines about a particular industry or group—often promote the interests of that industry or group. For example, information in trade publications for loggers or environmentalists might be biased. If you doubt the authority of a book or journal, ask a reference librarian or a professor.	Can you determine the publisher's identity from headers or footers? Is the publisher reputable? If the site comes from a personal account on an Internet service provider, the author might be writing outside his or her field of expertise. Many Internet sites exist largely for public relations or advertising. For instance, Web sites of corporations and other organizations are unlikely to contain self-critical information. For blogs, examine the *blogroll*, a list of links to other blogs and Web sites. Credible blogs are likely to link to blogs already known to be credible. If a blog links only to friends, blogs hosted by the same corporation, or blogs that share the same beliefs, be very cautious.

Criteria	For printed sources	For online sources
Knowledge of the literature	Does the author appear to be knowledgeable about the major literature? Is there a bibliography? Are there notes throughout the document?	Analyze the Internet source as you would any other source. Often, references to other sources will take the form of links.
Accuracy and verifiability of the information	Is the information based on reasonable assumptions? Does the author clearly describe the methods and theories used in producing the information, and are they appropriate to the subject? Has the author used sound reasoning? Has the author explained the limitations of the information?	Is the site well constructed? Is the information well written? Is it based on reasonable assumptions? Are the claims supported by appropriate evidence? Has the author used sound reasoning? Has the author explained the limitations of the information? Are sources cited? Online services such as BlogPulse help you evaluate how active a blog is, how the blog ranks compared to other blogs, and who is citing the blog. Active, influential blogs that are frequently linked to and cited by others might be more likely to contain accurate, verifiable information.
Timeliness	Does the document rely on recent data? Was the document published recently?	Was the document created recently? Was it updated recently? If a site is not yet complete, be wary.

On the Web

Evaluating sources is easier if you start searching from a reputable list of links, such as that of the WWW Virtual Library, sponsored by the World Wide Web Consortium. Click on Links Library for Ch. 5 on <bedfordstmartins.com/ps>.

CONDUCTING PRIMARY RESEARCH

Although the library and the Internet offer a wealth of secondary sources, in the workplace you will often need to conduct primary research to acquire new information. There are seven major categories of primary research: observations and demonstrations, inspections, experiments, field research, interviews, inquiries, and questionnaires.

Observations and Demonstrations

When you *observe*, you simply watch some activity to understand some aspect of it. For instance, if you are trying to determine whether the location of the break room is interfering with work on the factory floor, you could observe the situation, preferably at different times of the day and on different days of the week. If you saw workers distracted by people moving in and out of the room or by sounds made in the room, you would record your observations by taking notes, taking still pictures, or videotaping events. An observation might lead to other forms of primary research. You might, for example, follow up by interviewing some employees who might help you understand what you observed.

DOCUMENT ANALYSIS ACTIVITY
Evaluating Information from Internet Sources

The following blog post appears in the Health Care Blog, which uses the subtitle "Everything you always wanted to know about the Health Care system. But were afraid to ask." The questions ask you to consider the guidelines for evaluating Internet sources (pp. 92–93).

1. The author of this blog post, Dr. Daniel Palestrant, is a guest blogger. If you considered using Dr. Palestrant as a source in a document you were writing, what information would you want to discover about him, and how would you discover it?

2. If you considered using this post as a source in a document you were writing, what information would you want to discover about the blog? How would you discover it?

3. Study the Guidelines box (pp. 92–93). Evaluate this passage about health-care reform on the basis of the "accuracy and verifiability of the information" criterion. Identify a claim in the post that might be strengthened by the addition of more evidence.

On the Web

To submit your responses to your instructor, click on Document Analysis Activities for Ch. 5 on <bedfordstmartins.com/ps>.

The Health Care Blog

Everything you always wanted to know about the Health Care system. But were afraid to ask.

FRONT PAGE : | TECH | Op-Ed Page | About | Advertise | List

THCB UPDATE Get email updates of new posts and industry

IN THE PRESS

"A must-read blog ..."
-The Wall Street Journal

(More) Madness in Massachusetts

By Daniel Palestrant, MD

Lately I have been watching with complete horror the events playing out in my home state of Massachusetts. A bill currently under review by the state legislature will make participation in the state and federal Medicare/Medicaid programs a condition of medical licensure, effectively making physicians employees of the state.

This is particularly alarming because Massachusetts is essentially a leading indicator of what will happen in the rest of the country. Several years ago the state passed a series of laws mandating health coverage. Like the recently passed national health reform bill, the Massachusetts law did not address any of the well known causes of runaway costs, including tort reform, drug costs, or insurance regulation.

Although the state now has one of the highest percentages of its population insured, it is grappling with exploding healthcare costs. In response, it is imposing capitation schedules, reductions in payment rates and now mandatory participation in the health programs by physicians. What most people don't understand is that the private insurers are also free to lower their physician payments, based on the Medicare/Medicaid benchmarks. This is all the more concerning given the fact that the Federal reimbursement rate is now scheduled to be reduced 21% on April 15.

We will no doubt see the same sequence of events play out across the country as the current versions of healthcare reform are implemented. The net effect of these laws is that it will make it close to impossible for physicians to stay in private practice. Patient access to physicians will suffer as more and more physicians retire and/or move to different states. For our academic colleagues who think this turn of events can only "help" them because they won't have to compete with physicians in private practice, just wait. 28 states are now imposing "comparability" laws that allow nurse practitioners and other allied healthcare professionals to work without the supervision of a physician with equal pay. Few academic departments can avoid hiring "physician extenders" if they want to stay competitive. As this gains momentum, physician payments will be pushed downwards. As the "going rate" goes lower, academic salaries will also get pushed downwards. I knew this reform effort would be bad for the practice of medicine and even worse for patient care. I just had no idea things would deteriorate this fast.

Daniel Palestrant, MD, is the CEO of Sermo.

Source: Palestrant, 2010 <http://thehealthcareblog.com/blog/2010/04/22/more-madness-in-massachusetts>.

When you witness a *demonstration* (or *demo*), you are watching someone carry out a process. For instance, if your company is considering buying a mail-sorting machine, you could arrange to visit a manufacturer's facility, where technicians would show how the machine works.

When you plan to observe a situation or witness a demo, prepare beforehand. Write down the questions you need answered or the factors you want to investigate. Prepare interview questions in case you have a chance to speak with someone. Think about how you are going to incorporate the information you acquire into the document you will write. Finally, bring whatever equipment you will need (pen and paper, computer, camera, etc.) to the site of the observation or demo.

Inspections

Inspections are like observations, but you participate more actively. For example, a civil engineer can determine what caused a crack in a foundation by inspecting the site: walking around, looking at the crack, photographing it and the surrounding scene, picking up the soil.

Inspection techniques often require only your knowledge and professional judgment, but sometimes they are more complicated. A civil engineer inspecting foundation cracking might want to test his or her hunches by bringing soil samples back to the lab for analysis.

When you carry out an inspection, do your homework beforehand. Think about how you will use the data in your document: will you need photographs or video files or computer data? Then prepare the materials and equipment you'll need to capture the data.

Experiments

Learning to conduct the many kinds of experiments used in a particular field can take months or even years. This discussion is a brief introduction. In many cases, conducting an experiment involves four phases.

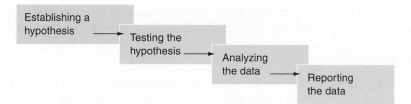

- *Establishing a hypothesis.* A hypothesis is an informed guess about the relationship between two factors. In a study relating gasoline octane and miles per gallon, a hypothesis might be that a car will get 10 percent better mileage with 89 octane gas than with 87 octane.

- *Testing the hypothesis.* Usually, you need an experimental group and a control group. These two groups would be identical except for the condition you are studying: in the above example, the gasoline. The control group would be a car running on 87 octane. The experimental group would be an identical car running on 89 octane. The experiment would consist of driving the two cars over an identical course at the same speed—preferably in some sort of controlled environment—over a given distance, such as 1,000 miles. Then, you would calculate the miles per gallon. The results would either support or refute your original hypothesis.

- *Analyzing the data.* Do your data show a correlation—one factor changing along with another—or a causal relationship? For example, we know that sports cars are involved in more fatal accidents than sedans (there is a stronger correlation for sports cars), but we don't know whether the car or the way it is driven is the important factor (causal relationship).

In This Book

For more about reports, see Chs. 12 and 13.

- *Reporting the data.* When researchers report their findings, they explain what they did, why they did it, what they saw, what it means, and what ought to be done next.

Field Research

Whereas an experiment yields quantitative data that typically can be measured precisely, most field research is qualitative; that is, it yields data that typically cannot be measured as precisely. Often in field research, you seek to understand the quality of an experience. For instance, you might want to understand how a new seating arrangement affects group dynamics in a classroom. You could design a study in which you observed and recorded the classes and interviewed the students and the instructor about their reactions to the new arrangement. Then you could do the same in a traditional classroom and compare the results.

Some kinds of studies have both quantitative and qualitative elements. In the case of classroom seating arrangements, you could include some quantitative measures, such as the number of times students talked with one another. You could also distribute questionnaires to elicit the opinions of the students and the instructor. If you used these same quantitative measures on enough classrooms, you could gather valid quantitative information.

Interviews

Interviews are extremely useful when you need information on subjects that are too new to have been discussed in the professional literature or are inappropriate for widespread publication (such as local political questions).

In choosing a respondent—a person to interview—answer three questions:

- *What questions do you want to answer?* Only then can you begin to search for a person who can provide the information.

- *Who could provide this information?* The ideal respondent is an expert willing to talk. Unless the respondent is an obvious choice, such as the professor carrying out the research you are studying, use directories, such as local industrial guides, to locate potential respondents.

- *Is the person willing to be interviewed?* On the phone or in writing, state what you want to ask about. The person might not be able to help you but might be willing to refer you to someone who can. Explain why you have decided to ask him or her. (A compliment works better than admitting that the person you really wanted to interview is out of town.) Explain what you plan to do with the information, such as write a report or give a talk. Then, if the person is willing to be interviewed, set up an appointment at his or her convenience.

Guidelines

Conducting an Interview

Preparing for the interview

▶ **Do your homework.** If you ask questions that are already answered in the professional literature, the respondent might become annoyed and uncooperative.

▶ **Prepare good questions.** Good questions are clear, focused, and open.

— Be clear. The respondent should be able to understand what you are asking.

UNCLEAR	Why do you sell Trane products?
CLEAR	What are the characteristics of Trane products that led you to include them in your product line?

The unclear question can be answered in a number of unhelpful ways: "Because they're too expensive to give away" or "Because I'm a Trane dealer."

— Be focused. The question must be narrow enough to be answered briefly. If you want more information, you can ask a follow-up question.

UNFOCUSED	What is the future of the computer industry?
FOCUSED	What will the American chip industry look like in 10 years?

— Ask open questions. Your purpose is to get the respondent to talk. Don't ask a lot of questions that have yes or no answers.

▶ On the Web

For an excellent discussion of interview questions, see Joel Bowman's *Business Communication: Managing Information and Relationships*. Click on Links Library for Ch. 5 on <bedfordstmartins.com/ps>.

	CLOSED	Do you think the federal government should create industrial partnerships?
	OPEN	What are the advantages and disadvantages of the federal government's creating industrial partnerships?

▶ **Check your equipment.** If you will be taping the interview, test your voice recorder or video camera to make sure it is operating properly.

Beginning the interview

▶ **Arrive on time.**

▶ **Thank the respondent for taking the time to talk with you.**

▶ **State the subject and purpose of the interview and what you plan to do with the information.**

▶ **If you wish to tape the interview, ask permission.**

Conducting the interview

▶ **Take notes.** Write down important concepts, facts, and numbers, but don't take such copious notes that you are still writing when the respondent finishes an answer.

▶ **Start with prepared questions.** Because you are likely to be nervous at the start, you might forget important questions. Have your first few questions ready.

▶ **Be prepared to ask follow-up questions.** Listen carefully to the respondent's answer and be ready to ask a follow-up question or request a clarification. Have your other prepared questions ready, but be willing to deviate from them if the respondent leads you in unexpected directions.

▶ **Keep the interview on track.** Gently return to the point if the respondent begins straying unproductively, but don't interrupt rudely or show annoyance.

Concluding the interview

▶ **Thank the respondent.**

▶ **Ask for a follow-up interview.** If a second meeting would be useful, ask to arrange it.

▶ **Ask for permission to quote the respondent.** If you think you might want to quote the respondent by name, ask for permission now.

After the interview

▶ **Write down the important information while the interview is fresh in your mind.** (This step is unnecessary, of course, if you have recorded the interview.) If you will be printing a transcript of the interview, make the transcript now.

> ▶ **Send a brief thank-you note.** Within a day or two, send a note that shows you appreciate the respondent's courtesy and that you value what you have learned. In the note, confirm any previous offers you have made, such as sending the respondent a copy of your final document.

When you wish to present the data from an interview in a document you are preparing, include a transcript of the interview (or an excerpt from the interview). You will probably present the transcript as an appendix so that readers can refer to it but are not slowed down when reading the body of the document. You might decide to present brief excerpts from the transcript in the body of the document as evidence for points you make.

Inquiries

A useful alternative to a personal interview is to send an inquiry. This inquiry can take the form of a letter, an e-mail, or a message sent through an organization's Web site. Although digital inquiries are more convenient for both the sender and the recipient, a physical letter is more formal and therefore might be more appropriate if the topic is important (concerning personnel layoffs, for instance) or related to safety.

▶ **In This Book**
For more about inquiry letters, see Ch. 9, p. 226.

If you are lucky, your respondent will provide detailed and helpful answers. However, the respondent might not clearly understand what you want to know or might choose not to help you. Although the strategy of the inquiry is essentially that of a personal interview, inquiries can be less successful because the recipient has not already agreed to provide information and might not respond. Also, an inquiry, unlike an interview, gives you little opportunity to follow up by asking for clarification.

Questionnaires

Questionnaires enable you to solicit information from a large group of people. You can send questionnaires through the mail, e-mail them, present them as forms on a Web site, or use survey software (such as SurveyMonkey).

Unfortunately, questionnaires rarely yield completely satisfactory results, for three reasons:

- *Some of the questions will misfire.* Respondents will misinterpret some of your questions or supply useless answers.

- *You won't obtain as many responses as you want.* The response rate will almost never exceed 50 percent. In most cases, it will be closer to 10 to 20 percent.

- *You cannot be sure the respondents are representative.* People who feel strongly about an issue are much more likely to respond to questionnaires than are those who do not. For this reason, you need to be careful in drawing conclusions based on a small number of responses to a questionnaire.

When you send a questionnaire, you are asking the recipient to do you a favor. Your goal should be to construct questions that will elicit the information you need as simply and efficiently as possible.

Asking Effective Questions   To ask effective questions, follow two suggestions:

- *Use unbiased language.* Don't ask, "Should U.S. clothing manufacturers protect themselves from unfair foreign competition?" Instead, ask, "Are you in favor of imposing tariffs on men's clothing?"

- *Be specific.* If you ask, "Do you favor improving the safety of automobiles?" only an eccentric would answer no. Instead, ask, "Do you favor requiring automobile manufacturers to equip new cars with electronic stability control, which would raise the price by an average of $300 per car?"

The Choices and Strategies box on page 101 explains common types of questions used in questionnaires.

Include an introductory explanation with the questionnaire. This explanation should clearly indicate who you are, why you are writing, what you plan to do with the information from the questionnaire, and when you will need it.

Testing the Questionnaire   Before you send out *any* questionnaire, show it and its accompanying explanation to a few people who can help you identify any problems. After you have revised the materials, test them on people whose backgrounds are similar to those of your real respondents. Revise the materials a second time, and, if possible, test them again. Once you have sent the questionnaire, you cannot revise it and resend it to the same people.

Administering the Questionnaire   Determining who should receive the questionnaire can be simple or difficult. If you want to know what the residents of a particular street think about a proposed construction project, your job is easy. But if you want to know what mechanical-engineering students in colleges across the country think about their curricula, you will need a background in sampling techniques to identify a representative sample.

Make it easy for respondents to present their information. For mailed questionnaires, include a self-addressed, stamped envelope.

Presenting Questionnaire Data in Your Document   To decide where and how to present the data that you acquire from your questionnaire, think about your audience and purpose. Start with this principle: important information is presented and analyzed in the body of a document, whereas less-important information is presented in an appendix (a section at the end that only some of your audience will read). Most often, some version of the information appears in both places, but in different ways.

CHOICES AND STRATEGIES   Choosing Types of Questions for Questionnaires

If you want to . . .	Consider using this question type	Example
Have respondents choose among alternatives	**Multiple choice.** The respondent selects one answer from a list.	Would you consider joining a company-sponsored sports team? Yes_____ No_____
Measure respondents' feelings about an idea or concept	**Likert scale.** The respondent ranks the degree to which he or she agrees or disagrees with the statement. Using an even number of possible responses (six, in this case) increases your chances of obtaining useful data. With an odd number, many respondents will choose the middle response.	The flextime program has been a success in its first year. strongly agree _ _ _ _ _ _ strongly disagree
Measure respondents' feelings about a task, an experience, or an object	**Semantic differentials.** The respondent registers a response along a continuum between a pair of opposing adjectives. As with Likert scales, an even number of possible responses yields better data.	simple _ _ _ _ _ _ difficult interesting _ _ _ _ _ _ boring
Have respondents indicate a priority among a number of alternatives	**Ranking.** When using ranking questions, be sure to give instructions about what method (in this case, numbering) the respondents should use to rank the items.	Please rank the following work schedules in order of preference. Put a 1 next to the schedule you would most like to have, a 2 next to your second choice, and so on. 8:00–4:30_____ 9:00–5:30_____ 8:30–5:00_____ flexible_____
Ask open-ended questions	**Short answer.** The respondent writes a brief answer using phrases or sentences.	What do you feel are the major advantages of the new parts-requisitioning policy? 1._____ 2._____ 3._____
Give respondents an opportunity to present fuller responses	**Short essay.** Although essay questions can yield information you never would have found using closed-ended questions, you will receive fewer responses because they require more effort. Also, essays cannot be quantified precisely, as data from other types of questions can.	The new parts-requisitioning policy has been in effect for a year. How well do you think it is working? _____ _____ _____ _____ _____

If you think your questionnaire data are relatively unimportant, present the questionnaire in an appendix. If you can, present the respondents' data—the answers they provided—in the questionnaire itself, as shown here:

If you think your reader will benefit from analyses of the data, present such analyses. For instance, you could calculate the percentage for each response: for question 1, "12 people—17 percent—say they do not eat in the cafeteria at all." Or you could present the percentage in parentheses after each number: "12 (17%)."

1. Approximately how many days per week do you eat lunch in the lunchroom?

   0 **12** 1 **16** 2 **18** 3 **12** 4 **9** 5 **4**

2. At approximately what time do you eat in the lunchroom?

   11:30–12:30 **3** 12:00–1:00 **26** 12:30–1:30 **7** varies **23**

If you think your questionnaire data are relatively important, present the full data in an appendix and interpret selected data in the body of the document. For instance, you might want to devote a few sentences or paragraphs to the data for one of the questions. The following example shows how one writer might discuss the data from question 2.

> Question 2 shows that 26 people say that they use the cafeteria between noon and 1:00. Only 10 people selected the two other times: 11:30–12:30 or 12:30–1:30. Of the 23 people who said they use the cafeteria at various times, we can conclude that at least a third—8 people—use it between noon and 1:00. If this assumption is correct, at least 34 people (26 + 8) use the cafeteria between noon and 1:00. This would explain why people routinely cannot find a table in the noon hour, especially between 12:15 and 12:30. To alleviate this problem, we might consider asking department heads not to schedule meetings between 11:30 and 1:30, to make it easier for their people to choose one of the less-popular times.

The body of a document is also a good place to discuss important nonquantitative data. For example, you might wish to discuss and interpret several representative textual answers to open-ended questions.

ETHICS NOTE

Reporting and Analyzing Data Honestly

When you put a lot of time and effort into a research project, it's frustrating when you can't find the information you need or when the information you find doesn't help you say what you want to say. As discussed in Chapter 2, your challenge as a professional is to tell the truth.

If the evidence suggests that the course of action you propose won't work, don't omit that evidence or change it. Rather, try to figure out the discrepancy between the evidence and your proposal. Present your explanation honestly.

If you can't find reputable evidence to support your claim that one device works better than another, don't just keep silent and hope your readers won't notice. Explain why you think the evidence is missing and how you propose to follow up by continuing your research.

If you make an honest mistake, you are a person. If you cover up a mistake, you're a dishonest person. If you get caught fudging the data, you could be an unemployed dishonest person. Even if you don't get caught, you're still a smaller person.

Writer's Checklist

☐ Did you determine the questions you need to answer for your document? (p. 80)

Did you choose appropriate secondary-research methods to answer those questions, including, if appropriate,
☐ online catalogs? (p. 86)
☐ reference works? (p. 86)
☐ periodical indexes? (p. 86)
☐ newspaper indexes? (p. 87)
☐ abstract services? (p. 87)
☐ government information? (p. 88)
☐ social media and other interactive resources? (p. 89)

In evaluating information, did you carefully assess
☐ the author's credentials? (p. 92)
☐ the publisher? (p. 92)

☐ the author's knowledge of literature in the field? (p. 93)
☐ the accuracy and verifiability of the information? (p. 93)
☐ the timeliness of the information? (p. 93)

Did you choose appropriate primary-research methods to answer your questions, including, if appropriate,
☐ observations and demonstrations? (p. 93)
☐ inspections? (p. 95)
☐ experiments? (p. 95)
☐ field research? (p. 96)
☐ interviews? (p. 96)
☐ inquiries? (p. 99)
☐ questionnaires? (p. 99)

☐ Did you report and analyze the data honestly? (p. 102)

Exercises

In This Book   For more about memos, see Ch. 9, p. 223.

1. Imagine that you are an executive working for a company that distributes books to bookstores in the Seattle, Washington, area. Your company, with a 20,000-square-foot warehouse and a fleet of 15 small delivery vans, employs 75 people. The following are three questions that an academic researcher specializing in energy issues might focus her research on. Translate each of these academic questions into workplace questions that your company might need to answer.

   a. What are the principal problems that need to be resolved before biomass (such as switchgrass) can become a viable energy source for cars and trucks?

   b. How much money will need to be invested in the transmission grid before windmills can become a major part of the energy solution for business and residential customers in the western United States?

   c. Would a federal program that enables companies to buy and sell carbon offsets help or hurt industry in the United States?

2. For each of the following questions, select a research technique that is likely to yield a useful answer. For

instance, if the question is "Which companies within a 20-mile radius of our company headquarters sell recycled paper?" a search of the Web is likely to provide a useful answer.

   a. Does the Honda CR-V include traction control as a standard feature?

   b. How much money has our company's philanthropic foundation donated to colleges and universities in each of the last three years?

   c. How does a tankless water heater work?

   d. Could our Building 3 support a rooftop green space?

   e. How can we determine whether we would save more money by switching to fluorescent or LED lighting in our corporate offices?

3. INTERNET EXERCISE Using a search engine, answer the following questions. Provide the URL of each site you mention. If your instructor requests it, submit your answers in an e-mail to him or her.

   a. What are the three largest or most important professional organizations in your field? (For example, if you are a construction management major, your field is construction management, civil engineering, or industrial engineering.)

b. What are three important journals read by people in your field?

c. What are three important online discussion lists or bulletin boards read by people in your field?

d. What are the date and location of an upcoming national or international professional meeting for people in your field?

e. Name and describe, in one paragraph for each, three major issues being discussed by practitioners or academics in your field. For instance, nurses might be discussing the effect of managed care on the quality of medical care delivered to patients.

4. Revise the following interview questions to make them more effective. In a brief paragraph for each question, explain why you have revised it as you have.

a. What is the role of communication in your daily job?

b. Do you think it is better to relocate your warehouse or go to just-in-time manufacturing?

c. Isn't it true that it's almost impossible to train an engineer to write well?

d. Where are your company's headquarters?

e. Is there anything else you think I should know?

5. Revise the following questions from questionnaires to make them more effective. In a brief paragraph for each, explain why you have revised the question as you have.

a. Does your company provide tuition reimbursement for its employees? Yes_____ No_____

b. What do you see as the future of bioengineering?

c. How satisfied are you with the computer support you receive?

d. How many employees work at your company? 5–10_____ 10–15_____ 15 or more_____

e. What kinds of documents do you write most often? memos_____ letters_____ reports_____

6. **GROUP/INTERNET EXERCISE** Form small groups, and describe and evaluate your college or university's Web site. A different member of the group might carry out each of the following tasks:

- In an e-mail to the site's webmaster, ask questions about the process of creating the site. For example, how involved was the webmaster with the content and design of the site? What is the webmaster's role in maintaining the site?

- Analyze the kinds of information the site contains, and determine whether the site is intended primarily for faculty, students, alumni, legislators, or prospective students.

- Determine the overlap between information on the site and information in printed documents published by the school. In those cases in which they overlap, is the information on the site merely a duplication of the printed information, or has it been revised to take advantage of the unique capabilities of the Web?

In a memo to your instructor, present your findings and recommend ways to improve the site.

On the Web

For a case assignment, "Revising a Questionnaire," see Cases on <bedfordstmartins.com/ps>.

6

Writing for Your Readers

iStockphoto. Photo composition by Jimmie Young.

Make sure the document is coherent and clear before it gets to the reader.

Writing for your readers means writing documents that are easy for readers to use and understand. It starts with making sure you present yourself effectively, as a professional whose writing is worth reading. In addition, writing for your readers involves creating a coherent document—one in which readers can easily find the information they need and can readily understand how that information relates to the rest of the document. If your document is coherent, your readers can concentrate on what it says rather than wonder what information it contains, how the information is organized, or how to find what they need. Finally, writing for your readers means choosing words carefully and crafting accurate, clear, concise, and forceful sentences. If a sentence doesn't say what you intended, misunderstandings can occur, and misunderstandings cost money.

More important, the ability to write for your readers—word by word and sentence by sentence—reflects positively on you and your organization.

PRESENTING YOURSELF EFFECTIVELY

A big part of presenting yourself effectively is showing that you know the appropriate information about your subject. However, you also need to come across as a professional.

Guidelines

Creating a Professional Persona

Your *persona* is how you appear to your readers. Demonstrating the following four characteristics will help you establish an attractive professional persona.

▶ **Cooperativeness.** Make clear that your goal is to solve a problem, not to advance your own interests.

▶ **Moderation.** Be moderate in your judgments. The problem you are describing will not likely spell doom for your organization, and the solution you propose will not solve all the company's problems.

▶ **Fair-mindedness.** Acknowledge the strengths of opposing points of view, even as you offer counterarguments.

▶ **Modesty.** If you fail to acknowledge that you don't know everything, someone else will be sure to volunteer that insight.

The following paragraph shows how a writer can demonstrate the qualities of cooperativeness, moderation, fair-mindedness, and modesty:

In the first three sentences, the writer acknowledges the problems with the plan.

The use of "I think" adds an attractive modesty; the recommendation might be unwise.

The recommendation itself is moderate; the writer does not claim that the plan will save the world.

In the last sentence, the writer shows a spirit of cooperativeness by focusing on the company's goals.

> This plan is certainly not perfect. For one thing, it calls for a greater up-front investment than we had anticipated. And the return on investment through the first three quarters is likely to fall short of our initial goals. However, I think this plan is the best of the three alternatives for the following reasons. . . . Therefore, I recommend that we begin implementing the plan. I am confident that this plan will enable us to enter the flat-screen market successfully, building on our fine reputation for high-quality advanced electronics.

USING BASIC ORGANIZATIONAL PATTERNS

Every document calls for its own organizational pattern. You should begin by asking yourself whether a conventional pattern for presenting your information already exists. A conventional pattern makes things easier for you as a writer because it serves as a template or checklist, helping you remember which information to include in your document and where to put it. For your audience, a conventional pattern makes your document easier to read and understand because the organization of information meets readers' expectations. When you write a proposal, for example, readers who are familiar with proposals can find the information they want in your document if you put it where others have put similar information. The Choices and Strategies box below explains the relationship between organizational patterns and the kinds of information you want to present.

Does this mean that technical communication is merely the process of filling in the blanks? No. You need to assess the writing situation continuously as you work. If you think you can communicate your ideas better by modifying a conventional pattern or by devising a new pattern, do so. Long, complex arguments often require several organizational patterns. For instance, one part of a document might be a causal analysis of a problem, and another might be a comparison and contrast of two options for solving that problem.

On the Web

For a discussion of organizing information, see Paradigm Online Writing Assistant. Click on Links Library for Ch. 6 on <bedfordstmartins.com/ps>.

CHOICES AND STRATEGIES   Choosing Effective Organizational Patterns

If you want to . . .	Consider using this organizational pattern	Example
Explain events that occurred or might occur, or tasks the reader is to carry out in sequence	**Chronological.** Most of the time, you present information in chronological order. Sometimes, however, you use reverse chronology.	You describe the process you used to diagnose the problem with the accounting software. In a job résumé, you describe your more-recent jobs before your less-recent ones.
Describe a physical object or scene, such as a device or a location	**Spatial.** You choose an organizing principle such as top-to-bottom, east-to-west, or inside-to-outside.	You describe the three buildings that will make up the new production facility.
Explain a complex situation or idea, such as the factors that led to a problem or the theory that underlies a process	**General to specific.** You present general information first, then specific information. Understanding the big picture helps readers understand the details.	You explain the major changes in and the details of the law mandating the use of a new refrigerant in cooling systems.
Present a set of factors	**More important to less important.** You discuss the most important issue first, then the next most-important issue, and so forth. In technical communication, you don't want to create suspense. You want to present the most important information first.	When you launch a new product, you discuss market niche, competition, and then pricing.

Choosing Effective Organizational Patterns (*continued*)

If you want to . . .	Consider using this organizational pattern	Example
Present similarities and differences between two or more items	**Comparison and contrast.** You choose from one of two patterns: discuss all the factors related to one item, then all the factors related to the next item, and so forth; or discuss one factor as it relates to all the items, then another factor as it relates to all the items, and so forth.	You discuss the strengths and weaknesses of three companies bidding on a contract your company is offering.
Assign items to logical categories, or discuss the elements that make up a single item	**Classification and partition.** Classification involves placing items into categories according to some basis. Partition involves breaking a single item into its major elements.	You group the motors your company manufactures according to the fuel they burn: gasoline or diesel. Or you explain the operation of each major component of one of your motors.
Discuss a problem you encountered, the steps you took to address the problem, and the outcome or solution	**Problem-methods-solution.** You can use this pattern in discussing the past, the present, or the future. Readers understand this organizational pattern because they use it in their everyday lives.	In describing how your company is responding to a new competitor, you discuss the problem (the recent loss in sales), the methods (how you plan to examine your product line and business practices), and the solution (which changes will help your company remain competitive).
Discuss the factors that led to (or will lead to) a given situation, or the effects that a situation led to or will lead to	**Cause and effect.** You can start from causes and speculate about effects, or start with the effect and work backward to determine the causes.	You discuss factors that you think contributed to a recent sales dip for one of your products. Or you explain how you think changes to an existing product will affect its sales.

WRITING COHERENT TITLES AND HEADINGS

The title of a document is crucial because it is your first chance to define your subject and purpose for your readers, giving them their first clue in deciding if the document contains the information they need. The title is an implicit promise to readers: "This document is about Subject A, and it was written to achieve Purpose B." Everything that follows has to relate clearly to the subject and purpose defined in the title; if it doesn't, then either the title is misleading or the document has failed to make good on the title's promise.

An effective title is precise. For example, if you are writing a feasibility study on the subject of offering free cholesterol screening at your company, the title should contain the key terms *free cholesterol screening* and *feasibility*. The following title would be effective:

> Offering Free Cholesterol Screening at Thrall Associates: A Feasibility Study

If your document is an internal report discussing company business, you might not need to identify the company. In that case, the following would be clear:

> Offering Free Cholesterol Screening: A Feasibility Study

Or you could present the purpose before the subject:

> A Feasibility Study of Offering Free Cholesterol Screening

Avoid substituting general terms, such as *health screening* for *cholesterol screening* or *study* for *feasibility study*; the more precise your terms, the more useful your readers will find the title. An added benefit of using precise terms is that your document can be more accurately and effectively indexed in databases and online libraries, increasing the chances that someone researching your subject will be able to find the document.

You'll notice that clear, comprehensive titles tend to be long. If you need eight or ten words to say what you want to say about your subject and purpose, use them.

Headings, which are lower-level titles for the sections and subsections in a document, do more than announce the subject that will be discussed in the document. Collectively, they create a *hierarchy of information*, dividing the document into major sections and subdividing those sections into subsections. In this way, coherent headings communicate the relative importance and generality of the information that follows, helping readers recognize major sections as *primary* (likely to contain more-important and more-general information) and subsections as *secondary* or *subordinate* (likely to contain less-important and more-specific information).

Coherent, well-designed headings communicate this relationship not only through their content, but also through their design. For this reason, you should ensure that the design of a primary heading (sometimes referred to as a *level 1 heading*, *1 heading*, or *A heading*) clearly distinguishes it from a subordinate heading (a *level 2 heading*, *2 heading*, or *B heading*), and that the design of that subordinate heading clearly distinguishes it from a subordinate heading at a lower level (a *level 3 heading*, *3 heading*, or *C heading*).

The headings used in this book illustrate this principle, as does the example below. Notice that the example uses both typography and indentation to distinguish one heading from another and to communicate visually how information at one level logically relates to information at other levels.

LEVEL 1 HEADING

Level 2 Heading

Level 3 Heading

Effective headings can help both reader and writer by forecasting not only the subject and purpose of the discussion that follows but also its scope and organization. When readers encounter the heading "Three Health Benefits of Yoga: Improved Muscle Tone, Enhanced Flexibility, Better Posture," they can reasonably assume that the discussion will consist of three parts (not two or four) and that it likely will begin with a discussion of muscle tone, followed by a discussion of flexibility and then posture.

Because headings introduce text that discusses or otherwise elaborates on the subject defined by the heading, you should avoid creating back-to-back headings. In other words, avoid following one heading directly with another heading:

3. Approaches to Neighborhood Policing

3.1 Community Policing

According to the COPS Agency (a component of the U.S. Department of Justice), "Community policing focuses on crime and social disorder." . . .

What's wrong with back-to-back headings? They are illogical, and they confuse readers. The heading "3. Approaches to Neighborhood Policing" announces to readers that you have something to say about neighborhood policing—but you don't say anything. Instead, another, subordinate heading appears, announcing to readers that you now have something to say about community policing.

To avoid confusing and frustrating readers, separate the headings with text, as in this example:

3. Approaches to Neighborhood Policing

Over the past decade, the scholarly community has concluded that community policing offers significant advantages over the traditional approach based on patrolling in police cars. However, the traditional approach has some distinct strengths. In the following discussion, we define each approach and then explain its advantages and disadvantages.

3.1 Community Policing

According to the COPS Agency (a component of the U.S. Department of Justice), "Community policing focuses on crime and social disorder." . . .

The text after the heading "3. Approaches to Neighborhood Policing" is called an *advance organizer*. It indicates the background, purpose, scope, and organization of the discussion that follows it. Advance organizers improve coherence by giving readers an overview of the discussion before they encounter the details in the discussion itself.

Guidelines

Revising Headings

Follow these four suggestions to make your headings more effective.

▶ **Avoid long noun strings.** The following example is ambiguous and hard to understand:

> Proposed Production Enhancement Strategies Analysis Techniques

Is the heading introducing a discussion of techniques for analyzing strategies that have been proposed? Or is it introducing a discussion that proposes using certain techniques to analyze strategies? Readers shouldn't have to ask such questions. Adding prepositions makes the heading clearer:

> Techniques for Analyzing the Proposed Strategies for Enhancing Production

This heading announces more clearly that the discussion describes techniques for analyzing strategies, that those strategies have been proposed, and that the strategies are aimed at enhancing production. It's a longer heading than the original, but that's okay because it's also much clearer.

▶ **Be informative.** In the preceding example, you could add information about how many techniques will be described:

> Three Techniques for Analyzing the Proposed Strategies for Enhancing Production

You can go one step further by indicating what you wish to say about the three techniques:

> Advantages and Disadvantages of the Three Techniques for Analyzing the Proposed Strategies for Enhancing Production

Again, don't worry if the heading seems too long; clarity is more important than conciseness.

▶ **Use a grammatical form appropriate to your audience.** The question form works well for less-knowledgeable readers (Benson, 1985) or for nonnative speakers:

> What Are the Three Techniques for Analyzing the Proposed Strategies for Enhancing Production?

The "how-to" form is best for instructional material, such as manuals:

> How to Analyze the Proposed Strategies for Enhancing Production

The gerund form (*-ing*) works well for discussions and descriptions of processes:

> Analyzing the Proposed Strategies for Enhancing Production

▶ **Avoid back-to-back headings.** Use advance organizers to separate the headings.

▶ In This Book
For more about how to format headings, see Ch. 7, p. 161.

WRITING COHERENT PARAGRAPHS

There are two kinds of paragraphs: body paragraphs and transitional paragraphs.

A *body paragraph*, the basic unit for communicating information, is a group of sentences (or sometimes a single sentence) that is complete and self-sufficient and that contributes to a larger discussion. In an effective paragraph, all the sentences clearly and directly articulate one main point, either by introducing the point or by providing support for it. In addition, the whole paragraph follows logically from the material that precedes it.

A *transitional paragraph* helps readers move from one major point to another. Like a body paragraph, it can consist of a group of sentences or be a single sentence. Usually it summarizes the previous point, introduces the next point, and helps readers understand how the two are related.

The following example of a transitional paragraph appeared in a discussion of how a company plans to use this year's net proceeds.

The first sentence contains the word then *to signal that it introduces a summary.*

The final sentence clearly indicates the relationship between what precedes it and what follows it.

> Our best estimate of how we will use these net proceeds, then, is to develop a second data center and increase our marketing efforts. We base this estimate on our current plans and on projections of anticipated expenditures. However, at this time we cannot precisely determine the exact cost of these activities. Our actual expenditures may exceed what we've predicted, making it necessary or advisable to reallocate the net proceeds within the two uses (data center and marketing) or to use portions of the net proceeds for other purposes. The most likely uses appear to be reducing short-term debt and addressing salary inequities among software developers; each of these uses is discussed below, including their respective advantages and disadvantages.

Structure Paragraphs Clearly

Most paragraphs consist of a topic sentence and supporting information.

The Topic Sentence   Because a topic sentence states, summarizes, or forecasts the main point of the paragraph, put it up front. Technical communication should be clear and easy to read, not suspenseful. If a paragraph describes a test you performed, include the result of the test in your first sentence:

> The point-to-point continuity test on Cabinet 3 revealed an intermittent open circuit in the Phase 1 wiring.

Then go on to explain the details. If the paragraph describes a complicated idea, start with an overview. In other words, put the "bottom line" on top:

> Mitosis is the usual method of cell division, occurring in four stages: (1) prophase, (2) metaphase, (3) anaphase, and (4) telophase.

ETHICS NOTE

Avoiding Burying Bad News in Paragraphs

The most emphatic location in a paragraph is the topic sentence, usually the first sentence in a paragraph. The second most emphatic location is the end of the paragraph. Do not bury bad news in the middle of the paragraph, hoping readers won't see it. It would be misleading to structure a paragraph like this:

> In our proposal, we stated that the project would be completed by May. In making this projection, we used the same algorithms that we have used successfully for more than 14 years. In this case, however, the projection was not realized, due to several factors beyond our control. . . . We have since completed the project satisfactorily and believe strongly that this missed deadline was an anomaly that is unlikely to be repeated. In fact, we have beaten every other deadline for projects this fiscal year.

The writer has buried the bad news in a paragraph that begins with a topic sentence that appears to suggest good news. The last sentence, too, suggests good news.

A more forthright approach would be as follows:

> We missed our May deadline for completing the project. Although we derived this schedule using the same algorithms that we have used successfully for more than 14 years, several factors, including especially bad weather at the site, delayed the construction. . . .
>
> However, we have since completed the project satisfactorily and believe strongly that this missed deadline was an anomaly that is unlikely to be repeated. In fact, we have beaten every other deadline for projects this fiscal year.

Here the writer forthrightly presents the bad news in a topic sentence. Then he creates a separate paragraph with the good news.

The Supporting Information The supporting information makes the topic sentence clear and convincing. Sometimes a few explanatory details provide all the support you need. At other times, however, you need a lot of information to clarify a difficult thought or defend a controversial idea. How much supporting information to provide also depends on your audience and purpose. Readers knowledgeable about your subject may require little supporting information compared to less-knowledgeable readers. Likewise, you may need to provide little supporting information if your purpose is merely to *state* a controversial point of view rather than *persuade* your reader to agree with it. In deciding such matters, your best bet is to be generous with your supporting information. Paragraphs with too little support are far more common than paragraphs with too much.

Supporting information is most often developed using the basic patterns of organization discussed on page 107, and it usually fulfills one of these five roles:

- It defines a key term or idea included in the topic sentence.
- It provides examples or illustrations of the situation described in the topic sentence.
- It identifies causes: factors that led to the situation.

- It defines effects: implications of the situation.
- It supports the claim made in the topic sentence.

Paragraph Length   How long should a paragraph be? In general, 75 to 125 words are enough for a topic sentence and four or five supporting sentences. Long paragraphs are more difficult to read than short paragraphs because they require more focused concentration. They can also intimidate some readers, who skip over them.

But don't let arbitrary guidelines about length take precedence over your own analysis of the audience and purpose. You might need only one or two sentences to introduce a graphic, for example. Transitional paragraphs are also likely to be quite short. If a brief paragraph fulfills its function, let it be. Do not combine two ideas in one paragraph simply to achieve a minimum word count.

You may need to break up your discussion of one idea into two or more paragraphs. An idea that requires 200 or 300 words to develop should probably not be squeezed into one paragraph.

When you think about paragraph length, consider how the information will be printed or displayed. If the information will be presented in a narrow column, such as in a newsletter, short paragraphs will be much easier to read. If the information will be presented in a wider column, readers will be able to handle a longer paragraph.

Use Coherence Devices Within and Between Paragraphs

In a coherent paragraph, ideas are linked together clearly and logically. Parallel ideas are expressed in parallel grammatical constructions. Even if the paragraph already moves smoothly from sentence to sentence, you can emphasize the coherence by adding transitional words and phrases, repeating key words, and using demonstrative pronouns followed by nouns.

Adding Transitional Words and Phrases   Transitional words and phrases help the reader understand a discussion by explicitly stating the logical relationship between two ideas. Table 6.1 lists the most common logical relationships between two ideas and some of the common transitions that express those relationships.

Transitional words and phrases benefit both readers and writers. When a transitional word or phrase explicitly states the logical relationship between two ideas, readers don't have to guess at what that relationship might be. As a writer, using transitional words and phrases forces you to think more deeply about the logical relationships between ideas than you might otherwise.

TABLE 6.1 ▶ Transitional Words and Phrases	
Relationship	**Transition**
addition	also, and, finally, first (second, etc.), furthermore, in addition, likewise, moreover, similarly
comparison	in the same way, likewise, similarly
contrast	although, but, however, in contrast, nevertheless, on the other hand, yet
illustration	for example, for instance, in other words, to illustrate
cause-effect	as a result, because, consequently, hence, so, therefore, thus
time or space	above, around, earlier, later, next, to the right (left, west, etc.), soon, then
summary or conclusion	at last, finally, in conclusion, to conclude, to summarize

To better understand how transitional words and phrases benefit both reader and writer, consider the following pairs of examples:

WEAK   Demand for flash-memory chips is down by 15 percent. We have laid off 12 production-line workers.

IMPROVED   Demand for flash-memory chips is down by 15 percent; *as a result*, we have laid off 12 production-line workers.

WEAK   The project was originally expected to cost $300,000. The final cost was $450,000.

IMPROVED   The project was originally expected to cost $300,000. *However*, the final cost was $450,000.

Whichever transitional words and phrases you use, place them as close as possible to the beginning of the second idea. As shown in the examples above, the link between two ideas should be near the start of the second idea, to provide context for it. Consider the following example:

The vendor assured us that the replacement parts would be delivered in time for the product release. The parts were delivered nearly two weeks after the product release, however.

The idea of Sentence 2 stands in contrast to the idea of Sentence 1, but the reader doesn't see the transition until the end of Sentence 2. Put the transition at the start of the second idea, where it will do the most good.

You should also use transitional words to maintain coherence *between* paragraphs, just as you use them to maintain coherence *within* paragraphs. The link between two paragraphs should be near the start of the second paragraph.

Repeating Key Words   Repeating key words—usually nouns—helps readers follow the discussion. In the following example, the first version could be confusing:

UNCLEAR	For months the project leaders carefully planned their research. The cost of the work was estimated to be over $200,000.
	What is the work: the planning or the research?
CLEAR	For months the project leaders carefully planned their research. The cost of the research was estimated to be over $200,000.

Using Demonstrative Pronouns Followed by Nouns   Demonstrative pronouns—*this*, *that*, *these*, and *those*—can help you maintain the coherence of a discussion by linking ideas securely. In almost all cases, demonstrative pronouns should be followed by nouns, rather than stand alone in the sentence. In the following examples, notice that a demonstrative pronoun by itself can be vague and confusing.

UNCLEAR	New screening techniques are being developed to combat viral infections. *These* are the subject of a new research effort in California.
	What is being studied in California: new screening techniques or viral infections?
CLEAR	New screening techniques are being developed to combat viral infections. *These techniques* are the subject of a new research effort in California.

STRUCTURING EFFECTIVE SENTENCES

Good technical communication consists of clear, correct, and graceful sentences that convey information economically. This section describes seven principles for structuring effective sentences:

- Use lists.
- Emphasize new and important information.
- Choose an appropriate sentence length.
- Focus on the "real" subject.
- Focus on the "real" verb.

- Use parallel structure.
- Use modifiers effectively.

Use Lists

Many sentences in technical communication are long and complicated:

> We recommend that more work on heat-exchanger performance be done with a larger variety of different fuels at the same temperature, with similar fuels at different temperatures, and with special fuels such as diesel fuel and shale-oil-derived fuels.

Here readers cannot concentrate fully on the information because they are trying to remember all the "with" phrases following "done." If they could *see* how many phrases they have to remember, their job would be easier:

> We recommend that more work on heat-exchanger performance be done
>
> - with a larger variety of different fuels at the same temperature
> - with similar fuels at different temperatures
> - with special fuels such as diesel fuel and shale-oil-derived fuels

In this version, the arrangement of the words on the page reinforces the meaning. The bullets direct readers to the three items in the series, and the fact that each item begins at the same left margin helps, too.

Guidelines

Creating Effective Lists

▶ **Set off each listed item with a number, a letter, or a symbol (usually a bullet).**

— Use numbered lists to suggest sequence (as in the steps in a set of instructions) or priority (the first item being the most important). Using numbers helps readers see the total number of items in a list. For sublists, use lowercase letters:

1. Item
   a. subitem
   b. subitem

2. Item
   a. subitem
   b. subitem

— Use bullets to avoid suggesting either sequence or priority, such as for lists of people (everyone except number 1 gets offended). For sublists, use dashes.

- Item
  – subitem
  – subitem

In This Book

For more about designing checklists, see Ch. 8, p. 204.

— Use an open (unshaded) box (☐) for checklists.

▶ **Break up long lists.** Because most people can remember only 5 to 9 items easily, break up lists of 10 or more items.

Original list	Revised list
Tool kit:	Tool kit:
• handsaw	• Saws
• coping saw	–handsaw
• hacksaw	–coping saw
• compass saw	–hacksaw
• adjustable wrench	–compass saw
• box wrench	• Wrenches
• Stillson wrench	–adjustable wrench
• socket wrench	–box wrench
• open-end wrench	–Stillson wrench
• Allen wrench	–socket wrench
	–open-end wrench
	–Allen wrench

In This Book

For more about parallelism, see p. 122.

▶ **Present the items in a parallel structure.** A list is parallel if all the items take the same grammatical form. For instance, in the parallel list below, each item is a verb phrase.

Nonparallel	Parallel
Here is the sequence we plan to follow:	Here is the sequence we plan to follow:
1. writing of the preliminary proposal	1. write the preliminary proposal
2. do library research	2. do library research
3. interview with the Bemco vice president	3. interview the Bemco vice president
4. first draft	4. write the first draft
5. revision of the first draft	5. revise the first draft
6. preparing the final draft	6. prepare the final draft

▶ **Structure and punctuate the lead-in correctly.** A lead-in introduces a list. As noted earlier, every list requires a lead-in; without one, readers are left to guess at how the list relates to the discussion and how the items in the list relate to each other. Although standards vary from organization to organization, the most common lead-in consists of a grammatically complete clause followed by a colon, as shown in the following examples:

Following are the three main assets:

The three main assets are as follows:

The three main assets are the following:

If you cannot use a grammatically complete lead-in, use a dash or no punctuation at all:

The committee found that the employee

- did not cause the accident
- acted properly immediately after the accident
- reported the accident according to procedures

▶ **Punctuate the list correctly.** Because rules for punctuating lists vary, you should find out whether people in your organization have a preference. If not, punctuate lists as follows:

— If the items are phrases, use a lowercase letter at the start. Do not use a period or a comma at the end. The white space beneath the last item indicates the end of the list.

The new facility will offer three advantages:

- lower leasing costs
- shorter commuting distance
- a larger pool of potential workers

— If the items are complete sentences, use an uppercase letter at the start and a period at the end.

The new facility will offer three advantages:

- The leasing costs will be lower.
- The commuting distance for most employees will be shorter.
- The pool of potential workers will be larger.

— If the items are phrases followed by complete sentences, use an initial uppercase letter and a final period. Begin the complete sentences with uppercase letters and end them with periods. Use italics to emphasize the main idea in each bullet point.

The new facility will offer three advantages:

- *Lower leasing costs.* The lease will cost $1,800 per month; currently we pay $2,300.
- *Shorter commuting distance.* Our workers' average commute of 18 minutes would drop to 14 minutes.
- *Larger pool of potential workers.* In the last decade, the population has shifted westward to the area near the new facility. As a result, we would increase our potential workforce in both the semiskilled and managerial categories.

— If the list consists of two kinds of items—phrases and complete sentences—capitalize each item and end it with a period.

The new facility will offer three advantages:

- Lower leasing costs.

- Shorter commuting distance. Our workers' average commute of 18 minutes would drop to 14 minutes.
- Larger pool of potential workers. In the last decade, the population has shifted westward to the area near the new facility. As a result, we would increase our potential workforce in both the semiskilled and managerial categories.

In most lists, the second and subsequent lines of each entry, called *turnovers*, align under the first letter of the first line, highlighting the bullet or number to the left of the text. This *hanging indentation* helps the reader see and understand the organization of the passage.

Emphasize New and Important Information

Sentences are often easier to understand and more emphatic if new information appears at the end. For instance, if your company has labor problems and you want to describe the possible results, structure the sentence like this:

Because of labor problems, we anticipate a three-week delay.

In this case, the "three-week delay" is the new information.

If your readers already expect a three-week delay but don't know the reason for it, reverse the structure:

We anticipate the three-week delay in production because of labor problems.

Here, "labor problems" is the new and important information.

Put orienters to time and space at the beginning of the sentence, where they can provide context for the idea that the main sentence expresses.

Since the last quarter of 2011, we have experienced an 8 percent turnover rate in personnel assigned to the project.

On the north side of the building, water from the leaking pipes has damaged the exterior siding and the sheetrock on some interior walls.

Choose an Appropriate Sentence Length

On the Web

For more about varying sentence length, search for "sentence variety" in Guide to Grammar & Writing. Click on Links Library for Ch. 6 on <bedfordstmartins.com/ps>.

Sometimes sentence length affects the quality of the writing. A series of 10-word sentences would be choppy. A series of 35-word sentences would probably be too demanding. And a succession of sentences of approximately the same length would be monotonous.

What length is best? There is no simple answer, because ease of reading depends on the vocabulary, sentence structure, and sentence length; the reader's motivation and knowledge of the topic; the purpose of the communication; and the conventions of the application you are using. For instance, you use shorter sentences in tweets and text messages than in reports. In general, sentences of about 15 to 20 words are appropriate for most technical communication.

Often a draft will include overly long sentences such as the following:

> The construction of the new facility is scheduled to begin in March, but it might be delayed by one or even two months by winter weather conditions, which can make it impossible or nearly impossible to begin excavating the foundation.

To avoid creating such long sentences, say one thing clearly and simply before moving on to the next idea. For instance, to make this difficult 40-word sentence easier to read, divide it into two sentences:

> The construction of the new facility is scheduled to begin in March. However, construction might be delayed until April or even May by winter weather conditions, which can make it impossible or nearly impossible to begin excavating the foundation.

Sometimes an overly long sentence can be fixed by creating a list (see the Guidelines box on page 117).

Focus on the "Real" Subject

The conceptual or "real" subject of the sentence should also be the grammatical subject. Don't disguise or bury the real subject in a prepositional phrase following a weak grammatical subject. In the following examples, the weak subjects obscure the real subjects. (The grammatical subjects are italicized.)

WEAK	The *use* of this method would eliminate the problem of motor damage.
STRONG	This *method* would eliminate the problem of motor damage.
WEAK	The *presence* of a six-membered lactone ring was detected.
STRONG	A six-membered lactone *ring* was detected.

In revising a draft, look for the real subject (the topic) and ask yourself whether the sentence would be more effective if the real subject was also the grammatical subject. Sometimes all that is necessary is to ask yourself this question: *What is the topic of this sentence?* The author of the first example above wasn't trying to say something about *using* a method; she was trying to say something about the method itself.

Focus on the "Real" Verb

A "real" verb, like a "real" subject, should stand out in every sentence. A common problem in technical communication is the inappropriate use of a *nominalized* verb—a verb that has been changed into a noun, then coupled with a

On the Web

For more about using "real" subjects, see the e-handout on revising prose from the Center for Communication Practices at Rensselaer Polytechnic Institute. Click on Links Library for Ch. 6 on <bedfordstmartins.com/ps>.

weaker verb. *To install* becomes *to effect an installation*; *to analyze* becomes *to conduct an analysis*. Notice how nominalizing the verbs makes the following sentences both awkward and unnecessarily long (the nominalized verbs are italicized).

WEAK	Each *preparation* of the solution is done twice.
STRONG	Each solution is prepared twice.

WEAK	*Consideration* should be given to an acquisition of the properties.
STRONG	We should consider acquiring the properties.

Nominalizations are not errors. In fact, many common nouns are nominalizations: *maintenance*, *requirement*, and *analysis*, for example. In addition, nominalizations often effectively summarize an idea from a previous sentence (in italics below).

Congress recently passed a bill that restricts how High-Definition Television (HDTV) can be marketed to consumers. The new *legislation* could delay our *entry* into the HDTV market. This *delay* could cost us millions.

Some software programs search for common nominalizations. With any word processor, however, you can identify most of them by searching for character strings such as *tion*, *ment*, *sis*, *ence*, *ing*, and *ance*, as well as the word *of*.

Use Parallel Structure

A sentence is parallel if its coordinate elements follow the same grammatical form: for example, all the clauses are either passive or active, all the verbs are either infinitives or participles, and so on. Parallel structure creates a recognizable pattern, making a sentence easier for the reader to follow. Nonparallel structure creates no such pattern, distracting and possibly confusing readers. For example, the verbs in the following example are nonparallel because they do not use the same verb form (verbs are italicized).

NONPARALLEL	Our present system *is costing* us profits and *reduces* our productivity.
PARALLEL	Our present system *is costing* us profits and *reducing* our productivity.

When using parallel constructions, make sure that parallel items in a series do not overlap, causing confusion or even changing the meaning of the sentence:

CONFUSING	The speakers will include partners of law firms, businesspeople, and civic leaders.
	"Partners of" appears to apply to "businesspeople" and "civic leaders," as well as to "law firms." That is, "partners of" carries

over to the other items in the series. The following revision solves the problem by rearranging the items so that "partners" can apply only to "law firms."

CLEAR | The speakers will include businesspeople, civic leaders, and partners of law firms.

Use Modifiers Effectively

Modifiers are words, phrases, and clauses that describe other elements in the sentence. To make your meaning clear, you must indicate whether a modifier provides necessary information about the word or phrase it refers to (its *referent*) or whether it simply provides additional information. You must also clearly identify the referent.

Distinguish Between Restrictive and Nonrestrictive Modifiers As the term implies, a *restrictive modifier* restricts the meaning of its referent; it provides information that the reader needs to identify the referent and is, therefore, crucial to understanding the sentence. Notice that the restrictive modifier—italicized in the following example—is not set off by commas:

> The airplanes *used in the exhibitions* are slightly modified.

> *The modifying phrase "used in the exhibitions" identifies which airplanes the writer is referring to. Presumably, there are at least two groups of airplanes: those that are used in the exhibitions and those that are not. The restrictive modifier tells readers which of the two is being discussed.*

In most cases, the restrictive modifier doesn't require a relative pronoun, such as *that*, but you can choose to use the pronoun *that* (or *who*, for people):

> Please disregard the notice *that* you recently received from us.

A *nonrestrictive modifier* does not restrict the meaning of its referent: the reader does not need the information to identify what the modifier is describing or referring to. If you omit the nonrestrictive modifier, the basic sentence retains its primary meaning.

> The Hubble telescope, *intended to answer fundamental questions about the origin of the universe*, was last repaired in 2002.

> *Here, the basic sentence is "The Hubble telescope was last repaired in 2002." Removing the modifier doesn't change the meaning of the basic sentence.*

If you use a relative pronoun with a nonrestrictive modifier, choose *which* (or *who* or *whom* for a person).

> Go to the Registration Area, *which is located on the second floor.*

▶ **In This Book**

For more about using commas,
see Appendix, Part B, p. 452.

Use commas to separate a nonrestrictive modifier from the rest of the sentence. In the Hubble example, a pair of commas separates the nonrestrictive modifier from the rest of the sentence. In that respect, the commas function much like parentheses, indicating that the modifying information is parenthetical. In the next example, the comma indicates that the modifying information is tacked on at the end of the sentence as additional information.

Avoid Misplaced Modifiers   *Misplaced modifiers*—those that appear to modify the wrong referent—are a common problem. Usually, the best solution is to place the modifier as close as possible to its intended referent.

MISPLACED	The subject of the meeting is the future of geothermal energy *in the downtown Webster Hotel.*
CORRECT	The subject of the meeting *in the downtown Webster Hotel* is the future of geothermal energy.

A *squinting modifier* falls ambiguously between two possible referents, so the reader cannot tell which one is being modified:

UNCLEAR	We decided *immediately* to purchase the new system.
	Did we decide immediately, or did we decide to make the purchase immediately?
CLEAR	We *immediately* decided to purchase the new system.
CLEAR	We decided to purchase the new system *immediately*.

A subtle form of misplaced modification can also occur with *correlative constructions,* such as *either . . . or, neither . . . nor,* and *not only . . . but also:*

MISPLACED	The new refrigerant *not only decreases* energy costs *but also* spoilage losses.

Here, the writer is implying that the refrigerant does at least two things to energy costs: it decreases them and then does something else to them. Unfortunately, that's not how the sentence unfolds. The second thing the refrigerant does to energy costs never appears.

CORRECT	The new refrigerant *decreases not only* energy costs *but also* spoilage losses.

In the revised sentence, the phrase "decreases not only" implies that at least two things will be decreased, and as the sentence develops that turns out to be the case. "Decreases" applies to both "energy costs" and "spoilage losses." Therefore, the first half of the correlative construction ("not only") follows the verb ("decreases"). Note that if the sentence contains two different verbs, each half of the correlative construction precedes a verb:

The new refrigerant *not only decreases* energy costs *but also reduces* spoilage losses.

Avoid Dangling Modifiers   A *dangling modifier* has no referent in the sentence and can therefore be unclear:

DANGLING   Trying to solve the problem, the instructions seemed unclear.

This sentence says that the instructions are trying to solve the problem. To correct the sentence, rewrite it, adding the clarifying information either within the modifier or next to it:

CORRECT   As I was trying to solve the problem, the instructions seemed unclear.

CORRECT   Trying to solve the problem, I thought the instructions seemed unclear.

CHOOSING THE RIGHT WORDS AND PHRASES

This section discusses four principles that will help you use the right words and phrases in the right places: select an appropriate level of formality, be clear and specific, be concise, and use inoffensive language.

Select an Appropriate Level of Formality

Although no standard definition of levels of formality exists, most experts would agree that there are three levels:

INFORMAL   The Acorn 560 is a real screamer. With 3.8 GHz of pure computing power, it slashes through even the thickest spreadsheets before you can say $2 + 2 = 4$.

MODERATELY   With its 3.8 GHz microprocessor, the Acorn 560 can handle even
FORMAL   the most complicated spreadsheets quickly.

HIGHLY FORMAL   With a 3.8 GHz microprocessor, the Acorn 560 is a high-speed personal computer appropriate for computation-intensive applications such as large, complex spreadsheets.

Technical communication usually requires a moderately formal or highly formal style.

To achieve the appropriate level and tone, think about your audience, your subject, and your purpose:

- *Audience.* You would probably write more formally to a group of retired executives than to a group of college students. You would likewise write more formally to the company vice president than to your co-workers, and you would probably write more formally to people from most other cultures than to people from your own.

- *Subject.* You would write more formally about a serious subject—safety regulations or important projects—than about plans for an office party.

▶ **In This Book**
For more about writing to a multicultural audience, see Ch. 4, p. 63.

- *Purpose.* You would write more formally in a report to shareholders than in a company newsletter.

In general, it is better to err on the side of formality.

Be Clear and Specific

Follow these seven guidelines to make your writing clear and specific:

- Use active and passive voice appropriately.
- Be specific.
- Avoid unnecessary jargon.
- Use positive constructions.
- Avoid long noun strings.
- Avoid clichés.
- Avoid euphemisms.

On the Web

For more on choosing an appropriate voice, see "The Passive Engineer" by Helen Moody. Click on Links Library for Ch. 6 on <**bedfordstmartins .com/ps**>.

Use Active and Passive Voice Appropriately   In a sentence using the active voice, the subject performs the action expressed by the verb: the "doer" of the action is the grammatical subject. By contrast, in a sentence using the passive voice, the recipient of the action is the grammatical subject. Compare the following examples (the subjects are italicized):

ACTIVE   *Dave Brushaw* drove the launch vehicle.

              The doer of the action is the subject of the sentence.

PASSIVE   The launch *vehicle* was driven by Dave Brushaw.

              The recipient of the action is the subject of the sentence.

In most cases, the active voice works better than the passive voice because it emphasizes the *agent* (the doer of the action). An active-voice sentence also is shorter because it does not require a form of the verb *to be* and the past participle, as a passive-voice sentence does. In the active version of the example sentence, the verb is "drove" rather than "was driven," and the word "by" does not appear.

The passive voice, however, is generally better in these four cases:

- When the agent is clear from the context:

    Students are required to take both writing courses.

    Here, the context makes it clear that the college sets the requirements.

- When the agent is unknown:

    The comet was first referred to in an ancient Egyptian text.

    We don't know who wrote this text.

- When the agent is less important than the action:

  The blueprints were hand-delivered this morning.

  It doesn't matter who the messenger was.

- When a reference to the agent is embarrassing, dangerous, or in some other way inappropriate:

  Incorrect figures were recorded for the flow rate.

  It might be unwise or tactless to specify who recorded the incorrect figures. Perhaps it was your boss. However, it is unethical to use the passive voice to avoid responsibility for an action.

▶ **In This Book**

For more about ethics, see Ch. 2.

Some people believe that the active voice is inappropriate in technical communication because it emphasizes the person who does the work rather than the work itself, making the writing less objective. In many cases, this objection is valid. Why write "I analyzed the sample for traces of iodine" if there is no ambiguity about who did the analysis or no need to identify who did it? The passive focuses on the action, not the actor: "The samples were analyzed for traces of iodine." But if in doubt, use the active voice.

Other people argue that the passive voice produces a double ambiguity. In the sentence "The samples were analyzed for traces of iodine," the reader is not quite sure who did the analysis (the writer or someone else) or when it was done (during the project or some time previously). Identifying the actor can often clarify both ambiguities.

The best approach is to recognize that the two voices differ and to use each one where it is most effective.

Be Specific   Being specific involves using precise words, providing adequate detail, and avoiding ambiguity.

- *Use precise words.* A Ford Focus is an automobile, but it is also a vehicle, a machine, and a thing. In describing the Focus, *automobile* is better than the less-specific *vehicle*, because *vehicle* can also refer to pickup trucks, trains, hot-air balloons, and other means of transport. As words become more abstract—from *machine* to *thing*, for instance—chances for misunderstanding increase.

- *Provide adequate detail.* Readers probably know less about your subject than you do. What might be perfectly clear to you might be too vague for them.

VAGUE	An engine on the plane experienced some difficulties.
	Which engine? What plane? What kinds of difficulties?
CLEAR	The left engine on the Cessna 310 temporarily lost power during flight.

- *Avoid ambiguity.* Don't let readers wonder which of two meanings you are trying to convey.

AMBIGUOUS	After stirring by hand for 10 seconds, add three drops of the iodine mixture to the solution.
	After stirring the iodine mixture or the solution?
CLEAR	Stir the iodine mixture by hand for 10 seconds. Then add three drops to the solution.
CLEAR	Stir the solution by hand for 10 seconds. Then add three drops of the iodine mixture.

If you don't have the specific data, you should approximate—and clearly tell readers you are doing so—or explain why the specific data are unavailable and indicate when they will be available:

The fuel leakage is much greater than we had anticipated; we estimate it to be at least five gallons per minute, not two.

The fuel leakage is much greater than we had anticipated; we expect to have specific data by 4 P.M. today.

Avoid Unnecessary Jargon   Jargon is shoptalk. To an audiophile, *LP* is a long-playing record; to an engineer, it is liquid propane; to a physician, it is a lumbar puncture; to a drummer, it is Latin Percussion, a drum maker.

Using unnecessary jargon is inadvisable for four reasons:

- *It can be imprecise.* If you ask a co-worker to review a document and provide *feedback*, are you asking for a facial expression, body language, a phone call, or a written evaluation?

- *It can be confusing.* If you ask a computer novice to *cold swap the drive*, he or she might have no idea what you're talking about.

- *It is often seen as condescending.* Many readers will react as if you are showing off—displaying a level of expertise that excludes them. If readers feel alienated, they will likely miss your message.

- *It is often intimidating.* People might feel inadequate or stupid because they do not know what you are talking about. Obviously, this reaction undermines communication.

If you are addressing a technically knowledgeable audience, use jargon recognized in that field. However, keep in mind that technical documents often have many audiences in addition to the primary audience. When in doubt, avoid jargon; use more-common expressions or simpler terms.

Use Positive Constructions   The term *positive construction* has nothing to do with being cheerful. It indicates that the writer is describing what something is instead of what it is not. In the sentence "I was sad to see this project com-

On the Web

For advice on positive constructions, see the Security and Exchange Commission's *A Plain English Handbook.* Click on Links Library for Ch. 6 on <bedfordstmartins.com/ps>.

pleted," "sad" is a positive construction. The negative construction would be "not happy."

Here are a few more examples of positive and negative constructions:

Positive Construction	Negative Construction
most	not all
few	not many
on time	not late, not delayed
positive	not negative
inefficient	not efficient

Readers understand positive constructions more quickly and more easily than negative constructions. Consider the following examples:

DIFFICULT   Because the team did not have sufficient time to complete the project, it was unable to produce a satisfactory report.

SIMPLER   Because the team had too little time to complete the project, it produced an unsatisfactory report.

Avoid Long Noun Strings   A noun string contains a series of nouns (or nouns, adjectives, and adverbs), all of which modify the last noun. For example, in the phrase *parking-garage regulations*, the first two words modify *regulations*. Noun strings save time, and if your readers understand them, they are fine. It is easier to write *passive-restraint system* than *a system that uses passive restraints*.

Hyphens can clarify noun strings by linking words that go together. For example, in the phrase *flat-panel monitor*, the hyphen links *flat* and *panel*. Together they modify *monitor*. In other words, it is not a *flat panel*, or a *panel monitor*, but a *flat-panel monitor*. However, noun strings are sometimes so long or so complex that hyphens can't ensure clarity. To clarify a long noun string, untangle the phrases and restore prepositions, as in the following example:

UNCLEAR   preregistration procedures instruction sheet update

CLEAR   an update of the instruction sheet for preregistration procedures

▶ **In This Book**
For more about hyphens, see Appendix, Part B, p. 463.

Noun strings can sometimes be ambiguous—they can have two or more plausible meanings, leaving readers to guess at which meaning you're trying to convey.

AMBIGUOUS   The building contains a special incoming materials storage area.

                What's special? Are the incoming materials special? Or is the area they're stored in special?

UNAMBIGUOUS   The building contains a special area for storing incoming materials.

UNAMBIGUOUS   The building contains an area for storing special incoming materials.

An additional danger is that noun strings can sometimes sound pomp-ous. If you are writing about a simple smoke detector, there is no reason to call it a *smoke-detection device* or, worse, a *smoke-detection system*.

Avoid Clichés   Good writing is original and fresh. Rather than use a cliché, say what you want to say in plain English. Current clichés include *pushing the envelope*; *synergy*; *mission critical*; *paradigm shift*; and *been there, done that*. The best advice is to avoid clichés: if you are used to hearing or reading a phrase, don't use it. Don't think outside the box, bring your "A" game, be a change agent, raise the bar, throw anyone under a bus, be proactive, put lipstick on a pig, or give 110 percent. And you can assume that everyone already knows that it is what it is.

Avoid Euphemisms   A euphemism is a polite way of saying something that makes people uncomfortable. For instance, a near miss between two air-planes is officially an "air proximity incident." Firing someone might be re-ferred to as "dehiring." The more uncomfortable the subject, the more often people resort to euphemisms. Dozens of euphemisms deal with drinking, bathrooms, sex, and death.

ETHICS NOTE

Euphemisms and Truth Telling

There is nothing wrong with using the euphemism *restroom*, even though few people visit one to rest. The British use the phrase *go to the toilet* in polite company, and nobody seems to mind. In this case, if you want to use a euphemism, no harm done.

But it is unethical to use a euphemism to gloss over an issue that has important im-plications for people or the environment. People get uncomfortable when discussing layoffs—and they should. It's an uncomfortable issue. But calling a layoff a *redundancy elimination initiative* or a *career-change-opportunity creation* ought to make you even more uncomfortable. Don't use language to cloud reality. It's an ethical issue.

Be Concise

To be concise, avoid unnecessary prepositional phrases, wordy phrases, and fancy words.

Avoid Unnecessary Prepositional Phrases   A prepositional phrase consists of a preposition followed by a noun or a noun equivalent, such as *in the summary*, *on the engine*, and *under the heading*. Unnecessary prepositional phrases, often used along with abstract nouns and nominalizations, can make your writing long and boring.

LONG	The increase *in* the number *of* students enrolled *in* the materials-engineering program *at* Lehigh University is suggestive *of* the regard *in* which that program is held *by* the university's new students.
SHORTER	The increased enrollment in Lehigh University's materials-engineering program suggests that the university's new students consider it a good program.

Avoid Wordy Phrases   Wordy phrases also make writing long and boring. For example, some people write *on a daily basis* rather than *daily*. The long phrase may sound more important, but *daily* says the same thing more concisely.

Table 6.2 lists common wordy phrases and their more concise equivalents.

TABLE 6.2 ▶ Wordy Phrases and Their Concise Equivalents

Wordy phrase	Concise phrase	Wordy phrase	Concise phrase
a majority of	most	in the event that	if
a number of	some, many	in view of the fact that	because
at an early date	soon	it is often the case that	often
at the conclusion of	after, following	it is our opinion that	we think that
at the present time	now	it is our recommendation that	we recommend that
at this point in time	now	it is our understanding that	we understand that
based on the fact that	because	make reference to	refer to
check out	check	of the opinion that	think that
despite the fact that	although	on a daily basis	daily
due to the fact that	because	on the grounds that	because
during the course of	during	prior to	before
during the time that	during, while	relative to	regarding, about
have the capability to	can	so as to	to
in connection with	about, concerning	subsequent to	after
in order to	to	take into consideration	consider
in regard to	regarding, about	until such time as	until

DOCUMENT ANALYSIS ACTIVITY
Revising for Conciseness and Simplicity

The following passage is from a request for proposals published by the National Science Foundation. (Sentence numbers have been added here.) The accompanying questions ask you to think about word choice (as discussed on pp. 125–31).

1. This passage contains many prepositional phrases. Identify two of them. For each one, is its use justified, or would the sentence be easier to understand if the sentence were revised to eliminate it?

2. Part of this passage is written in the passive voice. Select one sentence in the passive voice that would be clearer in the active voice, and rewrite it in the active voice.

3. This passage contains a number of examples of fancy words. Identify two of them. How can they be translated into plain English?

On the Web

To submit your responses to your instructor, click on Document Analysis Activities for Ch. 6 on <bedfordstmartins .com/ps>.

National Science Foundation
WHERE DISCOVERIES BEGIN

SEARCH
NSF Web Site

HOME | FUNDING | AWARDS | DISCOVERIES | NEWS | PUBLICATIONS | STATISTICS | ABOUT | FastLane

Grant Proposal Guide

NSF 08-1 January 2008
Chapter I - Pre-Submission Information

A. NSF Proposal Preparation and Submission Mechanisms

1. Grants.gov, part of the President's Management Agenda to improve government services to the public, provides a single Government-wide portal for finding and applying for Federal grants online.

2. Proposals submitted via Grants.gov must be prepared and submitted in accordance with the *NSF Grants.gov Application Guide*, available through Grants.gov as well as on the NSF website at: http://www.nsf.gov/bfa/dias/policy/docs/grantsgovguide.pdf.

3. The Grants.gov Application Guide contains important information on:

- general instructions for submission via Grants.gov, including the Grants.gov registration process and Grants.gov software requirements;
- NSF-specific instructions for submission via Grants.gov, including creation of PDF files;
- grant application package instructions;
- required SF 424 (R&R) forms and instructions; and
- NSF-specific forms and instructions.

4. Upon successful insertion of the Grants.gov submitted proposal in the NSF FastLane system, no further interaction with Grants.gov is required.

5. All further interaction is conducted via the NSF FastLane system.

Source: National Science Foundation, 2008 <www.nsf.gov/pubs/policydocs/pappguide/nsf08_1 /gpg_1.jsp#IA1>.

Compare the following wordy sentence and its concise translation:

WORDY   I am of the opinion that, in regard to profit achievement, the statistics pertaining to this month will appear to indicate an upward tendency.

CONCISE   I think this month's statistics will show an increase in profits.

Avoid Fancy Words   Writers sometimes think they will impress their readers by using fancy words—*utilize* for *use*, *initiate* for *begin*, *perform* for *do*, *due to* for *because*, and *prioritize* for *rank*. In technical communication, plain talk is best. Compare the following fancy sentence with its plain-English version:

FANCY   The purchase of a database program will enhance our record-maintenance capabilities.

PLAIN   Buying a database program will help us maintain our records.

Table 6.3 lists commonly used fancy words and their plain equivalents.

Use Inoffensive Language

Writing to avoid offense is not merely a matter of politeness; it is a matter of perception. Language reflects attitudes, but it also helps to form attitudes. Writing inoffensively is one way to break down such stereotypes.

TABLE 6.3 ▶ Fancy Words and Their Plain Equivalents

Fancy word	Plain word	Fancy word	Plain word
advise	tell	herein	here
ascertain	learn, find out	impact (verb)	affect
attempt (verb)	try	initiate	begin
commence	start, begin	manifest (verb)	show
demonstrate	show	parameters	variables, conditions
due to	because of	perform	do
employ (verb)	use	prioritize	rank
endeavor (verb)	try	procure	get, buy
eventuate	happen	quantify	measure
evidence (verb)	show	terminate	end, stop
finalize	end, settle, agree, finish	utilize	use
furnish	provide, give		

On the Web

For more about sexist language, see the e-handout from the Center for Communication Practices. Click on Links Library for Ch. 6 on <bedfordstmartins .com/ps>.

Use Nonsexist Language   Sexist language suggests that some kinds of work are appropriate for women and some kinds for men. Policy manuals that consistently use *she* to refer to administrative assistants suggest that most or all administrative assistants are female. Manuals that use *he* to refer to engineers suggest that most or all engineers are male. In this way, sexist language stereotypes people. In almost all cases of sexist language, women are assigned to duties and jobs that are less prestigious and lower paid than those to which men are assigned.

Guidelines

Avoiding Sexist Language

Follow these five suggestions for writing gender-neutral text.

▶ **Replace the male-gender words with non-gender-specific words.** *Chairman*, for instance, can become *chairperson* or *chair*. *Firemen* are *firefighters*; *policemen* are *police officers*.

▶ **Switch to a different form of the verb.**

SEXIST	The operator must pass rigorous tests before he is promoted.
NONSEXIST	The operator must pass rigorous tests before being promoted.

▶ **Switch to the plural.**

NONSEXIST	Operators must pass rigorous tests before they are promoted.

Some organizations accept the use of plural pronouns with singular nouns, particularly in memos and other informal documents:

If an employee wishes to apply for tuition reimbursement, they should consult Section 14.5 of the Employee Manual.

Careful writers and editors, however, resist this construction because it is grammatically incorrect (it switches from singular to plural).

▶ **Switch to *he or she, he/she, s/he,* or *his or her*.** *He or she*, *his or her*, and related constructions are awkward, especially if overused, but at least they are clear and inoffensive.

▶ **Address the reader directly.** Use *you* and *your*, or the understood *you* (as in "[You] Enter the serial number in the first text box").

On the Web

For books about nonsexist writing, see the Selected Bibliography on <bedfordstmartins .com/ps>.

Use Inoffensive Language When Referring to People with Disabilities   One in six Americans—some 50 million people—has a physical, sensory, emotional, or mental impairment that interferes with daily life (U.S. Department of Labor, 2010). In writing about people with disabilities, use the "people-first" approach: treat the person as someone with a disability, not as someone defined by that disability. The disability is a condition the person has, not what the person is.

Guidelines

Using the People-First Approach

When writing about people with disabilities, follow these five guidelines, which are based on Snow (2009).

▶ **Refer to the person first, the disability second.** Write "people with mental retardation," not "the mentally retarded."

▶ **Don't confuse *handicap* with *disability*.** *Disability* refers to the impairment or condition; *handicap* refers to the interaction between the person and his or her environment. A person can have a disability without being handicapped.

▶ **Don't refer to victimization.** Write "a person with AIDS," not "an AIDS victim" or "an AIDS sufferer."

▶ **Don't refer to a person as "wheelchair bound" or "confined to a wheelchair."** People who use wheelchairs to get around are not confined.

▶ **Don't refer to people with disabilities as abnormal.** They are atypical, not abnormal.

Writer's Checklist

☐ Did you consider using a conventional pattern of organization? (p. 106)

Titles and Headings

Did you revise the title of your document so that it

☐ clearly states the subject and purpose of your document? (p. 108)

☐ is precise and informative? (p. 108)

☐ Did you avoid back-to-back headings by including an advance organizer? (p. 110)

Did you revise the headings to

☐ avoid long noun strings? (p. 111)

☐ be informative? (p. 111)

☐ use a grammatical form appropriate to your audience? (p. 111)

Paragraphs

Did you revise your paragraphs so that each one

☐ begins with a clear topic sentence? (p. 112)

☐ has adequate and appropriate support? (p. 112)

☐ is not too long for readers? (p. 113)

☐ uses coherence devices such as transitional words and phrases, repetition of key words, and demonstrative pronouns followed by nouns? (p. 114)

Lists

☐ Is each list of the appropriate kind: numbered, lettered, bulleted, or checklist? (p. 117)

☐ Does each list contain an appropriate number of items? (p. 118)

☐ Are all the items in each list grammatically parallel? (p. 118)

☐ Is the lead-in to each list structured and punctuated properly? (p. 119)

☐ Are the items in each list punctuated properly? (p. 000)

Sentences

☐ Are the sentences structured with the new or important information near the end? (p. 120)

☐ Are the sentences the appropriate length? (p. 120)

☐ Does each sentence focus on the "real" subject? (p. 121)

☐ Does each sentence focus on the "real" verb, without weak nominalizations? (p. 121)

☐ Have you used parallel structure in your sentences? (p. 122)

☐ Have you used restrictive and nonrestrictive modifiers appropriately? (p. 123)

☐ Have you eliminated misplaced modifiers, squinting modifiers, and dangling modifiers? (p. 124)

Words and Phrases

Did you

☐ select an appropriate level of formality? (p. 125)
☐ use active and passive voice appropriately? (p. 126)
☐ use precise words? (p. 127)
☐ provide adequate detail? (p. 127)
☐ avoid ambiguity? (p. 128)
☐ avoid unnecessary jargon? (p. 128)

☐ use positive rather than negative constructions? (p. 128)
☐ avoid long noun strings? (p. 129)
☐ avoid clichés? (p. 130)
☐ avoid euphemisms? (p. 130)
☐ avoid unnecessary prepositional phrases? (p. 130)
☐ use the most concise phrases? (p. 131)
☐ avoid fancy words? (p. 133)

☐ Did you use nonsexist language? (p. 134)
☐ Did you use the people-first approach in referring to people with disabilities? (p. 134)

Exercises

▷ **In This Book** For advice about how to critique a draft effectively, see Ch. 3, pp. 40–42.

1. Identify the best organizational pattern for a discussion of each of the subjects that follow. For example, a discussion of distance education and on-campus courses could be organized using the comparison-and-contrast pattern. Write a brief explanation supporting your selection. (Use each of the organizational patterns discussed in this chapter at least once.)

   a. how to register for courses at your college or university

   b. how you propose to reduce the time required to register for classes or to change your schedule

   c. your car's dashboard

   d. the current price of gasoline

   e. the reasons you chose your college or major

   f. two music-streaming services

   g. MP3 players

   h. college courses

   i. increased security in airports

   j. how to prepare for a job interview

2. The following titles fall short of incorporating the advice found in this chapter. Write a one-paragraph evaluation of each title. How clearly does the title indicate the subject and purpose of the document? In what ways does it fall short of incorporating this chapter's advice about titles? On the basis of your analysis, rewrite each title.

   a. Recommended Forecasting Techniques for Haldane Company

   b. A Study of Digital Cameras

   c. Agriculture in the West: A 10-Year View

3. The following headings fall short of incorporating the advice found in this chapter. Write a one-paragraph evaluation of each heading. How clearly does the heading indicate the subject and purpose of the text that will follow it? In what ways does it fall short of incorporating this chapter's advice about headings? On the basis of your analysis, rewrite each heading to make it clearer and more informative. Invent any necessary details.

   a. Multigroup Processing Technique Review Board Report Findings

   b. The Great Depression of 1929

   c. Intensive-Care Nursing

4. Revise the following list so that the lead-in is clear, easy to understand, and punctuated correctly. In addition, be sure the bullet items are grammatically parallel with one another.

   There are several goals being pursued by the Natural and Accelerated Bioremediation Research office;

   • the development of cost-effective *in situ* bioremediation strategies for subsurface radionuclides and metals;

   • an understanding of intrinsic bioremediation as well as accelerated bioremediation using nutrient amendments to immobilize contaminants;

   • identifying societal issues associated with bioremediation research, and communication of bioremediation research findings to stakeholders.

5. Provide a topic sentence for this paragraph.

> The reason for this difference is that a larger percentage of engineers working in small firms may be expected to hold high-level positions. In firms with fewer than 20 engineers, for example, the median income was $62,200. In firms of 20 to 200 engineers, the median income was $60,345. For the largest firms, the median was $58,600.

6. In the following paragraph, transitional words and phrases have been removed. Add an appropriate transition in each blank space. Where necessary, add punctuation.

> One formula that appeared foolproof for selling computers was direct sales by the manufacturer to the consumer. Dell, _____, climbed to number two in PC sales by selling customized products directly on its Web site. _____, the recent success of Acer, now number three in sales, suggests that the older formula of distributing commodity items through retailers might be best for today's PC industry. Acer's success can be attributed to three decisions it made. First, it sold off its division that manufactured components for other PC brands. _____, it correctly concluded that consumers, who generally prefer preconfigured PCs, would outnumber business customers. And _____, it decided to expand its line of inexpensive netbooks (small PCs for surfing the Web) just when the economic downturn increased the demand for cheaper PC products. These decisions appear to have paid off for Acer: last year, its market share rose 3 percentage points, from 8 to 11. _____, Dell rose only 0.1 point, from 14.8 to 14.9.

7. In each of the following exercises, the second sentence begins with a demonstrative pronoun. Add a noun after the demonstrative to enhance coherence.

   a. The Zoning Commission has scheduled an open hearing for March 14. This _____ will enable concerned citizens to voice their opinions on the proposed construction.

   b. The university has increased the number of parking spaces, instituted a shuttle system, and increased parking fees. These _____ are expected to ease the parking problems.

NOTE: In Exercises 8–29, pay close attention to what you are being asked to do, and do only as much revising as is necessary. Take special care to preserve the meaning of the original material. If necessary, invent reasonable details.

8. Refer to the advice on pages 117–20, and rewrite the following sentence in the form of a list.

> The causes of burnout can be studied from three perspectives: physiological—the roles of sleep, diet, and physical fatigue; psychological—the roles of guilt, fear, jealousy, and frustration; and environmental—the role of physical surroundings at home and at work.

9. The following sentences might be too long for some readers. Refer to the advice on pages 120–21, and break each sentence into two or more sentences.

   a. If we get the contract, we must be ready by June 1 with the necessary personnel and equipment, so with this in mind a staff meeting, which all group managers are expected to attend, is scheduled for February 12.

   b. Once we get the results of the stress tests on the 125-Z fiberglass mix, we will have a better idea of whether the project is on schedule, because if the mix isn't suitable we will really have to hurry to find and test a replacement by the Phase 1 deadline.

10. In the following sentences, the real subjects are buried in prepositional phrases or obscured by expletives. Refer to the advice on page 121, and revise the sentences so that the real subjects appear prominently.

    a. There has been a decrease in the number of students enrolled in our training sessions.

    b. The use of in-store demonstrations has resulted in a dramatic increase in business.

11. In the following sentences, unnecessary nominalization obscures the real verb. Refer to the advice on page 121, and revise the sentences to focus on the real verb.

    a. Pollution constitutes a threat to the Matthews Wildlife Preserve.

    b. Evaluation of the gumming tendency of the four tire types will be accomplished by comparing the amount of rubber that can be scraped from the tires.

12. Refer to the advice on pages 122–23, and revise the following sentences to eliminate nonparallelism.

    a. The next two sections of the manual discuss how to analyze the data, the conclusions that can be drawn from your analysis, and how to decide what further steps are needed before establishing a journal list.

b. In the box, we should include a copy of the documentation, the cables, and the docking station.

13. Refer to the advice on pages 123–25, and revise the following sentences to correct punctuation or pronoun errors related to modifiers.

a. Press the Greeting Record button to record the greeting that is stored on a microchip inside the machine.

b. This problem that has been traced to manufacturing delays, has resulted in our losing four major contracts.

14. Refer to the advice on page 124, and revise the following sentences to eliminate the misplaced modifiers.

a. Information provided by this program is displayed at the close of the business day on the information board.

b. The computer provides a printout for the Director that shows the likely effects of the action.

15. Refer to the advice on page 125, and revise the following sentences to eliminate the dangling modifiers.

a. By following these instructions, your computer should provide good service for many years.

b. To examine the chemical homogeneity of the plaque sample, one plaque was cut into nine sections.

16. Refer to the advice on pages 125–26, and revise the following informal sentences to make them moderately formal.

a. The learning modules were put together by a couple of profs in the department.

b. If the University of Arizona can't figure out where to dump its low-level radioactive waste, Uncle Sam could pull the plug on millions of dollars of research grants.

17. Refer to the advice on pages 126–27, and rewrite the following sentences to remove inappropriate use of the passive voice.

a. Mistakes were made.

b. Come to the reception desk when you arrive. A packet with your name on it can be picked up there.

18. Refer to the advice on pages 126–33, and revise the following sentences to remove the redundancies.

a. In grateful appreciation of your patronage, we are pleased to offer you this free gift as a small token gesture of our gratitude.

b. An anticipated major breakthrough in storage technology will allow us to proceed ahead in the continuing evolution of our products.

19. Refer to the advice on pages 127–28, and revise the following sentences by replacing the vague elements with specific information. Make up any reasonable details.

a. The results won't be available for a while.

b. The chemical spill in the lab caused extensive damage.

20. Refer to the advice on page 128, and revise the following sentences to remove unnecessary jargon.

a. We need to be prepared for blowback from the announcement.

b. The mission-critical data on the directory will be migrated to a new server on Tuesday.

21. Refer to the advice on pages 128–29, and revise the following sentences to convert the negative constructions to positive constructions.

a. Management accused Williams of filing trip reports that were not accurate.

b. We must make sure that all our representatives do not act unprofessionally to potential clients.

22. General readers might find the following sentences awkward or difficult to understand. Refer to the advice on pages 129–30, and rewrite the following sentences to eliminate the long noun strings.

a. The corporate-relations committee meeting location has been changed.

b. The research team discovered a glycerin-initiated, alkylene-oxide-based, long-chain polyether.

23. Refer to the advice on page 130, and revise the following sentences to eliminate clichés.

a. If we are to survive this difficult period, we are going to have to keep our ears to the ground and our noses to the grindstone.

b. At the end of the day, if everyone is on the same page and it turns out to be the wrong page, you're really up a creek without a paddle.

24. Refer to the advice on page 130, and revise the following sentences to eliminate euphemisms.

    a. Downsizing our workforce will enable our division to achieve a more favorable cash-flow profile.

    b. Of course, accident statistics can be expected to show a moderate increase in response to a streamlining of the training schedule.

25. Refer to the advice on page 130–31, and revise the following sentences to eliminate unnecessary prepositional phrases.

    a. The complexity of the module will hamper the ability of the operator in the diagnosis of problems in equipment configuration.

    b. The purpose of this test of your aptitudes is to help you with the question of the decision of which major to enroll in.

26. Refer to the advice on pages 130–33, and revise the following sentences to make them more concise.

    a. The instruction manual for the new copier is lacking in clarity and completeness.

    b. We remain in communication with our sales staff on a weekly basis.

27. Refer to the advice on page 133, and revise the following sentences to eliminate fancy words.

    a. This state-of-the-art soda-dispensing module is to be utilized by Marketing Department personnel.

    b. We have failed to furnish the proposal to the proper agency by the mandated date by which such proposals must be in receipt.

28. Refer to the advice on pages 133–34, and revise the following sentences to eliminate sexist language.

    a. Each doctor is asked to make sure he follows the standard procedure for handling Medicare forms.

    b. Policemen are required to live in the city in which they work.

29. Refer to the advice on page 134, and revise the following sentences to eliminate the offensive language.

    a. This year, the number of female lung-cancer victims is expected to rise because of increased smoking.

    b. Mentally retarded people are finding greater opportunities in the service sector of the economy.

▶ On the Web

For two case assignments, "Organizing a Document for Clarity—and Diplomacy" and "Highlighting the Coherence of a Passage," see Cases on <bedfordstmartins.com/ps>.

PART 3

Designing User-Friendly Documents and Web Sites

7

Designing Documents and Web Sites

Courtesy Mayo Clinic.

Good design helps readers accomplish a task simply and easily.

The design of a page or a screen can help a writer achieve many goals: to entertain, to amaze, to intrigue, to sell. In technical communication, that goal is typically to help the reader accomplish a task. The Mayo Clinic page shown here is a good example of an effective design. Each link is clearly labeled to enable users to get where they want to go, quickly and easily. From this page, users can learn about medical issues, set up appointments, refer patients, look for a job or an educational opportunity, or search the Mayo Clinic site. When you look at a well-designed page or site, you intuitively understand how to use it.

Design refers to the physical appearance of documents and Web sites. For printed documents, design features include page layout, typography, and use of color. For Web sites, many of the same design elements apply, but there are unique elements, too, such as the use of navigation bars, the design of hyperlinks, and tables of contents on long pages.

The effectiveness of a document or Web site largely depends on how well it is designed, because readers *see* the document or site before they actually *read* it. In less than a second, the document or site makes an impression on them, one that might determine how well they read it—or even whether they decide to read it at all.

GOALS OF DOCUMENT AND WEB DESIGN

In designing a document or Web site, you have five major goals:

- *To make a good impression on readers.* Your document or site should reflect your own professional standards and those of your organization.

- *To help readers understand the structure and hierarchy of the information.* As they navigate a document or site, readers should know where they are and how to get where they are headed. They should also be able to see the hierarchical relationship between one piece of information and another.

- *To help readers find the information they need.* Usually, people don't read printed technical documents from cover to cover. Design elements (such as tabs, icons, and color), page design, and typography help readers find the information they need quickly and easily. On Web sites, helping readers find information is critical because they can see only the page that is currently displayed on the screen.

- *To help readers understand the information.* Effective design can clarify information. For instance, designing a set of instructions so that the text describing each step is next to the accompanying graphic makes the instructions easier to understand. A Web site in which the main sections are clearly displayed on a navigation bar is easier to understand than a site that doesn't have this feature.

- *To help readers remember the information.* An effective design helps readers create a visual image of the information, making it easier to remember. Text boxes, pull quotes, and similar design elements help readers remember important explanations and passages.

PLANNING THE DESIGN OF DOCUMENTS AND WEB SITES

The first step in designing a technical document or Web site is planning. Analyze your audience and purpose, and then determine your resources.

In This Book

For more about analyzing your audience and purpose, see Ch. 4.

On the Web

See Roger C. Parker's design site and Webmonkey's Web Typography Tutorial. Click on Links Library for Ch. 7 on <bedfordstmartins.com/ps>.

Guidelines

Planning Your Design

Follow these four suggestions as you plan your design.

▶ **Analyze your audience.** Consider factors such as your readers' knowledge of the subject, their attitudes, their reasons for reading, the way they will be using the document, and the kinds of tasks they will perform. Think too about your audience's expectations. Readers expect to see certain kinds of information presented in certain ways. Plan to fulfill those expectations. For example, hyperlinks in Web sites are often underscored and presented in blue type.

▶ **Consider multicultural readers.** If you are writing for multicultural readers, keep in mind that many aspects of design vary from one culture to another. In memos, letters, reports, and manuals, you may see significant differences in design practice. The best advice, therefore, is to study documents from the culture you are addressing. Look for differences in paper size, text direction, typeface preferences, and color preferences.

▶ **Consider your purpose.** For example, if you are creating a Web site for a new dental office, do you merely want to provide information on the hours and location, or do you also want to present dental information for patients? Let patients set up or change appointments? Ask a question? Each of these purposes affects the site design.

▶ **Determine your resources.** Think about your resources of time, money, and equipment. Short, informal documents and Web sites are usually produced in-house; more-ambitious projects are often subcontracted to specialists. If your organization has a technical-publications department, consult the people there about scheduling and budgeting. A sophisticated design might require professionals at service bureaus and print shops, and their services can require weeks or months and cost thousands of dollars.

UNDERSTANDING DESIGN PRINCIPLES

To design effective documents and Web sites, you need to understand a few basic design principles. The following discussion is based on Robin Williams's *The Non-designer's Design Book* (2008), which describes four principles of design: proximity, alignment, repetition, and contrast.

Proximity

The principle of proximity is simple: group related items together. If two items appear close to each other, the reader will interpret them as related to each other. If they are far apart, the reader will interpret them as unrelated. Text describing a graphic should be positioned close to the graphic, as shown in Figure 7.1.

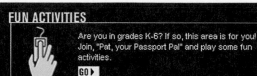

FUN ACTIVITIES

Are you in grades K-6? If so, this area is for you!
Join, "Pat, your Passport Pal" and play some fun
activities.

GO ▶

PARENTS AND EDUCATORS

Parents and Educators are the most important
influencing factors on youth. Here are some
resources to help you share the exciting world of
foreign affairs with your children and students.

GO ▶

MY FUTURE WITH THE STATE DEPARTMENT

Learn how you can join the U.S. Department of
State. Help develop a free, secure, and peaceful
world. Create, represent, and implement U.S. foreign
policy. Experience the world of a Foreign Service
Officer. Explore opportunities for students at the
Department of State.

GO ▶

*Text and graphics are clearly
related by the principle of proximity. The textual descriptions
are placed next to the drawings
to which they refer.*

Figure 7.1   Effective Use of Proximity
Source: U.S. Department of State, 2011 <http://future.state.gov>.

Alignment

The principle of alignment is that you should con-
sciously place text and graphics on the page so
that the reader can understand the relationships
among these elements. Figure 7.2 shows how
alignment works to help organize information.

Repetition

The principle of repetition is that you should treat
the same kind of information in the same way to
create consistent patterns. For example, all first-
level headings should have the same typeface,
type size, spacing above and below, and so forth.
This repetition signals a connection between
headings, making the content easier to understand. Other elements that are used to create consistent visual patterns are colors, icons, rules, and
screens. Figure 7.3 on page 146 shows an effective
use of repetition.

First Floor

SciQuest
Step inside a wind tunnel, feel an earthquake
or control a four-foot tornado as you explore
the forces of nature, the physics of flight and
sound and the science of light and waves.

Rangos Omnimax Theater
A four-story, domed screen and hundreds of
speakers allow you to take a leading role in this
Omnimax Theater — the only one of its kind in
Western Pennsylvania. Journey through new
lands, be in the center of nature, or see popular
feature films on this giant film screen. The
OMNIMAX experience is incredible every
time you come to the movies.

XPLOR Carnegie Science Center Store
Visitors can take the Science Center home when
they choose from a wide selection of books,
games, toys, microscopes and a variety of
telescopes selected by our expert Buhl
Planetarium staff.

Highmark Science Stage
Get into the act as science comes alive in this
participation demonstration theater.

Second Floor

Miniature Railroad & Village®
Speeding locomotives travel Western
Pennsylvania's landscape, winding through
2,000 miniature replicas and 100 animated
characters and scenes. (Closed June 14–18
and September 27–November 18, 2004.)

Henry Buhl, Jr. Planetarium And Observatory
This 50-foot domed planetarium literally takes
visitors into space. Explore Mars, navigate the
stars or journey through the mysteries of the
Cosmos. Come at night for a live Laser Fantasy
show where color and music surround you every
Friday and Saturday evening.

*This panel from a museum
brochure uses alignment to help
organize the information.*

*The writer is using three levels
of importance, signaled by the
three levels of alignment.*

*Writers often use more than one
technique at a time to help organize information. In this case,
the first level of information is
also presented in a larger-size
type.*

*The second level of information
is presented in a different color
than the rest of the text.*

Figure 7.2   Effective Use of Alignment
Source: Carnegie Science Center, n.d.

This page shows repetition used effectively as a design element.

Different colors, typefaces, and type sizes are used for the headings, figures, and definitions in the margin. For instance, the two graphics use the same beige background and the same typeface, style, and color for the titles and captions.

In the main text, the two headings and subheadings use the same typefaces, sizes, and colors.

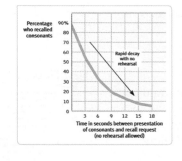

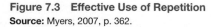

Figure 7.3   Effective Use of Repetition
Source: Myers, 2007, p. 362.

Contrast

The principle of contrast works in several different ways in technical documents and Web sites. For example, black print is easiest to see against a white background; larger letters stand out among smaller ones; information printed in a color, such as red, grabs readers' attention better than information printed in black. Figure 7.4 shows effective use of contrast.

Figure 7.4　Effective Use of Contrast
Source: Lambert Coffin, 2010 <www.lambertcoffin.com/index.php?sid=2>.

The light-colored text at the top of this screen contrasts most effectively with the dark blue of the night sky. In the navigation buttons on the left, the dark text contrasts well against the light background. The text "About the Firm" uses negative type—light text against a green background—but in this case the contrast is less sharp because the background color is lighter.

UNDERSTANDING LEARNING THEORY

A page of technical communication is effectively designed if the reader can recognize a pattern, such as where to look for certain kinds of information. See the Guidelines box beginning on page 148 for more about understanding learning theory and page design.

DESIGNING DOCUMENTS

To design effective technical documents, start by thinking about accessing aids to help readers find the information they seek. Then think about how to design the document pages.

Accessing Aids

In a well-designed document, readers can easily find the information they seek. Most accessing aids use the design principles of repetition and contrast to help readers navigate the document. The Choices and Strategies box on page 150 explains six common kinds of accessing aids.

Guidelines

Understanding Learning Theory and Page Design

In designing the page, create visual patterns that help readers find, understand, and remember information. Three principles of learning theory, the result of research into how people learn, can help you design effective pages: chunking, queuing, and filtering.

▶ **Chunking.** People understand information best if it is delivered to them in chunks—small units—rather than all at once. For single-spaced type, chunking involves double-spacing between paragraphs, as shown in Figure 7.5.

During the 18th century, there were many wars in Europe caused by the ambition of various kings to make their domains larger and to increase their own incomes. King Louis XIV of France had built up a very powerful kingdom. Brave soldiers and skillful generals spread his rule over a great part of what is Belgium and Luxembourg, and annexed to the French kingdom the part of Germany between the Rhine River and the Vosges (Vozh) Mountains.

Finally, the English joined with the troops of the Holy Roman Empire to curb the further growth of the French kingdom, and at the battle of Blenheim (1704), the English Duke of Marlborough, aided by the emperor's army, put an end to the further expansion of the French.

The 18th century also saw the rise of a new kingdom in Europe. You will recall that there was a county in Germany named Brandenburg, whose count was one of the seven electors who chose the emperor. The capital of this county was Berlin. It so happened that a number of Counts of Brandenburg, of the family of Hohenzollern, had been men of ambition and ability. The little county had grown by adding small territories around it. One of these counts, called "the Great Elector," had added to Brandenburg the greater part of the neighboring county of Pomerania. His son did not have the ability of his father, but was a very proud and vain man.

He happened to visit King William III of England, and was very much offended because during the interview, the king occupied a comfortable arm chair, while the elector, being simply a count, was given a chair to sit in which was straight-backed and had no arms. Brooding over this insult, as it seemed to him, he went home and decided that he too should be called a king. The question was, what should his title be. He could not call himself "King of Brandenburg," for Brandenburg was part of the Empire, and the emperor would not allow it. It had happened some one hundred years before, that, through his marriage with the daughter of the Duke of Prussia, a Count of Brandenburg had come into possession of the district known as East Prussia, at the extreme southeastern corner of the Baltic Sea.

The son of this elector who first called himself king had more energy and more character than his father. He ruled his country with a rod of iron, and built up a strong, well-drilled army. He was especially fond of tall soldiers, and had agents out all over Europe, kidnapping men who were over six feet tall to serve in his famous regiment of Guards. He further increased the size of the Prussian kingdom.

His son was the famous Frederick the Great, one of the most remarkable fighters that the world has ever seen. This prince had been brought up under strict discipline by his father. The old king had been insistent that his son should be no weakling. It is told that one day, finding Frederick playing upon a flute, he seized the instrument and snapped it in twain over his son's shoulder.

France in the 18th Century
During the 18th century, there were many wars in Europe caused by the ambition of various kings to make their domains larger and to increase their own incomes. King Louis XIV of France had built up a very powerful kingdom. Brave soldiers and skillful generals spread his rule over a great part of what is Belgium and Luxembourg, and annexed to the French kingdom the part of Germany between the Rhine River and the Vosges (Vozh) Mountains.

Finally, the English joined with the troops of the Holy Roman Empire to curb the further growth of the French kingdom, and at the battle of Blenheim (1704), the English Duke of Marlborough, aided by the emperor's army, put an end to the further expansion of the French.

Prussia
The 18th century also saw the rise of a new kingdom in Europe. You will recall that there was a county in Germany named Brandenburg, whose count was one of the seven electors who chose the emperor. The capital of this county was Berlin. It so happened that a number of Counts of Brandenburg, of the family of Hohenzollern, had been men of ambition and ability. The little county had grown by adding small territories around it. One of these counts, called "the Great Elector," had added to Brandenburg the greater part of the neighboring county of Pomerania. His son did not have the ability of his father, but was a very proud and vain man.

He happened to visit King William III of England, and was very much offended because during the interview, the king occupied a comfortable arm chair, while the elector, being simply a count, was given a chair to sit in which was straight-backed and had no arms. Brooding over this insult, as it seemed to him, he went home and decided that he too should be called a king. The question was, what should his title be. He could not call himself "King of Brandenburg," for Brandenburg was part of the Empire, and the emperor would not allow it. It had happened some one hundred years before, that, through his marriage with the daughter of the Duke of Prussia, a Count of Brandenburg had come into possession of the district known as East Prussia, at the extreme southeastern corner of the Baltic Sea.

The son of this elector who first called himself king had more energy and more character than his father. He ruled his country with a rod of iron, and built up a strong, well-drilled army. He was especially fond of tall soldiers, and had agents out all over Europe, kidnapping men who were over six feet tall to serve in his famous regiment of Guards. He further increased the size of the Prussian kingdom.

a. Without chunking   b. With chunking

Figure 7.5   Chunking

Chunking emphasizes units of related information. Note how the use of headings creates clear chunks of information.

▶ **Queuing.** Queuing refers to creating visual distinctions to indicate levels of importance. More-emphatic elements—those with bigger type or boldface type—are more important than less-emphatic ones. Another visual element of queuing is alignment. Designers start more-important information closer to the left margin and indent less-important information. (An exception is titles, which are often centered in reports in the United States.) Figure 7.6 shows queuing.

▶ **Filtering.** Filtering is the use of visual patterns to distinguish various types of information. Introductory material might be displayed in larger type, and notes might appear in italics, another typeface, and a smaller size. Figure 7.7 shows filtering.

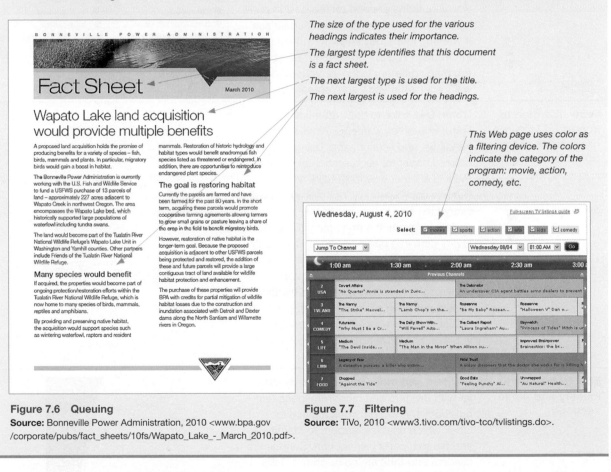

The size of the type used for the various headings indicates their importance.

The largest type identifies that this document is a fact sheet.

The next largest type is used for the title.

The next largest is used for the headings.

This Web page uses color as a filtering device. The colors indicate the category of the program: movie, action, comedy, etc.

Figure 7.6   Queuing
Source: Bonneville Power Administration, 2010 <www.bpa.gov /corporate/pubs/fact_sheets/10fs/Wapato_Lake_-_March_2010.pdf>.

Figure 7.7   Filtering
Source: TiVo, 2010 <www3.tivo.com/tivo-tco/tvlistings.do>.

CHOICES AND STRATEGIES   Creating Accessing Aids

If you want to . . .	Try using this accessing aid	Example
Symbolize actions or ideas	**Icons.** Icons are pictures that symbolize actions or ideas. An hourglass or a clock tells you to wait while the computer performs a task. Perhaps the most important icon is the stop sign, which alerts you to a warning. Icons depend on the design principle of repetition: every time readers see a warning icon, they know what kind of information you are presenting. Don't use too many different icons, or your readers will forget what each one represents.	**Explore groups** Find out what people are doing with Google Groups [Search for a group] Arts & Entertainment Groups / Business Groups / Computer Groups / Health Groups / Home Groups / News Groups / People Groups / Recreation Groups / School & University Groups / Sci/Tech Groups / Society & Humanities Groups / Browse group categories... **Source:** Google, 2010 <http://groups.google.com /grphp?hl=en>.
Draw attention to important features or sections of the document	**Color.** Use color to draw attention to features such as warnings, hints, major headings, and section tabs. Using different-colored paper for each section of a document is another way to simplify access. But use color sparingly, or it will overpower everything else in the document. Color exploits the principles of repetition (every item in a particular color is logically linked) and contrast (items in one color contrast with items in another color). Use color logically. Third-level headings should not be in color, for example, if first- and second-level headings are printed in black. For more about using color, see Chapter 8, page 186.	**Source:** *Discover*, 2005.
Enable readers to identify and flip to sections	**Dividers and tabs.** You are already familiar with dividers and tabs from loose-leaf notebooks. A tab provides a place for a label, which enables readers to identify and flip to a particular section. Sometimes dividers and tabs are color-coded. Tabs work according to the design principle of contrast: the tabs literally stick out.	
Refer readers to related information within the document	**Cross-reference tables.** These tables, which exploit the principle of alignment, refer readers to related discussions.	*Read . . .* *To learn to . . .* Ch. 1 connect to the router Ch. 2 set up a firewall

Creating Accessing Aids (*continued*)

If you want to . . .	Try using this accessing aid	Example
Help readers see where they are in the document	**Headers and footers.** Headers and footers work according to the principle of repetition: readers learn where to look on the page to see where they are. In a book, for example, the headers on the left-hand pages might repeat the chapter number and title; those on the right-hand pages might contain the most recent first-level heading. Sometimes writers build other identifying information into the headers. For example, your instructor might ask you to identify your assignments with a header like the following: "Smith, Progress Report, English 302, page 6."	Chapter 1 Microsoft Word: Getting Started **ters** ı variety of symbols and r example, if you want to add a he Symbol dialog box to specify : at the position of the insertion ıu want to repeat the text (in the same or in a +Y or F4. Word will automatically insert the peatedly to insert multiple copies of this text. Discovering Microsoft Office XP 35 **Source:** Microsoft, 2001.
	Page numbering. For one-sided documents, use Arabic numerals in the upper right corner. (The first page of most documents is unnumbered.) For two-sided documents, put the page numbers near the outside margins. Complex documents often use two number sequences: lowercase Roman numerals (i, ii, and so on) for the front matter and Arabic numerals for the body. The title page is unnumbered; the page following it is ii. Appendixes are often paginated with a letter and number combination: Appendix A begins with page A-1, followed by A-2, and so on; Appendix B starts with page B-1. Sometimes documents list the total number of pages in the document (so recipients can be sure they have all of them). The second page is "2 of 17," and the third page is "3 of 17." Documents that will be updated are sometimes numbered by section: Section 3 begins with page 3-1, followed by 3-2; Section 4 begins with 4-1. This way, a complete revision of one section does not affect the page numbering of subsequent sections.	DOCUMENTING YOUR SOURCES 4.9.1 Documentation identifies the sources of the ideas and the quotations in your document. Integrated throughout your document, documentation consists of citations in the text and a reference list (or list of works cited) at the back of your document. Documentation serves three basic functions: • It help... 4.9.2 IEEE STYLE When you cite a reference in the text, you treat the citation similarly to how you would treat endnotes; however, the reference number appears on the line, in square brackets, inside the punctuation. Use *et al.* if there are three or more author names. DOCUMENTING YOUR SOURCES 4.9.3 The following guidelines will help you prepare IEEE-style references. For additional information on formatting entries, consult the latest edition of *The Chicago Manual of Style*. For a sample IEEE-style reference list, see p. 695. • Arranging entries. Arrange and number the entries in the order in which they first appear in the text, much like endnotes. Place the numbers in square brackets and set them flush left in a column of their own, separate from the body of the references. Place the entries in their own column with no indents for turnovers.

TECH TIP

How to Set Up Pages

When designing a page to meet your audience's needs and expectations, you can control many design elements by using the **Page Setup** dialog box or the drop-down menus in the **Page Setup** group on the **Page Layout** tab.

In the **Page Setup** group, use the **Page Setup** dialog box launcher to display the **Page Setup** dialog box.

Use the **Margins**, **Paper**, and **Layout** tabs to specify such design elements as page margins, paper orientation, paper size, starting locations for new sections, and header and footer placement.

You can also use the drop-down menus on the **Page Setup** group to control many of the same design elements.

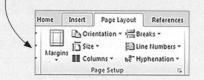

KEYWORDS: page layout tab, page setup group, page setup, margins, paper, layout

---

On the Web

For information on design principles and software, see the discussion about document design at About.com. Click on Links Library for Ch. 7 on <bedfordstmartins.com/ps>.

Page Layout

Every page has two kinds of space: white space and space devoted to text and graphics. The best way to design a page is to make a grid—a drawing of what the page will look like. In making a grid, you decide how to use white space and determine how many columns to have on the page.

Page Grids As the phrase suggests, a *page grid* is like a map on which you plan where the text, the graphics, and the white space will go. Many writers like to begin with a *thumbnail sketch*, a rough drawing that shows how the text and graphics will look on the page. Figure 7.8 shows several thumbnail sketches for a page from the body of a manual.

Experiment by sketching the different kinds of pages of your document: body pages, front matter, and so on. When you are satisfied, make page grids. You can use either a computer or a pencil and paper, or you can combine the two techniques.

Figure 7.9 shows two simple grids: one using picas (the unit that printing professionals use, which equals one-sixth of an inch) and one using inches.

Create different grids until the design is attractive, meets the needs of your readers, and seems appropriate for the information you are conveying. Figure 7.10 on page 154 shows some possibilities.

▶ On the Web

For more information on page layout, see the Document Design Tutorial on <bedfordstmartins.com/ps>.

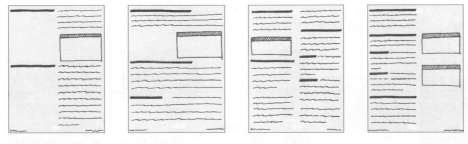

Figure 7.8 Thumbnail Sketches

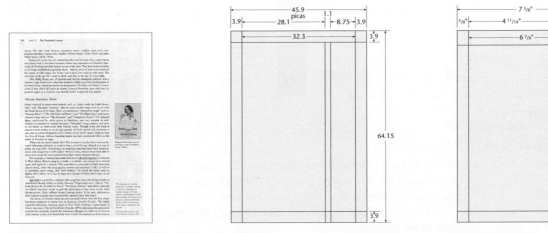

Figure 7.9 Sample Grids Using Picas and Inches
Source: Kerman and Tomlinson, 2004, p. 388.

a. **Double-column grid**
Source: Williams and Miller, 2002, p. 70.

b. **Two-page grid, with narrow outside columns for notes**
Source: Myers, 2003, pp. 10–11.

c. **Three-panel brochure**
Source: Norman Rockwell Museum, 2005.

Figure 7.10   Popular Grids

White Space   Sometimes called *negative space*, white space is the area of the paper with no writing or graphics: the space between two columns of text, the space between text and graphics, and, most obviously, the margins.

Margins, which make up close to half the area on a typical page, serve four main purposes:

- They reduce the amount of information on the page, making the document easier to read and use.

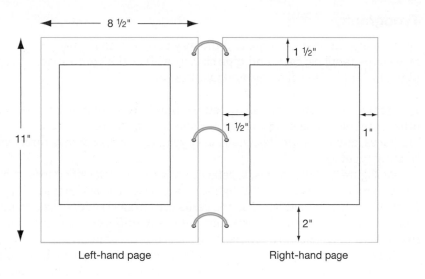

Figure 7.11   Typical Margins for a Document That Is Bound Like a Book

8 ½"

11"

1 ½"

1 ½"

1"

2"

Left-hand page

Right-hand page

Increase the size of the margins if the subject is difficult or if your readers are not knowledgeable about it.

- They provide space for binding and allow readers to hold the page without covering up the text.
- They provide a neat frame around the type.
- They provide space for marginal glosses.

Figure 7.11 shows common margin widths for an 8.5 × 11-inch document.

White space can also set off and emphasize an element on the page. For instance, white space around a graphic separates it from the text and draws readers' eyes to it. White space between columns helps readers read the text easily. And white space between sections of text helps readers see that one section is ending and another is beginning.

In This Book
For more about marginal glosses, see p. 164.

Columns

Many workplace documents have multiple columns. A multicolumn design offers three major advantages:

- Text is easier to read because the lines are shorter.
- Columns allow you to fit more information on the page, because many graphics can fit in one column or extend across two or more columns. In addition, a multicolumn design can contain more words on a page than a single-column design.
- Columns let you use the principle of repetition to create a visual pattern, such as text in one column and accompanying graphics in an adjacent column.

Typography

Typography, the study of type and the way people read it, encompasses typefaces, type families, case, and type size, as well as the white space of typography: line length, line spacing, and justification.

On the Web

Webmonkey's Web Typography Tutorial offers excellent advice about typography for both online and print applications. Click on Links Library for Ch. 7 on <bedfordstmartins.com/ps>.

Typefaces   A typeface is a set of letters, numbers, punctuation marks, and other symbols, all bearing a characteristic design. There are thousands of typefaces, and more are designed every year. Figure 7.12 shows three contrasting typefaces.

As Figure 7.13 illustrates, typefaces are generally classified into two categories: *serif* and *sans serif*. Although scholars used to think that serif typefaces are easier to read because the serifs encourage readers' eyes to move along the line, most now believe that there is no difference in readability between serif and sans-serif typefaces, either in print or online.

Most of the time you will use a handful of standard typefaces such as Times New Roman and Arial, which are included in your software and which your printer can reproduce.

Type Families   Each typeface belongs to a family of typefaces, which consist of variations on the basic style, such as italic and boldface. Figure 7.14, for example, shows the Helvetica family.

This paragraph is typed in French Script typeface. You are unlikely to see this style of font in a technical document because it is too ornate and too hard to read. It is better suited to wedding invitations and other formal announcements.

This paragraph is Times Roman. It looks like the kind of type used by the *New York Times* and other newspapers in the nineteenth century. It is an effective typeface for text in the body of technical documents.

This paragraph is Univers, which has a modern, high-tech look. It is best suited for headings and titles in technical documents.

Figure 7.12   Three Contrasting Typefaces

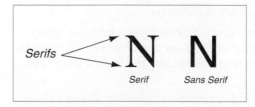

Figure 7.13   Serif and Sans-Serif Typefaces

Helvetica Light

Helvetica Light Italic

Helvetica Regular

Helvetica Regular Italic

Helvetica Bold

Helvetica Bold Italic

Helvetica Heavy

Helvetica Heavy Italic

Helvetica Regular Condensed

Helvetica Regular Condensed Italic

Figure 7.14　Helvetica Family of Type

Individual variations are greater in lowercase words

THAN THEY ARE IN UPPERCASE WORDS.

Figure 7.15　Individual Variations in Lowercase and Uppercase Type
Lowercase letters are easier to read than uppercase because the individual variations from one letter to another are greater.

Be careful not to overload your text with too many different members of the same family. Used sparingly and consistently, they can help you with filtering: calling attention to various kinds of text, such as warnings and notes. Use italics for book titles and other elements, and use bold type for emphasis and headings. Stay away from outlined and shadowed variations. You can live a full, rewarding life without ever using them.

Case　To make your document easy to read, use uppercase and lowercase letters as you would in any other kind of writing (see Figure 7.15). The average person requires 10 to 25 percent more time to read text using all uppercase letters than to read text using both uppercase and lowercase. In addition, uppercase letters take up as much as 35 percent more space than lowercase letters (Haley, 1991). And if the text includes both cases, readers will find it easier to see where new sentences begin (Poulton, 1968).

Type Size　Type size is measured with a unit called a *point*. There are 12 points in a *pica* and 72 points in an inch. In most technical documents 10-, 11-, or 12-point type is used for the body of the text:

▷ **On the Web**

For more information on typography, see the Document Design Tutorial on <bedfordstmartins.com/ps>.

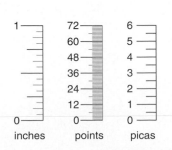

This paragraph is printed in 10-point type. This size is easy to read, provided it is reproduced on a high-quality ink-jet printer or laser printer.

This paragraph is printed in 12-point type. If the document will be read by people over age 40, 12-point type is a good size because it is more legible than a smaller size.

This paragraph is printed in 14-point type. This size is appropriate for titles or headings.

Type sizes used in other parts of a document include the following:

footnotes	8- or 9-point type
indexes	2 points smaller than body text
slides or transparencies	24- to 36-point type

In general, aim for at least a 2- to 4-point difference between the headings and the body. Too many size variations, however, suggest a sweepstakes advertisement rather than a serious text.

ETHICS NOTE

Using Type Sizes Responsibly

Text set in large type contrasts with text set in small type. It makes sense to use large type to emphasize headings and other important information. But be careful with small type. It is unethical (and, according to some court rulings, illegal) to use excessively small type (such as 6 points or smaller) to disguise information that you *don't* want to stand out. You get annoyed when you have to read the fine print in an ad for cell-phone service to learn that the low rates are guaranteed for only three months or that you are committing to a long-term contract. You *should* get annoyed. Very fine print is annoying. Don't use it.

Line Length   The line length most often used on an 8.5 × 11-inch page— about 80 characters—is somewhat difficult to read. A shorter line of 50 to 60 characters is easier, especially in a long document (Biggs, 1980).

Line Spacing   Sometimes called *leading* (pronounced "ledding"), *line spacing* refers to the white space between lines or between a line of text and a graphic. If lines are too far apart, the page looks diffuse, the text loses coherence, and readers tire quickly. If lines are too close together, the page looks crowded and becomes difficult to read. Some research suggests

a. Excessive line spacing

Aronomink Systems has been contracted by Cecil Electric Cooperative, Inc.

(CECI) to design a solid waste management system for the Cecil County plant,

Units 1 and 2, to be built in Cranston, Maryland. The system will consist

of two 600 MW pulverized coal-burning units fitted with high-efficiency

electrostatic precipitators and limestone reagent FGD systems.

b. Appropriate line spacing

Aronomink Systems has been contracted by Cecil Electric Cooperative, Inc.
(CECI) to design a solid waste management system for the Cecil County plant,
Units 1 and 2, to be built in Cranston, Maryland. The system will consist of two
600 MW pulverized coal-burning units fitted with high-efficiency electrostatic
precipitators and limestone reagent FGD systems.

c. Inadequate line spacing

Aronomink Systems has been contracted by Cecil Electric Cooperative, Inc.
(CECI) to design a solid waste management system for the Cecil County plant,
Units 1 and 2, to be built in Cranston, Maryland. The system will consist of two
600 MW pulverized coal-burning units fitted with high-efficiency electrostatic
precipitators and limestone reagent FGD systems.

Figure 7.16   Line Spacing

that smaller type, longer lines, and sans-serif typefaces all benefit from extra line spacing. Figure 7.16 shows three variations in line spacing.

Line spacing is usually determined by the kind of document you are writing. Memos and letters are single-spaced; reports, proposals, and similar documents are often double-spaced or one-and-a-half-spaced.

Figure 7.17 on page 160 shows how line spacing can be used to distinguish one section of text from another and to separate text from graphics.

Justification   Justification refers to the alignment of words along the left and right margins. In technical communication, text is often *left-justified* (also called *ragged right*). Except for paragraph indentations, the lines begin along a uniform left margin but end on an irregular right border. Ragged right is most common in word-processed text (even though word processors can justify the right margin).

Net (Cost)/Income (Dollars in Millions)	FY 2005	FY 2006	FY 2007	FY 2008	FY 2009
Earned Revenue	$ 1,372.8	$ 1,594.4	$ 1,735.7	$ 1,862.2	$ 1,927.1
Program Cost	(1,424.0)	(1,514.2)	(1,769.6)	(1,892.6)	(1,981.9)
Net (Cost)/Income	$ (51.2)	$ 80.2	$ (33.9)	$ (30.4)	$ (54.8)

The line spacing between two sections is greater than the line spacing within a section.

STATEMENT OF NET COST

The Statement of Net Cost presents the USPTO's results of operations by the following responsibility segments – Patent, Trademark, and Intellectual Property Protection and Enforcement Domestically and Abroad. The above table presents the total USPTO's results of operations for the past five fiscal years. In FY 2005, the USPTO's operations resulted in a net cost. In FY 2006, the USPTO generated a net income due to the increased maintenance fees received and revenue recognition of previously deferred revenue collected subsequent to the fee increase on December 8, 2004. During FY 2007, FY 2008, and FY 2009 the USPTO's operations resulted in a net cost of $33.9 million, $30.4 million, and $54.8 million, respectively.

The Statement of Net Cost compares fees earned to costs incurred during a specific period of time. It is not necessarily an indicator of net income or net cost over the life of a patent or trademark. Net income or net cost for the fiscal year is dependent upon work that has been completed over the various phases of the production life cycle. The net income calculation is based on fees earned during the fiscal year being reported, regardless of when those fees were collected. Maintenance fees also play a large part in whether a total net income or net cost is recognized. Maintenance fees collected in FY 2009 are a reflection of patent issue levels 3.5, 7.5, and 11.5 years ago, rather than a reflection of patents issued in FY 2009. Therefore, maintenance fees can have a significant impact on matching costs and revenue.

During FY 2009, with the number of patent filings decreasing by 2.3 percent over the prior year, the backlog for patent applica-

tions likewise decreased, decreasing deferred revenue and increasing earned revenue. This was evidenced by the Patent organization disposing of 22.9 percent more applications than were disposed of during FY 2008.

During FY 2009, with the number of trademark applications decreasing by 12.3 percent over the prior year, the Trademark organization was able to continue to address the existing inventory and reduce pendency by 0.3 months from FY 2008. The Trademark organization was able to do this while recognizing a slight decrease in revenue earned.

EARNED REVENUE

The USPTO's earned revenue is derived from the fees collected for patent and trademark products and services. Fee collections are recognized as earned revenue when the activities to complete the work associated with the fee are completed. The table below presents the earned revenue for the past five years.

Earned revenue totaled $1,927.1 million for FY 2009, an increase of $64.9 million, or 3.5 percent, over FY 2008 earned revenue of $1,862.2 million. Of revenue earned during FY 2009, $454.3 million related to fee collections that were deferred for revenue recognition in prior fiscal years, $546.7 million related to maintenance fees collected during FY 2009, which were considered earned immediately, $920.7 million related to work performed for fees collected during FY 2009, and $5.4 million were not fee-related.

Line spacing is also used to separate the text from the graphics.

Earned Revenue (Dollars in Millions)	FY 2005	FY 2006	FY 2007	FY 2008	FY 2009
Patent	$ 1,197.8	$ 1,384.2	$ 1,507.0	$ 1,625.0	$ 1,697.4
Percentage Change in Patent Earned Revenue	9.6%	15.6%	8.9%	7.8%	4.5%
Trademark	175.0	210.2	228.7	237.2	229.7
Percentage Change in Trademark Earned Revenue	19.5%	20.1%	8.8%	3.7%	(3.2)%
Total Earned Revenue	$ 1,372.8	$ 1,594.4	$ 1,735.7	$ 1,862.2	$ 1,927.1
Percentage Change in Earned Revenue	10.8%	16.1%	8.9%	7.3%	3.5%

48   PERFORMANCE AND ACCOUNTABILITY REPORT: FISCAL YEAR 2009

Figure 7.17   Line Spacing Used to Distinguish One Section from Another
Source: U.S. Patent and Trademark Office, 2010 <www.uspto.gov/about/stratplan/ar/2009/2009annualreport.pdf>.

In *justified text*, also called *full-justified text*, both the left and right margins are justified. Justified text is seen most often in formal documents, such as books. The following passage (U.S. Department of Agriculture, 2002) is presented first in left-justified form and then in justified form:

Notice that the space between words is uniform in left-justified text.

We recruited participants to reflect the racial diversity of the area in which the focus groups were conducted. Participants had to meet the following eligibility criteria: have primary responsibility or share responsibility for cooking in their household; prepare food and cook in the home at least three times a week; eat meat and/or poultry; prepare meat and/or poultry in the home at least twice a week; and not regularly use a digital food thermometer when cooking at home.

We recruited participants to reflect the racial diversity of the area in which the focus groups were conducted. Participants had to meet the following eligibility criteria: have primary responsibility or share responsibility for cooking in their household; prepare food and cook in the home at least three times a week; eat meat and/or poultry; prepare meat and/or poultry in the home at least twice a week; and not regularly use a digital food thermometer when cooking at home.

In justified text, the spacing between words is irregular, slowing down the reader. Because a big space suggests a break between sentences, not a break between words, readers can become confused, frustrated, and fatigued.

Notice that the irregular spacing not only slows down reading but also can create "rivers" of white space. Readers are tempted to concentrate on the rivers running south rather than on the information itself.

Full justification can make the text harder to read in one more way. Some word processors and typesetting systems automatically hyphenate words that do not fit on the line. Hyphenation slows down and distracts the reader. Left-justified text does not require as much hyphenation as full-justified text.

Titles and Headings

Titles and headings should stand out visually on the page because they present a new idea.

Titles   Because a title is the most important heading in a document, it should be displayed clearly and prominently. If it is on a cover page or a title page, use boldface in a large size, such as 18 or 24 points. If it also appears at the top of the first page, make it slightly larger than the rest of the text—perhaps 16 or 18 points for a document printed in 12 point—but smaller than it is on the cover or title page. Many designers center titles on the page between the right and left margins.

> **In This Book**
> For more about titling your document, see Ch. 6, p. 108.

Headings   Readers should be able to tell when you are beginning a new topic. The most effective way to distinguish one level of heading from another is to use size variations (Williams & Spyridakis, 1992). Most readers will notice a 20 percent size difference between a first-level heading and a second-level heading. Boldface also sets off headings effectively. The *least* effective way to set off headings is underlining, because the underline obscures the *descenders*, the portions of letters that extend below the body of the letters, such as in *p* and y.

> **In This Book**
> For more about using headings, see Ch. 6, p. 108.

In general, the more important the heading level, the closer it is to the left margin: first-level headings usually begin at the left margin, second-level headings are often indented a half inch, and third-level headings are often indented an inch. Indented third-level headings can also be run into the text.

> **On the Web**
> For more information on designing headings, see the Document Design Tutorial on <bedfordstmartins.com/ps>.

TECH TIP

How to Modify and Create Styles

As you write, you can use the **Styles** group to modify and create styles to address your specific writing situation.

1. To modify a style, right-click the style you wish to modify in the **Styles** group on the **Home** tab. Select **Modify** from the drop-down menu that appears.

   Use the **Modify Style** dialog box to make changes.

   For additional formatting options for elements such as fonts, paragraphs, and numbering, select the **Format** button.

2. To create a new style, apply the desired character formatting to some text or the desired paragraph formatting to a paragraph. Next, select the desired text or paragraph and then right-click it.

   Choose **Styles** and then **Save Selection as a New Quick Style**.

Use the **Create New Style from Formatting** dialog box to name your new style. Apply additional formatting to the style by selecting the **Modify** button.

3. You can also create a new style by selecting the **Styles** dialog box launcher and then selecting the **New Style** button. Use the dialog box that appears to create a new style.

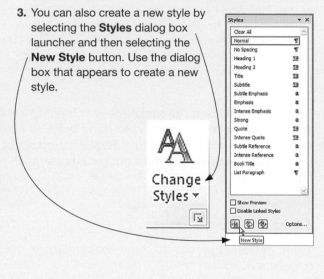

KEYWORDS: styles group, quick styles, create new quick styles, modify styles, new styles

---

In designing headings, use line spacing carefully. A perceivable distance between a heading and the following text increases the impact of the heading. Consider these three examples:

Summary

In this example, the writer has skipped a line between the heading and the text that follows it. The heading stands out clearly.

Summary
In this example, the writer has not skipped a line between the heading and the text that follows it. The heading stands out, but not as emphatically.

Summary. In this example, the writer has begun the text on the same line as the heading. This run-in style makes the heading stand out the least.

Other Design Features

Table 7.1 shows five other design features that are used frequently in technical communication: rules, boxes, screens, marginal glosses, and pull quotes.

TABLE 7.1 ▶ Rules, Boxes, Screens, Marginal Glosses, and Pull Quotes

Two types of rules are used here: the vertical rules to separate the columns, and the blue horizontal rules to separate the items. Rules enable you to fit a lot of information on a page, but when overused they make the page look cluttered.

Source: Institute of Scientific and Technical Communicators, 2005, p. 43.

Rules. A *rule* is a design term for a straight line. Using the drawing tools in a word processor, you can add rules. Horizontal rules can separate headers and footers from the body of the page or divide two sections of text. Vertical rules can separate columns on a multicolumn page or identify revised text in a manual. Rules exploit the principles of alignment and proximity.

Source: Valley, 2005, p. 61.

Boxes. Adding rules on all four sides of an item creates a box. Boxes can enclose graphics or special sections of text, or form a border for the whole page. Boxed text is often positioned to extend into the margin, giving it further emphasis. Boxes exploit the principles of contrast and repetition.

TABLE 7.1 ▶ Rules, Boxes, Screens, Marginal Glosses, and Pull Quotes *(continued)*

The three different colors of screens clearly distinguish the three sets of equations.

Source: Purves, Sadava, Orians, and Heller, 2004, p. 466.

Screens. Shading behind text or graphics for emphasis is called a *screen*. The density can range from 1 percent to 100 percent; 5 to 10 percent is usually enough to provide emphasis without making the text illegible. You can use screens with or without boxes. Screens exploit the principles of contrast and repetition.

This author uses marginal glosses for presenting definitions of key words.

Source: Myers, 2003, p. 603.

Marginal glosses. A marginal gloss is a brief comment on the main discussion. Marginal glosses are usually set in a different typeface—and sometimes in a different color—from the main discussion. Although marginal glosses can be helpful in providing a quick overview of the main discussion, they can also compete with the text for readers' attention. Marginal glosses exploit the principles of contrast and repetition.

This pull quote is placed in the margin, but it can go anywhere on the page, even spanning two or more columns or the whole page.

Source: Roark et al., 2005, p. 115.

Pull quotes. A pull quote is a brief quotation (usually just a sentence or two) that is pulled from the text, displayed in a larger type size and usually in a different typeface, and sometimes enclosed in a box. Newspapers and magazines use pull quotes to attract readers' attention. Pull quotes are inappropriate for reports and similar documents because they look too informal. They are increasingly popular, however, in newsletters. Pull quotes exploit the principles of contrast and repetition.

TECH TIP

How to Create Borders and Screens

To emphasize page elements by enclosing them in a box or including background shading, use the **Borders and Shading** dialog box.

To create a **border** around a page element or an entire page, select the area you want to format. Select the **Page Layout** tab, and then select **Page Borders** in the **Page Background** group.

> 🔲 Watermark ▾
> 🔲 Page Color ▾
> 🔲 Page Borders
> Page Background

Select the **Borders** or **Page Border** tab.

You can specify the type of border, line style, color, and line width.

To create **shading**, also called a screen, select the area you want to format, and then select **Page Borders** in the **Page Background** group. Select the **Shading** tab.

You can specify the color within the box as well as the style of the pattern.

KEYWORDS: borders, page borders, shading, page background group

TECH TIP

How to Create Text Boxes

To emphasize graphics or special sections of text or to position such elements independently of your margins, use the **Text Box** feature in the **Text** group on the **Insert** tab.

To **create** a text box, select **Draw Text Box** from the **Text Box** drop-down menu.

Click and drag your cursor to create your text box.

Click inside the text box and begin typing.

You can select the text box and move it around your page.

You can also insert a **built-in** text box from the **Text Box** drop-down menu.

To **format** your text box, select the box and then select the **Format Shape** dialog box launcher from the **Shape Styles** group on the **Format** tab.

The **Arrange** group allows you to specify design elements such as the text box's position in relation to other objects and the wrapping style of the surrounding text.

After selecting the box, you can also use buttons on the **Format** tab to specify such design elements as fill color, line color, font color, line style, and other effects.

KEYWORDS: text box, drawing toolbar, fill color, line color

ANALYZING PAGE DESIGNS

Figures 7.18 and 7.19 show typical page designs used in technical documents. These figures illustrate the concepts discussed in this chapter.

A multicolumn design can be flexible. Here, the writer emphasizes the "Purpose" section by breaking the three-column design, using a screen, and using a larger typeface than that used for the text.

SECURITY SECTOR REFORM (SSR)

PURPOSE

This document provides Department of State, DoD, and USAID practitioners with guidelines for coordinating, planning, and implementing SSR programs with foreign partner nations. The objective of this paper is to provide guidance on how best to design, develop, and deliver foreign assistance such that it promotes effective, legitimate, transparent, and accountable security sector development in partner states.

INTRODUCTION

SSR emerged as a discipline over the last decade in recognition of the changing international security environment and the limitations of existing donor approaches. SSR builds on the USG's longstanding tradition of working in partnership with foreign governments and organizations to support peace, security, and democratic governance globally.

The 2006 U.S. National Security Strategy stated that the goal of U.S. statecraft is "to help create a world of democratic, well-governed states that can meet the needs of their citizens and conduct themselves responsibly in the international system." SSR can help achieve that objective, reinforce U.S. diplomatic, development, and defense priorities, and reduce long-term threats to U.S. security by helping to build stable, prosperous, and peaceful societies beyond our borders. SSR enables U.S. foreign assistance providers to respond to national strategic guidance and transform our approaches towards cooperation, partnership capacity building, stabilization and reconstruction, and engagement. Accordingly, the principles contained in this paper guide relevant actors to conduct security-related engagement in more holistic, integrated ways.

The U.S. foreign assistance framework[1] identifies SSR as a key program area in support of the *Peace and Security* foreign policy objective and security sector governance as a program element in support of the *Governing Justly and Democratically* foreign policy objective. SSR is an ongoing process and may be an appropriate engagement for countries in each of the foreign assistance country categories. SSR may include activities in support of security force and intelligence reform; justice sector reform; civilian oversight and management of military and intelligence services; community security; and disarmament, demobilization, and reintegration (DDR). Program design–including sequencing and prioritization–should be undertaken with full consideration of country context and circumstance.

The USG is not alone in its pursuit of comprehensive approaches to SSR. The United Nations (UN) is integrating SSR across different UN offices and agencies, including the United Nations Development Program (UNDP) and the United Nations Department of Peacekeeping Operations (UNDPKO).[2] The North Atlantic Treaty Organization (NATO), the European Union (EU), the Organization for Economic Cooperation and Development (OECD), and major bilateral donors have advanced a more holistic SSR concept through combined funding mechanisms and enhanced collaboration among defense and development agencies. In April 2004, USAID endorsed the OECD/Development Assistance Committee's publication, *Security System Reform and Governance: Policy and Good Practice* on behalf of the U.S. Government.[3]

OBJECTIVE

The Department of State, DoD, and USAID should pursue integrated SSR strategies and programs. The objective is to design, develop, and deliver foreign assistance such that it promotes effective, legitimate, transparent, and accountable security and development in partner states.

2

Figure 7.18   A Multicolumn Design
Source: U.S. Agency for International Development, U.S. Department of Defense, and U.S. Department of State, 2009 <www.usaid.gov/our_work/democracy_and_governance/publications /pdfs/SSR_JS_Mar2009.pdf>.

HUMAN TRAFFICKING FOR ORGAN REMOVAL

INTRODUCTION

Mohammad Salim Khan woke up in a strange house and felt an excruciating pain in his abdomen. Unsure where he was, Khan asked a man wearing a surgical mask what had happened. "We have taken your kidney," the stranger said, according to a January 2008 Associated Press report. "If you tell anyone, we'll shoot you."

Six days earlier, Khan, a 33-year-old Indian day laborer from New Delhi, had been approached by a bearded man offering a construction job. The man explained that the work would pay $4 a day – not unusual in India – and would last three months. Khan, a father of five, jumped at the chance for work.

He traveled with the man to a small town several hours away. Once there, Khan was locked in a room and forced at gunpoint to give a blood sample and take drugs that made him unconscious. He didn't wake up until after surgery. Police raided the illegal clinic afterward, rescuing Khan and two other men. Khan never received money for his kidney, and it took months to recover physically. Indian authorities pursued charges against the doctor involved.

Khan was trafficked for the purpose of organ removal.

The UN TIP Protocol prohibits the use of human trafficking for the purpose of organ removal. This may include situations in which a trafficker causes the involuntary removal of another living person's organ, either for profit or for another benefit, such as to practice traditional medicine or witchcraft.

A far greater number of organs are obtained from people in the developing world, sometimes through exploitative means, and sold in a highly lucrative international market. The UN TIP Protocol does not cover this voluntary sale of organs for money, which is considered lawful in most countries.

But the demand for organs is rising as the world's rich are growing older. At the same time, the world's poor are growing poorer, and the potential for more human trafficking cases like Khan's is increasing. The World Health Organization (WHO) estimates that 10 percent of the 70,000 kidneys transplanted each year may originate on the black market.

or recruiters unlawfully exploit an initial debt the worker assumed as part of the terms of employment.

Workers may also inherit debt in more traditional systems of bonded labor. Traditional bonded labor in South Asia, for example, enslaves huge numbers of people from generation to generation. A January 2009 report by Anti-Slavery International, a London-based NGO, concluded that this form of forced labor, traditionally more prevalent in villages, is expanding into urban areas of the region, rather than diminishing on an aggregate level, as the result of development and modernization.

Debt Bondage Among Migrant Laborers

The vulnerability of migrant laborers to trafficking schemes is especially disturbing because the population is sizeable in some regions. There are three potential contributing factors: (1) abuse of contracts; (2) inadequate local laws governing the recruitment and employment

of migrant laborers; and (3) intentional imposition of exploitative and often illegal costs and debts on these laborers in the source country, often with the support of labor agencies and employers in the destination country.

Abuses of contracts and hazardous conditions

"We are blind to trafficking all around us, and we should be more alert to the fact that trafficking is not a 'remote' issue but rather something that is local to us and impacts on our communities."

Nick Kinsella, Chief Executive Officer of the UK Human Trafficking Centre.

of employment do not in themselves constitute involuntary servitude. But the use or threat of physical force or restraint to keep a person working may convert a situation into one of forced labor. Costs imposed on laborers for the "privilege" of working abroad can make laborers

17

Figure 7.19   A Complex Page Design

Source: U.S. Department of State, 2009 <www.state.gov/documents/organization/123360.pdf>.

Annotations:

This page is a two-column design, with several embellishments.

The dark red bar functions as a header or footer, including the part title and the page number.

The "Human Trafficking for Organ Removal" section is distinguished from the main text by its single-column design, its screen, and the flush-left text with no paragraph indentations.

The pull quote uses reverse type: light text on a dark background. In addition, the pull quote extends to the edge of the page, giving it additional emphasis.

The headings use the same color as the bar at the edge of the page.

DOCUMENT ANALYSIS ACTIVITY

Analyzing a Page Design

The following page is from a government report. The accompanying questions ask you to think about page design (as discussed on pp. 147–65).

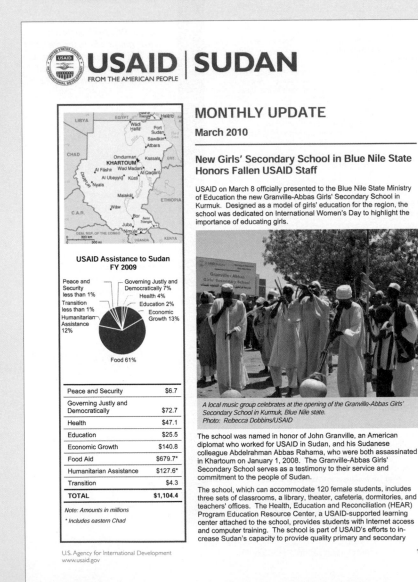

1. Describe the use of proximity as a design principle on this page. How effective is it?

2. Describe the use of alignment as a design principle on this page. How effective is it?

3. Describe the use of repetition as a design principle on this page. How effective is it?

4. Describe the use of contrast as a design principle on this page. How effective is it?

On the Web

To submit your responses to your instructor, click on Document Analysis Activities for Ch. 7 on <bedfordstmartins.com/ps>.

Source: U.S. Agency for International Development, 2010 <www.usaid.gov/locations/sub-saharan _africa/countries/sudan/docs/mar10_monthly_update.pdf>.

DESIGNING WEB SITES

Accessing tools are vitally important in Web sites because if you can't figure out how to find the information you want on a Web site, you're out of luck. With a printed document, you can at least flip through the pages, hoping that you'll find what you're looking for.

The following discussion focuses on seven principles that can help you make it easy for readers to find and understand the information you provide:

- Create informative headers and footers.
- Help readers navigate the site.
- Include extra features your readers might need.
- Help readers connect with others.
- Design for readers with disabilities.
- Design for multicultural audiences.
- Design simple, clear Web pages.

Create Informative Headers and Footers

Headers and footers help readers understand and navigate your site, and they help establish your credibility. You want readers to know that they are visiting the official site of your organization and that it was created by professionals. Figure 7.20 shows a typical Web site header, and Figure 7.21 shows a typical Web site footer.

Notice that a header in a Web site provides much more accessing information than a header in a printed document. This header from Ford lets readers search the site or link directly to the major sections of the site.

Figure 7.20   Web Site Header
Source: Ford Motor Company, 2010 <www.ford.com>.

Dealer Directory | Site Map | Contact Ford | Site Feedback

Privacy | Your California Privacy Rights | Corporate Governance
Copyright 2010 Ford Motor Company. All rights reserved.

This simply designed footer presents all the links as text. Readers with impaired vision who use text-to-speech devices are able to understand these textual links; they would not be able to understand them if they were graphical links. The links to the left lead to a dealer directory, a site map, a contact page, and a feedback form. The links on the right lead to some of the site's legal and privacy information.

Figure 7.21   Web Site Footer
Source: Ford Motor Company, 2010 <www.ford.com>.

Help Readers Navigate the Site

Because readers of a Web site can view only the page that appears on the screen, each page should help them see where they are in the site and get where they want to go. One important way to help readers navigate is to create and sustain a consistent visual design on every page. Make the header, footer, background color or pattern, typography (typeface, type size, and color), and placement of the navigational links the same on every page. That way, readers will know where to look for these items.

On the Web

For advice on how to design an effective site map, see Jakob Nielsen's "Site Map Usability." Click on Links Library for Ch. 7 on <bedfordstmartins .com/ps>.

Guidelines

Making Your Site Easy to Navigate

Follow these five suggestions to make it easy for readers to find what they want on your site.

▶ **Include a site map or index.** A site map, which lists the pages on the site, can be a graphic or a textual list of the pages, classified according to logical categories. An index is an alphabetized list of the pages. Figure 7.22 on page 171 is a portion of the genome.gov site map.

▶ **Use a table of contents at the top of long pages.** If your page extends for more than a couple of screens, include a table of contents—a set of links to the items on that page—so that your readers do not have to scroll down to find the topic they want. Tables of contents can link to information further down on the same page or to information on separate pages. Figure 7.23 on page 171 shows an excerpt from the table of contents at the top of a frequently asked questions (FAQ) page.

▶ **Help readers get back to the top of long pages.** If a page is long enough to justify a table of contents, include a "Back to top" link (a textual link or a button or icon) before the start of each new chunk of information.

▶ **Include a link to the home page on every page.** This link can be a simple "Back to home page" textual link, a button, or an icon.

▶ **Include textual navigational links at the bottom of the page.** If you are using buttons or icons for links, include textual versions of those links at the bottom of the page. Readers with impaired vision might be using special software that reads the information on the screen. This software interprets text only, not graphics.

Include Extra Features Your Readers Might Need

Because readers with a range of interests and needs will visit your site, consider adding some or all of the following five features:

- *An FAQ.* A list of frequently asked questions helps new readers by providing basic information, explaining how to use the site, and directing them to more-detailed discussions.

- *A search page or engine.* A search page or search engine lets readers enter a keyword or phrase and find all the pages on the site that contain it.

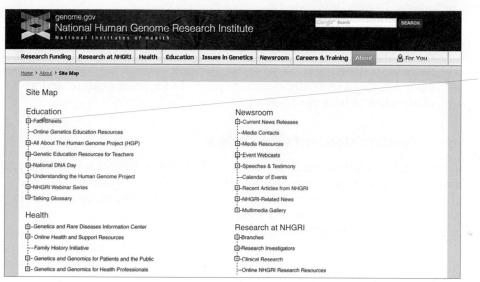

In this site map, plus signs indicate pages that have subordinate pages.

Figure 7.22   Site Map
Source: National Institutes of Health, 2010 <www.genome.gov/sitemap.cfm>.

Frequently Asked Questions about Copyright

The Copyright Office offers introductory answers to frequently asked questions about copyright, registration, and services of the Office. Click on a subject heading below to view questions and answers relating to your selection. Links throughout the answers will guide you to further information on our website or from other sources. Should you have any further questions, please consult our Contact Us page.

NEW! Tip of the month!

Also see our FAQs for eCO online registration.

Preguntas frecuentes

Copyright in General

- What is copyright?
- What does copyright protect?
- How is a copyright different from a patent or a trademark?
- When is my work protected?
- Do I have to register with your office to be protected?
- Why should I register my work if copyright protection is automatic?
- I've heard about a "poor man's copyright." What is it?
- Is my copyright good in other countries?

The reader clicks on a red question to go to its answer.

Figure 7.23   Table of Contents
Source: U.S. Copyright Office, 2010 <www.copyright.gov/help/faq>.

- *Resource links.* If one of the purposes of your site is to educate readers, provide links to other sites.
- *A printable version of your site.* A Web site is designed for a screen, not a page. A printable version of your site, with black text on a white

background, and all the text and graphics consolidated into one big file, saves readers paper and toner.

- A *text-only version of your site*. Many readers with impaired vision rely on text because their specialized software cannot interpret graphics. Consider creating a text-only version of your site for these readers, and include a link to it on your home page.

Help Readers Connect with Others

An organization's Web site is the main way for clients, customers, suppliers, journalists, government agencies, and the general public to learn about and interact with the organization. For this reason, most organizations use their Web sites to connect with their various stakeholders through social media such as discussion boards and blogs.

Use your Web site to direct readers to interactive features on your own site, as well as to your pages on social-media sites such as Facebook or Twitter. Figure 7.24 shows Volvo's "Community" page.

Design for Readers with Disabilities

The Internet has proved to be a terrific technology for people with disabilities because it brings a world of information to their computers, allowing them to work from home and participate in virtual communities. However,

On the Web

For a detailed look at accessibility issues, see the Web Accessibility Initiative, from the World Wide Web Consortium. Click on Links Library for Ch. 7 on <bedfordstmartins.com/ps>.

Volvo's "Community" page directs readers to various events, videos, and blogs on the Volvo site, as well as to four external social-media sites.

Figure 7.24   Helping Readers Connect with Others
Source: Volvo Cars, 2010 <www.volvocars.com/us/top/community/pages/followus.aspx>.

most sites on the Internet are not designed to accommodate people with disabilities.

The following discussion highlights several ways to make your site easier to use for people with disabilities. Consider three main types of disabilities as you design your site:

- *Vision impairment.* People who cannot see, or cannot see well, rely on text-to-speech software. Provide either a text-only version of the site or textual equivalents of all your graphics. Use the "alt" (alternate) tag to create a textual label that appears when the reader holds the mouse over the graphic.

    Do not rely on color or graphics alone to communicate information. For example, if you use a red icon to signal a warning, also use the word *warning*. If you use tables to create columns on the screen, label each column clearly using a text label rather than just an image.

    Use 12-point type or larger throughout your site, and provide audio feedback—for example, having a button beep when the reader presses it.

- *Hearing impairment.* If you use video, provide captions and, if the video includes sound, a volume control. Also use visual feedback techniques; for example, make a button flash when the reader presses it.

- *Mobility impairment.* Some people with mobility impairments find it easier to use the keyboard than a mouse. Therefore, build in keyboard shortcuts wherever possible. If readers have to click on an area of the screen using a pointing device, make the area large so that it is easy to see and click.

Design for Multicultural Audiences

About 75 percent of the people using the Internet are nonnative speakers of English, and that percentage continues to grow as more people from developing nations go online (Internet World Stats, 2010). Therefore, it makes sense to plan your site as if many of your readers will not be proficient in English.

Planning for a multicultural Web site is similar to planning for a multicultural printed document:

- *Use common words and short sentences and paragraphs.*

- *Avoid idioms, both verbal and visual, that might be confusing.* For instance, don't use sports metaphors, such as *full-court press*, or a graphic of an American-style mailbox to suggest an e-mail link.

- *If a large percentage of your readers speak a language other than English, consider creating a version of your site in that language.* The expense can be considerable, but so can the benefits.

> **On the Web**
>
> Color Vision Simulator, from Vischeck, lets you see what graphics look like to people with different color disabilities. Click on Links Library for Ch. 7 on <bedfordstmartins.com/ps>.

Design Simple, Clear Web Pages

Well-designed Web pages are simple, with only a few colors and nothing extraneous. In addition, the text is easy to read and chunked effectively, and the links are written carefully to help readers decide whether to follow them.

When you create a site, it doesn't cost anything to use all the colors in the rainbow, to add sound effects and animation, to make text blink on and off. Most of the time, however, these effects only slow the download and annoy the reader. If a special effect serves no useful function, avoid it.

▶ **On the Web**

For examples of excellent Web design, see the Links Library for Ch. 7 on <bedfordstmartins.com/ps>.

▶ **On the Web**

For an introduction to color theory as it applies to the Web, see Dmitry's Design Lab. Click on Links Library for Ch. 7 on <bedfordstmartins.com/ps>.

▶ **On the Web**

For more on writing for the Web, see "Concise, SCANNABLE, and Objective" by John Morkes and Jakob Nielsen. Click on Links Library for Ch. 7 on <bedfordstmartins.com/ps>.

▶ **In This Book**

For more about chunking, see p. 148.

Guidelines

Designing Simple, Clear Web Pages

Follow these eight suggestions to make your design attractive and easy to use.

▶ **Use conservative color combinations to increase text legibility.** The greater the contrast between the text color and the background color, the more legible the text. The most legible color combination is black text against a white background. Bad idea: black on purple.

▶ **Avoid decorative graphics.** Don't waste space using graphics that convey no useful information. Think twice before you use clip art.

▶ **Use thumbnail graphics.** Instead of a large graphic, which takes up space and requires a long time to download, use a thumbnail so that readers can click on it if they wish to open a larger version.

▶ **Keep the text short.** Web pages are harder to read than paper documents because screen resolution is much less sharp: usually, 72 dots per inch (dpi) versus 1200 dpi on a printout from a basic laser printer and 2400 dpi in some books. Poor resolution makes reading long stretches of text difficult. In general, pages should contain no more than two or three screens of information.

▶ **Chunk information.** When you write for the screen, chunk information to make it easier to understand. Use frequent headings, brief paragraphs, and lists.

▶ **Make the text as simple as possible.** Use common words and short sentences to make the information as simple as the subject allows.

▶ **Structure your sentences as if there were no links in your text.**

AWKWARD	Click here to go to the Rehabilitation Center page, which links to research centers across the nation.
SMOOTH	The Rehabilitation Center page links to research centers across the nation.

▶ **Indicate what information a linked page contains.** Readers get frustrated if they wait for a Web file to download and then discover that it doesn't contain the information they expected.

UNINFORMATIVE	See the Rehabilitation Center.
INFORMATIVE	See the Rehabilitation Center's hours of operation.

Writer's Checklist

Did you

- ☐ analyze your audience: their knowledge of the subject, their attitudes, their reasons for reading, and the kinds of tasks they will be carrying out? (p. 144)
- ☐ consider the purpose or purposes you are trying to achieve? (p. 144)
- ☐ determine your resources in time, money, and equipment? (p. 144)

Designing Printed Documents and Pages

Did you

- ☐ think about which accessing tools would be most appropriate, such as icons, color, dividers and tabs, and cross-reference tables? (p. 150)
- ☐ use color, if you have access to it, to highlight certain items, such as warnings? (p. 150)
- ☐ devise a style for headers and footers? (p. 150)
- ☐ devise a style for page numbers? (p. 151)
- ☐ draw thumbnail sketches and page grids that define columns and white space? (p. 153)
- ☐ choose typefaces that are appropriate for your subject? (p. 156)
- ☐ use appropriate styles from the type families? (p. 156)
- ☐ use type sizes that are appropriate for your subject and audience? (p. 157)
- ☐ choose a line length that is suitable for your subject and audience? (p. 158)
- ☐ choose line spacing that is suitable for your line length, subject, and audience? (p. 158)
- ☐ decide whether to use left-justified text or full-justified text? (p. 159)

- ☐ design your title for clarity and emphasis? (p. 159)
- ☐ devise a logical, consistent style for each heading level? (p. 159)
- ☐ use rules, boxes, screens, marginal glosses, and pull quotes where appropriate? (p. 163)

Designing Web Sites and Pages

Did you

- ☐ create informative headers and footers? (p. 169)
- ☐ help readers navigate the site by including a site map, a table of contents, back-to-top links, and textual navigation buttons? (p. 170)
- ☐ include extra features your readers might need, such as an FAQ, a search page or engine, resource links, a printable version of your site, or a text-only version? (p. 170)
- ☐ help readers connect with others through links to interactive portions of your site and to social-media sites? (p. 172)
- ☐ design for readers with vision, hearing, or mobility impairment? (p. 172)
- ☐ design for multicultural audiences? (p. 173)
- ☐ aim for simplicity in Web page design by using conservative color combinations and by avoiding decorative graphics? (p. 174)
- ☐ make the text easy to read and understand by keeping it short, chunking information, and writing simply? (p. 174)
- ☐ create clear, informative links? (p. 174)

Exercises

In This Book For more about memos, see Ch. 9, p. 223.

1. Study the first and second pages of an article in a journal in your field. Describe ten design features you identify on these two pages. Which design features are most effective for the audience and purpose? Which are least effective?

2. **GROUP EXERCISE** Form small groups for this collaborative exercise in analyzing design. Photocopy or scan a page from a book or a magazine. Choose a page that does not contain advertisements. Each person works independently for the first part of this project:

- One person describes the design elements.
- One person evaluates the design. Which aspects of the design are effective, and which could be improved?
- One person creates a new design using thumbnail sketches.

Then, meet as a group and compare notes. Do all members of the group agree with the first member's description of the design? With the second member's evaluation of the design? Do all members like the third member's redesign? What have your discussions taught you about design? Write a memo to your instructor presenting your findings, and include the photocopied page with your memo.

3. Study the excerpt from the Micron data flyer (2010, p. 9). Describe the designer's use of alignment as a design principle. How effective is it? How would you modify it? Present your analysis and recommendations in a brief memo to your instructor.

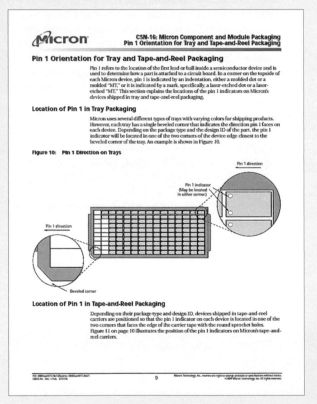

4. **INTERNET EXERCISE** Find the sites of three manufacturers within a single industry, such as personal watercraft, cars, computers, or medical equipment. Study the three sites, focusing on one of these aspects of site design:

- use of color
- quality of the writing
- quality of the site map or index
- navigation, including the clarity and placement of links to other pages in the site
- accommodation of multicultural readers
- accommodation of people with disabilities
- phrasing of the links

Which of the three sites is most effective? Which is least effective? Why? Compare and contrast the three sites in terms of their effectiveness.

5. **INTERNET EXERCISE** Using a search engine, find a site that serves the needs of people with a physical disability (for example, the Glaucoma Foundation, <www.glaucomafoundation.org>). What attempts have the designers made to accommodate the needs of visitors to the site? How effective do you think those attempts have been?

On the Web

For a case assignment, "Designing a Flyer," see Cases on <bedfordstmartins.com/ps>.

8

Creating Graphics

NTL/Landov.

Graphics offer benefits that words alone cannot.

A typical commercial jet contains literally thousands of labeled graphics throughout the passenger compartment and the cockpit, but Kulula, a South African airline, was the first to label the exterior of some of its jets. Although the airline chose Flying 101 as a humorous theme, the graphics inside the aircraft, and on the laminated safety-information cards help the crew operate the aircraft safely. In addition, graphics help passengers with everything from finding their seats to determining whether the restroom is occupied to understanding what to do in an emergency.

Graphics are the "pictures" in technical communication: drawings, maps, photographs, diagrams, charts, graphs, and tables. Graphics range from realistic, such as photographs, to highly abstract, such as organization charts. In terms of function, graphics range from the decorative, such as clip art that shows people seated at a conference table, to highly informative, such as a schematic diagram of an electronic device.

Graphics are important in technical communication because they do the following:

- catch readers' attention and interest

- help writers communicate information that is difficult to communicate with words

- help writers clarify and emphasize information

- help nonnative speakers of English understand information

- help writers communicate information to multiple audiences with different interests, aptitudes, and reading habits

THE FUNCTIONS OF GRAPHICS

We have known for decades that graphics motivate people to study documents more closely. Some 83 percent of what we learn derives from what we see, whereas only 11 percent derives from what we hear (Gatlin, 1988). Because we are good at acquiring information through sight, a document that includes a visual element beyond words on the page is more effective than one that doesn't. People studying a text with graphics learn about one-third more than people studying a text without graphics (Levie & Lentz, 1982). And people remember 43 percent more when a document includes graphics (Morrison & Jimmerson, 1989). In addition, readers like graphics. According to one survey, readers of computer documentation consistently want more graphics and fewer words (Brockmann, 1990, p. 203).

Graphics offer benefits that words alone cannot:

- *Graphics are indispensable in demonstrating logical and numerical relationships.* For example, an organization chart effectively represents the lines of authority in an organization. And if you want to communicate the number of power plants built in each of the last 10 years, a bar graph works better than a paragraph.

- *Graphics can communicate spatial information more effectively than words alone.* If you want to show the details of a bicycle derailleur, a diagram of the bicycle with a close-up of the derailleur is more effective than a verbal description.

- *Graphics can communicate steps in a process more effectively than words alone.* A troubleshooter's guide, a common kind of table, explains what might be causing a problem in a process and how you might fix it. And a diagram can show clearly how acid rain forms.

- *Graphics can save space.* Consider the following paragraph:

  In the Wilmington area, some 80 percent of the population aged 18 to 24 have watched streamed movies on their computers. They watch an average of 1.86 movies a week. Among 25- to 34-year-olds, the percentage is 76, and the average number of movies is 1.52. Among 35- to 49-year-olds, the percentage is 62, and the average number of movies is 1.19. Finally, among the 50 to 64 age group, the percentage is 47, and the average number of movies watched weekly is 0.50.

  Presented as a paragraph, this information is uneconomical and hard to remember. Presented as a table, however, the information is more concise and more memorable.

Age	Percentage watching streaming movies	Number of movies watched per week
18–24	80	1.86
25-34	76	1.52
35-49	62	1.19
50-64	47	0.50

- *Graphics can reduce the cost of documents intended for international readers.* Translation costs can reach 30 to 40 cents per word. Used effectively, graphics can reduce the number of words you have to translate (Corante, 2005).

As you plan and draft your document, look for opportunities to use graphics to clarify, emphasize, summarize, and organize information.

THE CHARACTERISTICS OF AN EFFECTIVE GRAPHIC

Effective graphics must be clear, understandable, and meaningfully related to the larger discussion. Follow these five principles:

- *A graphic should serve a purpose.* Don't include a graphic unless it will help readers understand or remember information. Avoid content-free clip art, such as drawings of businesspeople shaking hands.

- *A graphic should be simple and uncluttered.* Three-dimensional bar graphs are easy to make, but they are harder to understand than two-dimensional ones, as shown in Figure 8.1 on page 180.

- *A graphic should present a manageable amount of information.* Presenting too much information can confuse readers. Consider audience and purpose: what kinds of graphics are readers familiar with, how much do they already know about the subject, and what do you want the document to do? Because readers learn best if you present information in small chunks, create several simple graphics rather than a single complicated one.

Unnecessary 3-D is one example of chartjunk, a term used by Tufte (1983) to describe the ornamentation that clutters up a graphic, distracting readers from the message.

The two-dimensional bar graph is clean and uncluttered, whereas the three-dimensional graph is more difficult to understand because the additional dimension obscures the main data points. The number of uninsured emergency-room visits in February, for example, is very difficult to see in the three-dimensional graph.

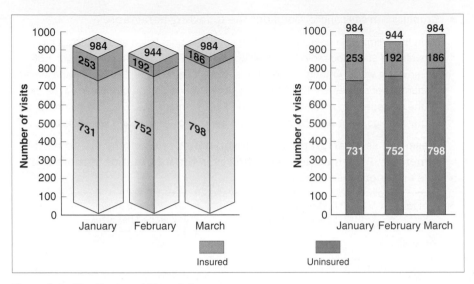

Figure 8.1   Chartjunk and Clear Art

- A *graphic should meet readers' format expectations.* Through experience, readers learn how to read different kinds of graphics. Follow the conventions—for instance, use diamonds to represent decision points in a flowchart—unless you have a good reason not to.
- A *graphic should be clearly labeled.* Give every graphic (except a brief, informal one) a unique, clear, informative title. Fully label the columns of a table and the axes and lines of a graph. Don't make readers guess whether you are using meters or yards, or whether you are also including statistics from the previous year.

ETHICS NOTE

Creating Honest Graphics

Follow these six suggestions to ensure that you represent data honestly in your graphics.

- If you did not create the graphic or generate the data, cite your source and, if you want to publish it, obtain permission. For more on citing graphics, see page 185.
- Include all relevant data. For example, if you have a data point that you cannot explain, do not change the scale to eliminate it.
- Begin the axes in your graphs at zero—or mark them clearly—so that you represent quantities honestly.
- Do not use a table to hide a data point that would be obvious in a graph.

- Show items as they really are. Do not manipulate a photograph of a computer monitor to make the screen look bigger than it is, for example.

- Do not use color or shading to misrepresent an item's importance. A light-shaded bar in a bar graph, for example, appears larger and nearer than a dark-shaded bar of the same size.

Common problem areas are pointed out in the discussions of various kinds of graphics throughout this chapter.

Guidelines

Integrating Graphics and Text

It is not enough to add graphics to your text; you have to integrate the two.

▶ **Place the graphic in an appropriate location.** If readers need the graphic to understand the discussion, put it directly after the relevant point in the discussion, or as soon after it as possible. If the graphic merely supports or elaborates a point, include it as an appendix.

▶ **Introduce the graphic in the text.** Whenever possible, refer to a graphic before it appears (ideally, on the same page). Refer to the graphic by number (such as "see Figure 7"). Do not refer to "the figure above" or "the figure below," because the graphic might be moved during the production process. If the graphic is in an appendix, cross-reference it: "For complete details of the operating characteristics, see Appendix, Part B, page 19."

▶ **Explain the graphic in the text.** State what you want readers to learn from it. Sometimes a simple paraphrase of the title is enough: "Figure 2 compares the costs of the three major types of coal gasification plants." At other times, however, you might need to explain why the graphic is important or how to interpret it. If the graphic is intended to make a point, be explicit:

> As Figure 2 shows, a high-sulfur bituminous coal gasification plant is more expensive than either a low-sulfur bituminous or anthracite plant, but more than half of its cost is cleanup equipment. If these expenses could be eliminated, high-sulfur bituminous would be the least expensive of the three types of plants.

Graphics often are accompanied by captions, explanations ranging from a sentence to several paragraphs.

▶ **Make the graphic clearly visible.** Distinguish the graphic from the surrounding text by adding white space or rules (lines), by putting a screen behind it, or by enclosing it in a box.

▶ **Make the graphic accessible.** If the document is more than a few pages long and contains more than four or five graphics, consider including a list of illustrations so that readers can find them easily.

In This Book

For more about white space, screens, boxes, and rules, see Ch. 7, pp. 154 and 163. For more about lists of illustrations, see Ch. 13, p. 325.

UNDERSTANDING THE PROCESS OF CREATING GRAPHICS

Creating graphics involves planning, producing, revising, and citing.

Planning Graphics

Whether you think first about the text or the graphics, consider the following four aspects of the document as you plan.

- *Audience.* Will readers understand the kinds of graphics you want to use? Will they know the standard icons in your field? Are they motivated to read your document, or do you need to enliven the text—for example, by adding color for emphasis—to hold their attention? General audiences know how to read common types of graphics, such as those that appear frequently in newspapers. A general audience, for example, could use this bar graph to compare two bottles of wine:

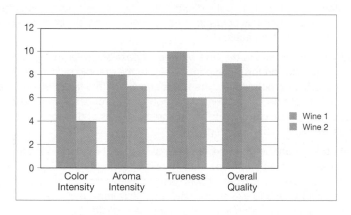

However, they would probably have trouble with the following radar graph:

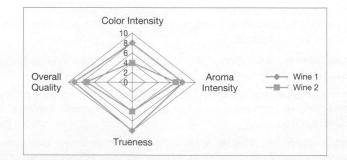

- *Purpose.* What point are you trying to make with the graphic? Imagine what you want your readers to know and do with the information. For example, if you want readers to know the exact dollar amounts spent on athletics by a college, use a table:

Year	Men's athletics ($)	Women's athletics ($)
2010	38,990	29,305
2011	42,400	30,080
2012	44,567	44,213

If you want readers to know how spending on athletics is changing over time, use a line graph:

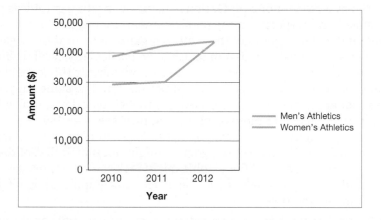

- *The kind of information you want to communicate.* Your subject will help you decide what type of graphic to include. For example, in writing about languages spoken by your state's citizens, you might use tables for the statistical data, maps for the patterns of language use, and graphs for statistical trends over time.
- *Physical conditions.* The physical conditions in which readers will use the document—amount of lighting, amount of surface space available, and so forth—will influence the type of graphic as well as its size and shape, the thickness of lines, the size of type, and the color.

As you plan how you are going to create the graphics, consider four important factors:

- *Time.* Because making a complicated graphic can take a lot of time, you need to establish a schedule.
- *Money.* A high-quality graphic can be expensive. How big is the project budget? How can you use that money effectively?
- *Equipment.* Determine what tools and software you will require, such as spreadsheets for tables and graphs or graphics software for diagrams.

- *Expertise*. How much do you know about creating graphics? Do you have access to the expertise of others?

Producing Graphics

Usually, you won't have all the resources you would like. You will have to choose one of the following four approaches:

- *Use existing graphics*. For a student paper that *will not be published*, some instructors allow the use of photocopies or scans of existing graphics; other instructors do not. For a document that *will be published*, whether written by a student or a professional, using an existing graphic is permissible if the graphic is in the public domain (that is, not under copyright), if it is the property of the writer's organization, or if the organization has obtained permission to use it. Be particularly careful about graphics you find on the Web. Many people mistakenly think that anything on the Web can be used without permission. The same copyright laws that apply to printed material apply to Web-based material, whether words or graphics. For more on citing graphics, see page 185.

  Aside from the issue of copyright, think carefully before you use existing graphics. The style of the graphic might not match that of the others you want to use, and the graphic might lack some features you want or include some you don't. If you use an existing graphic, assign it your own number and title.

- *Modify existing graphics*. You can redraw an existing graphic or scan it and then modify it electronically with graphics software.
- *Create graphics on a computer*. You can create many kinds of graphics using your spreadsheet software and the drawing tools on your word processor.
- *Have someone else create the graphics*. Professional-level graphics software can cost hundreds of dollars and require hundreds of hours of practice. Some companies have technical-publications departments with graphics experts, but others subcontract this work. Many print shops and service bureaus have graphics experts on staff or can direct you to them.

▶ **On the Web**

For a list of books about graphics, see the Selected Bibilography on <bedfordstmartins .com/ps>.

▶ **In This Book**

For more about work made for hire, see Ch. 2, p. 23.

Revising Graphics

As with any other aspect of technical communication, schedule enough time and budget enough money to revise the graphics. Create a checklist and evaluate each graphic for effectiveness. The Writer's Checklist at the end of this chapter is a good starting point. Show your graphics to people whose backgrounds are similar to your intended readers' and ask them for suggestions. Revise the graphics, and then solicit more reactions.

TECH TIP

How to Insert and Modify Graphics

To highlight, clarify, summarize, and organize information, you can insert and modify graphics by using the **Picture** button and the **Format** tab.

To **insert a graphic** that you have on file—such as a photograph, drawing, chart, or graph—place your cursor where you want to insert the

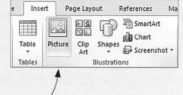

graphic and then select the **Picture** button in the **Illustrations** group on the **Insert** tab.

You can also insert clip art, shapes, charts, screenshots, and SmartArt.

To **modify an image** that is already in your document, double-click on it and then use the **Picture Tools Format** tab. This tab allows you to modify the appearance, size, and layout of a picture.

Buttons in the **Adjust** group allow you to modify many aspects of the picture's appearance.

Buttons in the **Arrange** group allow you to position your graphic and control how text wraps around it.

KEYWORDS: format tab, arrange group, picture style, size, adjust, insert picture, format picture, modify picture, picture style, picture toolbar

Citing Graphics

If you wish to publish a graphic that is protected by copyright (even if you have revised it), you need to obtain written permission from the copyright holder. Related to the issue of permission is the issue of citation. Of course, you do not have to cite a graphic if you created it yourself, from scratch, or if your organization owns the copyright.

In all other cases, however, you should include a citation, even if the document is a course assignment and will not be published. Citing graphics, even those you have revised substantially, shows your instructor that you understand professional conventions and your ethical responsibilities.

If you are following a style manual, check to see whether it presents a format for citing graphics. In addition to citing a graphic in the reference list, most style manuals call for a source statement in the caption:

In This Book
For more about copyright, see Ch. 2, p. 22.

Print Source

Source: Verduijn, 2010, p. 14. Copyright 2010 by Tedopres International B.V. Reprinted with permission.

Online Source

Source: Johnson Space Center Digital Image Collection. Copyright 2010 by NASA. Reprinted with permission.

If your graphic is based on an existing graphic, the source statement should state that your graphic is "based on" or "adapted from" your source:

> Source: Adapted from Jonklaas et al., 2008, p. 771. Copyright 2008 by American Medical Association. Reprinted with permission.

USING COLOR EFFECTIVELY

▶ **In This Book**
For guidelines for citing graphics, see Appendix, Part A.

Color draws attention to information you want to emphasize, establishes visual patterns to promote understanding, and adds interest. But it is also easy to misuse. The following discussion is based on Jan V. White's excellent text, *Color for the Electronic Age* (1990).

In using color in graphics and page design, keep these five principles in mind:

▶ **On the Web**
See the Tips section of the Xerox Small Business Resource Center for articles about color theory. Click on Links Library for Ch. 8 on <bedfordstmartins .com/ps>.

- *Don't overdo it.* Readers can interpret only two or three colors at a time. Use colors for small items, such as portions of graphics and important words. And don't use colors where black and white will work better.

- *Use color to emphasize particular items.* People interpret color before they interpret shape, size, or placement on the page. Color effectively draws readers' attention to a particular item or group of items on a page. In Figure 8.2, for example, color adds emphasis to several different kinds of information.

- *Use color to create patterns.* The principle of repetition—readers learn to recognize patterns—applies in graphics as well as document design. In creating patterns, also consider shape. For instance, use red for safety comments but place them in octagons resembling a stop sign. This way, you give your readers two visual cues to help them recognize the pattern. Figure 8.3 shows an illustration from a psychology textbook that uses color to establish patterns.

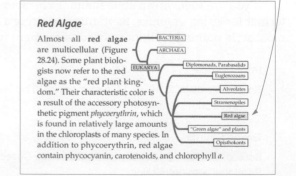

a. Color used to set off a title and the totals row in a table
Source: Bonneville Power Administration, 2009 <www.bpa.gov/corporate /Finance/A_Report/09/AR2009.pdf>.

b. Color used to emphasize one item among others
Source: Purves, Sadava, Orians, and Heller, 2004, p. 560.

Figure 8.2　Color Used for Emphasis

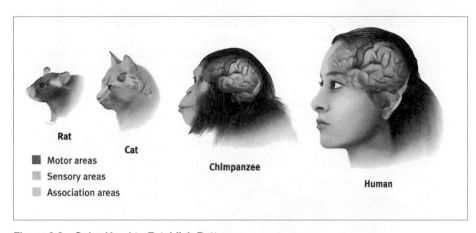

Figure 8.3   Color Used to Establish Patterns
Source: Myers, 2010, p. 72.

Color is also an effective way to emphasize design features such as text boxes, rules, screens, and headers and footers.

- *Use contrast effectively.* The visibility of a color is a function of the background against which it appears (see Figure 8.4). The strongest contrasts are between black and white and between black and yellow.

Notice that a color washes out if the background color is too similar.

⌕ **In This Book**
For more about designing your document, see Ch. 7. For more about presentation graphics, see Ch. 15, p. 396.

Figure 8.4   The Effect of Background in Creating Contrast

The need for effective contrast also applies to graphics used in presentations, as shown here:

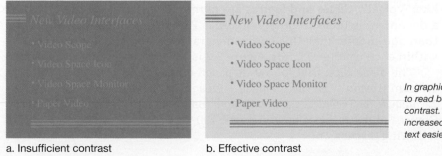

a. Insufficient contrast   b. Effective contrast

In graphic (a), the text is hard to read because of insufficient contrast. In graphic (b), the increased contrast makes the text easier to read.

In This Book
For more about cultural patterns, see Ch. 4, p. 63.

- *Take advantage of any symbolic meanings colors may already have.* In American culture, for example, red signals danger, heat, or electricity; yellow signals caution; and orange signals warning. Using these warm colors in ways that depart from these familiar meanings could be confusing. The cooler colors—blues and greens—are more conservative and subtle. (Figure 8.5 illustrates these principles.) Keep in mind, however, that different cultures interpret colors differently.

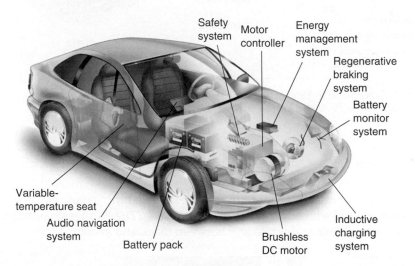

The batteries are red. The warm red contrasts effectively with the cool green of the car body.

Safety system   Motor controller   Energy management system
Regenerative braking system
Battery monitor system

Variable-temperature seat
Audio navigation system
Battery pack
Brushless DC motor
Inductive charging system

Figure 8.5   Colors Have Clear Associations for Readers

CHOOSING THE APPROPRIATE KIND OF GRAPHIC

As Figure 8.6 shows, even a few simple facts can yield a number of different points. Your responsibility when creating a graphic is to determine what point you want to make and how best to make it. Don't rely on your software to do your thinking; it can't.

Graphics used in technical documents fall into two categories: tables and figures. Tables are lists of data, usually numbers, arranged in columns. Figures are everything else: graphs, charts, diagrams, photographs, and the like. Typically, tables and figures are numbered separately: the first table in a document is Table 1; the first figure is Figure 1. In documents of more than one chapter (like this book), the graphics are usually numbered within each chapter. That is, Figure 3.2 is the second figure in Chapter 3.

The discussion that follows is based on the classification system in William Horton's "Pictures Please—Presenting Information Visually," in *Techniques for Technical Communicators* (Barnum & Carliner, 1993). The Choices and Strategies box on pages 190–91 presents an overview of the following discussion.

Rail Line	November		December		January	
	Disabled by electrical problems (%)	Total disabled	Disabled by electrical problems (%)	Total disabled	Disabled by electrical problems (%)	Total disabled
Bryn Mawr	19 (70)	27	17 (60)	28	20 (76)	26
Swarthmore	12 (75)	16	9 (52)	17	13 (81)	16
Manayunk	22 (64)	34	26 (83)	31	24 (72)	33

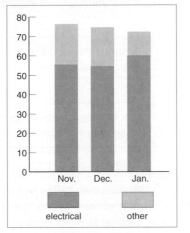

a. Number of railcars disabled, November–January

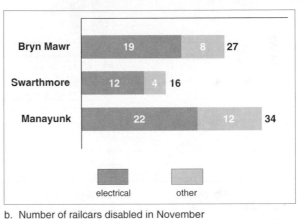

b. Number of railcars disabled in November

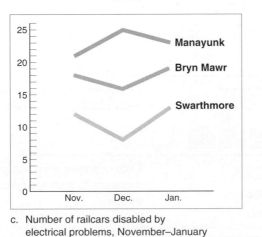

c. Number of railcars disabled by electrical problems, November–January

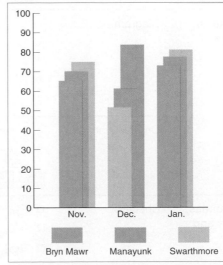

d. Range in percentage of railcars, by line, disabled by electrical problems, November–January

Figure 8.6 Different Graphics Emphasizing Different Points

Each of these four graphs emphasizes a different point derived from the data in the table. Graph (a) focuses on the total number of railcars disabled each month, classified by cause; graph (b) focuses on the three rail lines during one month; and so forth. For information on bar graphs, see pages 194–97; for information on line graphs, see pages 199–200.

CHOICES AND STRATEGIES   Choosing the Appropriate Kind of Graphic

If you want to . . .	Try this type of graphic	What the graphic does best
Illustrate numerical information	Table	Shows large amounts of numerical data, especially when there are several variables for a number of items.
	Bar graph	Shows the relative values of two or more items.
	Pictograph	Enlivens statistical information for the general reader.
	Line graph	Shows how the quantity of an item changes over time. A line graph can accommodate much more data than a bar graph can.
	Pie chart	Shows the relative size of the parts of a whole. Pie charts are instantly familiar to most readers.
Illustrate logical relationships	Diagram	Represents items or properties of items.
	Organization chart	Shows the lines of authority and responsibility in an organization.
Illustrate process descriptions and instructions	Checklist	Lists or shows what equipment or materials to gather, or describes an action.
	Table	Shows numbers of items or indicates the state (on/off) of an item.

Choosing the Appropriate Kind of Graphic (*continued*)

If you want to . . .	Try this type of graphic	What the graphic does best
Illustrate process descriptions and instructions (*continued*)	Flowchart	Shows the stages of a procedure or a process.
	Logic tree	Shows which of two or more paths to follow.
Illustrate visual and spatial characteristics	Photograph	Shows precisely the external surface of objects.
	Screen shot	Shows what appears on a computer screen.
	Line drawing	Shows simplified representations of objects.
	Map	Shows geographic areas.

Source: Based on Horton, 1993.

The data in this table consist of numbers, but tables can also present textual information or a combination of numbers and text.

Tables are usually titled at the top because readers scan them from top to bottom.

Include a stub head. The stub—the left-hand column—lists the items for which data are displayed. The stub head in this table should be titled "Category."

A screen behind every other data row would help the reader scan across the row.

Numerical data are right-aligned.

Note that tables often contain one or more source statements and footnotes.

Table 1. Clean Energy Spending by Category

Category	Appropriations[a]	Through the end of 2009:Q4		Through the end of 2010:Q1	
		Obligations[b]	Outlays[b]	Obligations[c]	Outlays[c]
	Millions of Dollars				
Energy Efficiency	19,935	11,903	1,152	15,559	2,203
Renewable Generation	26,598	2,028	1,994	2,970	2,934
Grid Modernization	10,453	2,666	72	3,283	101
Advanced Vehicles and Fuels Technologies	6,142	3,149	450	3,608	617
Traditional Transit and High-Speed Rail	18,113	8,834	1,804	10,056	2,733
Carbon Capture and Sequestration	3,400	425	4	963	13
Green Innovation and Job Training	3,549	2,197	123	3,015	428
Clean Energy Equipment Manufacturing	1,624	13	13	61	61
Other	408	148	12	239	36
Total[d]	90,222	31,363	5,624	39,754	9,127

Sources: Appropriations estimates from the Office of Management and Budget (OMB); agency Financial and Activity Reports to OMB through March 31, 2010; simulations from the Department of the Treasury (Office of Tax Analysis) based on the FY2011 budget.
Notes: a. Appropriations include estimated cost of tax provisions through 2019:Q3.
b. Include estimated costs of tax provisions through December 31, 2009.
c. Include estimated costs of tax provisions through March 31, 2010.
d. Items may not add to total due to rounding.

Figure 8.7   Parts of a Table
Source: Council of Economic Advisers, 2010 <www.whitehouse.gov/sites/default/files/image/arra_%20 and_clean_energy_transformation_3Q_supplement.pdf>.

Illustrating Numerical Information

The kinds of graphics used most often to display numerical values are tables, bar graphs, pictographs, line graphs, and pie charts.

Tables   Tables convey large amounts of numerical data easily, and they are often the only way to present several variables for a number of items. For example, if you want to show how many people are employed in six industries in 10 states, a table would probably be most effective. Although tables lack the visual appeal of other kinds of graphics, they can handle much more information.

Figure 8.7 illustrates the standard parts of a table. Tables are identified by number ("Table 1") and an informative title that includes the items being compared and the basis (or bases) of comparison:

Table 3. Mallard Population in Rangeley, 2009–2011

Table 4.7. The Growth of the Robotics Industry in Japan and the United States, 2010

Guidelines

Creating Effective Tables

Follow these nine suggestions to make sure your tables are clear and professional.

▶ **Indicate the units of measure.** If all the data are expressed in the same unit, indicate that unit in the title:

Farm Size in the Midwestern States (in Hectares)

If the data in different columns are expressed in different units, indicate the units in the column heads:

Population   Per Capita Income
(in Millions)   (in Thousands of U.S. Dollars)

If all the *data cells* in a column use the same unit, indicate that unit in the column head, not in each data cell:

Speed (in Knots)

15
18
14

You can express data in both real numbers and percentages. A column head and the first data cell under it might read as follows:

Number of Students (Percentage)

53 (83)

▶ **In the stub—the left-hand column—list the items being compared.** Arrange the items in a logical order: big to small, more-important to less-important, alphabetical, chronological, geographical, and so forth. If the items fall into several categories, include the names of the categories in the stub:

    Snowbelt States . . . .
       Connecticut . . . .
       New York . . . .
       Vermont . . . .

    Sunbelt States . . . .
       Arizona . . . .
       California . . . .
       New Mexico . . . .

If the items in the stub cannot be grouped in logical categories, skip a line after every five rows to help the reader follow the rows across the table. Or use a screen (a colored background) for every other set of five rows. Also useful are *dot leaders*: a row of dots that links the stub and the next column.

▶ **In the columns, arrange the data clearly and logically.** Use the decimal-tab feature to line up the decimal points:

    3,147.4
      365.7
46,803.5

In general, don't change units unless the quantities are so dissimilar that your readers would have a difficult time understanding them if expressed in the same units.

    3.4 hr
12.7 min
  4.3 sec

This list would probably be easier for most readers to understand than one in which all quantities were expressed in the same unit.

In This Book

For more about screens, see
Ch. 7, p. 163.

▶ **Do the math.** If your readers will need to know the totals for the columns or the rows, provide them. If your readers will need to know percentage changes from one column to the next, present them:

Number of Students (Percentage Change from Previous Year)

2010	2011	2012
619	644 (+4.0)	614 (−4.7)

▶ **Use dot leaders if a column contains a "blank" spot—a place where there are no appropriate data:**

3,147
. . .
46,803

But don't substitute dot leaders for a quantity of zero.

▶ **Don't make the table wider than it needs to be.** The reader should be able to scan across a row easily. As White (1984) points out, there is no reason to make the table as wide as the text column in the document. If a column head is long—more than five or six words—stack the words:

Computers Sold Without
a Memory-Card Reader

▶ **Minimize the use of rules.** Grimstead (1987) recommends using rules only when necessary: to separate the title and the heads, the heads and the body, and the body and the notes. When you use rules, make them thin rather than thick.

▶ **Provide footnotes where necessary.** All the information your readers need to understand the table should accompany it.

▶ **If you did not generate the information yourself, indicate your source.** See the discussion of citing graphics on pages 185–86.

Bar Graphs   Like tables, *bar graphs* can communicate numerical values, but they are better at showing the relative values of two or more items. Figure 8.8 on page 196 shows typical horizontal and vertical bar graphs that you can make easily using your spreadsheet software. Figure 8.9 on page 196 shows an effective bar graph that uses grid lines.

Guidelines

Creating Effective Bar Graphs

To present information effectively in a bar graph, follow these six suggestions.

▶ **Make the proportions fair.** Make your vertical axis about 25 percent shorter than your horizontal axis. An excessively long vertical axis exaggerates the differences in quantities; an excessively long horizontal axis minimizes the differences. Make all the bars the same width, and make the space between them about half as wide as a bar. Here are two poorly proportioned graphs:

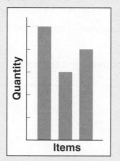

a. Excessively long vertical axis

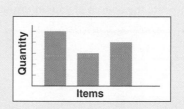

b. Excessively long horizontal axis

▶ **If possible, begin the quantity scale at zero.** Doing so ensures that the bars accurately represent the quantities. Notice how misleading a graph can be if the scale doesn't begin at zero.

On the Web

For a tutorial on creating effective charts and graphs from a spreadsheet program, see Tutorials on <bedfordstmartins .com/ps>.

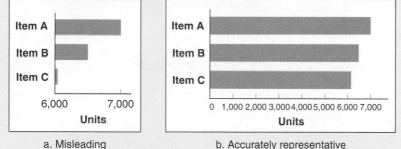

a. Misleading

b. Accurately representative

If it is not practical to start the quantity scale at zero, break the quantity axis clearly at a common point on all the bars.

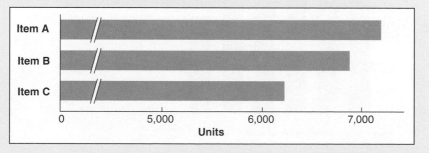

▶ **Use tick marks—marks along the axis—to signal the amounts.** Use grid lines—tick marks that extend through the bars—if the graph has several bars, some of which are too far away from the tick marks to allow readers to gauge the quantities easily. (See Figure 8.9 on page 196.)

► **Arrange the bars in a logical sequence.** For a vertical bar graph, use chronology if possible. For a horizontal bar graph, arrange the bars in order of descending size, beginning at the top of the graph, unless some other logical sequence seems more appropriate.

► **Place the title below the figure.** Unlike tables, which are usually read from top to bottom, figures are usually read from the bottom up.

► **Indicate the source of your information if you did not generate it yourself.**

Horizontal bars are best for showing quantities such as speed and distance. Vertical bars are best for showing quantities such as height, size, and amount. However, these distinctions are not ironclad; as long as the axes are clearly labeled, readers should have no trouble understanding the graph.

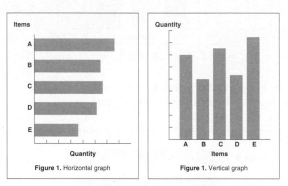

Figure 8.8   Structures of Horizontal and Vertical Bar Graphs

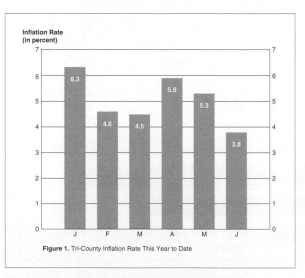

Figures 8.9   Effective Bar Graph with Grid Lines

e-Pages

To analyze an interactive graphic, visit <bedfordstmartins.com/ps/epages>.

The five variations on the basic bar graph shown in Table 8.1 can help you accommodate different communication needs. You can make all these types using your spreadsheet software.

TABLE 8.1 ► Variations on the Basic Bar Graph

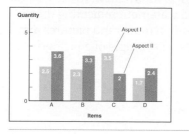

Grouped bar graph. The *grouped bar graph* lets you compare two or three quantities for each item. Grouped bar graphs would be useful, for example, for showing the numbers of full-time and part-time students at several universities. One bar could represent full-time students; the other, part-time students. To distinguish between the bars, use hatching (striping), shading, or color, and either label one set of bars or provide a key.

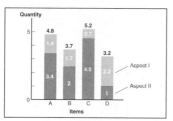

Subdivided bar graph. In the *subdivided bar graph*, Aspect I and Aspect II are stacked like wooden blocks placed on top of one another. Although totals are easy to compare in a subdivided bar graph, individual quantities are not.

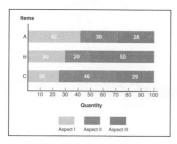

100-percent bar graph. The *100-percent bar graph*, which shows the relative proportions of the elements that make up several items, is useful in portraying, for example, the proportion of full-scholarship, partial-scholarship, and no-scholarship students at a number of colleges.

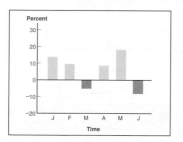

Deviation bar graph. The *deviation bar graph* shows how various quantities deviate from a norm. Deviation bar graphs are often used when the information contains both positive and negative values, such as profits and losses. Bars on the positive side of the norm line represent profits; bars on the negative side, losses.

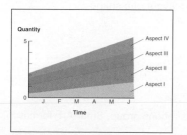

Stratum graph. The *stratum graph*, also called an *area graph*, shows the change in quantities of several items over time. Although stratum graphs are used frequently in business and scientific fields, general readers sometimes have trouble understanding how to read them.

Pictographs   Pictographs—bar graphs in which the bars are replaced by a series of symbols—are used primarily to present statistical information to the general reader. The quantity scale is usually replaced by a statement indicating the numerical value of each symbol. Thousands of clip-art symbols and pictures are available for use in pictographs. Figure 8.10 shows an example of a pictograph.

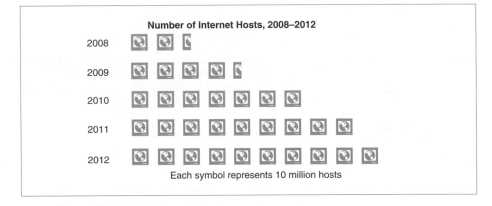

Clip-art pictures and symbols are available online for use in pictographs. Arrange pictographs horizontally rather than vertically.

Figure 8.10   Pictograph

TECH TIP

How to Use Drawing Tools

Although you can make many types of graphics using a spreadsheet, some types, such as pictographs, call for drawing tools. Your word processor includes basic drawing tools.

To create **shapes** and **SmartArt**, use the **Illustrations** group on the **Insert** tab.

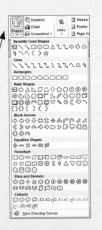

Use the **Shapes** drop-down menu to select a simple shape, such as a line, arrow, rectangle, or oval. Then drag your cursor to create the shape.

You can select complex shapes from the **SmartArt** drop-down menu in the **Illustrations** group.

Once you have created a shape, you can position the shape on your document by selecting and dragging it.

To **modify a shape**, select it and use the **Drawing Tools Format** tab.

Groups on the **Format** tab let you modify the appearance, size, and layout of a shape.

KEYWORDS: shapes, illustrations group, SmartArt, format tab

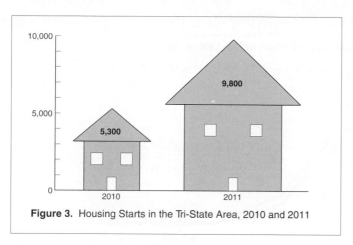

The reader sees the total area of the symbol rather than its height.

Figure 3. Housing Starts in the Tri-State Area, 2010 and 2011

Figure 8.11   Misleading Pictograph

Represent quantities in a pictograph honestly. Figure 8.11 shows an inherent problem: a picture drawn to scale can appear many times larger than it should.

Line Graphs   *Line graphs* are used almost exclusively to show changes in quantity over time, for example, the month-by-month production figures for a product. A line graph focuses readers' attention on the change in quantity, whereas a bar graph emphasizes the quantities themselves.

You can plot three or four lines on a line graph. If the lines intersect, use different colors or patterns to distinguish them. If the lines intersect too often, however, the graph will be unclear; in this case, draw separate graphs. Figure 8.12 on page 200 shows a line graph.

Guidelines

Creating Effective Line Graphs

Follow these three suggestions to create line graphs that are clear and easy to read.

▶ **If possible, begin the quantity scale at zero.** Doing so is the best way to portray the information honestly. If you cannot begin at zero, clearly indicate a break in the axis.

▶ **Use reasonable proportions for the vertical and horizontal axes.** As with bar graphs, make the vertical axis about 25 percent shorter than the horizontal axis.

▶ **Use grid lines—horizontal, vertical, or both—rather than tick marks when your readers need to read the quantities precisely.**

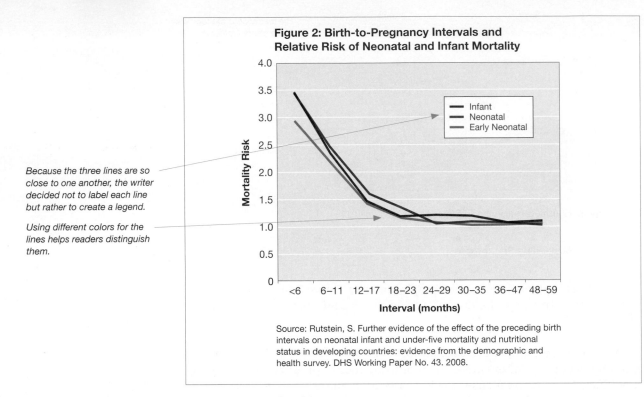

Because the three lines are so close to one another, the writer decided not to label each line but rather to create a legend.

Using different colors for the lines helps readers distinguish them.

Figure 8.12   Line Graph
Source: U.S. Agency for International Development, 2009 <http://pdf.usaid.gov/pdf_docs/PDACN515.pdf>.

Pie Charts   The *pie chart* is a simple but limited design used for showing the relative size of the parts of a whole. You can make pie charts with your spreadsheet software. Figure 8.13 shows typical examples.

You can set your software so that the slices use different saturations of the same color. This way, the slices are easy to distinguish from one another—without any distractions or misrepresentations caused by a rainbow of colors.

You can set your software to emphasize one slice by separating it from the rest of the pie.

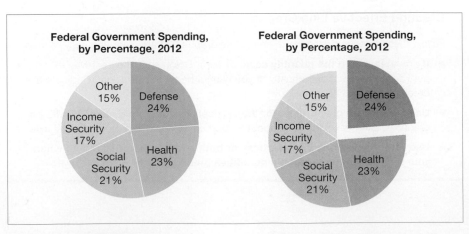

Figure 8.13   Pie Charts

Guidelines

Creating Effective Pie Charts

Follow these eight suggestions to ensure that your pie charts are easy to understand and professional looking.

▶ **Restrict the number of slices to no more than seven.** As the slices get smaller, judging their relative sizes becomes more difficult.

▶ **Begin with the largest slice at the top and work clockwise in order of decreasing size, unless you have a good reason to arrange them otherwise.**

▶ **Include a miscellaneous slice for very small quantities that would make the chart unclear.** Explain its contents in a footnote. This slice, sometimes called "other," follows the other slices.

▶ **Label the slices (horizontally, not radially) inside the slice, if space permits.** Include the percentage that each slice represents and, if appropriate, the raw numbers.

▶ **To emphasize one slice, use a bright, contrasting color or separate the slice from the pie.** Do this, for example, when you introduce a discussion of the item represented by that slice.

▶ **Check to see that your software follows the appropriate guidelines for pie charts.** Some spreadsheet programs add fancy visual effects that can impair comprehension. For instance, many programs portray the pie in three dimensions, as shown here.

In this three-dimensional pie chart, the sophomore slice looks bigger than the freshman slice, even though it isn't, because it appears closer to the reader. A two-dimensional pie chart would communicate these numbers more clearly.

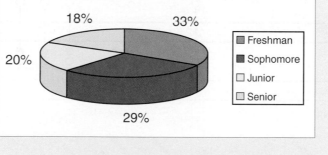

▶ **Don't overdo fill patterns.** Fill patterns are designs, shades, or colors that distinguish one slice from another. In general, use simple, understated patterns, or none at all.

▶ **Check that your percentages add up to 100.** If you are doing the calculations yourself, check your math.

Illustrating Logical Relationships

Graphics can help you present logical relationships among items. For instance, in describing a piece of hardware, you might want to show its major components. The two kinds of graphics that best show logical relationships are diagrams and organization charts.

Diagrams   A *diagram* is a visual metaphor that uses symbols to represent items or their properties. In technical communication, common kinds of diagrams are blueprints, wiring diagrams, and schematics. Figure 8.14 is a diagram.

Organization Charts   A popular form of diagram is the *organization chart*, in which simple geometric shapes, usually rectangles, suggest logical relationships, as shown in Figure 8.15 on page 204. You can create organizational charts with your word processor.

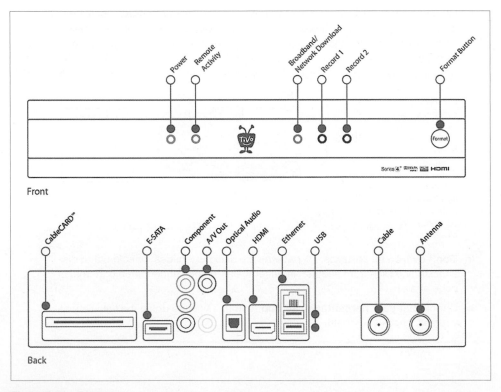

The purpose of this diagram is to help people understand how to connect the cables and use a TiVo box. The diagram itself is very simple—because it doesn't need to be complicated.

Figure 8.14   Diagram
Source: TiVo, 2010 <www.tivo.com/products/tivo-premiere/premiere-specs.html#tab>.

DOCUMENT ANALYSIS ACTIVITY

Analyzing a Graphic

The following diagram is from a government report (Defense Intelligence Agency, 2003, p. 16). The accompanying questions ask you to think about diagrams, as discussed on page 202.

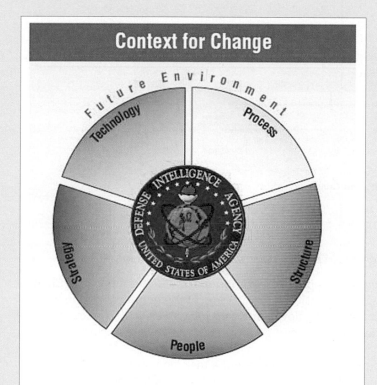

The graphic above illustrates the components of change that the Defense Intelligence Agency will consider as it embraces transformation. In the sections that follow, we discuss each component in turn, beginning with the Future Environment, progressing around the circle and ending with Recommendations.

Source: Defense Intelligence Agency, 2003 <www.dia.mil/thisisdia/DIA _Workforce_of_the_Future.pdf>.

1. This design resembles a pie chart, but it does not have the same function as a pie chart. What message does this design communicate? Is it effective?

2. Do the colors communicate any information, or are they merely decorative? If you think they are decorative, would you revise the design to change them in any way?

3. What does the phrase "Future Environment," above the graphic, mean? Is it meant to refer only to the "Technology" and "Process" shapes?

4. Is the explanation below the graphic clear? Would you change it in any way?

▶ On the Web

To submit your responses to your instructor, click on Document Analysis Activities for Ch. 8 on <bedfordstmartins .com/ps>.

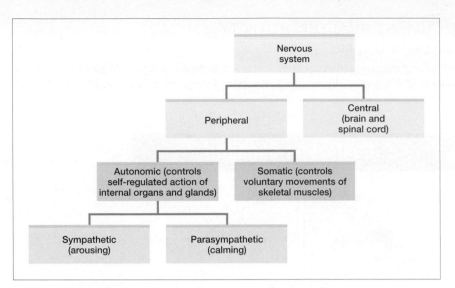

An organization chart is often used to show the hierarchy in an organization, with the president of a company, for example, in the box at the top.

Alternatively, as shown here, an organization chart can show the functional divisions of a system, such as the human nervous system.

Figure 8.15   Organization Chart
Source: Myers, 2007, p. 61.

Illustrating Process Descriptions and Instructions

Graphics often accompany process descriptions and instructions (see Chapter 14). The following discussion looks at some of the graphics used in writing about actions: checklists, flowcharts, and logic trees. It also discusses techniques for showing motion in graphics.

Checklists   In explaining how to carry out a task, you often need to show the reader what equipment or materials to gather, or describe an action or a series of actions to take. A *checklist* is a list of items, each preceded by a check box. If readers might be unfamiliar with the items you are listing, include drawings of the items, as shown in Figure 8.16. You can use the list function in your word processor to create checklists.

Often you need to indicate that readers are to carry out certain tasks at certain intervals. A table is a useful graphic for this kind of information, as shown in Figure 8.17.

Flowcharts   A *flowchart*, as the name suggests, shows the various stages of a process or a procedure. Flowcharts are useful, too, for summarizing instructions. On a basic flowchart, stages are represented by labeled geometric shapes. Flowcharts can portray open systems (those that have a "start" and a "finish") or closed systems (those that end where they began). Figure 8.18 on page 206 shows an open-system flowchart and a closed-system flowchart.

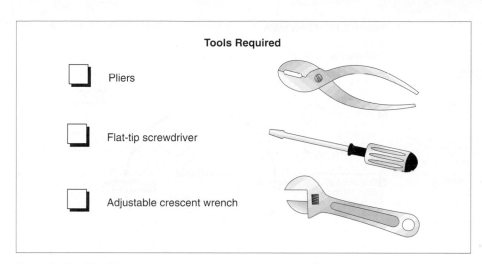

Figure 8.16   Checklist

Regular Maintenance, First 40,000 Miles

	Mileage							
	5,000	10,000	15,000	20,000	25,000	30,000	35,000	40,000
Change oil, replace filter	✓	✓	✓	✓	✓	✓	✓	✓
Rotate tires	✓	✓	✓	✓	✓	✓	✓	✓
Replace air filter				✓				✓
Replace spark plugs				✓				✓
Replace coolant fluid								✓
Replace ignition cables								✓
Replace timing belt								✓

Figure 8.17   A Table Used to Illustrate a Maintenance Schedule

Logic Trees   *Logic trees* use a branching metaphor. The logic tree shown in Figure 8.19 on page 206 helps students think through the process of registering for a course.

Techniques for Showing Motion   In some types of process descriptions and instructions, you will want to show motion. For instance, in an instruction manual for helicopter technicians, you might want to illustrate the process of removing an oil dipstick or tightening a bolt, or you might want to show a

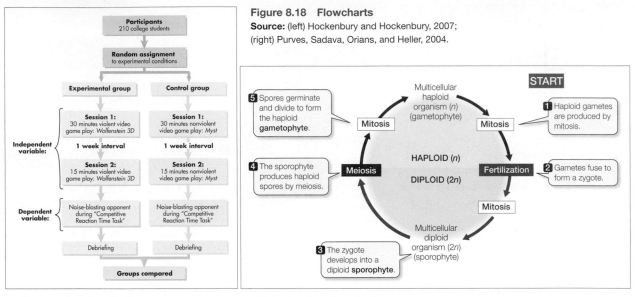

Figure 8.18　Flowcharts
Source: (left) Hockenbury and Hockenbury, 2007;
(right) Purves, Sadava, Orians, and Heller, 2004.

a. Open-system flowchart　　　　　b. Closed-system flowchart

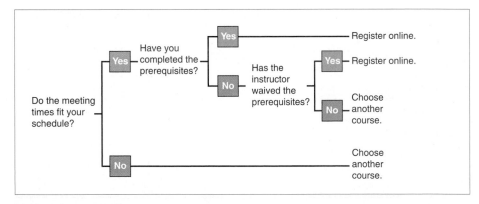

Figure 8.19　Logic Tree

warning light flashing. Although document designers frequently use animation or video, printed graphics are still needed to communicate this kind of information.

If the reader is to perform the action, show the action from the reader's point of view, as in Figure 8.20.

Figure 8.21 illustrates four additional techniques for showing motion. These techniques are conventional but not universal. If you are addressing readers from another culture, consult a qualified person from that culture to make sure your symbols are clear and inoffensive.

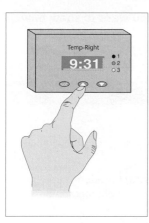

Figure 8.20　Showing Action from the Reader's Perspective

In many cases, you need to show only the person's hands, not the whole body.

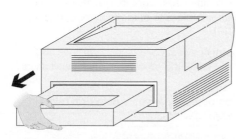

a. Use arrows or other symbols to suggest the direction in which something is moving or should be moved.

c. Shake lines suggest vibration.

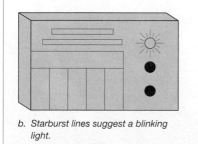

b. Starburst lines suggest a blinking light.

d. An image of an object both before and after the action suggests the action.

Figure 8.21　Showing Motion

Illustrating Visual and Spatial Characteristics

To illustrate visual and spatial characteristics, use photographs, screen shots, line drawings, and maps.

Photographs　Photographs are unmatched for reproducing visual detail. Sometimes, however, a photograph can provide too much information. In a sales brochure for an automobile, a glossy photograph of the dashboard might be very effective. But in an owner's manual, if you want to show how to use the trip odometer, use a diagram that focuses on that one item.

Guidelines

Presenting Photographs Effectively

Follow these five suggestions to make sure your photographs are clear, honest, and easy to understand.

▶ **Eliminate extraneous background clutter that can distract readers.** Crop the photograph to delete unnecessary detail. Figure 8.22 shows a photograph before and after cropping.

▶ **Do not electronically manipulate the photograph.** There is nothing unethical about removing blemishes or cropping a digital photograph. However, manipulating a photograph—for example, enlarging the size of the monitor that comes with a computer system—*is* unethical.

▶ **Help readers understand the perspective.** Most objects in magazines and journals are photographed at an angle to show the object's depth as well as its height and width.

▶ **If appropriate, include some common object, such as a coin or a ruler, in the photograph to give readers a sense of scale.**

▶ **If appropriate, label components or important features.**

Figure 8.22   Cropping a Photograph
Source: AP Photo/Samsung Electronics, HO.

Sometimes a photograph can provide too little information; the item you want to highlight might be located inside the mechanism or obscured by another component.

Screen Shots   Screen shots—images of what appears on a computer monitor—are often used in software manuals to show users what the screen looks like at various points during the use of a program. Figure 8.23 is an example of how a screen shot might be used.

This Web site from a university media lab uses a screen shot to show what the user of a 3-D simulation program will see.

Figure 8.23   Screen Shot
Source: Carnegie Mellon University, 2010 <www.panda3d.org/showss.php?shot=ssg-code3d/code3D01>.

Line Drawings   Line drawings are simplified visual representations of objects. Line drawings offer three possible advantages over photographs:

- Line drawings can focus readers' attention on desired information better than a photograph can.

- Line drawings can highlight information that might be obscured by bad lighting or a bad angle in a photograph.

- Line drawings are sometimes easier for readers to understand than photographs are.

Figure 8.24 on page 210 shows the effectiveness of line drawings. You have probably seen the three variations on the basic line drawing shown in Figure 8.25 on page 211.

TECH TIP

How to Create and Insert Screen Shots

To show your reader what appears in a window on your computer monitor, you can insert a **screen shot**.

Select **Screenshot** from the **Illustrations** group on the **Insert** tab. You will see a small version of each window you have open on your desktop. Click the screen you want to show your readers, and Word will insert the picture into your document.

If your active screen has a dialog box open, you will see it pictured under **Available Windows**. Click on the picture of the dialog box to insert it.

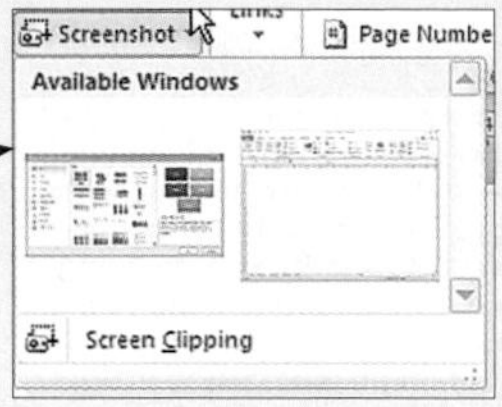

To insert part of an active screen other than a dialog box, select **Screen Clipping**. You will see the active screen with a white shade over it. Use your cursor to draw a rectangular box around the part that you want in your screen shot.

You can modify screen shots by using the **Picture Tools Format** tab. For example, you can use the **Crop** tool in the **Size** group to hide unnecessary details.

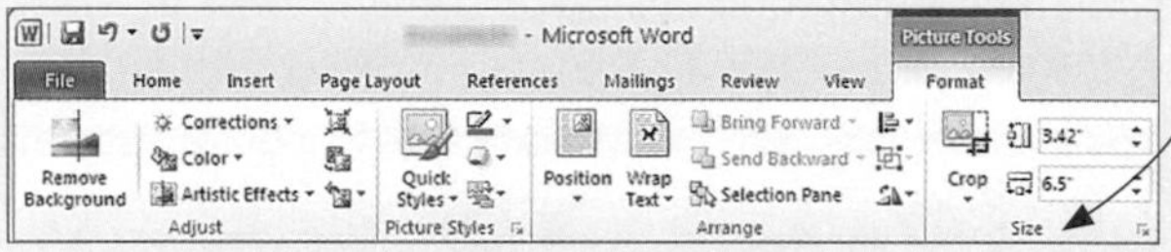

If you plan to create many screen shots, consider using software designed to capture and edit screen images efficiently. Search the Internet for "screen capture software," such as TechSmith's Snagit.

KEYWORDS: screen shot, format tab, crop

This drawing, which accompanies a manual about the Americans with Disabilities Act, illustrates the idea that "wheelchair seating locations must provide lines of sight comparable to those provided to other spectators." A photograph could not show this concept as clearly as this drawing does.

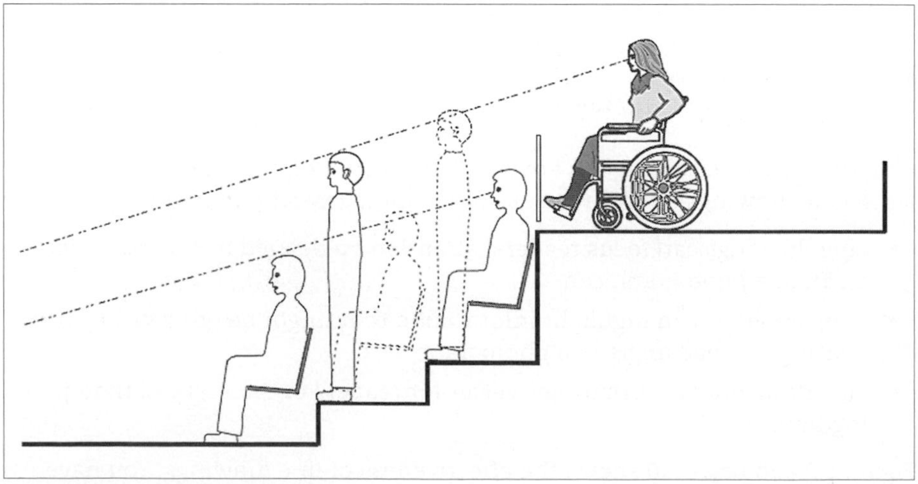

Figure 8.24 Line Drawing
Source: U.S. Department of Justice, 2010 <www.ada.gov/stadium.pdf>.

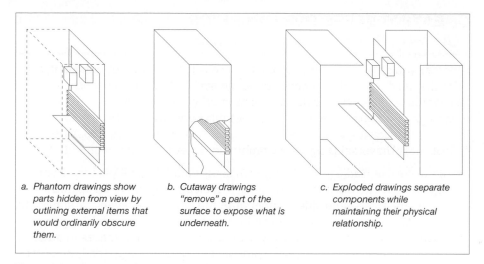

a. *Phantom drawings show parts hidden from view by outlining external items that would ordinarily obscure them.*

b. *Cutaway drawings "remove" a part of the surface to expose what is underneath.*

c. *Exploded drawings separate components while maintaining their physical relationship.*

Figure 8.25   Phantom, Cutaway, and Exploded Views

Maps   Maps are readily available as clip art that can be modified with a graphics program. Figure 8.26 shows a map derived from clip art.

Include a scale and a legend if the map is one that is not thoroughly familiar to your readers. Also, use conventional colors, such as blue for water.

Figure 8.26   Map

CREATING EFFECTIVE GRAPHICS FOR MULTICULTURAL READERS

Whether you are writing for people within your organization or outside it, consider the needs of readers whose first language is different from your own. Like words, graphics have cultural meanings. If you are unaware of these meanings, you could communicate something very different from what you intend. The following guidelines are based on William Horton's (1993) article "The Almost Universal Language: Graphics for International Documents."

- *Be aware that reading patterns differ.* In some countries, people read from right to left or from bottom to top. In some cultures, direction signifies value: the right-hand side is superior to the left, or the reverse. You need to think about how to sequence graphics that show action, or where you put "before" and "after" graphics. If you want to show a direction, as in an informal flowchart, consider using arrows to indicate how to read the chart.

- *Be aware of varying cultural attitudes toward giving instruction.* Instructions for products made in Japan are highly polite and deferential: "Please attach the cable at this time." Some cultures favor spelling out general principles but leaving the reader to supply the details. For people in these cultures, instructions containing a detailed close-up of how to carry out a task might appear insulting.

- *Deemphasize trivial details.* Because common objects, such as plugs on the ends of power cords, come in different shapes around the world, draw them to look generic rather than specific to one country.

- *Avoid culture-specific language, symbols, and references.* Don't use a picture of a mouse to symbolize a computer mouse because the device is not known by that name everywhere. Avoid the casual use of national symbols (such as the maple leaf or national flags); any error in a detail might offend your readers. Use colors carefully: red means danger to most people from Western cultures, but it is a celebratory color to the Chinese.

- *Portray people very carefully.* Every aspect of a person's appearance, from clothing to hairstyle to features, is culture- or race-specific. A photograph of a woman in casual Western attire seated at a workstation would be ineffective in an Islamic culture where only the hands and eyes of a woman may be shown. Horton (1993) recommends using stick figures or silhouettes that do not suggest any one culture, race, or sex.

- *Be particularly careful in portraying hand gestures.* Many Western hand gestures, such as the "okay" sign, are considered obscene in other cultures, and long red fingernails are inappropriate to some. Use hands in graphics only when necessary—for example, carrying out a task—and obscure the person's sex and race.

Cultural differences are many and subtle. Learn as much as possible about your readers and about their culture and outlook, and have the graphics reviewed by a native of the culture.

Writer's Checklist

☐ Does the graphic have a purpose? (p. 179)

☐ Is the graphic simple and uncluttered? (p. 179)

☐ Does the graphic present a manageable amount of information? (p. 179)

☐ Does the graphic meet readers' format expectations? (p. 180)

☐ Is the graphic clearly labeled? (p. 180)

☐ Is the graphic honest? (p. 180)

☐ Does the graphic appear in a logical location in the document? (p. 181)

☐ Is the graphic introduced clearly in the text? (p. 181)

☐ Is the graphic explained in the text? (p. 181)

☐ Is the graphic clearly visible in the text? (p. 181)

☐ Is the graphic easily accessible to your readers? (p. 181)

☐ For an existing graphic, do you have the legal right to use it? (p. 185) If so, have you cited it appropriately? (p. 185)

☐ Is the graphic inoffensive to your readers? (p. 212)

Exercises

In This Book   For more about memos, see Ch. 9, p. 223.

1. Find out from the Admissions Department at your college or university the number of students enrolled from the different states or from the different counties in your state. Present this information in four different kinds of graphics:

   a. map

   b. table

   c. bar graph

   d. pie chart

   In three or four paragraphs, explain why each graphic is appropriate for a particular audience and purpose and how each emphasizes different aspects of the information.

2. Design a flowchart for a process you are familiar with, such as applying for a summer job, studying for a test, preparing a paper, or performing some task at work. Your audience is someone who will be carrying out the process.

3. The following table provides statistics on injuries (U.S. Census Bureau, 2010, p. 197). Study the table, then perform the following tasks:

   a. Create two different graphics, each of which communicates information about the cost of lost wages and productivity.

   b. Create two different graphics, each of which compares wage and productivity losses to the total of other losses due to unintentional injuries.

Table 197. Costs of Unintentional Injuries: 2007

[684.4 represents $684,400,000,000. Covers costs of deaths or disabling injuries together with vehicle accidents and fires]

Cost	Amount (bil. dol.)					Percent distribution				
	Total [1]	Motor vehicle	Work	Home	Other	Total [1]	Motor vehicle	Work	Home	Other
Total	684.4	257.7	175.3	164.7	108.3	100.0	100.0	100.0	100.0	100.0
Wage and productivity losses [2]	344.4	88.5	84.1	104.4	71.1	50.3	34.3	48.0	63.4	65.7
Medical expense	134.0	38.5	35.3	38.1	24.3	19.6	14.9	20.1	23.1	22.4
Administrative expenses [3]	129.2	86.1	40.4	8.3	8.1	18.9	33.4	23.0	5.0	7.5
Motor vehicle damage	42.6	42.6	1.7	(NA)	(NA)	6.2	16.5	1.0	(NA)	(NA)
Employer uninsured cost [4]	19.5	2.0	10.4	4.8	2.6	2.8	0.8	5.9	2.9	2.4
Fire loss	14.7	(NA)	3.4	9.1	2.2	2.1	(NA)	1.9	5.5	2.0

NA Not available.   [1] Excludes duplication between work and motor vehicle; $21.6 billion in 2007.   [2] Actual loss of wages and household production, and the present value of future earnings lost.   [3] Home and other costs may include costs of administering medical treatment claims for some motor-vehicle injuries filed through health insurance plans.   [4] Estimate of the uninsured costs incurred by employers, representing the money value of time lost by noninjured workers.

Source: National Safety Council, Itasca, IL, *Injury Facts*, annual (copyright); <http://www.nsc.org/lrs/statstop.aspx>.

4. For each of the following four graphics, write a paragraph evaluating its effectiveness and describing how you would revise it.

a. **Majors**

	2009	2010	2011
Civil Engineering	236	231	253
Chemical Engineering	126	134	142
Comparative Literature	97	86	74
Electrical Engineering	317	326	401
English	714	623	592
Fine Arts	112	96	72
Foreign Languages	608	584	566
Materials Engineering	213	227	241
Mechanical Engineering	196	203	201
Other	46	42	51
Philosophy	211	142	151
Religion	86	91	72

b. **Number of Members of the U.S. Armed Forces in 2009 (in Thousands)**

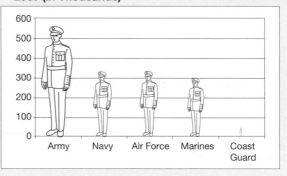

c. **Expenses at Hillway Corporation**

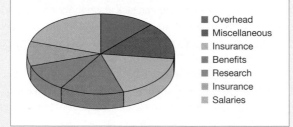

- Overhead
- Miscellaneous
- Insurance
- Benefits
- Research
- Insurance
- Salaries

d. **Costs of the Components of a PC**

5. The following three graphs illustrate the sales of two products—Series 1 and Series 2—for each quarter of 2011. Which is the most effective in conveying the information? Which is the least effective? What additional information would make the most effective graph better?

a. 2011 Sales of Series 1 and 2, by Quarters

Quarters

b. 2011 Sales of Series 1 and 2, by Quarters

Quarters

c.

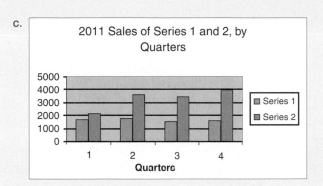

6. The following table from a report on the federal response to Hurricane Katrina presents data on the damage done by five hurricanes (Townsend, 2006). After studying the table, write a paragraph in which you explain the data to general readers interested in comparing the damage done by Hurricane Katrina with the damage done by other major hurricanes in U.S. history.

Table 1   Hurricane Katrina Compared to Hurricanes San Felipe, Camille, Andrew, and Ivan

Hurricane (year)	Homes damaged or destroyed	Property damage (in billions of dollars)	Deaths
San Felipe (1928)	*	<1	2,750
Camille (1969)	22,008	6	335
Andrew (1992)	79,663	33	61
Ivan (2004)	27,772	15	57
Katrina (2005)	300,000	96	1,330

*Data not available.

7. **INTERNET EXERCISE** Locate a graphic on the Web that you consider inappropriate for an international audience because it might be offensive or unclear in some cultures. Imagine an intended audience for the graphic, such as people from the Middle East, and write a brief statement explaining the potential problem. Finally, revise the graphic so that it would be appropriate for its intended audience.

On the Web

For a case assignment, "Creating Appropriate Graphics to Accompany a Report," see Cases on <bedfordstmartins .com/ps>.

PART 4

Learning Important Applications

9

Writing Correspondence

AP Photo/Paul Sakuma.

You will communicate every day on the job.

A s this photograph shows, new media make it simple and inexpensive to add a visual dimension to business correspondence. Here, two people are using a videoconferencing product to confirm information that they will put into writing using the product's instant-messaging feature.

Regardless of whether you use microblogs, instant messaging, text messaging, or more traditional applications, you will communicate in writing every day on the job. This chapter discusses the four major formats used for producing workplace correspondence: letters, memos, e-mails, and microblogs. Throughout this chapter, the word *correspondence* refers to all these forms.

Focus on Process

When writing correspondence, pay special attention to these steps of the writing process. For a complete process for writing technical documents, see page 14.

- **Planning.** You will need to choose the appropriate type of correspondence for your writing situation. See the Choices and Strategies box for help.

- **Drafting.** For letters, memos, and e-mail, clearly state your purpose, use headings to help your readers, summarize your message, provide adequate background, organize the discussion, and highlight action items. For microblogs, state your message or question clearly.

- **Proofreading.** You might need to write correspondence quickly, but you still need to write carefully. Proofread *everything* before you publish or send it. See Appendix, Part B, for help.

SELECTING A TYPE OF CORRESPONDENCE

When you need to correspond with others in the workplace, your first task is to decide on the appropriate application. You have four major choices: letters, memos, e-mail, and microblogs.

CHOICES AND STRATEGIES   Choosing a Type of Correspondence

If the situation is ...	And you are writing to ...	Try this type of correspondence
Formal	People outside or within your organization	**Letters.** Because letters use centuries-old conventions such as the salutation and complimentary close, they are the most formal of the four types of correspondence.
Moderately formal	People outside your organization	**Letters or e-mail.** Letters are more formal than e-mail, but consider how your readers will need to use the information. Recipients can store and forward an e-mail easily, as well as capture the text and reuse it in other documents. In addition, you can attach other files to an e-mail.
Moderately formal	People within your organization	**Memos or e-mail.** Memos are moderately formal and can be sent in the body of an e-mail or as an attachment.
Informal	People outside or within your organization	**E-mail or microblogs.** E-mail is good for quick, relatively informal communication with one or many recipients. Microblog posts such as Twitter tweets or Facebook status updates can be useful for quick questions addressed to a group. Microblogs are the most informal type of correspondence.

PRESENTING YOURSELF EFFECTIVELY IN CORRESPONDENCE

When you write business correspondence, follow these five suggestions for presenting yourself as a professional:

- Use the appropriate level of formality.
- Communicate correctly.
- Project the "you attitude."
- Avoid correspondence clichés.
- Communicate honestly.

Use the Appropriate Level of Formality

People are sometimes tempted to use informal writing in informal digital applications such as e-mail and microblogs. Don't. Remember that everything you write on the job is legally the property of the organization for which you work, and messages are almost always archived digitally, even after recipients have deleted them. Remember, too, that they might be read by the company president, or they might appear in a newspaper or in a court of law. Therefore, use a moderately formal tone to avoid potential embarrassment.

TOO INFORMAL	Our meeting with United went south right away when they threw a hissy fit, saying that we blew off the deadline for the progress report.
MODERATELY FORMAL	In our meeting, the United representative expressed concern that we had missed the deadline for the progress report.

Communicate Correctly

In This Book

For more about editing and proofreading, see Appendix, Part B, pp. 445–68.

As discussed in Chapter 1, correct writing is free of grammar, punctuation, style, usage, and spelling errors. Sending correspondence that contains such errors is unprofessional because it suggests a lack of respect for your reader—and for yourself. It also causes your reader to think that you are careless about your job.

Project the "You Attitude"

Correspondence should be courteous and positive. The key to accomplishing this task is using the "you attitude"—that is, looking at the situation from the reader's point of view and adjusting the content, structure, and tone to meet his or her needs. For example, if you are writing to a supplier who has failed to deliver some merchandise on time, the "you attitude" dictates that you not discuss problems you are having with other suppliers; those problems don't concern your reader. Instead, concentrate on explaining clearly and politely that the reader has violated your agreement and that not having the merchandise is costing you money. Then propose ways to expedite the shipment.

SARCASTIC   You'll need two months to deliver those parts? Who do you think you are, the post office?

BETTER   Surely you would find a two-month delay for the delivery of parts unacceptable in your business. That's how I feel, too.

A calm, respectful tone makes the best impression and increases the chances that you will achieve your goal.

Avoid Correspondence Clichés

Over the centuries, a set of words and phrases has come to be associated with business correspondence; one common example is *as per your request*. These phrases sound stilted and insincere. Don't use them.

Figure 9.1 lists common clichés and their more natural equivalents. Figure 9.2 on page 222 shows two versions of the same letter: one written in clichés, the other in plain language.

Communicate Honestly

You should communicate honestly when you write any kind of document, and business correspondence is no exception. Communicating honestly shows respect for your reader and for yourself.

In This Book

For more about choosing the right words and phrases, see Ch. 6, p. 125.

Letter clichés	Natural equivalents
attached please find	attached is
enclosed please find	enclosed is
pursuant to our agreement	as we agreed
referring to your ("Referring to your letter of March 19, the shipment of pianos . . .")	"As you wrote in your letter of March 19, the shipment of pianos . . ." (or subordinate the reference at the end of your sentence)
wish to advise ("We wish to advise that . . .")	(The phrase doesn't say anything. Just say what you want to say.)
the writer ("The writer believes that . . .")	"I believe . . ."

Figure 9.1 Letter Clichés and Natural Equivalents

Figure 9.2 Sample Letters with and Without Clichés

The letter on the right side avoids clichés and shows an understanding of the "you attitude." Instead of focusing on the violation of the warranty, it presents the conclusion as good news: the snowmobile is not ruined, and it can be repaired and returned in less than a week for a small charge.

Letter containing clichés

Dear Mr. Smith:

Referring to your letter regarding the problem encountered with your new Trailrider Snowmobile, our Customer Service Department has just submitted its report.

It is their conclusion that the malfunction is caused by water being present in the fuel line. It is our conclusion that you must have purchased some bad gasoline. We trust you are cognizant of the fact that while we guarantee our snowmobiles for a period of not less than one year against defects in workmanship and materials, responsibility cannot be assumed for inadequate care. We wish to advise, for the reason mentioned hereinabove, that we cannot grant your request to repair the snowmobile free of charge.

Permit me to say, however, that the writer would be pleased to see that the fuel line is flushed at cost, $30. Your Trailrider would then give you many years of trouble-free service.

Enclosed please find an authorization card. Should we receive it, we shall perform the above-mentioned repair and deliver your snowmobile forthwith.

Sincerely yours,

Letter in natural language

Dear Mr. Smith:

Thank you for writing to us about the problem with your new Trailrider Snowmobile.

Our Customer Service Department has found water in the fuel line. Apparently some of the gasoline was bad. While we guarantee our snowmobiles for one year against defects in workmanship and materials, we cannot assume responsibility for problems caused by bad gasoline. We cannot, therefore, grant your request to repair the snowmobile free of charge.

However, no serious harm was done to the snowmobile. We would be happy to flush the fuel line at cost, $30. Your Trailrider would then give you many years of trouble-free service. If you will authorize us to do this work, we will have your snowmobile back to you within four working days. Just fill out the enclosed authorization card and drop it in the mail.

Sincerely yours,

ETHICS NOTE

Writing Honest Business Correspondence

Why is dishonesty a big problem in correspondence? Perhaps because the topics discussed in business correspondence often relate to the writer's professionalism and the quality of his or her work. For instance, when a salesperson working for a supplier writes to a customer explaining why the product did not arrive on time, he is tempted to make it seem as if his company—and he personally—is blameless. The most professional thing to do is tell the truth. If you mislead a reader in explaining why the shipment didn't arrive on time, the reader will likely double-check the facts, conclude that you are trying to avoid responsibility, and end your business relationship.

WRITING LETTERS

Letters are still a basic means of communication between organizations, with millions written each day. To write effective letters, you need to understand the elements of a letter, its format, and the common types of letters sent in the business world.

Elements of a Letter

Most letters include a heading, inside address, salutation, body, complimentary close, and signature. Some letters also include one or more of the following: attention line, subject line, enclosure notation, and copy line. Figure 9.3 on pages 224–25 shows the elements of a letter. This letter uses the full-block format, in which all the elements except the heading are aligned on the left margin.

Common Types of Letters

Organizations send out many different kinds of letters. This section focuses on three types of letters written frequently in the workplace: inquiry, claim, and adjustment letters.

Inquiry Letter   Figure 9.4 on page 226 shows an inquiry letter, in which you ask questions.

Claim Letter   Figure 9.5 on page 227 is an example of a claim letter that the writer faxed to the reader.

Adjustment Letter   Figures 9.6 and 9.7 on pages 228 and 229 show "good news" and "bad news" adjustment letters. The first is a reply to the claim letter shown in Figure 9.5.

WRITING MEMOS

Even in the age of e-mail and microblogs, memos are likely to survive because sometimes writers want a slightly more formal document. Like letters, memos have a characteristic format, which consists of the elements shown in Figure 9.8 on page 230.

Print the second and all subsequent pages of a memo on plain paper rather than on letterhead. Include three items in the upper right-hand or

▶ On the Web

For more about letter writing, search for "business letters" at Purdue University's OWL. Click on Links Library for Ch. 9 on <bedfordstmartins.com/ps>.

▶ In This Book

Two other types of letters are discussed in this book: the transmittal letter in Ch. 13, p. 323, and the job-application letter in Ch. 10, p. 262.

Heading. *Most organizations use letterhead stationery with their heading printed at the top. This preprinted information and the date the letter is sent make up the heading. If you are using blank paper rather than letterhead, your address (without your name) and the date form the heading. Use letterhead for the first page and do not number it. Use blank paper for the second and all subsequent pages.*

Inside Address. *If you are writing to an individual who has a professional title—such as Professor, Dr., or, for public officials, Honorable—use it. If not, use Mr. or Ms. (unless you know the recipient prefers Mrs. or Miss). If the reader's position fits on the same line as the name, add it after a comma; otherwise, drop it to the line below. Spell the name of the organization the way the organization itself does: for example, International Business Machines calls itself IBM. Include the complete mailing address: street number and name, city, state, and zip code.*

Attention Line. *Sometimes you will be unable to address a letter to a particular person because you don't know (and cannot easily find out) the name of the individual who holds that position in the company.*

DAVIS TREE CARE
1300 Lancaster Avenue
Berwyn, PA 19092
www.davisfortrees.com

May 11, 2013

Fairlawn Industrial Park
1910 Ridgeway Drive
Rollins, MO 84639

Attention: Director of Maintenance

Subject: Fall pruning

Dear Director of Maintenance:

Do you know how much your trees are worth? That's right—your trees. As a maintenance director, you know how much of an investment your organization has in its physical plant. And the landscaping is a big part of your total investment.

Most people don't know that even the hardiest trees need periodic care. Like shrubs, trees should be fertilized and pruned. And they should be protected against the many kinds of diseases and pests that are common in this area.

At Davis Tree Care, we have the skills and experience to keep your trees healthy and beautiful. Our diagnostic staff is made up of graduates of major agricultural and forestry universities, and all of our crews attend special workshops to keep current with the latest information on tree maintenance. Add to this our proven record of 43 years of continuous service in the Berwyn area, and you have a company you can trust.

Subject Line. *The subject line is an optional element in a letter. Use either a project number (for example, "Subject: Project 31402") or a brief phrase defining the subject (for example, "Subject: Price quotation for the R13 submersible pump").*

Salutation. *If you decide not to use an attention line or a subject line, put the salutation, or greeting, two lines below the inside address. The traditional salutation is Dear, followed by the reader's courtesy title and last name, followed by a colon (not a comma):*
Dear Ms. Hawkins:

Figure 9.3　Elements of a Letter

Letter to Fairlawn Industrial Park
Page 2
May 11, 2013

May we stop by to give you an analysis of your trees—
absolutely without cost or obligation? A few minutes with one
of our diagnosticians could prove to be one of the wisest moves
you've ever made. Just give us a call at 555-9187, and we'll be
happy to arrange an appointment at your convenience.

Sincerely yours,

Jasmine Brown

Jasmine Brown
President

Enclosure: Davis Tree Care brochure

c: Darrell Davis, Vice President

Header *for second page.*

Body. *In most cases, the body contains at least three paragraphs: an introductory paragraph, a concluding paragraph, and one or more body paragraphs.*

Complimentary Close. *The conventional phrases* Sincerely, Sincerely yours, Yours sincerely, Yours very truly, *and* Very truly yours *are interchangeable.*

Signature. *Type your full name on the fourth line below the complimentary close. Sign the letter, in ink, above the typed name. Most organizations prefer that you include your position under your typed name.*

Copy Line. *If you want the primary recipient to know that other people are receiving a copy of the letter, include a copy line. Use the symbol* c *(for "copy") followed by the names of the other recipients (listed either alphabetically or according to organizational rank). If appropriate, use the symbol* cc *(for "courtesy copy") followed by the names of recipients who are less directly affected by the letter.*

Enclosure Notation. *If the envelope contains documents other than the letter, include an enclosure notation that indicates the number of enclosures. For more than one enclosure, add the number: "Enclosures (2)." In determining the number of enclosures, count only separate items, not pages. A three-page memo and a 10-page report constitute only two enclosures. Some writers like to identify the enclosures:*

> *Enclosure: 2012 Placement Bulletin*
> *Enclosures (2): "This Year at Ammex"*
> *2012 Annual Report*

Figure 9.3   (continued)

You write an inquiry letter to acquire information. Explain who you are and why you are writing. Make your questions precise, clear, and therefore easy to answer. Explain what you plan to do with the information and how you can compensate the reader for answering your questions.

This writer's task is to motivate the reader to provide some information. That information is not likely to lead to a sale because the writer is a graduate student doing research, not a potential customer.

Notice the flattery in the first sentence. ──▶

The writer presents specific questions in a list format, making the questions easy to read and understand. ──▶

In the final paragraph, the writer politely indicates his schedule and requests the reader's response. Note that he offers to send the reader a copy of his report. ──▶

If the reader provides information, the writer should send a thank-you letter. The letter is in modified-block format, in which the inside address and complimentary close begin at the center margin.

---

14 Hawthorne Avenue
Belleview, TX 75234

November 2, 2013

Dr. Andrea Shakir
Director of Technical Services
Orion Corporation
721 West Douglas Avenue
Maryville, TN 31409

Dear Dr. Shakir:

I am writing to you because of Orion's reputation as a leader in the manufacture of adjustable x-ray tables. I am a graduate student in biomedical engineering at the University of Texas, and I am working on an analysis of diagnostic equipment for a seminar paper. Would you be able to answer a few questions about your Microspot 311?

1. Can the Microspot 311 be used with lead oxide cassettes, or does it accept only lead-free cassettes?
2. Are standard generators compatible with the Microspot 311?
3. What would you say is the greatest advantage, for the operator, of using the Microspot 311? For the patient?

Because my project is due on January 15, I would greatly appreciate your assistance in answering these questions by January 10. Of course, I would be happy to send you a copy of my report when it is completed.

Yours very truly,

Albert K. Stern

Albert K. Stern

Figure 9.4   Inquiry Letter

ROBBINS CONSTRUCTION, INC.

255 Robbins Place, Centerville, MO 65101 | (417) 555-1850 | www.robbinsconstruction.com

August 17, 2013

Mr. David Larsyn
Larsyn Supply Company
311 Elmerine Avenue
Anderson, MO 63501

Dear Mr. Larsyn:

As steady customers of yours for over 15 years, we came to you first when we needed a quiet pile driver for a job near a residential area. On your recommendation, we bought your Vista 500 Quiet Driver, at $14,900. We have since found, much to our embarrassment, that it is not substantially quieter than a regular pile driver.

We received the contract to do the bridge repair here in Centerville after promising to keep the noise to under 90 dB during the day. The Vista 500 (see enclosed copy of bill of sale for particulars) is rated at 85 dB, maximum. We began our work and, although one of our workers said the driver didn't seem sufficiently quiet to him, assured the people living near the job site that we were well within the agreed sound limit. One of them, an acoustical engineer, marched out the next day and demonstrated that we were putting out 104 dB. Obviously, something is wrong with the pile driver.

I think you will agree that we have a problem. We were able to secure other equipment, at considerable inconvenience, to finish the job on schedule. When I telephoned your company that humiliating day, however, a Mr. Meredith informed me that I should have done an acoustical reading on the driver before I accepted delivery.

I would like you to send out a technician—as soon as possible—either to repair the driver so that it performs according to specifications or to take it back for a full refund.

Yours truly,

Jack Robbins

Jack Robbins, President

Enclosure

Figure 9.5 Claim Letter

A claim letter is a polite, reasonable complaint. If you purchase a defective or falsely advertised product or receive inadequate service, you write a claim letter. If the letter is convincing, your chances of receiving an equitable settlement are good because most organizations realize that unhappy customers are bad for business. In addition, claim letters help companies identify weak points in their product or service.

The writer indicates clearly in the first paragraph that he is writing about an unsatisfactory product. Note that he identifies the product by model name.

The writer presents the background, filling in specific details about the problem. Notice how he supports his earlier claim that the problem embarrassed him professionally.

The writer states that he thinks the reader will agree that there was a problem with the equipment.

Then the writer suggests that the reader's colleague did not respond satisfactorily.

The writer proposes a solution: that the reader take appropriate action. The writer's clear, specific account of the problem and his professional tone increase his chances of receiving the solution he proposes. This letter is in block format, in which all elements are aligned on the left margin.

An adjustment letter, a response to a claim letter, tells the customer how you plan to handle the situation. Your purpose is to show that your organization is fair and reasonable and that you value the customer's business.

If you can grant the request, the letter is easy to write. Express your regret, state the adjustment you are going to make, and end on a positive note by encouraging the customer to continue doing business with you.

The writer wisely expresses regret about the two problems cited in the claim letter.

The writer describes the actions he has already taken and formally states that he will do whatever the reader wishes.

The writer expresses empathy in making the offer of adjustment. Doing so helps to create a bond: you and I are both professionals who rely on our good reputations.

This polite conclusion appeals to the reader's sense of fairness and good business practice.

On the Web

For excellent advice on adjustment letters, see Business Communication: Managing Information and Relationships. Click on Links Library for Ch. 9 on <bedfordstmartins.com/ps>.

Larsyn Supply Company

311 Elmerine Avenue
Anderson, MO 63501
(417) 555-2484
www.larsynsupply.com

August 22, 2013

Mr. Jack Robbins, President
Robbins Construction, Inc.
255 Robbins Place
Centerville, MO 65101

Dear Mr. Robbins:

I was very unhappy to read your letter of August 17 telling me about the failure of the Vista 500. I regretted most the treatment you received from one of my employees when you called us.

Harry Rivers, our best technician, has already been in touch with you to arrange a convenient time to come out to Centerville to talk with you about the driver. We will of course repair it, replace it, or refund the price. Just let us know your wish.

I realize that I cannot undo the damage that was done on the day that a piece of our equipment failed. To make up for some of the extra trouble and expense you incurred, let me offer you a 10 percent discount on your next purchase or service order with us, up to a $1,000 total discount.

You have indeed been a good customer for many years, and I would hate to have this unfortunate incident spoil that relationship. Won't you give us another chance? Just bring in this letter when you visit us next, and we'll give you that 10 percent discount.

Sincerely,

Dave Larsyn

Dave Larsyn, President

Figure 9.6   "Good News" Adjustment Letter

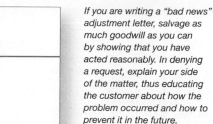

Quality Storage Media

2077 Highland, Burley, ID 84765
208 · 555 · 1613
www.qualstorage.com

February 4, 2013

Ms. Dale Devlin
1903 Highland Avenue
Glenn Mills, NE 69032

Dear Ms. Devlin:

Thank you for writing us about the external hard drive you purchased on January 11, 2013. I know from personal experience how frustrating it is when a drive fails.

According to your letter, you used the drive to store the business plan for your new consulting business. When you attempted to copy that file to your internal hard drive, the external drive failed, and the business plan was lost. You have no other copy of that file. You are asking us to reimburse you $1,500 for the cost of re-creating that business plan from notes and rough drafts.

As you know, our drives carry a lifetime guarantee covering parts and workmanship. We will gladly replace the defective external drive. However, the guarantee states that the manufacturer and the retailer will not assume any incidental liability. Thus we are responsible only for the retail value of the external drive, not for the cost of duplicating the work that went into making the files stored on the drive.

However, your file might still be recoverable. A reputable data-recovery firm might be able to restore the data from the file at a very reasonable cost. To prevent such problems in the future, we always recommend that you back up all valuable files periodically.

We have already sent out your new external drive by overnight delivery. It should arrive within the next two days.

Please contact us if we can be of any further assistance.

Sincerely yours,

Paul R. Blackwood

Paul R. Blackwood, Manager
Customer Relations

If you are writing a "bad news" adjustment letter, salvage as much goodwill as you can by showing that you have acted reasonably. In denying a request, explain your side of the matter, thus educating the customer about how the problem occurred and how to prevent it in the future.

The writer does not begin by stating that he is denying the reader's request. Instead, he begins politely by trying to form a bond with the reader. In trying to meet the customer on neutral ground, be careful about admitting that the customer is right. If you say "We are sorry that the engine you purchased from us is defective," it will bolster the customer's claim if the dispute ends up in court.

The writer summarizes the facts of the incident, as he sees them.

The writer explains that he is unable to fulfill the reader's request. Notice that the writer never explicitly denies the request. It is more effective to explain why granting the request is not appropriate. Also notice that the writer does not explicitly say that the reader failed to make a backup copy of the plan and therefore the problem is her fault.

The writer shifts from the bad news to the good news. The writer explains that he has already responded appropriately to the reader's request.

The writer ends with a polite conclusion. A common technique is to offer the reader a special discount on another, similar product.

Figure 9.7   "Bad News" Adjustment Letter

Write out the month instead of using the all-numeral format (6/12/12); multicultural readers might use a different notation for dates and could be confused.

AMRO   MEMO

To: B. Pabst
From: J. Alonso *J. A.*
Subject: MIXER RECOMMENDATION FOR PHILLIPS
Date: June 12, 2013

INTEROFFICE

To: C. Cleveland   c: B. Aaron
From: H. Rainbow *H. R.*   K. Lau
Subject: Shipment Date of Blueprints   J. Manuputra
          to Collier   W. Williams
Date: October 2, 2013

List the names of persons receiving copies of the memo, either alphabetically or in descending order of organizational rank.

NORTHERN PETROLEUM COMPANY
INTERNAL CORRESPONDENCE

Date: January 3, 2013
To: William Weeks, Director of Operations
From: Helen Cho, Chemical Engineering Dept. *H. C.*
Subject: Trip Report—Conference on Improved Procedures
          for Chemical Analysis Laboratory

Most writers put their initials or signature next to the typed name (or at the end of the memo) to show that they have reviewed the memo and accept responsibility for it.

Figure 9.8   Identifying Information in a Memo

Some organizations prefer the full names of the writer and reader; others want only the first initials and last names. Some prefer job titles; others do not. If your organization does not object, include your job title and your reader's. The memo will then be informative for anyone who refers to it after either of you has moved on to a new position, as well as for others in the organization who might not know you.

left-hand corner of each page: the name of the recipient, the date of the memo, and the page number.

Figure 9.9, a sample memo, is a trip report, a record of a business trip written after the employee returned to the office. Readers are less interested in an hour-by-hour narrative of what happened than in a carefully structured discussion of what was important. Although writer and reader appear to be relatively equal in rank, the writer has gone to the trouble of organizing the memo to make it easy to read and refer to later.

Dynacol Corporation

INTEROFFICE COMMUNICATION

To: G. Granby, R&D
From: P. Rabin, Technical Services   *P.R.*
Subject: Trip Report—Computer Dynamics, Inc.
Date: September 21, 2013

The purpose of this memo is to present my impressions of the Computer Dynamics technical seminar of September 19. The goal of the seminar was to introduce their new PQ-500 line of high-capacity storage drives.

Summary
In general, I was impressed with the technical capabilities and interface of the drives. Of the two models in the 500 series, I think we ought to consider the external drives, not the internal ones. I'd like to talk to you about this issue when you have a chance.

Discussion
Computer Dynamics offers two models in its 500 series: an internal drive and an external drive. Both models have the same capacity (100 G of storage), and they both work the same way: they extend the storage capacity of a server by integrating an optical disk library into the file system. The concept is that they move files between the server's faster, but limited-capacity, storage devices (hard disks) and its slower, high-capacity storage devices (magneto-optical disks). This process, which they call data migration and demigration, is transparent to the user.

For the system administrator, integrating either of the models would require no more than one hour. The external model would be truly portable; the user would not need to install any drivers, as long as his or her device is docked on our network. The system administrator would push the necessary drivers onto all the networked devices without the user having to do anything.

Although the internal drive is convenient—it is already configured for the computer—I think we should consider only the external drive. Because so many of our employees do teleconferencing, the advantage of portability outweighs the disadvantage of inconvenience. The tech rep from Computer Dynamics walked me through the process of configuring both models. A second advantage of the external drive is that it can be salvaged easily when we take a computer out of service.

Recommendation
I'd like to talk to you, when you get a chance, about negotiating with Computer Dynamics for a quantity discount. I think we should ask McKinley and Rossiter to participate in the discussion. Give me a call (x3442) and we'll talk.

Figure 9.9   Sample Memo

The subject line is specific: the reader can tell at a glance that the memo reports on a trip to Computer Dynamics, Inc. If the subject line read only "Computer Dynamics, Inc.," the reader would not know what the writer is going to discuss about that company.

The memo begins with a clear statement of purpose, as discussed in Ch. 4, p. 59.

Note that the writer has provided a summary, even though the memo is less than a page. The summary gives the writer an opportunity to convey his main request: he would like to meet with the reader.

The main section of the memo is the discussion, which conveys the detailed version of the writer's message. Often the discussion begins with the background: the facts that readers will need to know to understand the memo. In this case, the background consists of a two-paragraph discussion of the two models in the company's 500 series. Presumably, the reader already knows why the writer went on the trip.

Note that the writer ends this discussion with a conclusion, or statement of the meaning of the facts. In this case, the writer's conclusion is that the company should consider only the external drive.

A recommendation is the writer's statement of what he would like the reader to do next. In this case, the writer would like to sit down with the reader to discuss how to proceed.

Guidelines

Organizing a Memo

When you write a memo, organize it so that it is easy to follow. Consider these five important organizational elements.

▶ **A specific subject line.** "Breast Cancer Walk" is too general. "Breast Cancer Walk Rescheduled to May 14" is better.

▶ **A clear statement of purpose.** As discussed in Chapter 4 (p. 59), the purpose statement is built around an infinitive verb that clearly states what you want the readers to know, believe, or do.

▶ **A brief summary.** Even if a memo fits on one page, consider including a summary. For readers who want to read the whole memo, the summary is an advance organizer; for readers in a hurry, reading the summary substitutes for reading the whole memo.

▶ **Informative headings.** Headings make the memo easier to read by enabling readers to skip sections they don't need and by helping them understand what each section is about. In addition, headings make the memo easier to write because they prompt the writer to provide the kind of information readers need.

▶ **A prominent recommendation.** Many memos end with one or more recommendations. Sometimes these recommendations take the form of action steps: bulleted or numbered lists of what the writer will do, or what the writer would like others to do. Here is an example:

> **Action Items:**
> I would appreciate it if you would work on the following tasks and have your results ready for the meeting on Monday, June 9.
> - Henderson: recalculate the flow rate.
> - Smith: set up meeting with the regional EPA representative for sometime during the week of May 13.
> - Falvey: ask Armitra in Houston for his advice.

WRITING E-MAILS

Before you write an e-mail in the workplace, find out your organization's e-mail policies. Most companies have written policies that discuss circumstances under which you may and may not use e-mail, principles you should use in writing e-mails, and the monitoring of employee e-mail. Figure 9.10 shows the basic elements of an e-mail.

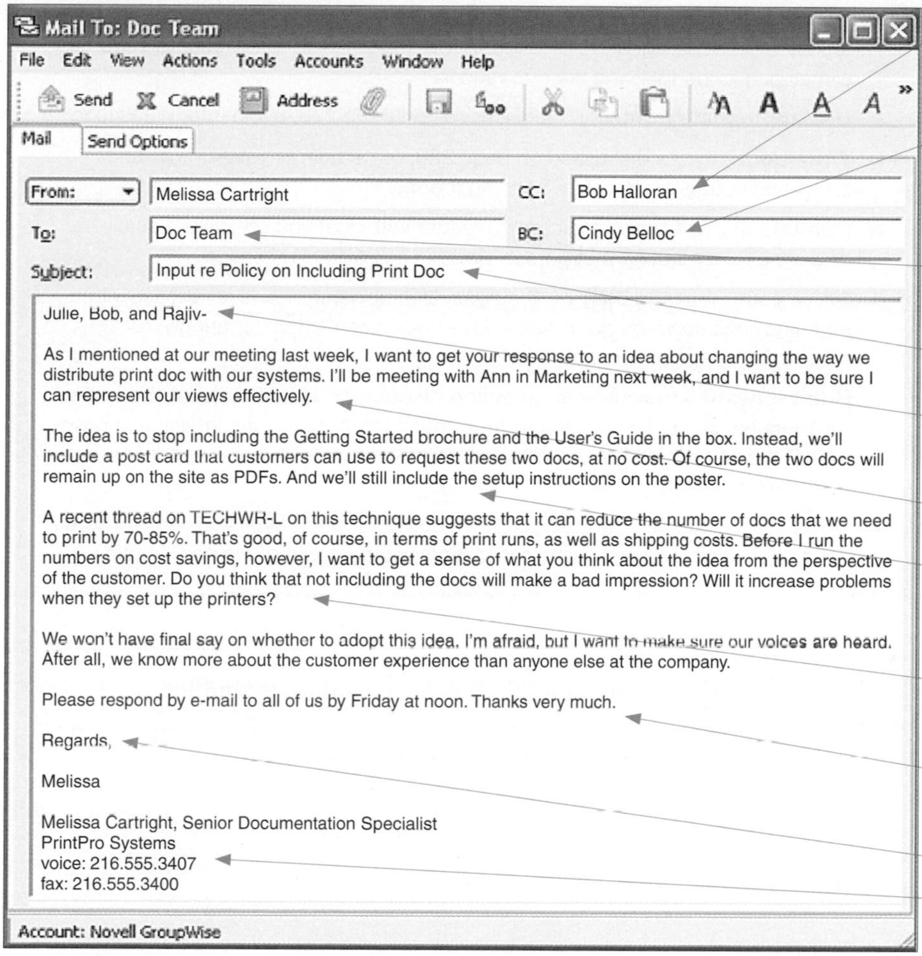

Figure 9.10   Elements of an E-mail

The annotations around the figure read:

"CC" stands for courtesy copy. All of your recipients will know that you are sending a copy to this person or group.

"BC" or "Bcc" stands for blind copy or blind courtesy copy. None of your readers will know that you are sending a copy to this person or group.

You can create a "group" for people whom you e-mail frequently.

Like a memo, an e-mail should have a specific subject line.

By naming her readers at the start, the writer is showing respect for them.

The first paragraph of the e-mail clarifies the writer's purpose.

The second paragraph describes the idea. You want to be sure your readers understand the context.

Notice that paragraphs are relatively brief and that the writer skips a line between paragraphs.

The writer explains what she would like her readers to do, and she states a deadline.

The writer ends politely.

The writer has created a signature, which includes her contact information. This signature is attached automatically to her e-mails.

The e-mail content shown in the figure:

Julie, Bob, and Rajiv-

As I mentioned at our meeting last week, I want to get your response to an idea about changing the way we distribute print doc with our systems. I'll be meeting with Ann in Marketing next week, and I want to be sure I can represent our views effectively.

The idea is to stop including the Getting Started brochure and the User's Guide in the box. Instead, we'll include a post card that customers can use to request these two docs, at no cost. Of course, the two docs will remain up on the site as PDFs. And we'll still include the setup instructions on the poster.

A recent thread on TECHWR-L on this technique suggests that it can reduce the number of docs that we need to print by 70-85%. That's good, of course, in terms of print runs, as well as shipping costs. Before I run the numbers on cost savings, however, I want to get a sense of what you think about the idea from the perspective of the customer. Do you think that not including the docs will make a bad impression? Will it increase problems when they set up the printers?

We won't have final say on whether to adopt this idea, I'm afraid, but I want to make sure our voices are heard. After all, we know more about the customer experience than anyone else at the company.

Please respond by e-mail to all of us by Friday at noon. Thanks very much.

Regards,

Melissa

Melissa Cartright, Senior Documentation Specialist
PrintPro Systems
voice: 216.555.3407
fax: 216.555.3400

Guidelines

Following Netiquette

When you write e-mail in the workplace, adhere to the following netiquette guidelines. *Netiquette* refers to etiquette on a network.

▶ **Stick to business.** Don't send jokes or other nonbusiness messages.

▶ **Don't waste bandwidth.** Keep the message brief. Don't quote long passages from another e-mail. Instead, paraphrase the other e-mail briefly or include a short quotation from it. When you quote, delete the routing information from the top as well as the signature block from the bottom. And make sure to send the e-mail only to people who need to read it.

▶ **Use appropriate formality.** As discussed on page 220, avoid informal writing.

▶ **Write correctly.** As discussed on page 220, remember to revise, edit, and proofread your e-mails before sending them.

▶ **Don't flame.** To *flame* is to scorch a reader with scathing criticism, usually in response to something that person wrote in a previous message.

▶ **Make your message easy on the eyes.** Use uppercase and lowercase letters, and skip lines between paragraphs. Use uppercase letters (sparingly) for emphasis.

▶ **Don't forward a message to an online discussion forum without the writer's permission.** Doing so is unethical and illegal; the e-mail is the intellectual property of the writer or (if it was written as part of the writer's work responsibilities) the writer's company.

▶ **Don't send a message unless you have something to say.** If you can add something new, do so, but don't send a message just to be part of the conversation.

On the Web

See Albion.com's discussion of netiquette. Click on Links Library for Ch. 9 on <bedfordstmartins.com/ps>.

Figure 9.11a shows an e-mail that violates netiquette guidelines. The writer is a technical professional working for a microchip manufacturer. Figure 9.11b shows a revised version of this e-mail message.

The writer does not clearly state his purpose in the subject line and the first paragraph.

Using all uppercase letters gives the impression that the writer is yelling at his readers.

The writer has not proofread.

The writer's tone is hostile.

With long lines and no spaces between paragraphs, this e-mail is difficult to read.

> **To:** Supers and Leads
> **Subject:** ➤
>
> LATELY, WE HAVE BEEN MISSING LASER REPAIR FILES FOR OUR 16MEG WAFERS. AFTER BRIEF INVESTIGATION, I HAVE FOUND THE MAIN REASON FOR THE MISSING DATA.
>
> OCCASIONALLY, SOME OF YOU HAVE WRONGLY PROBED THE WAFERS UNDER THE CORRELATE STEP AND THE DATA IS THEN COPIED INTO THE NONPROD STEP USING THE QTR PROGRAM. THIS IS REALLY STUPID. WHEN DATE IS COPIED THIS WAY THE REPAIR DATA IS NOT COPIED. IT REMAINS UNDER THE CORRELATE STEP.
>
> TO AVOID THIS PROBLEM, FIRST PROBE THE WAFERS THE RIGHT WAY. IF A WAFER MUST BE PROBED UNDER A DIFFERENT STEP, THE WAFER IN THE CHANGE FILE MUST BE RENAMED TO THE *.* FORMAT.
>
> EDITING THE WAFER DATA FILE SHOULD BE USED ONLY AS A LAST RESORT, IF THIS BECOMES A COMMON PROBLEM, WE COULD HAVE MORE PROBLEMS WITH INVALID DATA THAT THERE ARE NOW.
>
> SUPERS AND LEADS: PLEASE PASS THIS INFORMATION ALONG TO THOSE WHO NEED TO KNOW.
>
> ROGER VANDENHEUVAL

a. E-mail that violates netiquette guidelines

Figure 9.11 Netiquette

```
| To:      Supers and Leads
| Subject:   Fix for Missing Laser Repair Files for 16MB Wafers   ◄

  Supers and Leads:

  Lately, we have been missing laser repair files for our 16MB wafers.
  In this e-mail I want to briefly describe the problem and recommend a
  method for solving it.

  Here is what I think is happening. Some of the wafers have been
  probed under the correlate step; this method copies the data into the
  nonprod step and leaves the repair data uncopied. It remains under
  the correlate step.

  To prevent this problem, please use the probing method outlined in
  Spec 344-012. If a wafer must be probed using a different method,
  rename the wafer in the CHANGE file to the *.* format. Edit the wafer
  data file only as a last resort.

  I'm sending along copies of Spec 344-012. Would you please pass
  along this e-mail and the spec to all of your operators.

  Thanks. Please get in touch with me if you have any questions.   ◄

  Roger Vandenheuval
```

The writer has edited and proofread the e-mail.

The subject line and first paragraph clearly state the writer's purpose.

Double-spacing between paragraphs and using short lines make the e-mail easier to read.

The writer concludes politely.

b. E-mail that adheres to netiquette guidelines

Figure 9.11   (continued)

WRITING MICROBLOGS

Microblogs are often extremely brief and quite informal in tone. Usually, you do not revise microblogs extensively. You just proofread and send them.

However, when you write microblogs, you are creating an archived communication that is subject to the same laws and regulations that pertain to all other kinds of documents. Many of the guidelines for following netiquette (see pages 233–34) apply to microblogs as well as e-mail. Take care, especially, not to flame. Become familiar with your microblog's privacy settings, and be aware of which groups of readers may view and share your posts.

The best way to understand your responsibilities when you write a microblog at work is to study your organization's guidelines. Sometimes, these guidelines are part of the organization's guidelines for all business practices or all digital communication. Sometimes, they are treated separately. Figure 9.12 on page 237 shows one company's microblogging guidelines.

DOCUMENT ANALYSIS ACTIVITY
Following Netiquette in an E-mail

This message was written in response to a question e-mailed to several colleagues by a technical communicator seeking advice on how to write meeting minutes effectively. A response to an e-mail message should adhere to the principles of effective e-mails and proper netiquette. The accompanying questions ask you to think about these principles (explained on pp. 233–35).

1. **How effectively has the writer conserved bandwidth?**

2. **How effectively has the writer stated her purpose?**

3. **How effectively has the writer projected a "you attitude" (explained on pages 220–21)?**

4. **How effectively has the writer made her message easy to read?**

▶ **On the Web**

To submit your responses to your instructor, click on Document Analysis Activities for Ch. 9 on <bedfordstmartins .com/ps>.

✉ Re: meeting minutes - Message (Rich Text)

File Edit View Insert Format Tools Actions Help

Type a question for help

Send

Arial 10

ⓘ This message has not been sent.

To...: jjensen@procom.com

Cc...:

Subject: Re: meeting minutes

<<For the past several months, I have been trying to capture the meeting minutes for the McKinley documentation team's weekly meetings. These meetings are well attended (about 10-15 participants) and are fast-paced, with a number of key participants talking very fast and interrupting each other. At first I tried to capture these exchanges with a paper and pen. Sadly, I don't know shorthand. It was impossible.

Now I use a recorder and transcribe the conversations after each meeting. Unfortunately, the recorder I currently use doesn't always pick up low voices but easily picks up rustling papers. The transcription is very time intensive: I spend a lot of time pushing the playback button. My supervisor keeps telling me to stop relying on the recorder and to go back to taking minutes by hand. I totally DISAGREE with her.

Do any of you take minutes and, if so, do you have any suggestions for how to deal with my situation? Your thoughts are most welcomed.

Jessi Jensen
Documentation Specialist II
ProCom, Inc.
jjensen@procom.com
(619) 692-1234>>

I always try to avoid taking minutes--it's a SECRETARY'S JOB. It's definitely not something a TECHNICAL COMMUNICATOR--especially a female tech communicator (we don't want to encourage gender stereotyping)--should be wasting time with. I think it's STUPID to transcribe WORD-FOR-WORD the talk that occurs in meetings. Is even 5% of the talk of value? I AGREE with your supervisor: you are WASTING a ton of time.

When I can't avoid taking meeting minutes, I bring my laptop to the meeting. I try to have the meeting agenda already open on my word processor. Then I enter points under those headings instead of having to type the headings. I note meeting details (date, team name, names of attendees, etc.), changes to (or approval of) previous meeting's minutes, main topics of discussion, and decisions/action items. If I miss something or am unclear whether a decision was made, I interrupt and ask, "So, let me confirm that I've got this straight." Later, I edit my notes into coherent minutes. Kelly

---

Microblogging Guidelines

Definition

Microblogging is social networking combined with short-message blogging. Author-owned content "updates" are delivered in short messages (typically 140 characters or less in length) distributed through online and mobile networks to the author's "followers."

The leading microblog is Twitter; however, there are additional microblogs such as Jaiku. Twitter interactions can be made via the Twitter website, or via mobile text messages, Instant Messaging, or desktop applications such as Twitterific, Twhirl, and others. Flexibility is further enhanced by the ability to subscribe to updates via RSS.

Best Practices

- Remember, Twitter is a public platform and can be indexed by search engines. This means that what is written can become part of your and Xerox's "permanent record."
- Be yourself. Losing the trust of your followers can damage a reputation.
- Don't create an account and have someone else post on your behalf.
- Know that what you Tweet can be ReTweeted by others and referenced on other sites. Give credit to others whose message you are ReTweeting.
- Respond in a timely fashion and be sure to always contact those reaching out to you.
- Too much pro-brand messaging or marketing hype will negatively impact the number of followers you attract and/or keep.
- If you decide to open an account, take the time to actively monitor your account and facilitate two-way conversation.
- Don't make a professional account too personal, but don't lack personal touch either.
- Avoid making your followers feel that "Big Brother" is watching. It is good to interact, but don't comment on every single post they make.

Figure 9.12   Guidelines for Microblogging
Source: Xerox, 2010 <www.xerox.com/downloads/usa/en/s/Social_Media_Guidelines.pdf>.

Note that some of these "best practices" apply only to the use of a public microblogging site such as Twitter, whereas others refer to all sites, public or private.

WRITING CORRESPONDENCE TO INTERCULTURAL READERS

The four applications of business correspondence discussed in this chapter are used differently in countries around the world. These differences fall into three categories:

- *Cultural practices.* As discussed in Chapter 4, cultures differ in a number of ways, such as the focus on individuals or groups, the distance between power ranks, and attitudes toward uncertainty. Typically, a culture's attitudes are reflected in its business communication. For example, in Japan, which has a high power distance—that is, people in top positions are treated with great respect by their subordinates—the reader might be addressed as "Most Esteemed Mr. Director." Some cultural practices, however, are not intuitively obvious even if you understand the culture. For example, in Japanese business culture, it is considered rude to reply to an e-mail by using the reply function in the e-mail software; it is polite to begin a new e-mail (Sasaki, 2010).

In This Book
For more about cultural variables, see Ch. 4, p. 63.

- *Language use and tone.* In the United States, writers tend to use contractions, the first names of their readers, and other instances of informal language. In many other countries, this informality is potentially offensive. Also potentially offensive is U.S. directness. A writer from the United States might write, for example, that "14 percent of the products we received from you failed to meet the specifications." A Korean would more likely write, "We were pleased to note that 86 percent of the products we received met the specifications." The writer either would not refer to the other 14 percent (assuming that the reader would get the point and replace the defective products quickly) or would write, "We would appreciate replacement of the remaining products." Many other aspects of business correspondence differ from culture to culture, such as preferred length, specificity, and the use of seasonal references in the correspondence.

- *Application choice and use.* In cultures in which documents tend to be formal, letters might be preferred to memos, or face-to-face meetings to phone calls or e-mail. In Asia, for instance, a person is more likely to walk down the hall to deliver a brief message in person because doing so shows more respect. In addition, the formal characteristics of letters, memos, and e-mails are different in different cultures. The French, for instance, use indented paragraphs in their letters, whereas in the United States, paragraphs are typically left-justified. The ordering of the information in the inside address and complimentary close of letters varies widely. In many countries, e-mails are structured like memos, with the "to," "from," "subject," and "date" information added at the top, even though this information is already present in the routing information.

Try to study business correspondence written by people from the culture you will be addressing. When possible, have important documents reviewed by a person from that culture before you send them.

Writer's Checklist

Letter Format

- [ ] Did you type the first page on letterhead stationery? (p. 224)
- [ ] Did you include the date? (p. 224)
- [ ] Is the inside address complete and correct? (p. 224)
- [ ] Did you use the appropriate courtesy title? (p. 224)
- [ ] If appropriate, did you include an attention line? (p. 224)
- [ ] If appropriate, did you include a subject line? (p. 224)
- [ ] Is the salutation appropriate? (p. 224)
- [ ] Did you capitalize only the first word of the complimentary close? (p. 224)

- [ ] Is the signature legible, and did you type your name beneath the signature? (p. 225)
- [ ] If appropriate, did you include an enclosure line? (p. 225)
- [ ] If appropriate, did you include a copy and/or courtesy-copy line? (p. 225)

Types of Letters

Does the inquiry letter

- [ ] explain why you chose the reader to receive the inquiry? (p. 226)

☐ explain why you are requesting the information and to what use you will put it? (p. 226)

☐ specify by what date you need the information? (p. 226)

☐ list the questions clearly and, if appropriate, provide room for the reader's responses? (p. 226)

☐ offer, if appropriate, the product of your research? (p. 226)

Does the claim letter

☐ identify specifically the unsatisfactory product or service? (p. 227)

☐ explain the problem(s) clearly? (p. 227)

☐ propose an adjustment? (p. 227)

☐ conclude courteously? (p. 227)

Does the "good news" adjustment letter

☐ express your regret? (p. 228)

☐ explain the adjustment you will make? (p. 228)

☐ conclude on a positive note? (p. 228)

Does the "bad news" adjustment letter

☐ meet the reader on neutral ground, expressing regret but not apologizing? (p. 229)

☐ explain why the company is not at fault? (p. 229)

☐ clearly imply that the reader's request is denied? (p. 229)

☐ attempt to create goodwill? (p. 229)

Memos

☐ Does the identifying information adhere to your organization's standards? (p. 231)

☐ Did you include a specific subject line? (p. 231)

☐ Did you clearly state your purpose at the start of the memo? (p. 231)

☐ Did you include informative headings to help your readers? (p. 231)

☐ If appropriate, did you summarize your message? (p. 231)

☐ Did you provide appropriate background for the discussion? (p. 231)

☐ Did you organize the discussion clearly? (p. 231)

☐ Did you highlight items requiring action? (p. 231)

E-mail

☐ Did you refrain from discussing nonbusiness subjects? (p. 233)

☐ Did you keep the e-mail as brief as possible and send it only to appropriate people? (p. 233)

☐ Did you use appropriate formality? (p. 234)

☐ Did you write correctly? (p. 234)

☐ Did you avoid flaming? (p. 234)

☐ Did you write a specific, accurate subject line? (p. 234)

☐ Did you use uppercase and lowercase letters? (p. 234)

☐ Did you skip lines between paragraphs? (p. 234)

☐ Did you check with the writer before forwarding his or her message? (p. 234)

Microblogs

☐ Did you study your organization's policy on which microblog sites you may use and how you should use them? (p. 235)

Exercises

1. As the head of research for a biological research organization, you recently purchased a $2,000 commercial refrigerator for storing research samples. Recently, you suffered a loss of more than $600 in samples when the thermostat failed and the temperature in the refrigerator rose to more than 48 degrees over the weekend. Inventing any reasonable details, write a claim letter to the manufacturer of the refrigerator.

2. As the recipient of the claim letter described in Exercise 1, write an adjustment letter granting the customer's request.

3. As the manager of an electronics retail store, you guarantee that you will not be undersold. If a customer finds another retailer selling the same equipment at a lower price within one month of his or her purchase, you will refund the difference. A customer has written to you and enclosed an ad from another store showing that it is selling a router for $26.50 less than he paid at your store. The advertised price at the other store was a one-week sale that began five weeks after the date of his purchase. He wants a $26.50 refund. Inventing any reasonable details, write an adjustment letter denying his request. You are willing, however, to offer him a 4GB USB drive worth $9.95 if he would like to come pick it up.

4. **GROUP EXERCISE** Form small groups for this exercise on claim and adjustment letters. Have each member of your group study the following two letters. Meet and discuss your reactions to the two letters. How effectively does the writer of the claim letter present his case? How effective is the adjustment letter? Does its writer succeed in showing that the company's procedures for ensuring hygiene are effective? Does its writer succeed in projecting a professional tone? Write a memo to your instructor discussing the two letters. Attach a revision of the adjustment letter to the memo.

Seth Reeves
19 Lowry's Lane
Morgan, TN 30610

April 13, 2013

Sea-Tasty Tuna
Route 113
Lynchburg, TN 30563

Gentlemen:

I've been buying your tuna fish for years, and up to now it's been OK.

But this morning I opened a can to make myself a sandwich. What do you think was staring me in the face? A fly. That's right, a housefly. That's him you see taped to the bottom of this letter.

What are you going to do about this?

Yours very truly,

Sea-Tasty Tuna
Route 113
Lynchburg, TN 30563
www.seatastytuna.com

April 20, 2013

Mr. Seth Reeves
19 Lowry's Lane
Morgan, TN 30610

Dear Mr. Reeves:

We were very sorry to learn that you found a fly in your tuna fish.

Here at Sea-Tasty we are very careful about the hygiene of our plant. The tuna are scrubbed thoroughly as soon as we receive them. After they are processed, they are inspected visually at three different points. Before we pack them, we rinse and sterilize the cans to ensure that no foreign material is sealed in them.

Because of these stringent controls, we really don't see how you could have found a fly in the can. Nevertheless, we are enclosing coupons good for two cans of Sea-Tasty tuna.

We hope this letter restores your confidence in us.

Truly yours,

5. Louise and Paul work for the same manufacturing company. Louise, a senior engineer, is chairing a committee to investigate ways to improve the hiring process at the company. Paul, a technical editor, also serves on the committee. The excerpts quoted in Louise's e-mail are from an e-mail written by Paul to all members of the committee in response to Louise's request that members describe their approach to evaluating job-application materials. How would you revise Louise's e-mail to make it more effective?

To: Paul

From: Louise

Sometimes I just have to wonder what you're thinking, Paul.

>Of course, it's not possible to expect perfect
>resumes. But I have to screen them, and
>last year I had to read over 200. I'm not looking for
>perfection, but as soon as I spot an error I make
>a mental note of it and, when I hit a second and
>then a third error I can't really concentrate on the
>writer's credentials.

Listen, Paul, you might be a sharp editor, but the rest of us have a different responsibility: to make the products and move them out as soon as possible. We don't have the luxury of studying documents to see if we can find errors. I suggest you concentrate on what you were hired to do, without imposing your "standards" on the rest of us.

>From my point of view, an error can include a
>misused tradmark.

Misusing a "tradmark," Paul? Is that Error Number 1?

6. **INTERNET EXERCISE** Because students use e-mail to communicate with other group members when they write collaboratively, your college or university would like to create a one-page handout on how to use e-mail responsibly. Using a search engine, find three or four netiquette guides on the Internet that focus on using e-mail. Study these guides and write a one-page student guide to using e-mail to communicate with other students. Somewhere in the guide, be sure to list the sites you studied, so that students can visit them for further information about netiquette..

On the Web

For a case assignment, "Employing the 'You Attitude' in a 'Bad News' Letter," see Cases on <bedfordstmartins.com/ps>.

10

Writing Job-Application Materials

Winston Davidian/Getty Images.

Getting hired always involves writing.

Getting hired has always involved writing. Whether you send a formal letter and résumé through the mail, apply online through a company's Web site, or reply to a posting on Craigslist, you will use words to make the case that the organization should offer you a position.

During your career, you will use your writing skills to apply for a job many times. According to the U.S. Department of Labor (2006), the typical American worker holds more than 10 different jobs while he or she is between the ages of 18 and 38. Every time you apply for a job you will need to change your résumé and your other job-application materials.

Preparing job-application materials requires weeks and months, not days, and there is no way to cut corners. You have to do a self-inventory and learn as much as you can about potential employers. Use a variety of resources, including the job-placement office on campus, published ads, company Web sites, and social media. Perform primary and secondary research on the organizations to which you will apply.

Next, you need to decide whether to write a chronological or skills résumé, each of which emphasizes different aspects of your credentials. You might create a portfolio to show your best work. You will want to revise, edit, and proofread your materials rigorously. Once you have completed your interviews, you will write a letter to each organization that interviewed you.

This chapter discusses how to prepare résumés, job-application letters, portfolios, and follow-up letters.

Focus on Process

In writing job-application materials, pay special attention to these steps in the writing process. For a complete process for writing technical documents, see page 14.

- **Planning.** Learn as much as you can about the organizations to which you will apply. See Chapter 5 for help with research.

- **Drafting.** Decide whether to write a chronological or skills résumé, and use traditional sections and headings. In your job-application letter, elaborate on key points from your résumé.

- **Revising, editing, and proofreading.** You want these documents to be perfect. Ask several people to review them. See the Writer's Checklist on page 271.

WRITING PAPER RÉSUMÉS

For a successful job search, you will likely need to present your credentials both on paper and online. This section discusses the fundamentals for preparing paper résumés. The next section discusses electronic résumés.

Many students wonder whether to write their résumé themselves or use a résumé-preparation agency. It is best to write your own résumé, for three reasons:

- *You know yourself better than anyone else does.* No matter how professional the work of a résumé-preparation agency, you can do a better job communicating important information about yourself.

- *Employment officers know the style of the local agencies.* Readers who recognize that you did not write your own résumé might wonder whether you are hiding any deficiencies.

- *If you write your own résumé, you will be more likely to adapt it to different situations.* You are unlikely to return to a résumé-preparation agency and pay an additional fee to make a minor revision.

A résumé communicates in two ways: through its appearance and through its content.

> **On the Web**
>
> To find job-related resources on the Web, click on Links Library for Ch. 10 on <bedfordstmartins.com/ps>.

Appearance of the Résumé

Your résumé has to look professional. When employers look at a résumé, they see the documents they will be reading if they hire you. Résumés should appear neat and professional. They should have

- *Generous margins.* Leave a one-inch margin on all four sides.
- *Clear type.* Use a good-quality laser printer.
- *Balance.* Arrange the information so that the page has a balanced appearance.
- *Clear organization.* Use adequate white space. The line spacing between items should be greater than the line spacing within an item. That is, there should be more space between your education section and your employment section than between items within either of those sections. You should be able to see the different sections clearly if you view it at 50 percent on your monitor or if you stand and look down at the printed résumé on the floor by your feet.

Indent appropriately. When you arrange items in a vertical list, indent *turnovers*, the second and subsequent lines of any item, a few spaces. The following list, from the computer-skills section of a résumé, could be confusing:

Computer Experience

Systems: PC, Macintosh, Linux, Andover AC–256, Prime 360
Software: Dreamweaver, XMetal, Flash, Visual dBASE 7.5, PlanPerfect, Micrografx
Designer, Adobe InDesign, Microsoft Office
Languages: C#, C++, Java, HTML, XHTML

▶ **In This Book**
For more about page design, see Ch. 7, p. 148.

When the second line of the long entry is indented, the arrangement is much easier to understand:

Computer Experience

Systems: PC, Macintosh, Linux, Andover AC–256, Prime 360
Software: Dreamweaver, XMetal, Flash, Visual dBASE 7.5, PlanPerfect, Micrografx
     Designer, Adobe InDesign, Microsoft Office
Languages: C#, C++, Java, HTML, XHTML

Figure 10.1 shows how an unattractive résumé creates a negative impression, whereas an attractive one creates a positive impression.

Content of the Résumé

Although experts advocate different approaches to résumé writing, they all agree that résumés must be informative as well as attractive.

- *The résumé must provide clear, specific information, without generalizations or self-congratulation.* Your résumé is a sales document, but you are both the

James K. Wislo	1628 Rossi Street
	Boise, ID 83706
	(208) 555 2697
	jameswislo@mail.boisestate.edu
Objective	Entry-level position as a general assistant
Education	Boise State University, Boise, ID
	BS in Biomechanical Engineering
	Current GPA: 3.1
	Expected date of graduation: August 2014
	Related course work Basic Mechanics I
	Skeletal Development and Evolution
	Biomechanics of Movement
	Technical Communication
Employment	1/2010–present (20 hours per week): Custodial and maintenance
	Boise State University, recreation center, Boise, ID
	Install and maintain soap dispenser machines.
	Treat all floors (wooden and linoleum) with appropriate chemicals.
	Pressure-wash showers and sauna using TENNANT 750 machine.
	Report damaged equipment in the building.
	Report any shortage or lack of cleaning detergent and equipment.
	Organize daily and weekly cleaning schedule.
	10/2009–1/2010: Food server
	Aramark Food Service, Boise, ID
	Serve food across counter. Prepare all condiments to be served.
	Clean kitchen and eating area after regular open hours.
	Act as a liaison between students and chef: report on likes and
	dislikes of students.
Honors	National Dean's List, 2009–2010
	Awarded $4,500 GEM scholarship from Boise State University
Activities	Member, Boise State University international student organization
	Certified CPR Instructor, American Red Cross
References	Available upon request

a. Unattractively designed résumé

Figure 10.1   Unattractive and Attractive Résumés

The unattractive résumé, with its inadequate margins, poor balance, and poor line spacing, is a chore to read. The attractive résumé is much easier to read and makes a much better impression on readers.

Figure 10.1 (continued)

James K. Wislo

1628 Rossi Street
Boise, ID 83706

(208) 555-2697
jameswislo@mail.boisestate.edu

Objective   Entry-level position as a general assistant

Education   Boise State University, Boise, ID
BS in Biomechanical Engineering
Current GPA: 3.1
Expected date of graduation: August 2014

Related course work
Skeletal Development and Evolution
Biomechanics of Movement
Basic Mechanics I
Technical Communication

Employment   1/2010–present (20 hours per week): Custodial and maintenance
Boise State University, recreation center, Boise, ID
- Install and maintain soap dispenser machines.
- Treat all floors (wooden and linoleum) with appropriate chemicals.
- Pressure-wash showers and sauna using TENNANT 750 machine.
- Report damaged equipment in the building.
- Report any shortage or lack of cleaning detergent and equipment.
- Organize daily and weekly cleaning schedule.

10/2009–1/2010: Food server
Aramark Food Service, Boise, ID
- Serve food across counter.
- Prepare all condiments to be served.
- Clean kitchen and eating area after regular open hours.
- Act as a liaison between students and chef: report on likes and dislikes of students.

Honors   - National Dean's List, 2009–2010
- Awarded $4,500 GEM scholarship from Boise State University

Activities   - Member, Boise State University international student organization
- Certified CPR Instructor, American Red Cross

References   Available upon request

b. Attractively designed résumé

salesperson and the product. You cannot gracefully say, "I am a terrific job candidate." Instead, you have to show the reader by providing the details that will lead the reader to conclude that you are a terrific job candidate.

- *The résumé must be free of errors.* Writing errors cast doubt on the accuracy of the information in the résumé. Ask for assistance after you have written the draft, and proofread the finished product at least twice. Then have someone else proofread it, too.

A résumé should be long enough to include all pertinent information but not so long that it bores or irritates the reader. A survey from Career-Builder.com found that 52 percent of executives prefer one-page résumés for the typical applicant, whereas 44 percent prefer two pages ("Résumés Redefined," 2008). If you have more experience, your résumé will be longer; if you have less experience, it will be shorter. If the information comes to just over a page, either eliminate or condense some of the material to make it fit onto one page, or modify the layout so that it fills a substantial part of a second page.

ETHICS NOTE

Writing Honest Job-Application Materials

Many résumés contain lies or exaggerations. Job applicants say they attended colleges they didn't and were awarded degrees they weren't, give themselves inflated job titles, say they were laid off when they were really fired for poor performance, and inflate their accomplishments. Companies take this problem seriously. Career-guidance specialist Michelle Goodman (2010) reports that, according to the Society for Human Resource Management, most employers run background checks on applicants, and about a third of these checks reveal significant lies. Employers hire agencies that verify the applicant's education and employment history and check for a criminal record. If the company finds any discrepancies, it does not offer the candidate a position. If the person is already working for the company, he or she is fired.

Two common résumé styles are *chronological* and *skills*. In a *chronological résumé*, you use time as the organizing pattern for each section, including education and experience, and discuss your responsibilities for each job you have held. In a *skills résumé*, you merely list your previous jobs but include a skills section in which you describe your talents and achievements.

Recent graduates usually use the chronological résumé because in most cases they lack the record of skills and accomplishments needed for a skills résumé. However, if you have a lot of professional work experience, consider the skills style.

Elements of the Chronological Résumé

Most chronological résumés have six basic elements: identifying information, objectives or summary of qualifications, education, employment history, interests and activities, and references.

Identifying Information   Include your full name, address, phone number, and e-mail address. Use your complete address, including the zip code. If your address during the academic year differs from your home address, list both and identify them clearly. An employer might call during an academic holiday to arrange an interview.

Objectives or Summary of Qualifications   After the identifying information, add a statement of objectives or a summary of qualifications.

A *statement of objectives*, used most often by candidates new to the field, is a brief phrase or sentence—for example, "Objective: Entry-level position as a hospital dietitian," or "A summer internship in manufacturing processes." When drafting your statement, follow these three suggestions:

- *State only the goals or duties explicitly mentioned, or clearly implied, in the job advertisement.* If you unintentionally suggest that your goals are substantially different from the job responsibilities, the reader might infer that you would not be happy working there and might not consider you further.

- *Focus on the reader's needs, not on your goals.* Instead of stating that you are looking for a position "with opportunities for advancement," find out what the company needs: for example, "Position in Software Engineering specializing in database-applications development that enables me to use my four years of experience developing large enterprise-database solutions based on a normalized relational design."

- *Be specific.* You accomplish little by writing, "Position offering opportunities in the field of health science, where I can use my communication and analytical skills." Specify what kind of position you want—nurse, physician, hospital administrator, pharmaceutical researcher.

Job candidates with more experience tend to write a *summary of qualifications.* This statement is usually a brief paragraph that highlights three or four important skills or accomplishments. For example:

Summary of Qualifications

Six years' experience creating testing documentation to qualify production programs that run on Automated Test and Handling Equipment. Four years' experience running QA tests on software, hardware, and semiconductor products. Bilingual English and Italian. Secret security clearance.

Education   If you are a student or a recent graduate, place the education section next. If you have substantial professional experience, place the employment-history section before the education section.

Include at least the following information in the education section:

- *The degree*. After the degree abbreviation (such as BS, BA, AA, or MS), list your academic major (and, if you have one, your minor)—for example, "BS in Materials Engineering, minor in General Business."

- *The institution*. Identify the institution by its full name: "Louisiana State University," not "LSU."

- *The location of the institution*. Include the city and state.

- *The date of graduation*. If your degree has not yet been granted, add "Anticipated date of graduation" or a similar phrase.

- *Information about other schools you attended*. List any other institutions you attended beyond high school, even those from which you did not earn a degree. The description for other institutions should include the same information as in the main listing. Arrange entries in reverse chronological order: that is, list first the school you attended most recently.

Guidelines

Elaborating on Your Education

The following four guidelines can help you develop the education section of your résumé.

▶ **List your grade-point average.** If your average is significantly above the median for the graduating class, list it. Or list your average in your major courses, or all your courses in the last two years. Calculate it however you wish, but be honest and clear.

▶ **Compile a list of courses.** Include courses that will interest an employer, such as advanced courses in your major, or communications courses, such as technical communication, public speaking, and organizational communication. For example, a list of business courses on an engineer's résumé shows special knowledge and skills. But don't bother listing required courses; everyone else in your major took the same courses. Include the substantive titles of listed courses; employers won't know what "Chemistry 450" is. Call it by its official title: "Chemistry 450. Organic Chemistry."

▶ **Describe a special accomplishment.** For a special senior design or research project, present the title and objective of the project, any special or advanced techniques or equipment you used, and, if you know them, the major results: "A Study of Shape Memory Alloys in Fabricating Actuators for Underwater Biomimetic Applications—a senior design project to simulate the swimming styles and anatomy of fish." A project discussion makes you seem more like a professional: someone who designs and carries out projects.

▶ **List honors and awards you received.** Scholarships, internships, and academic awards suggest exceptional ability. If you have received a number of such honors, or some that were not exclusively academic, you might list them separately (in a section called "Honors" or "Awards") rather than in the education section. Decide where this information will make the best impression.

The education section is the easiest part of the résumé to adapt in applying for different positions. For example, a student majoring in electrical engineering who is applying for a position requiring strong communications skills can list communications courses in one version of the résumé and advanced electrical engineering courses in another version. As you compose the education section, emphasize those aspects of your background that meet the requirements for the particular job.

Employment History   Present at least the basic information about each job you have held: the dates of employment, the organization's name and location, and your position or title. Then, add carefully selected details. Readers want to know what you did and accomplished. Provide at least a two- to three-line description for each position. For particularly important or relevant jobs, write more, focusing on one or more of the following factors:

- *Skills.* What technical skills did you use on the job?
- *Equipment.* What equipment did you operate or oversee? In particular, mention computer equipment or software with which you are familiar.
- *Money.* How much money were you responsible for? Even if you considered your data-entry position fairly easy, the fact that the organization grossed, say, $2 million a year shows that the position involved real responsibility.
- *Documents.* What important documents did you write or assist in writing, such as brochures, reports, manuals, proposals, or Web sites?
- *Personnel.* How many people did you supervise?
- *Clients.* What kinds of, and how many, clients did you do business with in representing your organization?

Whenever possible, emphasize *results*. If you reorganized the shifts of the weekend employees you supervised, state the results:

> Reorganized the weekend shift, resulting in a cost savings of more than $3,000 per year.

In This Book
For more about using strong verbs, see Ch. 6, p. 121.

When you describe positions, functions, or responsibilities, use the active voice ("supervised three workers") rather than the passive voice ("three workers were supervised by me"). The active voice highlights action. Note that writers often omit the *I* at the start of sentences: "Prepared bids," rather than "I prepared bids." Whichever style you use, be consistent. Figure 10.2 lists some strong verbs to use in describing your experience.

Here is a sample listing of employment history:

> June–September 2012: Student Dietitian
> Millersville General Hospital, Millersville, TX
>
> Gathered dietary histories and assisted in preparing menus for a 300-bed hospital. Received "excellent" on all seven items in evaluation by head dietitian.

administered	coordinated	evaluated	maintained	provided
advised	corresponded	examined	managed	purchased
analyzed	created	expanded	monitored	recorded
assembled	delivered	hired	obtained	reported
built	developed	identified	operated	researched
collected	devised	implemented	organized	solved
completed	directed	improved	performed	supervised
conducted	discovered	increased	prepared	trained
constructed	edited	instituted	produced	wrote

Figure 10.2 Strong Verbs Used in Résumés

In just a few lines, you can show that you sought and accepted responsibility and that you acted professionally. Do not write, "I accepted responsibility"; instead, present facts that lead the reader to that conclusion.

Naturally, not all jobs entail professional skills and responsibilities. Many students find summer work as laborers, sales clerks, and so forth. If you have not held a professional position, list the jobs you have held, even if they were unrelated to your career plans. If the job title is self-explanatory, such as waitperson or service-station attendant, don't elaborate. If you can write that you contributed to your tuition or expenses, such as by earning 50 percent of your annual expenses through a job, employers will be impressed by your self-reliance.

One further suggestion: if you have held a number of nonprofessional as well as several professional positions, group the nonprofessional ones:

> Other Employment: cashier (summer 2008), salesperson (part-time, 2009), clerk (summer 2010).

This strategy prevents the nonprofessional positions from drawing the reader's attention away from the more important positions.

List jobs in reverse chronological order on the résumé to highlight the most recent employment.

Two common circumstances call for some subtlety:

- *You have gaps in your employment history.* If you were not employed for several months or years because you were raising children, attending school, recovering from an accident, or for other reasons, consider using a skills résumé, which focuses more on your skills and less on your job history. Also, you can explain the gaps in the cover letter. For instance, you could write, "I spent 2008 and part of 2010 caring for my elderly parent, but during that time I was able to do some substitute teaching and study at home to prepare for my A+ and Network+ certification, which I earned in late 2010." Do not lie or mislead about your dates of employment.

- *You have had several positions with the same employer.* If you want to show that you have had several positions with the same employer, you can present one description that encompasses all the positions or present a separate description for each position.

Presenting One Description

> **Blue Cross of Iowa**, Ames, Iowa (January 2004–present)
>
> - *Internal Auditor II (2008–present)*
> - *Member Service Representative/Claims Examiner II (2006–2008)*
> - *Claims Examiner II (2004–2006)*
>
> As Claims Examiner II, processed national account inquiries and claims in accordance with . . . After promotion to Member Service Representative/ Claims Examiner II position, planned policies and procedures . . . As Internal Auditor II, audit claims, enrollment, and inquiries; run dataset population and sample reports . . .

This format enables you to mention your promotions and to create a clear narrative that emphasizes your progress within the company.

Presenting Separate Descriptions

> **Blue Cross of Iowa**, Ames, Iowa (January 2004–present)
>
> - *Internal Auditor II (2008–present)*
>
>   Audit claims, enrollment, and inquiries . . .
>
> - *Member Service Representative/Claims Examiner II (2006–2008)*
>
>   Planned policies and procedures . . .
>
> - *Claims Examiner II (2004–2006)*
>
>   Processed national account inquiries and claims in accordance with . . .

This format, which enables you to create fuller descriptions of each position, is effective if you are trying to show that each position is distinct and you wish to describe the more-recent positions more fully.

Interests and Activities   The interests-and-activities section of the résumé is the appropriate place for several kinds of information about you:

- participation in community-service organizations (such as Big Brothers/ Big Sisters) or volunteer work in a hospital
- hobbies related to your career (for example, electronics for an engineer)
- sports, especially those that might be socially useful in your professional career, such as tennis, racquetball, and golf
- university-sanctioned activities, such as membership on a team, work on the college newspaper, or election to a responsible position in an academic organization or a residence hall

Do not include activities that might create a negative impression, such as gambling or performing in a rock band. And always omit such activities as meeting people and reading: everybody does these things.

References   Potential employers will want to learn more about you from your professors and previous employers. These people who are willing to speak or write on your behalf are called *references*.

Choose your references carefully. Solicit references only from those who know your work best and for whom you have done your best work—for instance, a previous employer with whom you worked closely or a professor from whom you received A's. Don't ask prominent professors who do not know your work well; they will be unable to write informative letters.

Do not simply assume that someone is willing to serve as a reference for you. Give the potential referee an opportunity to decline gracefully. Sometimes the person has not been as impressed with your work as you think. If you simply ask the person to serve as a reference, he or she might accept and then write a lukewarm letter. It is better to ask, "Would you be able to write an enthusiastic letter for me?" or "Do you feel you know me well enough to write a strong recommendation?" If the person shows any signs of hesitation or reluctance, withdraw the request. It may be a little embarrassing, but it is better than receiving a weak recommendation.

Once you have secured your references' permission to list them, create a references page. This page begins with your name and contact information, just as you present this information at the top of the résumé itself. Some job applicants add, for each reference, a sentence or two describing their relationship with the reference, such as, "Dr. Willerton was my adviser and my instructor for two courses; one in technical editing and one in document design." Figure 10.3 on page 254 shows a references page.

Other Elements   The sections discussed so far appear on almost everyone's résumé. Other sections are either optional or appropriate for only some job seekers.

- *Computer skills.* Classify your skills in categories such as hardware, software, languages, and operating systems. List any professional certifications you have earned.

- *Military experience.* If you are a veteran, describe your military service as if it were a job, citing dates, locations, positions, ranks, and tasks. List positive job-performance evaluations.

- *Language ability.* A working knowledge of another language can be very valuable, particularly if the potential employer has international interests and you could be useful in translation or foreign service. List your proficiency, using terms such as *beginner*, *intermediate*, and *advanced*. Some applicants distinguish among reading, writing, and speaking abilities.

- *Willingness to relocate.* If you are willing to relocate, say so. Many organizations will find you a more attractive candidate.

Samantha Breveux   5986 Center Street   Boise, ID 83703
                              208.555.8693   sbreveux@gmail.com

Professional References

Dr. Dale Cletis   Dr. Cletis was my instructor in three
Professor of English   literature courses, as well as my adviser.
Boise State University
Boise, ID 83725
208.555.2637
dcletis@boisestate.edu

Dr. Miriam Finkelstein   Dr. Finkelstein encouraged me to study
Professor of Economics   for a minor in economics, which I did. She
Boise State University   was my instructor in two courses.
Boise, ID 83725
208.555.9375
mfinkel@boisestate.edu

Dr. Charles Tristan   Dr. Tristan, my instructor in two courses,
Professor of English   encouraged me to study abroad. I spent my
Boise State University   junior year in Paris.
Boise, ID 83725
208.555.1355
ctristan@boisestate.edu

Personal References

Mr. Heiko Yamamoto   For three summers, beginning after my
Yamamoto Paving   high-school graduation, I worked in
1450 Industrial Drive   Mr. Yamamoto's office as a bookkeeper.
Eagle, ID 83467
208.555.2387
heiko@yamamotopaving.com

Mr. Paul Engels   I volunteered my services writing and
Yellow House Literary Cabin   distributing press releases and advertising
1877 Capitol Boulevard   for the Yellow House Literary Cabin.
Boise, ID 83703
208.555.3827
pengels@yellowhouse.org

Martha Cummings, RN   For many years, my family has trained
St. Luke's Regional Medical Center   service dogs for hospital visitations. I
322 Bannock Street   worked with Ms. Cummings during high
Boise, ID 83604   school and my first two years in college in
208.555.3489   helping other service-dog trainers.
mcummings@stlukesrmc.org

Less-advanced job applicants are more likely than more-advanced job applicants to list personal references.

Figure 10.3   References Page

Elements of the Skills Résumé

A skills résumé differs from a chronological résumé in that it includes a separate section, usually called "Skills" or "Skills and Abilities," that emphasizes job skills and knowledge. In a skills résumé, the employment section becomes a brief list of information about your employment history: company, dates of employment, and position. Here is an example of a skills section.

Skills and Abilities

Management
  Served as weekend manager of six employees in a retail clothing business. Also trained three summer interns at a health-maintenance organization.

Writing and Editing
  Wrote status reports, edited performance appraisals, participated in assembling and producing an environmental impact statement using desktop publishing.

Teaching and Tutoring
  Tutored in the University Writing Center. Taught a two-week course in electronics for teenagers. Coach youth basketball.

In a skills section, you choose the headings, the arrangement, and the level of detail. Your goal, of course, is to highlight the skills the employer is seeking.

Figures 10.4, 10.5, and 10.6 on pages 256–58 show three examples of effective résumés.

WRITING ELECTRONIC RÉSUMÉS

Although paper résumés continue to be popular, especially after a company has decided to interview you, electronic résumés are more popular, especially for organizations that receive many applications and especially for a candidate's first contact with the organization. According to CareerBuilder.com, 94 percent of the 500 largest U.S. companies use software for the first look at résumés ("Résumés Redefined," 2008). For this reason, you will need an electronic résumé in addition to your traditional formatted paper résumé.

Most companies use computerized *applicant-tracking systems* to evaluate the dozens, hundreds, or even thousands of job applications they receive every day. Companies store the information from these applications in databases, which they search electronically for desired keywords to generate a pool of applicants for specific positions.

An electronic résumé can take several forms:

- *A formatted résumé attached to an e-mail message*. You attach the word-processing file to an e-mail message. Or you save your résumé as a Portable Document Format (PDF) file and attach it. (A PDF of your résumé retains the formatting of your original and prevents others from modifying

The writer uses design to emphasize his name and provides his contact information, including his e-mail address.

The writer could modify his objective to name the company to which he is applying.

The writer chooses to emphasize his advanced engineering courses. For another position, he might emphasize other courses.

The writer wisely creates a category that calls attention to his academic awards and his membership in his field's major professional organization.

The writer lists his references on a separate page and includes this page in his application materials only if an employer requests it. For each reference, the writer provides complete contact information and a statement describing his relationship to the person, as shown in Fig. 10.3 on p. 254.

CARLOS RODRIGUEZ
3109 Vista Street   Philadelphia, PA 19136   (215) 555-3880   crodrig@dragon.du.edu

Objective
Entry-level position in signal processing

Education
BS in Electrical Engineering
Drexel University, Philadelphia, PA
Anticipated 6/2013
Grade-Point Average: 3.67 (on a scale of 4.0)
Senior Design Project: "Enhanced Path-Planning Software for Robotics"

Advanced Engineering Courses
Digital Signal Processing   Computer Hardware
Introduction to Operating Systems I, II   Systems Design
Digital Filters   Computer Logic Circuits I, II

Employment
6/2010–1/2011 Electrical Engineering Intern II
RCA Advanced Technology Laboratory, Moorestown, NJ
Designed ultra-large-scale integrated circuits using VERILOG and VHDL hardware description languages. Assisted senior engineer in CMOS IC layout, modeling, parasitic capacitance extraction, and PSPICE simulation operations.

6/2009–1/2010 Electrical Engineering Intern I
RCA Advanced Technology Laboratory, Moorestown, NJ
Verified and documented several integrated circuit designs. Used CAD software and hardware to simulate, check, and evaluate these designs. Gained experience with Mathcad.

Honors and Organizations
Eta Kappa Nu (Electrical Engineering Honor Society)
Tau Beta Pi (General Engineering Honor Society)
IEEE

References
Available upon request

Figure 10.4   Chronological Résumé of a Traditional Student

Alice P. Linder

1781 Weber Road
Warminster, PA 18974
(215) 555-3999
linderap423@aol.com

The writer uses a table format for her résumé. Notice that all her headings are contained within the left-hand column.

Objective

An internship in molecular research that uses my computer skills ◄

The writer indicates that she is interested in an internship, not a continuing position.

Education

Harmon College, West Yardley, PA
BS in Bioscience and Biotechnology
Expected Graduation Date: 6/2013

Related Course Work

General Chemistry I, II, III	Biology I, II, III
Organic Chemistry I, II	Statistical Methods for Research
Physics I, II	Technical Communication
Calculus I, II	

The writer's list of courses includes several outside her technical subject area to emphasize the skills she has demonstrated in her career.

Employment Experience

6/2010–present (20 hours per week): Laboratory Assistant Grade 3 ◄
GlaxoSmithKline, Upper Merion, PA
Analyze molecular data on E&S PS300, Macintosh, and IBM PCs. Write programs in C#, and wrote a user's guide for an instructional computing package. Train and consult with scientists and deliver in-house briefings.

All of the writer's positions show an interest in working with people.

8/2007–present: Volunteer, Physical Therapy Unit ◄
Children's Hospital of Philadelphia, Philadelphia, PA
Assist therapists and guide patients with their therapy. Use play therapy to enhance strengthening progress.

The volunteer position says something about the writer's character.

6/1999–1/2002: Office Manager ◄
Anchor Products, Inc., Ambler, PA
Managed 12-person office in $1.2 million company. Also performed general bookkeeping and payroll.

Before attending college, the writer worked as an office manager. Notice how the description of her position suggests that she is a skilled and responsible worker.

Honors

Awarded three $5,000 tuition scholarships (2009–2011) from the Gould Foundation.

Additional Information

Member, Harmon Biology Club, Yearbook Staff
Raising three school-age children ◄
Tuition 100% self-financed

The writer believes that the skills required in raising children are relevant in the workplace. Others might think that because a résumé describes job credentials, this information should be omitted.

References

Available upon request

Figure 10.5   Chronological Résumé of a Nontraditional Student

This is another version of the résumé in Fig. 10.5.

Alice P. Linder   1781 Weber Road   (215) 555-3999
Warminster, PA 18974   linderap423@aol.com

___

Objective   An internship in molecular research that uses my computer skills

___

In a skills résumé, you present the skills section at the start. This organization lets you emphasize your professional attributes. Notice that the writer uses specific details—names of software, number of credits, types of documents, kinds of activities—to make her case.

Skills and Abilities

Laboratory Skills
• Analyze molecular data on E&S PS300, Macintosh, and IBM PCs. Write programs in C#.
• Have taken 12 credits in biology and chemistry labs.

Communication Skills
• Wrote a user's guide for an instructional computing package.
• Train and consult with scientists and deliver in-house briefings.

Management Skills
• Managed 12-person office in $1.2 million company.

___

Education   Harmon College, West Yardley, PA
BS in Bioscience and Biotechnology
Expected Graduation Date: 6/2013

Related Course Work
General Chemistry I, II, III   Biology I, II, III
Organic Chemistry I, II   Statistical Methods for Research
Physics I, II   Technical Communication
Calculus I, II

___

The employment section now contains a list of positions rather than descriptions of what the writer did in each position.

Employment Experience   6/2010–present (20 hours per week)
GlaxoSmithKline, Upper Merion, PA
Laboratory Assistant Grade 3

8/2007–present
Children's Hospital of Philadelphia, Philadelphia, PA
Volunteer, Physical Therapy Unit

6/1999–1/2002
Anchor Products, Inc., Ambler, PA
Office Manager

___

Honors   Awarded three $5,000 tuition scholarships (2009–2011) from the Gould Foundation.

___

Additional Information   Member, Harmon Biology Club, Yearbook Staff
Raising three school-age children
Tuition 100% self-financed

___

References   Available upon request

Figure 10.6   Skills Résumé of a Nontraditional Student

it.) Or you save your file in Rich Text Format (RTF) with the file extension .rtf. An RTF file retains some formatting and makes the information compatible across platforms (Apple, IBM, and UNIX) and word-processing programs (Word, WordPerfect, and others). Attaching an RTF file is a good choice when you do not know which file format the employer prefers. Follow the instructions the company offers on which file type to use and how to submit your materials. If the job ad requests, for example, "a plain-text document sent in the body of the message," do not attach a file.

- A *text résumé*. Also referred to as a *plain-text résumé* or an *ASCII résumé*, a text résumé uses the limited ASCII character set and is saved as a .txt file, which can be entered directly into the organization's keyword-searchable database. You can also paste text résumés piece-by-piece into Web-based forms, which often do not allow you to paste your complete résumé all at once.

- A *scannable résumé (one that will be scanned into an organization's database)*. There are dozens of database programs for this purpose, such as ResTrac or Resumix. Because most employers now prefer electronic submissions, scannable résumés are less common. However, if you submit a printed résumé to a company, you should consider how well the document will scan electronically.

- A *Web-based résumé*. You can put your résumé on your own Web site and hope that employers will come to you, or you can post it to a job board on the Web. As with any information you post on the Internet, you should carefully consider which personal details you reveal on your Web-based résumé.

Ways of creating and sending résumés will undoubtedly change as the technology changes. For now, you need to know that the traditional printed résumé is only one of several ways to present your credentials, and you should keep abreast of new techniques for applying for positions. Which form should your résumé take? Whichever form the organization prefers. If you learn of a position from an ad on the organization's own site, the notice will tell you how to apply.

Content of the Electronic Résumé

Most of the earlier discussion of the content of a printed résumé also applies to an electronic résumé. The résumé must be honest and free of errors, and it must provide clear, specific information.

However, if the résumé is to be entered into a database instead of read by a person, include industry-specific jargon: all the keywords an employment officer might use in searching for qualified candidates. If an employment officer is looking for someone with experience writing Web pages, be sure you include the terms "Web page," "Internet," "XHTML," "Java," "CSS," and any other relevant keywords. If your current position requires an understanding of programming languages, list the languages you know. Also use keywords that refer to your communication skills, such as "public speaking," "oral communication," and "communication skills." In short, whereas a traditional printed résumé focuses on *verbs*—tasks you have done—an electronic résumé focuses on *nouns*.

One hiring consultant puts it this way: "The bottom line is that if you apply for a job with a company that searches databases for keywords, and your résumé doesn't have the keywords the company seeks for the person who fills that job, you are pretty much dead in the water" (Hansen, 2008).

Format of the Electronic Résumé

Because electronic résumés must be easy to read and scan, they require a very simple design. Consequently, they are not as attractive as paper-based résumés, and they are longer, because they use only a single narrow column of text.

▶ On the Web

For more information on formatting electronic résumés, see The Riley Guide: Résumés, Cover Letters. Click on Links Library for Ch. 10 on <bedfordstmartins.com/ps>.

▶ On the Web

To analyze an electronic résumé, see Document Analysis Activities for Ch. 10 on <bedfordstmartins.com/ps>.

Guidelines

Preparing a Plain-Text Résumé

Follow these three suggestions to ensure that your plain-text résumé is formatted correctly.

▶ **Use ASCII text only.** ASCII text includes letters, numbers, and basic punctuation marks. Avoid boldface, italics, underlining, and special characters such as "smart quotation marks" and math symbols. Also avoid horizontal or vertical lines or graphics. To be sure you are using only ASCII characters, save your file as "plain text." Then open it up using your software's text editor, such as Notepad, and check to be sure it contains only ASCII characters: non-ASCII characters will appear as garbage text.

▶ **Left-align the information.** Do not try to duplicate the formatting of a traditional paper résumé. You can't. Instead, left align each new item. For example, here is a sample listing from an employment-experience section:

    6/2009-present
    (20 hours per week)
    GlaxoSmithKline
    Upper Merion, PA
    Laboratory Assistant Grade 3
    Analyze molecular data on E&S PS300, Macintosh, and IBM PCs. Write programs in C#, and wrote a user's guide for an instructional computing package. Train and consult with scientists and deliver in-house briefings.

▶ **Send yourself a test version of the résumé.** When you finish writing and formatting the résumé, send yourself a copy, then open it in your text editor and see if it looks professional.

If you are mailing a paper résumé that will be scanned, follow the seven additional guidelines outlined in the box "Preparing a Scannable Résumé." Figure 10.7 is an example of a scannable résumé.

Alice P. Linder
1781 Weber Road
Warminster, PA 18974
(215) 555-3999
linderap423@aol.com

Objective: An internship in molecular research that uses my computer skills

Skills and Abilities:
Laboratory Skills. Analyze molecular data on E&S PS300, Macintosh, and IBM PCs.
Write programs in C#. Have taken 12 credits in biology and chemistry labs.

Communication Skills. Wrote a user's guide for an instructional computing package.
Train and consult with scientists and deliver in-house briefings.

Management Skills. Managed 12-person office in $1.2 million company.

Education:
Harmon College, West Yardley, PA
BS in Bioscience and Biotechnology
Expected Graduation Date: June 2013

Related Course Work:
General Chemistry I, II, III
Organic Chemistry I, II
Physics I, II
Calculus I, II
Biology I, II, III
Statistical Methods for Research
Technical Communication

Employment Experience:
June 2010-present (20 hours per week)
GlaxoSmithKline, Upper Merion, PA
Laboratory Assistant Grade 3

August 2007-present
Children's Hospital of Philadelphia, Philadelphia, PA
Volunteer, Physical Therapy Unit

June 1999-January 2002
Anchor Products, Inc., Ambler, PA
Office Manager

Honors:
Awarded three $5,000 tuition scholarships (2009-2011) from the Gould Foundation.

Additional Information:
Member, Harmon Biology Club, Yearbook Staff
Raising three school-age children
Tuition 100% self-financed

References:
Available upon request

Figure 10.7   Scannable Résumé

This is an electronic version of the résumé in Fig. 10.6. Notice that the writer uses ASCII text and left justification.

Throughout, the writer includes keywords such as C#, IBM, PC, Macintosh, bioscience, biotechnology, molecular research, laboratory assistant, management, volunteer, and physical therapy.

Guidelines

Preparing a Scannable Résumé

Follow these seven suggestions to make sure your résumé will scan correctly.

- ▶ **Use a good-quality laser printer.** The better the resolution, the better the scanner will work.

- ▶ **Use white paper.** Even a slight tint to the paper can increase the chances that the scanner will misinterpret a character.

- ▶ **Do not fold the résumé.** The fold line can confuse the scanner.

- ▶ **Use a simple sans-serif typeface.** Scanners can easily interpret large, open typefaces such as Arial.

- ▶ **Use a single-column format.** A double-column text will scan inaccurately. Left-align everything.

- ▶ **Use wide margins.** Instead of an 80-character width, set your software for 65. This way, regardless of the equipment the reader is using, the lines will break as you intend them.

- ▶ **Use the space bar instead of the tab key.** Tabs will be displayed according to the settings on the reader's equipment, not the settings on yours. Therefore, use the space bar to move text horizontally.

WRITING JOB-APPLICATION LETTERS

Whether you send a formal letter in the mail or upload a statement to a Web site, you will need to write a job-application letter. The letter is crucial not only because it enables you to argue that you should be considered for a position but also because it shows your writing skills. Make your letter appeal as directly and specifically as possible to a particular person, and make sure it shows your best writing.

Selectivity and Development

The keys to a good letter are selectivity and development. *Select* two or three points of greatest interest to the potential employer and *develop* them into paragraphs. Emphasize results, such as improved productivity or quality or decreased costs. If one of your previous part-time positions called for skills that the employer is looking for, write a substantial paragraph about that position, even though the résumé devotes only a few lines to it.

For most candidates, a job-application letter should fill the better part of a page. For more-experienced candidates, it might fill up to two pages. Regardless, if you write at length on a minor point, you become boring and appear to have poor judgment. Employers seek candidates who can say a lot in a small space.

▶ **In This Book**
For more about letters, see Ch. 9, p. 223.

Elements of the Job-Application Letter

The inside address—the name, title, organization, and address of the recipient—is important because you want to be sure your materials get to the right person. And you don't want to offend that person with a misspelling or an incorrect title. If you are uncertain about any of the information—the reader's name, for example, might have an unusual spelling—verify it by researching the organization on the Internet or by phoning.

When you do not know who should receive the letter, phone the company to find out who manages the department. If you are unsure of the appropriate department or division to write to, address the letter to a high-level executive, such as the president. The letter will get to the right person. Also, because the application includes both a letter and a résumé, use an enclosure notation.

The four-paragraph example discussed here is only a basic model, consisting of an introductory paragraph, two body paragraphs, and a concluding paragraph. At a minimum, your letter should include these four paragraphs, but there is no reason it cannot have five or six.

▶ **In This Book**
For more about developing paragraphs, see Ch. 6, p. 112.

Plan the letter carefully. Draft it and then revise it. Let it sit for a while, then revise it again, and edit and proofread. Spend as much time on it as you can.

The Introductory Paragraph   The introductory paragraph has four specific functions:

- It *identifies your source of information*. In an unsolicited application, all you can do is ask if a position is available. For a solicited application, however, state how you heard about the position.

- It *identifies the position you are interested in*. Often, the organization you are applying to is advertising several positions; if you omit the title of the position you are interested in, your reader might not know which one you seek.

- It *states that you wish to be considered for the position*. Although the context makes your wish obvious, you should mention it because the letter would be awkward without it.

- It *forecasts the rest of the letter*. Choose a few phrases that forecast the body of the letter so that the letter flows smoothly. For example, if you use the phrase "retail experience" in the opening paragraph, you are preparing your reader for the discussion of your retail experience later in the letter.

These four points need not appear in any particular order, nor does each need to be covered in a single sentence. The following sample paragraphs demonstrate different ways of providing the necessary information:

Response to a Job Ad

I am writing in response to your notice in the online May 13 *New York Times.* I would like to be considered for the position in system programming. I hope you find that my studies in computer science at Eastern University, along with my programming experience at Airborne Instruments, qualify me for the position.

Unsolicited Job Application

My academic training in hotel management and my experience with Sheraton International have given me a solid background in the hotel industry. Would you please consider me for any management trainee position that might be available?

Unsolicited Personal Contact

Mr. Howard Alcott of your Research and Development Department suggested that I write to you. He thinks that my organic chemistry degree and my practical experience with Brown Laboratories might be of value to XYZ Corporation. Do you have an entry-level position in organic chemistry for which I might be considered?

The Education Paragraph For most students, the education paragraph should come before the employment paragraph because the education paragraph will be stronger. However, if your employment experience is stronger, present it first.

In writing your education paragraph, take your cue from the job ad (if you are responding to one). What aspect of your education most directly fits the job requirements? If the ad stresses versatility, you might structure your paragraph around the range and diversity of your courses. Also, you might discuss course work in a subject related to your major, such as business or communication skills. Extracurricular activities are often very valuable; if you were an officer in a student organization, you could discuss the activities and programs that you coordinated. Perhaps the most popular strategy for developing the education paragraph is to discuss skills and knowledge gained from advanced course work in your major field.

Example About a Project Based on a Course Assignment

At Eastern University, I have taken a wide range of science courses, but my most advanced work has been in chemistry. In one laboratory course, I developed a new aseptic brewing technique that lowered the risk of infection by more than 40 percent. This new technique was the subject of an article in the *Eastern Science Digest.* Representatives from three national breweries have visited our laboratory to discuss the technique with me.

Note that the writer identifies the date of the ad, the name of the publication, and the name of the position. Then, she forecasts the main points she will make in the body of the letter.

The writer politely requests that the reader consider his application.

Notice the tone in all three of these samples: quiet self-confidence. Don't oversell yourself ("I am the candidate you have been hoping for") or undersell yourself ("I don't know that much about computers, but I am willing to learn").

Note that the writer develops one idea, presenting enough information about it to interest the reader. Paragraphs that merely list a number of courses that the writer has taken are ineffective: everyone takes courses.

Example About Writing a Document

To broaden my education at Southern University, I took eight business courses in addition to my requirements for a degree in civil engineering. Because your ad mentions that the position will require substantial client contact, I believe that my work in marketing, in particular, would be of special value. In an advanced marketing seminar, I used InDesign to produce a 20-page sales brochure describing the various kinds of building structures for sale by Oppenheimer Properties to industrial customers in our section of the city. That brochure is now being used at Oppenheimer, where I am an intern.

The writer elaborates on a field other than his major. Note how he develops an idea based on a detail in the job ad. This strategy shows that he studied the ad carefully and wrote a custom letter. This initiative makes this the sort of candidate most hiring officials would like to interview.

Example About a Competition

The most rewarding part of my education at Western University occurred outside the classroom. My entry in a fashion-design competition sponsored by the university won second place. More important, through the competition I met the chief psychologist at Western Regional Hospital, who invited me to design clothing for people with disabilities. I have since completed six different outfits, which are now being tested at the hospital. I hope to be able to pursue this interest once I start work.

The writer develops an effective paragraph about a small aspect of her credentials. She sounds like a focused, intelligent person who wants to do some good.

An additional point: if you haven't already specified your major and your college or university in the introductory paragraph, be sure to do so here.

The Employment Paragraph Like the education paragraph, the employment paragraph should begin with a topic sentence and develop a single idea. That idea might be that you have a broad background or that one job in particular has given you special skills that make you especially well suited for the available job.

Example About Advancement on the Job

For the past three summers and part-time during the academic year, I have worked for Redego, Inc., a firm that specializes in designing and planning industrial complexes. I began as an assistant in the drafting room. By the second summer, I was accompanying a civil engineer on field inspections. Most recently, I have used Auto-CAD to assist an engineer in designing and drafting the main structural supports for a 15-acre, $30 million chemical facility.

The writer makes the point that he is being promoted within the company because of his good work. Notice his reference to the specialized software and the size of the project.

Example About Experience Working Collaboratively

Although I have worked every summer since I was 15, my most recent position, as a technical editor, was the most rewarding. I was chosen by Digital Systems, Inc., from among 30 candidates because of my dual background in computer science and writing. My job was to coordinate the editing of computer manuals. Our copy editors, most of whom were not trained in computer science, needed someone to help verify the technical accuracy of their revisions. When I was unable to answer their questions, I was responsible for interviewing our systems analysts to find the correct answers and to make sure the computer novice could follow them. This position gave me a good understanding of the process of creating operating manuals.

The writer starts by suggesting that he is hardworking. Notice that he doesn't say it explicitly; rather, he provides evidence to lead the reader to that conclusion.

Another theme in this paragraph is that the writer knows how to work with people effectively. Again, he doesn't say it; he implies it.

In this paragraph, the writer suggests that she has technical and interpersonal skills and that her company thought she did an excellent job on a project she coordinated.

The theme of all these samples is that an effective paragraph has a sharp focus and specific evidence and that it clearly suggests the writer's qualifications.

Example Based on Project-Based Experience

I have worked in merchandising for three years as a part-time and summer salesperson in men's fashions and accessories. I have had experience running inventory-control software and helped one company switch from a manual to an online system. Most recently, I assisted in clearing $200,000 in closeout men's fashions: I coordinated a campaign to sell half of the merchandise at cost and was able to convince the manufacturer's representative to accept the other half for full credit. For this project, I received a certificate of appreciation from the company president.

Although you will discuss your education and experience in separate paragraphs, try to link these two halves of your background. If an academic course led to an interest that you were able to pursue in a job, make that point in the transition from one paragraph to the other. Similarly, if a job experience helped shape your academic career, tell the reader about it.

The Concluding Paragraph   The purpose of the concluding paragraph is to motivate the reader to invite you for an interview. In the preceding paragraphs, you provided the information that you hope has convinced the reader to give you another look. In the last paragraph, you want to make it easy for him or her to do so. The concluding paragraph contains three main elements:

- A *reference to your résumé*. If you have not yet referred to it, do so now.
- A *polite but confident request for an interview*. Use the phrase *at your convenience*. Don't make the request sound as if you're asking a personal favor.
- *Your phone number and e-mail address*. State the time of day you can be reached. Adding an e-mail address gives the employer one more way to get in touch with you.

Example 1

The enclosed résumé provides more information about my education and experience. Could we meet at your convenience to discuss the skills and experience I could bring to Pentamax? You can leave a message for me anytime at (303) 555-5957 or cfilli@claus.cmu.edu.

Example 2

All job letters end with a paragraph that urges the reader to contact the writer and provides the contact information that makes it easy to do so.

More information about my education and experience is included on the enclosed résumé, but I would appreciate the opportunity to meet with you at your convenience to discuss my application. You can reach me after noon on Tuesdays and Thursdays at (212) 555-4527 or anytime at rforster@psu.edu.

The examples of effective job-application letters in Figures 10.8 and 10.9 on pages 267–68 correspond to the résumés in Figures 10.4 and 10.5.

Figure 10.8
Job-Application Letter

3109 Vista Street
Philadelphia, PA 19136

January 20, 2013

Mr. Stephen Spencer, Director of Personnel
Department 411
Boeing Naval Systems
103 Industrial Drive
Wilmington, DE 20093

Dear Mr. Spencer:

I am writing in response to your advertisement in the January 16 *Philadelphia Inquirer*. Would you please consider me for the position in Signal Processing? I believe that my academic training in electrical engineering at Drexel University, along with my experience with the RCA Advanced Technology Laboratory, would qualify me for the position.

My education at Drexel has given me a strong background in computer hardware and system design. I have concentrated on digital and computer applications, developing and designing computer and signal-processing hardware in two graduate-level engineering courses. For my senior design project, I am working with four other undergraduates in using OO programming techniques to enhance the path-planning software for an infrared night-vision robotics application.

While working at the RCA Advanced Technology Laboratory, I was able to apply my computer experience to the field of DSP. I designed ultra-large-scale integrated circuits using VERILOG and VHDL hardware description languages. In addition, I assisted a senior engineer in CMOS IC layout, modeling, parasitic capacitance extraction, and PSPICE simulation operations.

The enclosed résumé provides an overview of my education and experience. Could I meet with you at your convenience to discuss my qualifications for this position? Please leave a message anytime at (215) 555-3880 or e-mail me at crodrig@dragon.du.edu.

Yours truly,

Carlos Rodriguez

Carlos Rodriguez

Enclosure (1)

Notice that the writer's own name does not appear at the top of his letter.

In the inside address, he uses the reader's courtesy title, "Mr."

The writer points out that he has taken two graduate courses. Notice that he discusses his senior design project, which makes him look more like an engineer solving a problem than a student taking a course.

Notice the use of "In addition" to begin the third sentence. This phrase breaks up the "I" openings of several sentences.

An enclosure notation refers to his résumé.

Figure 10.9
Job-Application Letter

The writer gracefully suggests that she would be an even better candidate this year than last year.

The writer is making two points: she is experienced in the lab, and she is an experienced communicator.

By mentioning her portfolio, she is suggesting that she would be happy to show the reader her documents. This statement is an example of understated self-confidence.

1781 Weber Road
Warminster, PA 18974

January 17, 2013

Ms. Hannah Gail
Fox Run Medical Center
399 N. Abbey Road
Warminster, PA 18974

Dear Ms. Gail:

Last April I contacted your office regarding the possibility of an internship as a laboratory assistant at your center. Your assistant, Mary McGuire, told me then that you might consider such a position this year. With the experience I have gained since last year, I believe I would be a valuable addition to your center in many ways.

At Harmon College, I have earned a 3.7 GPA in 36 credits in chemistry and biology; all but two of these courses had laboratory components. One skill stressed at Harmon is the ability to communicate effectively, both in writing and orally. Our science courses have extensive writing and speaking requirements; my portfolio includes seven research papers and lab reports of more than 20 pages each, and I have delivered four oral presentations, one of 45 minutes, to classes.

At GlaxoSmithKline, where I currently work part-time, I analyze molecular data on an E&S PS300, a Macintosh, and an IBM PC. I have tried to remain current with the latest advances; my manager at GlaxoSmithKline has allowed me to attend two different two-day in-house seminars on computerized data analysis using SAS. My experience as the manager of a 12-person office for four years helped me acquire interpersonal skills that would benefit Fox Run.

More information about my education and experience is included on the enclosed résumé, but I would appreciate the opportunity to meet with you at your convenience to discuss my application. If you would like any additional information about me or Harmon's internship program, please call me at (215) 555-3999 or e-mail me at linderap423@aol.com.

Very truly yours,

Alice P. Linder

Alice P. Linder

Enclosure

PREPARING A PORTFOLIO

A *portfolio* is a collection of your best work. You can give a prospective employer a copy of the portfolio to showcase your skills. For technical communicators, the portfolio will include a variety of documents made in courses and in previous positions. For technical professionals, it might include proposals and reports as well as computer simulations, Web sites, or presentation graphics. A portfolio can be presented in a loose-leaf notebook, with each item preceded by a statement that describes the item, explains the context in which it was written, and evaluates it.

Often, a portfolio is digital, presented on a CD or on a Web site. Items typically presented in an electronic portfolio include a résumé, letters of recommendation, transcripts and professional certifications, and reports, papers, Web sites, slides of oral presentations, and other types of documents you have written or created as a student or an employee.

Because the portfolio is electronic, it can include all kinds of media, from simple word-processed documents to HTML files, video, audio, and animation. And it's relatively easy to update an electronic portfolio. Just add the new items as you create them. One important point comes across clearly in a carefully prepared electronic portfolio: you know how to create a Web site.

e-Pages

To analyze a sample online portfolio by a student, visit <bedfordstmartins.com/ps/epages>.

On the Web

For more on online portfolios, see "Developing Your Online Portfolio" by Kevin M. Barry and Jill C. Wesolowski. Click on Links Library for Ch. 10 on <bedfordstmartins.com/ps>.

WRITING FOLLOW-UP LETTERS OR E-MAILS AFTER AN INTERVIEW

After an interview, you should write a letter or e-mail of appreciation. If you are offered the job, you also may have to write a letter accepting or rejecting the position.

- *Letter of appreciation after an interview.* Thank the interviewer for taking the time to see you, and emphasize your particular qualifications. You can also restate your interest in the position. A follow-up letter can do more good with less effort than any other step in the job-application procedure because so few candidates bother to write one.

Dear Mr. Weaver:

Thank you for taking the time yesterday to show me your facilities and to introduce me to your colleagues.

Your advances in piping design were particularly impressive. As a person with hands-on experience in piping design, I can appreciate the advantages your design will have.

The vitality of your projects and the good fellowship among your employees further confirm my initial belief that Cynergo would be a fine place to work. I would look forward to joining your staff.

Sincerely yours,

Harriet Bommarito

Harriet Bommarito

- *Letter accepting a job offer*. This one is easy: express appreciation, show enthusiasm, and repeat the major terms of your employment.

  Dear Mr. Weaver:

  Thank you very much for the offer to join your staff. I accept.

  I look forward to joining your design team on Monday, July 19. The salary, as you indicate in your letter, is $48,250.

  As you have recommended, I will get in touch with Mr. Matthews in Personnel to get a start on the paperwork.

  I appreciate the trust you have placed in me, and I assure you that I will do what I can to be a productive team member at Cynergo.

  Sincerely yours,

  Mark Greenberg

  Mark Greenberg

- *Letter rejecting a job offer*. If you decide not to accept a job offer, express your appreciation and, if appropriate, explain why you are declining the offer. Remember, you might want to work for this company sometime in the future.

  Dear Mr. Weaver:

  I appreciate very much the offer to join your staff.

  Although I am certain that I would benefit greatly from working at Cynergo, I have decided to take a job with a firm in Baltimore, where I have been accepted at Johns Hopkins to pursue my master's degree at night.

  Again, thank you for your generous offer.

  Sincerely yours,

  Cynthia O'Malley

  Cynthia O'Malley

- *Letter acknowledging a rejection*. Why write back after you have been rejected for a job? To maintain good relations. You might get a phone call the next week explaining that the person who accepted the job has had to change her plans and offering you the position.

  Dear Mr. Weaver:

  I was disappointed to learn that I will not have a chance to join your staff, because I feel that I could make a substantial contribution. However, I realize that job decisions are complex, involving many candidates and many factors.

  Thank you very much for the courtesy you have shown me.

  Sincerely yours,

  Paul Goicochea

  Paul Goicochea

Writer's Checklist

Printed Résumé

- ☐ Does the résumé have a professional appearance, with generous margins, a balanced layout, adequate white space, and effective indentation? (p. 244)
- ☐ Is the résumé honest? (p. 247)
- ☐ Is the résumé free of errors? (p. 247)
- ☐ Does the résumé meet the needs of its readers? (p. 248)
- ☐ Does the identifying information contain your name, address(es), phone number(s), and e-mail address(es)? (p. 248)
- ☐ Does the résumé include a clear statement of your job objectives or a summary of your qualifications? (p. 248)
- ☐ Does the education section include your degree, your institution and its location, and your (anticipated) date of graduation, as well as any other information that will help a reader appreciate your qualifications? (p. 249)
- ☐ Does the employment section include, for each job, the dates of employment, the organization's name and location, and (if you are writing a chronological résumé) your position or title, as well as a description of your duties and accomplishments? (p. 250)
- ☐ Does the interests-and-activities section include relevant hobbies or activities, including extracurricular interests? (p. 252) Have you omitted any personal information that might reflect poorly on you? (p. 253)
- ☐ Does the references section include the names, job titles, organizations, mailing addresses, and phone numbers of three or four references? (p. 253) If you are not listing this information, does the strength of the rest of the résumé offset the omission? (p. 253)
- ☐ Does the résumé include any other appropriate sections, such as skills and abilities, military service, language abilities, or willingness to relocate? (p. 253)

Electronic Résumé

In addition to the items mentioned in the checklist for the printed résumé, did you

- ☐ use plain text? (p. 259)
- ☐ use a simple sans-serif typeface? (p. 262)
- ☐ use a single-column format? (p. 262)
- ☐ use wide margins? (p. 262)
- ☐ use the space bar instead of the tab key? (p. 262)

Job-Application Letter

- ☐ Does the letter meet your reader's needs? (p. 262)
- ☐ Does the letter look professional? (p. 263)
- ☐ Is the letter honest? (p. 263)
- ☐ Does the introductory paragraph identify your source of information and the position you are applying for, state that you wish to be considered, and forecast the rest of the letter? (p. 263)
- ☐ Does the education paragraph respond to your reader's needs with a unified idea introduced by a topic sentence? (p. 264)
- ☐ Does the employment paragraph respond to your reader's needs with a unified idea introduced by a topic sentence? (p. 265)
- ☐ Does the concluding paragraph include a reference to your résumé, a request for an interview, your phone number, and your e-mail address? (p. 266)
- ☐ Does the letter include an enclosure notation? (p. 267)

Follow-up Letters

- ☐ Does your letter of appreciation for a job interview thank the interviewer and briefly restate your qualifications? (p. 269)
- ☐ Does your letter accepting a job offer show enthusiasm and repeat the major terms of your employment? (p. 270)
- ☐ Does your letter rejecting a job offer express your appreciation and, if appropriate, explain why you are declining the offer? (p. 270)
- ☐ Does your letter acknowledging a rejection have a positive tone that will help you maintain good relations? (p. 270)

Exercises

▶ **In This Book**   For more about memos, see Ch. 9, p. 223.

1. **INTERNET EXERCISE** Using a job board on the Web, list and briefly describe five positions in your field in your state. What skills, experience, and background does each position require? What is the salary range for each position?

2. **INTERNET EXERCISE** Locate and provide the URLs of three job boards that provide interactive forms for creating a résumé automatically. In a brief memo to your instructor, describe the strengths and weaknesses of each. Which job board appears to be the easiest to use? Why?

3. The following résumé was submitted in response to an ad describing the following duties: "CAM Technician to work with other technicians and manage some GIS and mapping projects. Also perform updating of the GIS database. Experience required." In a brief memo to your instructor, describe how effective the résumé is. What are some of its problems?

Kenneth Bradley

530 Maplegrove   Bozeman, Mont. 59715 (406)-484-2916

Objective	Entry level position as a CAM Technician. I am also interested in staying with the company until after graduation, possibly moving into a position as a Mechanical Engineer.
Education	Enrolled at Montana State University August 2011- Present
Employment	Fred Meyer 65520 Chinden Garden City, MT (208)-323-7030 ***Janitor- 7/10-6/11*** Responsible for cleaning entire store, as well as equipment maintenance and floor maintenance and repair. ***Assistant Janitorial Manager- 6/11-9/11*** Responsible for cleaning entire store, equipment maintenance, floor maintenance and repair, scheduling, and managing personnel ***Head of Freight- 9/11-Present*** In charge of braking down all new freight, stocking shelves, cleaning the stock room, and managing personnel **Montana** State University Bozeman, MT ***Teachers Aide ME 120- 1/10-5/10*** ***Teachers Aide ME 120*** In charge of keeping students in line and answering any questions related to drafting.

References   Timothy Rayburn
Janitorial Manager
(406)-555-8571

Eduardo Perez
Coworker
(406)-555-2032

4. The following application letter responds to an ad describing the following duties: "CAM Technician to work with other technicians and manage some GIS and mapping projects. Also perform updating of the GIS database. Experience required." In a brief memo to your instructor, describe how effective the letter is and how it could be improved.

530 Maplegrove
Bozeman, Mont. 59715
November 11, 2013

Mr. Bruce Hedley
Adecco Technical
Bozeman, Mont. 59715

Dear Mr. Hedley,

I am writing you in response to your ad on Monsterjobs .com. Would you please consider me for the position of CAM technician? I believe that my academic schooling at Montana State University, along with my work experience would make me an excellent candidate for the position.

While at Montana State University, I took one class in particular that applies well to this job. It was a CAD drafting class, which I received a 97% in. The next semester I was a Teachers Aid for that same class, where I was responsible for answering questions about drafting from my peers. This gave me a much stronger grasp on all aspects of CAD work than I could have ever gotten from simply taking the class.

My employment at Fred Meyer is also a notable experience. While there is no technical aspects of either positions I have held, I believe that my experience there will shed light on my work ethic and interpersonal skills. I started out as a graveyard shift janitor, with no previous experience. All of my coworkers were at least thirty years older than me, and had a minimum of five years of janitorial experience. However after working there for only one year I was promoted to assistant manager. Three months after I received this position, I was informed that Fred Meyer was going to contract out the janitorial work and that all of us would be losing our jobs. I decided that I wanted to stay within the company, and I was able to receive a position as head of freight.

The enclosed resumé provides an overview of my education and work experience. I would appreciate an opportunity to meet with you at your convience to disscuss my qualifications for this position. Please write me at the above address or leave a message anytime. If you would like to contact me by e-mail, my e-mail address is kbradley @montanastate.edu.

Yours truly,

Ken Bradley

5. How effective is the following letter of appreciation? How could it be improved? Present your findings in a brief memo to your instructor.

914 Imperial Boulevard
Durham, NC 27708

November 13, 2013

Mr. Ronald O'Shea
Division Engineering
Safeway Electronics, Inc.
Holland, MI 49423

Dear Mr. O'Shea:

Thanks very much for showing me around your plant. I hope I was able to convince you that I'm the best person for the job.

Sincerely yours,

Robert Harad

6. In a newspaper or journal or on the Internet, find a job ad for a position in your field for which you might be qualified. Write a résumé and a job-application letter in response to the ad; include a copy of the ad. You will be evaluated not only on the content and appearance of the materials, but also on how well you have targeted them to the job ad.

On the Web

For a case assignment, "Adding 'Social' to 'Networking,'" see Cases on <bedfordstmartins.com/ps>.

11

Writing Proposals

U.S. Air Force photo by Don Lindsey.

Whether the project is small or big, it is likely to call for a proposal.

This photo shows an Air Force airman piloting a cockpit simulator at a symposium attended by military personnel and defense contractors. The military buys almost everything it uses—from food and water to uniforms, equipment, weapons systems, and security—from suppliers who compete for the contracts by writing proposals.

A proposal is an offer to carry out research or to provide a product or service. For instance, a physical therapist might write a proposal to her supervisor for funding to attend a convention to learn about current rehabilitation practices. The director of a homeless shelter might write a proposal for funding to expand the services offered by the shelter. Whether the project is small or big, within your own company or outside it, it is likely to call for a proposal.

THE LOGISTICS OF PROPOSALS

Proposals can be classified as either internal or external; external proposals are either solicited or unsolicited. Figure 11.1 shows the relationship among these four terms.

Internal and External Proposals

Proposals are either internal (submitted to the writer's own organization) or external (submitted to another organization).

Internal Proposals   An internal proposal is an argument, submitted within an organization, for carrying out an activity that will benefit the organization. An internal proposal might recommend that the organization conduct research, purchase a product, or change some aspect of its policies or procedures.

For example, one day, while working on a project in the laboratory, you realize that if you had a fiber-curl measurement system, you could do your job better and faster. The increased productivity would save your company the cost of the system

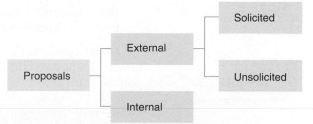

Figure 11.1   The Logistics of Proposals

in a few months. Your supervisor asks you to write a memo describing what you want, why you want it, what you're going to do with it, and what it costs; if your request seems reasonable and the money is available, you'll likely get the new system.

Often, the scope of the proposal determines its format. A request for a small amount of money might be conveyed orally or by e-mail or a brief memo. A request for a large amount, however, is likely presented in a formal document such as a report.

External Proposals   No organization produces all the products or provides all the services it needs. Web sites need to be designed, written, and maintained; inventory databases need to be created; facilities need to be constructed. Sometimes projects require unusual expertise, such as sophisticated market analyses. Because many companies supply these products and services, most organizations require that a prospective supplier compete for the business by submitting a proposal, a document arguing that it deserves the business.

Solicited and Unsolicited Proposals

External proposals are either solicited or unsolicited. A *solicited proposal* is submitted in response to a request from the prospective customer. An *unsolicited proposal* is submitted by a supplier who believes that the prospective customer has a need for goods or services.

Solicited Proposals   When an organization wants to purchase a product or service, it publishes one of two basic kinds of statements:

- An *information for bid (IFB)* is used for standard products. When a state agency needs desktop computers, for instance, it informs computer manufacturers of the configuration it needs. All other things being equal, the supplier that offers the lowest bid wins the contract.

- A *request for proposal (RFP)* is used for more-customized products or services. For example, if the Air Force needs an "identification of friend from foe" device, the RFP it publishes might be a long and detailed set of technical specifications. The supplier that can design, produce, and deliver the device most closely resembling the specifications—at a reasonable price—will probably win the contract.

Most organizations issue RFPs and IFBs in print and online. Government RFPs and IFBs are published on the FedBizOpps Web site. Figure 11.2 shows a portion of an RFP.

Unsolicited Proposals   An unsolicited proposal is like a solicited proposal except that it does not refer to an RFP. Even though the potential customer never formally requested the proposal, in most cases, the supplier was

On the Web
For links to FedBizOpps, click on Links Library for Ch. 11 on <bedfordstmartins.com/ps>.

WETLAND CONSTRUCTION INSPECTOR SVCS.

Solicitation Number: NRCS-FL-10-07
Agency: Department of Agriculture
Office: Natural Resources Conservation Service
Location: Florida State Office

Synopsis:

The USDA Natural Resources Conservation Service (NRCS) in Florida requires the services of a qualified Wetland Construction Inspector to perform construction inspection services in the State of Florida and is issuing a Request for Proposal. This acquisition process is being conducted in accordance with FAR Subparts 12 & 15. This is a combined synopsis/solicitation for commercial items prepared in accordance with the format in Subpart 12.6, as supplemented with additional information in this notice. This announcement constitutes the only solicitation; proposals are being requested and a written solicitation will not be issued. The primary North American Industrial Classification System Code (NAICS) is 541690. Successful Offeror must be registered in the Central Contractor Registration (CCR) database prior to award.

Statement of Work: The Inspector must be a qualified construction inspector, preferably with experience in wetland restoration projects. This item includes providing construction inspection services to ensure the wetland restoration project is installed in accordance with the engineering plans and specifications. Qualified construction inspectors will be required to perform construction inspection services on a variety of construction practices including but not limited to: construction layout, checking elevations and grades of works of improvement, areas requiring clearing and grubbing, structure removal, excavation, earthfill, pipe installation, vegetative measures, and pest management. Practices requiring construction inspection services will be identified in the site specific Quality Assurance Plan (example attached). Other duties include maintaining timely communication with the Contracting Officer's Technical Representative (COTR) and contractor, keeping daily job diaries, computing quantities as per the bid schedule and construction specifications, reviewing shop drawings, taking photographs of critical work and maintaining a photograph log, construction checkout, and developing as-built construction drawings. (See attached Design and Engineering Services Specifications.) . . .

Contracting Office Address:

2614 NW 43rd Street
Gainesville, Florida 32606

Place of Performance:

Throughout state of Florida, Various, Florida, United States

Figure 11.2   Excerpt from an RFP
Source: FedBizOpps.gov, 2010 <www.fbo.gov/?s=opportunity&mode=form&id
=7d54e4cc37cd00c29bcddc2a2cfc2715&tab=core&_cview=1>.

invited to submit the proposal after people from the two organizations met and discussed the project. Because proposals are expensive to write, suppliers are reluctant to submit them without assurances that they will be considered carefully. Thus, the word *unsolicited* is only partially accurate.

THE "DELIVERABLES" OF PROPOSALS

A *deliverable* is what the supplier will deliver at the end of the project. Deliverables can be classified into two major categories: research or goods and services.

Research Proposals

On the Web

For sample proposals and writing checklists, see Writing Guidelines for Engineering and Science Students. Click on Links Library for Ch. 11 on <bedfordstmartins.com/ps>.

In a research proposal, you are promising to perform research and then provide a report about it. For example, a biologist for a state bureau of land management writes a proposal to the National Science Foundation requesting resources to build a window-lined tunnel in the forest to study tree and plant roots and the growth of fungi. The biologist also wishes to investigate the relationship between plant growth and the activity of insects and worms. The deliverable will be a report submitted to the National Science Foundation and, perhaps, an article published in a professional journal.

Research proposals often lead to two other applications: progress reports and completion reports.

After a proposal has been approved and the researchers have begun work, they often submit one or more *progress reports*, which tell the sponsor of the project how the work is proceeding. Is it following the plan of work outlined in the proposal? Is it going according to schedule? Is it staying within budget?

In This Book

For more about progress reports and recommendation reports, see Ch. 12, p. 302, and Ch. 13.

At the end of the project, researchers prepare a *completion report*, often called a *final report*, a *project report*, a *recommendation report*, or simply a *report*. A completion report tells the whole story of the research project, beginning with the problem or opportunity that motivated it, the methods used in carrying it out, and the results, conclusions, and recommendations.

People carry out research projects to satisfy their curiosity and to advance professionally. Organizations often require that their professional employees carry out research and publish in appropriate reports, journals, or books. Government researchers and university professors, for instance, are expected to remain active in their fields. Writing proposals is one way to get the resources—time and money for travel, equipment, and assistants—to carry out the research.

Goods and Services Proposals

A *goods and services proposal* is an offer to supply a tangible product (a fleet of automobiles), a service (building maintenance), or some combination of the two (the construction of a building).

A vast network of goods and services contracts spans the working world. The U.S. government, the world's biggest customer, spent $297 billion in 2007 buying military equipment from organizations that submitted proposals (U.S. Department of Commerce, 2010, p. 494). But goods and services contracts are by no means limited to government contractors. An auto manufacturer might buy its engines from another manufacturer; a company that makes spark plugs might buy its steel from another company.

Another kind of goods and services proposal requests funding to support a local organization. For example, a homeless shelter might receive some of its funding from a city or county but might rely on grants from private philanthropies. Typically, an organization such as a shelter would apply for a grant to fund increased demand for its services due to a natural disaster or an economic slowdown in the community. Or it might apply for a grant to fund a pilot program to offer job training at the shelter. Most large corporations have philanthropic programs offering grants to help local colleges and universities, arts organizations, and social services.

PERSUASION AND PROPOSALS

A proposal is an argument. You must convince readers that the future benefits will outweigh the immediate and projected costs. Basically, you must persuade your readers of three things:

- that you understand their needs
- that you have already determined what you plan to do and that you are able to do it
- that you are a professional and are committed to fulfilling your promises

Understanding Readers' Needs

The most crucial element of the proposal is the definition of the problem or opportunity to which the proposed project responds. Although this point seems obvious, people who evaluate proposals agree that the most common weakness they see is an inadequate or inaccurate understanding of the problem or opportunity.

In This Book

For more about analyzing your audience, see Ch. 4.

Readers' Needs in an Internal Proposal   Writing an internal proposal is both simpler and more complicated than writing an external one. It is simpler because you have greater access to internal readers than you do to external readers, and you can get information more easily. However, it is more complicated because you might find it hard to understand the situation in your organization. Some colleagues will not tell you that your proposal is a long shot or that your ideas might threaten someone in the organization. Before you write an internal proposal, discuss your ideas with as many potential readers as you can to learn what the organization really thinks of them.

Readers' Needs in an External Proposal   Most readers will reject a proposal as soon as they realize that it doesn't address their needs. When you receive an RFP, study it thoroughly. If you don't understand something in it, contact the organization. They will be happy to clarify it, because a poor proposal wastes everyone's time.

When you write an unsolicited proposal, analyze your audience carefully. How can you define the problem or opportunity so that readers will understand it? Keep in mind readers' needs and, if possible, their backgrounds. Concentrate on how the problem has decreased productivity or quality or how your ideas would create new opportunities. When you submit an unsolicited proposal, your task in many cases is to convince readers that a need exists. Even when you have reached an understanding with some of your customer's representatives, your proposal will still have to persuade other officials in the company.

When you are preparing a proposal to be submitted to an organization in another culture, keep in mind the following six suggestions (Newman, 2006):

- *Understand that what makes an argument persuasive can differ from one culture to another*. Paying attention to the welfare of the company or the community might be more persuasive than a low bottom-line price. An American company was surprised to learn that the Venezuelan readers of its proposal had selected a French company that "had been making personal visits for years, bringing their families, and engaging in social activities long before there was any question of a contract" (Thrush, 2000).

- *Budget enough time for translating*. If your proposal has to be translated into another language, build in plenty of time. Translating long technical documents is a lengthy process because, even though some of the work can be done by computer software, the machine translation needs to be reviewed by native speakers of the target language.

▶ **In This Book**
For more about graphics, see Ch. 8.

- *Use simple graphics, with captions*. To reduce the chances of misunderstanding, use a lot of simple graphics, such as pie charts and bar graphs. Be sure to include captions so that readers can understand the graphics easily, without having to look through the text to see what each graphic means.

- *Write short sentences, using common vocabulary*. Short sentences are easier to understand than long sentences. Choose words that have few meanings. For example, use the word *right* as the opposite of *left*; use *correct* as the opposite of *incorrect*.

- *Use local conventions regarding punctuation, spelling, and mechanics*. Be aware that these conventions differ from place to place, even in the English-speaking world. For instance, the Australian state of New South Wales uses a different dictionary for spelling than all the other Australian states.

- *Ask if the prospective customer will do a read-through*. A read-through is the process of reading a draft of the proposal to determine whether it reveals any misunderstandings due to language or cultural differences. Why do prospective customers do this? Because it's in everyone's interest if the proposal responds clearly to the customer's needs.

Describing What You Plan to Do

Once you have shown that you understand what needs to be done and why, describe what you plan to do. Convince your readers that you can respond effectively to the situation you have just described. Discuss procedures and equipment you would use. If appropriate, justify your choices. For example, if you say you want to do ultrasonic testing on a structure, explain why, unless the reason is obvious.

Present a complete picture of what you would do from the first day of the project to the last. You need more than enthusiasm and good faith; you need a detailed plan showing that you have already started to do the work. Although no proposal can anticipate every question about what you plan to do, the more planning you have done before you submit the proposal, the greater the chances you will be able to do the work successfully if it is approved.

Demonstrating Your Professionalism

Once you have shown that you understand readers' needs and can offer a well-conceived plan, demonstrate that you are the kind of person (or that yours is the kind of organization) that is committed to delivering what you promise. Convince readers that you have the pride, ingenuity, and perseverance to solve the problems that are likely to occur. In short, show that you are a professional.

On the Web

For proposal-writing advice, see Joseph Levine's "Guide for Writing a Funding Proposal." Click on Links Library for Ch. 11 on <bedfordstmartins.com/ps>.

Guidelines

Demonstrating Your Professionalism in a Proposal

In your proposal, demonstrate your ability to carry out the project by providing four kinds of information.

▶ **Credentials and work history.** Show that you know how to do this project because you have done similar ones. Who are the people in your organization with the qualifications to carry out the project? What equipment and facilities do you have that will enable you to do the work? What management structure will you use to coordinate the activities and keep the project running smoothly?

▶ **Work schedule.** Sometimes called a *task schedule*, a work schedule is a graph or chart that shows when the various phases of the project will be carried out. The work schedule reveals more about your attitudes toward your work than about what you will be doing on any given day. A detailed work schedule shows that you have tried to foresee problems that might threaten the project.

▶ **Quality-control measures.** Describe how you would evaluate the effectiveness and efficiency of your work. Quality-control procedures might consist of technical evaluations carried out periodically by the project staff, on-site evaluations by recognized authorities or by the prospective customer, or progress reports.

▶ **Budget.** Most proposals conclude with a detailed budget, a statement of how much the project will cost. Including a budget is another way of showing that you have done your homework on a project.

ETHICS NOTE

Writing Honest Proposals

When an organization approves a proposal, it needs to trust that the people who will carry out the project will do it professionally. Over the centuries, however, dishonest proposal writers have perfected a number of ways to trick prospective customers into thinking the project will go smoothly:

- saying that certain qualified people will participate in the project, even though they will not
- saying that the project will be finished by a certain date, even though it will not
- saying that the deliverable will have certain characteristics, even though it will not
- saying that the project will be completed under budget, even though it will not

Copying from another company's proposal is another common dishonest tactic. Proposals are protected by copyright law. An employee may not copy from a proposal he or she wrote while working for a different company.

There are three reasons to be honest in writing a proposal:

- to avoid serious legal trouble stemming from breach-of-contract suits
- to avoid acquiring a bad reputation, thus ruining your business
- to do the right thing

THE STRUCTURE OF THE PROPOSAL

On the Web

To view the proposal submission checklist of the Society for Human Resource Management Foundation, click on Links Library for Ch. 11 on <bedfordstmartins.com/ps>.

Proposal structures vary greatly from one organization to another. A long, complex proposal might have 10 or more sections, including introduction, problem, objectives, solution, methods and resources, and management. If the authorizing agency provides an IFB, an RFP, or a set of guidelines, follow it closely. If you have no guidelines, or if you are writing an unsolicited proposal, use the structure shown here as a starting point. Then modify it according to your subject, your purpose, and the needs of your audience. An example of a proposal is presented on pages 290–95.

Summary

In This Book

For more about summaries, see Ch. 13, p. 323.

For a proposal of more than a few pages, provide a summary. Many organizations impose a length limit—such as 250 words—and ask the writer to present the summary, single-spaced, on the title page. The summary is crucial, because it might be the only item that readers study in their initial review of the proposal.

The summary covers the major elements of the proposal but devotes only a few sentences to each. Define the problem in a sentence or two. Next, describe the proposed program and provide a brief statement of your qualifications and experience. Some organizations wish to see the completion date and the final budget figure in the summary; others prefer that this information be presented separately on the title page along with other identifying information about the supplier and the proposed project.

Introduction

The purpose of the introduction is to help readers understand the context, scope, and organization of the proposal.

Guidelines

Introducing a Proposal

The introduction to the proposal should answer the following seven questions.

▶ **What is the problem or opportunity?** Describe the problem or opportunity in specific monetary terms, because the proposal itself will include a budget, and you want to convince your readers that spending money on what you propose is smart. Don't say that a design problem is slowing down production; say that it is costing $4,500 a day in lost productivity.

▶ **What is the purpose of the proposal?** The purpose of the proposal is to describe a problem or opportunity and propose activities that will culminate in a deliverable. Be specific in explaining what you want to do.

▶ **What is the background of the problem or opportunity?** Although you probably will not be telling your readers anything they don't already know, show them that you understand the problem or opportunity: the circumstances that led to its discovery, the relationships or events that will affect the problem and its solution, and so on.

▶ **What are your sources of information?** Review the relevant literature, ranging from internal reports and memos to published articles or even books, so that readers will understand the context of your work.

▶ **What is the scope of the proposal?** If appropriate, indicate what you are—and are not—proposing to do.

▶ **What is the organization of the proposal?** Explain the organizational pattern you will use.

▶ **What are the key terms that you will use in the proposal?** If you will use any specialized or unusual terms, define them in the introduction.

Proposed Program

In the proposed program, sometimes called the *plan of work*, explain what you want to do. Be specific. You won't persuade anyone by saying that you plan to "gather the data and analyze it." *How* will you gather and analyze the data? Justify your claims. Every word you say—or don't say—will give your readers evidence on which to base their decision.

On the Web

For a sample literature review, see Writing Guidelines for Engineering and Science Students. Click on Links Library for Ch. 11 on <bedfordstmartins.com/ps>.

If your project concerns a subject written about in the professional literature, show your familiarity with the scholarship by referring to the pertinent studies. However, don't just string together a bunch of citations. For example, don't write, "Carruthers (2010), Harding (2011), and Vega (2011) have all researched the relationship between global warming and groundwater contamination." Rather, use the recent literature to sketch the necessary background and provide the justification for your proposed program. For instance:

> Carruthers (2010), Harding (2011), and Vega (2011) have demonstrated the relationship between global warming and groundwater contamination. None of these studies, however, included an analysis of the long-term contamination of the aquifer. The current study will consist of . . .

▶ In This Book
For more about researching a subject, see Ch. 5.

You might include only a few references to recent research. However, if your topic is complex, you might devote several paragraphs or even several pages to recent scholarship.

Whether your project calls for primary research, secondary research, or both, the proposal will be unpersuasive if you haven't already done a substantial amount of the research. For instance, say you are writing a proposal to do research on industrial-grade lawn mowers. You are not being persuasive if you write that you are going to visit Walmart, Lowe's, and Home Depot to see what kinds of lawn mowers they carry. This statement is unpersuasive for two reasons:

- You need to justify why you are going to visit those three retailers rather than others. Anticipate your readers' questions: Why did you choose these three retailers? Why didn't you choose specialized dealers?

- You should already have visited the appropriate stores and completed any other preliminary research. If you haven't done the homework, readers have no assurance that you will in fact do it or that it will pay off. If your supervisor authorizes the project and then learns that none of the lawn mowers on the market meets your organization's needs, you will have to go back and submit a different proposal—an embarrassing move.

Unless you can show in your proposed program that you have done the research—and that the research indicates that the project is likely to succeed—the reader has no reason to authorize the project.

Qualifications and Experience

After you have described how you would carry out the project, show that you can do it. The more elaborate the proposal, the more substantial the discussion of your qualifications and experience has to be. For a small project, include a few paragraphs describing your technical credentials and those of

DOCUMENT ANALYSIS ACTIVITY
Writing the Proposed Program

The following project description is excerpted from a sample grant proposal seeking funding to begin a project to help police officers stay healthy (Ohio Office of Criminal Justice Services, 2003). The accompanying questions ask you to think about how to describe the project in a proposal.

1. The writer has used a lettering system to describe the four main tasks that he will undertake if he receives funding. What are the advantages of a lettering system?

2. How effective is the description of Task A? What factors contribute to the description's effectiveness or lack of effectiveness?

3. The descriptions of the tasks do not include cost estimates. Where would those estimates be presented in the proposal? Why would they be presented there?

4. How effective is the description of Task D? What additional information would improve its effectiveness?

On the Web

To submit your responses to your instructor, click on Document Analysis Activities for Ch. 11 on <bedfordstmartins .com/ps>.

PROJECT DESCRIPTION

The proposed project is comprised of several different, but related activities:

A. Physical Evaluation of the Officers

The first component of this project is the physical examination of all Summerville P.D. sworn employees. Of special interest for purposes of the project are resting pulse rate, target pulse rate, blood pressure, and percentage of body fat of the program participants. Dr. Feinberg will perform the physical examinations of all participating officers. The measurement of body fat will be conducted at the University of Summerville's Health Center under the direction of Dr. Farron Updike.

B. Renovation of Basement

Another phase of this project involves the renovation of the basement of police headquarters. The space is currently being used for storing Christmas decorations for City Hall.

The main storage room will be converted into a gym. This room will accommodate the Universal weight machine, the stationary bike, the treadmill, and the rowing machine. Renovation will consist of first transferring all the Christmas decorations to the basement of the new City Hall. Once that is accomplished, it will be necessary to paint the walls, install indoor/outdoor carpeting and set up the equipment.

A second, smaller room will be converted into a locker room. Renovation will include painting the floors and the installation of lockers and benches.

To complete the fitness center, a third basement room will be equipped as a shower room. A local plumber will tap into existing plumbing to install several showerheads.

C. Purchase of Fitness Equipment

The Department of Public Safety has identified five vendors of exercise equipment in the greater Summerville area. Each of these vendors submitted bids for the following equipment:

- Universal Weight Machine
- Atlas Stationary Bike
- Yale Rowing Machine
- Speedster Treadmill

D. Training of Officers

Participating officers must be trained in the safe, responsible use of the exercise equipment. Dr. Updike of the University of Summerville will hold periodic training sessions at the Department's facility.

your co-workers. For larger projects, include the résumés of the project leader, often called the *principal investigator*, and the other important participants.

External proposals should also discuss the qualifications of the supplier's organization, describing similar projects the supplier has completed successfully. For example, a company bidding on a contract to build a large suspension bridge should describe other suspension bridges it has built. It should also focus on the equipment and facilities the company already has and on the management structure that will ensure the project will go smoothly.

Budget

Good ideas aren't good unless they're affordable. The budget section of a proposal specifies how much the proposed program will cost.

Budgets vary greatly in scope and format. For simple internal proposals, add the budget request to the statement of the proposed program: "This study will take me two days, at a cost of about $400" or "The variable-speed recorder currently costs $225, with a 10 percent discount on orders of five or more." Or present a brief budget such as the following:

Budget

Following is an itemized budget for our proposed research.

Name	Hours	Hourly rate ($)	Cost ($)
Jessie Pritiken	10	17	170
Megan Turner	10	15	150
		Total	**320**

For more-complicated internal proposals and for all external proposals, include a more-explicit and complete budget.

Most budgets are divided into two parts: direct costs and indirect costs.

- *Direct costs* include such expenses as salaries and fringe benefits of program personnel, travel costs, and necessary equipment, materials, and supplies.
- *Indirect costs* cover the intangible expenses that are sometimes called *overhead*: general secretarial and clerical expenses not devoted exclusively to any one project, as well as operating expenses such as utilities and maintenance. Indirect costs are usually expressed as a percentage—ranging from less than 20 percent to more than 100 percent—of the direct expenses.

Appendixes

Many types of appendixes might accompany a proposal. Most organizations have boilerplate descriptions of the organization and of the projects they have completed. Another popular kind of appendix is the supporting letter: a testimonial to the supplier's skill and integrity written by a reputable and well-known person in the field. Two other kinds of appendixes deserve special mention: the task schedule and the description of evaluation techniques.

Task Schedule   The *task schedule* is almost always drawn in one of three graphical formats: a table, bar chart, or network diagram.

Tables   The simplest but least informative way to present a schedule is in a table, as shown in Figure 11.3. As with all graphics, provide a textual reference that introduces and, if necessary, explains the table.

Although displaying information in a table is better than writing it out in sentences, readers still cannot "see" the information. They have to read it to figure out how long each activity will last, and they cannot tell whether any of the activities are interdependent. They have no way of determining what would happen to the overall project schedule if one of the activities faced delays.

Bar Charts   Bar charts, also called *Gantt charts* after the early twentieth-century civil engineer who first used them, are more informative than tables. The basic bar chart shown in Figure 11.4 allows readers to see how long each task will take and whether different tasks will occur simultaneously. Like tables, however, bar charts do not indicate the interdependence of tasks.

TASK SCHEDULE

Figure 11.3   Task Schedule as a Table

Activity	Start date	Finish date
Design the security system	4 Oct. 12	19 Oct. 12
Research available systems	4 Oct. 12	3 Jan. 13
Etc.		

Schedule for Parking Analysis Project

Figure 11.4   Task Schedule as a Bar Chart

Number	Task	1/14	1/21	1/28	2/4	2/11
1	Perform research	▓				
2	Identify options		▓			
3	Analyze options			▓		
4	Test options			▓		
5	Collect and analyze data				▓	
6	Formulate recommendations					▓
7	Prepare report					▓

TECH TIP

How to Create a Gantt Chart

If you want to show how activities occur over time, you can create a simple **Gantt chart** using the **Table** feature in Word.

1. Create a **table** with enough cells to include your tasks and dates.

Task							
Task 1: Review Policies							
Task 2: Research Trends							
Task 3: Identify Criteria							
Task 4: Interview Experts							
Task 5: Evaluate Options							
Task 6: Prepare report							
	24	31	1	7	12	19	22

Enter the tasks in rows.

Enter the dates in columns.

If you need to add or remove rows or columns, you can use the buttons in the **Rows & Columns** group on the **Table Tools Layout** tab.

2. To create cells that span several columns, select the cells you wish to merge, right-click, and then select **Merge Cells** on the pop-up menu.

    To create column headings and horizontal bars, merge cells.

Task		Dates of Tasks					
Task 1: Review Policies							
Task 2: Research Trends							
Task 3: Identify Criteria							
Task 4: Interview Experts							
Task 5: Evaluate Options							
Task 6: Prepare report							
	24	31	1	8	15	19	22
	March			April			

3. To differentiate completed tasks (black bars) from tasks yet to be completed (gray bars) or to hide borders, select the cells you wish to modify and then choose the **Borders** button on the **Table Tools Design** tab. Then select **Borders and Shading**.

    The **Borders and Shading** dialog box will appear.

The **Borders** tab allows you to hide borders of selected cells.

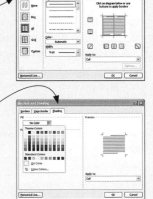

The **Shading** tab allows you to shade selected cells.

KEYWORDS: table, cells, merge cells, borders, shading

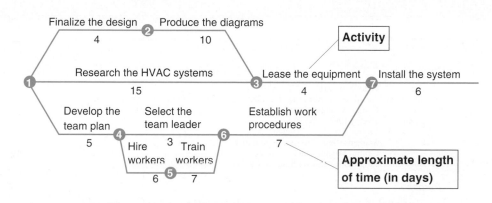

Figure 11.5 Task Schedule as a Network Diagram

A network diagram provides more useful information than either a table or a bar chart.

Network Diagrams Network diagrams show interdependence among various activities, clearly indicating which must be completed before others can begin. However, even a relatively simple network diagram, such as the one shown in Figure 11.5, can be difficult to read. You probably would not use this type of diagram in a document intended for general readers.

Description of Evaluation Techniques Although *evaluation* can mean different things to different people, an *evaluation technique* typically refers to any procedure used to determine whether the proposed program is both effective and efficient. Evaluation techniques can range from simple progress reports to sophisticated statistical analyses. Some proposals call for evaluation by an outside agent, such as a consultant, a testing laboratory, or a university. Other proposals describe evaluation techniques that the supplier will perform, such as cost-benefit analyses.

The issue of evaluation is complicated by the fact that some people think in terms of *quantitative evaluations*—tests of measurable quantities, such as production increases—whereas others think in terms of *qualitative evaluations*—tests of whether a proposed program is improving, say, the workmanship of a product. And some people include both qualitative and quantitative testing when they refer to evaluation. An additional complication is that projects can be tested while they are being carried out (*formative evaluations*) as well as after they have been completed (*summative evaluations*).

When an RFP calls for "evaluation," experienced proposal writers contact the prospective customer's representatives to determine precisely what the word means.

SAMPLE INTERNAL PROPOSAL

The following example of an internal proposal has been formatted as a memo rather than as a formal proposal. (See Chapter 12, pages 305–11, for the progress report written after this project was under way and Chapter 13, pages 331–55, for the recommendation report.)

On the Web

To see other sample proposals—one about selecting a table saw for a woodworking company, and one about selecting portable music players—click on Links Library for Ch. 11 on <bedfordstmartins.com/ps>.

In most professional settings, writers use letterhead stationery for memos, but because the writers are students, they decided to use plain stationery.

Proposals can be presented as memos or as reports.

The writers include their titles and that of their primary reader. This way, future readers will be able to more readily identify the reader and writers.

The subject line indicates the subject of the memo (the clicker study at CMSU) and the purpose of the memo (proposal).

Memos of more than one page should begin with a clear statement of purpose. Here, the writers communicate the purpose of the document in one sentence.

Memos of more than one page should contain a summary to serve as an advance organizer or to help readers who want only an overview of the document.

Although the students are writing to Dr. Bremerton, they refer to her in the third person to suggest the formality of their relationship.

The background of the problem. Don't assume that your reader knows what you are discussing, even if it was the reader who suggested the project in the first place.

The problem at the heart of the project.

The proposal. The writers have already begun to plan what they will do if the proposal is accepted, but they use the conditional tense ("would") because they cannot assume that their proposal will be authorized.

A summary of the schedule and the credentials of the writers. Because the reader will likely want to read this entire proposal, the summary functions as an advance organizer.

Memo

Date:	October 6, 2011
To:	Dr. Jill Bremerton, Vice President for Student Affairs
	Central Montana State University
From:	Jeremy Elkins, Co-chair
	Eloise Carruthers, Co-chair
	Student Affairs Advisory Committee
	Central Montana State University
Subject:	Proposal for Clicker Study at CMSU

Purpose

The purpose of our proposal is to request authorization to study the baseline requirements, including faculty and student attitudes and lecture-hall infrastructure, for adopting clickers at CMSU.

Summary

On September 6, 2011, Dr. Jill Bremerton, Vice President for Student Affairs at CMSU, invited the CMSU Student Affairs Advisory Committee (SAAC) to participate in a feasibility study about the use of clickers at CMSU.

Currently, Academic Technologies has only a handful of sets of clickers for checkout by faculty for occasional use. Because there is an increasing consensus among scholars that clickers improve the classroom learning environment and can improve learning in large lecture courses, Dr. Bremerton has allocated resources for a large feasibility study of whether CMSU should select a particular clicker system for use by CMSU instructors and establish a policy to provide technical support for clicker use and a method for students to acquire clickers through the university. The research that Dr. Bremerton invited SAAC to perform will be part of this large feasibility study.

Dr. Bremerton asked the committee to perform research that would determine whether instructors and students would support a single clicker system campus-wide and whether the physical characteristics of the lecture halls or the existing computer infrastructure in the lecture halls would restrict the university's technical choices in selecting a clicker system.

We propose to research clicker use in higher education, answer these questions, and present our findings to Dr. Bremerton. To answer these questions, we would create questionnaires (for Questions 1 and 2) and perform interviews (for Questions 3 and 4).

To perform this research and present a recommendation report, we estimate that we would each require approximately 50–60 hours over the next two months. Jeremy Elkins and Louise Carruthers are both upper-division students with successful academic records at CMSU, including backgrounds in survey design. Upon submission of a satisfactory report, Dr. Bremerton would authorize each of the authors to receive one credit of 497 Internship.

If this proposal were authorized, we would begin our research immediately, submitting to Dr. Bremerton a progress report on November 7, 2011, and a recommendation report on December 14, 2011. The recommendation report would include the details of our research and recommendation regarding whether and how to proceed with the feasibility study.

Introduction

On September 6, 2011, Dr. Jill Bremerton, Vice President for Student Affairs at Central Montana State University (CMSU), invited the CMSU Student Affairs Advisory Committee (SAAC) to participate in a feasibility study about the use of student response systems, commonly called *clickers*, at CMSU.

A brief statement of the context for the proposal.

Currently, Academic Technologies, which oversees all the computing functions in CMSU classrooms, has three sets of 100 clickers from Turning Technologies and two sets of 100 clickers from eInstruction. These clickers are available for instructors to check out for occasional use but may not be reserved for every meeting of an instructor's course. On the basis of an increasing consensus in the scholarly community that clickers improve the classroom learning environment and can improve learning in large lecture courses, Dr. Bremerton has allocated resources for a large feasibility study of whether CMSU should select a particular clicker system for use by CMSU instructors and establish a policy to provide technical support for clicker use and a method for students to acquire clickers through the university. The research that Dr. Bremerton invited SAAC to perform will be part of this large feasibility study.

An explanation of the problem: the current situation is inadequate because the university's administrators believe that clickers might be a useful educational tool for CMSU students. However, a number of important questions need to be answered before the administration decides to devote more resources to clickers.

Specifically, Dr. Bremerton asked the committee to perform research that would answer the following four questions:

1. Would instructors approve of a university policy that selects and provides technical support for a clicker system that they could use in large lecture courses?
2. Would students approve of a requirement that they purchase clickers as part of a university policy on clickers?
3. Would the physical characteristics of any of the large lecture halls affect the decision whether to adopt clickers or restrict the university to a particular technology or brand of clicker?
4. Would the computer platforms and operating systems used in the instructor stations in the large lecture halls affect the decision whether to adopt clickers or restrict the university to a particular technology or brand of clicker?

The writers quote from a memo Dr. Bremerton had written to them. Often in technical communication, you will quote your reader's words to remind him or her of the context and to show that you are carrying out your tasks professionally.

Dr. Bremerton explained that an understanding of faculty and student attitudes toward the adoption of a formal policy on clickers is fundamentally important because if faculty or students express no interest in their use or have serious reservations about their use, the university would need to consider whether and how to proceed with the feasibility study. Dr. Bremerton further explained that, for the university to study adopting a clicker policy, it would need to know whether the physical characteristics of the lecture halls and the existing computer environment in the lecture halls might influence the technical choices that need to be made.

The writers show that they understand the relationship between their work and the larger feasibility study of which it is a part.

A formal statement of the task that Dr. Bremerton asked the committee to perform.

▶ For these reasons, Dr. Bremerton asked SAAC to present our findings and recommend whether the university should proceed with the clicker project and, if so, how the computing environment in the lecture halls would affect the direction of the feasibility study.

The introduction concludes with an advance organizer for the rest of the proposal.

▶ The following sections of this memo include the proposed tasks, the schedule, our experience, and the references cited.

Proposed Tasks

By presenting the project as a set of tasks, the writers show that they are well organized. This organization by tasks will be used in the progress report (see Ch. 12, pages 305–11) and the recommendation report (see Ch. 13, pages 331–55).

With Dr. Bremerton's approval, we would perform the following tasks to determine the baseline requirements for adopting clickers at CMSU:

▶ *Task 1. Acquire a basic understanding of clicker use in higher education.*
We have already begun our research by surveying general introductions to clicker use in higher-education trade magazines and general periodicals, scholarly articles on student and faculty attitudes and on learning effects, technical specifications of clickers provided on the sites of the various manufacturers, and best practices presented on sites of colleges and universities that have adopted clickers.

Following the recommendation from Dr. Bremerton, the writers start by outlining the secondary research they plan to do. The logic is obvious: if the students are to contribute to the project, they need to understand the subject they will study.

Clickers, also called *classroom response systems*, *student response systems*, and *audience response systems*, are "wireless in-class electronic polling systems used by students to answer questions during lectures" (Ohio State, 2005, p. 2). In a clicker system, each student has an electronic device called a *clicker*, which looks like a TV remote control. The instructor poses a question, usually by embedding the question beforehand in a PowerPoint presentation, and students respond by inputting information using their clickers. Software on the instructor's computer tabulates the responses and presents them in a display, such as a bar graph, which appears on the instructor's screen, and (in some systems) on a screen on each student's clicker. Clickers are often used to engage students in learning, to give quizzes, and to take attendance (Vanderbilt University, 2010).

The proposal sounds credible because the writers have already begun their secondary research. Readers are reluctant to approve proposals unless they are sure that the writers have at least begun their research.

▶ Anecdotal and scholarly evidence suggests clearly that instructors like using clickers because they improve classroom dynamics by encouraging active learning. Whereas a traditional lecture can be a passive experience, with the instructor talking to students, clickers encourage interaction not only between the instructor and the students but also between students (Draper & Brown, 2004). In a traditional lecture, students are often unwilling to participate because they are afraid of embarrassment or disapproval by their peers, or simply because they have learned not to participate in a lecture (Caldwell, 2007). In a typical lecture, a small number of students dominate the questioning, often giving the instructor an inaccurate impression of how many students understand the material (Simpson & Oliver, 2006).

The writers explain what they still need to do to complete this task.

▶ We would still need to determine whether there is a consensus that clicker use affects student learning.

Task 2. Research faculty attitudes toward a formal policy on clicker use.
We would seek to answer the following question: "Would instructors approve of a university policy that selects and provides technical support for a clicker system that they could use in large lecture courses?"

We would need to determine whether CMSU instructors are like those nationwide. We have spoken informally with about a dozen instructors, most of whom have never used clickers. Because those who have used them are highly positive about the experience but those who have not used them do not understand much about how they work or what their purpose is, we think we should create two questionnaires: one for each category of instructor. That way, we would be able to pay appropriate attention to the attitudes of the relatively small number of CMSU instructors experienced with clickers and therefore learn whether our instructors are essentially similar to those across the country in their attitudes and experiences.

We think it would be most convenient if we could use an online survey program, such as Qualtrics, for distributing our questionnaires. Qualtrics, which is free, would enable us to transfer data to Excel, thus making it simple to tabulate and analyze.

Task 3. Research student attitudes toward a requirement to purchase a clicker.
We would seek to answer the following question: "Would students approve of a requirement that they purchase clickers as part of a university policy on clickers?"

Several research studies suggest that most students, across the country and across various course subjects, like using clickers. One study (Caldwell, 2007), at West Virginia University, found that some 88 percent of students "frequently" or "always" enjoyed using clickers in their introductory biology course. An aggregate of several studies shows that the percentage of student who approve of using clickers always exceeds 70 percent. Students comment that instructors who use clickers appear to be more aware of students' needs and employ a more responsive teaching style than those who don't use them.

One study (Caldwell, 2007) summarizing student perceptions notes that there are two main problems: some instructors do not know how to integrate the clickers effectively into their lectures, and the clickers cost students money. The first problem is something that the administration can address as part of an overall policy on clicker use. However, the cost problem is something we can learn about by performing primary research.

Task 4. Research the physical characteristics of the lecture halls.
We would seek to answer the following question: "Would the physical characteristics of any of the large lecture halls affect the decision whether to adopt clickers or restrict the university to a particular technology or brand of clicker?"

The writers show that they have applied the insights they gathered from their secondary research. Now they propose doing primary research to determine whether instructors at CMSU share the attitudes of instructors across the country. The logic is clear: if they do, the university administrators will know that they should proceed with the feasibility study.

Each task begins with the question that the writers seek to answer.

Here, again, the writers explain the logic of their decision. They decide to focus on the one concern that they can investigate effectively: the cost of the clicker.

The writers cite their sources throughout the proposal.

Our preliminary research indicates that there are two major technologies used in clicker systems: infrared (IR) and radio frequency (RF) (Ohio State University, 2005). IR, the technology used in television remote controls, requires a clear line of sight and has a limited range (40–80 feet). If IR is to be used for greater distances, the room would need to have additional receivers installed on the walls and connected either by wires or wirelessly to the instructor podium. In addition, IR signals can be disrupted by some classroom lighting systems.

By contrast, RF systems do not require a clear line of sight, have no range limitations, and are not subject to electronic interference. An RF system uses a receiver built into a USB device that attaches easily to the computer in the podium or to the instructor's laptop. For these reasons, RF systems are simpler and are becoming the industry standard.

The writers present just enough information about the two technologies to help the reader understand their logic. Writers sometimes present too much information; write only as much as necessary to get the job done.

However, IR systems are less expensive, with clickers costing less than $10. Therefore, if CMSU lecture halls meet the line-of-sight and range requirements, already have receivers installed, and pose no interference risk, IR systems would be an option. But if any of the lecture halls does not meet one or more of these criteria, CMSU should consider only RF systems.

The writers have already determined whom they need to interview to get the information they need.

We would meet with Marvin Nickerson, the Director of Physical Plant, to explain our project and to give him a list of the questions we need to answer.

Task 5. Research the existing computer environment in the lecture halls.
We would seek to answer the following question: "Would the computer platforms and operating systems used in the instructor stations in the large lecture halls affect the decision whether to adopt clickers or restrict the university to a particular technology or brand of clicker?"

We would need to determine which platforms (Windows, Macintosh, or other) and which operating systems (for example, Windows XP, Vista, or 7, or Macintosh OSX) are used in the computers in each podium in the large lecture halls identified by Mr. Nickerson. This information would be necessary to ensure that any clicker system CMSU selects is compatible with the existing computer technology in the lecture halls.

We would meet with Arlene Matthews, the Director of Academic Technologies, to explain our project and to give her a list of the questions we needed to answer. As Director of AT, Ms. Matthews has a database of this information because AT participated in installing all the instructor podiums and related systems in all the lecture halls.

Preparing the recommendation report is part of the project because the report is the deliverable.

Task 6. Analyze our data and prepare the recommendation report.
We would prepare a recommendation report that explains the questions we sought to answer, our research methods, and our findings.

Memo to Dr. Jill Bremerton   October 6, 2011   Page 6

Schedule

Figure 1 is a schedule of the tasks we would complete for this project.

Tasks	Date of Tasks (by Weeks)									
Task 1: Research clicker use										
Task 2: Research instructor attitudes										
Task 3: Research student attitudes										
Task 4: Research lecture halls										
Task 5: Research computer environment										
Task 6: Prepare report										
	10	17	24	31	7	14	21	28	5	12
	Oct.				Nov.				Dec.	

Figure 1. Schedule of Project Tasks

Experience

We are academically successful students who are qualified to perform this research and present our findings and recommendation:

- Jeremy Elkins, Co-chair of the Student Affairs Advisory Committee at CMSU, is a technical-communication major in the English Department and an honor student each of his three years at CMSU. He has used clickers in two of his courses.
- Eloise Carruthers, Co-chair of the Student Affairs Advisory Committee, is a civil-engineering major and a CMSU Top Ten Scholar. She has studied statistics in several courses and is an experienced writer of Web-based questionnaires.

References

Caldwell, J. E. (2007). Clickers in the large classroom: Current research and best-practice tips. *CBE Life Sciences Education, 6*(1): 9–20. doi:10.1187/cbe.06-12-0205

Draper, S. W., & Brown, M. I. (2004). Increasing interactivity in lectures using an electronic voting system. *Journal of Computer Assisted Learning, 20,* 81–94.

Ohio State University. (2005). *Committee on classroom response systems: Final report,* March 2, 2005. Retrieved September 2, 2011, from http://lt.osu.edu/assets/resources/clickers/crsfinalreport.pdf

Simpson, V., & Oliver, M. (2006). *Using electronic voting systems in lectures.* Retrieved September 5, 2011, from www.ucl.ac.uk/learningtechnology/examples/ElectronicVotingSystems.pdf

Vanderbilt University Center for Teaching. (2010). *Classroom response systems ("clickers").* Retrieved September 3, 2011, from www.vanderbilt.edu/cft/resources/teaching_resources/technology/crs.htm

---

Organizing the project by tasks makes it easy for the writers to present a Gantt chart. In addition, the task organization will help the writers stay on track if the proposal is approved and they continue their research.

Each task is presented with parallel grammar, which helps make the writers seem careful and professional.

Some tasks overlap in time: researchers often work on several tasks simultaneously.

The Tech Tip on p. 288 explains how to create a Gantt chart.

The writers summarize their credentials. Strong credentials help reinforce the writers' professionalism.

This proposal lacks a budget. Because the writers are students, they are being compensated with internship credits that Dr. Bremerton is overseeing.

This list of references follows the APA documentation style, which is discussed in Appendix, Part A, p. 419. The APA documentation system calls for References to begin a new page. Check with your instructor.

Writer's Checklist

The following checklist covers the basic elements of a proposal. Guidelines established by the recipient of the proposal should take precedence over these general suggestions.

Does the summary provide an overview of

☐ the problem or the opportunity? (p. 283)
☐ the proposed program? (p. 283)
☐ your qualifications and experience? (p. 283)

Does the introduction indicate

☐ the problem or opportunity? (p. 283)
☐ the purpose of the proposal? (p. 283)
☐ the background of the problem or opportunity? (p. 283)
☐ your sources of information? (p. 283)
☐ the scope of the proposal? (p. 283)
☐ the organization of the proposal? (p. 283)
☐ the key terms that you will use in the proposal? (p. 283)

☐ Does the description of the proposed program provide a clear, specific plan of action and justify the tasks you propose performing? (p. 283)

Does the description of qualifications and experience clearly outline

☐ your relevant skills and past work? (p. 284)
☐ the skills and background of the other participants? (p. 284)
☐ your department's (or organization's) relevant equipment, facilities, and experience? (p. 284)

Is the budget

☐ complete? (p. 286)
☐ correct? (p. 286)
☐ accompanied by an in-text reference? (p. 286)

☐ Do the appendixes include the relevant supporting materials, such as a task schedule, a description of evaluation techniques, and evidence of other successful projects? (p. 287)

Exercises

▶ **In This Book** For more about memos, see Ch. 9, p. 223.

1. **INTERNET EXERCISE** Study the National Science Foundation's (NSF) Grant Proposal Guide (click on Links Library for Chapter 11 on <bedfordstmartins.com/ps>). In what important ways does the NSF's guide differ from the advice provided in this chapter? What accounts for these differences? Present your findings in a 500-word memo to your instructor.

2. **INTERNET/GROUP EXERCISE** Form groups according to major. Using the FedBizOpps Web site (click on Links Library for Chapter 11 on <bedfordstmartins.com/ps>), find a request for proposal for a project related to your academic field. Study the RFP. What can you learn about the needs of the organization that issued it? How effectively does the RFP describe what the issuing organization expects to see in the proposal? Is the RFP relatively general or specific? What sorts of evaluation techniques does the RFP call for? In your response, include a list of questions that you would ask the issuing organization if you were considering responding to the RFP. Present your results in a memo to your instructor.

3. Write a proposal for a research project that will constitute a major assignment in this course. Your instructor will tell you whether the proposal is to be written individually or collaboratively. Start by defining a technical subject that interests you. (This subject could be one that you are involved with at work or in another course.) Using abstract services and other bibliographic tools, compile a bibliography of articles and books on the subject. (See Chapter 5 for a discussion of finding information.) Create a reasonable real-world context. Here are three common scenarios from the business world:

   • Our company uses Technology X to perform Task A. Should we instead be using Technology Y to perform Task A? For instance, our company uses traditional surveying tools in its contracting business. Should we be using GPS surveying tools instead?

   • Our company has decided to purchase a tool to perform Task A. Which make and model of the tool should we purchase, and from which supplier should we buy or lease it? For instance, our company has decided to purchase 10 multimedia computers. Which brand and model should we buy, and from whom should we buy them?

- Our company does not currently perform Function X. Is it feasible to perform Function X? For instance, we do not currently offer day care for our employees. Should we? What are the advantages and disadvantages of doing so? What forms can day care take? How is it paid for?

Following are some additional ideas for topics:

- the need to provide legal file-sharing access to students
- the value of using social media to form ties with a technical-communication class on another campus
- the need for expanded opportunities for internships in your major
- the need to create an advisory board of industry professionals to provide expertise about your major
- the need to raise money to keep the college's computer labs up-to-date
- the need to evaluate your major to ensure that it is responsive to students' needs

- the advisability of starting a campus branch of a professional organization in your field
- the need to improve parking facilities on campus
- the need to create or improve organizations for minorities or women on campus

These topics can be approached from different perspectives. For instance, the first one—on providing file-sharing access to students—could be approached in at least three ways:

- Our college currently purchases journals but does not provide legal file-sharing access for students. Should we consider reducing the library's journal budget to subsidize legal file-sharing access?
- Our college has decided to provide legal file-sharing access for students. How should it do so? What vendors provide such services? What are the strengths and weaknesses of each vendor?
- Our college does not offer legal file-sharing access for students. Should we make it a goal to do so? What are the advantages of doing so? The disadvantages?

▶ **On the Web**

For a case assignment, "Revising a Brief Proposal," see Cases on <bedfordstmartins.com/ps>.

12

Writing Informational Reports

Bloomberg/Getty Images.

Complex, expensive projects call for lots of informational reports.

Complex, expensive projects, such as building and installing wind turbines, as shown here, call for a lot of documents. Before a project begins, a vendor might write a *proposal* to interest prospective clients in the work. After a project is completed, an organization might write a *completion report* to document the project or a *recommendation report* to argue for a future course of action. In between, many people will write various *informational reports.* For example, after this blade is installed on the wind turbine, the contractor will likely write and submit an informational report updating management on the status of the project.

Informational reports share one goal: to describe something that has happened or is happening now. Their main purpose is to communicate clear, accurate, specific information. Sometimes, informational reports also analyze a situation. An *analysis* is an explanation of why something happened or how it happened. For instance, in an incident report about an accident on the job, the writer might speculate about how and why the accident occurred.

This chapter discusses four kinds of informational reports: directive, field report, progress report, and incident report. Here are examples of how each might be used in the workplace:

- A supervisor writes a *directive* explaining the company's new recycling policy and describing informational sessions that the company will offer on how to implement the policy.

- An insurance adjuster writes a *field report* describing his inspection of a building after a storm caused extensive damage.

- A research team writes a *progress report* explaining what the team has accomplished in the first half of the project, speculating on whether it will finish on time and on budget, and describing how it has responded to unexpected problems.

- A worker at a manufacturing company writes an *incident report* after a toxic-chemical spill.

Another type of informational report is a *recommendation report* (see Chapter 13).

Focus on Process

In writing informational reports, pay special attention to these steps in the writing process. For a complete process for writing technical documents, see page 14.

- **Planning.** In some cases, determining your audience and to whom to address the report is difficult. Choosing the appropriate format for your report can also be difficult. Consider whether your organization has a preferred format for reports and whether your report will be read by readers from other cultures who might expect a formal style and application. See Chapter 4 for more about analyzing your audience.

- **Drafting.** Some informational reports are drafted on-site. For instance, an engineer might use a handheld computer to "draft" a report as she walks around a site. For routine reports, you can sometimes use sections of previous reports or *boilerplate*. In a status report, for instance, you can copy the description of your current project from the previous report and then update it as necessary. See Chapter 2, page 24, for more about boilerplate.

- **Editing and proofreading.** Informal does not mean careless. Even informal reports should be free of errors.

WRITING DIRECTIVES

On the Web

To analyze a persuasive directive, see Document Analysis Activities for Ch.12 on <bedfordstmartins.com/ps>.

In a *directive*, you explain a policy or a procedure you want your readers to follow. Even though you can simply require your readers to follow the new policy, you want to explain why the new policy is desirable or at least necessary. You are most persuasive when you present clear, compelling evidence (in the form of commonsense arguments, numerical data, and examples); when you consider opposing arguments effectively; and when you present yourself as cooperative, moderate, fair-minded, and modest. If appropriate, include arguments that appeal to your readers' broader goals of security, recognition, personal and professional growth, and connectedness. Figure 12.1 is an example of a directive.

The writer begins with a clear explanation of the problem the directive addresses. Presenting the reasons for the new policy shows respect for the readers and therefore makes the directive more persuasive.

The writer's polite but informal tone throughout the memo is likely to motivate readers to cooperate. Notice the use of "please" and "thanks" in the second paragraph.

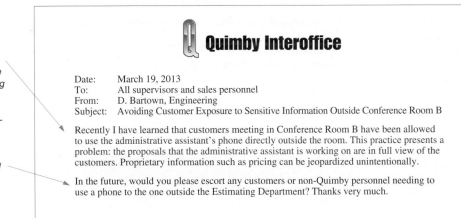

Figure 12.1   A Directive

WRITING FIELD REPORTS

A common kind of informational report describes inspections, maintenance, and site studies. These reports, often known as *field reports*, explain the problem, methods, results, and conclusions, but they deemphasize methods and can include recommendations. The report in Figure 12.2 illustrates a possible variation on this standard report structure.

Figure 12.2
A Field Report

LOBATE CONSTRUCTION
3311 Industrial Parkway
Speonk, NY 13508

Quality Construction Since 1957

April 11, 2013

Ms. Christine Amalli, Head
Civil Engineering
New York Power
Smithtown, NY 13507

Dear Ms. Amalli:

We are pleased to report the results of our visual inspection of the Chemopump after Run #9, ◀
a 30-day trial on Kentucky #10 coal.

The inspection was designed to determine if the new Chemopump is compatible with ◀
Kentucky #10, the lowest-grade coal that you anticipate using. In preparation for the 30-day
test run, the following three modifications were made by your technicians:

• New front-bearing housing buffer plates of tungsten carbide were installed.
• The pump-casting volute liner was coated with tungsten carbide.
• New bearings were installed.

Our summary is as follows. A number of small problems with the pump were observed, but ◀
nothing serious and nothing surprising. Normal break-in accounts for the wear. The pump
accepted the Kentucky #10 well.

The following four minor problems were observed:

• The outer lip of the front-end bell was chipped along two-thirds of its circumference.
• Opposite the pump discharge, the volute liner received a slight wear groove along one-
  third of its circumference.
• The impeller was not free-rotating.
• The holes in the front-end bell were filled with insulating mud.

Our conclusion is that the problems can be attributed to normal break-in for a new
Chemopump. The Kentucky #10 coal does not appear to have caused any extraordinary
problems. In general, the new Chemopump seems to be operating well.

*Because the writer and the
reader work for different
companies, a letter is the
appropriate format for this brief
informational report.*

The word visual *describes the
methods.*

*The writer states the purpose of
the inspection.*

*The writer has chosen to
incorporate the words* summary
and conclusion *in the body
of the letter rather than use
headings as a method of
organization.*

Figure 12.2 (continued)

page 2

Informational reports sometimes include recommendations.

We would recommend, however, that the pump be modified as follows:

1. Replace the front-end bell with a tungsten carbide-coated front-end bell.
2. Replace the bearings on the impeller.
3. Install insulation plugs in the holes in the front-end bell.

Further, we recommend that the pump be reinspected after another 30-day run on Kentucky #10.

The writer concludes politely.

If you have any questions or would like to authorize these modifications, please call me at 555-1241. As always, we appreciate the trust you have placed in us.

Sincerely,

Marvin Littridge

Marvin Littridge
Director of Testing and Evaluation

---

e-Pages

To analyze an informational report presented as a Web site, visit <bedfordstmartins.com/ps/epages>.

Guidelines

Responding to Readers' Questions in a Field Report

Be sure to answer the following six questions.

▶ What is the purpose of the report?

▶ What are the main points covered in the report?

▶ What were the problems leading to the decision to perform the procedure?

▶ What methods were used?

▶ What were the results?

▶ What do the results mean?

If appropriate, also discuss what you think should be done next.

WRITING PROGRESS AND STATUS REPORTS

In This Book

For more about proposals, see Ch. 11. For more about completion reports and recommendation reports, see Ch. 13.

A *progress report* describes an ongoing project. A *status report*, sometimes called an *activity report*, describes the entire range of operations of a department or division. For example, the director of marketing for a manufacturing company might submit a monthly status report.

A progress report is an intermediate communication between the proposal (the argument that a project be undertaken) and the completion report (the comprehensive record of a completed project) or recommendation report (an argument to take further action). Progress reports let you check in with your audience.

Regardless of how well the project is proceeding, explain clearly and fully what has happened and how it will affect the overall project. Your tone should be objective, neither defensive nor casual. Unless ineptitude or negligence caused the problem, you're not to blame. Regardless of the news you are delivering—good, bad, or mixed—your job is the same: to provide a clear and complete account of your activities and to forecast the next stage of the project.

When things go wrong, you might be tempted to cover up problems and hope that you can solve them before the next progress report. This course of action is unwise and unethical. Chances are that problems will multiply, and you will have a harder time explaining why you didn't alert your readers earlier.

ETHICS NOTE

Reporting Your Progress Honestly

Withholding bad news is unethical because it can mislead readers. As sponsors or supervisors of the project, readers have a right to know how it is going. If you find yourself faced with any of the following three common problems, consider responding in these ways.

- *The deliverable—the document or product you will submit at the end of the project—won't be what you thought it would be.* Without being defensive, describe the events that led to the situation and explain how the deliverable will differ from what you described in the proposal.

- *You won't meet your schedule.* Explain why you are going to be late, and state when the project will be complete.

- *You won't meet the budget.* Explain why you need more money, and state how much more you will need.

Organizing Progress and Status Reports

The time pattern and the task pattern, two organizational patterns frequently used in progress and status reports, are illustrated in Figure 12.3. A status report is usually organized according to task; by its nature, this type of report covers a specified time period.

In the time pattern, you describe all the work that you have completed in the present reporting period and then sketch in the work that remains. Some writers include a section on present work, which enables them to focus on a long or complex task still in progress.

The time pattern

Discussion
    A. Past Work
    B. Future Work

The task pattern

Discussion
    A. Task 1
        1. Past work
        2. Future work
    B. Task 2
        1. Past work
        2. Future work

The task pattern allows you to describe, in order, what has been accomplished on each task. Often, a task-oriented structure incorporates the chronological structure.

Figure 12.3   Organizational Patterns in Reports

Concluding Progress and Status Reports

In the conclusion of a progress or status report, evaluate how the project is proceeding. In the broadest sense, there are two possible messages: things are going well, or things are not going as well as anticipated.

If appropriate, use appendixes for supporting materials, such as computations, schematics, diagrams, or a revised task schedule. Cross-reference these appendixes in the body of the report, so that readers can find them easily.

Guidelines

Projecting an Appropriate Tone in a Progress or Status Report

Whether the news is positive or negative, these two suggestions will help you sound like a professional.

▶ **If the news is good, convey your optimism but avoid overstatement.**

OVERSTATED	We are sure the device will do all that we ask of it, and more.
REALISTIC	We expect that the device will perform well and that, in addition, it might offer some unanticipated advantages.

Beware of promising early completion. It is embarrassing to have to report a failure to meet an optimistic deadline.

▶ **Don't panic if the preliminary results are not as promising as you had planned or if the project is behind schedule.** Even the best-prepared proposal writers cannot anticipate all problems. As long as the original proposal was well planned and contained no wildly inaccurate computations, don't feel responsible. Just do your best to explain unanticipated problems and the status of the project. If your news is bad, at least give the reader as much time as possible to deal with it effectively.

▶ **On the Web**
To see other sample progress reports—one about selecting a table saw for a woodworking company, and one about selecting portable music players for a gym—click on Links Library for Ch. 12 on <bedfordstmartins .com/ps>.

Find other progress reports at Writing Guidelines for Engineering and Science Students. Click on Links Library for Ch. 12 on <bedfordstmartins.com/ps>.

Sample Progress Report

The following progress report was written for the project proposed on pages 289–95 in Chapter 11. (The recommendation report for this study is on page 331 in Chapter 13.)

Memo

Date: November 7, 2011
To: Dr. Jill Bremerton, Vice President for Student Affairs
           Central Montana State University
From: Jeremy Elkins, Co-chair
           Eloise Carruthers, Co-chair
           Student Affairs Advisory Committee
           Central Montana State University
Subject: Progress Report for Clicker Study at CMSU

Purpose

This is a progress report on our research on the baseline requirements, including faculty and student attitudes and lecture-hall infrastructure, for adopting clickers at CMSU.

Summary

On October 10, 2011, Dr. Jill Bremerton, Vice President for Student Affairs at CMSU, authorized our study of the baseline requirements for adopting clickers at CMSU. We have completed the first three tasks of our project: acquiring a basic understanding of clicker use in higher education, determining whether instructors would support clicker use, and determining whether students would support clicker use.

Our study is currently on schedule, and we expect to submit a recommendation report on December 14, 2011, as indicated in our proposal dated October 6, 2011.

Introduction

On October 10, 2011, Dr. Jill Bremerton, Vice President for Student Affairs at Central Montana State University (CMSU), approved our proposal to participate in a feasibility study about the use of clickers at CMSU.

Currently, Academic Technologies has only three sets of 100 clickers from Turning Technologies and two sets of 100 clickers from eInstruction. These clickers are available for instructors to check out for occasional use but may not be reserved for every meeting of an instructor's course. On the basis of an increasing consensus in the scholarly community that clickers improve the classroom learning environment and can improve learning in large lecture courses, Dr. Bremerton has allocated resources for a large feasibility study of whether CMSU should select a particular clicker system for use by CMSU instructors and establish a policy to provide technical support for clicker use and a method for students to acquire clickers through the university. The research that Dr. Bremerton invited SAAC to perform will be part of this large feasibility study.

Dr. Bremerton approved our proposal to perform research and present our recommendation on whether the university should proceed with the clicker study and, if so, how the physical characteristics of the lecture halls and the existing computer environment in the lecture halls would affect the direction of the feasibility study.

In most professional settings, writers use letterhead stationery for memos, but because the writers are students, not employees, they decided to use plain stationery.

Progress reports can be presented as memos or as reports.

The writers include their titles and that of their primary reader. This way, future readers will be able to more readily identify the reader and writers.

The subject line indicates the subject of the memo (the clicker study at CMSU) and the purpose of the memo (progress report).

Memos should begin with a clear statement of purpose. Here, the writers communicate the purpose of the document in one sentence.

Memos of more than one page should include a summary.

Readers of progress reports want to know whether the project is proceeding according to schedule and (if appropriate) on budget.

A brief statement of the context for the proposal. Note that the writers refer to the reader's having authorized their proposal.

A formal statement of the task that Dr. Bremerton asked the committee to perform.

Most of the information in the introduction is taken directly from the proposal. This reuse of text is ethical.

The writers begin by describing the organization of the results section. For a progress report, a chronological organization makes good sense.

The writers follow the task structure that they used in the proposal.

The writers skillfully integrate their secondary research into their discussion of the criteria. By doing so, they enhance their credibility.

Results of Research

In this progress report, we present our completed work on Tasks 1–3. Then we discuss our future work: Tasks 4–6.

Completed Work

Task 1. Acquire a basic understanding of clicker use in higher education.

Clickers, also called *classroom response systems*, *student response systems*, and *audience response systems*, are "wireless in-class electronic polling systems used by students to answer questions during lectures" (Ohio State, 2005, p. 2). In a clicker system, each student has an electronic device called a *clicker*, which looks like a TV remote control. The instructor poses a question, usually by embedding the question beforehand in a PowerPoint presentation, and students respond by inputting information on their clickers. Software on the instructor's computer tabulates the responses and presents them in a display, such as a bar graph, which appears on the instructor's screen, and (in some systems) on a screen on each student's clicker.

Clickers are often used to engage students in learning, to give quizzes, and to take attendance.

Clickers can help instructors improve the classroom atmosphere in a number of ways (Vanderbilt University, 2010):
- promote active student engagement during a lecture
- promote discussion and collaboration among students during class
- encourage participation from every student in a class
- check for student understanding during class
- teach in a way that adapts to the immediate learning needs of students

Anecdotal and scholarly evidence suggests clearly that using clickers improves classroom dynamics by encouraging active learning. Whereas a traditional lecture can be a passive experience, with the instructor talking to students, clickers encourage interaction not only between the instructor and the students but also between students (Draper & Brown, 2004). In a traditional lecture, students are often unwilling to participate because they are afraid of embarrassment or disapproval by their peers, or simply because they have learned not to participate in a lecture (Caldwell, 2007). In a typical lecture, a small number of students dominate the questioning, often giving the instructor an inaccurate impression of how many students understand the material (Simpson & Oliver, 2006).

Although it makes sense to assume that a more active learning environment leads to better learning, measuring learning is very challenging, and therefore there is not yet complete consensus that clickers improve learning. There are some studies that do suggest improved learning. For instance, a study (Ohio State, 2008) of a large, multi-section physics course found that students in clicker sections outperformed those in non-clicker sections by 10 points on a final exam, and that female students did as well as males in the clicker sections (but not in non-clicker sections). And a meta-analysis by Fies and Marshall (2006) shows that 11 of 26 studies show clear evidence of improved comprehension of complex concepts.

The bulk of scholarly literature, however, is consistent with Beatty et al. (2006), who see great potential for improved student learning. As Caldwell (2007) puts it,

> Most reviews agree that "ample converging evidence" suggests that clickers generally cause improved student outcomes such as improved exam scores or passing rates, student comprehension, and learning and that students like clickers. The reviews of the literature, however, also agree that much of the research so far is not systematic enough to permit scientific conclusions about what causes the benefits. (n.p.)

At the very least, as Knight and Wood (2005) argue, students with clickers almost always do at least as well in exam scores as students who don't use clickers.

Task 2. Research faculty attitudes toward a formal policy on clicker use.
Because student attendance, engagement, and participation increase with the use of clickers, it makes sense that many instructors would like clickers. Anecdotal evidence reported in Caldwell (2007) suggests that instructors do enjoy the improved student engagement and perceive that students learn more effectively in clicker courses.

However, the literature suggests (see Vanderbilt, 2010) that instructors have cited problems with clicker use:
- Technical problems with the hardware or software can occur during a class.
- It takes time for an instructor to learn a system and use it effectively.
- It takes time for an instructor to embed clicker questions in teaching materials (such as PowerPoint slides).
- Using clickers in class takes time away from other instructional activities.
- Changing a lesson "on the fly" or conducting a discussion in response to clicker responses can disrupt the flow of a lesson.

We considered these findings in devising our questionnaires for CMSU instructors. We wrote the two questionnaires, and then field-tested them with three faculty members from different colleges at CMSU. Then, we uploaded the survey to Qualtrics and sent an e-mail to the instructors, inviting them to respond to the appropriate questionnaire.

The 16 instructors who had taught with clickers at least two semesters were directed to the Faculty Questionnaire 1, which is presented in Appendix A, page 9.

The cross-references to the questionnaires help readers find the information quickly. The questionnaires are presented in Ch. 13, pp. 341–47.

The writers have created and distributed the two questionnaires but have not yet collected and analyzed the data that the questionnaires will provide. They will report on these data in the recommendation report to be submitted on December 14.

The 56 instructors who had never taught with clickers (or taught with them for only one semester) but who regularly teach lectures with more than 100 students were directed to Faculty Questionnaire 2, which is presented in Appendix B, page 10. Both questionnaires have a deadline of November 20, 2011.

Task 3. Research student attitudes toward a requirement to purchase a clicker.
Several research studies suggest that most students, across the country and across various course subjects, like using clickers. One study (Caldwell, 2007), at West Virginia University, found that some 88 percent of students "frequently" or "always" enjoyed using clickers in their introductory biology course. Aggregating several studies, the percentage of students who approve of using clickers always exceeds 70 percent. Students comment that instructors who use clickers are more aware of students' needs and employ a more responsive teaching style than those who don't use them.

The writers cite their sources throughout the report.

However, students do not always approve of clicker use. The principal complaints reported nationally (Caldwell, 2007) relate to the following problems:
- Some clickers cost too much.
- Some instructors do not explain the purpose of using the clickers.
- Some instructors spend too much class time using the clickers.
- Some instructors let clicker use drive the course content.
- Some students are anxious about having their course grades depend, to some extent, on their use of an electronic device.

Of these concerns, all but the one related to the cost of the clicker refer to how instructors integrate the clickers into the course content. As many commentators suggest, schools need to provide training for instructors that covers not only technical questions about how to operate clickers and related software but also about how to use them effectively in teaching the course.

We concluded that the most useful data we could obtain would relate to what price our students thought was reasonable. A review of the sites of the four leading manufacturers of clicker systems (Turning Technologies, eInstruction, iClicker, and Qwizdom) shows that pricing can vary, depending on the pricing model the vendor uses. For instance, some companies (such as Turning Technologies) charge a one-time price, with no fees for registering the clicker each semester. Other companies (such as eInstruction) charge once for the clicker but have a per-semester registration fee. In addition, commentators (University of Wisconsin-Eau Claire, n.d.) point out that some vendors have established relationships with textbook manufacturers so that the clickers are packaged with selected textbooks. Finally, some schools have entered into contractual relationships with clicker vendors that call for a particular price for students at that school. Therefore, it is impossible to answer the cost question simply.

We therefore decided to try to determine the one-time price that students would find reasonable for a clicker. Although CMSU might not in fact be able to achieve a one-time price contract for the clicker, the answer to this question would at least give the university an idea of student attitudes about price. We selected a price ranging from zero (for students who wish to express an opposition to having to buy a clicker at any price) to approximately $60. (At this time, Quizdom's clicker, at $66.55, represents the high end of prices.)

We wrote the following one-question questionnaire for the 11,324 currently enrolled undergraduate students.

The writers explain the logic of their decision. They decided to focus on what they think is the most appropriate information: student attitudes toward the price of the clickers. Questions related to how instructors use clickers will be addressed in Dr. Bremerton's larger study.

As you may know, Vice President for Student Affairs Bremerton is conducting a study to determine whether CMSU should select a single brand of clicker to be used in some lecture courses at CMSU. Clickers are used by students to respond to questions posed by instructors in large lecture courses. If such a choice were made, you might be required to purchase a clicker for use in some of your lecture courses. Following are some details:

1. The university would seek to enter into a two-year contract with a manufacturer of the clicker systems. Although the university would hope to renew that contract so that the one clicker you buy would last for your entire career at CMSU, it is possible that you would need to buy a new clicker as often as every two years.
2. You would be responsible for purchasing the batteries for your clicker. Batteries generally last from six months to a year, and replacement batteries cost approximately $3–6.
3. You would be responsible for replacing your clicker if you lose it.

We would appreciate your telling us what price you think would be reasonable for the clicker unit. Please select one of the following responses, and then hit the Submit button.

○ $0. I don't want to have to buy any clicker.
○ Up to $20.
○ Up to $40.
○ Up to $60.

Thank you!

Writers often need to decide where to present information in a technical document. This questionnaire could have appeared in an appendix, as the two instructor questionnaires did. However, because it is relatively brief, the writers decided to include it in the body of the report.

We made this questionnaire available for all undergraduate students because, of the 11,324 students currently enrolled, only 832 had ever used a clicker at CMSU. Because that number constituted only some 7 percent of the total undergraduate population, we felt that it was not worth the expense of separating out those who had used a clicker on campus.

We then field-tested the question with the three other members of SAAC. Next, we uploaded the survey to Qualtrics and sent an e-mail to students, inviting them to respond to the question. The deadline for this questionnaire is November 27.

Future Work

We are now at work on Task 4: researching the physical characteristics of the lecture halls.

Task 4. Research the physical characteristics of the lecture halls.
We will seek to answer the following question: "Would the physical characteristics of any of the large lecture halls affect the decision whether to adopt clickers or restrict the university to a particular technology or brand of clicker?" We have scheduled a meeting for November 9 with Mr. Marvin Nickerson, the Director of Physical Plant, to explain our project and to give him a list of the questions we need to answer.

Task 5. Research the existing computer environment in the lecture halls.
We will seek to answer the following question: "Would the computer platforms and operating systems used in the instructor stations in the large lecture halls affect the decision whether to adopt clickers or restrict the university to a particular technology or brand of clicker?" We have scheduled a meeting with Dr. Arlene Matthews, the Director of Academic Technologies, on November 14, 2011, to explain our project and to give her a list of the questions we need to answer.

Task 6. Analyze our data and prepare a recommendation report.
We will prepare a recommendation report that explains the questions we sought to answer, our research methods, and our findings.

Updated Schedule

The dark blue bars represent completed tasks. The light blue bars represent tasks yet to be completed.

The Gantt chart shows the progress toward completing each of the project tasks. See the Tech Tip in Ch. 11, p. 288, for advice on how to create Gantt charts.

Tasks	Date of Tasks (by Weeks)									
Task 1: Research clicker use										
Task 2: Research instructor attitudes										
Task 3: Research student attitudes										
Task 4: Research lecture halls										
Task 5: Research computer environment										
Task 6: Prepare report										
	10	17	24	31	7	14	21	28	5	12
	Oct.				Nov.				Dec.	

Figure 1. Schedule of Project Tasks

Conclusion

We have successfully completed Tasks 1–3 and begun Tasks 4 and 5. We are on schedule to complete Tasks 4–6 by the December 14 deadline. We have acquired an understanding of how clickers are used in higher education and gone live with the questionnaires for instructors and students. We are currently preparing for our interviews to better understand the infrastructure of our lecture halls. In the report we will present on December 14, we will include our recommendation on how this background information should affect the larger feasibility study on clicker use at CMSU.

Please contact Jeremy Elkins at jelkins@cmsu.edu or at 444-3967 if you have questions or comments or would like to discuss this project further.

The conclusion summarizes the status of the project.

The writers end with a polite offer to provide additional information.

This progress report lacks a budget. Because the writers are students, they are being compensated with internship credits that Dr. Bremerton is overseeing.

References

Beatty, I. D., Gerace, W. J., Leonar, W. J., & Dufresne, R. J. (2006). Designing effective questions for classroom response system teaching. *American Journal of Physics, 74*(1), 31–39.

Caldwell, J. E. (2007). Clickers in the large classroom: Current research and best-practice tips. *CBE Life Sciences Education, 6*(1): 9–20. doi:10.1187/cbe.06-12-0205

Draper, S. W., & Brown, M. I. (2004). Increasing interactivity in lectures using an electronic voting system. *Journal of Computer Assisted Learning, 20,* 81–94.

Fies, C., & Marshall, J. (2006). Classroom response systems: A review of the literature. *Journal of Science Education & Technology, 15,* 101–109.

Knight, J. K., & Wood, W. B. (2005). Teaching more by lecturing less. *Cell Biology Education, 4,* 298–310.

Ohio State University. (2005). *Committee on classroom response systems: Final report*, March 2, 2005. Retrieved September 2, 2011, from http://lt.osu.edu/assets /resources/clickers/crsfinalreport.pdf

Ohio State University. (2008, July 18). Students who use "clickers" score better on physics tests. *ScienceDaily*. Retrieved September 4, 2011, from www.sciencedaily .com/releases/2008/07/080717092033.htm

Simpson, V., & Oliver, M. (2006). *Using electronic voting systems in lectures.* Retrieved September 5, 2011, from www.ucl.ac.uk/learningtechnology/examples /ElectronicVotingSystems.pdf

University of Wisconsin-Eau Claire. (n.d.). *Comparison of student response system vendors.* Retrieved September 3, 2011, from www.uwec.edu/evansmm/SRS /clickerDecision.pdf

Vanderbilt University Center for Teaching. (2010). *Classroom response systems ("clickers").* Retrieved September 3, 2011, from www.vanderbilt.edu/cft /resources/teaching_resources/technology/crs.htm

This list of references follows the APA documentation style, which is discussed in Appendix, Part A, p. 419.

The appendixes for this report are presented in Ch. 13, pp. 354–55.

WRITING INCIDENT REPORTS

An incident report describes events such as workplace accidents, health or safety emergencies, and equipment problems. (Specialized kinds of incident reports go by other names, such as *accident reports* or *trouble reports*.) The purpose of an incident report is to explain what happened, why it happened, and what the organization did (or is going to do) to follow up on the incident. Incident reports often contain a variety of graphics, including tables, drawings, diagrams, and photographs, as well as videos.

Incident reports can range from forms that are filled out on paper or online to substantial reports hundreds of pages long. Figure 12.4 shows an accident form used at a university.

UNC – Chapel Hill – Facilities Services – Safety Plan

APPENDIX A

Employee's Accident Report Form
University of North Carolina at Chapel Hill

This form is to be completed by the employee and forwarded to the Health and Safety office as soon as practicable after the injury. (See Human Resources Manual)

Accident Date:

1. Name of employee:
2. Date and time of injury:
3. Descibe how the injury occurred:
4. Describe what job duty you were doing at the time of your injury:
5. Describe what part of your body was injured:
6. Describe what you would recommend to prevent a reoccurrence:
7. Further information you would like to include regarding your injury:

Employee signature　　　Date

HTTP://www.fac.unc.edu

Figure 12.4 An Accident Report Form

Source: University of North Carolina at Chapel Hill, 2010 <www.fac.unc.edu/Employees/Safety/SafetyDocuments/tabid/233/Default.aspx>.

Writer's Checklist

☐ Did you choose an appropriate application for the informational report? (p. 299)

Does the directive
☐ clearly and politely explain your message? (p. 300)
☐ explain your reasoning, if appropriate? (p. 300)

Does the field report
☐ clearly explain the important information? (p. 300)
☐ use, if appropriate, a problem-methods-results-conclusion-recommendations organization? (p. 300)

Does the progress or status report
☐ clearly announce that it is a progress or status report? (p. 302)
☐ use an appropriate organization? (p. 303)

☐ clearly and honestly report on the subject and forecast the problems and possibilities of the future work? (p. 303)
☐ append supporting materials that substantiate the discussion? (p. 304)

Does the incident report
☐ explain what happened? (p. 312)
☐ explain why it happened? (p. 312)
☐ explain what the organization did about it or will do about it? (p. 312)

Exercises

▶ **In This Book** For more about memos, see Ch. 9, p. 223.

1. As the manager of Lewis, Lewis, and Wollensky Law, LPC, you have been informed by some clients that tattoos on the arms and chests of your employees create a negative impression. Write a directive in the form of a memo defining a new policy: employees are required to wear clothing that covers any tattoos on their arms and chests.

2. Write a progress report about the research project you are working on in response to Exercise 3 on page 296 in Chapter 11. If the proposal was a collaborative effort, collaborate with the same group members on the progress report.

▶ **On the Web**
For a case assignment, "Writing a Directive About Using Agendas for Meetings," see Cases on <bedfordstmartins.com/ps>.

13

Writing Recommendation Reports

Zilvinas Narvydas/Alamy.

What should we do next?

When the London Millennium Footbridge across the River Thames opened in 2000, it was a big hit. With some 2,000 people on the bridge, it began to sway, causing what engineers called *synchronous lateral excitation*: when the bridge swayed, people on the bridge began to sway in rhythm as they walked, which amplified the movement. Three days later, the bridge, newly nicknamed the Wobbly Bridge, was closed for study and repair. Engineers studied two options for fixing the problem: increasing the stiffness of the bridge or increasing its damping. Eventually, they wrote a report recommending the installation of 89 dampers, shown in the photo, to control horizontal and vertical movement. The bridge reopened in 2002 after repairs, but Londoners still call it the Wobbly Bridge.

Chapter 12 discussed informational reports: those in which the writer's main purpose is to present information. This chapter discusses recommendation reports. A *recommendation report* also presents information but goes one step further by offering suggestions about what the readers ought to do next.

■ ■ ■ ■

Focus on Process

When writing a recommendation report, pay special attention to **planning**. You need a problem-solving model for conducting the analysis that will enable you to write the recommendation report. See pages 316–19 for a discussion of the problem-solving model. For a complete process for writing technical documents, see page 14.

UNDERSTANDING THE ROLE OF RECOMMENDATION REPORTS

A recommendation report can be the final link in a chain of documents that begins with a proposal and continues with one or more progress reports. This last, formal report is often called a *final report*, *project report*, *recommendation report*, *completion report*, or simply a *report*. The sample report beginning on page 331 is the recommendation report in the series about clickers at CMSU presented in Chapters 11 and 12. A recommendation report can also be a freestanding document, one that was not preceded by a proposal or by progress reports.

Here are examples of the kinds of questions a recommendation report might address:

- *What should we do about Problem X?* What should we do about the synchronous lateral excitation on the bridge?

- *Should we do Function X?* Although we cannot afford to reimburse tuition for all courses our employees wish to take, can we reimburse them for courses directly related to their work?

- *Should we use Technology A or Technology B to do Function X?* Should we buy several high-output copiers or a larger number of low-output copiers?

- *We currently use Method A to do Function X. Should we be using Method B?* We sort our bar-coded mail by hand; should we buy an automatic sorter?

Each of these questions can lead to a wide variety of recommendations, ranging from "do nothing" to "study this some more" to "take the following actions immediately."

Most recommendation reports discuss questions of feasibility. *Feasibility* is a measure of the practicality of a course of action. For instance, a company might conduct a *feasibility study* of whether it should acquire a competing company. In this case, the two courses of action are to acquire the competing company or not to acquire it. Or a company might do a study to determine which make and model of truck to buy for its fleet.

A feasibility report is a report that answers three kinds of questions:

- *Questions of possibility.* We would like to build a new rail line to link our warehouse and our retail outlet, but if we cannot raise the money, the project is not possible. Even if we have the money, do we have government authorization? If we do, are the soil conditions appropriate for the rail link?

- *Questions of economic wisdom.* Even if we can afford to build the rail link, should we do so? If we use all our resources on this project, what other projects will have to be postponed or canceled? Is there a less expensive or a less financially risky way to achieve the same goals?

- *Questions of perception.* Because our company's workers have recently accepted a temporary wage freeze, they might view the rail link as an inappropriate use of funds. The truckers' union might see it as a threat to truckers' job security. Some members of the public might also be interested parties, because any large-scale construction might affect the environment.

USING A PROBLEM-SOLVING MODEL FOR PREPARING RECOMMENDATION REPORTS

To write a recommendation report, start by using a problem-solving model to conduct your analysis.

Identify the Problem or Opportunity

What is not working or is not working as well as it might? What situation presents an opportunity to decrease costs or improve the quality of a product or service? Without a clear statement of your problem or opportunity, you cannot plan your research.

For example, your company has found that employees who smoke are absent and ill more often than those who don't smoke. Your supervisor has asked you to investigate whether the company should offer a free smoking-cessation program. The company can offer the program only if the company's insurance carrier will pay for it. The first thing you need to do is talk with the insurance agent; if the insurance carrier will pay for the program, you can proceed with your investigation. If the agent says no, you have to determine whether another insurance carrier offers better coverage or whether there is some other way to encourage employees to stop smoking.

Establish Criteria for Responding to the Problem or Opportunity

Criteria are standards against which you measure your options. Criteria can be classified into two categories: *necessary* and *desirable*. For example, if you want to buy a photocopier for your business, necessary criteria might be that each copy cost less than two cents to produce and that the photocopier be able to handle oversized documents. If the photocopier doesn't fulfill those two criteria, you will not consider it further. By contrast, desirable criteria might include that the photocopier do double-sided copying and stapling. Desirable criteria let you make distinctions among a variety of similar objects, objectives, actions, or effects. If a photocopier does not fulfill a desirable criterion, you will still consider it, although it will be less attractive.

Determine the Options

After you establish your criteria, you determine your options. *Options* are potential courses of action you can take in responding to a problem or opportunity. Determining your options might be simple or complicated.

For example, your department's photocopier is old and breaking down. Your first decision is whether to repair it or replace it. Once you have answered that question, you might have to make more decisions. If you are going to replace it, what features should you look for in a new one? Each time you make a decision, you have to answer more questions until, eventually, you arrive at a recommendation. For a complicated scenario like this, you might find it helpful to use logic boxes or flowcharts to sketch the logic of your options, as shown in Figure 13.1.

Study Each Option According to the Criteria

Once you have identified your options (or series of options), study each one according to the criteria. For the photocopier project, secondary research would include studying articles about photocopiers and specification sheets

In This Book
For more about research techniques, see Ch. 5.

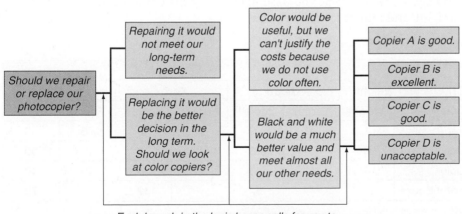

Each branch in the logic boxes calls for you to make a decision.

Figure 13.1   Using Logic Boxes to Plot a Series of Options

from the manufacturers. Primary research might include observing product demonstrations as well as interviewing representatives from different manufacturers and managers who have purchased different brands.

To make the analysis of the options as objective as possible, professionals sometimes create a *decision matrix*, a tool for systematically evaluating each option according to each criterion. A decision matrix is a table (or a spreadsheet), as shown in Figure 13.2. Here the writer is nearly at the end of his series of options: he is evaluating three similar photocopiers according to three criteria. Each criterion has its own weight, which suggests how important it is. The greater the weight, the more important the criterion.

As shown in Figure 13.2, the criterion of pages per minute is relatively unimportant: it receives a weight of 1. For this reason, the Ricoh, even though it receives a high rating for pages per minute (9), receives only a modest score of 9 ($1 \times 9 = 9$). However, the criterion of color copying is quite important, with a weight of 4. On this criterion, the Ricoh, with its rating of 10, achieves a very high score ($4 \times 10 = 40$).

But a decision matrix cannot stand on its own. You need to explain your methods. That is, in the discussion or in footnotes to the matrix, you need to explain the following decisions:

- *Why you chose each criterion—or didn't choose a criterion the reader might have expected to see included.* For instance, why did you choose duplexing but not image storing?

- *Why you assigned a particular weight to each criterion.* For example, why is the ability to do color copying four times more important than speed?

- *Why you assigned a particular rating to each option.* For example, why does one copier receive a rating of 1 on duplexing, but another receives a 3?

A decision matrix is helpful only if your readers understand your methods and agree with the logic you used in choosing the criteria and assigning weights and ratings for each option.

Criteria and Weight		Options					
		Ricoh		Xerox		Sharp	
Criterion	Weight	Rating	Score[1]	Rating	Score[1]	Rating	Score[1]
Pages/min.	1	9	**9**	6	**6**	3	**3**
Duplex	3	1	**3**	3	**9**	10	**30**
Color	4	10	**40**	1	**4**	10	**40**
Total Score			**52**		**19**		**73**

[1]Score = weight × rating.

Figure 13.2 A Decision Matrix
Spreadsheet programs often contain templates for creating decision matrices.

Draw Conclusions About Each Option

Whether you use a decision matrix or a less-formal means of recording your evaluations, the next step is to draw conclusions about your options—by interpreting your results and writing evaluative statements about the options.

For the study of photocopiers, your conclusion might be that the Sharp model is the best copier: it meets all your necessary criteria and the greatest number of desirable criteria, or it scores highest on your matrix. Depending on your readers' preferences, you can rank the options, classify them as either acceptable or unacceptable, or present a compound conclusion: that the Sharp offers the most technical features but that the Ricoh is the best value, for example.

Formulate Recommendations Based on the Conclusions

If you conclude that Option A is better than Option B—and you see no obvious problems with Option A—recommend Option A. But if the problem has changed or your company's priorities or resources have changed, you might decide to recommend a course of action that is inconsistent with the conclusions you derived. Use your judgment, and then recommend the best course of action.

WRITING RECOMMENDATION REPORTS

The following discussion presents a basic structure for a recommendation report. Remember that every document you write should reflect its audience, purpose, and subject. Therefore, you might need to modify, add to, or delete some of the elements discussed here.

The easiest way to draft a report is to think of it as consisting of three sections: the front matter, the body, and the back matter. Table 13.1 on page 320 shows the purposes of and typical elements in these three sections.

You will probably draft the body before the front and back matter. This sequence is easiest because you think through what you want to say in the body, and then draft the front and back matter based on it.

If you are writing your recommendation report for readers from another culture, keep in mind that conventions differ from one culture to another. In the United States, reports are commonly organized from general to specific. That is, the most general information (the abstract and the executive summary) appears early in the report. In many cultures, however, reports are organized from specific to general. Detailed discussions of methods and results precede discussions of the important findings.

Similarly, elements of the front and back matter are rooted in culture. For instance, in some cultures—or in some organizations—writers do not create

TABLE 13.1 ▶ Elements of a Typical Report		
Section of the report	**Purposes of the section**	**Typical elements in the section**
Front matter	• to orient the reader to the subject • to provide summaries for technical and managerial readers • to help readers navigate the report • to help readers decide whether to read the document	• letter of transmittal (p. 323) • cover (p. 323) • title page (p. 323) • abstract (p. 323) • table of contents (p. 324) • list of illustrations (p. 325) • executive summary (p. 326)
Body	• to provide the most comprehensive account of the project, from the problem or opportunity that motivated it, to the methods and the most important findings	• introduction (p. 320) • methods (p. 321) • results (p. 321) • conclusions (p. 322) • recommendations (p. 322)
Back matter	• to present supplementary information, such as more-detailed explanations than are provided in the body • to enable readers to consult the secondary sources the writers used	• glossary (p. 328) • list of symbols (p. 328) • references (p. 330) • appendixes (p. 330)

executive summaries, or their executive summaries differ in length or organization from those discussed here. According to interface designer Pia Honold (1999), German users of high-tech products rely on the table of contents in a manual because they like to understand the scope and organization of the manual. Therefore, writers of manuals for German readers should include comprehensive, detailed tables of contents.

Study samples of writing produced by people from the culture you are addressing to see how they organize their reports and use front and back matter.

Writing the Body of the Report

The elements that make up the body of a report are discussed here in the order in which they usually appear in a report. However, you should draft the elements in whatever order you prefer. The sample recommendation report on pages 331–55 includes these elements.

Introduction   The introduction helps readers understand the technical discussion that follows. Start by analyzing who your readers are, then consider these questions:

- *What is the subject of the report?* If the report follows a proposal and a progress report, you can probably copy this information from one of those documents, modifying it as necessary. Reusing this information is efficient and ethical.

- *What is the purpose of the report?* The purpose of the report is not the purpose of the project. The purpose of the report is to present information and offer recommendations.

In This Book
For more about purpose statements, see Ch. 4, p. 72.

- *What is the background of the report?* Include this information, even if you have presented it before; some of your readers might not have read your previous documents or might have forgotten them.

- *What are your sources of information?* Briefly describe your primary and secondary research, to prepare your readers for a more detailed discussion of your sources in subsequent sections of the report.

- *What is the scope of the report?* Indicate the topics you are including, as well as those you are not.

- *What are the most significant findings?* Summarize the most significant findings of the project.

- *What are your recommendations?* In a short report containing a few simple recommendations, include those recommendations in the introduction. In a lengthy report containing many complex recommendations, briefly summarize them in the introduction, then refer readers to the more detailed discussion in the recommendations section.

- *What is the organization of the report?* Indicate your organizational pattern so that readers can understand where you are going and why.

- *What key terms are you using in the report?* The introduction is an appropriate place to define new terms. If you need to define many terms, place the definitions in a glossary and refer readers to it in the introduction.

Methods   The methods section answers the question "What did you do?" In drafting the methods section, consider your readers' knowledge of the field, their perception of you, and the uniqueness of the project, as well as their reasons for reading the report and their attitudes toward the project. Provide enough information to help readers understand what you did and why you did it that way. If others will be using the report to duplicate your methods, include sufficient detail.

Results   Whereas the methods section answers the question "What did you do?" the results section answers the question "What did you see?"

Results are the data you have discovered or compiled. Present the results objectively, without comment. Save the interpretation of the results—your conclusions—for later. If you combine results and conclusions, your readers might be unable to follow your reasoning and might not be able to tell whether the evidence justifies your conclusions.

Your audience's needs will help you decide how to structure the results. How much they know about the subject, what they plan to do with the report, what they expect your recommendation(s) to be—these and many other factors will affect how you present the results. For instance, suppose that your company is considering installing a VoIP phone system that will allow you to make telephone calls over the Internet. In the introduction, you explain the disadvantages of the company's current phone system. In the methods section, you describe how you established the criteria you applied to the available phone systems, as well as your research procedures. In the results section, you provide the details of each phone system you are considering, as well as the results of your evaluation of each system.

In This Book

For more about evaluating evidence and drawing conclusions, see Ch. 5, pp. 90–93.

Conclusions   Conclusions answer the question "What does it mean?" They are the implications of the results. To draw conclusions, you need to think carefully about your results, weighing whether they point clearly to a single meaning.

Recommendations   Recommendations answer the question "What should we do?" As discussed earlier in this chapter, recommendations do not always flow directly from conclusions. Always consider recommending that the organization take no action, or no action at this time.

Methods	**Results**	**Conclusions**	**Recommendations**
What did you do?	What did you see?	What does it mean?	What should we do?

Guidelines

Writing Recommendations

As you draft your recommendations, consider the following four factors.

▶ **Content.** Be clear and specific. If the project has been unsuccessful, don't simply recommend that your readers "try some other alternatives." What alternatives do you recommend, and why?

▶ **Tone.** When you recommend a new course of action, be careful not to offend whoever formulated the earlier course. Do not write that following your recommendations will "correct the mistakes" that have been made. Instead, your recommendations should "offer great promise for success." A restrained, understated tone is more persuasive because it shows that you are interested only in the good of your company, not personal rivalries.

▶ **Form.** If the report leads to only one recommendation, use traditional paragraphs. If the report leads to more than one recommendation, consider a numbered list.

▶ **Location.** Consider including a summary of the recommendations—or, if they are brief, the full list—after the executive summary or in the introduction as well as at the end of the body of the report.

Writing the Front Matter

Front matter is common in reports, proposals, and manuals. As discussed in Table 13.1 on page 320, front matter helps readers understand the whole report and find the information they seek. Most organizations have established formats for front matter. Study the style guide used in your company or, if there isn't one, examples from the files to see how other writers have assembled their reports.

Letter of Transmittal   The letter of transmittal, which can take the form of a letter or a memo, introduces the primary reader to the purpose and content of the report. It is attached to the report, bound in with it, or simply placed on top of it. Even though the letter likely contains no information that is not included elsewhere in the report, it is important because it is the first thing the reader sees. It establishes a courteous and professional tone. Letters of transmittal are customary even when the writer and the reader both work for the same organization. See page 331 in the sample recommendation report for an example of a transmittal letter in the form of a memo.

In This Book
For more about formatting a letter, see Ch. 9, p. 223.

Cover   The cover protects the report from normal wear and tear and from harsher environmental conditions, such as water or grease. The cover usually contains the title of the report, the name and position of the writer, the date of submission, and the name or logo of the writer's company. Sometimes the cover also includes a security notice or a statement of proprietary information.

Title Page   A title page includes at least the title of the report, the name of the writer, and the date of submission. A more complex title page might also include a project number, a list of additional personnel who contributed to the report, and a distribution list. See page 332 in the sample recommendation report for an example of a title page.

Abstract   An abstract is a brief technical summary of the report, usually no more than 200 words. It addresses readers who are familiar with the technical subject and who need to decide whether they want to read the full report. In an abstract, you can use technical terminology and refer to advanced concepts in the field. Abstracts are sometimes published by abstract services, which are useful resources for researchers.

In This Book
For more about abstract services, see Ch. 5, p. 87.

Abstracts often contain a list of half a dozen or so keywords, which are entered into electronic databases. As the writer, one of your tasks is to think of the various keywords that will lead people to the information in your report.

There are two types of abstracts: descriptive and informative. A *descriptive abstract*—sometimes called a *topical*, *indicative*, or *table-of-contents abstract*—describes the kinds of information contained in the report. It does not provide the major findings (important results, conclusions, or recommendations). It simply lists the topics covered, giving equal emphasis to each. Figure 13.3 is a

ABSTRACT

"Design of a Radio-Based System for Distribution Automation"

by Brian D. Crowe

At this time, power utilities' major techniques of monitoring their distribution systems are after-the-fact indicators such as interruption reports, meter readings, and trouble alarms. These techniques are inadequate because they are expensive and they fail to provide the utility with an accurate picture of the dynamics of the distribution system. This report describes a project to design a radio-based system for a pilot project. This report describes the criteria we used to design the system, then describes the hardware and software of the system.

Keywords: distribution automation, distribution systems, load, meters, radio-based systems, utilities

This abstract is descriptive rather than informative because it does not explain the criteria or describe the system.

Figure 13.3　Descriptive Abstract

descriptive abstract from a report by a utility company about its pilot program for measuring how much electricity its customers are using. A descriptive abstract is used most often when space is at a premium. Some government proposals, for example, call for a descriptive abstract to be placed at the bottom of the title page.

An *informative abstract* presents the major findings. If you don't know which kind of abstract the reader wants, write an informative one.

The distinction between descriptive and informative abstracts is not absolute. Sometimes you might have to combine elements of both in a single abstract. For instance, if there are 15 recommendations—far too many to list—you might simply note that the report includes numerous recommendations.

See page 333 in the sample recommendation report for an example of an informative abstract.

Table of Contents　The table of contents, the most important guide to navigating the report, has two main functions: to help readers find the information they want and to help them understand the scope and organization of the report.

A table of contents uses the same headings as the report itself. Therefore, to create an effective table of contents, you must first make sure that the headings are clear and that you have provided enough of them. If the table of contents shows no entry for five or six pages, you probably need to partition that section of the report into additional subsections. In fact, some tables of contents have one entry, or even several, for every report page.

The following table of contents, which relies exclusively on generic headings (those that describe an entire class of items), is too general to be useful.

Table of Contents

◄——— *This methods section, which goes from page 4 to page 18, should have subentries to break up the text and to help readers find the information they seek.*

For more-informative headings, combine the generic and the specific:

Recommendations: Five Ways to Improve Information-Retrieval Materials Used in the Calcification Study

Results of the Commuting-Time Analysis

Then build more subheadings into the report itself. For instance, in the "Recommendations" example above, you could create a subheading for each of the five recommendations. Once you establish a clear system of headings within the report, use the same text attributes—capitalization, boldface, italics, and outline style (traditional or decimal)—in the table of contents. Note that the table of contents should not contain an entry for itself.

When adding page numbers to your report, remember two points:

▶ **In This Book**

For more about text attributes, see Ch. 7, p. 156.

- Front matter is numbered using lowercase Roman numerals (i, ii, and so forth), often centered at the bottom of the page. The title page of a report is not numbered, although it represents page i. The abstract is usually numbered page ii. The table of contents is usually not numbered, although it represents page iii.

- The body of the report is numbered with Arabic numerals (1, 2, and so on), typically in the upper outside corner of the page.

See page 334 in the sample recommendation report for an example of a table of contents.

List of Illustrations   A *list of illustrations* is a table of contents for the figures and tables. List the figures first, then the tables. (If the report contains only figures, call it a *list of figures*. If it contains only tables, call it a *list of tables*.) You may begin the list of illustrations on the same page as the table of contents, or you may begin the list on a separate page and include it in the table of contents. Figure 13.4 on page 326 shows a list of illustrations.

LIST OF ILLUSTRATIONS

Figure 13.4   List of Illustrations

Executive Summary   The executive summary (sometimes called the *epitome, executive overview, management summary*, or *management overview*) is a brief condensation of the report addressed to managers. Most managers need only a broad understanding of the projects that the organization undertakes and how they fit together into a coherent whole.

An executive summary for a report under 20 pages is typically one page (double-spaced). For longer reports, the maximum length is often calculated as a percentage of the report, such as 5 percent.

The executive summary presents information to managers in two parts:

- *Background.* This section explains the problem or opportunity: what was not working or was not working effectively or efficiently; or what potential modification of a procedure or product had to be analyzed.

- *Major findings and implications.* This section might include a brief description—only one or two sentences—of the methods, followed by a full paragraph about the conclusions and recommendations.

An executive summary differs from an informative abstract. An abstract focuses on the technical subject (such as whether the new radio-based system monitors energy usage effectively); an executive summary concentrates on whether the system can improve operations at a particular company.

TECH TIP

How to Format Headers, Footers, and Page Numbers

In writing a report, you might want to use different headers, footers, and page-numbering schemes and styles in different sections of the report. To do this, you will create different sections in your Word file. Within each section, you can modify the headers, footers, and page numbers by using the **Header & Footer** group.

To **insert**, **remove**, or **edit the format** of headers, footers, and page numbers, use the drop-down menus in the **Header & Footer** group on the **Insert** tab.

The **Header & Footer** drop-down menus allow you to insert headers and footers with **built-in** styles and to edit and remove headers and footers.

You can also add and modify header and footer text, insert page numbers and dates, and choose the format of page numbers by double-clicking the header or footer in **Print Layout View** and using the groups on the **Design** tab.

The **Options** group allows you to specify different headers and footers for odd and even pages, as well as the first page.

The **Page Number** drop-down menu allows you to change the format of page numbers.

KEYWORDS: header & footer group, options group, header, footer, print layout view, design tab, page number, format page numbers

TECH TIP

How to Create a Table of Contents

You can make a table of contents automatically in Word. You can then use the **Styles** feature to format the headings in your report.

Place your cursor where you want to create the table of contents.

Use the **Table of Contents** drop-down menu in the **Table of Contents** group on the **Reference** tab to insert a table of contents with a **built-in** style.

You may also select **Insert Table of Contents** to choose the format for the table of contents, select the level of detail to show, and preview the appearance of the table.

If you select **Insert Table of Contents**, you can also **modify** the text attributes of the table levels to match the text attributes in your report.

If you later change your report and its pagination, you can update the page numbers or the entire table of contents by selecting the table of contents and then selecting **Update Table of Contents**.

In the **Update Table of Contents** dialog box, select the option you want: **update page numbers only**, or **update entire table**.

KEYWORDS: table of contents, table of contents group, update fields, update table of contents

Guidelines

Writing an Executive Summary

Follow these five suggestions in writing executive summaries.

▶ **Use specific evidence in describing the background.** For most managers, the best evidence includes costs and savings. Instead of writing that the equipment you are now using to cut metal foil is ineffective, write that the equipment jams once every 72 hours on average, costing $400 in materials and $2,000 in productivity. Then add up these figures for a monthly or an annual total.

▶ **Be specific in describing the research.** For instance, research suggests that if your company had a computerized energy-management system you could cut your energy costs by 20 to 25 percent. If your energy costs last year were $300,000, you could save $60,000 to $75,000.

▶ **Describe the methods briefly.** If you think your readers are interested, include a brief description—no more than a sentence or two.

▶ **Describe the findings according to your readers' needs.** If your readers want to know your results, provide them. If your readers are unable to understand the technical data or are uninterested, go directly to the conclusions and recommendations.

▶ **Ask an outside reader to review your draft.** Give it to someone who has had no connection to the project. That person should be able to read your summary and understand what the project means to the organization.

See page 335 in the sample recommendation report for an example of an executive summary.

Writing the Back Matter

The back matter of a recommendation report might include the following items: glossary, list of symbols, references, and appendixes.

Glossary and List of Symbols   A *glossary*, an alphabetical list of definitions, is particularly useful if some of your readers are unfamiliar with the technical vocabulary in your report. Instead of slowing down your discussion by defining technical terms as they appear, you can use boldface, or some similar method of highlighting words, to indicate that the term is defined in the glossary. The first time a boldfaced term appears, explain this system in a footnote. For example, the body of the report might say, "Thus the **positron*** acts as the . . . ," while a note at the bottom of the page explains:

*This and all subsequent terms in boldface are defined in the Glossary, page 26.

Although the glossary is usually placed near the end of the report, before the appendixes, it can also be placed immediately after the table of contents if the glossary is brief (less than a page) and if it defines essential terms. Figure 13.5 on page 330 shows an excerpt from a glossary.

DOCUMENT ANALYSIS ACTIVITY

Analyzing an Executive Summary

The following executive summary comes from a corporate report on purchasing Black-Berry devices for employees. The accompanying questions ask you to think about the discussion of executive summaries (beginning on page 326).

Executive Summary

On May 11, we received approval to study whether BlackBerry devices could help our 20 engineers receive e-mail, monitor their schedules, take notes, and store files they need in the field. In our study, we addressed these problems experienced by many of our engineers:

- They have missed deadlines and meetings and lost client information.
- They have been unable to access important files from the field.
- They have complained about the weight of the binders and other materials— sometimes weighing more than 40 pounds—that they have to carry.
- They have to spend time keyboarding notes that they took in the field.

In 2011, missed meetings and other schedule problems cost the company over $400,000 in lost business. And our insurance carrier settled a claim for $50,000 from an engineer who experienced back and shoulder problems due to the weight of his pack.

We researched the capabilities of BlackBerry devices, and then established these criteria for our analysis:

- The device must weigh less than four ounces.
- It must be compatible with Windows back to 98.
- It must have a full keyboard.
- It must have built-in GPS.
- It must have 3G connectivity.
- It must have Wi-Fi capability.
- It must have a 3.2 MP camera.
- It must have at least 512 MB of flash memory.
- It must have Bluetooth capability.
- It must cost $500 or less.

On the basis of our analysis, we recommend that the company purchase five BlackBerry Bold devices, for a total cost of $2,500. These devices best meet all our technical and cost criteria. We further recommend that after a six-month trial period, the company decide whether to purchase an additional 15 devices for the other engineers.

1. How clearly do the writers explain the background? Identify the problem or opportunity they describe in this executive summary.

2. Do the writers discuss the methods? If so, identify the discussion.

3. Identify the findings: the results, conclusions, and recommendations. How clearly have the writers explained the benefits to the company?

▶ On the Web

To submit your responses to your instructor, click on Document Analysis Activities for Ch. 13 on <bedfordstmartins .com/ps>.

Glossary

Applicant: A state agency, local government, or eligible private nonprofit organization that submits a request to the Grantee for disaster assistance under the state's grant.

Case Management: A systems approach to providing equitable and fast service to applicants for disaster assistance. Organized around the needs of the applicant, the system consists of a single point of coordination, a team of on-site specialists, and a centralized, automated filing system.

Cost Estimating Format (CEF): A method for estimating the total cost of repair for large, permanent projects by use of construction industry standards. The format uses a base cost estimate and design and construction contingency factors, applied as a percentage of the base cost.

Declaration: The President's decision that a major disaster qualifies for federal assistance under the Stafford Act.

Hazard Mitigation: Any cost-effective measure that will reduce the potential for damage to a facility from a disaster event.

Figure 13.5   Glossary

List of Symbols

β	beta
CRT	cathode-ray tube
γ	gamma
Hz	hertz
rcvr	receiver
SNR	signal-to-noise ratio
uhf	ultra high frequency
vhf	very high frequency

Figure 13.6   List of Symbols

A list of symbols is formatted like a glossary, but it defines symbols and abbreviations rather than terms. It, too, may be placed before the appendixes or after the table of contents. Figure 13.6 shows a list of symbols.

References   Many reports contain a list of references (sometimes called a *bibliography* or *list of works cited*) as part of the back matter. References and the accompanying textual citations throughout the report are called *documentation*. Documentation acknowledges your debt to your sources, establishes your credibility as a writer, and helps readers locate and review your sources. See Appendix, Part A, for a detailed discussion of documentation. See page 353 in the sample recommendation report for an example of a reference list.

Appendixes   An *appendix* is any section that follows the body of the report (and the glossary, list of symbols, or reference list). Appendixes (or *appendices*) convey information that is too bulky for the body of the report or that will interest only a few readers. Appendixes might include maps, large technical diagrams or charts, computations, computer printouts, test data, and texts of supporting documents.

Appendixes, usually labeled with letters rather than numbers (Appendix A, Appendix B, and so on), are listed in the table of contents and are referred to at appropriate points in the body of the report. Therefore, they are accessible to any reader who wants to consult them. See pages 354–55 in the sample recommendation report for examples of appendixes.

e-Pages
To analyze a recommendation report presented as an audio podcast, visit <bedfordstmartins.com/ps/epages>.

SAMPLE RECOMMENDATION REPORT

The following example is the recommendation report on the CMSU clicker project proposed in Chapter 11 on page 289. The progress report for this project appears in Chapter 12 on page 305.

Memo

Date: December 14, 2011
To: Dr. Jill Bremerton, Vice President for Student Affairs
             Central Montana State University
From: Jeremy Elkins, Co-chair
             Eloise Carruthers, Co-chair
             Student Affairs Advisory Committee
             Central Montana State University
Subject: Recommendation Report for Clicker Study at CMSU

Attached is the report for our study, "Establishing Baseline Requirements for Adopting Clickers at CMSU: A Recommendation Report." We completed the tasks described in our proposal of October 6, 2011: familiarizing ourselves with clicker use in higher education, assessing instructor and student attitudes toward clickers, and determining whether the current infrastructure of the large lecture halls on campus would affect whether and how the university should pursue its feasibility study.

To perform these tasks, we performed secondary and primary research. We studied the literature on clicker use, conducted interviews, and distributed questionnaires to appropriate CMSU stakeholders. Then, we collected and analyzed our data and wrote the report.

Our findings suggest that instructors probably will be very receptive to your feasibility study. In addition, if CMSU adopts a formal policy of clicker use, faculty will be positive about it—provided that the university chooses a good clicker system and provides effective technical support. Further, we found that most CMSU students are willing to pay up to $40 for a clicker. The infrastructure of our 17 large lecture halls presents no special difficulties for clicker use, provided that we restrict our study to radio-frequency-based systems. Although an older technology—infrared-based systems—offers cheaper clickers, it would require upgrading the lecture halls with additional hardware. Further, we found that the existing computer systems in the lecture halls include both Macs and PCs with operating systems back to Windows XP. Any clicker system selected would need to work with these operating systems.

On the basis of these findings, we recommend that CMSU proceed with its feasibility study of the costs and benefits of adopting a clicker policy on campus.

We appreciate the trust you have shown in inviting us to participate in the initial stages of the feasibility study, and we would look forward to working with you on other portions of the study. If you have any questions or comments, please contact Jeremy Elkins at jelkins@cmsu.edu or at 444-3967.

In most professional settings, writers use letterhead stationery for memos, but because the writers are students, they decided to use plain stationery.

Transmittal "letters" can be presented as memos.

The writers include their titles and that of their primary reader. This way, future readers will be able to more readily identify the reader and writers.

The subject line indicates the subject of the report (the clicker study at CMSU) and the purpose of the report (recommendation report).

The purpose of the study. Notice that the writers link the recommendation report to the proposal, giving them an opportunity to state the main tasks they carried out in the study.

The methods the writers used to carry out the research.

The principal findings—the results and conclusions of the study.

The major recommendation.

A polite offer to participate further or to provide more information.

A good title indicates the subject and purpose of the document. One way to indicate the purpose is to use a generic term—such as *analysis, recommendation, summary,* or *instructions*—in a phrase following a colon. For more about titles, see Ch. 6, p. 108.

The names and positions of the principal reader and the writers of the document.

The date the document was submitted.

The name or logo of the writers' organization often is presented at the bottom of the title page. In this case, the writers are students who have chosen not to use the university logo because they are not formal employees of the university.

Establishing Baseline Requirements for Adopting Clickers at CMSU: A Recommendation Report

Prepared for: Dr. Jill Bremerton, Vice President for Student Affairs
Central Montana State University

Prepared by: Jeremy Elkins, Co-chair
Eloise Carruthers, Co-chair
Student Affairs Advisory Committee
Central Montana State University

December 14, 2011

Abstract

"Establishing Baseline Requirements for Adopting Clickers at CMSU: A Recommendation Report"

Prepared by: Jeremy Elkins, Co-chair
Eloise Carruthers, Co-chair
Student Affairs Advisory Committee
Central Montana State University

On September 6, 2011, Dr. Jill Bremerton, Vice President for Student Affairs at Central Montana State University (CMSU), formally asked the CMSU Student Affairs Advisory Committee (SAAC) to participate in a feasibility study about the use of student response systems, commonly called *clickers*, at CMSU by assessing instructor and student attitudes toward clickers and determining whether the current infrastructure of the large lecture halls on campus would affect whether and how the university should pursue its feasibility study. To perform this research, SAAC devised interview questions and questionnaires to distribute to appropriate CMSU stakeholders. We found that faculty—both those experienced with clickers and those without experience—are very receptive to a careful feasibility study. Faculty's most important concern is that, if CMSU adopts a formal policy of clicker use, the university choose a good clicker system and provide effective technical support. More than half of the students expressed a willingness to pay up to $40 for a clicker, with 23 percent willing to pay only $20 and 19 percent willing to pay up to $60. The lecture halls are not equipped to handle infrared-based clicker systems. We recommend that CMSU consider only radio-frequency-based systems. In addition, because our large lecture halls use both PCs and Macs, we should consider only those vendors that offer systems that are cross-platform and (for PCs) that are compatible back to the Windows XP operating system.

Keywords: clickers, student response systems, classroom response systems, student attitudes, faculty attitudes

The title of the report is often enclosed in quotation marks because the abstract might be placed outside the report, in which case the report is a separate document.

Abstracts are often formatted as a single paragraph.

The background and purpose of the report.

The methods.

The major findings.

The major recommendations.

The writers provide some technical information about student attitudes, about the system they are recommending, and about the infrastructure of the large lecture halls.

A keywords list ensures that if the report is searched electronically, it will register "hits" for each of the terms listed.

Note that the typeface and design of the headings in the table of contents match the typeface and design of the headings in the report itself.

In this table of contents, the two levels of headings are distinguished by type size, type style (boldface versus italic), and indentation.

Table of Contents

1

Executive Summary

On September 6, 2011, Dr. Jill Bremerton, Vice President for Student Affairs at Central Montana State University (CMSU), formally invited the CMSU Student Affairs Advisory Committee (SAAC) to participate in a feasibility study about the use of student response systems, commonly called *clickers*, at CMSU.

Currently, CMSU has only a few sets of clickers that instructors can check out for occasional use in their large lecture courses. Because of an increasing consensus in the scholarly community that clickers improve the classroom learning environment and can improve learning in large lecture courses, Dr. Bremerton has allocated resources for a large feasibility study of whether CMSU should select a particular clicker system for use on campus. The research that Dr. Bremerton asked SAAC to perform will be part of this large feasibility study.

Dr. Bremerton invited us to perform research that would assess instructor and student attitudes toward clickers and determine whether the current infrastructure of the large lecture halls on campus would affect whether and how the university should pursue its feasibility study. She further asked us to present our findings and recommendations.

To perform this research, we familiarized ourselves with the basics of clicker use in postsecondary schools. Then, we devised interview questions and questionnaires to distribute to appropriate CMSU stakeholders.

We found that instructors will likely be very receptive to this feasibility study. In addition, if CMSU adopts a formal policy of clicker use, faculty will be positive about it—provided the university chooses a good clicker system and provides effective technical support. Further, we found that more than half (56 percent) of the CMSU students who responded to our questionnaire expressed a willingness to pay up to $40 for a clicker. A quarter (23 percent) are willing to pay only $20, but a fifth (19 percent) are willing to pay up to $60. The infrastructure of our 17 large lecture halls presents no special difficulties for clicker use, provided that we restrict our study to radio-frequency-based systems, which is becoming the standard technology for clickers. Further, we found that the existing computer systems in the lecture halls include both Macs and PCs with operating systems back to Windows XP.

On the basis of these conclusions, we recommend that CMSU proceed with its feasibility study of the costs and benefits of adopting a clicker policy on campus.

The executive summary describes the project with a focus on the managerial aspects, particularly the recommendation. Note the writers' emphasis on the problem at CMSU.

Here the writers present a brief statement of the subject of their report.

The background of the feasibility study that Dr. Bremerton is funding.

A statement of the assignment that Dr. Bremerton gave the writers. This statement helps the reader remember the context for the report she is reading. Don't assume that your readers remember what they asked you to do weeks or months earlier.

A brief statement of the methods the writers used to carry out their research. Throughout this report, the writers use the active voice ("We familiarized ourselves . . ."). See Ch. 6, p. 126, for more on the active voice. Note, too, that the discussion of the methods is brief: most executive readers are not very interested in the details of the methods you used.

Findings are the important results and conclusions of a study. Here, the writers devote a few sentences to the findings related to instructor and student attitudes and a few sentences to the findings related to the infrastructure.

The writers use the word *recommend*. Using key generic terms such as *problem, methods, results, conclusions,* and *recommendations* helps readers understand the role that each section plays in the document.

2

In some organizations, all first-level headings begin a new page.

A brief statement of the context for the report.

Introduction

On September 6, 2011, Dr. Jill Bremerton, Vice President for Student Affairs at Central Montana State University (CMSU), invited the CMSU Student Affairs Advisory Committee (SAAC) to participate in a feasibility study about the use of student response systems, commonly called *clickers*, at CMSU.

The word currently *is used to introduce the background of the study: the current situation is inadequate because the university is not taking advantage of a potentially useful educational tool: clickers.*

Currently, Academic Technologies, which oversees all the computing functions in CMSU classrooms, has three sets of 100 clickers from Turning Technologies and two sets of 100 clickers from eInstruction. These clickers are available for instructors to check out for occasional use but may not be reserved for every meeting of an instructor's course. On the basis of an increasing consensus in the scholarly community that clickers improve the classroom learning environment and can improve learning in large lecture courses, Dr. Bremerton has allocated resources for a large feasibility study of whether CMSU should select a particular clicker system for use by CMSU instructors and establish a policy to provide technical support for clicker use and a method for students to acquire clickers through the university. The research that Dr. Bremerton invited SAAC to perform will be part of this large feasibility study.

Specifically, Dr. Bremerton asked the committee to perform research that would answer the following four questions:

The writers quote from the memo Dr. Bremerton had written to them. Often in technical communication, you will quote your reader's words to remind him or her of the context and to show that you are carrying out your tasks professionally.

1. Would instructors approve a university policy that selects and provides technical support for a clicker system that they could use in large lecture courses?

2. Would students approve a requirement that they purchase clickers as part of a university policy on clickers?

3. Would the physical characteristics of any of the large lecture halls affect the decision whether to adopt clickers or restrict the university to a particular technology or brand of clicker?

4. Would the computer platforms and operating systems used in the instructor stations in the large lecture halls affect the decision whether to adopt clickers or restrict the university to a particular technology or brand of clicker?

The writers show that they understand the relationship between their work and the larger feasibility study of which it is a part.

Dr. Bremerton explained that an understanding of faculty and student attitudes toward the adoption of a formal policy on clickers was fundamentally important because if faculty or students expressed no interest in their use or held serious reservations about their use, the university would need to consider whether and how to proceed with the feasibility study. Dr. Bremerton further explained that, for the university to study adopting a clicker policy, the administration would need to understand whether the physical characteristics of the lecture halls and the existing computer environment in the lecture halls would influence the technical choices that needed to be made.

3

For these reasons, Dr. Bremerton asked SAAC to present our findings and recommend whether the university should proceed with the clicker project and, if so, how the computing environment in the lecture halls would affect the direction of the feasibility study.

A formal statement of the task that Dr. Bremerton asked the committee to perform.

First, we sought to understand the basics of clicker use in higher education to inform our further research. Next, we wrote the interview questions and the questionnaires that we used to gather our data, field-tested the questions, and performed the interviews and distributed the questionnaires. Finally, we collected and analyzed the data, and then wrote this report.

The methods the writers used to carry out their study.

We wish to thank the three other members of the SAAC—Melissa Otheridge, Larry Wilins, and Rebecca Phillips—for reviewing the draft and offering valuable suggestions for revision.

The writers politely acknowledge the assistance they received from their colleagues on the committee.

We found that instructors likely will be very receptive to a feasibility study. In addition, if CMSU adopts a formal policy of clicker use, faculty will be positive about it—provided that the university chooses a good clicker system and provides effective technical support. Further, we found that more than half (56 percent) of the CMSU students who responded to our questionnaire expressed a willingness to pay up to $40 for a clicker. A quarter (23 percent) were willing to pay only $20, but a fifth (19 percent) were willing to pay up to $60.

The writers devote two paragraphs to their principal findings. Introductions can present the major findings of a report; technical communication is not about drama and suspense.

The infrastructure of our 17 large lecture halls presents no special difficulties for clicker use, provided that we restrict our study to radio-frequency-based systems. Although an older technology—infrared-based systems—offers cheaper clickers, it would require upgrading the lecture halls with additional hardware. Further, we found that the existing computer systems in the lecture halls include both Macs and PCs with operating systems back to Windows XP. Therefore, the selected system would need to work with all those operating systems.

On the basis of these findings, we recommend that CMSU proceed with its feasibility study of the costs and benefits of adopting a clicker policy on campus.

Notice the writers' use of the phrase "we recommend." Repeating key terms in this way helps readers understand the logic of a report and concentrate on the technical information it contains.

In the following sections, we provide additional details about our research methods, the results we obtained, the conclusions we drew from those results, and our recommendation.

An advance organizer for the rest of the report.

4

Research Methods

The writers use the same task organization as in the proposal and progress report.

To acquire the information requested by Dr. Bremerton, we broke the project into six tasks:

1. acquire a basic understanding of clicker use in higher education
2. research faculty attitudes toward a formal policy on clicker use
3. research student attitudes toward a requirement to purchase a clicker
4. research the physical characteristics of the lecture halls
5. research the existing computer environment in the lecture halls
6. analyze our data and prepare this recommendation report

In the following discussion of how we performed each task, we explain the reasoning that guided our research.

Task 1. Acquire a basic understanding of clicker use in higher education

Dr. Bremerton pointed us to a number of resources on clicker use in higher education. In addition, we conducted our own literature review. Most of the research we studied fell into one of four categories:

- general introductions to clicker use in higher-education trade magazines and general periodicals
- scholarly articles on student and faculty attitudes and on learning effects
- technical specifications of clickers provided on the sites of the various manufacturers
- best practices presented on sites of colleges and universities that have adopted clickers

By stating that they know that their sources are a mixture of different kinds of information, not all of which is equally useful for every one of their questions, the writers suggest that they are careful analysts.

As we expected, the information we acquired about this commercial technology contained a mixture of research findings and marketing. We relied most heavily on manufacturers' Web sites for technical information on system capabilities and compatibility issues; we relied most heavily on university Web sites for information on instructor attitudes and experiences and best practices for implementing clicker programs. Finally, we relied most heavily on research literature for information about how clickers might affect classroom atmosphere and student learning.

Task 2. Research faculty attitudes toward a formal policy on clicker use

In performing Task 2, we sought to answer the following question posed by Dr. Bremerton: "Would instructors approve a university policy that selects and provides technical support for a clicker system that they could use in large lecture courses?"

5

Because our review of the research suggested that instructors across the country who have used clickers are generally quite positive about them, we wanted to ensure that we paid appropriate attention to the attitudes of the relatively small number of CMSU instructors experienced with clickers. This way, we could get a sense of whether our instructors are essentially similar to those across the country in their attitudes and experiences. We decided to use a slightly different questionnaire for instructors who have not used clickers.

We created Faculty Questionnaire 1 (see Appendix A, on page 20) for instructors who had taught with clickers at least two semesters. We chose two semesters as a minimum because we wanted to ensure that we were gathering data from instructors who are reasonably comfortable using clickers. Instructors who are new to clickers or who had taught with them only once and then abandoned them might not provide valid data. Of the 25 instructors who have used clickers at CMSU, 16 had used them at least two semesters and therefore received the questionnaire.

We created Faculty Questionnaire 2 (see Appendix B, on page 21) for the 56 instructors who regularly teach lectures with more than 100 students who had never used clickers or who had used them only one semester.

We field-tested the two questionnaires with the three other members of SAAC and, for each questionnaire, three faculty members from English, Physics, and Chemistry. We reviewed the comments from these field tests and incorporated changes in the two questionnaires.

With the authorization of Dr. Bremerton, we uploaded the questionnaires to Qualtrics, and then sent an e-mail to appropriate faculty inviting them to respond.

Task 3. Research student attitudes toward a requirement to purchase a clicker

In performing Task 3, we sought to answer the following question: "Would students approve a requirement that they purchase clickers as part of a university policy on clickers?"

Several research studies suggest that most students, across the country and across various course subjects, like using clickers. One study (Caldwell, 2007), at West Virginia University, found that some 88 percent of students "frequently" or "always" enjoyed using clickers in their introductory biology course. Aggregating several studies, the percentage of students who approve of using clickers always exceeds 70 percent. Students comment that instructors who use clickers are more aware of students' needs and employ a more responsive teaching style than those who don't use them.

The writers carefully explain the logic of their methods. Do not assume that your readers will automatically understand why you did what you did. Sometimes it is best to explain your thinking. Technical communication contains a lot of facts and figures, but like other kinds of writing it relies on clear, logical arguments.

Including a page number in the cross-reference to Appendix A is a convenience to the reader. When you insert cross-references, remember to add the correct page number after you determine where the referenced material will appear in your report.

As discussed in Ch. 5, p. 99, some questions will misfire. Therefore, it is smart to field-test a questionnaire before you distribute it.

Note that these tasks begin with the question that the writers sought to answer. Don't be afraid to repeat information. Technical communication often calls for presenting different versions of the same information in different places in a document or in a set of documents.

The writers cite their sources throughout the report.

6

However, students do not always approve of clicker use. The principal complaints reported nationally (Caldwell, 2007) relate to the following problems:

- Some clickers cost too much.
- Some instructors do not explain the purpose of using the clickers.
- Some instructors spend too much class time using the clickers.
- Some instructors let clicker use drive the course content.
- Some students are anxious about having their course grades depend, to some extent, on their use of an electronic device.

Of these concerns, all except the one related to the cost of the clicker refer to how instructors integrate the clickers into the course content. As many commentators suggest, schools need to provide training for instructors that covers technical questions not only about how to operate clickers and related software but also about how to use them effectively in teaching the course.

We concluded that the most useful data we could obtain would relate to what price CMSU students thought was reasonable. A review of the sites of the four leading manufacturers of clicker systems (Turning Technologies, eInstruction, iClicker, and Qwizdom) shows that pricing can vary, depending on the pricing model the vendor uses. For instance, some companies (such as Turning Technologies) charge a one-time price, with no fees for registering the clicker so that it can be used. Other companies (such as eInstruction) charge once for the clicker but have a per-semester registration fee. In addition, commentators (University of Wisconsin-Eau Claire, n.d.) point out that some vendors have established relationships with textbook manufacturers so that the clickers are packaged with selected textbooks. Finally, some schools have entered into contractual relationships with clicker vendors that call for a particular price for students at that school. Therefore, it is impossible to answer the cost question simply.

Here, again, the writers explain the logic of their methods. They decided to focus on what they think is the most appropriate information: student attitudes toward the price of the clickers. Questions related to how instructors use clickers will be addressed in Dr. Bremerton's larger study.

We therefore decided to try to determine the one-time price that students would find reasonable for a clicker. Although CMSU might not in fact be able to achieve a one-time price contract for the clicker, the answer to this question will at least give the university an idea of student attitudes about price. We selected a price ranging from zero (for students who wish to express an opposition to having to buy a clicker at any price) to approximately $60. (At this time, Qwizdom's clicker, at $66.55, represents the high end of prices.)

We wrote the following one-question questionnaire for the 11,324 currently enrolled undergraduate students.

7

As you may know, Vice President for Student Affairs Bremerton is conducting a study to determine whether CMSU should select a single brand of clicker to be used in some lecture courses at CMSU. Clickers are used by students to respond to questions posed by instructors in large lecture courses. If such a choice were made, you might be required to purchase a clicker for use in some of your lecture courses. Following are some details:

1. The university would seek to enter into a two-year contract with a manufacturer of the clicker systems. Although the university would hope to renew that contract so that the one clicker you purchase would last for your entire career at CMSU, it is possible that you would need to purchase a new clicker as often as every two years.
2. You would be responsible for purchasing the batteries for your clicker. Batteries generally last from six months to a year, and replacement batteries cost approximately $3–6.
3. You would be responsible for replacing your clicker if you lose it.

We would appreciate your telling us what price you think would be reasonable for the clicker unit. Please select one of the following responses, and then hit the Submit button.

- ○ $0. I don't want to have to buy any clicker.
- ○ Up to $20.
- ○ Up to $40.
- ○ Up to $60.

Thank you!

We made this questionnaire available for all undergraduate students because, of the 11,324 students currently enrolled, only 832 had ever used a clicker at CMSU. Because that number constituted only some 7 percent of the total undergraduate population, we felt that it was not worth the expense of separating out those who had used a clicker on campus.

We then field-tested the question with the three other members of SAAC. With the authorization of Dr. Bremerton, we uploaded the survey to Qualtrics, and then sent an e-mail to students, inviting them to respond to the question.

Task 4. Research the physical characteristics of the lecture halls

In performing Task 4, we sought to answer the following question: "Would the physical characteristics of any of the large lecture halls affect the decision whether to adopt clickers or restrict the university to a particular technology or brand of clicker?"

Writers often need to decide where to present information in a technical document. This questionnaire could have appeared in an appendix, as the two instructor questionnaires did. However, because it is relatively brief and readers are very interested in student attitudes, the writers decided to include it in the body of the report.

8

The writers present just enough information about the two technologies to help the reader understand their logic. Writers sometimes present too much information; write only as much as you need to get the job done.

Our research indicated that there are two major technologies used in clicker systems: infrared (IR) and radio frequency (RF) (Ohio State University, 2005). IR, which is the technology used in television remote controls, requires a clear line of sight and has a limited range (40–80 feet). If IR is to be used for greater distances, the room would need to have additional receivers installed on the walls and connected either by wires or wirelessly to the instructor podium. In addition, IR signals can be disrupted by some classroom lighting systems.

By contrast, RF systems do not require a clear line of sight, have no range limitations, and are not subject to electronic interference. An RF system uses a receiver built into a USB device that attaches easily to the computer in the podium or to the instructor's laptop. For these reasons, RF systems are simpler and are becoming the industry standard.

However, IR systems are less expensive, with clickers costing less than $10. Therefore, if CMSU lecture halls meet the line-of-sight and range requirements, already have receivers installed, and pose no interference risk, IR systems would be an option. But if any of the lecture halls does not meet one or more of these criteria, CMSU should consider only RF systems.

We began by meeting with Marvin Nickerson, the Director of Physical Plant, on November 8, 2011, to explain our project and to give him a list of the questions we needed to answer. Table 1 shows the questions we posed, as well as the rationale for each question:

Table 1.   Questions About the Physical Characteristics of the Lecture Halls

Question	Rationale
1. Which lecture halls have more than 100 seats?	Although clickers can be used in any size classroom, they are used most frequently in large lecture halls, where the effect they can have in increasing interactivity between the instructor and the students is most valuable.
2. For each of these lecture halls, what is the distance from the podium to the farthest student seat?	Because IR systems have a range of only 40–80 feet, we wanted to know whether CMSU would need to install extra IR receivers for the systems to work effectively.

The table is an appropriate graphic for presenting the questions and their rationales economically. Again, the writers are explaining the logic of their decisions.

9

Question	Rationale
3. Do any of these lecture halls have pillars or other obstructions between the podium and any of the student seats?	IR systems cannot function if there is a line-of-sight obstruction.
4. Do any of these lecture halls already have infrared receivers and transmission lines installed?	Because IR systems would require the installation of IR receivers and transmission lines, we wanted to know if such hardware is already in place.
5. Do any of these lecture halls have any technical characteristics that might interfere with either IR or RF transmission between the podium and any student seat?	We wanted to know if there was anything else about any of the lecture halls that we needed to consider. Although we are unaware of any other factors that might be relevant, we thought it appropriate to ask Mr. Nickerson, who has vast experience with the physical infrastructure of the classroom buildings.

Mr. Nickerson responded in an e-mail to us dated November 11, 2011. We thanked him in an e-mail the next day.

Task 5. Research the existing computer environment in the lecture halls

In performing Task 5, we sought to answer the following question: "Would the computer platforms and operating systems used in the instructor stations in the large lecture halls affect the decision whether to adopt clickers or restrict the university to a particular technology or brand of clicker?"

We wanted to determine which platform (Windows, Macintosh, or other) and which operating system (for example, Windows XP, Vista, or 7 or Macintosh OSX) are used in the computers used in each podium in the large lecture halls identified by Mr. Nickerson. This information would be necessary to ensure that any clicker system CMSU selects would work with the existing computer technology in the lecture halls.

We met with Dr. Arlene Matthews, the Director of Academic Technologies, on November 14, 2011, to explain our project and to give her a list of the questions we needed to answer. As Director of AT, Dr. Matthews would have a database of this information because AT participated in installing all the instructor podiums and related systems in all the lecture halls. We exchanged several phone calls during that week, and she responded in an e-mail dated November 17, 2011. We thanked her in an e-mail later that day.

10

On the basis of Dr. Matthews's e-mail, we made follow-up phone calls to the network administrators for three departments to obtain information that Dr. Matthews lacked or that we thought might be out of date.

Because analyzing their data and writing this report is part of the writers' study, it is appropriate to include it as one of the steps. In some organizations, however, this task is assumed to be part of the study and is therefore not presented in the report.

Task 6. Analyze our data and prepare this recommendation report
We drafted this report and uploaded it to a wiki that we created to make it convenient for the other SAAC members to help us revise it. We incorporated most of our colleagues' suggestions and then presented a final draft of this report on the wiki to gather any final editing suggestions.

Results

The writers present an advance organizer for the results section.

In this section, we present the results of our research. For each of the tasks we carried out, we present the most important data we acquired.

Task 1. Acquire a basic understanding of clicker use in higher education

The writers continue to use the task structure that they used in the methods section.

Clickers, which are also called *classroom response systems*, *student response systems*, and *audience response systems*, are "wireless in-class electronic polling systems used by students to answer questions during lectures" (Ohio State University, 2005, p. 2). In a clicker system, each student has an electronic device called a *clicker*, which looks like a TV remote control. The instructor poses a question, usually by embedding the question beforehand in a PowerPoint presentation, and students respond by inputting information on their clickers. Software on the instructor's computer tabulates the responses and presents them in a display, such as a bar graph, which appears on the instructor's screen, and (in some systems) on a screen on each student's clicker.

Clickers are often used to engage students in learning, to give quizzes, and to take attendance.

Figure 1 shows students using clickers.

This photograph is the only one in the report. If the purpose of the report were to recommend which clicker system to use, the report would likely contain photos of each of the various brands of clickers. In this report, the photograph of students enthusiastically using the clickers is appropriate. The photo was first published in a student blog. Be sure to consider the intellectual-property issues related to your use of any copyrighted information, as discussed in Ch. 2, p. 28.

Figure 1.   Students using clickers (Brilling, 2008)

11

Clickers can help instructors improve the classroom atmosphere in a number of ways (Vanderbilt University, 2010):

- promote active student engagement during a lecture
- promote discussion and collaboration among students during class
- encourage participation from every student in a class
- check for student understanding during class
- teach in a way that adapts to the immediate learning needs of students

Anecdotal and scholarly evidence suggests clearly that using clickers improves classroom dynamics by encouraging active learning. Whereas a traditional lecture can be a passive experience, with the instructor talking to students, clickers encourage interaction not only between the instructor and the students but also between students (Draper & Brown, 2004). In a traditional lecture, students are often unwilling to participate because they are afraid of embarrassment or disapproval by their peers, or simply because they have learned not to participate in a lecture (Caldwell, 2007). In a typical lecture, a small number of students dominate the questioning, often giving the instructor an inaccurate impression of how many students understand the material (Simpson & Oliver, 2006).

Although it makes sense to assume that a more active learning environment leads to better learning, measuring learning is more challenging and therefore there is not yet complete consensus that clickers improve learning. There are some studies that do suggest improved learning. For instance, a study (Ohio State University, 2008) of a large, multi-section physics course found that students in clicker sections outperformed those in non-clicker sections by 10 points on a final exam, and that female students did as well as males in the clicker sections (but not in non-clicker sections). And a meta-analysis by Fies and Marshall (2006) shows that 11 of 26 studies show clear evidence of improved comprehension of complex concepts.

The bulk of scholarly literature, however, is consistent with Beatty et al. (2006), who see great potential for improved student learning. As Caldwell (2007) puts it,

> Most reviews agree that "ample converging evidence" suggests that clickers generally cause improved student outcomes such as improved exam scores or passing rates, student comprehension, and learning and that students like clickers. The reviews of the literature, however, also agree that much of the research so far is not systematic enough to permit scientific conclusions about what causes the benefits. (n.p.)

At the very least, as Knight and Wood (2005) argue, students with clickers almost always do at least as well in exam scores as students who don't use clickers.

This is probably the most important point for this reader: no scholarly studies have found that clickers hurt the learning process.

12

Task 2. Research faculty attitudes

Because student attendance, engagement, and participation increase with
the use of clickers, it makes sense that many instructors would like clickers.
Anecdotal evidence reported in Caldwell (2007) suggests that instructors do
enjoy the improved student engagement and perceive that students learn more
effectively in clicker courses.

However, the literature suggests (see Vanderbilt, 2010) that instructors have
cited problems with clicker use:

- Technical problems with the hardware or software can occur during a class.
- It takes time for an instructor to learn a system and use it effectively.
- It takes time for an instructor to embed clicker questions in teaching
  materials (such as PowerPoint slides).
- Using clickers in class takes time away from other instructional activities.
- Changing a lesson "on the fly" or conducting a discussion in response to
  clicker responses can disrupt the flow of a lesson.

We considered these findings in devising our questionnaires for CMSU
instructors.

We distributed Faculty Questionnaire 1 to the 16 instructors who had taught
with clickers at least two semesters. Of that number, 14 responded. Figure 2
shows the mean responses to the five questions (with 1 = "strongly disagree"
and 6 = "strongly agree"):

Q1. I find it easy to use clickers in my lecture courses.
Q2. Using clickers in my lecture classes improves student attendance and
     engagement.
Q3. Using clickers in my lecture classes improves student learning.
Q4. It is very important to me that CMSU select a versatile, dependable clicker
     and provide adequate technical support for faculty who choose to use it.
Q5. If CMSU selects a good clicker and provides good technical support, I
     will use it in my lecture courses.

*Even though the reader could
flip to Appendix A to read the
questions, it is more convenient
to read the questions here,
along with the data they elicited.*

13

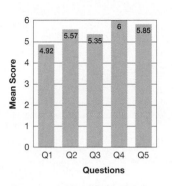

Figure 2.   Attitudes of Faculty Experienced with Clickers

Appendix A, page 20, presents the raw data that are summarized in Figure 2.

We distributed Faculty Questionnaire 2 to the 56 instructors who had never taught with clickers (or taught with them for only one semester) but who regularly teach lectures with more than 100 students. Of the 56, 42 responded. Figure 3 shows the mean responses to the five questions (with 1 = "strongly disagree" and 6 = "strongly agree"):

Q1. I would like to make my lectures a more active learning experience for students.
Q2. I would like to improve my ability to know how many students understand the concepts I am trying to present during my lectures.
Q3. I would like to be able to automate tasks such as taking attendance or delivering quizzes quickly and accurately using clickers.
Q4. It is very important to me that CMSU select a versatile, dependable clicker and provide adequate technical support for faculty who choose to use it.
Q5. I would be very interested in learning more about how I could use clickers in my lecture courses.

14

Note that the writers use a conservative design for their bar graphs, with simple two-dimensional bars, labels presenting the data clearly, and same-color bars. If there is no reason to use different colors, don't.

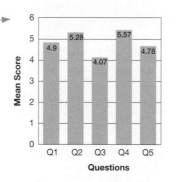

Figure 3. **Attitudes of Faculty Not Experienced with Clickers**

Appendix B, page 21, presents the raw data that are summarized in Figure 3.

Task 3. Research student attitudes

We received 8,576 responses to the questionnaire we made available to the 11,324 enrolled undergraduates. Figure 4 shows the responses:

A pie chart is a good choice for showing the relative proportions of a small set of data that add up to a whole. Again, note that the writers set their software so that the chart is a conservative design. For the colors, they chose different saturations of the same hue. For the data, they chose to present the maximum dollar figures and the percentage for each possible response to the question.

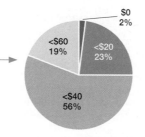

Figure 4. **Students' Attitudes Toward Reasonable Price for a Clicker**

Task 4. Research the physical characteristics of the lecture halls

Table 2 shows the questions we posed to Mr. Nickerson, the rationale for each question, and Mr. Nickerson's replies.

15

**Table 2.   Questions and Answers About the Physical Characteristics of the
Lecture Halls** ◄——————   *The writers adapted the table
from the methods section by
adding the right-hand column
for Mr. Nickerson's reply.*

Question	Rationale	Mr. Nickerson's reply
1. Which lecture halls have more than 100 seats?	Although clickers can be used in any size classroom, they are used most frequently in large lecture halls, where the effect they can have in increasing interactivity between the instructor and the students is most valuable.	There are 17 such rooms on campus: [here is the list of the rooms]
2. For each of these lecture halls, what is the distance from the podium to the farthest student seat?	Because IR systems have a range of only 40–80 feet, we wanted to know whether CMSU would need to install extra IR receivers for the systems to work effectively.	Of the 17, 15 have a distance of over 80 feet.
3. Do any of these lecture halls have pillars or other obstructions between the podium and any of the student seats?	IR systems cannot function if there is a line-of-sight obstruction.	Of the 17, 4 have pillars that obstruct up to 12 seats.
4. Do any of these lecture halls already have infrared receivers and transmission lines installed?	Because IR systems would require the installation of IR receivers and transmission lines, we wanted to know if such hardware is already in place.	No.
5. Do any of these lecture halls have any technical characteristics that might interfere with either IR or RF transmission between the podium and any student seat?	We wanted to know if there was anything else about any of the lecture halls that we needed to consider in evaluating the two main types of systems. Although we are unaware of any other factors that might be relevant, we thought it appropriate to ask Mr. Nickerson, who has vast experience with the physical infrastructure of the classroom buildings.	No.

16

Task 5. Research the computers used in the lecture halls

From our meeting with Dr. Matthews, the Director of Academic Technologies, and some follow-up phone calls to her and representatives of three academic departments, we determined that the 17 large lecture halls in which we might use clicker systems use the following computer platforms and operating systems:

Platform	Operating system	Number of lecture halls
Macintosh	OSX	3
PC	XP	7
PC	Vista	7
PC	Windows 7	4

Small, informal tables like this one often are not numbered or titled. See Ch. 8, p. 192, for more on tables.

Conclusions

In this section, we present our conclusions based on our research related to the four questions we were asked to answer.

The function of a conclusion is to explain what the data mean. Here the writers explain how their results can help their readers determine whether and how to proceed with the clicker study. Notice that a conclusion is not the same as a recommendation, which explains what the writers think should be done next.

The writers present an advance organizer for the conclusions section.

Faculty attitudes

Faculty who have taught with clickers at least two semesters have very positive attitudes toward the technology. On a scale of 1–6 (with 1 = "strongly disagree" and 6 = "strongly agree"), they feel that systems were easy to use, improve student attendance and engagement, and improve learning. They were unanimous that it was important for CMSU to select a versatile, dependable clicker and provide adequate technical support and suggested very clearly that they would use a clicker system. In short, our instructors with experience using clickers want to proceed with the project.

At this point in the document, the writers have decided to abandon the "task" labels. Their thinking is that they are focusing less on what they did and more on the meaning of the information they have gathered. However, they are retaining the headings that help readers understand the topic they are discussing.

Instructors who lacked significant experience with clickers but who regularly teach lectures with more than 100 students were somewhat less enthusiastic but still very positive. They feel that clickers would make their lectures a more active learning experience for students and help them understand the concepts presented in the lectures. They were less enthusiastic about using clickers to automate tasks such as taking attendance or delivering quizzes, but they echo the experienced instructors in feeling it important to select a versatile, dependable clicker and provide adequate technical support. Most importantly,

17

they expressed a strong desire to learn more about using clickers in their large lecture courses. In short, these data suggest that instructors inexperienced with clickers wish to learn more about them and are at least open to the possibility that clickers will enhance the learning environment and improve student learning.

On the basis of the results of these two questionnaires, we think that instructors will be very receptive to a feasibility study. In addition, if CMSU adopts a formal policy of clicker use, faculty probably will be positive about it—provided that the university chooses a good clicker system and provides effective technical support.

Student attitudes

More than half (56 percent) of the CMSU students who responded to our questionnaire expressed a willingness to pay up to $40 for a clicker. A quarter (23 percent) are willing to pay only $20, but a fifth (19 percent) are willing to pay up to $60. Two percent do not wish to pay anything for a clicker.

We therefore conclude that price is an important factor that the university should consider during the feasibility study. CMSU students make considerable sacrifices to attend the university, with the majority of them earning most, if not all, of their college expenses. For a clicker program to be received positively by students here, they will need to believe that the cost to them is modest and that the advantages to them outweigh that cost.

Physical characteristics of the lecture halls

Although IR systems use cheaper clickers than RF systems do, our large lecture halls are not already equipped to handle IR systems. Therefore, we should consider only those vendors that offer RF systems.

If a point can be made in only a few sentences, use only a few sentences.

Computers used in the lecture halls

Because our large lecture halls use both PCs and Macintoshes, we should consider only those vendors that offer systems that are cross-platform. In addition, we should ensure that the system we are considering is compatible with Windows XP (the oldest operating system on campus). If the system is not, we would need to upgrade the podium computers in seven of our large lecture halls.

18

Recommendation

We recommend that CMSU proceed with its feasibility study of the costs and benefits of adopting a clicker policy on campus. Instructors, both those experienced with clickers and those who are not, are strongly positive toward the possibility of being able to use clickers, especially if the best one is selected and it is supported effectively by the university. Students are positive toward the possibility, especially if they are asked to spend no more than $40 for a clicker. The existing infrastructure of the large lecture halls poses no particular problems, but we would need to adopt an RF-based system that is compatible with our current PC and Macintosh systems.

This recommendation states explicitly what the writers think the reader should do next.

The recommendation largely repeats information presented in other places in the report. In technical communication, repetition can reinforce important information and increase your chances of reaching readers who read only selected portions of long documents.

19

References

Beatty, I. D., Gerace, W. J., Leonar, W. J., & Dufresne, R. J. (2006). Designing effective questions for classroom response system teaching. *American Journal of Physics, 74*(1), 31–39.

Brilling, S. (2008, October 22). Using clickers in class. *My Hearing Life.* Retrieved September 2, 2011, from http://samshearinglife.blogspot.com/

Caldwell, J. E. (2007). Clickers in the large classroom: Current research and best-practice tips. *CBE Life Sciences Education, 6*(1): 9–20. doi:10.1187/cbe.06-12-0205

Draper, S. W., & Brown, M. I. (2004). Increasing interactivity in lectures using an electronic voting system. *Journal of Computer Assisted Learning, 20*, 81–94.

Fies, C., & Marshall, J. (2006). Classroom response systems: A review of the literature. *Journal of Science Education & Technology, 15*, 101–109.

Knight, J. K., & Wood, W. B. (2005). Teaching more by lecturing less. *Cell Biology Education, 4*, 298–310.

Ohio State University. (2005). *Committee on classroom response systems: Final report,* March 2, 2005. Retrieved September 2, 2011, from http://lt.osu.edu/assets/resources/clickers/crsfinalreport.pdf

Ohio State University. (2008, July 18). Students who use "clickers" score better on physics tests. *ScienceDaily.* Retrieved September 4, 2011, from www.sciencedaily.com/releases/2008/07/080717092033.htm

Simpson, V., & Oliver, M. (2006). *Using electronic voting systems in lectures.* Retrieved September 5, 2011, from www.ucl.ac.uk/learningtechnology/examples/ElectronicVotingSystems.pdf

University of Wisconsin-Eau Claire. (n.d). *Comparison of student response system vendors.* Retrieved September 3, 2011, from www.uwec.edu/evansmm/SRS/clickerDecision.pdf

Vanderbilt University Center for Teaching. (2010). *Classroom response systems ("clickers").* Retrieved September 3, 2011, from www.vanderbilt.edu/cft/resources/teaching_resources/technology/crs.htm

This list of references follows the APA documentation style, which is discussed in Appendix, Part A, p. 419.

Presenting the raw data in boldface after each question is a clear way to communicate how the respondents voted. Although most readers will not be interested in the raw data, some will.

20

Appendix A: Faculty Questionnaire 1

This is the questionnaire we distributed to the 16 CMSU instructors who had taught with clickers for at least two semesters. Of the 16, 14 responded. The numbers in the responses represent the number of faculty who selected each response.

Questionnaire on Clicker Use at CMSU

Directions: As you may know, Vice President for Student Affairs Bremerton is conducting a study to determine whether to institute a formal mechanism for using clickers in large lecture courses at CMSU. We are asking you to participate in this study because you are an experienced user of clickers. We greatly appreciate your answering the following five questions.

1. I find it easy to use clickers in my lecture courses.
    Strongly disagree ___ ___ ___ **4** **7** **3** Strongly agree

2. Using clickers in my lecture classes improves student attendance and engagement.
    Strongly disagree ___ ___ ___ ___ **6** **8** Strongly agree

3. Using clickers in my lecture classes improves student learning.
    Strongly disagree ___ ___ **2** **5** **7** Strongly agree

4. It is very important to me that CMSU select a versatile, dependable clicker and provide adequate technical support for faculty who choose to use it.
    Strongly disagree ___ ___ ___ ___ ___ **14** Strongly agree

5. If CMSU selects a good clicker and provides good technical support, I will use it in my lecture courses.
    Strongly disagree ___ ___ ___ ___ **2** **12** Strongly agree

Thank you!

21

Appendix B: Faculty Questionnaire 2

This is the questionnaire we distributed to the 56 CMSU instructors who had *not* taught with clickers for at least two semesters. Of the 56 faculty, 42 responded. The numbers in the responses represent the number of faculty who selected each response.

Questionnaire on Clicker Use at CMSU

Directions: As you may know, Vice President for Student Affairs Bremerton is conducting a study to determine whether to institute a formal mechanism for using clickers in large lecture courses at CMSU. Students use clickers to respond to multiple-choice questions posed by faculty. Instructors use clickers for such tasks as assessing student understanding, prompting discussions, giving quizzes, and taking attendance.

In the introductory text before the five questions, the writers present a slightly more detailed explanation of clickers, because most of their respondents have not used them.

We are asking you to participate in this study because we want to gauge your interest in using clickers in your lecture courses. We greatly appreciate your answering the following five questions.

1. I would like to make my lectures a more active learning experience for students.
    Strongly disagree ___ ___ **7** **4** **17** **14** Strongly agree

2. I would like to improve my ability to know how many students understand the concepts I am trying to present during my lectures.
    Strongly disagree ___ ___ ___ **9** **12** **21** Strongly agree

3. I would like to be able to automate tasks such as taking attendance or delivering quizzes quickly and accurately using clickers.
    Strongly disagree ___ **8** **3** **16** **8** **7** Strongly agree

4. It is very important to me that CMSU select a versatile, dependable clicker and provide adequate technical support for faculty who choose to use it.
    Strongly disagree ___ ___ ___ ___ **18** **24** Strongly agree

5. I would be very interested in learning more about how I could use clickers in my lecture courses.
    Strongly disagree **4** **2** **3** **9** **12** **12** Strongly agree

Thank you!

Writer's Checklist

In planning your recommendation report, did you

☐ identify the questions that need to be answered? (p. 316)

☐ carry out appropriate research? (p. 317)

☐ draw valid conclusions about the results (if appropriate)? (p. 319)

☐ formulate recommendations based on the conclusions (if appropriate)? (p. 319)

Does the transmittal letter

☐ clearly state the title and, if necessary, the subject and purpose of the report? (p. 323)

☐ clearly state who authorized or commissioned the report? (p. 323)

☐ briefly state the methods you used? (p. 323)

☐ summarize your major results, conclusions, and recommendations? (p. 323)

☐ acknowledge any assistance you received? (p. 323)

☐ courteously offer further assistance? (p. 323)

Does the cover include

☐ the title of the report? (p. 323)

☐ your name and position? (p. 323)

☐ the date of submission? (p. 323)

☐ the company name or logo? (p. 323)

Does the title page

☐ include a title that clearly states the subject and purpose of the report? (p. 323)

☐ list the names and positions of both you and your principal reader(s)? (p. 323)

☐ include the date of submission of the report and any other identifying information? (p. 323)

Does the abstract

☐ list the report title, your name, and any other identifying information? (p. 323)

☐ clearly define the problem or opportunity that led to the project? (p. 323)

☐ briefly describe (if appropriate) the research methods? (p. 323)

☐ summarize the major results, conclusions, and recommendations? (p. 324)

Does the table of contents

☐ clearly identify the executive summary? (p. 324)

☐ contain a sufficiently detailed breakdown of the major sections of the body of the report? (p. 324)

☐ reproduce the headings as they appear in your report? (p. 324)

☐ include page numbers? (p. 325)

☐ Does the list of illustrations (or list of tables or list of figures) include all the graphics found in the body of the report? (p. 325)

Does the executive summary

☐ clearly state the problem or opportunity that led to the project? (p. 326)

☐ explain the major results, conclusions, recommendations, and managerial implications of your report? (p. 326)

☐ avoid technical vocabulary and concepts that a managerial audience is not likely to know? (p. 326)

Does the introduction

☐ explain the subject of the report? (p. 321)

☐ explain the purpose of the report? (p. 321)

☐ explain the background of the report? (p. 321)

☐ describe your sources of information? (p. 321)

☐ indicate the scope of the report? (p. 321)

☐ briefly summarize the most significant findings of the project? (p. 321)

☐ briefly summarize your recommendations? (p. 321)

☐ explain the organization of the report? (p. 321)

☐ define key terms used in the report? (p. 321)

☐ Does the methods section describe your methods in sufficient detail? (p. 321)

☐ Have you justified your methods where necessary, explaining, for instance, why you chose one method over another? (p. 321)

Are the results presented

☐ clearly? (p. 321)

☐ objectively? (p. 321)

☐ without interpretation? (p. 321)

Are the conclusions

☐ presented clearly? (p. 322)

☐ drawn logically from the results? (p. 322)

Are the recommendations

- ☐ clear? (p. 322)
- ☐ objective? (p. 322)
- ☐ polite? (p. 322)
- ☐ in an appropriate form (list or paragraph)? (p. 322)
- ☐ in an appropriate location? (p. 322)

☐ Does the glossary include definitions of all the technical terms your readers might not know? (p. 328)

☐ Does the list of symbols include all the symbols and abbreviations your readers might not know? (p. 328)

☐ Does the list of references include all your sources and adhere to an appropriate documentation system? (p. 330)

☐ Do the appendixes include supporting materials that are too bulky to present in the report body or are of interest to only a small number of your readers? (p. 330)

Exercises

▶ **In This Book** For more about memos, see Ch. 9, p. 223.

1. An important element in carrying out a feasibility study is determining the criteria by which to judge each option. For each of the following topics, list five necessary criteria and five desirable criteria you might apply in assessing the options.
   a. buying a cell phone
   b. selecting a major
   c. choosing a company to work for
   d. buying a car
   e. choosing a place to live while you attend college

2. **INTERNET EXERCISE** Using the Links Library for Chapter 5 on <bedfordstmartins.com/ps>, find a site that links to government agencies and departments. Then find a recommendation report on a subject that interests you. In what ways does the structure of the report differ from the structure described in this chapter? In other words, does it lack some of the elements described in this chapter, or does it have additional elements? Are the elements arranged in the same order in which they are described in this chapter? In what ways do the differences reflect the audience, purpose, and subject of the report?

3. **GROUP EXERCISE** Write the recommendation report for the research project you proposed in response to Exercise 3 on page 000 in Chapter 11. Your instructor will tell you whether the report is to be written individually or collaboratively, but either way, work closely with a partner to review and revise your report. A partner can be very helpful during the planning phase, too, as you choose a topic, refine it, and plan your research.

4. **INTERNET EXERCISE** Secure a recommendation report for a project subsidized by a city or federal agency, a private organization, or a university committee or task force. (Be sure to check your university's Web site; universities routinely publish strategic planning reports and other sorts of self-study reports. Also check <www.nas.edu>, which is the site for the National Academy of Sciences, the National Academy of Engineering, the Institute of Medicine, and the National Research Council, all of which publish reports on the Web.) In a memo to your instructor, analyze the report. Overall, how effective is the report? How could the writers have improved it? If possible, submit a copy of the report along with your memo.

▶ On the Web

For a case assignment, "Analyzing Decision Matrices," see Cases on <bedfordstmartins.com/ps>.

14

Writing Definitions, Descriptions, and Instructions

fotog/Getty Images.

Do everything you can to ensure that your readers won't get hurt.

Instructions are all around us. This photo from the inside of a passenger train shows instructions explaining what to do in case of various kinds of emergencies. Notice that these instructions use images, words, and colors to help people understand how to make the right decisions quickly.

This chapter discusses definitions, descriptions, and instructions. We need to start by defining these three terms:

- A *definition* is typically a brief explanation of an item or concept using words and (sometimes) graphics. You could write a definition of *file format* or of *regenerative braking*.

- A *description* is typically a longer explanation—usually accompanied by graphics—of an object, mechanism, or process. You could write a description of a *wind turbine*, of *global warming*, or of *shale-oil extraction*.

- A set of *instructions* is a kind of process description, usually accompanied by graphics, intended to enable a person to carry out a task. You could write a set of instructions for laying a brick patio or for making a playlist for your MP3 player.

Regardless of your field, you will write definitions, descriptions, and instructions frequently. Whether you are communicating with other technical professionals, with managers, or with the public, you must be able to define and describe your topic and explain how to carry out tasks.

Focus on Process

In writing definitions, descriptions, and instructions, pay special attention to these steps in the writing process. For a complete process for writing technical documents, see page 14.

- **Planning.** For definitions, you will need to decide where to place the definition. Parenthetical and sentence definitions can be placed in the text, in a marginal gloss, in a separate hyperlinked file, in a footnote, or in a glossary (an alphabetized list of definitions). An extended definition can be a section in the body of the larger document or can be placed in an appendix.

- **Drafting.** For descriptions, you will need to indicate clearly the nature and scope of the description, introduce the description clearly, provide additional detail, and conclude the description. For instructions, you will need to design the instructions based on how your readers will be using them, and you should include appropriate graphics. Do everything you can to ensure readers' safety.

- **Revising.** If you can, carry out usability testing on any instructions you write.

WRITING DEFINITIONS

The world of business and industry depends on clear definitions. Suppose you learn at a job interview that the employer pays tuition and expenses for employees' job-related education. You'll need to study the employee-benefits manual to understand just what the company will pay for. Who, for instance, is an *employee*? Is it anyone who works for the company, or is it someone who has worked for the company full-time (40 hours per week) for at least six uninterrupted months? What is *tuition*? Does it include laboratory or student fees? What is *job-related education*? Does a course about time management qualify? What, in fact, constitutes *education*?

Definitions are common in communicating policies and standards "for the record." Definitions also have many uses outside legal or contractual contexts. Two such uses occur frequently:

- *Definitions clarify a description of a new development or a new technology in a technical field.* For instance, a zoologist who has discovered a new animal species names and defines it.

- *Definitions help specialists communicate with less knowledgeable readers.* A manual explaining how to tune up a car includes definitions of parts and tools.

Definitions, then, are crucial in many kinds of technical communication. All readers, from the general reader to the expert, need effective definitions to carry out their jobs.

Analyzing the Writing Situation for Definitions

In This Book

For more about audience and purpose, see Ch. 4.

The first step in writing effective definitions is to analyze the writing situation: the audience and the purpose of the document. Physicists wouldn't need a definition of *entropy*, but lawyers might. Builders know what a molly bolt is, but many insurance agents don't. When you write for people whose first language is not English, consider adding a *glossary* (a list of definitions), using Simplified English and easily recognizable terms in your definitions, and using graphics to help readers understand a term or concept.

Think, too, about your purpose. For readers who need only a basic understanding of a concept—say, *time-sharing vacation resorts*—a brief, informal definition is usually sufficient. However, readers who need to understand an object, process, or concept thoroughly and be able to carry out related tasks need a more formal and detailed definition. For example, the definition of a "Class 2 Alert" written for operators at a nuclear power plant must be comprehensive, specific, and precise.

The appropriate type of definition depends on your audience and purpose. You have three major choices: parenthetical, sentence, and extended.

CHOICES AND STRATEGIES   Choosing the Appropriate Type of Definition

If the term is . . .	And the document is . . .	Try this type of definition
Relatively simple	Relatively informal	**Parenthetical.** A *parenthetical definition* is a brief clarification within an existing sentence. Sometimes, a parenthetical definition is simply a word or phrase enclosed in parentheses or commas or introduced by a colon or a dash. For example, "The computers were infected by a *Trojan horse* (a destructive program that appears to be benign)."

Choosing the Appropriate Type of Definition (*continued*)

If the term is . . .	And the document is . . .	Try this type of definition
Relatively simple	Relatively formal	**Sentence.** A *sentence definition* usually follows a standard pattern: the item to be defined is placed in a category of similar items and then distinguished from them. For instance, "Crippleware is shareware in which some features of the program are disabled until the user buys a license to use the program." Here, "shareware" is the category and the words that follow "shareware" are the distinguishing information. Writers often use sentence definitions to present a working definition for a particular document: "In this report, *electron microscope* refers to any microscope that uses electrons rather than visible light to produce magnified images." This type of definition is called a *stipulative definition.* See the Guidelines box below for more about writing sentence definitions.
Relatively complex	Informal or formal	**Extended.** An *extended definition* is a detailed explanation—usually one or more paragraphs—of an object, process, or idea. Often an extended definition begins with a sentence definition, which is then elaborated. For instance, the sentence definition "An electrophorus is a laboratory instrument used to generate static electricity" tells you the basic function of the device, but it doesn't explain how it works, what it is used for, and its strengths and limitations. An extended definition would address these and other topics. See pages 362–66 for more about extended definitions.

Writing Sentence Definitions

The following Guidelines box presents more advice on sentence definitions.

Guidelines

Writing Effective Sentence Definitions

The following five suggestions can help you write effective sentence definitions.

▶ **Be specific in stating the category and the distinguishing characteristics.**
If you write, "A Bunsen burner is a burner that consists of a vertical metal tube connected to a gas source," the imprecise category—"a burner"—ruins the definition: many types of large-scale burners use vertical metal tubes connected to gas sources.

▶ **Don't describe a specific item if you are defining a general class of items.** If you wish to define *catamaran*, don't describe a particular catamaran. The one you see on the beach in front of you might be made by Hobie and have a white hull and blue sails, but those characteristics are not essential to all catamarans.

▶ **Avoid writing circular definitions, that is, definitions that merely repeat the key words or the distinguishing characteristics of the item being defined in the category.** The definition "A required course is a course that is required" is useless: required of whom, by whom? However, in defining electron microscopes, you can repeat *microscope* because *microscope* is not the difficult part of the term. The purpose of defining *electron microscope* is to clarify *electron* as it applies to a particular type of microscope.

▶ **Be sure the category contains a noun or a noun phrase rather than a phrase beginning with *when*, *what*, or *where*.**

INCORRECT	A brazier is what is used to . . .
CORRECT	A brazier is a metal pan used to . . .
INCORRECT	Hypnoanalysis is when hypnosis is used to . . .
CORRECT	Hypnoanalysis is a psychoanalytical technique in which . . .

▶ **Consider including a graphic.** A definition of an electron microscope would probably include photographs, diagrams, or drawings, for example.

Writing Extended Definitions

There is no one way to "extend" a definition. Your analysis of your audience and the purpose of your communication will help you decide which method to use. In fact, an extended definition sometimes employs several of the eight techniques discussed here.

Graphics   Perhaps the most common way to present an extended definition in technical communication is to present and explain a graphic. Graphics are useful in defining not only physical objects but also concepts and ideas. A definition of *temperature inversion*, for instance, might include a diagram showing the forces that create temperature inversion.

The following passage from an extended definition of *additive color* shows how graphics can complement words in an extended definition.

> Additive color is the type of color that results from mixing colored light, as opposed to mixing pigments such as dyes or paints. When any two colored lights are mixed, they produce a third color that is lighter than either of the two original colors, as shown in this diagram. And when green, red, and blue lights are mixed together in equal parts, they form white light.
>
> We are all familiar with the concept of additive color from watching TV monitors. A TV monitor projects three beams of electrons—one each for red, blue, and green—onto a fluorescent screen. Depending on the combinations of the three colors, we see different colors on the screen.

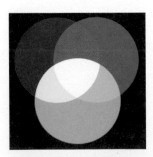

The graphic effectively and economically clarifies the concept of additive color.

Examples   Examples are particularly useful in making an abstract term easier to understand. The following paragraph is an extended definition of *hazing activities* (Fraternity, 2003).

> No chapter, colony, student or alumnus shall conduct or condone hazing activities. Hazing activities are defined as: "Any action taken or situation created, intentionally, whether on or off fraternity premises, to produce mental or physical discomfort, embarrassment, harassment, or ridicule. Such activities may include but are not limited to the following: use of alcohol; paddling in any form; creation of excessive fatigue; physical and psychological shocks; quests, treasure hunts, scavenger hunts, road trips or any other such activities carried on outside or inside of the confines of the chapter house; wearing of public apparel which is conspicuous and not normally in good taste; engaging in public stunts and buffoonery; morally degrading or humiliating games and activities; and any other activities which are not consistent with academic achievement, fraternal law, ritual or policy or the regulations and policies of the educational institution or applicable state law."

This extended definition is effective because the writer has presented a clear sentence definition followed by numerous examples.

Partition   Partitioning is the process of dividing a thing or an idea into smaller parts so that readers can understand it more easily. The following example (Brain, 2005) uses partition to define *computer infection*.

Types of Infection

When you listen to the news, you hear about many different forms of electronic infection. The most common are:

- **Viruses**—A virus is a small piece of software that piggybacks on real programs. For example, a virus might attach itself to a program such as a spreadsheet program. Each time the spreadsheet program runs, the virus runs, too, and it has the chance to reproduce (by attaching to other programs) or wreak havoc.

- **E-mail viruses**—An e-mail virus moves around in e-mail messages, and usually replicates itself by automatically mailing itself to dozens of people in the victim's e-mail address book.

- **Worms**—A worm is a small piece of software that uses computer networks and security holes to replicate itself. A copy of the worm scans the network for another machine that has a specific security hole. It copies itself to the new machine using the security hole, and then starts replicating from there, as well.

- **Trojan horses**—A Trojan horse is simply a computer program. The program claims to do one thing (it may claim to be a game) but instead does damage when you run it (it may erase your hard disk). Trojan horses have no way to replicate automatically.

Principle of Operation   Describing the principle of operation—the way something works—is an effective way to develop an extended definition, especially for an object or a process. The following excerpt from an extended definition of *adaptive cruise control* (U.S. Department of Transportation, 2007) is based on the mechanism's principle of operation.

Without target vehicle

With target vehicle

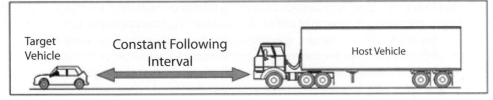

The system maintains the host vehicle's following interval by adjusting its speed. If the target vehicle speeds up, increasing the following interval between the two vehicles, the system informs the engine control module to accelerate and increase the vehicle's speed until either the set following interval or the cruise control preset speed are reached. However, if the gap between the target and the host vehicles is decreasing, the system informs the engine control module to reduce the vehicle's speed. The engine control module then issues a command to dethrottle the engine (e.g., by reducing fuel), apply the engine brake, and, when available, downshift the automated transmission.

Comparison and Contrast   Using comparison and contrast, a writer discusses the similarities or differences between the item being defined and an item with which readers are more familiar. The following definition of VoIP (Voice over Internet Protocol) contrasts this new form of phone service to the form we all know.

Voice over Internet Protocol is a form of phone service that lets you connect to the Internet through your cable or DSL modem. VoIP service uses a device called a telephony adapter, which attaches to the broadband modem, transforming phone pulses into IP packets sent over the Internet.

In this excerpt, the second and third paragraphs briefly compare VoIP and traditional phone service. Notice that this passage is organized according to the comparison-and-contrast pattern.

VoIP is considerably cheaper than traditional phone service: for as little as $20 per month, users get unlimited local and domestic long-distance service. For international calls, VoIP service is only about three cents per minute, about a third the rate of traditional phone service. In addition, any calls from one person to another person with the same VoIP service provider are free.

However, sound quality on VoIP cannot match that of a traditional land-based phone. On a good day, the sound is fine on VoIP, but frequent users comment on clipping and dropouts that can last up to a second. In addition, sometimes the sound has the distant, tinny quality of some of today's cell phones.

Analogy   An *analogy* is a specialized kind of comparison. In a traditional comparison, the writer compares one item to a similar item: an electron microscope to a common microscope, for example. In an analogy, however, the item being defined is compared to an item that is in some ways completely different but that shares some essential characteristic. For instance, the central processing unit of a computer is often compared to a brain. Obviously, these two items are very different, except that the relationship of the central processing unit to the computer is similar to that of the brain to the body.

The following example from a definition of *decellularization* (Falco, 2008) shows an effective use of an analogy.

> Researchers at the University of Minnesota were able to create a beating [rat] heart using the outer structure of one heart and injecting heart cells from another rat. Their findings are reported in the journal *Nature Medicine*. Rather than building a heart from scratch, which has often been mentioned as a possible use for stem cells, this procedure takes a heart and breaks it down to the outermost shell. It's similar to taking a house and gutting it, then rebuilding everything inside. In the human version, the patient's own cells would be used.

The writer of this passage uses the analogy of gutting a house to clarify the meaning of decellularization.

Negation   A special kind of contrast is sometimes called *negation* or *negative statement*. Negation clarifies a term by distinguishing it from a different term with which readers might confuse it. The following example uses negation to distinguish the term *ambulatory* from *ambulance*.

> An ambulatory patient is not a patient who must be moved by ambulance. On the contrary, an ambulatory patient is one who can walk without assistance from another person.

Negation is rarely the only technique used in an extended definition; in fact, it is used typically in a sentence or two at the start. Once you have explained what the item is not, you need to explain what it is.

Etymology   *Etymology*, the derivation of a word, is often a useful and interesting way to develop a definition. The following example uses the etymology of *spam*—unsolicited junk e-mail—to define it.

> For many decades, Hormel Foods has manufactured a luncheon meat called Spam, which stands for "Shoulder Pork and hAM"/"SPiced hAM." Then, in the 1970s, the English comedy team Monty Python's Flying Circus broadcast a skit about a restaurant that served Spam with every dish. In describing each dish, the waitress repeats the word *Spam* over and over, and several Vikings standing in the corner chant the word repeatedly. In the mid-1990s, two businessmen hired a programmer to write a program that would send unsolicited ads to thousands of electronic newsgroups. Just as Monty Python's chanting Vikings drowned out other conversation in the restaurant, the ads began drowning out regular communication online. As a result, people started calling unsolicited junk e-mail *spam*.

Etymology is a popular way to begin definitions of *acronyms*, which are abbreviations pronounced as words:

> RAID, which stands for redundant array of independent (or inexpensive) disks, refers to a computer storage system that can withstand a single (or, in some cases, even double) disk failure.

Etymology, like negation, is rarely used alone in technical communication, but it is an effective way to introduce an extended definition.

A Sample Extended Definition   Figure 14.1 is an example of an extended definition addressed to a general audience.

WRITING DESCRIPTIONS

Technical communication often requires descriptions: verbal and visual representations of objects, mechanisms, and processes.

- *Objects.* An object is anything ranging from a physical site, such as a volcano, to an artifact, such as a hammer, or a tomato plant.
- *Mechanisms.* A mechanism is a synthetic object consisting of a number of identifiable parts that work together such as a cell phone, a voltmeter, or a submarine.
- *Processes.* A process is an activity that takes place over time: species evolve; steel is made; plants perform photosynthesis. *Descriptions of processes*, which explain how something happens, differ from *instructions*, which explain how to do something. Readers of a process description want to *understand* the process; readers of instructions want a step-by-step guide to help them *perform* the process.

Descriptions of objects, mechanisms, and processes appear in virtually every kind of technical communication, typically as part of a larger document. For example, an employee who wants to persuade management to buy some equipment includes a mechanism description of the equipment in the proposal to buy it. A company manufacturing a consumer product provides a description and a graphic on its Web site to attract buyers. A maintenance manual for an air-conditioning system might begin with a description of the system to help the reader understand first how it operates and then how to fix or maintain it.

Analyzing the Writing Situation for Descriptions

Before you begin to write a description, consider carefully how the audience and the purpose of the document will affect what you write.

THE GREENHOUSE EFFECT

Energy from the sun drives the earth's weather and climate, and heats the earth's surface; in turn, the earth radiates energy back into space. Atmospheric greenhouse gases (water vapor, carbon dioxide, and other gases) trap some of the outgoing energy, retaining heat somewhat like the glass panels of a greenhouse.

The first paragraph of this extended definition of the greenhouse effect begins with a general description and ends with a sentence that explains the etymology of the term.

Without this natural "greenhouse effect," temperatures would be much lower than they are now, and life as known today would not be possible. Instead, thanks to greenhouse gases, the earth's average temperature is a more hospitable 60°F. However, problems may arise when the atmospheric concentration of greenhouse gases increases.

Since the beginning of the industrial revolution, atmospheric concentrations of carbon dioxide have increased nearly 30%, methane concentrations have more than doubled, and nitrous oxide concentrations have risen by about 15%. These increases have enhanced the heat-trapping capability of the earth's atmosphere. Sulfate aerosols, a common air pollutant, cool the atmosphere by reflecting light back into space; however, sulfates are short-lived in the atmosphere and vary regionally.

The body of this extended definition is a discussion of the factors that have increased the greenhouse effect.

Why are greenhouse gas concentrations increasing? Scientists generally believe that the combustion of fossil fuels and other human activities are the primary reason for the increased concentration of carbon dioxide. Plant respiration and the decomposition of organic matter release more than 10 times the CO_2 released by human activities; but these releases have generally been in balance during the centuries leading up to the industrial revolution with carbon dioxide absorbed by terrestrial vegetation and the oceans.

Questions are effective in topic sentences, particularly in discussions aimed at general readers.

What has changed in the last few hundred years is the additional release of carbon dioxide by human activities. Fossil fuels burned to run cars and trucks, heat homes and businesses, and power factories are responsible for about 98% of U.S. carbon dioxide emissions, 24% of methane emissions, and 18% of nitrous oxide emissions. Increased agriculture, deforestation, landfills, industrial production, and mining also contribute a significant share of emissions. In 1997, the United States emitted about one-fifth of total global greenhouse gases.

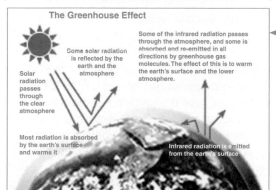

The Greenhouse Effect

Some solar radiation is reflected by the earth and the atmosphere

Solar radiation passes through the clear atmosphere

Some of the infrared radiation passes through the atmosphere, and some is absorbed and re-emitted in all directions by greenhouse gas molecules. The effect of this is to warm the earth's surface and the lower atmosphere.

Most radiation is absorbed by the earth's surface and warms it

Infrared radiation is emitted from the earth's surface

This diagram aids the reader by visually summarizing the principle of operation of the greenhouse effect.

Estimating future emissions is difficult, because it depends on demographic, economic, technological, policy, and institutional developments. Several emissions scenarios have been developed based on differing projections of these underlying factors. For example, by 2100, in the absence of emissions control policies, carbon dioxide concentrations are projected to be 30–150% higher than today's levels.

Figure 14.1   An Extended Definition
Source: U.S. Environmental Protection Agency, 2001 <www.epa.gov/globalwarming/climate.index/html>.

Your sense of your audience will determine not only how technical your vocabulary should be but also how long your sentences and paragraphs should be. Another audience-related factor is your use of graphics. Less-knowledgeable readers need simple graphics; they might have trouble understanding sophisticated schematics or decision charts. Also consider whether any of your readers are from other cultures and might therefore expect different topics, organization, or writing style in the description.

Consider, too, your purpose. If you want your readers to understand how a personal computer works, write a *general description* that applies to several varieties of computers. If you want your readers to understand how a specific computer works, write a *particular description*. Your purpose will determine every aspect of the description, including its length, the amount of detail, and the number and type of graphics.

Drafting Effective Descriptions

There is no single structure or format used for descriptions. Because descriptions are written for different audiences and different purposes, they can take many shapes and forms. However, the following four suggestions will guide you in most situations:

- Indicate clearly the nature and scope of the description.
- Introduce the description clearly.
- Provide appropriate detail.
- Conclude the description.

In This Book

For more about titles and headings, see Ch. 6, p. 108.

Indicate Clearly the Nature and Scope of the Description　If the description is to be a separate document, give it a title. If the description is to be part of a longer document, give it a section heading. In either case, clearly state the subject and indicate whether the description is general or particular. For instance, a general description of an object might be entitled "Description of a Minivan," and a particular description, "Description of the 2012 Honda Odyssey." A general description of a process might be called "Description of the Process of Designing a New Production Car," and a particular description, "Description of the Process of Designing the Chevrolet Malibu."

Introduce the Description Clearly　Start with a general overview: you want to give readers a broad understanding of the object, mechanism, or process. Consider adding a graphic that introduces the overall concept. For example, in describing a process, you might include a flowchart summarizing the steps in the body of the description; in describing an object, such as a bicycle, you might include a photograph or a drawing showing the major components you will describe in detail in the body.

Table 14.1 shows some of the basic kinds of questions you might want to answer in introducing object, mechanism, and process descriptions. Figure

TABLE 14.1 ▶ Questions to Answer in Introducing a Description

For object and mechanism descriptions	For process descriptions
• *What is the item?* Start with a sentence definition.	• *What is the process?* Start with a sentence definition.
• *What is the function of the item?* If the function is not implicit in the sentence definition, state it: "Electron microscopes magnify objects that are smaller than the wavelengths of visible light."	• *What is the function of the process?* Unless the function is obvious, state it: "The main purpose of performing a census is to obtain current population figures, which government agencies use to revise legislative districts and determine revenue sharing."
• *What does the item look like?* Include a photograph or drawing if possible. (See Chapter 8 for more about incorporating graphics with text.) If not, use an analogy or comparison: "The USB drive is a plastic- or metal-covered device, about the size of a pack of gum, with a removable cap that covers the type-A USB connection." Mention the material, texture, color, and the like, if relevant. Sometimes an object is best pictured with both graphics and words.	• *Where and when does the process take place?* "Each year the stream is stocked with hatchery fish in early March." Omit these facts only if your readers already know them.
• *How does the item work?* In a few sentences, define the operating principle. Sometimes objects do not "work"; they merely exist. For instance, a ship model has no operating principle.	• *Who or what performs the process?* If there is any doubt about who or what performs the process, state it.
• *What are the principal parts of the item?* Limit your description to the principal parts. A description of a bicycle, for instance, would not mention the dozens of nuts and bolts that hold the mechanism together; it would focus on the chain, gears, pedals, wheels, and frame.	• *How does the process work?* "The four-treatment lawn-spray plan is based on the theory that the most effective way to promote a healthy lawn is to apply different treatments at crucial times during the growing season. The first two treatments—in spring and early summer—consist of . . ."
	• *What are the principal steps of the process?* Name the steps in the order in which you will describe them. The principal steps in changing an automobile tire, for instance, include jacking up the car, replacing the old tire with the new one, and lowering the car back to the ground. Changing a tire also includes secondary steps, such as placing chocks against the tires to prevent the car from moving once it is jacked up. Explain or refer to these secondary steps at the appropriate points in the description.

14.2 on page 371 shows the introductory graphic accompanying a description of an electric bicycle.

Provide Appropriate Detail   In the body of a description, treat each major part or step as a separate item. In describing an object or a mechanism, define each part and then, if applicable, describe its function, operating principle, and appearance. In discussing the appearance, include shape, dimensions, material, and physical details such as texture and color (if essential). In describing a process, treat each major step as if it were a separate process.

A description can have not only parts and steps but also subparts and substeps. A description of a computer system includes a keyboard as one of its main parts, and the description of the keyboard includes the numeric keypad as one of its subparts. And the description of the numeric keypad includes the arrow keys as one of its subparts. The same principle applies in describing processes: a step might have substeps.

Guidelines

Providing Appropriate Detail in Descriptions

Use the following techniques to flesh out your descriptions.

For mechanism and object descriptions

- **Choose an appropriate organizational principle.** Two organizational principles are common:
  - — Functional: how the item works or is used. In a radio, the sound begins at the receiver, travels into the amplifier, and then flows out through the speakers.
  - — Spatial: based on the physical structure of the item (from top to bottom, east to west, outside to inside, and so forth).

  Descriptions can be organized in various ways. For instance, the description of a house could be organized functionally (the different electrical and mechanical systems) or spatially (top to bottom, inside to outside, east to west, and so on). A complex description can use a combination of patterns at different levels in the description.

- **Use graphics.** Present a graphic for each major part. Use photographs to show external surfaces, drawings to emphasize particular items on the surface, and cutaways and exploded diagrams to show details beneath the surface. Other kinds of graphics, such as graphs and charts, are often useful supplements (see Chapter 8).

For process descriptions

- **Structure the step-by-step description chronologically.** If the process is a closed system—such as the cycle of evaporation and condensation—and thus has no first step, begin with any principal step.

- **Explain causal relationships among steps.** Don't present the steps as if they have nothing to do with one another. In many cases, one step causes another. In the operation of a four-stroke gasoline engine, for instance, each step creates the conditions for the next step.

- **Use the present tense.** Discuss steps in the present tense unless you are writing about a process that occurred in the historical past. For example, use the past tense in describing how the Snake River aquifer was formed: "The molten material condensed . . ." However, use the present tense in describing how steel is made: "The molten material is then poured into . . ." The present tense helps readers understand that, in general, steel is made this way.

- **Use graphics.** Whenever possible, use graphics to clarify each point. Consider flowcharts or other kinds of graphics, such as photographs, drawings, and graphs. For example, in a description of how a four-stroke gasoline engine operates, use diagrams to illustrate the position of the valves and the activity occurring during each step.

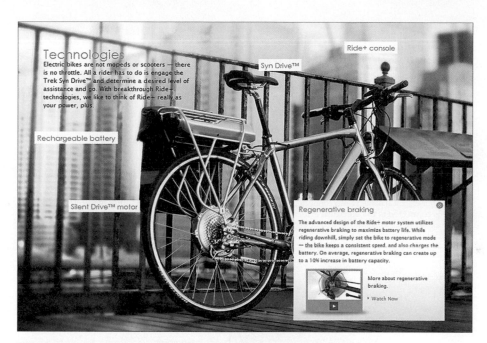

This Web-based description includes five labels. When you click on a label, you see an expanded description, complete with an embedded video, that explains more about the system. Here we see the expanded description of the regenerative braking system. Videos are used frequently in Web-based descriptions and instructions.

Figure 14.2   Graphic with Linked Detailed Graphics and Descriptions
Source: Trek Bicycle, 2011 <www.trekbikes.com/us/en/rideplus/technology>.

Conclude the Description   A typical description has a brief conclusion that summarizes it and prevents readers from overemphasizing the part or step discussed last.

A common technique for concluding descriptions of mechanisms and of some objects is to state briefly how the parts function together. A process description usually has a brief conclusion: a short paragraph summarizing the principal steps or discussing the importance or implications of the process.

A Look at Several Sample Descriptions

A look at some sample descriptions will give you an idea of how different writers adapt basic approaches for a particular audience and purpose.

Figure 14.3 on page 372 shows the extent to which a process description can be based on a graphic. The topic is a household solar array. The audience is the general reader.

Figure 14.4 on page 373 shows an excerpt from a set of specifications.

Figure 14.5 on page 374 is a description of the process of turning biomass into useful fuels and other products.

:e **e-Pages**

To analyze a mechanism description that uses animated graphics, visit <bedfordstmartins.com/ps/epages>.

Figure 14.3 A Process Description Based on a Graphic
Source: Vanguard Energy Partners, 2010 <www .vanguardenergypartners.com /howsolarworks.html>.

This description begins with an informal definition of "direct grid-tie system."

In the next section, the writer presents the steps of the process in chronological order.

The description uses boldfaced text to emphasize key terms, most of which appear in the graphic.

The description focuses on the operating principle of the system. It does not seek to explain the details of how the system works. Accordingly, the graphic focuses on the logic of the process, not on the particulars of what the components look like or where they are located in the house.

How Our Solar Electric System Works

Your solar electric system is most likely to be what is called a **direct grid-tie system.** This means it is connected into the electricity system provided by your utility company.

Here's how it works . . .

The sun strikes the panels of your **solar array** and a flow of **direct current (DC) electricity** is produced. This is the only type of current produced by solar cells.

Appliances and machinery, however, are run on higher voltage **alternating current (AC) electricity** as supplied by your utility.

The lower voltage DC is fed into an **inverter** that transforms it into alternating current. The AC feeds into the **main electrical panel** from which it powers your household's or your business's electrical needs.

Your electrical panel is also connected to a **specially installed bi-directional utility meter.** This is **connected to the electrical grid,** which is the utility's means of delivering electricity. This setup allows AC electricity to flow both into, and out of, your home or business.

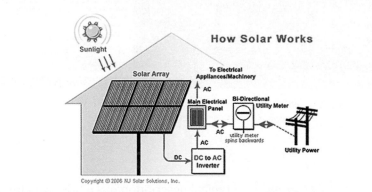

During the day, your solar electric system will be providing some, or all, of your electrical needs.

How much will depend, firstly, on the intensity of the sunlight; the system produces less power on cloudy days and during the winter months. It will also depend on the appliances or machinery you are running at the time.

If your solar system is not providing all the power you need at any time, the **balance is automatically provided by your utility.**

On days when sunlight is intense, **your system may well produce more than you need.** The excess is automatically fed into the grid. This is registered on your bi-directional meter which will spin backwards, **giving you credit for the electricity you are providing.** (This is known as net metering.)

At night, your utility company automatically provides your electrical needs.

If there is a utility power outage, your grid-tie system will shut down immediately for safety reasons. Your power will be reinstated moments after grid power is restored.

A grid-tie solar electric system does not provide power during outages **unless it incorporates a battery storage system.** If your home or business has critical needs that require an uninterrupted power supply, we'll be happy to take you through the various alternatives available to you.

Off-grid, or stand-alone, solar systems produce power independently of the utility grid. They are most appropriate for remote or environmentally sensitive areas; stand-alone systems may effectively provide farm lighting, fence charging or solar water pumps. Most of these systems rely on battery storage so that power produced during the day can be used at night.

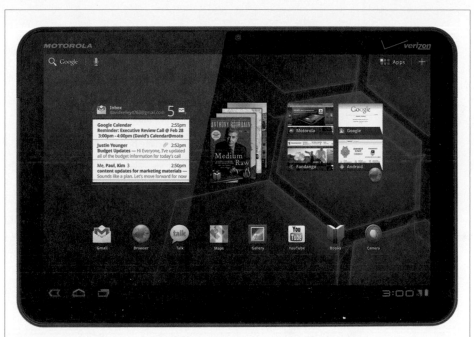

Figure 14.4 Specifications
Source: Motorola, 2011 <http:
//mediacenter.motorola.com
/Fact-Sheets/Motorola-XOOM
-Fact-Sheet-3537.aspx>.

An important kind of description is called a specification. *A typical specification consists of a graphic and a set of statistics about the device and its performance characteristics. Specifications help readers understand the capabilities of an item. You will see specifications on devices as small as transistors and as large as aircraft carriers.*

Motorola XOOM Tablet

OS	Android 3.0 Honeycomb
Differentiation	Larger display in smaller form-factor, 1080p HD support, first tablet with Honeycomb software, dual-core 1GHz processor, and a wide range of docking options
Dimensions	249.1mm (h) x 167.8mm (w) x 12.9mm (d)
Display	10.1" 1280x800 resolution
Weight	730 g
Processor	NVIDIA® Tegra™ 2: 1GHz dual-core processor
Battery	Up to 10 hour video playback
Connectivity	3.5mm, micro USB 2.0 HS, Corporate Sync, Wi-Fi 2.4GHz & 5GHz 802.11b/g/n, Bluetooth 2.1 + EDR + HID
Network	3G, 4G LTE upgradeable, 802.11n w/Personal Hotspot
Messaging/Web/Apps	Email (Corporate Sync, Google Mail, POP3/IMAP embedded, Push Email, Yahoo Mail), WebKit w/ Flash
Audio	AAC, AAC+, AMR NB, AMR WB, MP3, XMF
Video	720p capture/1080p playback/streaming, H.263, H.264, MPEG4
Camera	5MP rear-facing camera with dual LED flash/2MP front-facing camera
Memory	32GB on board user memory, SD card support after software update, 1GB DDR2 RAM

Because this Web-based spec sheet accompanies a consumer product, the specs are classified into categories geared toward the interests of the likely purchasers.

Figure 14.5 An Effective Process Description

Source: U.S. Department of Energy, 2010 <www1.eere .energy.gov/biomass/pdfs /biochemical_four_pager.pdf>.

This description begins with an overview of the process of biochemical conversion: the process of using fermentation and catalysis to make fuels and products.

The description includes a flowchart explaining the major steps in the process. The designers included photographs to add visual interest to the flowchart.

The lettered steps in the flowchart correspond to the textual descriptions of each step in the process.

Most of the description is written in the passive voice (such as "Feedstocks for biochemical processes are selected . . ."). The passive voice is appropriate because the focus of this process description is on what happens to the materials, not on what a person does. By contrast, in a set of instructions the focus is on what a person does.

e-Pages

To analyze a process description that uses video animation, visit <bedfordstmartins.com/ps /epages>.

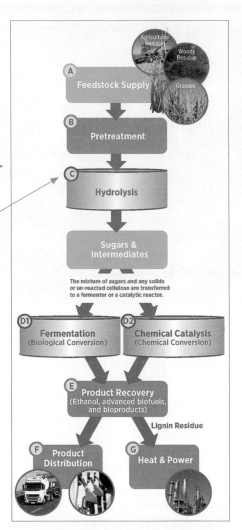

Biochemical conversion uses biocatalysts, such as enzymes, in addition to heat and other chemicals, to convert the carbohydrate portion of the biomass (hemicellulose and cellulose) into an intermediate sugar stream. These sugars are intermediate building blocks that can then be fermented or chemically catalyzed into ethanol, other advanced biofuels, and value-added chemicals. The overall process can be broken into the following essential steps:

A. **Feedstock Supply:** Feedstocks for biochemical processes are selected for optimum composition, quality, and size. Feedstock handling systems tailored to biochemical processing are essential to cost-effective, high-yield operations.

B. **Pretreatment:** Biomass is heated (often combined with an acid or base) to break the tough, fibrous cell walls down and make the cellulose easier to hydrolyze (see next step).

C. **Hydrolysis:** Enzymes (or other catalysts) enable the sugars in the pretreated material to be separated and released over a period of several days.

D1. **Fermentation:** Microorganisms are added to the mixture to ferment the sugars into alcohol or other fuels, much like the centuries-old process for winemaking.

D2. **Chemical Catalysis:** Instead of fermentation, the sugars can be converted to fuel or an entire suite of other useful products using chemical catalysis.

E. **Product Recovery:** Products are separated from water, solvents, and any residual solids.

F. **Product Distribution:** Fuels are transported to blending facilities, while other products and intermediates may be sent to traditional refineries or processing facilities for use in a diverse slate of consumer products.

G. **Heat & Power:** The remaining solids are mostly lignin, which can be burned for heat and power.

WRITING INSTRUCTIONS

This section discusses *instructions*, which are process descriptions written to help readers perform a specific task—for instance, installing a water heater in a house.

When you write instructions, you use the same planning, drafting, revising, editing, and proofreading process that you use with other kinds of technical documents. In addition, you might perform one other task—usability testing—to ensure that the instructions are accurate and easy to follow.

On the Web

For links to sites on usability testing, click on Links Library for Ch. 14 on <bedfordstmartins .com/ps>.

Designing a Set of Instructions

As you plan to write a set of instructions, think about how readers will be using it. Analyzing your audience and purpose and gathering and organizing your information will help you decide whether you should write a one-page set of instructions or a longer document that needs to be bound. You might realize that the information would work better as a Web-based document that allows readers to link to the information they need and that enables you to include videos. Or you might decide to write several versions of the information: a brief paper-based set of instructions and a longer, Web-based document with links. You will need to consider your resources, especially your budget: long documents cost more than short ones; color costs more than black and white; heavy paper costs more than light paper; secure bindings cost more than staples.

Designing a set of instructions is much like designing any other kind of technical document. As discussed in Chapter 7, you want to create a document that is attractive and easy to use. When you design a set of instructions, you need to consider a number of issues related to document design and page design:

- *What are your readers' expectations?* For instructions that accompany a simple, inexpensive product, such as a light switch, readers will expect instructions written on the back of the package or, at most, printed in black and white on a small sheet of paper folded inside the package. For instructions that accompany an expensive consumer product, such as a high-definition TV, readers will expect a more sophisticated full-color document printed on high-quality paper.

- *Do you need to create more than one set of instructions for different audiences?* If you are writing about complex devices such as electronic thermostats, you might decide to create one set of instructions for electricians (who will install and maintain the device) and one set for homeowners (who will operate the device). You might decide to create a paper-based document that can also be read easily on the Internet, as well as a brief video of the tasks you describe.

- *Will readers be anxious about the information?* If readers will find the information intimidating, make the design unintimidating. See the Guidelines box on page 377 for advice on designing clear, attractive pages.

- *Will the environment in which the instructions are read affect the document design?* If people will be using the instructions outdoors, you will need to use a coated paper that can tolerate a little water. If people will be reading the instructions while sitting in a small, enclosed area, you might select a small size of paper and a binding that allows the reader to fold the pages over to save space. If people have a lot of room, you might decide to create poster-size instructions that can be taped to the wall and that are easy to read from across the room.

If your instructions will be used by multicultural readers, you need to consider three additional questions.

- *What languages should you use?* In most countries, including the United States, several or many languages are spoken. You might decide to include instructions in two or more languages. Doing so will help you communicate better with more people, and it can help you avoid legal problems. In liability cases, U.S. courts sometimes find that if a company knows that many of its customers speak only Spanish, for example, the instructions should appear in Spanish as well as in English. You have two choices for design: simultaneous or sequential. In a *simultaneous design*, you might create a multi-column page. One column presents the graphics; another presents the text in English; another presents the text in Spanish. Obviously, this won't work if you have more than two or three languages. But it is efficient because you can present each graphic only once. In a *sequential design*, you present all the information in English (say, on pages 1–8), then all the information in Spanish (on pages 9–16). The sequential design is easier for readers to use because they are not distracted by text in other languages, but you will have to present the graphics more than once, which will make the instructions longer.

- *Do the text or graphics need to be modified?* As discussed in Chapter 4, communicators need to be aware of cultural differences. For example, a printer manual for an Italian audience presented nude models with strategically placed rectangles showing the various colors the machine could reproduce. Nudity would be inappropriate in almost all other countries. A software manual in the United States showed an illustration of a person's left hand. Because the left hand is considered unclean in many countries in the Middle East, the manual would need to be modified for those countries (Delio, 2002).

- *What is the readers' technological infrastructure?* If your readers don't have Internet access, there is no point in making a Web version of the information. If your readers pay by the minute for Internet access, you will want to create Web-based information that downloads quickly.

▷ On the Web
Read Michelle Delio's article about cultural factors and manuals in *Wired News*. Click on Links Library for Ch. 14 on <bedfordstmartins.com/ps>.

Guidelines

Designing Clear, Attractive Pages

To design pages that are clear and attractive, follow these two guidelines.

▶ **Create an open, airy design.** Do not squeeze too much information onto the page. Build in space for wide margins and effective line spacing, use large type, and chunk the information effectively.

▶ **Clearly relate the graphics to the text.** In the step-by-step portion of a set of instructions, you will want to present graphics to accompany every step or almost every step. Create a design that makes it clear which graphics go with each text passage. One easy way to do this is to use a table, with the graphics in one column and the text in the other. Use a horizontal rule or extra line spacing to separate the text and graphics for one step from the text and graphics for the next step.

Figure 14.6 illustrates these points.

In This Book
For more about chunking, see Ch. 7, p. 148.

a. Cluttered design

This page is cluttered, containing far too much information. In addition, the page is not chunked effectively. As a result, the reader's eyes don't know where to focus. Would you look forward to using these instructions to assemble a cabinet?
Source: Slide-Lok, 2005 <www.slide-lok.com /assembly/P2468/P2468.pdf>.

b. Attractive design

This page is well designed, containing an appropriate amount of information presented in a simple two-column format. Notice the effective use of white space and the horizontal rules separating the steps.
Source: Anthro, 2005 <www.anthro.com/downloads /assemblyinstructions/300-5237-00.pdf>.

Figure 14.6   Cluttered and Attractive Page Designs in a Set of Instructions

Planning for Safety

If the subject you are writing about involves safety risks, your most important responsibility is to do everything you can to ensure your readers' safety.

ETHICS NOTE

Protecting Your Readers' Safety

To a large extent, the best way to keep your readers safe is to be honest and write clearly. If readers will encounter safety risks, explain what those risks are and how to minimize them. Doing so is a question of rights. Readers have a right to the best information they can get.

Protecting your readers' safety is also a question of law. People who get hurt can sue the company that made the product or provided the service. This field of law is called *liability*. Your company is likely to have legal professionals on staff or on retainer whose job is to ensure that the company is not responsible for putting people at unnecessary risk.

When you write safety information, be clear and concise. Avoid complicated sentences.

COMPLICATED	It is required that safety glasses be worn when inside this laboratory.
SIMPLE	You must wear safety glasses in this laboratory.
SIMPLE	Wear safety glasses in this laboratory.

Sometimes a phrase works better than a sentence: "Safety Glasses Required."

Because a typical manual or set of instructions can contain dozens of comments—some related to safety and some not—experts have devised *signal words* to indicate the seriousness of the advice. Unfortunately, signal words are not used consistently. For instance, the American National Standards Institute (ANSI) and the U.S. military's MILSPEC publish definitions that differ significantly, and many private companies have their own definitions. Figure 14.7 presents the four most popular signal words. The first three signal words are accompanied by symbols showing the color combinations endorsed by ANSI in its standard Z535.4.

Whether the safety information is printed in a document or on machinery or equipment, it should be prominent and easy to read. Many organizations use visual symbols to represent levels of danger, but these symbols are not standardized.

Organizations that create products that are used only in the United States use safety information that conforms with standards published by ANSI and with the federal Occupational Safety and Health Administration (OSHA). Organizations that create products that are also used outside the United States use safety information that conforms with standards pub-

Signal Word	Explanation	Example
Danger **⚠ DANGER**	*Danger* is used to alert readers about an immediate and serious hazard that will likely be fatal. Writers often use all-uppercase letters for danger statements.	DANGER: EXTREMELY HIGH VOLTAGE. STAND BACK.
Warning **⚠WARNING**	*Warning* is used to alert readers about the potential for serious injury or death or serious damage to equipment. Writers often use all-uppercase letters for warning statements.	WARNING: TO PREVENT SERIOUS INJURY TO YOUR ARMS AND HANDS, YOU MUST MAKE SURE THE ARM RESTRAINTS ARE IN PLACE BEFORE OPERATING THIS MACHINE.
Caution **⚠ CAUTION**	*Caution* is used to alert readers about the potential for anything from moderate injury to serious equipment damage or destruction.	Caution: Do not use nonrechargeable batteries in this charging unit; they could damage the charging unit.
Note	*Note* is used for a tip or suggestion to help readers carry out the procedure successfully.	Note: Two kinds of washers are provided—regular washers and locking washers. Be sure to use the locking washers here.

Figure 14.7   Signal Words

lished by the International Organization for Standardization (ISO). Figure 14.8 shows a safety label that incorporates both ANSI and ISO standards.

Part of planning for safety is determining the best location for the safety information. This question has no easy answer because you cannot control how your audience reads your document. Be

Figure 14.8   A Typical Safety Label
Source: HCS, 2004 <www.safetylabel.com/ search/index.php?pn=H6010-CDDHPL>.

The yellow triangle is consistent with the ISO approach. Because ISO creates standards for international use, its safety labels use icons, not words, to represent safety dangers.

The Danger signal word and the text are consistent with the ANSI approach. The information is presented in English.

conservative: put safety information wherever you think the reader is likely to see it, and don't be afraid to repeat yourself. A reasonable amount of repetition—such as including the same safety comment at the top of each page—is effective. But don't repeat the same piece of advice in each of 20 steps, because readers will stop paying attention to it. If your company's format for instructions calls for a safety section near the beginning of the document, place the information there and repeat it just before the appropriate step in the step-by-step section.

Figure 14.9 on page 380 shows one industry association's guidelines for placing safety information on conveyor belts.

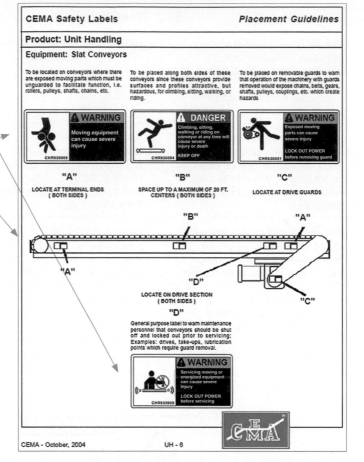

This page shows the four safety labels that the industry association recommends for use on conveyor belts.

The diagram of the conveyor belt shows where the organization recommends placing the safety labels.

Figure 14.9 **Placement of Safety Information on Equipment**
Source: Conveyor Equipment Manufacturers Association, 2004 <http://cemanet
.org/safety/uh6.pdf>.

Drafting Effective Instructions

Instructions can be brief (a small sheet of paper) or extensive (up to 20 pages or more). Brief instructions might be produced by a writer, a graphic artist, and a subject-matter expert. Longer instructions might call for the assistance of others, such as marketing and legal personnel.

Regardless of the size of the project, most instructions are organized like process descriptions. The main difference is that the conclusion of a set of instructions is not a summary but an explanation of how to make sure readers have followed the instructions correctly. Most sets of instructions contain four elements: a title, a general introduction, step-by-step instructions, and a conclusion.

Drafting Titles   A good title for instructions is simple and clear. Two forms are common:

- *How-to.* This is the simplest: "How to Install the J112 Shock Absorber."
- *Gerund.* The gerund form is the *-ing* form of the verb: "Installing the J112 Shock Absorber."

One form to avoid is the noun string, which is awkward and difficult for readers to understand: "J112 Shock Absorber Installation Instructions."

▶ **In This Book**
For more about noun strings, see Ch. 6, p. 111.

Drafting General Introductions   The general introduction provides the preliminary information that readers will need to follow the instructions safely and easily.

Guidelines

Drafting Introductions for Instructions

Every set of instructions is unique and therefore calls for a different introduction. Where appropriate, consider answering the following six questions.

▶ **Who should carry out this task?** Sometimes you need to identify or describe the person or persons who are to carry out a task. Aircraft maintenance, for example, may be performed only by those certified to do it.

▶ **Why should the reader carry out this task?** Sometimes the reason is obvious: you don't need to explain why a backyard barbecue grill should be assembled. But you do need to explain the rationale for many tasks, such as changing radiator antifreeze in a car.

▶ **When should the reader carry out this task?** Some tasks, such as rotating tires or planting crops, need to be performed at particular times or at particular intervals.

▶ **What safety measures or other concerns should the reader understand?** In addition to the safety measures that apply to the whole task, mention any tips that will make the job easier:

   NOTE: For ease of assembly, leave all nuts loose. Give only 3 or 4 complete turns on bolt threads.

▶ **What items will the reader need?** List necessary tools, materials, and equipment so that readers will not have to interrupt their work to hunt for something. If you think readers might not be able to identify these items easily, include drawings next to the names.

▶ **In This Book**
For more about graphics, see Ch. 8.

▶ **How long will the task take?** Consider stating how long the task will take readers with no experience, some experience, and a lot of experience.

Drafting Step-by-Step Instructions   The heart of a set of instructions is the step-by-step information.

Guidelines

Drafting Steps in Instructions

Follow these six suggestions for writing steps that are easy to understand.

On the Web

For examples of instructions, see Knowledge Hound. Click on Links Library for Ch. 14 on <bedfordstmartins.com/ps>.

▶ **Number the instructions.** For long, complex instructions, use two-level numbering, such as a decimal system:

   1

      1.1
      1.2

   2

      2.1
      2.2

   etc.

If you need to present a long set of steps, such as 50, group them logically into, say, six sets of eight or nine steps, and begin each set with a clear heading.

▶ **Present the right amount of information in each step.** Each step should define a single task the reader can carry out easily, without having to refer back to the instructions.

TOO MUCH INFORMATION	1. Mix one part cement with one part water, using the trowel. When the mixture is a thick consistency without any lumps bigger than a marble, place a strip of the mixture about 1″ high and 1″ wide along the face of the brick.
TOO LITTLE INFORMATION	1. Pick up the trowel.
RIGHT AMOUNT OF INFORMATION	1. Mix one part cement with one part water, using the trowel, until the mixture is a thick consistency without any lumps bigger than a marble.
	2. Place a strip of the mixture about 1″ high and 1″ wide along the face of the brick.

In This Book

For more about the passive voice, see Ch. 6, p. 126.

▶ **Use the imperative mood.** For example, "Attach the red wire . . ." The imperative is more direct and economical than the indicative mood ("You should attach the red wire . . ." or "The operator should attach the red wire . . ."). Avoid the passive voice ("The red wire is attached . . ."), because it can be ambiguous: is the red wire already attached?

▶ **Do not confuse steps and feedback statements.** A *step* is an action that the reader is to perform. A *feedback statement* describes an event that occurs in response to a step. For instance, a step might read, "Insert the disk in the drive." That step's feedback statement might read, "The system will now update your user information." Do not make a feedback statement a numbered step. Present it as part of the step to which it refers. Some writers give all feedback statements their own design.

> ▶ **Include graphics.** When appropriate, add a photograph or a drawing to show the reader what to do. Some activities, such as adding a drop of a reagent to a mixture, do not need an illustration, but they might be clarified by charts or tables.
>
> ▶ **Do not omit articles (*a, an, the*) to save space.** Omitting articles can make the instructions unclear and hard to read. In the sentence "Locate midpoint and draw line," for example, the reader cannot tell if "draw line" is a noun (as in "locate the draw line") or a verb and its object (as in "draw a line").

Drafting Conclusions   Instructions often conclude by stating that the reader has now completed the task or by describing what the reader should do next. For example:

> Now that you have replaced the glass and applied the glazing compound, let it sit for at least five days so that the glazing can cure. Then, prime and paint the window.

Some conclusions end with *maintenance tips* or a *troubleshooting guide*. A troubleshooting guide, usually presented as a table, identifies common problems and explains how to solve them.

Revising, Editing, and Proofreading Instructions

You will want to revise, edit, and proofread all the documents you write to make sure they are honest, clear, accurate, comprehensive, accessible, concise, professional in appearance, and correct. When you write instructions, you should be extra careful, for two reasons.

First, your readers rely on your instructions to carry out the task. If they can't complete it—or they do complete it, but the device doesn't work correctly—they'll be unhappy. Nobody likes to spend a few hours assembling a garage-door opener, and then find a half dozen parts left over. Second, your readers rely on you to help them complete the task safely. To prevent injuries—and liability actions—build time into the budget to revise, edit, and proofread the instructions carefully. Then, if you can, carry out usability testing on the instructions.

A Look at Several Sample Instructions

Figure 14.10 on page 384 is an excerpt from a set of instructions. Figure 14.11 on page 385 shows a list of tools and materials from a set of instructions. Figure 14.12 on page 386 is an excerpt from the troubleshooting guide in a set of instructions for a lawnmower.

▶ **On the Web**

For links to sites on usability testing, click on Links Library for Ch. 14 on <bedfordstmartins .com/ps>.

 e-Pages

To analyze three examples of instructions that use video and screen capture techniques, visit <bedfordstmartins.com/ps /epages>.

This page from the user's manual for a Sony Reader discusses how to transfer a downloaded book from a computer to a Sony Reader.

The writer uses gerunds (-ing phrases) to describe the actions ("importing and transferring content") and uses the imperative mood ("Slide the POWER switch") for steps.

The typography varies with the type of information the writer is presenting. The action the reader is to perform is in large, boldfaced type, following the step number. Non-boldfaced type is used for the feedback statement: what the device does in response to the action that has just been described. The Note is presented in even smaller type.

Step 2 includes a cross-reference to a different section of the instructions to help readers who might need help carrying out a portion of the task.

A labeled screenshot helps readers recognize what they will see on their computer.

The ample white space makes the information seem less overwhelming.

The footer contains a continued symbol (telling the reader that the instructions continue on the next page) and the page number.

Importing and Transferring Content

1 **Slide the POWER switch.**
The Reader is turned on.

Note

- If the Reader does not turn on, the battery has been fully depleted. In this case, go to the next step. Although charging is in progress (charge indicator lights up in red), the Reader will not turn on until ▬ (indicating connection via USB) appears on the screen (it takes at least 40 minutes).

---

2 **Connect the Reader to your computer using the supplied USB cable. (▷ page 11)**
eBook Library starts automatically and "Reader" appears in the Source view of eBook Library.

— Reader

— Source view

Continued   27

Figure 14.10   Excerpt from a Set of Instructions
Source: Sony, 2009 <http://www.docs.sony.com/release/PRS300RCB.pdf>.

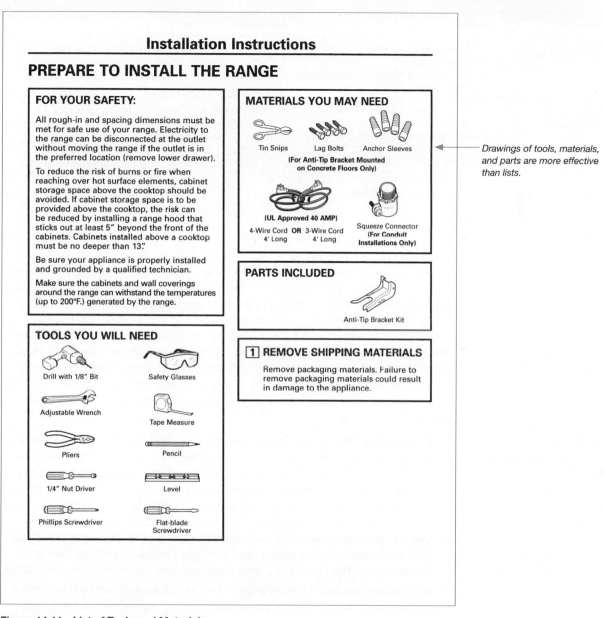

Installation Instructions

PREPARE TO INSTALL THE RANGE

FOR YOUR SAFETY:

All rough-in and spacing dimensions must be met for safe use of your range. Electricity to the range can be disconnected at the outlet without moving the range if the outlet is in the preferred location (remove lower drawer).

To reduce the risk of burns or fire when reaching over hot surface elements, cabinet storage space above the cooktop should be avoided. If cabinet storage space is to be provided above the cooktop, the risk can be reduced by installing a range hood that sticks out at least 5" beyond the front of the cabinets. Cabinets installed above a cooktop must be no deeper than 13".

Be sure your appliance is properly installed and grounded by a qualified technician.

Make sure the cabinets and wall coverings around the range can withstand the temperatures (up to 200°F.) generated by the range.

TOOLS YOU WILL NEED

Drill with 1/8" Bit   Safety Glasses

Adjustable Wrench

Tape Measure

Pliers   Pencil

1/4" Nut Driver   Level

Phillips Screwdriver   Flat-blade Screwdriver

MATERIALS YOU MAY NEED

Tin Snips   Lag Bolts   Anchor Sleeves

(For Anti-Tip Bracket Mounted on Concrete Floors Only)

(UL Approved 40 AMP)

4-Wire Cord **OR** 3-Wire Cord
4' Long   4' Long

Squeeze Connector
(For Conduit Installations Only)

PARTS INCLUDED

Anti-Tip Bracket Kit

1 **REMOVE SHIPPING MATERIALS**

Remove packaging materials. Failure to remove packaging materials could result in damage to the appliance.

Drawings of tools, materials, and parts are more effective than lists.

Figure 14.11   List of Tools and Materials
Source: General Electric, 2003.

Problem	Cause	Correction
The mower does not start.	1. The mower is out of gas. 2. The gas is stale. 3. The spark plug wire is disconnected from the spark plug.	1. Fill the gas tank. 2. Drain the tank and refill it with fresh gas. 3. Connect the wire to the plug.
The mower loses power.	1. The grass is too high. 2. The air cleaner is dirty. 3. There is a buildup of grass, leaves, or trash in the underside of the mower housing.	1. Set the mower to a "higher cut" position. See page 10. 2. Replace the air cleaner. See page 11. 3. Disconnect the spark plug wire, attach it to the retainer post, and clean the underside of the mower housing. See page 8.

Figure 14.12   Excerpt from a Troubleshooting Guide

WRITING MANUALS

There is no absolute distinction between a set of instructions and a manual. Typically, the two share a main purpose: to explain how to carry out a task safely, effectively, and efficiently. A set of instructions is typically shorter (usually 1 to 20 pages) and more limited in its subject. For example, a set of instructions might discuss how to use an extension ladder, whereas a manual might discuss how to use a laptop computer. Both kinds of documents can include safety information. The main difference between a manual and a set of instructions is that a manual has more-elaborate front matter and back matter:

In This Book
For more about typography, see Ch. 7, p. 156.

- *Front matter.* The introduction, sometimes called a *preface*, often contains an *overview of the contents*, frequently in the form of a table, which explains the main contents of each section and chapter. It also contains a *conventions* section, which explains the typography of the manual. For instance, *italics* are used for the titles of books, **boldface** for keyboard keys, and so forth. It also might include a *where to get help* section, referring readers to other sources of information, such as the company's Web site and customer-support center. And it might contain a section listing the *trademarks* of the company's own products and those of other companies.

In This Book
For more about specifications, see p. 373.

- *Back matter.* Manuals typically include a set of *specifications* of the device or system, a list of relevant government *safety regulations* and *industry standards* that the device or system supports, *tips on maintaining and servicing* the device, a *copyright page* listing bibliographic information about the manual, and an *index.* Many manuals also include *glossaries*.

DOCUMENT ANALYSIS ACTIVITY
Presenting Clear Instructions

The following page is from a set of instructions in a user's manual. The accompanying questions ask you to think about the discussion of instructions on pages 375–86.

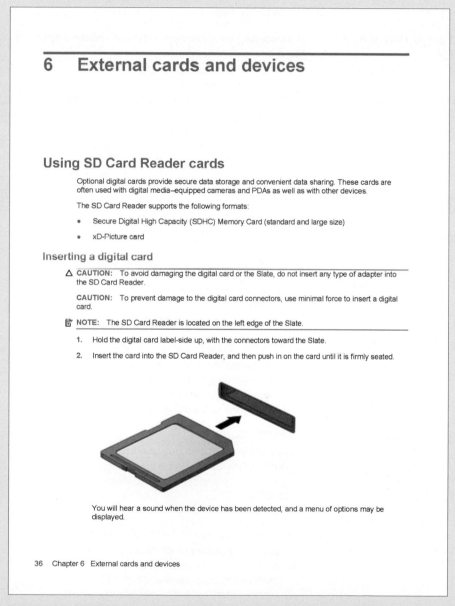

6   External cards and devices

Using SD Card Reader cards

Optional digital cards provide secure data storage and convenient data sharing. These cards are often used with digital media–equipped cameras and PDAs as well as with other devices.

The SD Card Reader supports the following formats:

- Secure Digital High Capacity (SDHC) Memory Card (standard and large size)
- xD-Picture card

Inserting a digital card

△ CAUTION: To avoid damaging the digital card or the Slate, do not insert any type of adapter into the SD Card Reader.

CAUTION: To prevent damage to the digital card connectors, use minimal force to insert a digital card.

NOTE: The SD Card Reader is located on the left edge of the Slate.

1.   Hold the digital card label-side up, with the connectors toward the Slate.

2.   Insert the card into the SD Card Reader, and then push in on the card until it is firmly seated.

You will hear a sound when the device has been detected, and a menu of options may be displayed.

36   Chapter 6   External cards and devices

1. How effectively has the designer helped readers recognize the distinction between cautions and notes?

2. Is the amount of information presented in each step appropriate?

3. How effective is the graphic in helping readers understand the information?

4. How effectively has the designer used typography to distinguish steps from feedback statements?

On the Web

To submit your responses to your instructor, click on Document Analysis Activities for Ch. 14 on <bedfordstmartins .com/ps>.

Source: Hewlett Packard, 2010 <http://bizsupport2.austin.hp.com/bc/docs/support/SupportManual /c02571793/c02571793.pdf>.

Writer's Checklist

Parenthetical, Sentence, and Extended Definitions

☐ Are all necessary terms defined? (p. 359)

☐ Are the definitions placed in the location most useful to readers? (p. 359)

Does each sentence definition

☐ contain a sufficiently specific category and distinguishing characteristics? (p. 361)

☐ avoid describing one particular item when a general class of items is intended? (p. 362)

☐ avoid circular definition? (p. 362)

☐ begin with a category that contains a noun or a noun phrase? (p. 362)

☐ Are the extended definitions developed logically and clearly? (p. 362)

Object and Mechanism Descriptions

☐ Did you clearly indicate the nature and scope of the description? (p. 368)

☐ Did you include a graphic identifying all the principal parts? (p. 368)

In introducing the description, did you answer, if appropriate, the following questions:

☐ What is the item? (p. 369)

☐ What is its function? (p. 369)

☐ What does it look like? (p. 369)

☐ How does it work? (p. 369)

☐ What are its principal parts? (p. 369)

In providing detailed information, did you

☐ answer, for each of the major components, the questions listed in the second item in this section? (p. 369)

☐ choose an appropriate organizational principle? (p. 370)

☐ include graphics for each of the components? (p. 370)

In concluding the description, did you

☐ summarize the major points in the part-by-part description? (p. 371)

☐ include (where appropriate) a description of the item performing its function? (p. 371)

Process Descriptions

☐ Did you clearly indicate the nature and scope of the description? (p. 368)

☐ Did you include a graphic identifying all the principal steps? (p. 368)

In introducing the description, did you answer, if appropriate, the following questions:

☐ What is the process? (p. 369)

☐ What is its function? (p. 369)

☐ Where and when does the process take place? (p. 369)

☐ Who or what performs it? (p. 369)

☐ How does the process work? (p. 369)

☐ What are its principal steps? (p. 369)

In providing detailed information, did you

☐ answer, for each of the major steps, the questions for introducing a description in Table 14.1? (p. 369)

☐ discuss the steps in chronological order or other logical sequence? (p. 370)

☐ make clear the causal relationships among the steps? (p. 370)

☐ include graphics for each of the principal steps? (p. 370)

☐ use the present tense? (p. 370)

In concluding the description, did you

☐ summarize the major points in the step-by-step description? (p. 371)

☐ discuss, if appropriate, the importance or implications of the process? (p. 371)

Instructions

☐ Are the instructions designed effectively, with adequate white space and a clear relationship between the graphics and the accompanying text? (p. 377)

☐ Do the instructions have a clear title? (p. 381)

Does the introduction to the set of instructions

☐ state the purpose of the task? (p. 381)

☐ describe safety measures or other concerns that readers should understand? (p. 381)

☐ list necessary tools and materials? (p. 381)

Are the step-by-step instructions

☐ numbered? (p. 382)

☐ expressed in the imperative mood? (p. 382)

☐ simple and direct? (p. 382)

☐ Are appropriate graphics included? (p. 383)

Does the conclusion

☐ include any necessary follow-up advice? (p. 383)

☐ include, if appropriate, a troubleshooting guide? (p. 383)

Exercises

▶ **In This Book** For more about memos, see Ch. 9, p. 223.

1. Add a parenthetical definition for the italicized term in each of the following sentences:

   a. Reluctantly, he decided to *drop* the physics course.

   b. Last week, the computer was *down*.

   c. The department is using *shareware* in its drafting course.

2. Write a sentence definition for each of the following terms:

   a. catalyst

   b. job interview

   c. Web site

3. Revise any of the following sentence definitions that need revision:

   a. A thermometer measures temperature.

   b. The spark plugs are the things that ignite the air-gas mixture in a cylinder.

   c. Parallel parking is where you park next to the curb.

   d. A strike is when the employees stop working.

   e. Multitasking is when you do two things at once while you're on the computer.

4. Write a 500- to 1,000-word extended definition of one of the following terms or of a term used in your field of study. If you do secondary research, cite your sources clearly and accurately. In addition, check that the graphics are appropriate for your audience and purpose. In a brief note at the start, indicate the audience and purpose for your definition.

   a. flextime

   b. binding arbitration

   c. robotics

   d. an academic major (don't focus on any particular major; instead, define what a major is)

   e. bioengineering

5. Write a 500- to 1,000-word description of one of the following items or of a piece of equipment used in your field. Include appropriate graphics, and be sure to cite them correctly if you did not create them. In a note preceding the description, specify your audience and indicate the type of description (general or particular) you are writing.

   a. GPS device

   b. MP3 player

   c. waste electrical and electronic equipment

   d. automobile jack

   e. camera phone

6. Write a 500- to 1,000-word description of one of the following processes or a similar process with which you are familiar. Include appropriate graphics. In a note preceding the description, specify your audience and indicate the type of description (general or particular) you are writing. If you use secondary sources, cite them properly (see Appendix, Part A, for documentation systems).

   a. how a wind turbine works

   b. how a food co-op works

   c. how a suspension bridge is constructed

   d. how we see

   e. how a baseball player becomes a free agent

7. **INTERNET EXERCISE** Study a set of instructions from Knowledge Hound <www.knowledgehound.com>. Write a memo to your instructor evaluating the quality of the instructions. Attach a screen shot or a printout of representative pages from the instructions.

8. You work in the customer-relations department of a company that makes plumbing supplies. The head of product development has just handed you the draft of installation instructions for a sliding tub door. She has asked you to comment on their effectiveness. Write a memo to her, evaluating the instructions and suggesting improvements.

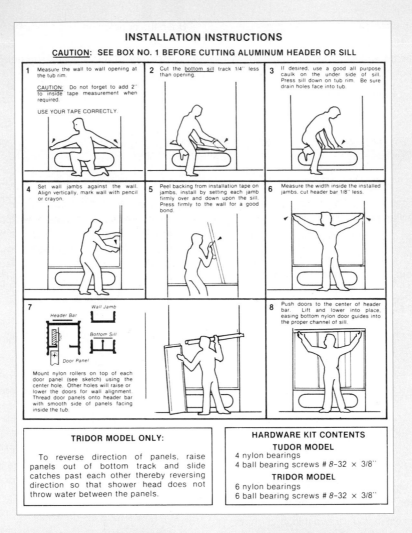

INSTALLATION INSTRUCTIONS
CAUTION: SEE BOX NO. 1 BEFORE CUTTING ALUMINUM HEADER OR SILL

1 Measure the wall to wall opening at the tub rim.

CAUTION: Do not forget to add 2" to inside tape measurement when required.

USE YOUR TAPE CORRECTLY.

2 Cut the bottom sill track 1/4" less than opening.

3 If desired, use a good all purpose caulk on the under side of sill. Press sill down on tub rim. Be sure drain holes face into tub.

4 Set wall jambs against the wall. Align vertically, mark wall with pencil or crayon.

5 Peel backing from installation tape on jambs, install by setting each jamb firmly over and down upon the sill. Press firmly to the wall for a good bond.

6 Measure the width inside the installed jambs, cut header bar 1/8" less.

7 Header Bar | Wall Jamb | Bottom Sill | Door Panel

Mount nylon rollers on top of each door panel (see sketch) using the center hole. Other holes will raise or lower the doors for wall alignment. Thread door panels onto header bar with smooth side of panels facing inside the tub.

8 Push doors to the center of header bar. Lift and lower into place, easing bottom nylon door guides into the proper channel of sill.

TRIDOR MODEL ONLY:

To reverse direction of panels, raise panels out of bottom track and slide catches past each other thereby reversing direction so that shower head does not throw water between the panels.

HARDWARE KIT CONTENTS
TUDOR MODEL
4 nylon bearings
4 ball bearing screws # 8–32 × 3/8"
TRIDOR MODEL
6 nylon bearings
6 ball bearing screws # 8–32 × 3/8"

9. Write a brief manual for a process familiar to you. Consider writing a procedures manual for a school activity or a part-time job, such as your work as the business manager of the school newspaper or as a tutor in the Writing Center.

10. **GROUP EXERCISE** Write instructions for one of the following activities or for a process used in your field. Include appropriate graphics. In a brief note preceding the instructions, indicate your audience and purpose. Exchange these materials with a partner. Observe your partner and take notes as he or she attempts to carry out the instructions. Then revise your instructions and share them with your partner; discuss whether the revised instructions are easier to understand and apply, and if so, how? Submit your instructions to your instructor.

a. how to change a bicycle tire

b. how to convert a WAV file to an MP3 file

c. how to find an online discussion board and subscribe to it

d. how to locate, download, and install a file from CNET's Shareware.com <www.shareware.com>, BrotherSoft <www.brothersoft.com>, or a similar site

On the Web

For a case assignment, "Balancing Clarity, Conciseness, and Usability in a Description," see Cases on <bedfordstmartins.com/ps>.

15

Making Oral Presentations

iStockphoto.

An oral presentation doesn't have to be deadly dull.

A search for "death by PowerPoint" on Google Images returned some 1,410,000 hits. Apparently, a lot of people have been on the receiving end of boring presentations built around bullet slides. But an oral presentation with slides doesn't have to be deadly dull.

And the process of creating and delivering a presentation doesn't have to be frightening. You might not have had much experience in public speaking, and perhaps your few attempts have been difficult. However, if you approach it logically, an oral presentation is simply another application you need to master in your role as a technical professional or technical communicator. Once you learn that the people in the room are there to hear what you have to say—not to stare at you or evaluate your clothing or catch you making a grammar mistake—you can calm down and deliver your information effectively while projecting your professionalism.

There are four basic types of presentations:

- *Impromptu presentations.* You deliver the presentation without advance notice. For instance, at a meeting, your supervisor calls on you to speak for a few minutes about a project you are working on.

- *Extemporaneous presentations.* You planned and rehearsed the presentation, and you might refer to notes or an outline, but you create the sentences as you speak. At its best, an extemporaneous presentation is clear and sounds spontaneous.

- *Scripted presentations.* You read a text that was written out completely in advance (by you or someone else). You sacrifice naturalness for increased clarity and precision.

- *Memorized presentations.* You speak without notes or a script. Memorized presentations are not appropriate for most technical subjects because most people cannot memorize presentations of more than a few minutes.

This chapter discusses extemporaneous and scripted presentations.

Focus on Process

When preparing an oral presentation, pay special attention to these steps.

- **Planning.** You will need to prepare effective presentation graphics that are visible, legible, simple, clear, and correct. Choose the appropriate technology based on the speaking situation and the available resources. See page 404.

- **Drafting.** Choose effective and memorable language. Your listeners will not be able to reread your presentation to help them understand your message. See pages 405–7.

- **Revising.** Rehearse at least three times, making any necessary changes to your transitions, the order of your slides, or your graphics.

PREPARING THE PRESENTATION

When you see an excellent 20-minute presentation, you are seeing only the last 20 minutes of a process that took many hours. Experts recommend devoting 20 to 60 minutes of preparation time for each minute of the finished presentation (Smith, 1991). That means that a 20-minute presentation takes an average of more than 13 hours to prepare. Obviously, there are many variables, including your knowledge of the subject and your experience creating graphics and giving presentations on that subject.

As you prepare a presentation, think about ways to enlist others to help you prepare and deliver it. If possible, you should rehearse the presentation in front of others. You can also call on others to help you think about your audience and purpose, the organization of the information, the types of graphics to use, appropriate designs for slides, and so forth. The more extensively you work with other people as you plan, assemble, and rehearse, the more successful the presentation is likely to be.

Preparing an oral presentation requires five steps:

- analyzing the speaking situation
- organizing and developing the presentation
- preparing presentation graphics
- choosing effective language
- rehearsing the presentation

Analyzing the Speaking Situation

An oral presentation has one big advantage over a written one: it enables a dialogue between the speaker and the audience. Listeners can make comments or simply ask questions, and the speaker and listeners can talk before and after the presentation. As a technical communicator, you can expect to give oral presentations to four types of audiences:

- *Clients and customers.* You present the features of your products and their advantages over the competition. After the sale or contract, you might present oral operating instructions and maintenance tips.
- *Colleagues in your organization.* You might instruct fellow workers on a subject you know well. After you return from an important conference, you might brief your supervisors. If you have an idea for improving operations at your organization, you might write an informal proposal and then present it orally to a small group of managers. Your presentation helps them determine whether to study the idea.
- *Fellow professionals at technical conferences.* You might speak about your own research project or about a team project to professionals in your field or in other fields.
- *The public.* You might deliver oral presentations to civic organizations and government bodies.

To prepare your presentation, you must first analyze your audience and purpose, and then determine how much information you can deliver in the allotted time.

Analyzing Your Audience and Purpose   In planning an oral presentation, consider audience and purpose, just as you would in writing a document.

- *Audience.* What does the audience know about your subject? Your answer will help you determine the level of technical vocabulary and concepts you will use, as well as the types of graphics. Why are audience members listening to your presentation? Are they likely to be hostile, enthusiastic, or neutral? A presentation on the benefits of free trade, for instance, will be received one way by conservative economists and another way by U.S. steelworkers. Does your audience include nonnative speakers of English? If so, prepare to slow down the pace of the delivery and use simple vocabulary.

- *Purpose.* Are you attempting to inform, or to both inform and persuade? If you are explaining how wind-turbine farms work, you might describe the process. If you are explaining why your wind turbines are an economical way to generate power, you might compare them with other power sources.

Your analysis of your audience and purpose will affect the content and the form of your presentation. For example, you might have to emphasize some aspects of your subject and ignore others altogether. Or you might have to arrange topics to accommodate an audience's needs.

TABLE 15.1 ▶ Time Allotment for a 20-Minute Presentation

Task	Time (minutes)
• Introduction	2
• Body	
– First Major Point	4
– Second Major Point	4
– Third Major Point	4
• Conclusion	2
• Questions	4

Budgeting Your Time   At most meetings, each speaker is given a maximum time, such as 20 minutes. If the question-and-answer period is part of your allotted time, plan accordingly. If you take more than your time, eventually your listeners will resent you or simply stop paying attention.

For a 20-minute presentation, the time allotment shown in Table 15.1 is typical. For scripted presentations, most speakers need a little over a minute to deliver a double-spaced page of text effectively.

Organizing and Developing the Presentation

The speaking situation will help you decide how to organize and develop the information you will present.

Start by considering the organizational patterns used typically in technical communication. For instance, if you are a quality-assurance engineer for a computer-chip manufacturer and must address your technical colleagues on why one of the company's products is experiencing a higher-than-normal failure rate, think in terms of cause and effect: the high failure rate is the effect, but what is the cause? Or think in terms of problem-method-solution: the high failure rate is the problem; the research you conducted to determine its cause is the method; your recommended action is the solution.

While you devise an effective organizational pattern for your presentation, note the kinds of information you will need for each section of the pre-

In This Book

For more about organizational patterns, see Ch. 6, p. 106.

sentation. Some of this information will be data; some of it will be graphics that you can use in your slides; some might be objects that you want to pass around in the audience. Prepare an outline of your presentation.

This is also a good time to plan the introduction and the conclusion. Like an introduction to a written document, an introduction to an oral presentation helps your audience understand what you are going to say, why you are going to say it, and how you are going to say it. The conclusion reinforces what you have said and looks to the future.

Guidelines

Introducing and Concluding the Presentation

In introducing a presentation, consider these five suggestions.

▶ **Introduce yourself.** Unless you are speaking to the colleagues you work with every day, begin with an introduction: "Good morning. My name is Omar Castillo, and I'm the Director of Facilities here at United." If you are using slides, include your name and position on the title slide.

▶ **State the title of your presentation.** Like all titles, titles of presentations should explain the audience and purpose, such as "Replacing the HVAC System in Building 3: Findings from the Feasibility Study." Include the title of your presentation on your title slide.

▶ **Explain the purpose of the presentation.** This explanation can be brief: "My purpose today is to present the results of the feasibility study carried out by the Facilities Group. As you may recall, last quarter we were charged with determining whether it would be wise to replace the HVAC system in Building 3."

▶ **State your main point.** An explicit statement can help your audience understand the rest of the presentation: "Our main finding is that the HVAC system should be replaced as soon as possible. Replacing it would cost approximately $120,000. The payback period would be 2.5 years. We recommend that we start soliciting bids now, for an installation date in the third week of November."

▶ **Provide an advance organizer.** Listeners need advance organizers: specific statements of where you are going: "First, I'd like to describe our present system, highlighting the recent problems we have experienced. Next, I'd like to . . . Then, I'd like to . . . Finally, I'd like to conclude and invite your questions."

In concluding a presentation, consider these four suggestions.

▶ **Announce that you are concluding.** For example, "At this point, I'd like to conclude my talk." This statement helps the audience focus on your conclusions.

▶ **Summarize the main points.** Because listeners cannot replay what you have said, you should briefly summarize your main points. If you are using slides, you should list each of your main points in one short phrase.

▶ **Look to the future.** If appropriate, speak briefly about what you think (or hope) will happen next: "If the president accepts our recommendation, you can expect the renovation to begin in late November. After a few hectic weeks, we'll have the ability to control our environment much more precisely than we can now—and start to reduce our expenses and our carbon footprint."

▶ **Invite questions politely.** You want to invite questions because they help you clarify what you said or communicate information that you did not cover in the formal presentation.

Preparing Presentation Graphics

Graphics clarify or highlight important ideas or facts. Statistical data, in particular, lend themselves to graphical presentation, as do abstract relationships and descriptions of equipment or processes. Research reported by speaking coach Terry C. Smith (1991) indicates that presentations that include graphics are judged more professional, persuasive, and credible than those that do not. In addition, Smith notes, audiences remember the information better:

	Retention after	
	3 hours	3 days
Without graphics	70%	10%
With graphics	85%	65%

One other advantage of using presentation graphics is that the audience is not always looking at you. Giving the audience another visual focus can reduce your nervousness.

Characteristics of an Effective Graphic   An effective presentation graphic has five characteristics:

In This Book
For more about creating graphics, see Ch. 8.

- *It presents a clear, well-supported claim.* In a presentation slide, the best way to present a claim and to support it is to put the claim in the headline section of the slide and the support in the body of the slide. Engineering professor and presentations specialist Michael Alley (2007) recommends the structure shown in Figure 15.1.

- *It is easy to see.* The most common problem with presentation graphics is that they are too small. In general, text has to be in 24-point type or larger to be visible on the screen. Figure 15.2 on page 398 shows a slide that contains so much information that most of it is too small to see easily.

- *It is easy to read.* Use clear, legible lines for drawings and diagrams: black on white works best. Use legible typefaces for text; a boldfaced sans-serif typeface such as Arial or Helvetica is effective because it reproduces clearly on a screen. Avoid shadowed and outlined letters.

> **Here you present the claim (in the form of a complete clause) that you will support with the graphics and words below and with the words you speak.**
>
> **Here you present the support for your claim. The support will consist of graphics, such as photographs, diagrams, and tables. Where appropriate, you should add brief clarifying comments in words. Some slides will include only one large graphic. Others will include several graphics.**

a. The structure of a typical slide

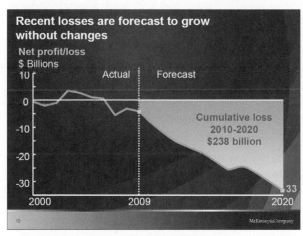

b. A slide with a claim and a single large graphic

This slide is structured like a paragraph. The words are the topic sentence; the graphic is the support.
Source: McKinsey & Company, 2010 <www.usps.com /strategicplanning/_pdf/McKinsey_March_2nd_Presentation2.pdf>.

c. A slide with a claim, several graphics, and textual callouts

In this slide, the headline functions as an advance organizer, introducing the three main options. Each option has its own graphic and its own key term, presented in yellow.
Source: McKinsey & Company, 2010 <www.usps.com /strategicplanning/_pdf/McKinsey_March_2nd_Presentation2.pdf>.

Figure 15.1   Michael Alley's Claim-and-Support Structure for Presentation Graphics

- *It is simple.* Text and drawings must be simple. Each graphic should present only one idea. Your listeners have not seen the graphic before and will not be able to linger over it.

- *It is correct.* Proofread your graphics carefully. Everyone makes mistakes of grammar, punctuation, or spelling, but mistakes are particularly embarrassing when they are 10 inches tall on a screen.

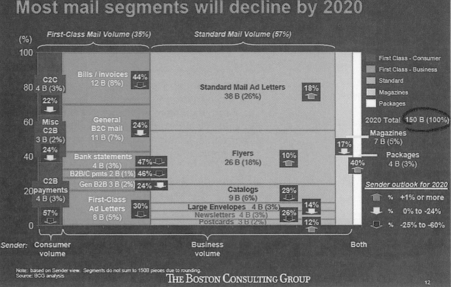

Figure 15.2 Too Much Information on a Slide
Source: Boston Group, 2010
<www.usps.com
/strategicplanning/_pdf/BCG
_Detailed%20presentation.pdf>.

When you use presentation software to create a set of graphics for a presentation, avoid the templates, many of which violate basic design principles. Instead, create a simple design using the Slide Master feature.

Presentation software programs contain many fancy sound and animation effects. For example, you can set the software so that when a new slide appears, it is accompanied by the sound of applause or of breaking glass, and the heading text spins around like a pinwheel. Do not use animation effects that are unrelated to your subject. They undercut your professionalism and will quickly become tiresome.

However, one animation effect, sometimes called *appear and dim*, is useful. When you need to create a bulleted list, you can set the software to make the next bullet item appear when you click the mouse. When you do so, the previous bullet item dims. This feature is useful because it focuses the audience's attention on the bullet item you are discussing.

One more point: you cannot use copyrighted material—images, text, music, video, or other material—in your presentation without written permission to do so. (Your presentations in class, however, do not require permission because they are covered by the fair-use exemption.)

▶ **In This Book**
For more about typefaces, see Ch. 7, p. 156. For more about using color in graphics, see Ch. 8, p. 186.

▶ **On the Web**
See the Copyright Clearance Center's materials on copyright. Click on Links Library for Ch. 15 on <bedfordstmartins .com/ps>.

TECH TIP

How to Create a Master Page Design in PowerPoint

To create a page design of your own, you can use the **Slide Master** feature to consistently apply design elements to your slides.

1. If a blank presentation does not open when you launch PowerPoint, select **New** from the **File** tab. Next, select **Blank Presentation**, and then select **Create**.

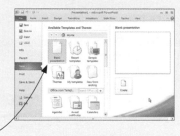

2. Select **Slide Master** from the **Master Views** group on the **View** tab.

By selecting elements on the master slide and then using the commands on the **Slide Master** tab, you can add a background, choose a color scheme, and choose type styles and sizes.

To add graphics to the master slide, use the **Images** and **Illustrations** groups on the **Insert** tab.

To modify the format, size, or position of placeholders for header and footer information, right-click on the header or footer box on the slide, and then make a selection from the pop-up menu.

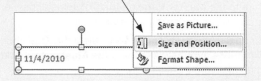

To make changes to the type of information displayed in placeholders, select the **Header & Footer** button in the **Text** group on the **Insert** tab, and then use the **Header and Footer** dialog box.

3. To save your page design so that you can use this design for another presentation, select **Save As** from the **File** tab, and then select **PowerPoint Template** from the drop-down menu.

KEYWORDS: slide master, presentation views, background, slide design, placeholder, header and footer, PowerPoint template, templates

TECH TIP

How to Set List Items to Appear and Dim During a Presentation

To help your audience focus on the point you are discussing, you can apply PowerPoint's **custom animation** feature to the **Master Page** so that list items appear and then dim when the next item appears.

1. To apply a **custom animation**, select the **Title and Content Layout** slide in the **Slide Master** view, and then highlight the list on the slide.

2. In the **Advanced Animation** group, select **Add Animation**, and then select the **Entrance** category and the **Appear** effect.

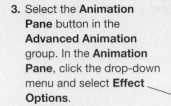

3. Select the **Animation Pane** button in the **Advanced Animation** group. In the **Animation Pane**, click the drop-down menu and select **Effect Options**.

4. On the **Effect** tab in the **Appear** dialog box, click the **After Animation** drop-down menu and select a dim color.

KEYWORDS: custom animation, slide master, effect options, entrance effects

---

Graphics and the Speaking Situation To plan your graphics, analyze four aspects of the speaking situation:

- *Length of the presentation.* How many slides should you have? Smith (1991) suggests showing a different slide approximately every 30 seconds of the presentation. This figure is only a guideline; base your decision on your subject and audience. Still, the general point is valid: it is far better to have a series of simple slides than to have one complicated one that stays on the screen for five minutes.

- *Audience aptitude and experience.* What kinds of graphics can your audience understand easily? You don't want to present scatter graphs, for example, if your listeners do not know how to interpret them.

- *Size and layout of the room.* Graphics to be used in a small meeting room differ from those to be used in a 500-seat auditorium. Think first about the size of the images, then about the layout of the room. For instance, will a window create glare that you will have to consider as you plan the type or placement of the graphics?

- *Equipment.* Find out what kind of equipment will be available in the presentation room. Ask about backups in case of equipment failure. If possible, bring your own equipment. That way, you know it works and you know how to use it. Some speakers bring graphics in two media just in case; that is, they have slides, but they also have transparencies of the same graphics.

Using Graphics to Signal the Organization of the Presentation Used effectively, graphics can help you communicate how your presentation is organized. For example, you can use the transition from one graphic to the next to indicate the transition from one point to the next. Figure 15.3 shows the slides for a presentation that accompanied the report in Chapter 13 on clickers at CMSU (see page 331).

> **On the Web**
>
> For excellent advice on designing slides, see Garr Reynolds's site. Click on Links Library for Ch. 15 on <bedfordstmartins.com/ps>.

Presentation software allows you to create two other kinds of documents—*speaking notes* and *handouts*—that can enhance a presentation. Figure 15.4 on page 403 shows a page of speaking notes. Figure 15.5 on page 403 shows a page from a handout.

Establishing Baseline Requirements for Adopting Clickers at CMSU: A Recommendation Report

Prepared by:
Jeremy Elkins, Co-chair
Eloise Carruthers, Co-chair
Student Affairs Advisory Committee
Central Montana State University

December 15, 2011

The first slide—the title slide—shows the title of the presentation and the name and affiliation of each speaker. You might also want to include the date of the presentation.

Recommendation Report Outline

➡ 1. Introduction
2. Major Results
   2.1 Instructor attitudes
   2.2 Student attitudes
   2.3 Lecture-hall requirements
   2.4 Existing computer infrastructure
3. Conclusions
4. Recommendation

December 15, 2011   Clicker-Use Recommendation Report   2

The next slide presents an outline of the presentation. The arrow identifies the point the speaker is addressing.

At the bottom of each slide in the body of the presentation is a footer with the date, a shortened presentation title, and the number of the slide. The slide numbers enable audience members to ask questions by referring to the number.

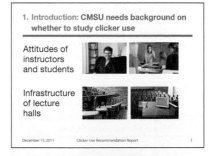

1. Introduction: **CMSU needs background on whether to study clicker use**

Attitudes of instructors and students

Infrastructure of lecture halls

December 15, 2011   Clicker-Use Recommendation Report   3

The title of the third slide uses the numbering system introduced in the previous slide. The cue helps the audience understand the structure of the presentation. Following the colon is an independent clause that presents the claim that will be supported in the slide.

If the images in your presentation are your own intellectual property or are clip art that comes with the software, you can legally display them anywhere.

Figure 15.3   Sample PowerPoint Presentation

The slide was made using SmartArt graphics, which are part of PowerPoint. SmartArt graphics help you show logical relationships. Here, the graphic shows that the questions the students are studying—about attitudes and about the infrastructure of the lecture halls—are the foundation on which the rest of the feasibility study will rest.

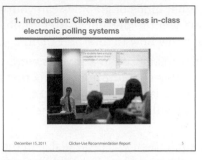

This photograph shows an instructor displaying the question he asked and a bar graph showing the students' clicker responses.

Even if an image is not your own intellectual property, you can display it in a class because it is covered by the fair-use provisions of U.S. copyright law. However, in a business presentation, you need formal written permission from the copyright holders. See Ch. 2, pp. 22–23, for more information.

Recommendation Report Outline

1. Introduction
➤ 2. Major Results
    2.1 Instructor attitudes
    2.2 Student attitudes
    2.3 Lecture-hall requirements
    2.4 Existing computer infrastructure
3. Conclusions
4. Recommendation

This slide is identical to Slide 2, except that the arrow has been moved. This slide helps the audience remember the overall organization of the presentation.

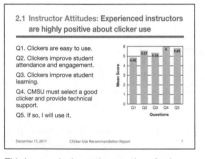

This bar graph shows the questions (and the mean scores) on the questionnaire for instructors experienced with clickers.

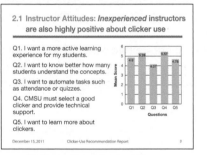

This slide presents the same kinds of information for the questionnaire completed by inexperienced instructors.

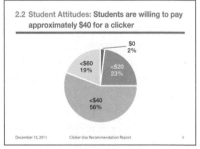

A pie chart is a logical choice for representing a small number of components that add up to 100 percent.

The speakers use conservative blues for all their graphics in the slide set.

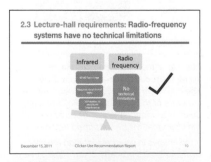

This is another SmartArt graphic, representing a balancing of two options. The speakers added the check mark to show that the radio-frequency system is preferable to the infrared system.

Figure 15.3   (continued)

2.4 Existing computer infrastructure: We have both platforms and many OSs

Platform	Operating system	Number of lecture halls
Macintosh	OSX	3
PC	XP	7
PC	Vista	7
PC	Win 7	4

When you use tables, keep them simple. If you have a lot of rows and columns, present the data on several slides.

Recommendation Report Outline

1. Introduction
2. Major Results
    2.1 Instructor attitudes
    2.2 Student attitudes
    2.3 Lecture-hall requirements
    2.4 Existing computer infrastructure
➤ 3. Conclusions
4. Recommendation

The speakers presented this organizing slide here to clarify the transition from Section 2 to Section 3. They did not present this slide at the start of each of the four subsections of Section 2.

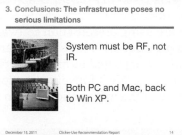

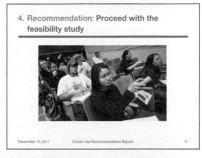

The formatting that appears throughout the slide set—the background color, the horizontal rule, and the footer—was created in the Slide Master view. This formatting will appear in every slide unless it is modified or deleted for that slide.

Note that the speakers use color—sparingly—for emphasis.

As discussed in Ch. 13, conclusions are inferences you draw from results. When you wish to cite sources, you have three choices: add source statements at the bottom of the appropriate slides, make a sources slide that you show at the end of the presentation, or make a paper copy of the sources to distribute.

Recommendations are statements about what you think should be done next. This final photograph underscores the speakers' recommendation: let's proceed with this study.

Some speakers make a final slide with the word "Questions?" on it to signal the end of the presentation. You can also display contact information to encourage audience members to get in touch with you.

Figure 15.3   (continued)

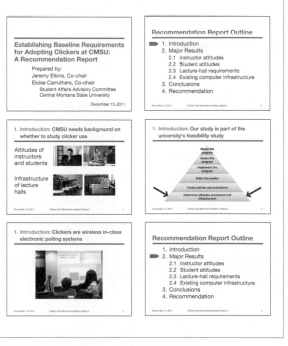

To create speaking notes for each slide, use your presentation software to type the notes in the box under the picture of the slide, and then print the notes pages. You can print the slides on your notes pages in color or black and white.

The problem with using speaking notes is that you cannot read your notes and maintain eye contact at the same time.

Figure 15.4   Speaking Notes

The software is set to display six slides on the page.

Figure 15.5   Handout

Typical Media Used to Present Graphics The Choices and Strategies box below describes the typical media used to present graphics.

If you are using presentation software, keep in mind that many of the templates provided with the software are unnecessarily ornate, full of fancy shading and designs and colors. If you choose a template, choose a simple one, and then modify it for your situation. You want the audience to focus on your delivery of the information, not on the complex design of the graphics.

CHOICES AND STRATEGIES   Choosing Media to Present Graphics

Medium	Advantages	Disadvantages
Computer presentations: images are projected from a computer to a screen	• Very professional appearance. • You can produce any combination of static or dynamic images, from simple graphs to sophisticated, three-dimensional animations, as well as sound and video. • You can embed links to videos or animations on the Web.	• The equipment is expensive and not available everywhere. • Preparing the graphics can be time-consuming. • Presentations prepared using one piece of software might not run on all systems.
Overhead projector: projects transparencies onto a screen	• Transparencies are inexpensive and easy to create. • You can draw transparencies "live." • You can create overlays by placing one transparency over another. • Lights can remain on during the presentation.	• Not as professional-looking as a computer presentation. • Each transparency must be loaded separately by hand.
Chalkboard or other hard writing surface	• Almost universally available. • You have complete control; you can add, delete, or modify the graphic easily.	• Complicated or extensive graphics are difficult to create. • Ineffective in large rooms. • Very informal appearance.
Objects: models or samples of material that can be held up or passed around the audience	• Interesting for the audience. • Provides a close look at the object.	• Audience members might not be listening while they are looking at the object. • It can take a long while to pass an object around a large room. • The object might be damaged.
Handouts: photocopies of written material given to each audience member	• Much material can fit on the page. • Audience members can write on their copies and keep them.	• Audience members might read the handout rather than listen to the speaker.

DOCUMENT ANALYSIS ACTIVITY

Integrating Graphics and Text on a Presentation Slide

The following slide is part of a presentation about the Human Genome Project. The accompanying questions ask you to think about the discussion of preparing presentation graphics (on pp. 396–404).

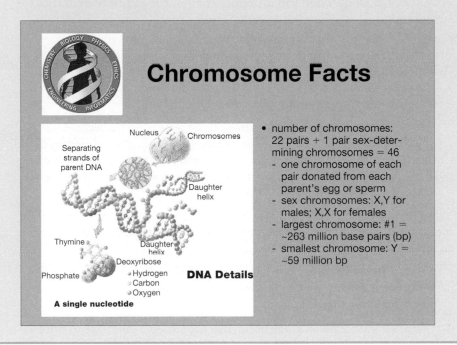

1. How effective is the Human Genome Project logo in the upper left-hand corner of the slide?

2. How well does the graphic of DNA support the accompanying text on chromosome facts?

3. Overall, how effective is the presentation graphic?

▶ On the Web

To submit your responses to your instructor, click on Document Analysis Activities for Ch. 15 on <bedfordstmartins .com/ps>.

In addition, set the software so that you use the mouse (or a colleague does) to advance from one graphic to the next. If you set the software so that the graphics advance automatically at a specified interval, such as 60 seconds, you will have to speed up or slow down your presentation to keep up with the graphics.

Choosing Effective Language

Delivering an oral presentation is more challenging than writing a document because listeners can't reread something they didn't understand. In addition, because you are speaking live, you must maintain your listeners' attention, even if they are hungry or tired or the room is too hot. Using language effectively helps you meet these two challenges.

Even if you use graphics effectively, listeners cannot "see" the organization of a presentation as well as readers can. For this reason, use language to alert your listeners to advance organizers, summaries, and transitions.

- *Advance organizers.* Use an advance organizer (a statement that tells the listener what you are about to say) in the introduction. In addition, use advance organizers when you introduce main ideas in the body of the presentation.

- *Summaries.* The major summary is in the conclusion, but you might also summarize at strategic points in the body of the presentation. For instance, after a three- to four-minute discussion of a major point, you might summarize it in one sentence before going on to the next major point. Here is a sample summary from a conclusion:

  > Let me conclude by summarizing my three main points about the implications of the new RCRA regulations on the long-range waste-management strategy for Radnor Township. The first point is . . . The second point is . . . The third point is . . . I hope this presentation will give you some ideas as you think about the challenges of implementing the RCRA.

- *Transitions.* As you move from one point to the next, signal the transition clearly. Summarize the previous point, and then announce that you are moving to the next point:

  > It is clear, then, that the federal government has issued regulations without indicating how it expects county governments to comply with them. I'd like to turn now to my second main point. . . .

To maintain your listeners' attention, use memorable language. A note about humor: only a few hundred people in the United States make a good living being funny. Don't plan to tell a joke. If something happens during the presentation that provides an opening for a witty remark, and you are good at making witty remarks, fine. But don't *prepare* to be funny.

Guidelines

Using Memorable Language in Oral Presentations

Draw on these three techniques to help make a lasting impression on your audience.

▶ **Involve the audience.** People are more interested in their own concerns than in yours. Talk to the audience about their problems and their solutions. In the introduction, establish a link between your topic and the audience's interests. For instance, a presentation to a city council about waste management might begin like this:

Picture yourself on the Radnor Township Council two years from now. After exhaustive hearings, proposals, and feasibility studies, you still don't have a waste-management plan that meets federal regulations. But you do have a mounting debt: the township is being fined $1,000 per day until you implement an acceptable plan.

▶ **Refer to people, not to abstractions.** People remember specifics; they forget abstractions. To make a point memorable, describe it in human terms:

> What could you do with that $365,000 every year? In each computer lab in each school in the township, you could replace each laptop every three years instead of every four years. Or you could expand your school-lunch program to feed every needy child in the township. Or …

▶ **Use interesting facts, figures, and quotations.** Search the Internet for interesting information about your subject. For instance, you might find a brief quotation from an authoritative figure in the field or a famous person not generally associated with the field (for example, Theodore Roosevelt on waste management and the environment).

Rehearsing the Presentation

Even the most gifted speakers need to rehearse. It is a good idea to set aside enough time to rehearse your speech at least three times.

- *First rehearsal.* Don't worry about posture or voice projection. Just present your presentation aloud with your presentation slides. Try to see if the speech makes sense—if you can explain all the points and create effective transitions. If you have trouble, stop and try to figure out the problem. If you need more information, get it. If you need a better transition, create one. You are likely to learn that you need to revise the order of your slides. Pick up where you left off and continue the rehearsal, stopping again where necessary to revise.

- *Second rehearsal.* The presentation now should flow more easily. Make any necessary changes to the slides. When you have complete control over the organization and flow, check to see if you are within the time limit.

- *Third rehearsal.* After a satisfactory second rehearsal, try the presentation under more realistic circumstances—if possible, in front of others. The listeners might offer questions or constructive advice about your speaking style. If people aren't available, record the presentation, and then evaluate your own delivery.

Rehearse again until you are satisfied with your presentation, but don't try to memorize it.

e-Pages

To analyze proposal delivered as an oral presentation by student Kerri Conley, visit <bedfordstmartins.com/ps/epages>.

On the Web

To download an oral-presentation evaluation form, see Forms for Technical Communication on <bedfordstmartins.com/ps>.

DELIVERING THE PRESENTATION

When giving your presentation, you will concentrate on what you have to say. However, you will have three additional concerns: staying calm, using your voice effectively, and using your body effectively.

Calming Your Nerves

Most professional actors admit to being nervous before a performance, so it is no wonder that most technical speakers are nervous. You might well fear that you will forget everything or that no one will be able to hear you. These fears are common. But keep in mind three facts about nervousness:

- *You are much more aware of your nervousness than the audience is.* They are farther away from your trembling hands.
- *Nervousness gives you energy and enthusiasm.* Without energy and enthusiasm, your presentation will be flat. If you seem bored and listless, your audience will become bored and listless.
- *After a few minutes, your nervousness will pass.* You will be able to relax and concentrate on the subject.

This advice is unlikely to make you feel much better if you are distracted by nerves as you wait to give your presentation. Experienced speakers offer three tips for coping with nervousness:

- *Realize that you are prepared.* If you have done your homework, prepared the presentation carefully, and rehearsed it several times, you'll be fine.
- *Realize that the audience is there to hear you, not to judge you.* Your listeners want to hear what you have to say. They are much less interested in your nervousness than you are.
- *Realize that your audience is made up of individual people who happen to be sitting in the same room.* You'll feel better if you realize that audience members also get nervous before making presentations.

When it is time to begin, don't jump up to the lectern and start speaking quickly. Walk up slowly and arrange your text, outline, or note cards before you. If water is available, take a sip. Look out at the audience for a few seconds before you begin. Begin with "Good morning" (or "Good afternoon" or "Good evening"), and refer to the officers and dignitaries present. If you have not been introduced, introduce yourself. In less-formal contexts, just begin your presentation.

So that the audience will listen to you and have confidence in what you say, use your voice and your body to project an attitude of restrained self-confidence. Show interest in your topic and knowledge about your subject.

Guidelines

Releasing Nervous Energy

Experienced speakers suggest the following four strategies for dealing with nervousness before a presentation.

▶ **Walk around.** A brisk walk of a minute or two can calm you by dissipating some of your nervous energy.

▶ **Go off by yourself for a few minutes.** Getting away can help you compose your thoughts and realize that you can handle your nervousness.

▶ **Talk with someone for a few minutes.** For some speakers, distraction works best. Find someone to talk to.

▶ **Take several deep breaths, exhaling slowly.** Doing so will help you control your nerves.

Using Your Voice Effectively

Inexperienced speakers often have problems with five aspects of vocalizing.

- *Volume.* Because acoustics vary greatly from room to room, you won't know how well your voice will carry in a particular setting until you have heard someone speaking there. In some rooms, speakers can use a conversational volume. Other rooms require greater voice projection. These circumstances aside, more people speak too softly than too loudly. After your first few sentences, ask if the people in the back of the room can hear you. When people speak into microphones, they tend to speak too loudly. Glance at your audience to see if you need to adjust your volume. The body language of audience members will be clear.

- *Speed.* Nervousness makes people speak quickly. Even if you think you are speaking at the right rate, you might be going a little too fast for some listeners. Although you know your subject well, your listeners are trying to understand new information. For particularly difficult points, slow down for emphasis. After finishing one major point, pause before introducing the next one.

- *Pitch.* In an effort to control their voices, many speakers end up flattening their pitch. The resulting monotone is boring and, for some listeners, distracting. Try to let the pitch of your voice go up or down as it would in a normal conversation.

- *Articulation.* Nervousness can accentuate sloppy pronunciation. If you want to say *environment*, don't say *envirament*. A related problem involves technical words and phrases, especially the important ones. When a speaker uses a phrase over and over, it tends to get clipped and becomes difficult to understand. Unless you articulate carefully, *Scanlon Plan* will end up as *Scanluhplah*.

- *Nonfluencies.* Avoid such meaningless fillers as *you know, like, okay, right, uh,* and *um.* These phrases do not hide the fact that you aren't saying anything. A thoughtful pause is better than an annoying verbal tic.

Using Your Body Effectively

Besides listening to you, the audience will be looking at you. Effective speakers use their body language to help listeners follow the presentation.

Guidelines

Facing an Audience

As you give a presentation, keep in mind these four guidelines about physical movement.

▶ **Maintain eye contact.** Eye contact helps you see how the audience is receiving the presentation. You will see, for instance, if listeners in the back are having trouble hearing you. For small groups, look at each listener randomly; for larger groups, look at each segment of the audience frequently during your speech. Do not stare at the screen, at the floor, or out the window.

▶ **Use natural gestures.** When people talk, they often gesture with their hands. Most of the time, gestures make the presentation look natural and improve listeners' comprehension. You can supplement your natural gestures by using your arms and hands to signal pauses and to emphasize important points. When referring to graphics, walk toward the screen and point to direct the audience's attention. Avoid mannerisms—physical gestures that serve no useful purpose, such as jiggling the coins in your pocket or pacing back and forth. Like verbal mannerisms, physical mannerisms are often unconscious. Constructive criticism from friends can help you pinpoint them.

▶ **Don't block the audience's view of the screen.** Stand off to the side of the screen. Use a pointer to indicate key words or images on the screen.

▶ **Control the audience's attention.** People will listen to and look at anything that is interesting. If you hand out photocopies at the start of the presentation, some people will start to read them and stop listening to you. If you leave an image on the screen after you finish talking about it, some people will keep looking at it instead of listening to you. When you want the audience to look at you and listen to you, remove the graphics or make the screen blank.

If your audience includes people of different cultures and native languages, keep in mind the following three suggestions:

- *Hire translators and interpreters if necessary.* If many people in the audience do not understand your language, hire interpreters (people who translate your words as you speak them) and translators (people who translate your written material in advance).

- *Use graphics effectively to reinforce your points for nonnative speakers.* Try to devise ways to present information using graphics—flowcharts, diagrams, and so forth—to help your listeners understand you. Putting more textual information on graphics will allow your listeners to see the accompanying text while you explain your points.

- *Be aware that gestures can have cultural meanings.* As discussed in Chapter 8, hand gestures (such as the thumbs-up sign or the "okay" gesture) have different—and sometimes insulting—meanings in other cultures. Therefore, it's a good idea to limit the use of these gestures. You can't go wrong with an arms-out, palms-up gesture that projects openness and inclusiveness.

ANSWERING QUESTIONS AFTER THE PRESENTATION

When you finish a presentation, thank the audience simply and directly: "Thank you for your attention." Then invite questions. Don't abruptly ask, "Any questions?" This phrasing suggests that you don't really want any questions. Instead, say something like this: "If you have any questions, I'll be happy to try to answer them now." If invited politely, people will be much more likely to ask, enabling you to communicate your information more effectively.

When you respond to questions, you might encounter any of these four situations:

- *You're unsure everyone heard the question.* Ask if people have heard it. If they haven't, repeat or paraphrase it, perhaps as an introduction to your response: "Your question is about the efficiency of these three techniques. . . ." Some speakers always repeat the question, which gives them an extra moment to prepare an answer.

- *You don't understand the question.* Ask for clarification. After responding, ask if you have answered the question adequately.

- *You have already answered the question during the presentation.* Restate the answer politely. Begin your answer with a phrase such as the following: "I'm sorry I didn't make that point clear in my talk. I wanted to explain how . . ." Never insult the person by pointing out that you already answered the question.

- *A belligerent member of the audience rejects your response and insists on restating his or her original point.* Politely offer to discuss the matter further after the session. This way, the person won't bore or annoy the rest of the audience.

If it is appropriate to stay after the session to talk individually with members of the audience, offer to do so.

ETHICS NOTE

Answering Questions Honestly

If an audience member asks a question to which you do not know the answer, admit it. Simply say, "I don't know" or "I'm not sure, but I think the answer is . . ." Smart people know that they don't know everything. If you have some ideas about how to find out the answer—by checking a particular reference source, for example—share them. If the question is obviously important to the person who asked it, you might offer to meet with him or her to discuss ways for you to give a more complete response, perhaps by e-mail.

Speaker's Checklist

☐ Did you analyze the speaking situation—the audience and purpose of the presentation? (p. 393)

☐ Did you determine how much information you can communicate in your allotted time? (p. 394)

☐ Did you organize and develop the presentation? (p. 394)

Does each presentation graphic have these five characteristics?

　☐ It presents a clear, well-supported claim. (p. 396)
　☐ It is easy to see. (p. 396)
　☐ It is easy to read. (p. 396)
　☐ It is simple. (p. 397)
　☐ It is correct. (p. 397)

☐ In planning your graphics, did you consider the length of your presentation, your audience's aptitude and experience, the size and layout of the room, and the equipment available? (p. 400)

☐ Did you plan your graphics to help the audience understand the organization of your presentation? (p. 401)

☐ Did you make sure that the presentation room will have the necessary equipment for the graphics? (p. 404)

☐ Did you choose appropriate media for your graphics? (p. 404)

☐ Did you use language to signal advance organizers, summaries, and transitions? (p. 406)

☐ Did you choose language that is vivid and memorable? (p. 406)

☐ Did you rehearse your presentation with a tape recorder, videocamera, or live audience? (p. 407)

Exercises

1. Learn some of the basic functions of a presentation software program. For instance, modify a template, create your own original design, add footer information to a master slide, insert a graphic on a slide, and set the animation feature to make each bullet item appear only after a mouse click.

2. Using presentation software, create a design to be used for the master slide of a computer presentation. Then, for the same information, create a design to be used for a transparency made on a black-and-white photocopier.

3. Prepare a five-minute presentation, including graphics, on one of the topics listed here. For each presentation, your audience will consist of the other students in your class, and your purpose is to introduce them to an aspect of your academic field.

    a. Define a key term or concept in your field.

    b. Describe how a particular piece of equipment is used in your field.

    c. Describe how to carry out a procedure common in your field.

The instructor and the other students will evaluate the presentation by filling out the oral-presentation evaluation form available from <bedfordstmartins.com/ps>.

4. **GROUP EXERCISE** Prepare a five-minute presentation based either on your proposal for a research report or on your completion report. Your audience will consist of the other students in your class, and your purpose is to introduce them to your topic. The instructor and the other students will evaluate the presentation by filling out the oral-presentation evaluation form available from <bedfordstmartins.com/ps>. If your instructor wishes, this assignment can be done collaboratively.

▷ On the Web

For a case assignment, "Understanding the Claim-and-Support Structure for Presentation Graphics," see Cases on <bedfordstmartins .com/ps>.

Appendix:
Reference Handbook

Part A: Documenting Your Sources

Documentation identifies the sources of the ideas and the quotations in your document. Integrated throughout your document, documentation consists of citations in the text and a reference list (or list of works cited) at the back of your document. Documentation serves three basic functions:

- *It helps you acknowledge your debt to your sources.* Complete and accurate documentation is a professional obligation, a matter of ethics. Failure to document a source, whether intentional or unintentional, is plagiarism. At most colleges and universities, plagiarism can mean automatic failure of the course and, in some instances, suspension or expulsion. In many companies, it is grounds for immediate dismissal.

- *It helps you establish credibility.* Effective documentation helps you place your document within the general context of continuing research and helps you define it as a responsible contribution to knowledge in the field. Knowing how to use existing research is one mark of a professional.

- *It helps your readers find your source in case they want to read more about a particular subject.*

To a large extent, your note taking will determine the quality of your finished product. Record information from your sources accurately and clearly. Mistakes made during note taking can be hard to catch later, and they can cause you to plagiarize unintentionally.

Three kinds of material should always be documented:

- Any quotation from a written source or an interview, even if it is only a few words.

- A paraphrased or summarized idea, concept, or opinion gathered from your reading.

- Any graphic from a written or an electronic source.

Just as organizations have their own preferences for formatting and punctuation, many organizations also have their own documentation styles. For documents prepared in the workplace, find out your organization's style and abide by it. Check with your instructor to see which documentation system to use in the documents you write for class. The documentation systems included in this section of the appendix are based on the following style manuals:

- *Publication manual of the American Psychological Association* (6th ed.). (2010). Washington, DC: APA.

- *IEEE editorial style manual* [PDF]. (2007). New York: IEEE.

- Modern Language Association. (2009). *MLA handbook for writers of research papers*. New York: Author.

▶ **On the Web**

For help with documenting sources in CSE style, download "CSE Documentation Style Guidelines" from <bedfordstmartins.com/ps>.

▶ **On the Web**

For a list of published style manuals, see the Selected Bibliography on <bedfordstmartins.com/ps>.

NOTE TAKING

Most note taking involves three kinds of activities: paraphrasing, quoting, and summarizing.

Paraphrasing

A paraphrase is a restatement, in your own words, of someone else's words. If you simply copy someone else's words — even a mere two or three in a row — you must use quotation marks.

In taking notes, what kind of material should you paraphrase? Any information that you think might be useful: background data, descriptions of mechanisms or processes, test results, and so forth.

Figure A.1 shows a paraphrased passage based on the following discussion. The author is explaining the concept of performance-centered design.

Original Passage

In performance-centered design, the emphasis is on providing support for the structure of the work as well as the information needed to accomplish it. One of the best examples is TurboTax®, which meets all the three main criteria of effective performance-centered design:

- *People can do their work with no training on how to use the system.* People trying to do their income taxes have no interest in taking any kind of training. They want to get their taxes filled out correctly and quickly, getting all the deductions they are entitled to. These packages, over the years, have moved the interface from a forms-based one, where the user had to know what forms were needed, to an interview-based one that fills out the forms automatically as you answer questions. The design of the interface assumes no particular computer expertise.

- *The system provides the right information at the right time to accomplish the work.* At each step in the process, the system asks only those questions that are relevant based on previous answers. The taxpayer is free to ask for more detail or may proceed through a dialog that asks more-detailed questions if the taxpayer doesn't know the answer to the higher-level question. If a taxpayer is married filing jointly, the system presents only those questions for that filing status.

- *Both tasks and systems change as the user understands the system.* When I first used TurboTax 6 years ago I found myself going to the forms themselves. Doing my taxes generally took about 2 days. Each year I found my need to go to the forms to be less and less. Last year, it took me about 2 hours to do my taxes, and I looked at the forms only when I printed out the final copy.

Lovgren, "Achieving Performance-Centered Design"
<www.reisman-consulting.com/pages/a-Perform.html>

example of performance-centered design:
TurboTax® meets three main criteria:

- People can do their work with no training on how to use the system.
- The system provides the right information at the right time to accomplish the work.
- Both tasks and systems change as the user understands the system.

This paraphrase is inappropriate because the three bulleted points are taken word for word from the original. The fact that the student omitted the explanations from the original is irrelevant. These are direct quotes, not paraphrases.

a. Inappropriate paraphrase

Lovgren, "Achieving Performance-Centered Design"
<www.reisman-consulting.com/pages/a-Perform.html>

example of performance-centered design:
TurboTax® meets three main criteria:

- You don't have to learn how to use the system.
- The system knows how to respond at the appropriate time to what the user is doing.
- As the user gets smarter about using the system, the system gets smarter, making it faster to complete the task.

This paraphrase is appropriate because the words are different from those used in the original.

When you turn your notes into a document, you are likely to reword your paraphrases. As you revise your document, check a copy of the original source document to be sure you haven't unintentionally reverted to the wording from the original source.

b. Appropriate paraphrase

Figure A.1   Inappropriate and Appropriate Paraphrased Notes
Source: Adapted from Lovgren, 2000 <www.reisman-consulting.com/pages/a-Perform.html>.

Guidelines

Paraphrasing Accurately

To be sure you do not introduce any errors into your paraphrase, follow these four suggestions.

▶ **Study the original until you understand it thoroughly.**

▶ **Rewrite the relevant portions of the original.** Use complete sentences, fragments, or lists, but don't compress the material so much that you'll have trouble understanding it later.

▶ **Title the information so that you'll be able to identify its subject at a glance.** The title should include the general subject and the author's attitude or approach to it, such as "Criticism of open-sea pollution-control devices."

▶ **Include the author's last name, a short title of the article or book, and the page number of the original.** You will need this information later in citing your source.

Quoting

▷ In This Book

For more about formatting quotations, see "Quotation Marks," "Ellipses," and "Square Brackets" in Appendix, Part B.

Sometimes you will want to quote a source, either to preserve the author's particularly well-expressed or emphatic phrasing or to lend authority to your discussion. Avoid quoting passages of more than two or three sentences, or your document will look like a mere compilation. Your job is to integrate an author's words and ideas into your own thinking, not merely to introduce a series of quotations.

Although you probably won't be quoting long passages in your document, recording a complete quotation in your notes will help you recall its meaning and context more accurately when you are ready to integrate it into your own work.

The simplest form of quotation is an author's exact statement:

As Jones states, "Solar energy won't make much of a difference for at least a decade."

To add an explanatory word or phrase to a quotation, use brackets:

As Nelson states, "It [the oil glut] will disappear before we understand it."

Use ellipses (three spaced dots) to show that you are omitting part of an author's statement:

| ORIGINAL STATEMENT | "The generator, which we purchased in May, has turned out to be one of our wisest investments." |
| ELLIPTICAL QUOTATION | "The generator . . . has turned out to be one of our wisest investments." |

According to the documentation style recommended by the Modern Language Association (MLA), if the author's original statement has ellipses, you should add brackets around the ellipses that you introduce:

| ORIGINAL STATEMENT | "I think reuse adoption offers . . . the promise to improve business in a number of ways." |
| ELLIPTICAL QUOTATION | "I think reuse adoption offers . . . the promise to improve business [. . .] ." |

Summarizing

Summarizing is the process of rewriting a passage in your own words to make it shorter while still retaining its essential message. Writers summarize to help them learn a body of information or create a draft of one or more of the summaries that will go into the document.

Guidelines

Summarizing

The following advice focuses on extracting the essence of a passage by summarizing it.

▶ **Read the passage carefully several times.**

▶ **Underline key ideas.** Look for them in the titles, headings, topic sentences, transitional paragraphs, and concluding paragraphs.

▶ **Combine key ideas.** Study what you have underlined. Paraphrase the underlined ideas. Don't worry about your grammar, punctuation, or style at this point.

▶ **Check your draft against the original for accuracy and emphasis.** Check that you have recorded statistics and names correctly and that your version of a complicated concept faithfully represents the original. Check that you got the proportions right; if the original devotes 20 percent of its space to a particular point, your draft should not devote 5 percent or 50 percent to that point.

▶ **Record the bibliographic information carefully.** Even though a summary might contain all your own words, you still must cite it, because the main ideas are someone else's. Record the author, title, publication data, call number or URL, and any other relevant information such as database name or retrieval data.

APA STYLE

APA style is used widely in the social sciences. It consists of two elements: citations in the text and a list of references at the end of the document.

▷ **On the Web**

For more information, see the APA Web site. Click on Links Library for Appendix, Part A, on <bedfordstmartins.com/ps>.

APA Style for Textual Citations

APA Style for Reference List Entries

APA Textual Citations

In APA style, a textual citation typically includes the name of the source's author and the date of its publication. Textual citations vary depending on the type of information cited, the number of authors, and the context of the citation. The following models illustrate a variety of common textual citations; for additional examples, consult the *Publication Manual of the American Psychological Association.*

1. Summarized or Paraphrased Material   For material or ideas that you have summarized or paraphrased, include the author's name and the publication date in parentheses immediately following the borrowed information.

> This phenomenon was identified more than 50 years ago (Wilkinson, 1948).

If your sentence already includes the source's name, do not repeat it in the parenthetical notation.

> Wilkinson (1948) identified this phenomenon more than 50 years ago.

2. Quoted Material or Specific Fact   If the reference is to a specific fact, idea, or quotation, add the page number(s) of the source to your citation.

> This phenomenon was identified more than 50 years ago (Wilkinson, 1948, p. 36).
> Wilkinson (1948) identified this phenomenon more than 50 years ago (p. 36).

3. Source with Multiple Authors   For a source written by two authors, cite both names. Use an ampersand (&) in the parenthetical citation itself, but use the word *and* in regular text.

> (Tyshenko & Paterson, 2010)
> Tyshenko and Paterson (2010) argued . . .

For a source written by three, four, or five authors, include all the names the first time you cite the reference; after that, include only the last name of the first author followed by *et al.*

First Reference

Cashman, Walls, and Thomas (2008) argued . . .

Subsequent References

Cashman et al. (2008) found . . .

For a source written by six or more authors, use only the first author's name followed by *et al.*

4. Source Issued by an Organization   If the author is an organization rather than a person, use the name of the organization.

There is currently ongoing discussion of the scope and practice of nursing informatics (American Nurses Association, 2010).

In a recent publication, the American Nurses Association (2010) discusses the scope and practice of nursing informatics.

If the organization name has a common abbreviation, you may include it in the first citation: (International Business Machines [IBM], 2011). Then use it in subsequent citations: (IBM, 2011).

5. Source with an Unknown Author   If the source does not identify an author, use a shortened version of the title in your parenthetical citation.

Hawking made the discovery that under precise conditions, thermal radiation could exit black holes ("World Scientists," 2007).

6. Multiple Authors with the Same Last Name   Use first initials if two or more sources have authors with the same last name.

B. Porter (2007) created a more stable platform for database transfers, while A. L. Porter (2007) focused primarily on latitudinal peer-to-peer outcome interference.

7. Multiple Sources in One Citation   Present the sources in alphabetical order, separated by a semicolon.

This phenomenon has been well documented (Houlding, 2011; Jessen, 2010).

8. Personal Communication   When you cite personal interviews, phone calls, letters, memos, and e-mails, include the words *personal communication* and the date of the communication. Do not include these sources in your list of references at the end of the document.

D. E. Walls (personal communication, April 3, 2011) provided the prior history of his . . .

9. Electronic Document   If the date is unknown, use *n.d.* (for *no date*).

> Interpersonal relationships are complicated by differing goals (Hoffman, n.d.).

If the document is posted as a PDF file, include a page number in the citation. If a page number is not available but the source contains paragraph numbers, give the paragraph number.

> (Tong, 2010, para. 4)

If no paragraph or page number is available and the source has headings, cite the appropriate heading and paragraph.

> The CDC (2007) warns that babies born to women who smoke during pregnancy are 30% more likely to be born prematurely (The Reality section, para. 3).

The APA Reference List

▶ **In This Book**
For a sample APA-style reference list, see p. 428.

A reference list provides the information your readers will need in order to find each source you have cited in the text. It should not include sources you read but did not use.

Following are some guidelines for an APA-style reference list.

- *Arranging entries.* Arrange the entries alphabetically by author's last name. If two or more works are by the same author, arrange them by date, earliest to latest. If two or more works are by the same author in the same year, list them alphabetically by title and include a lowercase letter after the date: Smith 2010a, Smith 2010b, and so on. Alphabetize works by an organization by the first significant word in the name of the organization.

- *Book titles.* Italicize titles of books. Capitalize only the first word of the book's title, the first word of the subtitle, and any proper nouns.

- *Publication information.* For books, give the publisher's full name, or consult your style guide for the preferred abbreviation. Include both the publisher's city and state (abbreviated) for all U.S. cities or the city and country (not abbreviated) for all non-U.S. cities; also include the province for Canadian cities.

- *Periodical titles.* Italicize titles of periodicals and capitalize all major words.

- *Article titles.* Do not italicize titles of articles or place them in quotation marks. Capitalize only the first word of the article's title and subtitle and any proper nouns.

- *Electronic sources.* Include as much information as you can about electronic sources, such as author, date of publication, identifying numbers, and retrieval information. Include the digital object identifier (DOI) when one exists. If there is the likelihood that the content could change, be sure to record the date you retrieved the information, because electronic information changes frequently.

- *Indenting*. Use a hanging indent, with the second and subsequent lines of each entry indented one-half inch:

  Sokolova, G. N. (2010). Economic stratification in Belarus and Russia: An experiment in comparative analysis. *Sociological Research, 49*(3), 25–26.

  Your instructor may prefer a paragraph indent, in which the first line of each entry is indented one-half inch:

  Sokolova, G. N. (2010). Economic stratification in Belarus and Russia: An experiment in comparative analysis. *Sociological Research, 49*(3), 25–26.

- *Spacing*. Double-space the entire reference list. Do not add extra spacing between entries.

- *Page numbers*. When citing a range of page numbers for articles, always give the complete numbers (for example, 121–124, *not* 121–24 or 121–4). If an article continues on subsequent pages interrupted by other articles or advertisements, use a comma to separate the page numbers. Use the abbreviation *p.* or *pp.* only with articles in newspapers, chapters in edited books, and articles from proceedings published as a book.

- *Dates*. Follow this format: year, month, day, with a comma after only the year (2011, October 31).

Following are models of reference list entries for a variety of sources. For further examples of APA-style citations, consult the *Publication Manual of the American Psychological Association*.

BOOKS

10. Book by One Author   Begin with the author's last name, followed by the first initial or initials. If the author has a first and a middle initial, include a space between the initials. Place the year of publication in parentheses, then give the title of the book, followed by the location and name of the publisher.

  Power, G. A. (2010). *Dementia beyond drugs: Changing the culture of care.* Baltimore, MD: Health Professions Press.

11. Book by Multiple Authors   When citing a work by two to seven authors, separate the authors' names with a comma or commas, and use an ampersand (&) instead of *and* before the final author's name.

  Tyshenko, M. G., & Paterson, C. (2010). *SARS unmasked: Risk communication of pandemics and influenza in Canada.* Montreal, Quebec, Canada: McGill-Queen's University Press.

To cite more than seven authors, list only the first six, followed by three ellipses dots and the last author's name.

12. Multiple Books by the Same Author List the entries by the author's name and then by date, with the earliest date first.

> Tabloski, P. A. (2007). *Clinical handbook for gerontological nursing.* Upper Saddle River, NJ: Pearson/Prentice Hall.

> Tabloski, P. A. (2010). *Gerontological nursing.* Upper Saddle River, NJ: Pearson.

If you use multiple works by the same author written in the same year, list the books alphabetically by title and include *a*, *b*, and so forth after the year—both in your reference list and in your parenthetical citations.

> Agger, B. (2007a). *Fast families, virtual children: A critical sociology of families and schooling.* Boulder, CO: Paradigm.

> Agger, B. (2007b). *Public sociology: From social facts to literary acts.* Lanham, MD: Rowman & Littlefield.

13. Book Issued by an Organization Use the full name of the organization in place of an author's name. If the organization is also the publisher, use the word *Author* in place of the publisher's name.

> American Nurses Association. (2010). *Nursing's social policy statement: The essence of the profession* (3rd ed.). Silver Spring, MD: Author.

14. Book by an Unknown Author If the author of the book is unknown, begin with the title in italics.

> *The PDR pocket guide to prescription drugs* (9th ed.). (2010). New York, NY: Pocket Books.

15. Edited Book Place the abbreviation *Ed.* (singular) or *Eds.* (plural) in parentheses after the name(s), followed by a period.

> Haugen, D., Musser, S., & Lovelace, K. (Eds.). (2010). *Global warming.* Detroit, MI: Greenhaven Press.

16. Chapter or Section in an Edited Book

> Jyonouchi, H. (2010). Possible impact of innate immunity in autism. In A. Chauhan, V. Chauhan, & W. T. Brown (Eds.), *Autism: Oxidative stress, inflammation, and immune abnormalities* (pp. 245–276). Boca Raton, FL: CRC Press.

17. Entry in a Reference Work Begin with the title of the entry if it has no author.

> Kohlrabi. (2010). In R. T. Wood, *The new whole foods encyclopedia: A comprehensive resource for healthy eating* (2nd ed., pp. 178–179). New York, NY: Penguin Books.

PERIODICALS

18. Journal Article   Follow the author's name and year with the article title; then give the journal title. For all journals, include the volume number (italicized). For journals that begin each issue with page 1, also include the issue number in parentheses (not italicized). Insert a comma, and end with the page number(s).

> Cumsille, P., Darling, N., & Martinez, M. L. (2010). Shading the truth: The pattern of adolescents' decisions to avoid issues, disclose, or lie to parents. *Journal of Adolescence, 33*, 285–296.

19. Magazine Article   Include the month after the year. If it's a weekly magazine, include the day. Give the volume and issue numbers, if any, after the magazine title.

> Stix, G. (2011, March). The neuroscience of true grit. *Scientific American, 304*(3), 28–33.

20. Newspaper Article   Include the specific publication date following the year.

> Seltz, J. (2010, December 26). Internet policies examined: Schools aim to clarify social rules. *Boston Globe*, p. 1.

21. Published Interview   If it is not clear from the title, or if there is no title, include the words *Interview with* and the subject's name in brackets.

> Jackson, L. (2010, December 6). The EPA is not the villain [Interview with Daniel Stone]. *Newsweek, 156*(23), 14.

ELECTRONIC SOURCES

Generally, include all the same elements for electronic sources as you would for print sources. Include any information required to locate the item. Many scholarly publishers are now assigning a digital object identifier (DOI) to journal articles and other documents. A DOI is a unique alphanumeric string assigned by a registration agency. It provides a persistent link to unchanging content on the Internet. When available, substitute the DOI for the URL. If the content is subject to change, include the retrieval date before the DOI or URL. Use the exact URL for open-source material; use the home page or menu page URL for subscription-only material or content presented in frames, which make exact URLs unworkable. Break URLs before most punctuation, and avoid punctuation after them so as not to confuse the reader.

22. Nonperiodical Web Document   To cite a nonperiodical Web document, provide as much of the following information as possible: author's name, date of publication or most recent update (use *n.d.* if there is no date), document title (in italics), and URL for the document.

> Centers for Disease Control and Prevention. (2010, June 1). *Teens behind the wheel: Graduated driver licensing.* Retrieved from http://www.cdc.gov /MotorVehicleSafety/Teen_Drivers/GDL/Teens_Behind_Wheel.html

If the author of a document is not identified, begin the reference with the title of the document. If the document is from a university program's Web site, identify the host institution and program or department, followed by a colon and the URL for the document.

> *Safety manual.* (2011, March 18). Retrieved from Harvard University, Center for Nanoscale Systems website: http://www.cns.fas.harvard.edu/users/Forms /CNS_Safety_Manual.pdf

23. Article with DOI Assigned

> Iemolo, F., Cavallaro, T., & Rizzuto, N. (2010). Atypical Alzheimer's disease: A case report. *Neurological Sciences, 31*, 643–646. doi:10.1007/s10072-010-0334-1

24. Article with No DOI Assigned

> Srivastava, R. K., & More, A. T. (2010). Some aesthetic considerations for over-the-counter (OTC) pharmaceutical products. *International Journal of Biotechnology, 11*(3–4), 267–283. Retrieved from http://www.inderscience.com

25. Online Magazine Content Not Found in Print Version

> Greenemeier, L. (2010, November 17). Buzz kill: FDA cracks down on caffeinated alcoholic beverages. *Scientific American.* Retrieved from http://www .scientificamerican.com/article.cfm?id=fda-caffeinated-alcohol

26. Electronic Book   Use "Retrieved from" if the URL leads to the information itself and "Available from" if the URL leads to information on how to obtain the content.

> Einstein, A. (n.d.). *Relativity: The special and general theory.* Retrieved from http:// www.gutenberg.org/etext/5001

27. Online Encyclopedia   Give the home or index page URL for reference works.

> Cross, M. S. (2011). Social history. In J. H. Marsh (Ed.), *The Canadian encyclopedia.* Retrieved from http://www.thecanadianencyclopedia.com

28. Wiki

> Tsunami. (n.d.). Retrieved March 20, 2011, from http://en.wikipedia.org/wiki/Tsunami

29. Graphic Representation of Data

U.S. Department of Labor, Bureau of Labor Statistics. (2011, April 4). Civilian unemployment rate (UNRATE) [Line graph]. Retrieved from Federal Reserve Bank of St. Louis website: http://research.stlouisfed.org/fred2/series/UNRATE

30. Audio Podcast   Include authority, if known; date; episode title; episode or show identifier in brackets, such as *[Show 13]*; show name; and retrieval information.

Cooper, Q. (Presenter). (2011, February 10). Science in Egypt. *The Material World* [Audio podcast]. Retrieved from http://www.bbc.co.uk/podcasts/series /material#playepisode8

31. Message Posted to an Electronic Mailing List, Online Forum, or Discussion Group   Use the screen name if the author's real name is not available. Provide a description of the post in brackets after the subject line or thread name.

Gomez, T. N. (2010, December 20). Food found in archaeological environments [Electronic mailing list message]. Retrieved from http://cool.conservation-us.org /byform/mailing-lists/cdl/2010/1297.html

32. Blog Post

Joseph j7uy5. (2010, May 11). Another rTMS update [Web log post]. Retrieved from http://scienceblogs.com/corpuscallosum/2010/05/another_rtms_update.php

OTHER SOURCES

33. Gray Literature

Wyominginspector. (2010). *Cell phone use in the mining industry* [PowerPoint slides]. Retrieved from http://www.slideshare.net/wyominginspector/cell-phone-use-in -the-mining-industry

Gray literature refers to print or electronic documents published by organizations such as businesses, government agencies, and scientific groups rather than by traditional publishers. Because gray literature is typically not cited in the popular bibliographic sources, it is often difficult to find and access.

34. Technical or Research Report   Include identifying numbers in parentheses after the report title. If appropriate, include the name of the service used to locate the item in parentheses after the publisher.

Arai, M., & Mazuka, R. (2010). *Linking syntactic priming to language development: A visual world eye-tracking study* (TL2010-18). Tokyo: Institute of Electronics, Information and Communication Engineers.

35. Government Document   For most government agencies, use the abbreviation *U.S.* instead of spelling out *United States*. Include any identifying document numbers after the publication title.

U.S. Department of State. (2010, June). *Trafficking in persons report* (10th ed.). Washington, DC: Government Printing Office.

36. Brochure or Pamphlet After the title of the document, include the word *Brochure* or *Pamphlet* in brackets.

> U.S. Department of Health and Human Services, Centers for Disease Control and Prevention. (2010, October). *How to clean and disinfect schools to help slow the spread of flu* [Pamphlet]. Washington, DC: Author.

37. Article from Conference Proceedings After the proceedings title, give the page numbers on which the article appears.

> Sebastianelli, R., Tamimi, N., Gnanendran, K., & Stark, R. (2010). An examination of factors affecting perceived quality and satisfaction in online MBA courses. In *Proceedings of the 41st Annual Meeting of the Decision Sciences Institute* (pp. 1641–1646). Atlanta, GA: Decision Sciences Institute.

38. Lecture or Speech

> Culicover, P. W. (2010, March 3). *Grammar and complexity: Language at the intersection of competence and performance.* Lecture presented at the Ohio State University, Columbus, OH.

Sample APA Reference List

Following is a sample reference list using the APA citation system.

References

Nonperiodical Web document → Centers for Disease Control and Prevention. (2010, June 1). *Teens behind the wheel: Graduated driver licensing.* Retrieved from http://www.cdc.gov /MotorVehicleSafety/Teen_Drivers/GDL/Teens_Behind_Wheel.html

Journal article, paginated by volume → Cumsille, P., Darling, N., & Martinez, M. L. (2010). Shading the truth: The pattern of adolescents' decisions to avoid issues, disclose, or lie to parents. *Journal of Adolescence, 33*, 285–296.

Online article with a DOI → Iemolo, F., Cavallaro, T., & Rizzuto, N. (2010). Atypical Alzheimer's disease: A case report. *Neurological Sciences, 31*, 643–646. doi:10.1007/s10072-010-0334-1

Chapter in an edited book → Jyonouchi, H. (2010). Possible impact of innate immunity in autism. In A. Chauhan, V. Chauhan, & W. T. Brown (Eds.), *Autism: Oxidative stress, inflammation, and immune abnormalities* (pp. 245–276). Boca Raton, FL: CRC Press.

Book in an edition other than the first → Quinn, G. R. (2010). *Behavioral science* (2nd ed.). New York, NY: McGraw-Hill Medical.

Online article, paginated by issue, with no DOI → Srivastava, R. K., & More, A. T. (2010). Some aesthetic considerations for over-the-counter (OTC) pharmaceutical products. *International Journal of Biotechnology, 11*(3–4), 267–283. Retrieved from http://www.inderscience.com

IEEE STYLE

IEEE style is often used for technical documents in areas ranging from computer engineering and biomedical technology to aerospace and consumer electronics. It consists of two elements: citations in the text and a reference list at the end of the document.

▶ **On the Web**

For more information, see the IEEE Web site. Click on Links Library for Appendix, Part A, on <bedfordstmartins.com/ps>.

IEEE Textual Citations

When you cite a reference in the text, you treat the citation similarly to how you would treat endnotes; however, the reference number appears on the line, in square brackets, inside the punctuation. Use *et al.* if there are three or more author names.

> A recent study by Goldfinkel [5] shows that this is not an efficient solution. Murphy [8]–[10] comes to a different conclusion.

You can also treat the citation as a noun.

> In addition, [5] shows that this is not an efficient solution; however, [8]–[10] come to a different conclusion.

Note: Because references are listed *in the order in which they first appear*, if you cite a new reference within the text while writing or editing, you will need to renumber the reference list as well as the citations in the text. If you were to add a new reference between the first times [8]–[10] appeared, the previous example might now read:

> Murphy [8], [10], [11] comes to a different conclusion.

To be more precise in citing a reference, you can provide extra information.

A recent study by Goldfinkel [5, pp. 12–19] shows that this is not an efficient solution.

The IEEE Reference List

▷ **In This Book**
For a sample IEEE-style reference list, see p. 434.

The following guidelines will help you prepare IEEE-style references. For additional information on formatting entries, IEEE recommends *The Chicago Manual of Style*.

- *Arranging entries.* Arrange and number the entries in the order in which they first appear in the text, much like endnotes. Place the numbers in square brackets and set them flush left in a column of their own, separate from the body of the references. Place the entries in their own column with no indents for turnovers.

- *Authors.* List the first initial (or initials, separated by spaces), and follow it with the last name. In the case of multiple authors, use all names; use *et al.* after the first author's name only if the other names are not given. If an editor or translator is used in place of an author, add the abbreviation *Ed.* (or *Eds.* for editors) or *Trans.*

- *Book titles.* Italicize titles of books. In English, capitalize the first word and all major words. In foreign languages, capitalize the first word of the title and subtitle, as well as any words that would be capitalized in that language.

- *Publication information.* For books, give the place (city) of publication, the country if it is not the United States, the abbreviated publisher's name, and the date (year) of publication. When two or more cities are given, include only the first. If the city is not well known, add the abbreviation of the state or province (if Canada). If the publisher's name indicates the state, no state abbreviation is necessary.

- *Periodical titles.* Italicize and abbreviate titles of periodicals. Capitalize all major words in the title.

- *Article titles.* Place titles of print articles in quotation marks; do not use quotation marks for articles found in electronic sources. Capitalize the first word. Do not capitalize the remaining words unless they are proper nouns.

- *Electronic sources.* The sequence of information for electronic sources is different from that for print material. Do not place article titles in quotation marks. In addition, give the medium and how to locate the source by including, for example, a URL. Dates are also handled differently. See the sample citations on pages 432–33.

- *Spacing.* The reference list is single-spaced. Do not add extra spacing between entries.

- *Page numbers.* If you are giving a range of pages for specific articles in books and periodicals, use the abbreviation *pp.* Write numbers in full (152–159, *not* 152–59 or 152–9).

- *Dates.* Follow this format for print sources: month (abbreviated), day, year (Apr. 3, 2010 or Feb. 22–23, 2011). Do not abbreviate May, June, or July. Follow this format for electronic sources: year, month (abbreviated), day (2011, Oct. 14).

BOOKS

1. Book by One Author   Include the author's first initial and middle initial (if available), the author's last name, the title (in italics), the edition (if applicable), the place of publication (city), the publisher, the year of publication, and the first and last pages of the material referenced.

> [1] B. Mehlenbacher, *Instruction and Technology: Designs for Everyday Learning.* Cambridge, MA: MIT Press, 2010, pp. 22–28.

2. Book by Multiple Authors   List all the authors' names. Use *et al.* after the first author's name only if the other names are not given. Use the format: Name1 and Name2, or Name1, Name2, and Name3.

> [2] S.-T. Yau and S. J. Nadis, *The Shape of Inner Space: String Theory and the Geometry of the Universe's Hidden Dimensions.* New York: Basic Books, 2010, pp. 254–255.

3. Book Issued by an Organization   The organization takes the place of the author.

> [3] World Bank, *World Development Report 2011: Conflict, Security, and Development.* Washington, DC: World Bank, 2011, pp. 25–31.

4. Edited Book   Include the word *Ed.* (singular) or *Eds.* (plural) after the name(s).

> [4] J. Dibbell, Ed., *The Best Technology Writing 2010.* New Haven: Yale University Press, 2010, pp. 157–162.

5. Chapter or Section in an Edited Book   Give the author and title of the chapter or section first, followed by the word *in*, the book title, and the book editor. Then give the publication information for the book and the page numbers on which the chapter or section appears.

> [5] E. Castronova, "The changing meaning of play," in *Online Communication and Collaboration: A Reader*, H. M. Donelan, K. L. Kear, and M. Ramage, Eds. New York: Routledge, 2010, pp. 184–189.

6. Book in an Edition Other Than the First   The edition number follows the title of the book and is preceded by a comma.

> [6] L. Xinju, *Laser Technology*, 2nd ed. Boca Raton, FL: CRC Press, 2010, pp. 203–205.

PERIODICALS

7. Journal Article   Include the author's name, the article title, and the abbreviated journal title, followed by the volume number, issue number, page number(s), abbreviated month, and year (or abbreviated month, day, and year for weekly periodicals).

> [7] R. C. Weber, P.-Y. Lin, E. J. Garnero, Q. Williams, and P. Lognonne, "Seismic detection of the lunar core," *Science*, vol. 331, no. 6015, pp. 309–312, Jan. 21, 2011.

8. Magazine Article   List the author's name, the article title, and the abbreviated magazine title, followed by the page number(s) and the issue date.

> [8] J. Villasenor, "The hacker in your hardware," *Scientific Amer.*, pp. 82–87, Aug. 2010.

9. Newspaper Article   List the author's name, the article title, and the newspaper name, followed by the section and the date.

> [9] M. Woolhouse, "For many, snow day is business as usual," *Boston Globe*, sec. B, Jan. 13, 2011.

ELECTRONIC SOURCES

10. Article in an Online Journal or Magazine   Place the medium in square brackets followed by a period: [Online]. After the expression *Available:* and a space, include the URL for the article.

> [10] R. Marani and A. G. Perri. (2010). An electronic medical device for preventing and improving the assisted ventilation of intensive care unit patients. *Open Elect. Electron. Eng. J.* [Online]. *4*, pp. 16–20. Available: http://www.benthamscience .com/open/toeej/openaccess2.htm

11. Article from a Database

> [11] Zhao, N. Huebsch, D. J. Mooney, and Z. Suo. (2010, Mar. 23). Stress-relaxation behavior in gels with ionic and covalent crosslinks. *J. App. Phys.* [Online]. *107(6)*. Available http://www.ncbi.nlm.nih.gov/pmc/articles/PMC3069988 /?tool=pmcentrez

12. Web Site

> [12] American Institute of Physics. (2011). American Institute of Physics [Online]. Available: http://www.aip.org

13. Government Site

[13] U.S. Department of Health and Human Services, Centers for Disease Control and Prevention. Preparation and planning for bioterrorism emergencies [Online]. Available: http://emergency.cdc.gov/bioterrorism/prep.asp

OTHER SOURCES

14. Thesis or Dissertation

[14] J. L. Beutler, "Frequency response and gain enhancement of solid-state impact-ionization multipliers (SIMs)," Ph.D. dissertation, Dept. Elect. Eng., Brigham Young Univ., Provo, UT, 2010.

15. Standard For standards, include the title in italics, the standard number, and the date.

[15] *Testing and Evaluation Protocol for Spectroscopic Personal Radiation Detectors (SPRDs) for Homeland Security*, ANSI Standard T&E Protocol N42.48, 2010.

16. Scientific or Technical Report

[16] E. G. Fernando, "Investigation of Rainfall and Regional Factors for Maintenance Cost Allocation," Texas Transportation Inst. Texas A&M, College Station, TX, Report 5-4519-01-1, Aug. 2010.

17. Paper Published in Conference Proceedings

[17] T. O'Brien, A. Ritz, B. J. Raphael, and D. H. Laidlaw, "Gremlin: An interactive visualization model for analyzing genomic rearrangements," in *Proc. IEEE Information Visualization Conf.*, 2010, vol. 16, no. 6, pp. 918–926.

18. Government Document

[18] W. R. Selbig and R. T. Bannerman, "Characterizing the size distribution of particles in urban stormwater by use of fixed-point sample-collection methods," U.S. Geological Survey, Open-File Report 2011–1052, 2011.

19. Unpublished Document

[19] S. Reed, "An approach to evaluating the autistic spectrum in uncooperative adolescents," unpublished.

Sample IEEE Reference List

Following is a sample reference list using the IEEE numbered reference system. The references are listed in the order in which they might appear in a fictional document.

Reference List

Article in an online magazine → [1] S. Schmidt. (2008, June). Arthur C. Clarke, 1917–2008. *Analogsf.com* [Online]. Available: http://www.analogsf.com/0806/Obitclarke.shtml

Chapter in an edited book → [2] E. Castronova, "The changing meaning of play," in *Online Communication and Collaboration: A Reader,* H. M. Donelan, K. L. Kear, and M. Ramage, Eds. New York: Routledge, 2010, pp. 184–189.

Book in an edition other than the first → [3] L. Xinju, *Laser Technology,* 2nd ed. Boca Raton, FL: CRC Press, 2010, pp. 203–205.

Online article → [4] R. Marani and A. G. Perri. (2010). An electronic medical device for preventing and improving the assisted ventilation of intensive care unit patients. *Open Elect. Electron. Eng. J.* [Online]. *4,* pp. 16–20. Available: http://www.benthamscience.com/open/toeej/openaccess2.htm

Standard → [5] *Testing and Evaluation Protocol for Spectroscopic Personal Radiation Detectors (SPRDs) for Homeland Security,* ANSI Standard T&E Protocol N42.48, 2010.

Journal article → [6] A. C. Mathieson, E. J. Hehre, C. J. Dawes, and C. D. Neefus, "An historical comparison of seaweed populations from Casco Bay, Maine," *Rhodora,* vol. 110, no. 941, pp. 1–10, 2008.

MLA STYLE

MLA style is used widely in the humanities. It consists of two elements: citations in the text and a list of works cited at the end of the document.

On the Web

For more information, see the MLA Web site. Click on Links Library for Appendix, Part A, on <bedfordstmartins.com/ps>.

MLA Textual Citations

In MLA style, the textual citation typically includes the name of the source's author and the number of the page being referred to. Textual citations vary depending on the type of information cited, the author's name, and the context of the citation. The following models illustrate a variety of common textual citations; for additional examples, consult the *MLA Handbook for Writers of Research Papers.*

1. Entire Work   If you are referring to the whole source, not to a particular page or pages, use only the author's name.

> Harwood's work gives us a careful framework for understanding the aging process and how it affects communication.

2. Specific Page(s)   Immediately following the borrowed material, include a parenthetical reference with the author's name and the page number(s) being referred to. Do not add a comma between the name and the page number, and do not use the abbreviation *p.* or *pp.*

> Each feature evolves independently, so there can't be a steady progression of fossils representing change (Prothero 27).

If your sentence already includes the author's name, include only the page number in the parenthetical notation.

> Prothero explains why we won't find a steady progression of human fossils approaching modern humans, as each feature evolves independently (27).

3. Work Without Page Numbers   Give a paragraph, section, or screen number, if provided. Use *par.* (singular) or *pars.* (plural) to indicate paragraph numbers. Either spell out or use standard abbreviations for other identifying words. Use a comma after the name if it begins the citation.

> Under the right conditions, humanitarian aid forestalls health epidemics in the aftermath of natural disasters (Bourmah, pars. 3–6).

> Maternal leave of at least three months has a significantly positive effect on the development of attachment in the infant (Ling, screen 2).

4. Multiple Sources by the Same Author   If you cite two or more sources by the same author, either include the full source title in the text or add a shortened title after the author's name in the parenthetical citation to prevent confusion.

> Chatterjee believes that diversification in investments can take many forms (*Diversification* 13).

> Risk is a necessary component of a successful investment strategy (Chatterjee, *Failsafe* 25).

5. Source with Multiple Authors   For a source written by two or three authors, cite all the names.

> Grendel and Chang assert that . . .

> This phenomenon was verified in the late 1970s (Grendel and Chang 281).

For a source written by four or more authors, either list all the authors or give only the first author, followed by the abbreviation *et al.* Follow the same format as in the works cited list.

6. Source Quoted Within Another Source   Give the source of the quotation in the text. In the parenthetical citation, give the author and page number(s) of the source in which you found the quotation, preceded by *qtd. in.*

> Freud describes the change in men's egos as science proved that the earth was not the center of the universe and that man was descended from animals (qtd. in Prothero 89–90).

Only the source by Prothero will appear in the list of works cited.

7. Source Issued by an Organization   If the author is an organization rather than a person, use the name of the organization. When giving the organization's name in parentheses, abbreviate common words in the name.

> In a recent booklet, the Association of Sleep Disorders discusses the causes of narcolepsy (2–3).

> The causes of narcolepsy are discussed in a recent booklet (Assn. of Sleep Disorders 2–3).

8. Source with an Unknown Author   If the source does not identify an author, use a shortened form of the title in your parenthetical citation.

> Multidisciplinary study in academia is becoming increasingly common ("Interdisciplinary" 23).

9. Multiple Sources in One Citation   To refer to two or more sources at the same point, separate the sources with a semicolon.

> Much speculation exists about the origin of this theory (Brady 42; Yao 388).

10. Multiple Authors with the Same Last Name   If two or more sources have authors with the same last name, spell out the first names of those authors in the text and use the authors' first initials in the parenthetical citation.

> In contrast, Albert Martinez has a radically different explanation (29).

> The economy's strength may be derived from its growing bond market (J. Martinez 87).

11. Electronic Source   When citing electronic sources in your document, follow the same rules as for print sources, providing author names and page numbers, if available. If an author's name is not given, use either the full title of the source in the text or a shortened version of the title in the parenthetical citation. If no page numbers are used, include any other identifying numbers, such as paragraph or section numbers. (See item 3 on page 436.)

> Twenty million books were in print by the early sixteenth century (Rawlins, ch. 3, sec. 2).

The MLA List of Works Cited

A list of works cited provides the information your readers will need to find each source you have cited in the text. It should not include background reading. Following are some guidelines for an MLA-style list of works cited.

▶ **In This Book**
For a sample MLA-style list of works cited, see p. 444.

- *Arranging entries.* Arrange the entries alphabetically by the author's last name. If two or more works are by the same author, arrange them alphabetically by title. Alphabetize works by an organization by the first significant word in the name of the organization.
- *Book titles.* Italicize titles of books and follow standard capitalization rules. Note that in MLA style, prepositions are not capitalized.
- *Publication information.* Shorten the publisher's name. For cities outside the United States, include the province (if Canada) or country, abbreviated, unless the city is well known (such as Tokyo or London).
- *Periodical titles.* Italicize titles of periodicals and capitalize all major words. Omit any initial article.
- *Article titles.* Place titles of articles and other short works in quotation marks and capitalize all major words.

- *Electronic sources.* Include as much information as you can about electronic sources, such as author, date of publication, identifying numbers, and retrieval information. Also, be sure to record the date you retrieved the information, because electronic information changes frequently. If no author is known, start with the title of the Web site. Italicize titles of entire Web sites; treat titles of works within Web sites, such as articles and video clips, as in print sources. In citations for online sources, include the sponsor or publisher, as well as the date of publication or update. If this information can't be located, use *N.p.* (for *No publisher*) or *n.d.* (for *no date*). Insert the word *Web* before the date of retrieval. Include the URL only if you feel that your reader will be unable to locate the source with a search engine. Place the URL in angle brackets at the end of the entry, after the date of retrieval.

- *Indenting.* Use a hanging indent, with the second and subsequent lines of each entry indented one-half inch.

- *Spacing.* Double-space the entire works cited list. Do not add extra spacing between entries.

- *Page numbers.* Do not use the abbreviation *p.* or *pp.* when giving page numbers. For a range of pages, give only the last two digits of the second number if the previous digits are identical (for example, 243–47, *not* 243–247 or 243–7). Use a plus sign (+) to indicate that an article continues on subsequent pages interrupted by other articles or advertisements.

- *Dates.* Follow this format: day, month, year, with no commas (20 Feb. 2009). Spell out *May*, *June*, and *July*; abbreviate all other months by using the first three letters (except *Sept.*) plus a period.

- *Medium.* With a few exceptions, explained below, list the medium of publication, followed by a period, as the last part of any entry. (See bullet item on electronic sources above.) Examples: *Print*; *Web*; *Radio*; *Television*; *CD*; *CD-ROM*; *Audiocassette*; *Film*; *Videocassette*; *DVD*; *Performance*; *Address*; *MS* (for *manuscript*); *TS* (for *typescript*); *E-mail*; *PDF file*; *Microsoft Word file*; *JPEG file*; *MP3 file*.

Following are models of works cited list entries for a variety of sources. For further examples of MLA-style citations, consult the *MLA Handbook for Writers of Research Papers*.

BOOKS

12. Book by One Author   Include the author's full name, in reverse order, followed by the book title. Next give the location and name of the publisher, followed by the year of publication and the medium.

> Gleick, James. *The Information: A History, a Theory, a Flood.* New York: Pantheon, 2011. Print.

13. Book by Multiple Authors For a book by two or three authors, present the names in the sequence in which they appear on the title page. Use reverse order for the name of the first author only. Use a comma to separate the names of the authors.

> Burt, Stephen, and David Mikics. *The Art of the Sonnet.* Cambridge: Belknap-Harvard UP, 2010. Print.

For a book by four or more authors, either name all the authors or use the abbreviation *et al.* after the first author's name.

14. Multiple Books by the Same Author For the second and subsequent entries by the same author, use three hyphens followed by a period in place of the name. Arrange the entries alphabetically by title.

> Hassan, Robert. *Empires of Speed: Time and the Acceleration of Politics and Society.* Leiden: Brill, 2009. Print.

> ---. *The Information Society: Cyber Dreams and Digital Nightmares.* Cambridge, UK: Polity, 2008. Print.

15. Book Issued by an Organization The organization takes the position of the author.

> World Bank. *Atlas of Global Development: A Visual Guide to the World's Greatest Challenges.* Washington: World Bank, 2011. Print.

16. Book by an Unknown Author If the author of the book is unknown, begin with the title.

> *The World Almanac Notebook Atlas.* Union: Hammond, 2010. Print.

17. Edited Book List the book editor's name, followed by *ed.* (or *eds.* if more than one editor), in place of the author's name.

> Levi, Scott Cameron, and Ron Sela, eds. *Islamic Central Asia: An Anthology of Historical Sources.* Bloomington: Indiana UP, 2010. Print.

18. Chapter or Section in an Edited Book Give the author and title of the article first, followed by the book title and editor. Present the editor's name in normal order, preceded by *Ed.* (for *Edited by*). After the publication information, give the pages on which the article appears.

> Marx, Karl. "Proletarians and Communists." *Marx Today: Selected Works and Recent Debates.* Ed. John F. Sitton. New York: Palgrave-Macmillan, 2010. 51–56. Print.

19. *Entry in a Reference Work*   If the work is well known, you do not need to include the publisher or place of publication. If entries are listed alphabetically, you do not need to include a page number.

> "Desdemona." *Women in Shakespeare: A Dictionary.* Ed. Alison Findlay. New York: Continuum, 2010. Print.

PERIODICALS

20. *Journal Article*   List the author's name, the article title (in quotation marks), and the journal title (italicized), followed by the volume number, issue number, year, page number(s), and medium.

> Mooney, William. "Sex, Booze, and the Code: Four Versions of *The Maltese Falcon*." *Literature-Film Quarterly* 39.1 (2011): 54–72. Print.

21. *Magazine Article*   List the author's name, the article title (in quotation marks), and the magazine title (italicized), followed by the issue date, page number(s), and medium.

> Seabrook, John. "Crush Point." *New Yorker* 7 Feb. 2011: 32–38. Print.

22. *Newspaper Article*   List the author's name, the article title (in quotation marks), and the newspaper name (italicized), followed by the issue date, page number(s) (which might include the section letter), and medium. If the newspaper appears in more than one edition, add a comma after the date and cite the edition (for example, *late ed.*). If sections are numbered, add a comma after the date, the word *sec.*, and the section number.

> Robertson, Campbell. "Beyond the Oil Spill, the Tragedy of an Ailing Gulf." *New York Times* 21 Apr. 2011: A17. Print.

23. *Article That Skips Pages*   Give the first page on which the article appears, followed by a plus sign (+) and a period.

> Kennicott, Philip. "Out-Vermeering Vermeer." *Washington Post* 10 Apr. 2011: E1+. Print.

ELECTRONIC SOURCES

24. *Entire Web Site*   If you are citing an entire Web site, begin with the name of the author or editor (if given) and the title of the site (italicized). Then give the name of the sponsoring institution or organization (or *N.p.*), the date of publication or most recent update (or *n.d.*), the medium, and your access date. Only if necessary, add the URL in angle brackets at the end, followed by a period.

> *Poets.org.* Academy of American Poets, 1997–2011. Web. 12 Jan. 2011.

25. Short Work from a Web Site   If you are citing a portion of a Web site, begin with the author, the title of the work (in quotation marks), and the title of the site (italicized). Then include the site's sponsor, the date of publication, the medium, and your access date.

> Ferenstein, Greg. "How Mobile Technology Is a Game Changer for Developing Africa." *Mashable.* Mashable, 19 July 2010. Web. 14 Jan. 2011.

26. Online Book   Begin with the author's name and the title of the work, along with publication information about the print source. If the book has not been published before, include the online publication date and publisher. Include the medium. End with your access date.

> Martín-Palma, Raúl J., and Akhlesh Lakhtakia. *Nanotechnology: A Crash Course.* Bellingham: SPIE, 2010. *SPIE Digital Library.* Web. 16 Jan. 2011.

27. Article in an Online Periodical   Begin with the author's name and include the title of the document, the name of the periodical, and the date of publication. If the periodical is a scholarly journal, include relevant identifying numbers, such as volume, issue, and page numbers (or *n. pag.* if there are no page numbers). For abstracts of articles, include the word *Abstract*, followed by a period, after the page number(s). End with the medium and your access date.

> Maas, Korey D. "Natural Law, Lutheranism, and the Public Good." *Lutheran Witness* 130.3 (2011): n. pag. Web. 14 Jan. 2011.

For magazine and newspaper articles found online, give the author, the title of the article (in quotation marks), the title of the magazine or newspaper (italicized), the sponsor or publisher of the site (use N.p. if there is none), the date of publication, the medium, and your date of access.

> Melia, Mike. "Atlantic Garbage Patch: Pacific Gyre Is Not Alone." *Huffington Post.* HuffingtonPost.com, 15 Apr. 2010. Web. 13 Feb. 2011.

28. Article from a Database or Subscription Service   After giving the print article information, give the name of the database (italicized), medium (*Web*), and your access date.

> Kunnan, Anthony John. "Publishing in the Era of Online Technologies." *Modern Language Journal* 94.4 (2010): 643–45. *Academic OneFile.* Web. 12 Feb. 2011.

29. E-mail Message   Include the author's name and the subject line (if any) in quotation marks, then the words *Message to* followed by the name of the recipient (if you, *the author*). End with the date the e-mail was sent and the medium (*E-mail*).

> Lange, Frauke. "Data for Genealogical Project." Message to the author. 26 Dec. 2010. E-mail.

30. Online Posting   List the author's name, the subject line (if any) in quotation marks, the name of the discussion group or newsgroup, the sponsor, the posting date, the medium (*Web*), and your access date. If there is no subject line, use the expression *Online posting* (not in quotation marks) in its place.

> Swallow, Bill. "Re: New Doc Group: FrameMaker or Flare?" *TECHWR-L*. RayComm, 5 Jan. 2010. Web. 10 Feb. 2011.

31. Other Online Sources   Follow the MLA guidelines, adapting them as appropriate to the electronic medium. The following examples are for a podcast and a blog, respectively. For a podcast, the medium might be *Web*, *MP3 file*, *MPEG-4 file*, *Video file*, and so on. If the blog doesn't have a title (in quotation marks), use the expression *Weblog entry* or *Weblog comment* in its place, not in quotation marks.

> "Hubble Marks 20 Years of Discovery." *NASACast Video*. NASA, 23 Apr. 2010. Web. 15 Jan. 2011.

> Raymo, Chet. "Divine Particulars." *Science Musings Blog*. Chet Raymo, 21 Jan. 2011. Web. 15 Feb. 2011.

OTHER SOURCES

32. Dissertation

> Zimmer, Kenyon. *The Whole World Is Our Country: Immigration and Anarchism in the United States, 1885–1940.* Diss. Pittsburgh: U of Pittsburgh, 2010. Print.

33. Government Document   Give the government name and agency as the author, followed by the publication title, the edition or identifying number (if any), the place and publisher, the date, and the medium.

> United States. National Commission on the Causes of the Financial and Economic Crisis. *The Financial Crisis Inquiry Report: Final Report of the National Commission on the Causes of the Financial and Economic Crisis in the United States.* Washington: GPO, 2011. Print.

For an online government publication, begin with the name of the country and the government agency. Follow with the document title and the name of the author (if known), preceded by the word By. If the author is not known, follow with the agency. Give the report number, the date of publication, and the medium. For an online source, include the publisher or sponsor and your date of access.

> United States. Dept. of the Interior. *A Refined Characterization of the Alluvial Geology of Yucca Flat and Its Effect on Bulk Hydraulic Conductivity.* By G. A. Phelps, A. Boucher, and K. J. Halford. Open-File Report 2010-1307. US Geological Survey, 2011. Web. 12 Feb. 2011.

34. *Article from Conference Proceedings*   List the author's name, the article title, the proceedings title, and the editor's name, followed by the publication information.

> Glicksman, Robert. "Climate Change Adaptation and the Federal Lands." *The Past, Present, and Future of Our Public Lands: Celebrating the 40th Anniversary of the Public Land Law Review Commission's Report.* Ed. Gary C. Bryner. Boulder: Natural Resources Law Center, 2010. Print.

35. *Report*   Cite a report as you would a book.

> Liebreich, Michael, et al. *Green Investing 2010: Policy Mechanisms to Bridge the Financing Gap.* Geneva: World Economic Forum, 2010. Print.

36. *Interview*   For a published interview, begin with the name of the person interviewed. If the interview has a title, enclose it in quotation marks. Insert the word *Interview* and give the interviewer's name, if relevant, followed by a period and the bibliographic information for the work in which it was published.

> Walcott, Derek. "Purple Prose." Interview by Alexander Newbauer. *Harper's Magazine* Feb. 2010: 24–26. Print.

If you conducted the interview yourself, give the interviewee's name, the words *Personal interview*, and the date.

> Youngblood, Adelaide. Personal interview. 5 Jan. 2011.

37. *Letter or Memo*   If the letter or memo was written to you, give the writer's name, the words *Letter* [or *Memo*] *to the author*, and the date it was written. End with the medium (e.g., *MS* for *manuscript* or *TS* for *typescript*).

> Jakobiak, Ursula. Letter to the author. 27 Oct. 2010. MS.

If the letter or memo was written to someone other than you, give the recipient's name in place of the words *the author.*

38. *Lecture or Speech*   Give the speaker's name, the title of the lecture or speech, and the place and date. If there is no title, use a descriptive label (such as *Lecture* or *Speech*), not enclosed in quotation marks. End with the medium.

> Wang, Samuel. "Neuroscience and Everyday Life." Freshman Assembly, Princeton University, Princeton, NJ. 12 Sept. 2010. Lecture.

39. *Map or Chart*   Give the author (if known), the title (in quotation marks), the word *Map* or *Chart*, the publication information, and the medium. For an online source, add the sponsor or publisher, and the date of access.

> "Aftershock Map Tohoku Earthquake." Map. *Earthquake Hazards Program.* US Geological Survey, 11 Mar. 2011. Web. 14 Apr. 2011.

Sample MLA List of Works Cited

Following is a sample list of works cited using the MLA citation system.

Works Cited

Book in an edition other than the first → Geary, Patrick, ed. *Readings in Medieval History.* 4th ed. North York, ON: U of Toronto P, 2010. Print.

Article from a database → Kunnan, Anthony John. "Publishing in the Era of Online Technologies." *Modern Language Journal* 94.4 (2010): 643–45. *Academic OneFile.* Web. 12 Feb. 2011.

Chapter in an edited book → Marx, Karl. "Proletarians and Communists." *Marx Today: Selected Works and Recent Debates.* Ed. John F. Sitton. New York: Palgrave-Macmillan, 2010. 51–56. Print.

Article in an online newspaper → Melia, Mike. "Atlantic Garbage Patch: Pacific Gyre Is Not Alone." *Huffington Post.* HuffingtonPost.com, 15 Apr. 2010. Web. 13 Feb. 2011.

Journal article → Mooney, William. "Sex, Booze, and the Code: Four Versions of *The Maltese Falcon.*" *Literature-Film Quarterly* 39.1 (2011): 54–72. Print.

Part B: Editing and Proofreading Your Documents

This part of the handbook contains advice on editing your documents for grammar, punctuation, and mechanics. If your organization or professional field has a style guide with different recommendations about grammar and usage, you should of course follow those guidelines.

Your instructor might use the following abbreviations to refer you to specific topics in this Appendix.

Abbreviation	Topic	Page Number	Abbreviation	Topic	Page Number
abbr	abbreviation	466	.	period	456
adj	adjective	450	!	exclamation point	457
agr p/a	pronoun-antecedent agreement	451	?	question mark	457
agr s/v	subject-verb agreement	450	,	comma	452
			;	semicolon	455
cap	capitalization	467	:	colon	456
comp	comparison of items	449	—	dash	457
cs	comma splice	446	( )	parentheses	458
frag	sentence fragment	446	-	hyphen	463
ital	italics (underlining)	462	'	apostrophe	458
num	numbers	464	" "	quotation marks	459
ref	ambiguous pronoun reference	448	. . .	ellipses	461
run	run-on sentence	447	< >	angle brackets	463
t	verb tense	451	[ ]	square brackets	462

GRAMMATICAL SENTENCES

frag   Avoid Sentence Fragments

A sentence fragment is an incomplete sentence, an error that occurs when a sentence is missing either a verb or an independent clause. To correct a sentence fragment, use one of the following two strategies:

1. **Introduce a verb.**

   FRAGMENT   The pressure loss caused by a worn gasket.

   This example is a fragment because it lacks a verb. (The word *caused* does not function as a verb here; rather, it introduces a phrase that describes the pressure loss.)

   COMPLETE   The pressure loss was caused by a worn gasket.

   Pressure loss has a verb: *was caused.*

   COMPLETE   We identified the pressure loss caused by a worn gasket.

   Pressure loss becomes the object in a new main clause: *We identified the pressure loss.*

2. **Link the fragment (a dependent element) to an independent clause.**

   FRAGMENT   The article was rejected for publication. Because the data could not be verified.

   Because the data could not be verified is a fragment because it lacks an independent clause: a clause that has a subject and a verb and could stand alone as a sentence. To be complete, it needs more information.

   COMPLETE   The article was rejected for publication because the data could not be verified.

   The dependent element is joined to the independent clause that precedes it.

   COMPLETE   Because the data could not be verified, the article was rejected for publication.

   The dependent element is followed by the independent clause.

cs   Avoid Comma Splices

A comma splice is an error that occurs when two independent clauses are joined, or spliced together, by a comma. Independent clauses in a comma splice can be linked correctly in three ways:

1. **Use a comma and a coordinating conjunction (*and*, *or*, *nor*, *but*, *for*, *so*, or *yet*).**

   SPLICE   The 909 printer is our most popular model, it offers an unequaled
                 blend of power and versatility.

   CORRECT   The 909 printer is our most popular model, for it offers an
                 unequaled blend of power and versatility.

                 The coordinating conjunction *for* explicitly states the rela-
                 tionship between the two clauses.

2. **Use a semicolon.**

   SPLICE   The 909 printer is our most popular model, it offers an unequaled
                 blend of power and versatility.

   CORRECT   The 909 printer is our most popular model; it offers an unequaled
                 blend of power and versatility.

                 The semicolon creates a somewhat more distant relation-
                 ship between the two clauses than the link created with
                 a comma and coordinating conjunction; the link remains
                 implicit.

3. **Use a period or another form of terminal punctuation.**

   SPLICE   The 909 printer is our most popular model, it offers an unequaled
                 blend of power and versatility.

   CORRECT   The 909 printer is our most popular model. It offers an unequaled
                 blend of power and versatility.

                 The two independent clauses are separate sentences. Of
                 the three ways to punctuate the two clauses correctly,
                 this punctuation suggests the most distant relationship
                 between them.

run   Avoid Run-on Sentences

In a run-on sentence (sometimes called a *fused sentence*), two independent
clauses appear together with no punctuation between them. A run-on
sentence can be corrected in the same three ways as a comma splice (see
page 446).

   RUN-ON   The 909 printer is our most popular model it offers an unequaled
                 blend of power and versatility.

   CORRECT   The 909 printer is our most popular model; it offers an unequaled
                 blend of power and versatility.

ref   Avoid Ambiguous Pronoun References

Pronouns must refer clearly to their antecedents—the words or phrases they replace. To correct ambiguous pronoun references, try one of these four strategies:

1. **Clarify the pronoun's antecedent.**

UNCLEAR	Remove the cell cluster from the medium and analyze it.
	Analyze what: the cell cluster or the medium?
CLEAR	Analyze the medium after removing the cell cluster from it.
CLEAR	Remove the cell cluster from the medium. Then analyze the cell cluster.

2. **Clarify the relative pronoun, such as *which*, introducing a dependent clause.**

UNCLEAR	She decided to evaluate the program, which would take five months.
	What would take five months: the program or the evaluation?
CLEAR	She decided to evaluate the program, a process that would take five months.
CLEAR	She decided to evaluate the five-month program.

3. **Clarify the subordinating conjunction, such as *where*, introducing a dependent clause.**

UNCLEAR	This procedure will increase the handling of toxic materials outside the plant, where adequate safety measures can be taken.
	Where can adequate safety measures be taken: inside the plant or outside?
CLEAR	This procedure will increase the handling of toxic materials outside the plant. Because adequate safety measures can be taken only in the plant, the procedure poses risks.
CLEAR	This procedure will increase the handling of toxic materials outside the plant. Because adequate safety measures can be taken only outside the plant, the procedure will decrease safety risks.

4. **Clarify the ambiguous pronoun that begins a sentence.**

UNCLEAR	Allophanate linkages are among the most important structural components of polyurethane elastomers. They act as cross-linking sites.
	What act as cross-linking sites: allophanate linkages or polyurethane elastomers?

CLEAR   Allophanate linkages, which are among the most important structural components of polyurethane elastomers, act as cross-linking sites.

The writer has rewritten part of the first sentence to add a clear nonrestrictive modifier and has combined it with the second sentence.

If you begin a sentence with a demonstrative pronoun that might be unclear to the reader, be sure to follow it immediately with a noun that clarifies the reference.

UNCLEAR   The new parking regulations require that all employees pay for parking permits. These are on the agenda for the next senate meeting.

What are on the agenda: the regulations or the permits?

CLEAR   The new parking regulations require that all employees pay for parking permits. These regulations are on the agenda for the next senate meeting.

comp   **Compare Items Clearly**

When comparing or contrasting items, make sure your sentence communicates their relationship clearly.

AMBIGUOUS   Trout eat more than minnows.

Do trout eat other food in addition to minnows, or do trout eat more than minnows eat?

CLEAR   Trout eat more than minnows do.

If you are introducing three items, make sure the reader can tell which two are being compared:

AMBIGUOUS   Trout eat more algae than minnows.

CLEAR   Trout eat more algae than they do minnows.

CLEAR   Trout eat more algae than minnows do.

Beware of comparisons in which different aspects of the two items are compared:

ILLOGICAL   The resistance of the copper wiring is lower than the tin wiring.

LOGICAL   The resistance of the copper wiring is lower than that of the tin wiring.

Resistance cannot be logically compared with *tin wiring*. In the revision, the pronoun *that* substitutes for *resistance* in the second part of the comparison.

adj   Use Adjectives Clearly

In technical communication, writers often need to use clusters of adjectives. To prevent confusion, follow two guidelines:

1. **Use commas to separate coordinate adjectives.**
    Adjectives that describe different aspects of the same noun are known as coordinate adjectives.

    > portable, programmable device
    >
    > adjustable, removable housings

    The comma is used instead of the word *and*.

    Sometimes an adjective is considered part of the noun it describes: *electric drill*. When one adjective modifies *electric drill*, no comma is required: *a reversible electric drill*. The addition of two or more adjectives, however, creates the traditional coordinate construction: *a two-speed, reversible electric drill*.

2. **Use hyphens to link compound adjectives.**
    A compound adjective is made up of two or more words. Use hyphens to link these elements when compound adjectives precede nouns.

    > a variable-angle accessory
    >
    > increased cost-of-living raises

    The hyphens in the second example prevent *increased* from being read as an adjective modifying *cost*.

    A long string of compound adjectives can be confusing even if you use hyphens appropriately. To ensure clarity, turn the adjectives into a clause or a phrase following the noun.

UNCLEAR	an *operator-initiated default-prevention* technique
CLEAR	a technique *initiated by the operator to prevent default*

agr s/v   Maintain Subject-Verb Agreement

The subject and verb of a sentence must agree in number, even when a prepositional phrase comes between them.

INCORRECT	The *result* of the tests *are* promising.
CORRECT	The *result* of the tests *is* promising.
INCORRECT	The *results* of the test *is* promising.
CORRECT	The *results* of the test *are* promising.

Don't be misled by the fact that the object of the preposition and the verb don't sound natural together, as in *tests is* or *test are*. Here, the noun *test(s)* precedes the verb, but it is not the subject of the verb. As long as the subject and verb agree, the sentence is correct.

agr p/a   Maintain Pronoun-Antecedent Agreement

A pronoun and its antecedent (the word or phrase being replaced by the pronoun) must agree in number. Often an error occurs when the antecedent is a collective noun—one that can be interpreted as either singular or plural, depending on its usage.

INCORRECT	The *company* is proud to announce a new stock option plan for *their* employees.
CORRECT	The *company* is proud to announce a new stock option plan for *its* employees.

Company acts as a single unit; therefore, the singular pronoun is appropriate.

When the individual members of a collective noun are emphasized, however, plural pronouns are appropriate.

CORRECT	The inspection team have prepared their reports.
CORRECT	The members of the inspection team have prepared their reports.

The use of *their* emphasizes that the team members have prepared their own reports.

t   Use Tenses Correctly

Two verb tenses are commonly used in technical communication: the present tense and the past perfect tense. It is important to understand the specific purpose of each.

1. **The present tense is used to describe scientific principles and recurring events.**

INCORRECT	In 1992, McKay and his coauthors argued that the atmosphere of Mars *was* salmon pink.
CORRECT	In 1992, McKay and his coauthors argued that the atmosphere of Mars *is* salmon pink.

   Although the argument was made in the historical past—1992—the point is expressed in the present tense because the atmosphere of Mars continues to be salmon pink.

   When the date of the argument is omitted, some writers express the entire sentence in the present tense.

CORRECT	McKay and his coauthors *argue* that the atmosphere of Mars *is* salmon pink.

2. **The past perfect tense is used to describe the earlier of two events that occurred in the past.**

CORRECT   We *had begun* excavation when the foreman *discovered* the burial remains.

               Had begun is the past perfect tense. The excavation began before the burial remains were discovered.

CORRECT   The seminar *had concluded* before I *got* a chance to talk with Dr. Tran.

PUNCTUATION

 Commas

The comma is the most frequently used punctuation mark, as well as the one about whose usage writers most often disagree. This section concludes with advice about editing for unnecessary commas.

1. **Use a comma in a compound sentence to separate two independent clauses linked by a coordinating conjunction (*and*, *or*, *nor*, *but*, *so*, *for*, or *yet*).**

INCORRECT   The mixture was prepared from the two premixes and the remaining ingredients were then combined.

CORRECT   The mixture was prepared from the two premixes, and the remaining ingredients were then combined.

2. **Use commas to separate items in a series composed of three or more elements.**

The manager of spare parts is responsible for ordering, stocking, and disbursing all spare parts for the entire plant.

Despite the presence of the conjunction *and*, most technical-communication style manuals require a comma after the second-to-last item. The comma clarifies the separation and prevents misreading.

CONFUSING   The report will be distributed to Operations, Research and Development and Accounting.

CLEAR   The report will be distributed to Operations, Research and Development, and Accounting.

3. **Use a comma to separate introductory words, phrases, and clauses from the main clause of the sentence.**

However, we will have to calculate the effect of the wind.

To facilitate trade, the government holds a yearly international conference.

NOTE: Writers sometimes make errors by omitting commas following introductory words, phrases, or clauses. A comma is optional only if the introductory text is brief and cannot be misread.

CORRECT   First, let's take care of the introductions.

CORRECT   First let's take care of the introductions.

INCORRECT   As the researchers sat down to eat the laboratory rats awakened.

CORRECT   As the researchers sat down to eat, the laboratory rats awakened.

4. **Use a comma to separate a dependent clause from the main clause.**

   Although most of the executive council saw nothing wrong with it, the advertising campaign was canceled.

   Most tablet computers use green technology, even though it is relatively expensive.

5. **Use commas to separate nonrestrictive modifiers (parenthetical clarifications) from the rest of the sentence.**

   Jones, the temporary chairperson, called the meeting to order.

▶ **In This Book**

For more about restrictive and nonrestrictive modifiers, see Ch. 6, p. 123.

6. **Use commas to separate interjections and transitional elements from the rest of the sentence.**

   Yes, I admit that your findings are correct.

   Their plans, however, have great potential.

7. **Use a comma to separate coordinate adjectives.**

   The finished product was a sleek, comfortable cruiser.

   The comma here takes the place of the conjunction *and*.

   If the adjectives are not coordinate—that is, if one of the adjectives modifies the combined adjective and noun—do not use a comma:

   They decided to go to the first general meeting.

   For more about coordinate adjectives, see page 450.

8. **Use a comma to signal that a word or phrase has been omitted from a sentence because it is implied.**

   Smithers is in charge of the accounting; Harlen, the data management; Demarest, the publicity.

9. **Use a comma to separate a proper noun from the rest of the sentence in direct address.**

> John, have you seen the purchase order from United?
>
> What I'd like to know, Betty, is why we didn't see this problem coming.

10. **Use a comma to introduce most quotations.**

> He asked, "What time were they expected?"

11. **Use commas to separate towns, states, and countries.**

> Bethlehem, Pennsylvania, is the home of Lehigh University.
>
> He attended Lehigh University in Bethlehem, Pennsylvania, and the University of California at Berkeley.

12. **Use a comma to set off the year in a date.**

> August 1, 2012, is the anticipated completion date.

If the month separates the date and the year, you do not need to use commas because the numbers are not next to each other:

> The anticipated completion date is 1 August 2012.

13. **Use a comma to clarify numbers.**

> 12,013,104

NOTE: European practice is to reverse the use of commas and periods in writing numbers: periods signify thousands, and commas signify decimals.

14. **Use a comma to separate names from professional or academic titles.**

> Harold Clayton, PhD

The comma also follows the title in a sentence:

> Harold Clayton, PhD, is the featured speaker.

UNNECESSARY COMMAS

Writers often introduce errors by using unnecessary commas. Do not insert commas in the following situations:

- Commas are not used to link two independent clauses without a coordinating conjunction (an error known as a "comma splice").

INCORRECT	All the motors were cleaned and dried after the water had entered, had they not been, additional damage would have occurred.
CORRECT	All the motors were cleaned and dried after the water had entered. Had they not been, additional damage would have occurred.

For more about comma splices, see page 446.

- Commas are not used to separate the subject from the verb in a sentence.

INCORRECT	Another of the many possibilities, is to use a "first in, first out" sequence.
CORRECT	Another of the many possibilities is to use a "first in, first out" sequence.

- Commas are not used to separate the verb from its complement.

INCORRECT	The schedules that have to be updated every month are, numbers 14, 16, 21, 22, 27, and 31.
CORRECT	The schedules that have to be updated every month are numbers 14, 16, 21, 22, 27, and 31.

- Commas are not used with a restrictive modifier.

INCORRECT	New and old employees who use the processed order form, do not completely understand the basis of the system.
	The phrase *who use the processed order form* is a restrictive modifier necessary to the meaning: it defines which employees do not understand the system.
CORRECT	New and old employees who use the processed order form do not completely understand the basis of the system.

- Commas are not used to separate two elements in a compound subject.

INCORRECT	Recent studies, and reports by other firms confirm our experience.
CORRECT	Recent studies and reports by other firms confirm our experience.

; Semicolons

Semicolons are used in the following instances:

1. **Use a semicolon to separate independent clauses not linked by a coordinating conjunction.**

   The second edition of the handbook is more up-to-date; however, it is also more expensive.

2. **Use a semicolon to separate items in a series that already contains commas.**

   The members elected three officers: Jack Resnick, president; Carol Wayshum, vice president; Ahmed Jamoogian, recording secretary.

MISUSE OF SEMICOLONS

Sometimes writers incorrectly use a semicolon when a colon is called for:

INCORRECT	We still need one ingredient; luck.
CORRECT	We still need one ingredient: luck.

Colons

Colons are used in the following instances:

1. **Use a colon to introduce a word, phrase, or clause that amplifies, illustrates, or explains a general statement.**

   We found three substances in excessive quantities: potassium, cyanide, and asbestos.

   The week was productive: 14 projects were completed, and another dozen were initiated.

   NOTE: The text preceding a colon should be able to stand on its own as a sentence.

▶ **In This Book**
For more about constructing lists, see Ch. 6, p. 117.

2. **Use a colon to introduce items in a vertical list if the sense of the introductory text would be incomplete without the list.**

   We found the following:

   - potassium
   - cyanide
   - asbestos

3. **Use a colon to introduce long or formal quotations.**

   The president began: "In the last year . . ."

MISUSE OF COLONS

Writers sometimes incorrectly use a colon to separate a verb from its complement:

INCORRECT	The tools we need are: a plane, a level, and a T square.
CORRECT	The tools we need are a plane, a level, and a T square.
CORRECT	We need three tools: a plane, a level, and a T square.

■ **Periods**

Periods are used in the following instances:

1. **Use a period at the end of sentences that do not ask questions or express strong emotion.**

   The lateral stress still needs to be calculated.

2. **Use a period with some abbreviations.**

   U.S.A.

   etc.

For more about abbreviations, see page 466.

3. **Use a period with decimal fractions.**

$6.75

75.6 percent

 ## Exclamation Points

The exclamation point is used at the end of a sentence that expresses strong emotion, such as surprise.

> The nuclear plant, which was originally expected to cost $1.6 billion, eventually cost more than $8 billion!

In technical documents, which require objectivity and a calm, understated tone, exclamation points are rarely used.

 ## Question Marks

The question mark is used at the end of a sentence that asks a direct question.

> What did the commission say about effluents?

NOTE: When a question mark is used within quotation marks, no other end punctuation is required.

> She asked, "What did the commission say about effluents?"

MISUSE OF QUESTION MARKS

Do not use a question mark at the end of a sentence that asks an indirect question.

> He wanted to know whether the procedure had been approved for use.

Dashes

To make a dash, use two uninterrupted hyphens (--). Do not add spaces before or after the dash. Some word-processing programs turn two hyphens into a dash, but with others, you have to use a special combination of keys to make a dash; there is no dash key on the keyboard.

Dashes are used in the following instances:

1. **Use a dash to set off a sudden change in thought or tone.**

> That's what she said—if I remember correctly.

2. **Use a dash to emphasize a parenthetical element.**

> The managers' reports—all 10 of them—recommend production cutbacks for the coming year.

3. **Use a dash to set off an introductory series from its explanation.**

   Wet suits, weight belts, tanks—everything will have to be shipped in.

MISUSE OF DASHES

Sometimes writers incorrectly use a dash as a substitute for other punctuation marks:

INCORRECT	The regulations—which were issued yesterday—had been anticipated for months.
CORRECT	The regulations, which were issued yesterday, had been anticipated for months.
INCORRECT	Many candidates applied—however, only one was chosen.
CORRECT	Many candidates applied; however, only one was chosen.

Parentheses

Parentheses are used in the following instances:

1. **Use parentheses to set off incidental information.**

   Please call me (x3104) when you get the information.

   Galileo (1564–1642) is often considered the father of modern astronomy.

2. **Use parentheses to enclose numbers and letters that label items listed in a sentence.**

   To transfer a call within the office, (1) place the party on HOLD, (2) press TRANSFER, (3) press the extension number, and (4) hang up.

Apostrophes

Apostrophes are used in the following instances:

1. **Use an apostrophe to indicate possession.**

the manager's goals	the employee's credit union
the workers' lounge	Charles's T square

   For joint possession, add an apostrophe and an s only to the last noun or proper noun:

   Watson and Crick's discovery

   For separate possession, add an apostrophe and an s to each of the nouns or pronouns:

   Newton's and Galileo's theories

NOTE: Do not add an apostrophe or an *s* to possessive pronouns: *his, hers, its, ours, yours, theirs.*

2. **Use an apostrophe to indicate possession when a noun modifies a gerund.**

   We were all looking forward to Bill's joining the company.

   The gerund *joining* is modified by the proper noun *Bill.*

3. **Use an apostrophe to form contractions.**

   I've   shouldn't

   can't   it's

   The apostrophe usually indicates an omitted letter or letters:

   can(no)t = can't

   it (i)s = it's

4. **Use an apostrophe to indicate special plurals.**

   three 9's

   two different JCL's

   the why's and how's of the problem

   NOTE: For plurals of numbers and abbreviations, some style guides omit the apostrophe: *9s, JCLs.* Because usage varies considerably, check with your organization.

MISUSE OF APOSTROPHES

Writers sometimes incorrectly use the contraction *it's* in place of the possessive pronoun *its.*

INCORRECT   The company does not feel that the problem is it's responsibility.

CORRECT   The company does not feel that the problem is its responsibility.

" " Quotation Marks

Quotation marks are used in the following instances:

1. **Use quotation marks to indicate titles of short works, such as articles, essays, or chapters.**

   Smith's essay "Solar Heating Alternatives" was short but informative.

2. **Use quotation marks to call attention to a word or phrase used in an unusual way or in an unusual context.**

> A proposal is "wired" if the sponsoring agency has already decided who will be granted the contract.

NOTE: Do not use quotation marks to excuse poor word choice:

INCORRECT The new director has been a real "pain."

In This Book

For more about quoting sources, see Appendix, Part A, p. 418.

3. **Use quotation marks to indicate a direct quotation.**

> "In the future," he said, "check with me before authorizing any large purchases."
>
> As Breyer wrote, "Morale *is* productivity."

NOTE: Quotation marks are not used with indirect quotations:

INCORRECT He said that "third-quarter profits will be up."

CORRECT He said that third-quarter profits will be up.

Also note that quotation marks are not used with quotations that are longer than four lines; instead, set the quotation in block format. In a word-processed manuscript, a block quotation is usually

- indented one-half inch from the left-hand margin
- typed without quotation marks
- introduced by a complete sentence followed by a colon

Different style manuals recommend variations on these basic rules; the following example illustrates APA style.

McFarland (2011) writes:

> The extent to which organisms adapt to their environment is still being charted. Many animals, we have recently learned, respond to a dry winter with an automatic birth control chemical that limits the number of young to be born that spring. This prevents mass starvation among the species in that locale. (p. 49)

Hollins (2012) concurs. She writes, "Biological adaptation will be a major research area during the next decade" (p. 2).

USING QUOTATION MARKS WITH OTHER PUNCTUATION

- If the sentence contains a *tag*—a phrase identifying the speaker or writer—a comma separates it from the quotation:

> Wilson replied, "I'll try to fly out there tomorrow."
>
> "I'll try to fly out there tomorrow," Wilson replied.

Informal and brief quotations require no punctuation before a quotation mark:

> She asked herself "Why?" several times a day.

- In the United States (unlike most other English-speaking nations), commas and periods at the end of quotations are placed within the quotation marks:

> The project engineer reported, "A new factor has been added."
>
> "A new factor has been added," the project engineer reported.

- Question marks, dashes, and exclamation points are placed inside quotation marks when they are part of the quoted material:

> He asked, "Did the shipment come in yet?"

- When question marks, dashes, and exclamation points apply to the whole sentence, they are placed outside the quotation marks:

> Did he say, "This is the limit"?

- When a punctuation mark appears inside a quotation mark at the end of a sentence, do not add another punctuation mark:

| INCORRECT | Did she say, "What time is it?"? |
| CORRECT | Did she say, "What time is it?" |

∎∎∎ Ellipses

Ellipses (three spaced periods) indicate the omission of material from a direct quotation.

| SOURCE | My team will need three extra months for market research and quality-assurance testing to successfully complete the job. |
| QUOTE | She responded, "My team will need three extra months . . . to successfully complete the job." |

Insert an ellipsis after a period if you are omitting entire sentences that follow:

> Larkin refers to the project as "an attempt . . . to clarify the issue of compulsory arbitration. . . . We do not foresee an end to the legal wrangling . . . but perhaps the report can serve as a definition of the areas of contention."

The writer has omitted words from the source after *attempt* and after *wrangling*. After *arbitration*, the writer has inserted an ellipsis after a period to indicate that a sentence has been omitted.

[ ] Square Brackets

Square brackets are used in the following instances:

1. **Use square brackets around words added to a quotation.**

   As noted in the minutes of the meeting, "He [Pearson] spoke out against the proposal."

   A better approach would be to shorten the quotation:

   The minutes of the meeting note that Pearson "spoke out against the proposal."

2. **Use square brackets to indicate parenthetical information within parentheses.**

   (For further information, see Charles Houghton's *Civil Engineering Today* [1997].)

MECHANICS

ital Italics

Although italics are generally preferred, you may use underlining in place of italics. Whichever method you choose, be consistent throughout your document. Italics (or underlining) are used in the following instances:

1. **Use italics for words used as words.**

   In this report, the word *operator* will refer to any individual who is in charge of the equipment, regardless of that individual's certification.

2. **Use italics to indicate titles of long works (books, manuals, and so on), periodicals and newspapers, long films, long plays, and long musical works.**

   See Houghton's *Civil Engineering Today*.

   We subscribe to the *Wall Street Journal*.

   Note that *the* is not italicized or capitalized when the title is used in a sentence.

   NOTE: The MLA style guide recommends that the names of Web sites be italicized.

   The Library of Congress maintains *Thomas*, a site for legislative information.

3. **Use italics to indicate the names of ships, trains, and airplanes.**

   The shipment is expected to arrive next week on the *Penguin*.

4. **Use italics to set off foreign expressions that have not become fully assimilated into English.**

> Grace's *joie de vivre* makes her an engaging presenter.

Check a dictionary to determine whether a foreign expression has become assimilated.

5. **Use italics to emphasize words or phrases.**

> *Do not* press the red button.

< > Angle Brackets

Some style guides advocate using angle brackets around URLs in print documents to set them off from the text.

> Our survey included a close look at three online news sites: the *New York Times* <www.nytimes.com>, the *Washington Post* <www.washingtonpost.com>, and CNN <www.cnn.com>.

Hyphens

Hyphens are used in the following instances:

1. **Use hyphens to form compound adjectives that precede nouns.**

> general-purpose register
>
> meat-eating dinosaur
>
> chain-driven saw

NOTE: Hyphens are not used after adverbs that end in -ly.

> newly acquired terminal

Also note that hyphens are not used when the compound adjective follows the noun:

> The Woodchuck saw is chain driven.

For more about compound adjectives, see page 450.

2. **Use hyphens to form some compound nouns.**

> once-over
>
> go-between

NOTE: There is a trend away from hyphenating compound nouns (*vice president*, *photomicroscope*); check your dictionary for proper spelling.

3. **Use hyphens to form fractions and compound numbers.**

   one-half

   fifty-six

4. **Use hyphens to attach some prefixes and suffixes.**

   post-1945

   president-elect

5. **Use hyphens to divide a word at the end of a line.**

   We will meet in the pavil-

   ion in one hour.

   Whenever possible, however, avoid such line breaks; they slow the reader down. When you do use them, check the dictionary to make sure you have divided the word between syllables. If you need to break a URL at the end of a line, do not add a hyphen. Instead, break it before a slash or a period:

   <http://www.stc.org

   /ethical.asp>

num   Numbers

Ways of handling numbers vary considerably. Therefore, in choosing between words and numerals, consult your organization's style guide. Many organizations observe the following guidelines:

1. **Technical quantities of any amount are expressed in numerals, especially if a unit of measurement is included.**

3 feet	43,219 square miles
12 grams	36 hectares

2. **Nontechnical quantities of fewer than 10 are expressed in words.**

   six whales

3. **Nontechnical quantities of 10 or more are expressed in numerals.**

   12 whales

4. **Approximations are written out.**

   about two million trees

5. **Round numbers over nine million are expressed in both words and numerals.**

   14 million light-years

   $64 billion

6. Decimals are expressed in numerals.

   3.14

   0.146

7. Fractions are written out, unless they are linked to technical units.

   two-thirds of the members

   3½ hp

8. Time of day is expressed in numerals if A.M. or P.M. is used; otherwise, it is written out.

   6:10 A.M.

   six o'clock

9. Page numbers and titles of figures and tables are expressed in numerals.

   Figure 1

   page 261

10. Back-to-back numbers are written using both words and numerals.

    six 3-inch screws

    3,012 five-piece starter units

    In general, the technical unit should be expressed with the numeral. If the nontechnical quantity would be cumbersome in words, use the numeral for it instead.

11. Numbers in legal contracts or in documents intended for international readers should be represented in both words and numerals.

    thirty-seven thousand dollars ($37,000)

    five (5) relays

12. Street addresses may require both words and numerals.

    3801 Fifteenth Street

SPECIAL CASES

- A number at the beginning of a sentence should be spelled out:

  Thirty-seven acres was the size of the lot.

  Many writers would revise the sentence to avoid spelling out the number:

  The lot was 37 acres.

- Within a sentence, the same unit of measurement should be expressed consistently in either numerals or words:

INCORRECT	On Tuesday the attendance was 13; on Wednesday, eight.
CORRECT	On Tuesday the attendance was 13; on Wednesday, 8.
CORRECT	On Tuesday the attendance was thirteen; on Wednesday, eight.

- In general, months should not be expressed as numbers. In the United States, 3/7/13 means March 7, 2013; in many other countries, it means July 3, 2013. The following forms, in which the months are written out, are preferable:

  March 7, 2013

  7 March 2013

abbr   Abbreviations

Abbreviations save time and space, but you should use them carefully because your readers may not understand them. Many companies and professional organizations provide lists of approved abbreviations.

Analyze your audience to determine whether and how to abbreviate. If your readers include a general audience unfamiliar with your field, either write out the technical terms or attach a list of abbreviations. If for any reason you are unsure about a term, write it out.

The following are general guidelines about abbreviations:

1. When an unfamiliar abbreviation is introduced for the first time, the full term should be given, followed by the abbreviation in parentheses. In subsequent references, the abbreviation may be used alone. For long works, the full term and its abbreviation may be written out at the start of major units, such as chapters.

   The heart of the new system is the self-loading cartridge (SLC).

2. To form the plural of an abbreviation, an *s* is added, either with or without an apostrophe, depending on the style preferred by your organization.

   GNP's or GNPs

   Most unit-of-measurement abbreviations do not take plurals:

   10 in.

   3 qt

3. Most abbreviations in scientific writing are not followed by periods.

> lb
>
> cos

If the abbreviation can be confused with another word, however, a period should be used:

> in.
>
> Fig.

4. **If no number is used with a measurement, an abbreviation should not be used.**

INCORRECT	How many sq meters is the site?
CORRECT	How many square meters is the site?

cap   Capitalization

For the most part, the conventions of capitalization in general writing apply in technical communication:

1. **Proper nouns, titles, trade names, places, languages, religions, and organizations should be capitalized.**

> William Rusham
>
> Director of Personnel
>
> Quick-Fix Erasers
>
> Bethesda, Maryland
>
> Italian
>
> Methodism
>
> Society for Technical Communication

In some organizations, job titles are not capitalized unless they refer to specific people.

> Alfred Loggins, Director of Personnel, is interested in being considered for vice president of marketing.

2. **Headings and labels should be capitalized.**

> Table 3
>
> Section One
>
> The Problem
>
> Figure 6

Proofreading Symbols and Their Meanings

Mark in margin	Instructions	Mark on manuscript	Corrected type
ℓ	Delete	$10 billion dollars	$10 billion
∧	Insert	enviroment	environment
(stet)	Let stand	let it stand	let it stand
(cap)	Capitalize	the english language	the English language
(lc)	Make lowercase	the English Language	the English language
—	Italicize	Technical Communication	*Technical Communication*
(tr)	Transpose	recieve	receive
◡	Close up space	diagnostic ultra sound	diagnostic ultrasound
(sp)	Spell out	(Pres) Smithers	President Smithers
#	Insert space	3amp light	3 amp light
¶	Start paragraph	. . . the results. These results	. . . the results. These results
run in	No paragraph	. . . the results. For this reason,	. . . the results. For this reason,
(sc)	Set in small capitals	Needle-nose pliers	NEEDLE-NOSE PLIERS
(bf)	Set in boldface	Needle-nose pliers	**Needle-nose pliers**
⊙	Insert period	Fig 21	Fig. 21
⌃	Insert comma	the plant which was built	the plant, which was built
=	Insert hyphen	menu driven software	menu-driven software
⊙	Insert colon	Add the following	Add the following:
⌃	Insert semicolon	. . . the plan however, the committee	. . . the plan; however, the committee
∨	Insert apostrophe	the users preference	the user's preference
❝/❞	Insert quotation marks	Furthermore, she said . . .	"Furthermore," she said . . .
(/)	Insert parentheses	Write to us at the Newark office	Write to us (at the Newark office)
[/]	Insert brackets	President John Smithers	President [John] Smithers
$\frac{1}{N}$	Insert en dash	1984 2001	1984–2001
$\frac{1}{M}$	Insert em dash	Our goal victory	Our goal—victory
∨	Insert superscript	4,000 ft2	4,000 ft^2
∧	Insert subscript	H2O	H_2O
//	Align	$123.05 $86.95	$123.05 $86.95
[	Move to the left	PVC piping	PVC piping
]	Move to the right	PVC piping	PVC piping
⌐	Move up	PVC piping	PVC piping
⌐	Move down	PVC piping	PVC piping

References

Chapter 1: Introduction to Technical Communication

About.com. (2008). *Self-service customer support.* Retrieved January 26, 2008, from http://onlinebusiness.about.com/cs/integration/a/selfsupport.htm

College Entrance Examination Board. (2004). *Writing: A ticket to work . . . or a ticket out: A survey of business leaders.* Retrieved January 25, 2008, from www.writingcommission.org/prod_downloads/writingcom/writing-ticket-to-work.pdf

Conference Board, Corporate Voices for Working Families, Partnership for 21st Century Skills, & Society for Human Resource Management. (2006). *Are they really ready to work? Employers' perspectives on the basic knowledge and applied skills of new entrants to the 21st century U.S. workforce.* Retrieved June 25, 2010, from www.p21.org/documents/FINAL_REPORT_PDF09-29-06.pdf

Marathon Technologies. (2010). *See the "Why Marathon" video.* Retrieved June 26, 2010, from www.marathon1.com/why_marathon_video.html

Plain English Network. (2002). *Writing and oral communication skills: Career-boosting assets.* Retrieved August 5, 2002, from www.plainlanguage.gov/Summit/writing.htm

Sage Software, Inc. (2009). *ACT! by Sage 2010: Delivering on usability and productivity.* Retrieved June 17, 2010, from http://download.act.com/act2010/docs/act_2010_usability_and_productivity_whitepaper.pdf

Teliris. (2011). Web site. Retrieved January 10, 2011, from www.teliris.com/teliris-telepresence-photos.html

Xerox Corporation. (2007). *Phaser® 6180/6180MFP.* Retrieved June 9, 2010, from www.office.xerox.com/latest/61CBR-01U.PDF

Chapter 2: Understanding Ethical and Legal Considerations

Alamy. (2011). *Image B2YKE4.* Retrieved January 10, 2011, from www.alamy.com

Donaldson, T. (1991). *The ethics of international business.* New York, NY: Oxford University Press.

Ethics Resource Center. (2010). *The importance of ethical culture: Increasing trust and driving down risks.* Arlington, VA: Author.

Kaptein, M. (2004). Business codes of multinational firms: What do they say? *Journal of Business Ethics, 50*(1), 13–31.

Lipus, T. (2006). International consumer protection: Writing adequate instructions for global audiences. *Journal of Technical Writing and Communication, 36*(1), 75–91.

Safety Label Solutions. (2010). *Other energy hazards.* Retrieved June 3, 2010, from http://safetylabelsolutions.com/store/page8.html

Texas Instruments. (2010). *Ethics.* Retrieved June 23, 2010, from www.ti.com/corp/docs/investor/gov/organize.shtml

U.S. Census Bureau. (2010). *The 2010 statistical abstract.* Washington, DC: U.S. Government Printing Office.

U.S. Consumer Product Safety Commission. (2009). *2009 annual report to the president and the Congress.* Bethesda, MD: Author. Retrieved June 27, 2010, from www.cpsc.gov/cpscpub/pubs/reports/2009rpt.pdf

Velasquez, M. G. (2006). *Business ethics: Concepts and cases* (6th ed.). Upper Saddle River, NJ: Pearson.

Chapter 3: Writing Collaboratively and Using Social Media

Chen, B. X. (2010, June 29). *How Microsoft crowdsourced the making of Office 2010*. Retrieved September 5, 2010, from www.wired.com/gadgetlab/2010/06/microsoft-office-2010

Cisco Systems, Inc. (2010). *Cisco 2010 midyear security report*. Retrieved July 22, 2010, from www.cisco.com/en/US/prod/collateral/vpndevc/security_annual_report_mid2010.pdf

Kaupins, G., & Park, S. (2010, June 2). Legal and ethical implications of corporate social networks. *Employee Responsibilities and Rights Journal*. Retrieved July 9, 2010, from www.springerlink.com/content/446x810tx0134588/fulltext.pdfDOI10.1007/s10672-010-9149-8

Matson, R. (1996, April). *The seven sins of deadly meetings*. Retrieved July 22, 1999, from www.fastcompany.com/online/02/meetings.html

Microsoft Corporation. (2011). *Halo: Reach Xbox forums*. Retrieved April 8, 2011, from http://forums.xbox.com/1496/ShowForum.aspx

National Aeronautics and Space Administration. (2011, June 11). *We're getting the band back together*. Retrieved June 17, 2011, from http://blogs.nasa.gov/cm/blog/fragileoasis/posts/post_1307836834103.html

Socialtext, Inc. (2010). *Products and services: Socialtext 4.5*. Retrieved November 8, 2010, from www.socialtext.com/products/desktop.php

wikiHow. (2010). *How to buy lenses for your digital SLR*. Retrieved July 8, 2010, from www.wikihow.com/Buy-Lenses-for-Your-Digital-SLR

Chapter 4: Analyze Your Audience and Purpose

Climate Savers Computing. (2010). *Three steps to go green*. Retrieved July 14, 2010, from www.climatesaverscomputing.org/component/option,com_surveys/act,view_survey/lang,en/survey,3%20Steps%20to%20Go%20Green

Google, Inc. (2010). *Technology overview*. Retrieved July 14, 2010, from www.google.com/corporate/tech.html

Hoft, N. L. (1995). *International technical communication: How to export information about high technology*. New York, NY: Wiley.

Indian Railways. (2010). *Report on restructuring of the probationary training for IRAS, IRPS and IRTS*. Retrieved July 14, 2010, from www.indianrailways.gov.in/indianrailways/directorate/mgt_ser/training_circulars/report_iras.pdf

Lovitt, C. R. (1999). Introduction: Rethinking the role of culture in international professional communication. In C. R. Lovitt & D. Goswami (Eds.), *Exploring the rhetoric of international professional communication: An agenda for teachers and researchers* (pp. 1–13). Amityville, NY: Baywood.

Markley, M. (2010a). *Mike Markley* [LinkedIn Web site]. Retrieved July 14, 2010, from www.linkedin.com/pub/mike-markley/0/244/64b

Markley, M. (2010b). *Mike Markley* [Twitter Web site]. Retrieved July 14, 2010, from http://twitter.com/mmboise

National Aeronautics and Space Administration. (2011). *NASA's Aeronautics Test Program: The right facility at the right time*. Retrieved May 23, 2011, from www.aeronautics.nasa.gov/atp/documents/B-1240.pdf

Ono, T. (2010). *Message from the president*. Retrieved July 14, 2010, from www.fdk.co.jp/company_e/message-e.html

Solomon, S., Qin, D., Manning, M., Marquis, M., Averyt, K., Tignor, M. M., & Miller, H. L. (2007). *Climate change 2007: The physical science basis*. New York, NY: Cambridge University Press.

Taser International, Inc. (2010). *Law enforcement FAQ's*. Retrieved July 16, 2010, from www.taser.com/research/Pages/LawEnforcementFAQs.aspx

Tebeaux, E., & Driskill, L. (1999). Culture and the shape of rhetoric: Protocols of international document design. In C. R. Lovitt & D. Goswami (Eds.), *Exploring the rhetoric of international professional communication: An agenda for teachers and researchers* (pp. 211–251). Amityville, NY: Baywood.

Chapter 5: Researching Your Subject

Eng-Tips Forums. (2010). *Earthwork/grading engineering forum*. Retrieved July 21, 2010, from www.eng-tips.com/viewthread.cfm?qid=274942&page=1

Garfein, R. S., Laniado-Laborin, R., Rodwell, T. C., Lozada, R., Deiss, R., Burgos, J. L., . . . & Strathdee, S. A. (2010). Abstract to Latent tuberculosis among persons at risk for infection with HIV, Tijuana, Mexico. *Emerging Infectious Diseases, 16*(5). Retrieved July 21, 2010, from www.cdc.gov/eid /content/16/5/757.htm

Palestrant, D. (2010). *(More) madness in Massachusetts.* Retrieved April 22, 2010, from http:// thehealthcareblog.com/blog/2010/04/22 /more-madness-in-massachusetts

U.S. Department of Health and Human Services. (2011, May 24). *Blog.AIDS.gov.* Retrieved May 24, 2011, from http://blog.aids.gov/

Chapter 6: Writing for Your Readers

Benson, P. (1985). Writing visually: Design considerations in technical publications. *Technical Communication, 32,* 35–39.

National Science Foundation. (2008). Pre-submission information. In *Grant proposal guide* (chap. 1). Retrieved March 12, 2008, from www.nsf.gov /pubs/policydocs/pappguide/nsf08_1/gpg _1.jsp#IA1

Snow, K. (2009). *People first language.* Retrieved August 2, 2010, from www.disabilityisnatural.com /images/PDF/pfl-sh09.pdf

U.S. Department of Labor. (2010). *Frequently asked questions.* Retrieved August 2, 2010, from www.dol .gov/odep/faqs/people.htm

Chapter 7: Designing Documents and Web Sites

Biggs, J. R. (1980). *Basic typography.* New York, NY: Watson-Guptill.

Bonneville Power Administration. (2010). *Wapato Lake land acquisition would provide multiple benefits.* Retrieved August 3, 2010, from www.bpa.gov /corporate/pubs/fact_sheets/10fs/Wapato_Lake _-_March_2010.pdf

Carnegie Science Center. (n.d.). *Carnegie Science Center* [Brochure]. Pittsburgh, PA: Author.

Discover. (2005, February). Letters. *Discover,* 6.

Ford Motor Company. (2010). Web site. Retrieved August 3, 2010, from www.ford.com

Google, Inc. (2010). *Google groups.* Retrieved August 3, 2010, from http://groups.google.com /grphp?hl=en

Haley, A. (1991). All caps: A typographic oxymoron. *U&lc, 18*(3), 14–15.

Institute of Scientific and Technical Communicators. (2005, Spring). Industry news. *Communicator,* 43.

Internet World Stats. (2010). *Internet world users by language.* Retrieved August 3, 2010, from www .internetworldstats.com/stats7.htm

Kerman, J., & Tomlinson, G. (2004). *Listen* (brief 5th ed.). Boston, MA: Bedford/St. Martin's.

Lambert Coffin. (2010). Web site. Retrieved August 3, 2010, from www.lambertcoffin.com/index .php?sid=2

Micron Technology, Inc. (2010). *CSN-16: Micron component and module packaging.* Retrieved August 3, 2010, from http://cache.micron.com/Protected /expiretime=1280866476;badurl=aHR0cDovL3d3d y5taWNyb24uY29tLy80MDQuaHRtbA== /98a94b45324cf1822dec1bdfb4abb0f8/1/43/CSN16 .pdf

Microsoft Corporation. (2001). *Discovering Microsoft Office XP Standard and Professional Version 2002.* Redmond, WA: Author.

Myers, D. G. (2003). *Exploring psychology* (5th ed. in modules). New York, NY: Worth Publishers.

Myers, D. G. (2007). *Psychology* (8th ed.). New York, NY: Worth Publishers.

National Institutes of Health. (2010). *National Human Genome Research Institute site map.* Retrieved April 14, 2010, from www.genome.gov/sitemap.cfm

Norman Rockwell Museum. (2005). *Norman Rockwell Museum* [Brochure]. Stockbridge, MA: Author.

Poulton, E. (1968). Rate of comprehension of an existing teleprinter output and of possible alternatives. *Journal of Applied Psychology, 52,* 16–21.

Purves, W. K., Sadava, D., Orians, G. H., & Heller, H. C. (2004). *Life: The science of biology* (7th ed.). Sunderland, MA: Sinauer.

Roark, J. L., Johnson, M. P., Cohen, P. C., Stage, S., Lawson, A., & Hartmann, S. M. (2005). *The American promise: A history of the United States: Vol. 1. To 1877.* Boston, MA: Bedford/St. Martin's.

TiVo. (2010). *TV listing guide.* Retrieved August 3, 2010, from www3.tivo.com/tivo-tco/tvlistings.do

U.S. Agency for International Development. (2010). *Sudan.* Retrieved August 3, 2010, from www.usaid .gov/locations/sub-saharan_africa/countries /sudan/docs/mar10_monthly_update.pdf

U.S. Agency for International Development, U.S. Department of Defense, & U.S. Department of State. (2009). *Security sector reform*, p. 2. Retrieved August 3, 2010, from www.usaid.gov/our_work /democracy_and_governance/publications/pdfs /SSR_JS_Mar2009.pdf

U.S. Copyright Office. (2010). *Frequently asked questions about copyright*. Retrieved on August 3, 2010, from www.copyright.gov/help/faq

U.S. Department of Agriculture. (2002, March 5). *Thermometer usage messages and delivery mechanisms for parents of young children*. Retrieved April 4, 2002, from www.fsis.usda.gov/oa/research/rti_thermy .pdf

U.S. Department of State. (2009). *Trafficking in persons report: June 2009*, p. 17. Retrieved July 11, 2010, from www.state.gov/documents/organization /123360.pdf

U.S. Department of State. (2011). *Future state*. Retrieved February 21, 2011, from http:// future.state.gov

U.S. Patent and Trademark Office. (2010). *Performance and accountability report: Fiscal year 2009*. Retrieved August 3, 2010, from www.uspto.gov/about /stratplan/ar/2009/2009annualreport.pdf

Valley, J. W. (2005, October). A cool early earth? *Scientific American*, 58–65.

Volvo Cars. (2010). *Follow us*. Retrieved August 21, 2010, from www.volvocars.com/us/top /community/pages/followus.aspx

Williams, G. A., & Miller, R. B. (2002, May). Change the way you persuade. *Harvard Business Review*, 65–73.

Williams, R. (2008). *The non-designer's design book* (3rd ed.). Berkeley, CA: Peachpit Press.

Williams, T., & Spyridakis, J. (1992). Visual discriminability of headings in text. *IEEE Transactions on Professional Communication, 35*, 64–70.

Chapter 8: Creating Graphics

Barnum, C. M., & Carliner, S. (1993). *Techniques for technical communicators*. New York, NY: Macmillan.

Bonneville Power Administration. (2009). *2009 annual report*, p. 73. Retrieved August 4, 2010, from www.bpa.gov/corporate/Finance/A_Report/09 /AR2009.pdf

Brockmann, R. J. (1990). *Writing better computer user documentation: From paper to hypertext*. New York, NY: Wiley.

Carnegie Mellon University. (2010). *Panda3D: Code3D™ by Sim Ops Studios screenshot*. Retrieved August 5, 2010, from www.panda3d.org/showss .php?shot=ssg-code3d/code3D01

Corante. (2005, June 21). *Going global: Translation*. Retrieved July 5, 2005, from www.corante.com /goingglobal/archives/cat_translation.php

Council of Economic Advisers. (2010). *The ARRA and the clean energy transformation*, p. 4. Retrieved August 4, 2010, from www.whitehouse.gov/sites /default/files/image/arra_%20and_clean_energy _transformation_3Q_supplement.pdf

Defense Intelligence Agency. (2003). *DIA workforce of the future: Creating the future of the Defense Intelligence Agency*, p. 16. Retrieved August 4, 2010, from www.dia.mil/thisisdia/DIA_Workforce _of_the_Future.pdf

Gatlin, P. L. (1988). Visuals and prose in manuals: The effective combination. In *Proceedings of the 35th International Technical Communication Conference* (pp. RET 113–115). Arlington, VA: Society for Technical Communication.

Grimstead, D. (1987). Quality graphics: Writers draw the line. In *Proceedings of the 34th International Technical Communication Conference* (pp. VC 66–69). Arlington, VA: Society for Technical Communication.

Hockenbury, D. H., & Hockenbury, S. E. (2007). *Discovering psychology* (4th ed.). New York, NY: Worth Publishers.

Horton, W. (1993). The almost universal language: Graphics for international documents. *Technical Communication, 40*, 682–693.

Levie, W. H., & Lentz, R. (1982). Effects of text illustrations: A review of research. *Journal of Educational Psychology, 73*, 195–232.

Morrison, C., & Jimmerson, W. (1989, July). Business presentations for the 1990s. *Video Manager, 4*, 18.

Myers, D. G. (2010). *Psychology* (9th ed.). New York, NY: Worth Publishers.

Purves, W. K., Sadava, D., Orians, G. H., & Heller, H. C. (2004). *Life: The science of biology* (7th ed.). Sunderland, MA: Sinauer.

TiVo, Inc. (2010). *TiVo-Premiere*. Retrieved August 4, 2010, from www.tivo.com/products/tivo-premiere/premiere-specs.html#tab

Townsend, F. F. (2006). *The federal response to Hurricane Katrina: Lessons learned*, p. 6. Retrieved February 27, 2008, from www.whitehouse.gov/reports/katrina-lessons-learned.pdf

Tufte, E. R. (1983). *The visual display of quantitative information*. Cheshire, CT: Graphics Press.

U.S. Agency for International Development. (2009). *Report to Congress: Health-related research and development activities at USAID: An update on the five-year strategy, 2006–2010*, p. 17. Retrieved August 4, 2010, from http://pdf.usaid.gov/pdf_docs/PDACN515.pdf

U.S. Census Bureau. (2010). *The 2010 statistical abstract*. Washington, DC: U.S. Government Printing Office.

U.S. Department of Justice. (2010). *Accessible stadiums*. Retrieved August 4, 2010, from www.ada.gov/stadium.pdf

White, J. V. (1984). *Using charts and graphs: 1000 ideas for visual persuasion*. New York, NY: R. R. Bowker.

White, J. V. (1990). *Color for the electronic age*. New York, NY: Watson-Guptill.

Chapter 9: Writing Correspondence

Sasaki, U. (2010). *Japanese business etiquette for email*. Retrieved September 3, 2010, from www.ehow.com/about_6523223_japanese-business-etiquette-email.html

Xerox Corporation. (2010). *Xerox social media guidelines*, pp. 4–5. Retrieved August 21, 2010, from www.xerox.com/downloads/usa/en/s/Social_Media_Guidelines.pdf

Chapter 10: Writing Job-Application Materials

Goodman, M. (2010, June 24). *Lying on your résumé: Why it won't work*. Retrieved August 23, 2010, from http://abcnews.go.com/Business/resume-fibbers-lying-bio-work/story?id=10994617&page=1

Hansen, K. (2008). *Tapping the power of keywords to enhance your resume's effectiveness*. Retrieved March 12, 2008, from www.quintcareers.com/resume_keywords.html

Résumés redefined. (2008). Retrieved August 24, 2010, from www.careerbuilder.com/Article/CB-977-Cover-Letters-and-Resumes-R%C3%A9sum%C3%A9s-Redefined

U.S. Department of Labor. (2006, August 25). *News* [Document 04-1678], p. 1. Retrieved February 29, 2008, from www.bls.gov/news.release/pdf/nlsoy.pdf

Chapter 11: Writing Proposals

FedBizOpps.gov. (2010). *Wetland construction inspector svcs*. (2010). Retrieved August 25, 2010, from www.fbo.gov/?s=opportunity&mode=form&id=7d54e4cc37cd00c29bcddc2a2cfc2715&tab=core&_cview=1

Newman, L. (2006). *Proposal guide for business and technical professionals* (3rd ed.). Farmington, UT: Shipley Associates.

Ohio Office of Criminal Justice Services. (2003). *Sample grant proposal*. Retrieved March 18, 2008, from www.graduate.appstate.edu/gwtoolbox/ocjs_sample_grant.pdf

Thrush, E. (2000, January 20). *Writing for an international audience: Part I. Communication skills*. Retrieved November 5, 2002, from www.suite101.com/article.cfm/5381/32233

U.S. Department of Commerce. (2010). *Statistical abstract of the United States: 2010*. Washington, DC: U.S. Government Printing Office. Page 494. Retrieved August 26, 2010, from www.census.gov/compendia/statab/2010/tables/10s0494.pdf

Chapter 12: Writing Informational Reports

University of North Carolina at Chapel Hill. (2010). *Facilities Services safety plan*, p. 8. Retrieved September 15, 2010, from www.fac.unc.edu/Employees/Safety/SafetyDocuments/tabid/233/Default.aspx

Chapter 13: Writing Recommendation Reports

Honold, P. (1999). Learning how to use a cellular phone: Comparison between German and Chinese users. *Technical Communication, 46*(2), 195–205.

Chapter 14: Writing Definitions, Descriptions, and Instructions

Anthro Corporation. (2005). *Anthro Space Pal* [Assembly instructions], p. 2. Retrieved September 29, 2005, from www.anthro.com/downloads /assemblyinstructions/300-5237-00.pdf

Brain, M. (2005). *How computer viruses work*. Retrieved June 20, 2005, from http://computer .howstuffworks.com/virus1.htm

Conveyor Equipment Manufacturers Association. (2004). *CEMA safety labels placement guidelines: Slat conveyors*. Retrieved January 28, 2010, from http:// cemanet.org/safety/uh6.pdf

Delio, M. (2002, June 4). Read the f***ing story, then RTFM. *Wired News*. Retrieved June 6, 2002, from www.wired.com/culture/lifestyle/news/2002 /06/52901

Falco, M. (2008, January 14). *New hope may lie in lab-created heart*. Retrieved March 21, 2008, from www .cnn.com/2008/HEALTH/01/14/rebuilt.heart

Fraternity Insurance and Purchasing Group. (2003). *Risk management* [Manual], p. 45. Retrieved June 20, 2005, from www.fipg.org/media /FIPGRiskMgmtManual.pdf

General Electric. (2003). *Installation instructions: Free-standing electric ranges* [Manual 229C4053P545-1 31-10556-1 04-03 JR], p. 2.

HCS, LLC. (2004). *HCS 2004 safety label catalog*. Retrieved January 28, 2005, from www.safetylabel .com/search/index.php?pn=H6010-CDDHPL

Hewlett Packard. (2010). *HP Slate* [Manual], p. 36. Retrieved April 8, 2011, from http://bizsupport2 .austin.hp.com/bc/docs/support/SupportManual /c02571793/c02571793.pdf

Motorola, Inc. (2011). *Motorola XOOM™ fact sheet*. Retrieved April 15, 2011, from http://mediacenter .motorola.com/Fact-Sheets/Motorola-XOOM-Fact -Sheet-3537.aspx

Slide-Lok Garage and Storage Cabinets. (2005). *P2468 pantry cabinet* [Assembly instructions], p. 2. Retrieved September 29, 2005, from www .slide-lok.com/assembly/P2468/P2468.pdf

Sony Corporation. (2009). *Sony Reader user's guide: PRS-300 digital book reader*, p. 50. Retrieved June 17, 2011, from http://www.docs.sony.com/release /PRS300RCB.pdf

Trek Bicycle Corporation. (2011). *Ride+ technology*. Retrieved September 1, 2010, from www.trekbikes .com/us/en/rideplus/technology

U.S. Department of Energy. (2010). *Using fermentation and catalysis to make fuels and products: Biochemical conversion*, p. 3. Retrieved April 8, 2011, from www1.eere.energy.gov/biomass/pdfs /biochemical_four_pager.pdf

U.S. Department of Transportation. (2007). *Description of the IVI Technologies and the FOT*. Retrieved February 20, 2008, from www.itsdocs.fhwa.dot.gov/JPODOCS /REPTS_TE/14352_files/2.0description.htm

U.S. Environmental Protection Agency. (2001). *Global warming*. Retrieved June 25, 2001, from www.epa .gov/globalwarming/climate/index.html

Vanguard Energy Partners, LLC. (2010). *How solar works*. Retrieved September 1, 2010, from www .vanguardenergypartners.com/howsolarworks .html

Chapter 15: Making Oral Presentations

Alley, M. (2007). *Rethinking the design of presentation slides*. Retrieved March 26, 2008, from www .writing.eng.vt.edu/slides.html

Boston Group. (2010). *Projecting US mail volumes to 2020: Final report—detail*. Retrieved September 3, 2010, from www.usps.com/strategicplanning /_pdf/BCG_Detailed%20presentation.pdf

McKinsey & Company. (2010). *Envisioning America's future postal service: Options for a changing environment*. Retrieved September 3, 2010, from www.usps.com/strategicplanning/_pdf/McKinsey _March_2nd_Presentation2.pdf

Smith, T. C. (1991). *Making successful presentations: A self-teaching guide*. New York, NY: Wiley.

Acknowledgments (continued from page iv)

Figure, p. 8: Courtesy of Xerox Corp.

Figure 1.2, p. 10: Reprinted by permission of Sage Software.

Figure 1.3, p. 11: Reprinted by permission of Marathon Technologies Corporation.

Figure 2.1, p. 21: Courtesy of Safety Label Solutions, Inc.

Figure 2.2, p. 30: Shaun Finch—Coyote—Photography. co.uk/Alamy.

Screen shots, p. 44: Used with permission from Microsoft.

Figure 3.2, p. 45: Socialtext, Socialtext Workspace, Miki, Socialtext Unplugged, SocialCalc, Socialtext Eventspace, Socialtext People, Socialtext Dashboard, and SocialPoint are trademarks of Socialtext Incorporated. © 2003–2010. All Rights Reserved.

Figure 3.3, p. 47: Reprinted by permission of wikiHow.

Figure 3.4, p. 49: Used with permission from Microsoft.

Figure 4.1, p. 62: Reprinted by permission of Mike Markley.

Figure 4.2, p. 64: Reprinted by permission of Mike Markley.

"Understanding the Cultural Variables 'Beneath the Surface,'" pp. 65–67: Based on "Culture and the Shape of Rhetoric: Protocols of International Document Design" by Elizabeth Tebeaux and Linda Driskill, from *Exploring the Rhetoric of International Professional Communication: An Agenda for Teachers and Researchers*, edited by Carl R. Lovitt. Copyright © 1999 by Baywood Publishing Company, Inc. Adapted with the permission of the publisher.

Figure 4.5b, p. 73: Reprinted by permission of TASER International, Inc.

Figure 4.6a, p. 74: Used by permission of Climate Savers Computing.

Figure 4.6b, p. 74: Copyright © 2003 Google Inc. Used with permission.

Figure 4.7, p. 75: *Climate Change 2007: The Physical Science Basis. Working Group I Contribution to the Fourth Assessment Report of the Intergovernmental Panel on Climate Change*, Table of Contents. Cambridge University Press.

Figure 5.2, p. 89: Reprinted by permission of Dave Murphy, Tecumseh Group, Inc.

Figure, p. 94: "(More) Madness in Massachusetts" by Daniel Palestrant, MD, from The Health Care Blog, April 22, 2010. Reprinted by permission.

Screen shot, p. 94: From The Health Care Blog, April 22, 2010. Reprinted by permission.

Figure 7.2, p. 145: Carnegie Science Center, 2004.

Figure 7.3, p. 146: From *Psychology*, Eighth Edition, by David C. Myers. Copyright © 2007 by Worth Publishers. Used with permission.

Figure 7.4, p. 147: Courtesy, Lambert Coffin.

Figure 7.6, p. 149: United States Department of Energy and the Bonneville Power Administration.

Figure 7.7, p. 149: TV Listings Guide, Friday, February 4, 2011. © McClatchy-Tribune Information Services. All Rights Reserved. Reprinted with permission.

Figure, p. 150: Copyright © Google Inc. Used with permission.

Figure, p. 150: From *Discover*, February 6, 2005 issue. Copyright © 2005 by Discover. All rights reserved. Used by permission and protected by the Copyright Laws of the United States. The printing, copying, redistribution, or retransmission of the material without express written permission is prohibited.

Figure, p. 151: Used with permission from Microsoft.

Screen shots, p. 152: Used with permission from Microsoft.

Figure 7.9b (left), p. 153: J. Kerman and G. Tomlinson, From *Listen, Brief Fifth Edition*. Copyright © 2004 by Bedford/St. Martin's. Reprinted with the permission of Bedford/St. Martin's.

Figure 7.10a, p. 154: G.A. Williams and R.B. Miller. "Disruptive Change: When Trying Harder Is Part of the Problem" (p. 96). From *Harvard Business Review* (May 2002). Copyright © 2002 by the Harvard Business School Publishing Corporation. Reprinted with the permission of Harvard Business Review. All rights reserved.

Figure 7.10b, p. 154: From David Myers, *Exploring Psychology, Fifth Edition in Modules*, Copyright © 2003. Used with permission of Worth Publishers.

Figure 7.10c, p. 154: Courtesy of The Norman Rockwell Museum.

Screen shots, p. 162: Used with permission from Microsoft.

Table 7.1a, p. 163: From *Communicator* (Spring 2005). Reprinted with the permission of the Institute of Scientific and Technical Communicators.

Table 7.1b, p. 163: From J.W. Valley, "A Cool Early Earth?" from *Scientific American* (October 2005): 58–65. Copyright © 2005 by Scientific American, Inc. All rights reserved. This figure includes all illustrations by Lucy Reading-Ikkanda, which are reprinted with the permission of the illustrator.

Table 7.1c, p. 164: From W.K. Purves, D. Sadava, G.H. Orians, and H.C. Heller, *Life: The Science of Biology*, Seventh Edition. Copyright © 2004. Reprinted with the permission of Sinauer Associates, Inc., Publishers.

Table 7.1d, p. 164: From David Myers, *Exploring Psychology, Fifth Edition in Modules*, Copyright © 2003. Used with permission of Worth Publishers.

Table 7.1e, p. 164: From J.L. Roark, M.P. Johnson, P.C. Cohen, S. Stage, A. Lawson, and S.M. Hartman, *The American Promise: A History of the United States, Volume I: to 1877*. Copyright © 2005 by Bedford/St. Martin's. Reprinted with the permission of Bedford/St. Martin's.

Screen shots, p. 165: Used with permission from Microsoft.

Figures 7.20 and 7.21, p. 169: Used by permission of Ford Motor Company.

Figure 7.24, p. 172: Courtesy, Volvo Cars of North America, LLC. Used with permission.

Figure, p. 176: Courtesy: Micron Technology, Inc.

Screen shots, p. 185: Used with permission from Microsoft.

Figure 8.2a, p. 186: United States Department of Energy and the Bonneville Power Administration.

Figure 8.2b, p. 186: From W.K. Purves, D. Sadava, G.H. Orians, and H.C. Heller, *Life: The Science of Biology*, Seventh Edition. Copyright © 2004. Reprinted with the permission of Sinauer Associates, Inc., Publishers.

Figure 8.3, p. 187: From *Psychology, Ninth Edition*, by David G. Myers. © 2010 by Worth Publishers. Used with permission.

Table, pp. 190–91: "Choosing the Appropriate Kind of Graphic" based on W. Horton, "The Almost Universal Language: Graphics for International Documentation" from *Technical Communication* 40 (1993): 682–93. Used with permission from Technical Journal, the Journal of the Society for Technical Communication, Arlington, VA U.S.A.

Screen shots, p. 196: Used with permission from Microsoft.

Figure 8.14, p. 202: Reprinted by permission of TiVo, Inc.

Figure 8.15, p. 204: From David Myers, *Exploring Psychology, Eighth Edition*, Copyright © 2007 by David Myers. Used with permission of Worth Publishers.

Figure 8.18a, p. 206: From Hockenbury and Hockenbury, *Discovering Psychology, Fourth Edition*, Copyright © 2007. Used with permission of Worth Publishers.

Figure 8.18b, p. 206: From W.K. Purves, D. Sadava, G.H. Orians, and H.C. Heller, *Life: The Science of Biology*, Eighth Edition. Copyright © 2007. Reprinted with the permission of Sinauer Associates, Inc., Publishers.

Figure 8.22, p. 208: AP Photo/Samsung Electronics, HO.

Figure 8.23, p. 209: Copyright © 2008, Carnegie Mellon University. All rights reserved.

Screen shots, p. 210: Used with permission from Microsoft.

Figure 9.12, p. 237: Courtesy of Xerox Corporation.

Figure, p. 285: Courtesy, Ohio Office of Criminal Justice Services.

Screen shots, p. 288: Used with permission from Microsoft.

Figure 12.4, p. 312: Courtesy, UNC-CH Environment, Health and Safety. Used by permission.

Screen shots, p. 327: Used with permission from Microsoft.

Figure 14.2, p. 371: Photo appears courtesy of Trek Bicycle.

Figure 14.3, p. 372: Courtesy, Vanguard Energy Partners LLC.

Figure 14.4, p. 373: Source: Motorola Mobility, Inc. Used by permission.

Figure 14.5, p. 374: Used by permission of the United States Environmental Protection Agency, ENERGY STAR Program.

Figure 14.6a, p. 377: Courtesy of SLIDE-LOK.

Figure 14.6b, p. 377: Courtesy of Anthro Corporation. www. anthro.com/downloads/assemblyinstructions/300-5237-00. pdf

Figure 14.8, p. 379: © 2012 Clarion Safety Systems.

Figure 14.9, p. 380: Reprinted with the permission of the Conveyor Equipment Manufacturers Association (CEMA).

Figure 14.10, p. 384: Used with permission from Sony Electronics, Inc.

Figure 14.11, p. 385: Courtesy of General Electric Company.

Figure, p. 387: Copyright 2012 Hewlett-Packard Development Company, L.P. Reproduced with permission.

Screen shots, p. 399: Used with permission from Microsoft.

Screen shots, p. 400: Used with permission from Microsoft.

Figure 15.3a, b, c, p. 401: Used with permission from Microsoft.

Figure 15.3d (photo of podium), p. 401: Tom Merton/Getty Images.

Figure 15.3e (photo of instructor with bar graph), p. 402: AP Photo/Stew Milne.

Figure 15.3f (photo of students using clickers), p. 403: AP Photo/Wisconsin State Journal, John Maniaci.

Figure A.1, p. 417: Courtesy of John Lovgren.

Index

Note: *f* indicates a figure and *t* indicates a table.

Selected Sample Documents and Examples

■ *To find more examples, search the index on pages 477–98.*